INTRODUCTION TO

SOCIAL WORK

THE PEOPLE'S PROFESSION

Related books of interest

Getting Your MSW: How to Survive and Thrive in a Social Work Program, Second Edition
Karen M. Sowers and Bruce A. Thyer

Food for Thought: A Two-Year Cooking Guide for Social Work Students
Kevin Corcoran

Women in Social Work Who Have Changed the World
Alice Lieberman

Introduction to Competence-Based Social Work: The Profession of Caring, Knowing, and Serving
Michael E. Sherr and Johnny M. Jones

The Practice of Social Work in North America: Culture, Context, and Competency Development
Kip Coggins

Essential Skills of Social Work Practice: Assessment, Intervention, and Evaluation, Second Edition
Thomas O'Hare

Navigating Human Service Organizations, Third Edition
Rich Furman and Margaret Gibelman

Straight Talk about Professional Ethics, Second Edition
Kim Strom-Gottfried

Modern Social Work Theory, Fourth Edition
Malcolm Payne

FOURTH EDITION

INTRODUCTION TO
SOCIAL WORK

THE PEOPLE'S PROFESSION

IRA COLBY
UNIVERSITY OF HOUSTON

SOPHIA F. DZIEGIELEWSKI
UNIVERSITY OF CENTRAL FLORIDA

OXFORD
UNIVERSITY PRESS

MT

OXFORD
UNIVERSITY PRESS

Oxford University Press is a department of the University of Oxford.
It furthers the University's objective of excellence in research, scholarship,
and education by publishing worldwide.

Oxford   New York
Auckland   Cape Town   Dar es Salaam   Hong Kong   Karachi
Kuala Lumpur   Madrid   Melbourne   Mexico City   Nairobi
New Delhi   Shanghai   Taipei   Toronto

With offices in
Argentina   Austria   Brazil   Chile   Czech Republic   France   Greece
Guatemala   Hungary   Italy   Japan   Poland   Portugal   Singapore
South Korea   Switzerland   Thailand   Turkey   Ukraine   Vietnam

Oxford is a registered trade mark of Oxford University Press
in the UK and certain other countries.

Published in the United States of America by
Oxford University Press
198 Madison Avenue, New York, NY 10016

© Oxford University Press 2016

Library of Congress Cataloging-in-Publication Data

Colby, Ira C. (Ira Christopher)
  Introduction to social work : the people's profession / Ira Colby, University of Houston,
Sophia F. Dziegielewski, University of Central Florida.—Fourth Edition.
    pages cm
  Revised edition of the authors' Introduction to social work, 2010.
    ISBN 978-0-19-061566-6 (pbk. : alk. paper)
  1. Social service—United States. 2. Social workers—United States. I. Dziegielewski,
Sophia F. II. Title.
  HV91.C597 2016
  361.3'20973—dc23
                                                                    2015019727

9 8 7 6 5 4 3

Printed in Canada
on acid-free paper

3/13/17

CONTENTS

Boxes and Tables

PREFACE

Your career should be personally rewarding. Feeling a sense of accomplishment when you make a difference in someone else's life provides a natural high that is both uplifting and fulfilling. Social work is a profession that provides ample opportunities to make positive differences in others' lives and to help make our communities better and safer for all people.

In the pages that follow, you will be introduced to the social work profession— its obvious strengths as well as its limitations. You will see how social work started and has grown from those early sixteenth- and seventeenth-century beginnings, working with poor and underserved populations, to the global profession of today. Each chapter introduces the aspiring professional to the context of social work and the variety of **roles** and associated tasks social workers perform. Although social work is an old profession, rich in tradition, it remains dynamic, flexible, nimble, and open to change. Indeed, with the field's focus on the **person-in-situation**, the need to address continuous and repeated change is ongoing. To facilitate this process, in addition to examining the field of social work in its present form, we make suggestions for future exploration and expansion. A review of the past, the present, and the future provides fertile ground for social workers to develop new services, allowing the best possible support and work with **clients**, be they individuals, a family, a neighborhood group, or even elected officials and **advocacy** groups.

By presenting the many different facets of social work, we attempt to provide a realistic and varied presentation to help you develop a more authentic understanding and appreciation of the profession. At a minimum you will be exposed to what social workers do and the importance of considering the environmental context that surrounds all decisions. Throughout the book are bios of social workers who are doing some amazing things while clearly reflecting the heart and soul of the profession. You will discover they come from all walks of life, enjoy working with and being with others, and, to be very honest, make us proud of the profession. As you read their statements, you will see many similarities in their work: they believe strongly in allowing ethical principles and a respect for cultural diversity to guide their practice; they recognize that differences in individuals are acknowledged and that concepts such as dignity, worth, and respect, along with a nonjudgmental attitude, provide the cornerstone for their work. Their work is being done on a global stage as well as in local neighborhoods, literally down the street from us.

It is our hope that the success of this book will be measured in part by whether it can help answer the following question: Is social work really the profession for me? If so, the book will introduce you to the field and the rewards and challenges that lie ahead. If not, we hope that you will gain increased awareness of the needs and struggles that people face, and the knowledge that most of these problems and issues are not self-perpetuated. And although you may not decide to become a social worker, what you learn in the chapters of this text will help to enrich any future experiences as a volunteer.

Part 1 provides a broad overview of the profession, in which we introduce professional terminology and acronyms. This is followed by a discussion of social workers' typical employment settings, responsibilities, and salaries. After that we explore, albeit briefly, the rich traditions within the field of social work, highlighting how the past clearly relates to the present and predicting what the future has in store.

In part 2, you will be introduced to the practice of social work at the micro, mezzo, and macro levels. We discuss concepts such as the client system and the notion that this system almost always involves more than one person. Although it is possible to view clients as individuals, they are most often addressed in terms of context or systems. This can involve individuals, families, groups, communities, or policies that either directly or indirectly affect client system well-being.

The chapters in part 3 present several examples of the various practice settings where social workers are employed, along with suggestions for expanding current activities and exploring further development of new areas.

This book is unique in that it will challenge you to synthesize information about successes and events in the field. Activities are included to give the beginning professional a sense of hands-on learning. These activities will help you develop a more in-depth understanding of the profession. There is also an emphasis on the use of the Internet, a tool that is now part of all of our lives. Case examples are used throughout to help you see the interface between what is written in the text and actual practice.

On a personal note, we would like to say that putting together this fourth edition, selecting and updating the topics most germane to the social work field, was not an easy task—nor should it have been. This book represents nearly eighty years of combined direct practice and teaching experience. We are both committed to using our passion for the profession to introduce others to this exciting and challenging field. As practitioners, we believe that much can be learned from the clients we serve. In fact, many of the examples we present have been drawn from our own practical, administrative, or academic experience. Using our actual experiences in direct practice and as educators helped us to decide how best to present information in a practical and informative way, one that is sensitive to students' interests and concerns while taking into account the important concepts central to a beginning social work course.

This book would not be complete if we did not acknowledge the individuals in our own support systems who have made this effort possible. Ira Colby thanks his wife and best friend for more than forty-five years, Deborah, who has honestly critiqued his teaching, writing, and thinking. Sophia Dziegielewski thanks her husband, family, friends, and colleagues, who respect and support her passion for the field and tolerate her workaholic ways.

Foremost, however, we would like to thank all the social workers who graciously allowed us to use their biographical sketches. Special thanks to our publisher, David Follmer, who supported us fully in making this the most accurate and updated depiction of the social work profession possible and Brent Jacocks for her editorial review.

Now, with all of that said, we invite you to begin this adventure in learning about one of the oldest helping professions ever developed. May this book and its description of the social work profession ignite a fire in you, as our careers in social work have done for us.

PART ONE

THE CONTEXT OF SOCIAL WORK

CHAPTER 1

SOCIAL WORK: THE PROFESSION

WHEN WRITING HIS CLASSIC WORK *MOBY DICK* IN 1851, HERMAN Melville began his work with a simple statement, "Call me Ishmael" (Melville, 1993, p. 3), followed by an incredible story depicting the quest of a sea-sailing captain to hunt down a great white whale. But what if Melville, sitting at his desk in his summer home in Pittsfield, Massachusetts, in 2015, started a new novel and began his work with the unpretentious words, "Call me a social worker" as he detailed the life of a social worker trying to help people and their communities? Melville would describe the social worker's life as rewarding and exciting with no two days alike. The worker's cases, Melville would write, run the gamut from simple to complex; whereas many are successfully resolved, some do not reach a positive outcome. Throughout the novel, Melville would time and again intimately describe the many challenges facing new and experienced social workers.

Herman Melville's social work novel might not make the *New York Times* best seller list nor be referenced centuries later, but it would be an honest attempt to portray the life and commitment necessary for today's social worker. The profession of social work is an old one whose story began in the mid-1880s, when professional helping and assistance, often referred to as *social casework*, was first introduced. At this time, social workers were active with all types of people, regardless of age, color, or creed, and this helping activity involved individuals, families, groups, and communities in both public and private social service settings.

These initial efforts at helping have come a long way. According to the 2010–13 United States Department of Labor's *Occupational Outlook Handbook*, there are approximately 607,300 professional social work jobs nationwide with a forecasted 19-percent increase in employment opportunities by the year 2022 (*see* U.S. Department of Labor, 2014). Approximately 132,000 individuals are members of the **National Association of Social Workers (NASW)**, the world's largest professional membership organization for social workers (NASW, 2014a). And in 2014, in addition to NASW, there were at least forty-one other professional social work membership associations in the United States that support specific interests or fields of practice such as research, gerontology, health care, and clinical social work (NASW, 2014b). The memberships of these various associations comprise professional social workers in all walks of life, from those who work with the elderly to those who work with infants.

For the professional education of all these social workers, there are 739 accredited baccalaureate and master's level social work education programs in 2015. There are also more than 80 doctoral programs in social work. And that's just in the United States! There is no precise figure or estimate of the number of social work educational programs in the world. In 2010 the International Association of Schools of Social Work (IASSW) conducted a "global census" of social work education programs and identified 2,500 social work education programs worldwide (**Council on Social Work Education [CSWE]**, 2014). No one knows for sure if this is an accurate number or an undercount of educational programs among the 190 nations (Leung Leung, Barretta-Herman, Littlechild, & Parada, 2013).

In 2013, the **International Federation of Social Workers (IFSW)** website claimed to represent 750,000 social workers around the world. We look at these numbers and must recognize that no one organization or group really knows the exact number of degreed (i.e., **BSW, MSW,** or **PhD**) social workers in the world.

One might suggest that simply totaling the members of different social work membership groups around the world would give us an accurate number, but this is simply not the case. Let's take the United States as an example. In 2014, the NASW, according to its website, totaled 132,000 members, yet the Department of Labor identified approximately 607,300 social work jobs in the United States. Where were the other 475,300 social workers? Maybe some belonged to other social work groups; the NASW identified forty-one different professional social work membership groups in the United States. However, we cannot just count the membership rolls of each association because social workers typically belong to multiple groups. Put another way, simply counting the membership lists results in double, triple, and even quadruple counting. Finally, there are social workers employed in positions that are not called social work, but these positions certainly require specific social work skills; employee assistance programs in corporations are an example.

So what can we conclude about the United States? We simply have no way to count the number of social workers in our country—and we recognize that this ambiguity is common to other nations around the world.

Let's approach the count now from a global perspective. China, for example, is currently in the midst of its *spring of social work* (Ting & Zhang, 2012, p. 201). After having been abolished during the so-called Cultural Revolution, the social work profession is once again growing with the support of the Chinese central government. In a 2010 government declaration, Memorandum on the Nation's Medium and Long-term Personnel Plan (Outline of China's National Plan, 2010),

the Chinese government stated that by the year 2015 there would be 2 million practicing social workers and by 2020 there would be 3 million social workers throughout the Mainland. From China alone we can easily deduce that the IFSW's claim
of 750,000 social workers worldwide is grossly inaccurate and we can recognize
that the social work profession is growing in all regions of the world.

So for a moment let's forget the numbers and look at what we do know. Social
work professionals are employed in more than 90 percent of the nations of the
world. Schools of social work can be found all regions of the world—in the north,
south, east, and west. Recognize that social work is not unique to the United States
or to the United Kingdom. We can conclude that social work is growing around the
world in both the number of social work educational programs and the number
of nation-based professional membership associations. This worldwide activity is
primarily represented by three global associations: the International Association of
Schools of Social Work, the International Consortium for Social Development,
and the International Federation of Social Workers. In addition, social workers
throughout the world are able to join social work membership associations in their
own countries, similar to those in the United States. In Canada, for example, social
workers may join Association Canadienne des Travailleuses et Travailleurs
Sociaux (Canadian Association of Social Workers); in the United Kingdom, the
British Association of Social Workers is the largest professional social work group;
and the National Association of Social Workers South Africa (NASWSA) is a nongovernmental organization (NGO) that supports social workers and the development of the profession in South Africa.

THE PROFESSIONAL SOCIAL WORKER

Considering the enduring popularity of the social work profession, you may ask
how and why this interest began and why it continues to grow in scope within the
global community. The answer is simple: people across the world and in our own
neighborhoods face similar problems and need the assistance that social workers
provide. When these problems are individual in nature they are referred to as
microsystem problems. Responsibility for finding solutions to microsystem problems often rests squarely on the shoulders of the individual client or family.

---

*Did You Know...According to the Substance Abuse and Mental Health Services
Administration (SAMHSA), professional social workers are the nation's largest group of
mental health services providers.*

For example, when a single older adult falls at home and breaks an arm, he or
she may need to be admitted to a local hospital for treatment. Often after admission,

the emergency room physician refers the case to the **hospital social worker**, who is tasked with assessing the client's situation. Suppose that, during the **assessment** process, the social worker learns that the client has no immediate family and lives alone. Taking into account the needs of the client, the social worker helps develop a plan with the elderly client that ensures provision of the appropriate support and services. In many cases, this includes arranging home health care so that the client can receive medical services in the home (Dziegielewski, 2013). It can also include ensuring that the client has access to nutritious meals by arranging contact with a **Meals on Wheels** program. To increase socialization and provide mealtime activity, the client can be referred to a local neighborhood center's senior citizens' program. Further, individual or group supportive counseling can be provided directly or by referral within the community. The role of the social worker through the micro perspective is essential because this role stresses the individual client's personal and social needs in the assessment and **intervention** processes.

Did You Know…Over 40% of all disaster mental health volunteers trained by the American Red Cross are professional social workers.

A second system often addressed in social work is the **mezzosystem**. Through the mezzo perspective, the social worker highlights the needs of the client by focusing primarily on the environmental systems that can provide assistance. The client is linked directly to support systems that enhance and maximize individual functioning. From a mezzo perspective, family and friends are paramount. This perspective also incorporates those social workers who work in administration as an **agency's** director/chief executive officer, a unit director, or a program supervisor. In both governmental and nonprofit social service agencies, we find that social workers lead many of the programs that a client will need and that they can either initiate or oversee service delivery.

Unfortunately, many problems have much wider roots in broader community or social institutions. Social workers need to be well versed in multiple roles "… from adding a few lines to a **policy** and procedures manual to altering the laws that guide how nations interact" (Ellis, 2008, p. 131). To address these problems a social worker would use what is called a **macrosystem** approach. From the macro perspective, solutions to the problems that clients face must be tied directly to larger systems. As a result, so-called macro practice ranges from working in politics to influence policy formulation to helping neighborhoods organize activities to directly address a local social issue.

For example, providing decent and safe places to sleep for people who are homeless may require advocacy with local and state government. The social worker may need to initiate and organize a citywide movement to open a shelter. Indeed, macro intervention for this population is not as simple to accomplish as an inexperienced observer may think. At a minimum, in order to initiate macro change, the social worker needs to understand housing policy as it affects the homeless. He or she must also be knowledgeable about housing options and shelter alternatives used elsewhere. In addition to this basic knowledge, the social worker must be aware of and anticipate resistance from the community that he or she is trying to serve. It is important to work with the larger community to get everyone to understand why a homeless shelter is needed and to mobilize agreement. However, caution must always be exercised when one is working within the macrosystem; providing a homeless shelter is much more complicated than simply securing the site and the funds to construct a building. In implementing this type of change, the social worker must be sensitive to current community concerns and political issues that can enhance or impede service assistance and progression.

Did You Know...March of each year is designated Social Work Month; recent themes are All People Matter (2014), Weaving Threads of Resilence and Advocacy (2013), Social Work Matters (2012), Social Workers Change Futures (2011), and Social Workers Inspire Community Action (2010).

This list of some of the most serious macrosystem social problems—homelessness, HIV/AIDS, physical and emotional **abuse**, mental health, substance abuse, **poverty**, immigration, health care, and community development—touches on only some of the areas that make up the domain of social work practice. As highlighted by Specht and Courtney (1994), the ultimate goal of the profession is to seek full and complete equality and **social justice** in all communities, whereby all people are given the opportunity to live their lives to the fullest and to achieve their own potential. On first sight, the concept of full and total equality without any form of prejudice or **discrimination** appears to represent a utopian goal that is unattainable. Evaluated more closely, however, the aim of such a community is not that unusual. Helping clients to improve their life situations and their capacity to achieve their full potential has been one of the central forces driving the profession since its modest mid-nineteenth-century beginnings.

TOWARD A DEFINITION OF SOCIAL WORK

What exactly is social work? Interestingly, although it is a well-established profession, any ten people will probably give you ten different answers. One weekend morning at a donut shop in Orlando, Florida, we asked ten people to describe what social workers do. We received the following responses:

- Social workers give out food stamps and money to freeloaders.
- I dunno.
- Don't they work at the welfare office?
- They help abused kids.
- My mom had one while she was in the hospital. She really liked that young gal!
- They work in mental hospitals.
- One helped my wife and I when we adopted our baby. He helped prepare us for parenting and has stayed in touch ever since. Now, some four years later, he still stays in touch.
- It is helping poor individuals to get services.
- Social workers are liberal thinkers that support programs for the poor.
- Help private and public agencies to help individuals in need.

One of the more interesting answers, however, was one from an older gentleman who said, "A social worker? I don't really know. Maybe they work at social events like the Wednesday night bingo game at the rec center." See the activity below, and try this yourself.

Activity…Select ten people either at a local mall or at any other shopping area and ask them, "What is social work?" Write down their answers. Also, take notes on their nonverbal reactions to the question.

The variety of responses illustrates two major points. First, the profession is a diverse one, and this diversity means that the roles and tasks that social workers perform are varied and often poorly defined. Second, our neighbors, members of the general public, are often confused about the profession. Many people simply do not understand exactly what the mission of this diverse profession really is. This confusion is deepened when social work professionals themselves define what they do on the basis of their scope of practice, using job-specific descriptions such as health care social worker, community organizer, adoptions worker, or mental health counselor. Today, the profession of social work remains flexible as it reflects a society where expectations are influenced by a market-driven, business-oriented service delivery system (Franklin, 2001). The diversity and broad purview of social work practice make it difficult to reach a simple all-inclusive definition of social work.

Social work is not the only profession that is difficult to define; however, professions whose tasks are easier to outline are generally received more positively by the community. For example, most people can describe accurately what a dentist, nurse, or physician does, or they can quickly describe the role of a stockbroker or a lawyer. Defining exactly what a social worker does and is expected to do is a lot more complicated. For a moment, think about a dentist. What picture comes to mind? What do you see the dentist doing? Can you describe what her/his office looks like? Now think about a nurse; again, what do you see in your mind's eye? Finally, think about a social worker. Can you visualize a social worker in his or her workplace? What is he or she doing? Do others share the same image?

There is so much confusion about what social workers do that you might have had an experience similar to that of a former student who is now an accomplished social worker: A woman at a holiday party asked what her college major was. She proudly announced, "social work." A disquieting hush spread over the room, and the party seemed to grind to a halt. Some of her relatives looked shocked and glanced around at other family members in astonishment. When her father noted the reaction, he simply shrugged his shoulders and said, "that's nice," noting that this career choice was "just a youthful phase" and that she would change her major before year's end. Today, although she has become a successful university professor of social work, her father and other relatives still refer to her as a psychologist! When asked why they keep making this mistake, they reply that they can usually explain to others what a psychologist does, but defining social work takes a lot more time and effort. "Besides," her father still asks, "is there really that much of a difference?" Although this question may at first seem alarming, it is one that those in the profession must face daily. What further complicates this distinction is the fact that many of these professions do perform many of the same functions, making it difficult to formulate an exact role for social workers, particularly those in what is generally referred to as *direct practice* (Dziegielewski, 2013; Franklin, 2001).

Did You Know...The member countries of the UN maintain missions in cities throughout the United States. You can learn from them about particular customs and cultural nuances that may affect your work with clients. Also, many international laws that affect practice pertain to individual visitors. If you're not sure about a particular situation, contact the relevant UN mission. Finally, a UN mission can provide you with a great deal of information about the welfare system of its home country.

Most social workers, old and new alike, have at least one or two similar stories about how their families reacted when they announced that they had selected social work as a career, and many of the stories will be parallel to the one above. The confusion surrounding what social workers do, as well as the image of them working primarily with the poor and disenfranchised in our communities, complicates efforts to define what social work is—or, indeed, what people perceive it to be. Now, despite the difficulties of making a simple definition, can we define social work?

Let us start by considering some of social work's key attributes. First, the profession generally involves addressing the needs of **at-risk populations** in a community. Second, in our society there is a common belief that people need to be helped and that the community **sanctions**, that is, approves, this helping activity. Third, most of the activity performed and services provided are agency based; social workers provide client services but also possess the business acumen to understand diverse administrative and profit-driven human service systems (Franklin, 2001). Fourth, social work is a profession and therefore requires a professional education as well as clearly defined ethical standards for practice. Becoming aware of and understanding these ethical standards, which are embodied in a professional code of **ethics**, is crucial to approaching professional practice regardless of the employment setting (Freud & Krug, 2002a). Now, let's explore these ideas more fully to develop an understanding of the breadth and depth of the profession.

Thinking about helping people focuses our attention on what social workers actually do. Through programs and intervention services, social workers help people—individuals, families, groups, communities, and organizations—in their day-to-day life situations (see Figure 1). A hallmark of social work helping is its focus on the interaction between person and social environment. Although a psychologist, for example, would consider primarily an individual's psychological state in trying to help, social workers go beyond this to include the interplay between the individual's life situation and social environment.

In the provision of social work services, at-risk populations comprise those people who, for any number of reasons, are vulnerable to any or all societal threats. Children and the elderly are often viewed as at-risk populations. Other people considered at risk are those who may be victimized by a person or group through a series of life events that leaves them susceptible to unwarranted pain and resulting problems. Certainly the larger context affects how we define at-risk populations. For example, the 2009 economic crisis led to home foreclosures and increased unemployment rates in all workforce sectors. Many middle-class individuals and families who had been financially secure found themselves, for reasons beyond their control, placed into significant at-risk situations. Basically we need to recognize that every individual, at any time, may unexpectedly become at risk. Being at risk is not limited to one or two population groups, but crosses all ages, racial and ethnic groups, and socioeconomic statuses.

Similar to other disciplines such as business and law, the social work profession is *sanctioned* to provide certain services. Sanction refers to the official, formal blessing or recognition of the need for a service or program. Professional sanctioning of services comes in many forms, but state licensing or state registration

Figure 1: A mother with her children and stepchildren is outside of a Boys & Girls Club. The club offers after-school, weekend, and summer programs and opportunities for children from first grade through high school.

and professional certification are among the more common types. Community funding agents, such as the United Way or private foundations, also sanction an activity by supporting it financially. When a funding entity such as the United Way supports a social service agency, it is indicating its belief that the services provided are important to the community good. This type of support is often called having *the gold stamp of approval*. Having the legitimacy that comes from such support is essential in gaining community approval. Formalized public (or community) sanctioning of the provision of social services can also protect the public by distinguishing between authorized and unauthorized service delivery.

Agency-based practice consists of social work services generally conducted by or delivered under the auspices of **social welfare** agencies. A social service agency can be public—funded by federal, state, or local tax dollars—or it can be private—funded by donations or foundations and commonly referred to as a nonprofit or in the international community as an NGO. Most practicing social workers are agency based; that is, they are employed by either a public or NGO social services agency. However, a small percentage of social workers do engage in full-time independent, or private practice, professional social work. Independent practitioners are generally educated at the master's degree level or beyond; some states allow bachelor's level social workers to engage in independent practice, but only in very limited situations and while under direct supervision. It is common for social workers, both students and practitioners alike, to want to become private practitioners in mental health and other health-related settings. As will be discussed later, launching a successful private practice is most difficult; the ideal of setting up a sole practitioner clinical practice is unrealistic due a variety of barriers such as restricted and reduced insurance reimbursements, the growth and resulting competitiveness of other helping professions, the significant costs of establishing and maintaining a private practice, and the difficulty of soliciting new clients. Even if one wishes to pursue a private clinical practice, he or she must be cognizant, as acknowledged by most professionals working in this area, that the old notion of long-term clinical therapy has been replaced with brief interventions that clearly focus the social worker-client relationship to emphasize outcomes that are obtained in the fastest, most efficient means possible (Dziegielewski, 2013; Franklin, 2001).

But we are putting the cart in front of the horse and must first identify the basic requirements to be a professional social worker. Being a professional requires, at a minimum, a formal four-year baccalaureate degree or a graduate degree in social work. College/university-based professional education provides the basic preparation for social work practice. Professional social work education takes place in baccalaureate and graduate level degree programs at colleges and universities. Such programs are accredited by the CSWE. Simply stated, a social worker must have a degree in social work from an academic program accredited by the CSWE. Don't worry; we will go into more detail about the council and its sanctioning authority. The bottom line to remember is that a degree in sociology, psychology, or any other course of study does not qualify a person to be a social worker.

Professional social work education begins in the classroom setting. This is expanded and strengthened by agency-based experiences through what is commonly called field education, field practicum, or internships. In the internship, students work in a specific field agency where they practice the skills, apply the theories taught in school, and begin the integration of the entire educational experience, both classroom and field, into the so-called professional self. To further advance their professional education, social workers, following graduation, typically begin working in a social work setting under the direct supervision of an experienced professional social worker while also completing **continuing education** (CE) programs each year. The ongoing CE requirement recognizes the profession's long-standing belief that a professional social worker's education is never ending as new ways of knowing and doing are discovered through research and practice.

The last area among the key components of social work practice has to do with ethics and expected conduct. Each profession is established and coordinated under a professional set of standards, often referred to as a code of ethics, that is designed to govern the moral behavior of those in the field. In social work, there is no one clear-cut code that all social workers must follow. Rather, the professional is bound to the code of a particular membership organization or state licensing board to which he or she belongs. For example, if you are a member of the National Association of Social Workers or the International Federation of Social Workers or the Association of Black Social Workers, you are bound to follow that organization's specified ethical standards; similarly, a licensed professional in Texas is required to abide by the state licensing board's code of conduct. What makes this complicated for the profession and the individual is that there are fifty different state licensing or regulatory boards with their own ethical codes. Recognize that there is no one unified code of ethics in social work. The Association of Social Work Boards (ASWB), similar to professional membership organizations, promotes its own version of an ethical code although the state licensing boards are not required to subscribe to this model. And, as you might have already guessed, the codes of the various state licensing boards differ from each other.

Even with the variety of ethical codes among social work member organizations and state licensing boards, there is a consensus among social workers that the NASW Code of Ethics is the most commonly referenced set of standards. Remember, however, that only NASW members are required to abide by this code unless of course the employing social service agency requires social workers to follow this standard. Through its National Delegate Assembly, the NASW Code of Ethics is updated every so often to ensure its currency and relevance to professional practice. The latest revision to the NASW Code of Ethics, approved by the Delegate Assembly and published in 2008, is included in appendix A of this book; because it is critical to understanding professional conduct, it will be discussed further in subsequent chapters.

In general, ethical and moral issues should always be evaluated in the definition of social work practice (Reamer, 2009). Social workers use the guidelines for professional practice given in the code of ethics to understand their moral and legal obligations in assisting their clients. Social workers entering the field must not only be aware of this document, but they must also agree to adhere to the standards it sets forth. Any questions about moral and ethical practice should be addressed by using the guidelines it provides. Therefore, the centrality of the code of ethics to all practice decisions is crucial to formulating a moral vision within our field that will help to determine both peripheral and procedural practices within the professional helping activities (Freud & Krug, 2002b).

Did You Know...In August 1996, the NASW delegate assembly met in Washington, DC, and updated social work's Code of Ethics to bring it more in line with social work practice. This was the first major revision since 1979. This updated and revised Code of Ethics went into effect on January 1, 1997. The current Code of Ethics was revised by the 2008 NASW Delegate Assembly, again to reflect the changes in practice.

SOCIAL WORK DEFINED

A definition of social work is not easy to formulate or apply. Most would agree, however, that the field of social work involves working actively to change the social, cultural, psychological, and larger societal conditions that most individuals, families, groups, and communities face (O'Hare, 2009). The helping process emphasizes the use of advocacy to create societal conditions that lead to a stronger sense of person-in-situation or person-in-environment; this promotes the community good, which benefits all individuals. According to this perspective, social work is directed to two ends: first, to help resolve the micro (individual) and mezzo (group) issues that clients face, and second to create societal macro (community) changes that prevent or ameliorate such problems for all individuals, families, groups, or communities.

To initiate the helping process, a social worker may begin by working with an individual or family on an issue. This micro level work will continue until the issue is resolved; however, the task of the social worker does not end here (see Figure 2). This is especially true when the social worker recognizes that the causes of the client's problems are not unique to that client. Many seemingly individual problems have deep roots in the policies and procedures of larger institutions. When these problems have the potential to affect others in the community, the social work practitioner must take a macro perspective. If current policies or programs may harm others unless certain changes take place, the social worker is called to action. The worker begins macro intervention and moves to promote changes in the larger system.

For example, Ellen, a social worker employed in a family agency, learned that her client had been evicted from his apartment. After helping the client to find a new apartment, Ellen discovered that the evicting landlord had not followed the procedures outlined in the city's ordinances. Ellen had to decide what to do next. For most social workers the task of helping the client would not be considered complete even though the client had a safe place to stay. The social worker might feel the need to continue helping this client and future potential clients who might

Figure 2: A respite house client writing a note to a social worker who is leaving for a new job. The respite house offers services and weekend-away-from-the-family programs for persons with physical and emotional disabilities. These programs give caregivers and parents a break from their caregiving duties.

also fall victim to this failed system enforcement. In this case, Ellen could begin working on macro issues by contacting city officials to ensure that local ordinances are enforced and to make them aware of the problems that can occur when ordinances are not enforced. Her advocacy efforts could prevent other people in similar circumstances from becoming homeless.

In sum, a social worker's immediate focus is usually on a particular client population, providing service to individuals, couples, or families. These immediate efforts take a micro or mezzo perspective; however, the macro perspective should never be ignored. Service provision in the field of social work cannot be defined simply—in order to be successful it often must go beyond the identified client and include the larger system. Social work is both science and art. A skilled social worker must be knowledgeable about all aspects and perspectives of client helping and flexible in their application. The best prepared social workers are those who recognize the importance of helping as a multifaceted process and who can easily move between microsystems, mezzosystems, and macrosystems with and on behalf of the client populations they serve.

BECOMING A SOCIAL WORKER

People sometimes call themselves social workers even when they do not possess the professional qualification (i.e., a social work degree from a CSWE accredited undergraduate or graduate social work program) needed to be a social worker. Many times newspaper articles, television news broadcasts, and talk radio hosts refer to a social worker whose mishandling of a case led to very negative consequences for an individual or family. The two following case examples are typical.

In the first case, a child abuse report was made to the state child protective services agency, but the child was not removed from the home. A few days later the child died after a severe beating by the caretaker. The media reported that the social worker responsible for the case did not follow through with a proper investigation and ignored a variety of information and signals. The community was given the impression that, if the social worker had done his job, the child would still be alive. Unfortunately, there is no simple formula for handling such situations or for avoiding them in the first place—even though we want there to be one. The glaring fact is that a child died and no one was able to help. This is disturbing to everyone, and it is difficult to look beyond the initial fact. However, if the event is not examined more deeply, other children may be placed in harm's way.

It is also important to look beyond the media's simplified portrayal of the situation: Due to cutbacks and limited funding, or for other reasons, the person responsible for the investigation may not be a social work professional at all. If you look closely, this person's formal title may be caseworker or child protective services worker but not social worker. This may be somewhat puzzling given that the work is typically associated with a social worker. Thus, it is fair to ask why this person is not called a social worker. In most states, the term social work is a *protected title* through state licensing; a protected title means that only a person licensed by the state may be called a social worker. This so-called title protection is essentially a consumer safeguard to inform the client that the practitioner meets standards set by the state and, in effect, is sanctioned to provide the service. In the case around the child's death, the college degree and professional training of the alleged social worker were not in the area of social work. His college education and training were in the liberal arts and he did not have the formal course work in the problem assessment and intervention methods essential to social work practice. Similarly, his education did not include the theories and practice frameworks necessary to understand and integrate the micro, mezzo, and macro perspectives required to address client situations and problems.

The second case involves a young family with a reported case of child neglect. The mother had been sending her children to school without their coats, and the weather was too cold for such attire. A state social service worker—a nondegreed social worker—visited the house and agreed that the mother seemed unfit to handle the needs of her children. The state worker reported that the mother's responses to questions were very basic and brief and that she did not appear to understand the seriousness of what she was allowing the children to do. He recommended that all the children be removed from the home before any harm came to them.

Now this case gets a bit complicated, but stay with us. One of this text's authors was involved in an unexpected request by a client who wanted to be discharged from a hospital against medical advice. The author met with the client, who had recently suffered a small stroke and had been immediately admitted to the hospital; he was the husband of the woman who was facing child neglect charges. The client feared that his wife could not care for their children properly and he needed to go home immediately. He stated that his wife is moderately retarded and that he had always handled most of the child care. After meeting with the client the author placed several phone calls to help secure child care coverage and, as a result, the client agreed to stay in the hospital for the remainder of his treatment.

Just as you might think this was successfully resolved, well, it turns out this was not the end of case.

Later that day, the client became very upset when a family friend, who stopped by the hospital for a visit, told him that his children were about to be removed from his home. The author was called by the floor staff. In working with the client, who was clearly angry and upset, the author received permission to release information about the situation (remember, the author's work was with the husband only); the author contacted the state social services worker who had decided to remove the children from their home. The author shared with the state worker the plan that had been developed to care for the children. The state social services worker reconsidered the removal decision, and because support was in place, decided that the children would not be removed from home.

In debriefing the case with the state social services worker, the author learned that he was obviously frustrated. His caseload did not give him time to explore disposition options. He was also concerned that a child had died several weeks before in a case very similar to this one. Because of the attention paid to that case, he felt it was best not to take a chance on this one. He also did not realize that the mother had a moderate developmental disability; he thought she might be on drugs or merely resistant to intervention. In trying to explain why he made such a limited assessment, the state social service worker said that he did not realize the significance of the client's behavior. He shared that he had limited on-the-job training and that he often used opportunities for in-service provision to catch up on his paperwork. Moreover, although he had a four-year professional degree, as required by his state, his degree was in physical education.

Cases like these are all too common. For whatever reason—be it a desire to cut costs or a lack of recognition for professional intervention—there is a widespread but false impression that anyone can be a social worker and that anyone can handle the tasks and responsibilities expected of a social worker. It is common for state governments to redefine or reclassify a position that was once titled social worker

I or social worker II under a different title such as child protective services worker I or mental health worker II. This is called *declassification*; it allows the public agency to hire an individual without a social work degree at a far lower salary, and as a result, to realize a cost savings for the state.

Sadly, there are even people who believe that they can be their own social workers. For example, a plumber working for one of the authors asked her what she did for a living. When he heard that she was a social worker, he smiled and said, "Oh, never needed one of them before; always do my own social work." When asked what he meant, he said, "Don't need somebody else to solve my problems. I can solve them for my family and myself. I had a lot of training on how to deal with people in school, and that helped." Such comments are very disturbing because they show that many people don't know what social workers do. Furthermore, it was very tempting for the social worker to reply with "Yes, I know—I used to do my own plumbing too, but your expertise is why you are here now." When people assume that social work is simply everyday problem solving, they conclude that anyone can do it, no matter one's education (in fact, a university education is not necessary). The irony in this statement is as pronounced as believing that everyone can do their own plumbing; but what happens when you try to fix your sink drain and you end up breaking the garbage disposal? You thought you knew what you were doing, but, in fact, you only made the problem worse. Just as plumbing requires a specific set of skills and knowledge, so too does social work. Simply thinking you can do it does not mean that you can.

Confusion also exists among helping and counseling professionals about who can be a qualified social worker. For example, at a public hearing held by the Florida Board of Mental Health Counselors, Marriage and Family Therapists, and Clinical Social Workers, a board member opposed the licensing of BSW and MSW social workers who do not do clinical social work. A marriage and family therapist added, "Anyone can do social work. There is such a thing as social work with a small *s* and *w*."

On the surface this statement seems to make sense, but it only reflects the idea around "anyone can do plumbing." Yes, all social workers must have good hearts, be compassionate, and willing to help others. But do these qualities alone make someone a professional social worker?

Let's make a comparison. Suppose you have a sore throat, feel somewhat congested, and have hot and cold sweats. Your roommate says, "You may be coming down with the flu. Why don't you take brand X over-the-counter cold pills, use some brand Y throat lozenges, and stay home and rest?" This could be very good helpful advice, but does this mean that your roommate is a medical doctor, albeit with a small *m* and *d*? Of course not—it seems crazy to even suggest that. Everyone knows that a medical doctor must have a formal education and supervised experience in a medical setting. You can't hang out a shingle that says *MD* just because you think you can diagnose some physical ailments. See Box 1 for a list of different definitions of social work by some of the profession's key leadership groups.

Box 1. Various Definitions of Social Work*

National Association of Social Workers

The professional activity of helping individuals, groups, or communities enhance or restore their capacity for social functioning and creating societal conditions favorable to this goal.

Council on Social Work Education, Commission on Educational Policy and Commission on Accreditation (2015), *2015 educational policy and accreditation standards for baccalaureate and master's social work programs* (p.5). Alexandria, VA: Author.

The purpose of the social work profession is to promote human and community well-being. Guided by a person-in-environment framework, a global perspective, respect for human diversity, and knowledge based on scientific inquiry, the purpose of social work is actualized through its quest for social and economic justice, the prevention of conditions that limit **human rights**, the elimination of poverty, and the enhancement of the quality of life for all persons, locally and globally.

International Federation of Social Workers and the International Association of Schools of Social Work

The social work profession promotes social change, problem solving in human relationships, and the empowerment and liberation of people to enhance well-being. Utilizing theories of human behavior and social systems, social work intervenes at the points where people interact with their environments. Principles of human rights and social justice are fundamental to social work.

Association of Social Work Boards, Model Practice Act

The practice of baccalaureate level social work means the application of social work theory, knowledge, methods, ethics, and the professional use of self to restore or enhance social, psychosocial, or biopsychosocial functioning of individuals, couples, families, groups, organizations, and communities. Baccalaureate level social work is basic **generalist practice** that includes assessment; planning; intervention; evaluation; case management; information and referral; counseling; supervision; consultation; education; advocacy; community organization; and the development, implementation, and administration of policies, programs, and activities.

The practice of master's level social work means the application of social work theory, knowledge, methods and ethics, and the professional use of self to restore or enhance social, psychosocial, or biopsychosocial functioning of individuals, couples, families, groups, organizations, and communities. Master's level social work practice includes the application of specialized knowledge and advanced practice skills in the areas of assessment, treatment planning, implementation and evaluation; case management; information and referral; counseling; supervision; consultation; education; research; advocacy; community organization; and the development, implementation, and administration of policies, programs and activities.

The Social Work Dictionary (Barker, 2003)

The applied science of helping people achieve an effective level of psychological functioning and effecting societal changes to enhance the well-being of all people.

*Visit the websites of various social work baccalaureate, master's, and doctoral programs to see how the various undergraduate and graduate programs define social work.

So what are the requirements for becoming a social worker? Certainly there are personal attributes that a social worker must have; many of these characteristics are common among people, no matter their education or chosen career. First, a social worker must like working with people. A social worker is involved with people from all walks of life. These people, who come from widely varying backgrounds, can have ideas and expectations very different from those of the social worker. Being aware of and sensitive to the beliefs of others is not always a simple task. In dealing with different people a social worker must really want to understand the troubles that others face. So first of all, a good social worker must genuinely like working with diverse individuals.

Second, a social worker must want to help people. A professional social worker encounters all sorts of client problems, ranging from abuse and neglect to homelessness and from mental health issues to community-based substance abuse problems. A good social worker wants to help his or her clients in their efforts to figure out what is going on and how best to resolve their problems.

Third, a social worker wants the community to be a better place for all people. Through his or her professional activities, a social worker helps a specific client while at the same time trying to better the community for all people. For example, ideally social workers want to end poverty and its debilitating effects on people and communities. Social workers envision communities where all people have access to decent housing and health care. They also strive to end unfair treatment of individuals, the *isms* that face millions of people today—racism, sexism, and

ageism. The personal traits that foster the desire to work with and to help individuals, families, and communities are critical ingredients in creating a social worker. To finish the mix, however, these personal traits must be complemented by professional education and training. In the United States, professional social work education takes place in baccalaureate or graduate level degree programs at specific colleges and universities.

Did You Know...The CSWE is the only national standard-setting and accrediting body for social work education in the United States. It was organized in 1952 through the merger of two professional educational associations that coordinated baccalaureate and graduate programs, respectively.

For any U.S. college or university to offer a recognized social work educational program, it must meet the **accreditation** standards of the Council on Social Work Education (CSWE). The accreditation standards build upon CSWE's **Educational Policy and Accreditation Standards (EPAS)**, which was updated in 2015 (CSWE, Commission on Educational Policy, 2015). The CSWE is authorized by the Council for Higher Education Accreditation (CHEA) to set and oversee educational standards for social work programs across the United States and is the sole social work accreditation authority in the United States. The CSWE was first established in 1952; at its inception there were 59 graduate schools (i.e., MSW programs) and 19 undergraduate (i.e., BSW) programs (Watkins & Holmes, 2008). By spring 2015, these numbers had increased to 504 BSW and 235 MSW programs.

Other countries have their own accrediting bodies for social work education. For example, the Joint University Council for Social and Public Administration oversees social work educational programs in the United Kingdom, Finnish programs of social work are associated with the Scandinavian Committee of Schools of Social Work, Brazilian schools of social work are members of the National Association of Schools of Social Work, and Indian social work educational programs are members of the Association of Schools of Social Work. International accreditation associations can be found in a number of different nations and, as might be expected, the accreditation standards generally vary by country because they reflect the unique cultural, historical, and regional differences of a particular nation-state. Although there are numerous accrediting associations throughout the world, in 2000 the International Association of Schools of Social Work created a joint initiative with the International Federation of Social Workers to establish global standards (http://www.iassw-aiets.org/index.php?option=com_content&task=blog category&id=28&Itemid=49). These standards attempt to develop consistency among social work educational programs around the world. The global standards, however, do not hold any authority from a particular nation or university. These are simply basic guidelines that are extremely useful for programs in nations that do not have an accrediting association such as the CSWE.

Regardless of where a professional social work program is located, it must withstand the rigorous scrutiny of an accreditation process, which entails the validation of explicit standards of practice (Barker, 2003). Curriculum format and delivery, which are the heart of the educational experience, must be coherent, built on a series of specific behavioral competencies and a supervised **field placement** or internship experience; through an internship the social work professional learns to apply in the field environment what has been taught in the classroom. Standards require that the faculty members who teach students possess certain types of degrees and in addition have professional work experience that can facilitate the education process. Accreditation standards also specify that a variety of institutional (e.g., college or university) resources be available. Finally, an accredited program must identify specific behavioral outcomes that all graduates are expected to demonstrate at the end of their course of study (see the activity below and look at the accreditation document from your own program).

Activity...Ask to review your social work program's latest self-study for accreditation. Compare this self-study to the CSWE's Educational Policy and Accreditation Standards and The Education Policy and Accreditation Standards Handbook. In order to be accredited, your program must conform to these standards. Being part of an accredited program is important for your future development.

Attending and graduating from an accredited social work program is crucial for the future social work professional. Remember that only a graduate of an accredited social work program is recognized as a professional social worker. Because CSWE accreditation standards apply nationally, the public recognizes that a graduate of a BSW program in California has completed the same minimum educational requirements as a graduate of a BSW program in New Hampshire or Georgia. Uniformity of foundation content throughout the country means that social workers can be hired in any state and meet specific educational requirements for employment and subsequent licensing in the field. This is particularly important for employers and supervisors of social work professionals because they can assume that a particular educational background implies familiarity with certain content. Many employers report that this standardization of course content across social work programs makes social workers predictable employees in regard to what they have and have not been trained to do.

A BSW education prepares individuals for entry or beginning level social work practice—commonly referred to as *generalist practice*. Baccalaureate studies occur in the junior and senior years of study. An MSW education prepares individuals for advanced practice, also called *specialization* or *concentration practice*. (We will explore advanced practice in more detail in chapters 5 and 6.) Although an MSW program typically requires two years of full-time study, a person with a BSW degree may be eligible for advanced standing in a graduate program, thus bypassing up to half of the graduate coursework through mastery of foundation competencies. The number of courses waived or exempted as a result of BSW study is different for each graduate program; the waived courses range from a maximum of one full year of full-time study to no courses waived. The decision on how to implement an advanced standing program and what courses to waive is made by the faculty of a particular social work program, not the CSWE.

Did You Know... The abbreviation BSW stands for baccalaureate social worker and MSW for master social worker. The abbreviations BSSW and MSSW also signify degrees in social work, bachelor of science in social work and master of science in social work. The most advanced degrees in social work are the DSW and the PhD. In most circles the MSW or the MSSW is considered the highest level needed to practice in the field.

Social work education is a very large enterprise in the United States. According to the CSWE Commission on Accreditation, in 2015 there were 744 total accredited programs, of which 596 were at the baccalaureate level and 235 offered the master's degree; there were an additional 32 BSW and MSW programs in candidacy, e.g., preaccreditation (CSWE, 2014). According to 2012 CSWE statistics, 10,929 full- and part-time faculty members were involved in the more than 700 baccalaureate and graduate programs (CSWE, 2014). In 2012, the CSWE reported that 116,340 individuals were enrolled in all levels of social work education, including full- and part-time students; there were 60,077 social work students working toward BSWs, 53,835 toward MSWs, and approximately 2,428 toward doctorates. In 2011–12, accredited social work programs awarded 38,694 social work degrees in the United States (for updated statistics, go to CSWE.org). In 2014, there were slightly more than 870 colleges and universities offering academic programs leading to a doctoral degree, either a PhD or a **DSW** (doctorate in social work); such programs are not accredited by the CSWE, however. As a result, doctoral education varies greatly from school to school, with a program's focus set by its faculty's values and beliefs. Individuals pursuing doctoral degrees in social work will for the most part be employed in academic settings, although some will work in agency settings, primarily in administration; supervisory positions; or research.

MEMBERSHIP ASSOCIATIONS FOR SOCIAL WORKERS

All professionals have the opportunity to belong to membership organizations or associations that represent their interests (see the activity below and consider attending an NASW meeting to see what it is like). Attending a meeting can be helpful because an association provides professional self-identity and an opportunity to meet colleagues in order to discuss ideas and share innovations in practice.

> *Activity...Gather information about your local unit of the NASW. Ask one of your instructors or a social worker in the community when your local unit of NASW will be meeting. Try to attend the next meeting. Also, find out when the state board of directors of the NASW meets next. These meetings occur several times each year and are held somewhere in the state. Try to attend one of these meetings to see the process firsthand.*

The NASW is the largest membership organization for social workers. According to NASW's website, its membership in 2015 totaled 132,000 persons, which makes the NASW the largest social work membership organization in the world. One important point to recognize is that membership is voluntary. Indeed, in the most recent edition of its annual publication, the *Occupational Outlook Handbook*, the U.S. Department of Labor reported that in 2014 there were about 607,300 professional social work positions in the United States, which means that slightly more than one-fifth (21.7%) of all social work professionals are members of the NASW.

The NASW is not the sole professional organization and, as its membership numbers indicate, it does not represent the majority of social workers in the United States. Nevertheless, it remains the largest social work membership organization in the world; consequently, social workers should understand its role and function. The NASW was first organized in 1955, with the merger of five special-interest organizations: the American Association of Group Workers, the American Association of Medical Social Workers, the American Association of Psychiatric Social Workers, the American Association of Social Workers, and the National Association of School Social Workers. In addition, two study groups joined the new organization: the Association for the Study of Community Organization and the Social Work Research Group. The ideas of all these groups were merged to unify the profession (Alexander, 1995). Today, the national offices of the NASW are located in Washington, DC, only a few blocks from the U.S. Capitol.

The NASW regards itself as a bottom-up members' organization. What this means is that governance and direction are established from below and responsibility lies with the units and chapters in each state. Each state has its own NASW

Name: Jacqueline Richardson-Melecio

Place of residence: Albany, NY

College/university degrees: University at Albany, Albany, NY, PhD candidate, BA, MSW

Present position: Assistant executive director, National Association of Social Workers, New York State chapter; president, New Heights Consulting, Provider: leadership development, diversity training, cultural competency, board training, and team building

Bio statement: Jacqueline Melecio is a master's level social worker and PhD candidate with over ten years of extensive experience in the administration and development of human and behavioral health service programs. Her work as a human service provider has afforded her experience in the development of programs and delivery of services aimed at addressing a broad range of service needs, such as youth at risk; housing; mental health; jail diversion; employment; mental health in the workplace; and adult, children, and family services. Throughout her career, she has worked with a broad range of providers, as well as various funding entities including county, state, federal, and private. These initiatives have included collaboration with diverse groups of service providers, populations, and communities. She has dedicated her career to serving those most in need and to addressing the existing disparities of current service delivery systems. She is the president of her own consulting service, New Heights Consulting, providing organizations with cultural competency training, strategic planning, and various tailored workshops aimed at meeting the needs of both private and public organizations. Please visit www.newheightscon.com for more information.

Previous work experience/volunteer experience

Management, human services: Managing director, Mental Health Association in New York State; program director, Hispanic Outreach Services Catholic Charities; president, New Heights Consulting; member of New York State Office of Mental Health, Multicultural Advisory Committee; training consultant: diversity training, leadership development, and strategic planning.

Teaching/training: Adjunct instructor, University at Albany, St. Rose College, Schenectady Community College. Courses (master's level): multicultural counseling, mental health policy, cultural competency presentations; (bachelor's level): Spanish for human service providers, sociology.

Diversity training experience: Providing workshops on integrating cultural competency in service delivery, assessment, and evaluation. Training programs have been developed and presented at for-profit and nonprofit agencies, statewide and national conferences, and college campuses.

Leadership development: Providing workshops with aid organizations to build their capacity through teaching, assessment, strategic planning, and building needed supports and services.

What is your favorite social work story? My favorite social work story occurred prior to my career as a social worker. When I reflect upon my community and the people who surrounded me my whole life, I do not have any doubt about what inspired me to be a social worker. Although predominately Hispanic, my community included a wonderful mix of various ethnic and racial groups. The early evenings of hot summer days were made up of unscheduled gatherings of young and old on the building steps. The crowd would usually extend out into the sidewalk; parked cars would sometimes be used as benches, and folding chairs and steps would also serve as seats. The grown-ups chattered while they rested from a long day at work. Some children played games like hopscotch, catch, or hide and seek while a few sat and talked and shared a joke or two. All the laughter, talking, screaming, music, and pitter-patter of little feet served as the backdrop to what I deem social work in its most natural state—resource sharing. At these gatherings, one saw resource sharing in many forms: referrals, housing assistance, job coaching and employment services, and counseling. It all happened so naturally every day and just because you were a part of the community, a neighbor in need, another human being. So my favorite social work story is also my inspiration for being a social worker: being part of a profession committed to making a difference in the lives of others because it is the right thing to do—being a good neighbor.

What would be the one thing you would change in the community if you had the power to do so? It is challenging to think of just one thing to change. Access to health care, homelessness, and hunger are all things at the top of my list. If I had the power to do so, I would aim to address each of these basic need areas. I would address the quality of services and access to care and would work toward ending hunger and homelessness in the world.

---

chapter, and each chapter is further subdivided into regional units. Each local unit covers a geographical area small enough to allow members to attend meetings and programs together.

After joining the NASW, each member is assigned to a state chapter and then to a local unit that reflects his or her home location. Most local units conduct quarterly or monthly meetings. These gatherings run the gamut of formality, from the very formal meeting with an invited speaker to the informal after-work get-together. Unit meetings offer social workers from the same geographical area an opportunity to meet on a regular basis and strengthen their professional networks.

The state chapter coordinates activities between the local units and offers ongoing educational opportunities, known as continuing education, around the state. A significant function of the state chapter is its political activity with state and local governments. The state chapter brings to the attention of its membership issues in the state legislature that could affect the profession or clients being served. Most state chapters provide their members with a monthly newsletter as well as professional and social activities such as an annual or biannual convention. The state chapter is staffed by a paid employee, generally a social worker, and is governed by a board of directors elected by the membership of the state and serving for a prescribed term.

Did You Know... NASW News, *the monthly newspaper of the NASW, is the primary source of news about opportunities for social workers across the United States. Each issue includes a classified section that lists job vacancies by state.*

The national office of the NASW comprises divisions ranging from membership services to political advocacy to publications. The national office's focus is on issues that affect the profession as a whole, thus leaving state-specific matters to the state chapters. The national office is responsible for carrying out the policy of the national board of directors, which is made up of elected social work members from across the country. The national office also publishes a monthly newspaper that provides an exhaustive overview of social work around the country. Other member benefits include opportunities to purchase life and malpractice insurance and reduced registration fees for national meetings (see box 2).

Box 2. Benefits of NASW Membership
- Subscription to the *Journal of Social Work*
- Subscription to *NASW News*
- State chapter and local unit memberships
- Credit and loan programs
- Hospital indemnity option
- Toll-free telephone to the NASW Information Center
- Representation on Capitol Hill in Washington, DC, and in state legislatures
- Discounts for NASW-sponsored continuing education programs
- Subscription discounts for specialty journals
- Car rental discounts
- Credit card option
- Term life insurance options
- Malpractice insurance
- Job link

Through local units, state chapters, and the national office of the NASW, individual social workers have numerous opportunities to affect the profession. Individual social workers mold the profession and give direction to future activities by holding leadership positions; serving on various committees; and attending local, state, and national meetings. Social workers belong to groups in order to support specific interests. Such groups provide the individual practitioner a connection with others who share similar professional interests and concerns while broadening the sphere of professional influence and encouraging the ongoing development of research in practice.

No one is quite sure how many different professional social work membership groups exist in the United States. In addition to the NASW, there are more than fifty other national membership or professional social work associations in the United States. These various groups are based on a variety of attributes ranging from race and ethnicity to practice interests (see box 3 for examples of professional associa-

---

Box 3. Examples of Social Work Membership Organizations

Advocacy Network for Social Work Education and Research
American Association of Industrial Social Workers
American Association for Psychoanalysis in Clinical Social Work
Association for Community Organization and Administration
Association of VA Social Workers
Council on Social Work Education
Influencing State Policy
International Federation of Social Work
Latino Social Work Organization
National Association of Black Social Workers
National Association of Oncology Social Workers
National Association of Puerto Rican/Hispanic Social Workers
National Federation of Societies of Clinical Social Work
National Indian Social Workers Association
North American Association of Christians in Social Work
Professional Association of Social Workers in HIV and AIDS
Rural Social Work Caucus
Social Welfare Alliance
Social Workers HELPING Social Workers
Society for Social Work Administrators in Health Care

For additional information on these and other social work organizations and links to their websites, go to http://www.socialworkers.org/swportal/swo1

---

tions), with total members ranging from a few hundred to a few thousand individuals. In 2002, the NASW convened a meeting of the presidents and chairs of these various associations, known as the Social Work Summit II, to meet and discuss common issues. The common feeling was that the profession could be strengthened if its membership groups had a better understanding of other such groups, their issues, and potential collaborations. In 2004 the CSWE brought together the leadership of the national educational associations, as well as the NASW, and this group has since met annually. Most special interest groups sponsor an annual meeting, and some publish a journal or newsletter. These organizations' membership rolls are much smaller than that of the NASW; they often do not have state or local units, and they generally do not have paid staff to run the organization.

One would think that the large number of social work membership groups combined with the low membership for the NASW would send a clear message that the profession needs to reorganize its efforts on behalf of individual practitioners and clients. As it is, there is no one organization that is able to claim that it represents all of social work. In effect the potential political clout and influence of a unified group—made up of over 600,000 persons, 700 undergraduate and graduate educational programs that are found in every state, and some 500 different public and private colleges and universities—are lost. Recognizing the potential gains and influence that social work might have as a unified group, eight social work associations—the NASW, the CSWE, Baccalaureate Program Directors, the Group for the Advancement of Doctoral Education in Social Work (GADE), the Institute for the Advancement of Social Work Research, the St. Louis Group, the Association of Social Work Boards, the National Association of Deans and Directors, and the Society for Social Work Research—met in 2007 at the Wingspread Conference Center in Racine, Wisconsin, to discuss unification of the profession. The question to be considered was whether it was necessary and possible for the various social work professional associations to come together as one professional association similar to those formed by other professions such as law, medicine, and psychology. Referred to simply as Wingspread, the meeting was historic in many ways. First, it provided a forum for open discussion on the social work profession and its relevancy in the twenty-first century in an increasingly turbulent world. Second, participants were forced to honestly assess their respective associations as well as those of others. Finally, participants had to move outside of their own interests and consider the best interests of the profession and the clients served. Meeting participants unanimously agreed on and signed a resolution calling for professional unification by 2012. A small work group was established to begin working on the details for creating a new professional association. Sadly, at the end of one year of work, the work group concluded that this would not happen because some associations felt that their organizational structures were too complex to fold into a new association. So today the profession remains disjointed, splintered into many special-interest groups and membership associations, some working together better than others.

SUMMARY

Social work is a diverse profession that is not easily defined and, as a result, is often misunderstood by the general public and the greater community. One thing remains evident: social work is a profession of people helping people. Despite possible confusion about the daily activities of social workers, there is growing recognition that social work plays an important role in today's society. Children, seniors, families, communities, the rich, the poor, and the middle class are all represented among the many clients who benefit directly from social work. Social work clients are found in all quarters of the country. Social work too is a global profession, similar to other professions, with many of its efforts designed to assist and stimulate an informed practice strategy rich in methods designed to incorporate strategy at the grassroots level.

Today thousands of people studying in colleges and universities are striving to become professional social workers. It is these new social work professionals who will steer the profession and support the mission of micro, mezzo, and macro intervention well into the twenty-first century.

Questions to Think About

1. What do you say to a friend who, after learning that you want to be a social worker, states, "You won't make any money doing that"?

2. What do you think a meeting of professional social workers, such as a local NASW unit meeting, would be like?

3. Do you know any professional social workers? What personal qualities do they have that you think might be useful for a social worker?

4. Do you think there should be one professional membership association that all social workers belong to or does the variety of special interest groups, as discussed in this chapter, create better opportunities for members?

5. Why do you think there is a general misunderstanding of social work?

6. What are some ways in which social workers could help to educate family and friends about what they do?

7. To what extent, if any, is social work different in other nations such as South Africa, India, or Viet Nam compared to the United States?

8. How will the growth of the social work profession in China (e.g., 3,000,000 degreed social workers by the year 2020) affect social work in the United States and other countries in the world?

REFERENCES

Alexander, C. (1995). Distinctive dates in social welfare history. In R. Edwards & J. G. Hopps (Eds.), *Encyclopedia of social work* (19th ed., pp. 2631–2647). Washington, DC: NASW Press.

Barker, R. L. (2003). *The social work dictionary* (5th ed.). Washington, DC: NASW Press.

Council on Social Work Education. (2014). *Accreditation.* Retrieved from http://www.cswe.org/Accreditation.aspx

Council on Social Work Education, Commission on Educational Policy and Commission on Accreditation. (2015). *2015 educational policy and accreditation standards for baccalaureate and master's social work programs.* Alexandria, VA: Author. Retrieved from http://cswe.org/Accreditation/EPASRevision.aspx

Dziegielewski, S. F. (2013). *The changing face of health care social work: Opportunities and challenges for professional practice* (3rd ed.). New York: Springer.

Ellis, R. A. (2008). Policy practice. In K. M. Sowers & C. N. Dulmus (Series Eds.) & I. C. Colby (Vol. Ed.), *Comprehensive handbook of social work and social welfare: Social policy and policy practice* (vol. 4, pp. 129–143). Hoboken, NJ: Wiley.

Franklin, C. (2001). Coming to terms with the business of direct practice social work. *Research on Social Work Practice, 11*, 235–244.

Freud, S., & Krug, S. (2002a). Beyond the code of ethics, Part 1: Complexities of ethical decision making in social work practice. *Families in Society, 83*, 474–482.

Freud, S., & Krug, S. (2002b). Beyond the code of ethics, Part 2: Dual relationships revisited. *Families in Society, 83*, 483–493.

Leung, P., Barretta-Herman, A., Littlechild, B., & Parada, H. (2013, June 24). Schools of social work in Asia Pacific Region: Challenges, trends and issues in 2010. Juried paper presented at the International Conference on Children and Youth, Phnom Penh, Cambodia.

Melville, H. (1993). *Moby Dick.* Hertfordshire, UK: Wordsworth Editions.

National Association of Social Workers. (2008). *Code of ethics of the National Association of Social Workers.* Washington, DC: Author. Retrieved from http://www.socialworkers.org/pubs/code/code.asp

National Association of Social Workers. (2014a). *NASW membership.* Retrieved from https://www.socialworkers.org/nasw/default.asp

National Association of Social Workers. (2014b). *Social work portal: A resource tool for social work.* Retrieved from: http://www.socialworkers.org/swportal/swo1/

O'Hare, T. (2009). *Essential skills of social work practice: Assessment, intervention, and education.* Chicago: Lyceum Books.

Outline of China's national plan for medium and long-term education reform and development (2010-2020). (2010). Beijing, China. Retrieved from http://r.search.yahoo.com/_ylt=A0SO8yNBrX1VR3wAnkJXNyoA;_ylu=X3oDMTByb2lvbXVuBGNvbG8Dz3ExBHB vcwMxBHZ0aWQDBHNlYwNzcg—/RV=2/RE=1434328513/RO=10/RU=http%3a%2f%2fplanipolis.iiep.unesco.org%2fupload%2fChina%2fChina_National_Long_Term_Educational_Reform_Development_2010-2020_eng.pdf/RK=0/RS=J0pVpFHFtBwWIlhgyYy5AnjkgWc-

Reamer, F. G. (2009). Ethical issues in social work. In A. Roberts (Ed.), *Social workers' desk reference* (2nd ed., pp. 115–120). New York: Oxford University Press.

Specht, H., & Courtney, M. (1994). *Unfaithful angels.* New York: Free Press.

Ting, W., & Zhang, H. (2012). Flourishing in the spring? Social work, social work education and field education in China. *China Journal of Social Work, 5,* 201–222.

U.S. Department of Labor. (2014). *Occupational outlook handbook, 2014–15 edition.* Retrieved from http://www.bls.gov/ooh/community-and-social-service/social-workers.htm#tab-6

Watkins, J. M., & Holmes, J. (2008). Educating for social work. In K. M. Sowers & C. N. Dulmus (Series Eds.) & B. W. White (Vol. Ed.), *Comprehensive handbook of social work and social welfare: The profession of social work* (vol. 1, pp. 25–36). Hoboken, NJ: Wiley.

CHAPTER 2

SOCIAL WELFARE: A SYSTEM'S RESPONSE TO PERSONAL ISSUES AND PUBLIC PROBLEMS

WHEN YOU HEAR THE WORDS *SOCIAL WELFARE*, WHAT COMES TO mind? Many people think of cash assistance to the poor, child protective services, food stamps (note—the **food stamp program** no longer exists, having been replaced by the Supplemental Nutritional Assistant Program (SNAP), or low-income housing. Before we begin to delve into social welfare, its meaning, and whether these examples are accurate, let's first test your knowledge of welfare with the following quiz. We expect that, as a beginning professional interested in this field, some of your answers will be right and others will be wrong; just give it your best guess.

WELFARE QUIZ

1. What is the Supplemental Nutrition Assistance Program?
    a. the former Food Stamp Program
    b. a prenatal food program
    c. federal government support for a food program limited to seniors
    d. faith-based food programs

2. Who makes up the majority (more than 50%) of people receiving public assistance?
    a. mothers and their children   b. unemployed adults
    c. senior citizens   d. single females

3. In the United States more minorities than Anglo/White individuals live in poverty.
    a. true   b. false

4. Many individuals who receive welfare benefits have children just to get more money from the government.

     a. true   b. false

5. When we talk about the unemployment rate, we are referring to those people who are not working at the present time.

     a. true   b. false

6. The amount given to the poor in a welfare check is the same in all states.

     a. true   b. true, but prorated for family size   c. false

7. More than half the people who receive welfare could be working but choose not to.

     a. true   b. false

8. Which of the following groups are not considered to be welfare recipients by the U.S. government (circle all that apply)?

    a. schoolchildren   b. seniors receiving social security
    c. armed forces veterans   d. Supplemental Nutritional Assistance
    e. college students receiving   recipients
        Pell grants   f. Medicare recipients

9. Temporary Assistance to Needy Families (TANF) is the only federal program that provides cash assistance to poor families.

     a. true   b. false

10. In your own words define *social welfare*.

Now turn to the back of this chapter to find the correct answers and see how you did. You'll find no answer to question 10. After you read this chapter, come back and answer question 10 again. Be sure to compare your two responses to see if your first response is different from your second.

Are you surprised by some of the answers? Think about which questions you got wrong and what you learned from this brief quiz. Clearly, social welfare is a very complicated system that is often misunderstood.

In this chapter we will discuss the dimensions of social welfare—in particular, what is meant by the term. We will also direct attention to the role of the social work profession as well as that of each individual social worker within our current social welfare system.

TOWARD A DEFINITION OF SOCIAL WELFARE

To begin our discussion of the current social welfare system, we would like you to try this exercise. To prepare, take a piece of paper and a pencil and get ready to write down some of your ideas. First, think of your hometown or the community where you were raised. Second, imagine that you have the ability to make it into what you consider the ideal place to live. What kinds of services would be needed to improve this neighborhood or community, bringing it to the perfection that Specht and Courtney (1994) suggest is the profession's goal?

Respect and Dignity: A Social Worker's Premise

Use the following list of questions to suggest possible ideas and guide your thinking on this topic:

Housing and employment

1. Would everyone have safe and affordable housing?
2. Would everyone be able to find employment?
3. Would employment pay well and include social and health benefits?

Education and services

4. Would the education of the young be given top priority?
5. Would the community help all schools to get the services and supplies they need (e.g., fully equipped classrooms and state-of-the-art technology), public and private alike?
6. Would a safe learning environment be provided?

Community safety and security

7. Would senior citizens be protected from abuse and neglect?
8. Would senior citizens have access to the services they need to complete their activities of daily living?
9. Would children be protected from exploitation and abuse?
10. Would **domestic violence** be tolerated, and what options would be available to those who are victimized?
11. Would discrimination based on race, color, age, sexual orientation, and the like be tolerated?
12. Would food services be provided to those who cannot afford to buy their own food?

Your own list probably includes many more considerations that you feel are essential to address. Nevertheless, we believe that if you compared your list with someone else's, you'd be surprised at how similar the two lists are. Most people agree that, in an ideal community, all people are treated with respect and dignity (see Figure 1). Further, most people agree that, for a community to be responsive, it needs to be a place where members are valued for who they are and what they can offer to their community.

> *Did You Know…According to the federal agency SAMHSA (Substance Abuse and Mental Health Services Administration), in 2011, 18.9 million adults in the United States had experienced substance use disorder and 41.4 million adults had experienced mental illness; 6.8 million adults experienced both.*

Seems too simple, doesn't it? And, it's true, some issues are much more difficult to address. Most people cannot agree on what services are needed in a community, who deserves these services, and how many services need to be provided. To further complicate things, communities are not static entities. A community needs to shift and change in response to current social, political, and economic conditions. Changing times can create and worsen social problems. For example,

Figure 1: Students in a self-contained public school classroom for persons with emotional disabilities. Biweekly sessions with the social worker help the students to discuss their feelings.

Did You Know...Domestic violence victims lose nearly 8 million days of paid work per year in the United States alone—the equivalent of 32,000 full-time jobs.

in 2011, the U.S. Bureau of the Census reported that 46.5 million people, about 15 percent of the U.S. population, were in poverty, and of those living in poverty many were women, children, and the elderly. The Brookings Institution, a think tank based in Washington, DC, reported that between 2005 and 2010 the number of people living in poverty worldwide dropped from 1.3 billion people to 900 million (Chandy, and Gertz, 2011, p. 3). The Brookings Institution calculated this number by using the World Bank definition of extreme poverty, which includes individuals living on less than $1.25 per day. For a moment consider what your life would be like if all you had in your pocket was $1.25 to buy food, pay for your transportation, purchase medicines, and pay your rent and utilities. Not surprisingly, living in poverty raises the susceptibility to other social issues such as poor health; low school attendance and graduation rates; increased crime rates; and sadly, an increase in the risk of abuse and neglect, both physical and emotional.

Did You Know...According to the federal Children's Bureau, nationally in 2012 the states' child protective service (CPS) agencies received an estimated 3.4 million referrals involving approximately 6.3 million children. Of these, 62 percent of referrals were screened in for further work, had a CPS response, and received a disposition.

Social Services for Social and Economic Justice

The United States is among the wealthiest countries in the world. It has abundant natural resources and technology, yet many American citizens battle daily with poverty as well as emotional and psychological difficulties that can impede their ability to function at home and in their communities. In 2014, the National Center for Children in Poverty (NCCP; 2014) reported that 22 percent of all children (16 million children) lived in poverty, defined as a family with an income below the federal poverty level. *The State of America's Children 2014* (Children's Defense Fund, 2014), concludes that ". . . child poverty has reached record levels and children of color are disproportionately poor." Every day millions of children are ill fed, live in unsafe environments, and have no access to high-quality health care services. And just who are these young people? The Children's Defense Fund offers a portrait of each day in the life of America's children in 2014 (see Table 1).

Did You Know...In 2013, there were 45.3 million people in poverty in the United States.

Did You Know…According to the Children's Defense Fund, Inc., in 2014, approximately 402,000 children were in foster care. And, on average more than 23,000 youth each year age out of the foster care system at age eighteen or older and are left on their own without ever finding a caring, permanent family connection.

Table 1. Each Day in America for All Children

- 2 mothers die in childbirth
- 4 children are killed by abuse or neglect
- 5 children or teens commit suicide
- 7 children or teens are killed by guns
- 24 children or teens die from accidents
- 66 babies die before their first birthdays
- 187 children are arrested for violent crimes
- 408 children are arrested for drug crimes
- 838 school students are corporally punished
- 847 babies are born to teen mothers
- 865 babies are born at low birth weight
- 1,241 babies are born without health insurance
- 1,392 babies are born into *extreme* poverty (e.g., families living on less than $1.25 per day)
- 1,837 children are confirmed as abused or neglected
- 2,723 babies are born into poverty
- 2,857 high school students drop out
- 4,028 children are arrested
- 4,408 babies are born to unmarried mothers
- 16,244 public school students are suspended

(*Source*: This material was created by the Children's Defense Fund, http://www.childrens defense.org/library/state-of-americas-children/documents/2014-SOAC_each-day-in-America.pdf)

In 2000, former surgeon general David Satcher (2000) reported that one of the greatest challenges for the U.S. health care system is to respond to both the physical and the mental health of our children, and quite clearly this challenge remains more than a decade later. Yet, children seemed to have slipped off of the nation's political and social agenda even in the face of these overwhelming problems.

The U.S. Census Bureau reported that in 2012, 15 percent of the U.S. population, or approximately 46.5 million people, lived in poverty (DeNavas-Walt and Proctor, 2014, p. 12); in addition, DeNavas-Walt and Proctor found that 9.1 percent of people over age sixty-five, approximately 3.9 million individuals, had an income below the **poverty threshold**. And what does that mean? It means that their annual income was below $11,720. Sherman and Shapiro (2005, p. 1) esti-mated that, without Social Security benefits, the incomes of nearly one in every two seniors would fall below the poverty threshold; with Social Security, the income for some 13 million seniors rises above the poverty threshold. There is now virtually universal agreement that the federal Social Security retirement program will not be able to meet the growing financial needs of our aging society as the baby boomers, born between 1946 and 1964, move into retirement.

> *Did You Know... The poverty rate for children under eighteen fell from 21.8 percent in 2012 to 19.9 percent in 2013. Even so, approximately 14.1 million children (under age eighteen) were in poverty in 2013.*

The list of social issues facing America today goes on and on. Education, health care, employment, and the environment are just a few, but also think of our global relations and obligations. The economic crisis that hit America with a vengeance in 2008 reverberated around the world. In the United States alone, some 8.4 million jobs were lost and nearly three million homes were foreclosed (Schoen, 2010).

> *Did You Know... In 2013, the poverty rate for families with a female head of house was 30.6%, whereas the poverty rate for families with a male head of house was 15.9%.*

Thus, we are left with a daunting question and task—how do we determine who should get service priority? Different people have different ideas about what is needed. With each member of a community asked for input, the list of sugges-tions will grow.

For social workers, whose primary mission is to help individuals in need, it is clear that challenging social injustice is critical. Their goals for helping vulner-able populations include (1) assessing and enhancing social resources, (2) acquir-ing and increasing economic resources, (3) increasing self-determined behavior, and (4) influencing the social policies and organizational and community prac-tices that affect the lives of vulnerable groups (Eamon, 2008). The role of the social worker is crucial in challenging systems that do not treat all individuals fairly. If social justice equates to *fairness* in terms of human relationships within the soci-ety, then conditions such as unemployment, poverty, starvation, and inadequate health care and education are only a few of the problems that will need to be addressed. Furthermore, what remains central is that the conditions that exist are often beyond the control of the individual. From a social work perspective, the existing conditions should not always be perceived as the fault of the individual based on his or her bad choices. Often circumstances develop because of coercion imposed by outside political and economic influences and the social order of systems.

Addressing social justice and encouraging social change are so important to the field of social work that the preamble to the National Association of Social Workers' Code of Ethics (NASW, 2008) clearly states that "social workers are sensitive to cultural and ethnic diversity and strive to end discrimination, oppression, poverty, and other forms of social injustice." Therefore, our purpose in this chapter is not merely to develop a laundry list of society's ills and social injustices; rather it is to identify how individuals within a community can begin to address these issues.

Social welfare may be best thought of as public and private programs and services that address social needs while promoting social justice. Our perceptions of social welfare vary. Social welfare conjures an array of images ranging from the homeless person walking to the shelter to the tornado victim receiving assistance from the Red Cross. From the varied perceptions of social welfare, two common but opposed threads emerge.

On one hand, many people believe that social welfare recipients are those who cannot make it on their own and need society's help and intervention. Some people also believe that most recipients are responsible for the misfortunes they are experiencing and in some cases have created their own problems. This misperception contributes to the view that welfare recipients are not worthy or lack the motivation to help themselves. It is important to note, however, that not everyone feels this way. Many people believe that some of the problems facing welfare recipients are not of their own making. They think that these problems should be regarded as similar to unexpected crises or traumas. In times of crisis, almost everyone expects victims to seek government assistance; such help is considered a right of citizenship.

The varying opinions that people can hold about government assistance and the wide range of social welfare services that can be provided make an accurate definition of social welfare essential. If the concept is defined too narrowly, people may focus on a few programs that account for only a small portion of welfare spending and decide that welfare policy is too specialized. If social welfare is defined too broadly, people may decide that entitlements are being given too freely and that society's limited resources cannot sustain this policy.

SOCIAL WELFARE DEFINED

Let's approach the concept of social welfare by examining several existing definitions. Later we will formulate a definition of our own (see Figure 2).

Name: Terry Werner

Place of residence: Lincoln, Nebraska

College/university degrees: University of Nebraska, BSW, Magna Cum Laude

Present position and title: Executive director of the Nebraska chapter of the National Association of Social Workers

Previous work experience:

2001–2005: At-large member of the Lincoln City Council and City Council chairperson from May 2004 to May 2005.

1977–1991: Vice president, Baker Hardware Co. Lincoln, Nebraska.

1991–present: President/owner, Werner Family Business Inc. In 1991, opened a Dairy Queen and later expanded to a second fast-food restaurant. In 1995, opened and operated Nebraska Discount Travel. In 1997, sold the restaurants and concentrated on the travel business.

Why did you choose social work as a career? When I discovered what social work is about, it was an aha moment. I was drawn to the profession because it was a way to contribute to and advocate for people less fortunate than me. My orientation was business and much of my career was in business, but my social work degree allowed me to succeed because all careers are about human relationships. I can think of no better college education for nearly any profession. This career has allowed me to continue my life's work of serving the public in a capacity that reflects my personal philosophies and beliefs. What I learned in social work school has enhanced my ability to be a public servant, a personnel manager, a volunteer, an executive director, a political advocate, and a business manager.

What is your favorite social work story? While serving on the Lincoln City Council I was able to pass an initiative called Ride for Five. This program allowed people living in poverty to have unlimited rides on the bus for $5.00 per month. When I was running for re-election, I received a campaign contribution in the mail from a man with mental illness and living on disability. In the envelope were three one dollar bills and a note. The note simply said that he wanted to support the person who started the Ride for Five. I was extremely moved by his contribution, knowing that he was truly giving until it hurt.

What is one thing you would change in the community if you had the power to do so? There are so many, but I'll limit it to one. Nebraska has more than 63,000 children living in poverty, equivalent to the population of our third largest city. We consistently rate in the top five states with children in poverty with at least one parent working full time. I would love to see living wage legislation pass in our state so that parents can raise their families with dignity.

Figure 2: Students with emotional disabilities posing in front of a mural they created during their study of insects.

Social welfare is . . .

◆ "The assignment of claims from one set of people who are said to produce or earn the national product to another set of people who may merit compassion and charity but not economic rewards for productive service" (Titmus, 1965).

◆ "Collective interventions to meet certain needs of the individual and/or to serve the wider interests of society" (Titmus, 1959, p. 42).

◆ "A system of social services and institutions, designed to aid individuals and groups to attain satisfying standards of life and health and personal social relationships which permit them to develop their full capacities and promote their well-being in harmony with the needs of their families and community" (Friedlander, 1955, p. 140).

◆ "A subset of social policy, which may be defined as the formal and consistent ordering of affairs" (Karger & Stoesz, 2010, p. 3).

◆ "A nation's system of programs, benefits, and services that help people meet those social, economic, educational, and health needs that are fundamental to the maintenance of society" (Barker, 2003, p. 221).

◆ "An encompassing and imprecise term but most often it is defined in terms of organizational activities, interventions, or some other element that suggests policy and programs to respond to recognized social problems or to improve the well-being of those at risk" (Reid, 1995, p. 2206).

◆ "A concept that encompasses people's health, economic condition, happiness, and quality of life" (Segal & Brzuzy, 1998, p. 8).

◆ "Society's organized way to provide for the persistent needs of all people—for health, education, socioeconomic support, personal rights, and political freedom" (Bloom, 1990, p. 6).

Close examination of these definitions shows that, while the phrasing differs, the content and focus are similar. Let's identify the common themes in these various statements as we develop a comprehensive definition of social welfare. First, social welfare includes a variety of programs and services that yield some type of benefit to their consumers. People participating in any type of welfare-based program benefit because they receive some form of assistance. Many times the assistance, or social provision, is given in cash. At other times a social provision is given **in-kind**, for example, as clothes, food, shelter, or counseling.

Second, social welfare, as a system of programs and services, is designed to meet the needs of people. The needs to be addressed can be all-encompassing, including economic and social well-being, health, education, and overall quality of life.

Third, the end result of social welfare is to improve the well-being of individuals, groups, and communities. Helping those systems in time of need will later benefit society at large.

RESIDUAL AND INSTITUTIONAL SOCIAL WELFARE

In their classic work *Industrial Society and Social Welfare,* Harold Wilensky and Charles Lebeaux (1965) attempt to answer a basic question: Is social welfare a matter of giving assistance only in emergencies, or is it a frontline service that society must provide? As part of their discussion, Wilensky and Lebeaux (1958) developed two important concepts that continue to frame and influence our understanding and discussions of social welfare: **residual social welfare** and **institutional social welfare** (see box 1 for examples). They defined the terms as follows:

◆ *Residual social welfare* institutions come into play only when the normal structures of supply, the family and the market, break down.

◆ *Institutional social welfare* services are normal, frontline functions of modern industrial society.

Box 1. Examples of Residual and Institutional Programs

Residual	Institutional
SNAP	Social security
Medicaid	**Medicare**
Head Start	Libraries
Temporary Assistance for Needy Families (TANF)	Health departments
Homeless shelters	Veteran's benefits

Residual Social Welfare

The residual conception of social welfare rests on the individualistic notion that people should take care of themselves and rely on government support only in times of crisis or emergency. People are not considered eligible for help until all of their own private resources, which may include assistance from the church, family wealth and inheritance, friends, and employers, have been exhausted. Only then do public welfare efforts at assistance come into play. Therefore, in order to access residual social welfare services, people must first prove their inability to provide for themselves and their families. As a result the help received often carries the **stigma** of failure.

Qualifying for this type of service is often referred to as **selective eligibility**. When eligibility is selective, social services are delivered only to people who meet certain defined criteria. When a person needs cash assistance as a service, the eligibility determination procedure is commonly called means testing. To access **means-tested programs**, people must demonstrate that they do not have the financial ability to meet their specific needs. When a residual type of program provides cash assistance, clients must recertify their eligibility every few months. The recertification process is designed primarily to ensure that clients are still unable to meet their needs through private or personal sources.

People who receive residual services are generally viewed as being different from people who receive other kinds of services. They are often regarded as failures because they do not show the rugged individualism that is a cornerstone ideal of our society. Many times beneficiaries of residual programs are labeled as lazy, immoral, and dishonest. They are often accused of making bad decisions and of needing constant monitoring because of their untrustworthiness. In short, people in residual programs carry a **stigma**.

Imagine for a moment that you are standing in the checkout line of your local grocery store. The person in front of you is paying for some items with food stamps. Noting this, would you feel compelled to look more closely at what is being purchased? In the grocery cart are potato chips, soda, some candy, and beer, as well as other food items. You have similar items in your own cart. On a piece of paper, write down your first thoughts about this; is it ok for the person with food stamps to purchase beer or liquor and potato chips, or should the money be spent on fruits and vegetables? Be honest and allow yourself to express any thoughts you might have. One response to this kind of situation is shown in box 2.

The response illustrated in box 2 is not unusual. In fact, it is fairly typical of the way many people view and react to beneficiaries of residual programs, and it raises some interesting questions. Do people receiving assistance have a right to entertainment? Or when they accept public assistance, do they give up their right to the luxuries available to others not dependent on this social welfare service? Look at it another way: Should the person on food stamps be treated any differently

---

Box 2. Welfare—Critics of Welfare 31 Years Apart; Nothing Really Changes

Example 1—January 1, 1983, *Dallas* (TX) *Morning News*, Letters to the Editor.

Last week I was passing through the checking line at a supermarket. In front of me was a young woman with two children about 5 and 6. She paid for her groceries with food stamps. On their way out they stopped by the store's video game machines. All three played the game, once each. In other words, the woman squandered 75 cents while letting taxpayers pay for the groceries. That money would have bought a dozen eggs for that "poor" family. I wonder if their color TV and stereo are working? I never have objected to my tax dollars being spent to help the truly poor, but I protest vehemently the idea of helping them pay for their entertainment or luxuries.

(Name Withheld)
Dallas, Texas

Example 2—September 23, 2014, *Modesto* (CA) *Bee*, Letters to the Editor

We constantly hear about how Social Security is going to run out of money. How come we never hear about welfare running out of money? What is interesting is the first group "worked for" their money; the second didn't. The Food Stamp Program, administered by the U.S. Department of Agriculture, is proud to be distributing this year the greatest amount of free meals and food stamps ever to 47 million people, according to the most recent figures in 2013. Meanwhile, the National Park Service asks us: "Please do not feed the animals." The stated reason is because "animals will grow dependent on handouts and will not learn to take care of themselves."

(Name Withheld)
Ceres, California

from you, your friends, or members of your family? As we will see in chapter 3, the history of social welfare is marred by a reluctance to help others in need. Residual programs and services are stigmatized, and those who need these types of services are constantly scrutinized. Many people believe that such services, although necessary as temporary forms of assistance or as last-resort charity, reinforce negative behaviors rather than promoting rugged individualism and a strong work ethic.

In summary, residual programs highlight narrow views of helping. Assistance is minimal and temporary and designed only to help people survive immediate problems or crises. These types of programs provide support only when no other options are available. In other words, a residual program is a program of last resort. In the 1980s, American public welfare programs were categorized as essentially residual in nature. Collectively referred to as *the safety net,* these programs could be accessed only after all other avenues of assistance had been exhausted.

There are three important points to keep in mind regarding residual programs. First, these programs are all means tested. To be eligible for benefits, people must document their inability to care financially for themselves and their families. In a typical residual program, clients are routinely means tested or recertified for continued eligibility every few months.

Second, residual programs can create barriers for those who seek assistance. The numerous eligibility criteria, which often force clients to produce a variety of supporting documents and evidence, can be disheartening. Continual recertification processes can thus encourage clients to give up, forgoing assistance even when their needs persist.

Third, residual programs carry a stigma, and recipients are not proud to receive services. The Supplemental Nutritional Assistance Program, more commonly referred to as the Food Stamp Program, is a typical residual program (see box 1). Recipients must qualify to receive program services, they must be recertified every few months by the state, and they are not viewed positively in the greater community.

Recall the SNAP recipient in our hypothetical grocery checkout line. How often do we look at what the person ahead of us is buying? Do we spend more time scrutinizing the purchases of those who pay with food stamps? If another person had been purchasing exactly the same items and paying with cash, would our reactions have been the same? Probably not. Why? Because both individuals have similar buying habits, why is there a difference in how these two people are viewed? The sad reality is that the Food Stamp recipient carries a stigma. Some people believe that beneficiaries of residual programs such as Food Stamps cannot be trusted, are morally weak, and do not make good decisions. They are often thought to be different from people who do not receive public aid.

Institutional Social Welfare

The second conception of social welfare described by Wilensky and Lebeaux (1965) is institutional social welfare. This definition of social welfare gives it much broader scope and function than the residual definition. In the institutional conception, the community is expected to assist individual members because problems are viewed not as failures, but instead as part of life in modern society. This broader community responsibility allows members in need to be provided services that go beyond immediate response to emergencies. Help is often provided before people exhaust all of their own resources, and preventive and rehabilitative services are stressed.

Therefore, an institutional program, as opposed to a residual program, is designed to meet the needs of all people. Eligibility is universal. Institutional programs have no stigma attached and are viewed as regular frontline programs in society. In fact, institutional programs are so widely accepted in society that many are not viewed as social welfare programs at all (see examples in box 1). Institutional programs are often called **entitlement programs**, meaning that services and benefits are available because of a person's earned status (see activities 1 and 2).

In concluding our discussion of residual and institutional provision of social welfare as outlined by Wilensky and Lebeaux, we must note the primary weakness of this framework. Specifically, not all programs and services are easily classified as institutional or residual; some programs have both institutional and residual attributes. The Head Start program, for example, is institutional in nature but it is means tested and restricted to a particular segment of the population. One solution is to expand the traditional dichotomy and classify social programs on a residual-institutional continuum. A program's position on the continuum reflects whether it is more residual or more institutional in design. Some questions to help guide the classification process include the following:

1. Is the program short or long term?
2. Is the program open to all people or a selected group of people?
3. Do program participants carry a stigma?
4. Does the public embrace the program?
5. Is the program controversial?
6. How would you feel if you were a program participant?

For all social programs, whether institutional or residual, the importance of ensuring social justice by addressing social stigma and misperception cannot be underestimated. The public does appear to openly support some forms of social welfare, but these feelings and expectations seem to vary based on individual perception and the service that is being received.

Activity...Ask fifteen to twenty people to define the term social welfare. *Then ask them to list five social welfare programs of which they are aware. Review these responses in light of the work of Wilensky and Lebeaux. Do you notice any patterns? How many of the programs would you identify as residual, institutional, or a mix of both types? In ana-lyzing these responses, do you find that people have a narrow or a broad view of social welfare? How do you feel about the responses you have received? Do you think your respon-dents' views are accurate?*

IS EVERYONE REALLY ON WELFARE?

Famed British social scientist Richard Titmus (1965) argued that social welfare was much more than aid to the poor and in fact represented a broad system of support to the middle and upper classes. In his model, social welfare has three branches:

1. Fiscal welfare: tax benefits and supports for the middle and upper classes.
2. Corporate welfare: tax benefits and supports for businesses.
3. Public welfare: assistance to the poor.

Abramowitz (1983) applied the Titmus model to American social welfare. She identified a *shadow welfare state* for the wealthy that parallels the social service system available to the poor. She concluded that poor and nonpoor alike benefit from government programs and tax laws that raise their disposable income. In other words, were it not for direct government support—whether through Food Stamps or through a child care tax exemption—people would have fewer dollars to spend and to support themselves and their families.

So, is everyone really on welfare? To address this question, let's focus first on college students. Did you know that college students are probably one of the largest groups of welfare recipients in the United States today? The vast majority of college students first attended public school, which was provided at no cost to them. Why? Because our government subsidizes the public school system. It is important for all children to have nutritious meals, and the daily school lunch is relatively inexpensive. In fact, try to buy the same meal in a restaurant and compare costs—the school lunch is much cheaper. Why? Because the government subsidies given to public schools lower the cost of these meals for all students. Okay, that's what happens in public school. Now consider the role of government in a public college. Compare tuition fees at a private college or university with those at a state- or community-supported institution. Why are tuition costs at the public college so much lower? Once again, the answer is simple: because of government subsidies. The government is very involved in subsidizing the educational needs of students at the elementary, secondary, and college levels. Students are very dependent on these subsidies in order to complete their education.

With all the support provided and the need for continuing support, don't these educational subsidies sound like welfare? Why then is there no stigma attached to this form of social provision? Some people may say, "I paid for my *welfare* through taxes on my earnings, which makes me different from those people who did not." There is no easy response to this statement, and such attitudes continue to disturb social work professionals who do not agree with the distinction between the worthy and the unworthy that is often applied to social services. Is there really a difference in the welfare service provided? Could most individuals and families afford to pay the full tuition for college that include the costs, such as but not limited to heating and cooling, building maintenance, and campus security? Government subsidies are important to the maintenance of society and are used by all people.

Mettler (2011) writes that there is "a system of social programs for the wealthy that is consuming the federal budget" although most of those who receive these benefits do not see themselves as welfare recipients. For example, 64 percent of veterans reported in 2008 that they had not participated in a government program even though they were directly receiving benefits from the tax advantaged 529 savings account for education. By 2011, the average amount of dollars returned to people through so-called tax loopholes reached $1 trillion per year; home mortgage deductions, pre-taxed employee pension plans, and employer-provided health benefits cost the nation $348.6 billion in 2011. The examples go on and on. The bottom line is that *everyone is on welfare*.

PUBLIC SOCIAL WELFARE

Social welfare is found in both public and private settings. *Public* refers to programs within the purview of state, federal, or local (city or county) government. Examples of public welfare include state agencies that deal with child protective services, adult protective services, housing services, Supplemental Nutrition Assistance Programs, mental health agencies, social security, and employment. *Private* refers to services provided for nonprofit agencies, voluntary services, and international nongovernmental organizations (NGOs). Agencies funded by the United Way and faith-based programs are types of private, nonprofit agencies.

Federal Welfare

One would think it would be easy to find out how much money the government spends each year on social welfare. That is not the case, and to make matters even more difficult, the published information is often badly out of date.

Why is it difficult to determine the government's welfare expenditures? The answer rests with how you define welfare and what programs you count as social welfare. For example, do you consider the reduced school meals program, veterans' affairs, and Section 8 housing as social welfare? The budgets for these three programs are in three different federal agencies; they are not part of one major federal welfare budget. What about Medicare and unemployment insurance? What about a library, a police or fire department, or a local waste management control agency—are they social welfare programs? As you can see, trying to identify all welfare programs and their budgets is problematic.

The federal government classifies social welfare into seven broad areas: social insurance, education, public aid, health and medical programs, veterans' programs, housing, and other social welfare (see box 3). Social insurance has been and continues to be the most costly area of federal welfare, followed by education. In fact, on average over the years, these two areas account for approximately 70 percent of total federal welfare expenses, whereas public aid accounts for only 14 percent of the federal welfare budget. It is interesting to note, however, that, when welfare cuts are discussed, the emphasis is on public aid. But what would happen, for example, if the federal appropriation for the basic welfare program, Temporary Assistance for Needy Families (TANF) were cut? In fiscal year 2013, the TANF allocation was 17.3 billion dollars; if we were to aggressively cut this allocation by 50 percent or $8.65 billion, the savings would be huge, right? Reducing TANF by $8.65 billion would reduce the total welfare federal budget ($422.3 trillion) by .02 percent.

Box 3. Federal Social Welfare Programs

◆ *Social insurance*: Old-age retirement (aka Social Security), workers' compensation, disability, unemployment assistance, railroad retirement, public employee retirement

◆ *Education*: Elementary, secondary, and higher education; vocational education

◆ *Public aid*: Cash payments under TANF and Women, Infants, and Children (WIC); general assistance; emergency assistance

◆ *Veterans' programs*: Assistance to veterans and their families, burial, health and medical programs, education, life insurance

◆ *Housing*: Public housing, Section 8 Housing vouchers

◆ *Health and medical programs*: Medicare, Medicaid, Affordable Health Care Act, maternal and child health programs, medical research, school health, other public health, medical facilities construction.

◆ Other social welfare: Vocational rehabilitation, institutional care, child nutrition, child welfare, ACTION programs, social welfare not classified elsewhere, SNAP

On the other hand, would the public support reducing federal expenditures on pre-primary through secondary education by 50 percent, thereby saving the government $29.95 billion? Probably not, even though the savings are nearly 3.5 times greater than those realized through a 50-percent reduction in TANF.

Any number of people and groups will advocate for the government to cut welfare to balance the budget. Yet, the numbers just do not add up and would do more harm to those in poverty by exacerbating the fragility of their day to day living circumstances.

Activity...For a moment, pretend to be a United States senator or a member of the United States House of Representatives. Your assignment is simple: balance the federal budget and eliminate the projected 2016 $426 billion deficit. Go the following website— www.buildabetterbudget.org—and follow the directions. You will be asked to increase, decrease, or maintain expenditures and revenues for the federal government.

State Welfare

State welfare programs differ across the country. Each state is able to develop its own set of social programs to augment the federal government's initiatives. Typically a state establishes rules and provides funds for statewide social agencies. State social welfare agencies include protective services for children and juvenile justice. Funding for state services comes from two sources: block grants from the federal government and state tax revenues. A **block grant** is a lump sum of funds given to a state, which then has the authority to determine how best to spend the dollars. The federal government imposes few rules on block grants, allowing each state to determine how programs will be structured. A state can also supplement block grant funding in order to expand services.

Local Welfare

City and county welfare programs depend on local taxes for funding. Such funds are primarily used for community protection and support, such as police, fire, and other basic local services. Funding and provision of most of these types of local social services are considered mandatory. By contrast, many government officials and community leaders see social welfare provision as a minimal, *fill the gap* measure. Those in power are usually reluctant to develop and sponsor costly local services. As with state government programs, the types and levels of local welfare programs vary by municipality. Because of their gap-filling status, local programs are generally residual in nature. Typical local programs include emergency food relief and housing and clothing vouchers.

PRIVATE SOCIAL WELFARE

Private social welfare consists of for-profit and not-for-profit agencies, also called voluntary agencies or nonprofits. Examples of nonprofits include the United Way, Red Cross, Salvation Army, Boys and Girls Clubs, Girl Scouts, YMCA, YWCA, Jewish Community Centers, Catholic Charities, and Family Services. Whereas in the United States such social service agencies are referred to as nonprofits, internationally these are called nongovernmental organizations or NGOs.

Karger and Stoesz write that confusion exists around the role of private social welfare and characterize it as "the forgotten sector" (p. 150). For the most part, American social welfare has rested within the public domain since the 1930s when the government implemented a series of welfare programs to combat the effects of the Great Depression. As the government took on greater welfare responsibility, the voluntary sector's activities lessened (Karger & Stoesz, 2010, p. 4). With financial cuts in federal welfare funding beginning in the early 1980s and continuing well into the twenty-first century, private welfare has taken on new importance. This forgotten sector is now recognized as a crucial player in the delivery of social services.

The nonprofit sector relies on donations from public foundations and, to a much lesser extent, federal, state, and local governments. In order for nonprofits to provide services, their fund-raising efforts must be successful. The success of fund-raising depends on three factors: (1) the agency's ability to provide a high-quality program, (2) the agency's ability to communicate its successes, and (3) the community's financial ability to support the program. Karger and Stoesz (2010) suggest that the voluntary sector, although well received by the public, faces many challenges including commercialization, an increase in faith-based services, and the growth of private independent practice (pp. 159–163). Therefore, in most instances, the level of private social welfare programming available depends directly on the financial well-being of the surrounding community. This dependence on private funding is particularly problematic during periods of economic turmoil, such as recession and rising unemployment. During these periods people have less money and time to donate to private charities, which in turn forces these organizations to make critical choices about which programs to close or cut.

According to the Social Security Administration, the role of the private sector in financing social welfare continues to grow, and this growth is needed to complement public social welfare expenditures and programs. Hoeffer and Colby (1998) referred to the private sector as the "mirror welfare state," a system of services that reflect public programs but are more supportive of the middle and upper classes than the poor.

SOCIAL WORK IN THE SOCIAL WELFARE SYSTEM

Social workers make up the primary professional group in the social welfare system. But social work is not the sole social welfare profession. Given the broad definition of social welfare used here and in the social work literature, many other professional groups are welfare providers as well. Although it is possible to lump the various professionals together and classify them all as welfare workers, it is more accurate to recognize that some professions are more concerned than others with people's social, health, wellness, and economic welfare needs. A useful way to differentiate among professions is to classify their level of involvement as either primary or secondary.

The primary category consists of professions whose principal efforts are in the provision of social, health, or economic services. The principal activities of professions in the secondary category are not directed toward welfare, but their work does at times involve social, health, or economic service provision (see box 4).

Look at the professionals listed in box 4. What is your opinion of who is included and where they have been placed? Do you think the professionals listed would agree with their classification? For example, how would an elementary schoolteacher react to being described as a welfare worker? We believe that many of the professionals listed below would openly disagree that they are welfare providers. It's possible that the stigma attached to programs and services offered under the rubric of welfare might influence their reactions. To explore this possibility, how do you think these professionals would reply to the following question: Do you as a professional provide a program, benefit, or service that helps people meet those social, economic, educational, health, and wellness needs that are fundamental to the maintenance of society?

Box 4. Examples of Social Welfare Professionals by Primary or Secondary Classification

Primary	Secondary
Social workers	Police officers
Mental health counselors	Librarians
Schoolteachers	Recreational specialists
Marriage and family therapists	Road crews
Psychologists	Government officials
Psychiatrists	Military personnel
Nurses	Sanitation workers

We believe that, as this question is framed—without openly addressing the concept of social welfare provision—the vast majority of the professionals listed in box 4, whether classified as primary or as secondary service providers, would answer yes. The simple truth is that, although few professionals think of their activities in this way, providing welfare services is an integral part of their jobs.

Our broad definition of social welfare also suggests some rethinking and challenging of the narrow, rigid ideas about social work. Social work began as a profession that primarily worked with the poor and disenfranchised (Hepworth, Rooney, & Larsen, 2002); sadly, today, in the twenty-first century, these groups of people are negatively stereotyped by the general public, and there are calls to reduce and eliminate services.

Although social work may have started out working with the poor and those generally cast off by society, the profession broadened its scope of work. Services and interventions were created to reach into new practice arenas such as mental health and health care. Reflecting this dynamic expanding purpose is the most recent revision of the NASW Code of Ethics:

> The primary mission of the social work profession is to enhance human well-being and help meet the basic human needs of all people, with particular attention to the needs and empowerment of people who are vulnerable, oppressed, and living in poverty. A historic and defining feature of social work is the profession's focus on individual well-being in a social context and the well-being of society. Fundamental to social work is the attention to the environmental forces that create, contribute to, and address problems in living.
>
> ... These activities may be in the form of direct practice, community organizing, supervision, consultation, administration, advocacy, social and political action, policy development and implementation, education, and research and evaluation. (NASW, 2008).

So today we find that the social welfare system and the social work profession address an array of diverse populations—such as the situationally and chronically homeless; victims of child and adult abuse and neglect; couples dealing with marital stress, unemployment, or underemployment; persons with behavioral health issues; individuals facing medical crises or addicted to a variety of substances, and juvenile delinquents—with a variety of public and private programs and services.

We also find that the term client is now used inclusively and can mean individuals, groups, families, organizations, and communities. Adopting, in essence, the institutional perspective, the social worker strives to restore and enhance client wellness and to provide preventive as well as basic services. Strategies to assist clients must address all of these areas because often the factors involved are intertwined and interdependent (Dziegielewski, 2013; Skidmore, Thackeray, & Farley, 1997).

The Fading Distinction between Public and Private

Changes in the social welfare environment have blurred once-clear distinctions in social work—for example, whether an agency that employs a social worker is public or private. For simplicity, public agencies are understood to be primarily, if not totally, funded through tax-supported dollars. It is the public agency that is regarded as most representative of social welfare services and programs (see activity below). Most people believe that these agencies have primary responsibility for residual or means-tested social welfare programs. Private agencies, on the other hand, are believed to be voluntarily supported and to rarely have tax-supported dollars as part of their basic budgets.

If public and private agencies were distinctly different, these straightforward definitions would suffice. However, in today's political world nothing could be further from the truth. There is no longer any clear distinction between public and private agencies because their funding and the services they deliver so often overlap. Many private agencies now actively seek public or tax-supported funds, and many public agencies now contract with private agencies and individual providers to serve their clients. Because private agencies can specialize in a way that public agencies with their broad responsibilities cannot, such contracts allow public agencies to secure services that they do not have the budget or the skilled personnel to offer on their own.

Activity...Go to your local (county or city) welfare or public assistance office. Look around and try to get a feel for the setting. What messages does the physical structure send to the clients? Does this environment seem like a typical business setting? Do the setting and staff suggest an interest in serving the clients, and are the clients made to feel important? How does this facility differ from a physician's office? What sorts of informational brochures are available to read? How long do clients wait before a worker sees them?

After you've visited a public agency, visit a private social service agency. What differences, if any, do you see between the two agencies? Why do you think they exist? Should there be any physical differences between public and private agencies?

In addition to this blurring of public and private agencies, a dispersion of social workers across both the public and private sectors has placed social work practitioners in new roles. Traditionally, social workers found jobs in public agencies because these agencies and programs assumed primary responsibility for the poor and the underserved. Today, however, social workers practice in diverse agency settings that have many different goals and allegiances.

Cost Containment versus Quality

For all social workers the current state of social work practice mirrors the turbulence in the general social welfare environment. There is little consistency in the delivery of social welfare services because primary emphasis is placed on cost containment, with each state designing and creating its unique services' structures. Social welfare program administrators, forced to justify each dollar billed for services, may reduce the provision of what some see as *expendable services*, designed to promote the mental health and well-being of clients. They may be tempted to regard the role of social workers as adjunct to the delivery of care and to cut back on professional staff or replace them with nonprofessionals simply to lower costs. These substitute professionals, or more appropriately *paraprofessionals*, have neither the depth nor the breadth of training of social work professionals, often resulting in substandard professional services.

The employment of these kinds of paraprofessionals, though cost effective, is not quality driven. When social services are rushed or minimized, issues such as the individual client's sense of well-being, ability to self-care, and family and environmental support may not be considered. The involvement of social work professionals is thus essential to ensuring that personal, social, and environmental issues are addressed and clients are not put at risk of harm.

For social workers, a client who is discharged home to a family that does not want him or her is at risk of abuse and neglect. A client who has a negative view of himself or herself and a hopeless and hapless view of his or her condition is more likely to attempt suicide or come to some other harm. Many paraprofessionals and members of other professional disciplines differ from social work professionals in that they do not recognize the paramount importance of culture and environmental factors to efficient and effective practice. Their outlook may enable the delivery of cheap service, at the cost of substandard care that has a direct negative impact on the client.

As social service administrators strive to cut costs by eliminating professional social work services, the overall philosophy of wellness may be sacrificed. It is important to note, however, that staff reorganizations and reductions in social welfare services are rarely personal attacks on social work professionals. The changes and cutbacks in services and those who provide them are responses to an immediate need to provide cost reduction. Fluctuating employment and downsizing of social work professionals, like other allied health professionals, simply reflects the fluctuating demands of the current market (Dziegielewski, 2013; Falck, 1990).

SUMMARY

So what is social welfare? The residual view suggests that welfare support should be temporary, only for the poor, and as little as possible. If we look at actual public welfare spending, however, it seems that social welfare as practiced is much broader. In fact, everyone in society is a welfare recipient of one type or another.

The role of the social work professional is broader than many people expect. Originally, social workers served the poor and disenfranchised; however, over the years the role of the social worker has expanded tremendously. Many social work professionals now provide services outside of the traditional social welfare realm. This diversity of style, task, and approach makes it difficult to define exactly what social workers do. Clarity of definition has been further complicated by changes in scope of practice, roles served, and expectations within the client-professional relationship.

In today's turbulent social welfare environment, social work professionals face a constant battle of quality of care issues versus cost containment measures for clients (Dziegielewski, 2013). In addition, they must strive to maintain a secure place as professional providers in the delivery of social welfare services.

Quiz Answers

1. a. the former Food Stamp Program.

2. a. mothers and their children. Approximately 60 percent of all welfare recipients, according to the U.S. Bureau of the Census, are mothers and their children.

3. b. false. The majority of people in poverty are White.

4. b. false. Under federal welfare rules, a family on welfare that has another baby will not receive any additional benefits.

5. b. false. The unemployment rate identifies only those people not working who actively looked for a job within the past thirty days.

6. c. false. Each state determines the amount a family receives on public assistance. As a result, the amount received by a person in Florida is a different amount from that received by someone in Alabama.

7. b. false. According to reports by the U.S. Bureau of Labor Statistics, more than 70 percent of public assistance recipients are women with children, children, and senior citizens.

8. All the groups listed are participants in programs the federal government defines as "social welfare." As a result, all of the groups are welfare recipients.

9. b. false. This is a trick question—AFDC was replaced by TANF—Temporary Assistance to Needy Families—in 1996.

10. Revise your answer to this question using the information presented in this chapter.

REFERENCES

Abramowitz, M. (1983). Everyone is on welfare: "The role of redistribution in social policy" revisited. *Social Work, 28*, 440–445.

Barker, R. L. (2003). *The social work dictionary* (5th ed.). Washington, DC: NASW Press.

Bloom, M. (1990). *Introduction to the social work drama.* Itasca, IL: Peacock.

Chandy, L., & Gertz, G. (2011), *Poverty in numbers: The change state of global poverty from 2005 to 2015.* Washington, DC: Brookings Institution.

Children's Defense Fund (2014). *The state of America's children 2014.* Washington, DC: Author. Available from http://www.childrensdefense.org/library/state-of-americas-children

DeNavas-Walt, C., & Proctor, B. (2014). *Income and poverty in the United States: 2013* (Current population reports, P60–249). Washington, DC: U.S. Government Printing Office.

Dziegielewski, S. F. (2013). *The changing face of health care social work: Opportunities and challenges for professional practice* (3rd ed.). New York: Springer.

Eamon, M. K. (2008). *Empowering vulnerable populations.* Chicago: Lyceum Books.

Falck, H. S. (1990). Maintaining social work standards in for-profit hospitals: Reasons for doubt. *Health & Social Work, 15*, 76–77.

Friedlander, W. (1955). *Introduction to social welfare.* Englewood Cliffs, NJ: Prentice-Hall.

Hepworth, D. H., Rooney, R. H., & Larsen, J. (2002). *Direct social work practice: Theory and skills.* Pacific Grove, CA: Brooks/Cole.

Hoeffer, R., & Colby, I. (1998). Private social welfare expenditures. In I. C. Colby, A. Garcia, R. G. McRoy, L. Videka-Sherman, & R. L. Edwards, (Eds.), *Encyclopedia of social work: 1997 supplement.* Washington, DC: NASW Press.

Karger, H. J., & Stoesz, D. (2010). *American social welfare policy: A pluralist approach* (6th ed.). Boston: Pearson Education/Allyn Bacon.

Mettler, S. (2011, July/August). 20,000 leagues under the state. *Washington Monthly.* Retrieved from: http://www.washingtonmonthly.com/magazine/julyaugust_2011/features/20000_leagues_under_the_state030498.php

National Association of Social Workers. (2008). *Code of ethics of the National Association of Social Workers.* Washington, DC: Author. Retrieved from http://www.socialworkers.org/pubs/code/code.asp

National Center for Children in Poverty. (2014). Child poverty. Retrieved from http://www.nccp.org/topics/childpoverty.html

Reid, P. N. (1995). Social welfare history. In R. Edwards & J. G. Hopps (Eds.), *Encyclopedia of social work* (19th ed.). Washington, DC: NASW Press.

Satcher, D. (2000). Foreword. In U.S. Public Health Service, *Report of the surgeon general's conference on children's mental health: A national action agenda* (pp. 1–2). Washington, DC: U.S. Department of Health and Human Services.

Schoen, J. W. (2010). *Study: 1.2 million households lost to recession.* MSNBC.com. Retrieved from http://www.msnbc.msn.com/id/36231884/ns/business-eye_on_the_economy/t/study-million-households-lost-recession

Segal, W., & Brzuzy, S. (1998). *Social welfare policy, programs, and practice.* Itasca, IL: Peacock.

Sherman, A., & Shapiro, I. (2005, February 24). *Social security lifts 13 million seniors above the poverty line: A state by state analysis.* Washington, DC: Center on Budget and Policy Priorities.

Skidmore, R. A., Thackeray, M. G., & Farley, O. W. (1997). *Introduction to social work* (7th ed.). Boston: Allyn and Bacon.

Specht, H., & Courtney, M. (1994). *Unfaithful angels*. New York: Free Press.

Titmus, R. (1959). *Essays on the welfare state*. New Haven, CT: Yale University Press.

Titmus, R. (1965). The role of redistribution in social policy. *Social Security Bulletin, 28*(6), 34–55.

Wilensky, H., & Lebeaux, C. (1958). *Industrial society and social welfare*. New York: Russell Sage Foundation.

Wilensky, H., & Lebeaux, C. (1965). *Industrial society and social welfare*. New York: Free Press.

CHAPTER 3
HOW DID WE GET HERE FROM THERE?

TIME FOR A BRIEF HISTORY QUIZ

1. Why is the year 1492 important in American history?
2. The **New Deal** was the name given to what set of programs?
3. What did the Emancipation Proclamation address?
4. What important event took place in Seneca Falls, New York, in 1848?
5. Where was an immigrant arriving at Ellis Island most likely to be from?
6. What is Salem, Massachusetts, perhaps best known for?
7. The United States acquired California, Nevada, Utah, and parts of Texas, Colorado, New Mexico, and Wyoming as part of what act or event?
8. What document preceded the U.S. Constitution?
9. What does the term Seward's Folly refer to?
10. What was at issue in the Dred Scott Case?

So, how did you do? (The answers are at the end of the chapter.) For most people taking this quiz, the results are mixed. A few of the questions seem easy whereas others are complete mysteries. Yet each of these questions addresses a meaningful part of our American history. The importance of being familiar with such events is twofold: (1) as informed citizens, we need to know about our history; and (2) knowledge of the past can help us to understand both present and future societal developments.

In the field of social work, as in other disciplines, knowing the history of the profession is essential to understanding its past, present, and future (Alexander, 1995). Social work has come a long way from its early beginnings, transcending its origins within religious orders to be adopted by public/private benefactors (Leighninger, 2008). Unfortunately, however, studying history and looking at what happened in the past may not seem as exciting as learning about direct social work practice, policy, or social action (see the activity below). When history is discussed in the classroom or in less formal situations, it is almost always received with an air of indifference and reluctance. As one student remarked, "It's over and done with, so why should I be concerned about it? I want to learn how to help people. What happened two hundred years ago won't help me today."

Is this statement valid? It's true that in social work practice, regardless of the model or technique employed, the emphasis is on the here and now. Nevertheless, most social workers recognize the importance of history in their practice. For example, when first meeting a client, the social worker asks probing, thoughtful questions about the client's past. This systematic accumulation of information is referred to as gathering a social history or a **psychosocial history**. A social work practitioner would never consider the social history that he completes on each client to be useless information. In particular, the social history is important to understand and explore the client's growth and development process as well as to identify possible effects of events and relations with others in the client's past.

The past offers valuable clues to interpreting the present and anticipating the future. History is essential to helping all of us better understand who we are and how we got here. It also influences our future decisions. Indeed, some people take the extreme position that we are so profoundly influenced by the past that it actually determines the future. This theory is called *determinism*.

Activity…Think about three people from social work history you would like to meet and invite to dinner. Maybe Nobel Peace Prize recipient Jane Addams or Queen Elizabeth I. What about Mary Richmond, who was a leader of the Charity Organization Society in the late nineteenth and early twentieth centuries, or Francis Perkins, the first woman to hold a president's cabinet position—you decide. What would you want to ask them and what do you think they would say?

Whatever degree of importance we place on history, it is obvious that people—sometimes intentionally, sometimes unintentionally—use past experiences as a frame of reference for current and future experiences. For example, a person has to burn his/her hand only once before learning not to put it on a hot stove. History can teach us if we allow it to do so—we do not put our hand on a hot stove because at some time in the past we learned that it hurt. Clearly, the importance of history cannot be underestimated. We hope we have sparked your interest in history as a way to understand the roots of social welfare and general aspects of social work practice. In many cases considering the experiences of the past can teach us valuable lessons worth remembering.

Did You Know…Harry Hopkins, a social worker, was one of President Franklin D. Roosevelt's closest friends and the administrator of a Great Depression program called the Federal Emergency Relief Administration.

Name: Darla Spence Coffey

Place of residence: Alexandria, VA

College/university degrees: Eastern College BSW; University of Pennsylvania, MSW; Bryn Mawr College, PhD

Present position: President and chief executive officer, Council on Social Work Education, Alexandria, Virginia

What do you do in your spare time? There is a lot of variability in the activities that I do outside of work—all of them sustain me in different ways. I'm an avid reader—and I can't actually capture what I like to read very succinctly. It runs the gamut from novels to history to professional literature to biographies. I need to work up a sweat on a regular basis, and do so by running, playing tennis, bicycle riding, and yoga (yes, you can get a sweat doing yoga!). I spend time with friends and family. I walk my dog (a golden retriever, the best dog in the world!). I love to cook and to experiment in the kitchen.

Why did you choose social work as a career? It sounds trite, but I chose social work as a very young person with a big dream of making a difference in the world. I still think that it's the best way to do that!

What is your favorite social work story? I am inspired by the stories of our historical social work leaders—Jane Addams, Bertha Capen Reynolds, Dorothy Height, Whitney Young, and others. But my favorite social work story is the story of change told to me by one of my very first clients. After I had spent months supporting her to act on her decision to leave an abusive relationship, she moved very quickly one weekend and left him. When she talked to me about it later, she told me that it was because of something that she heard on a daytime talk show. She hadn't considered any of the things that we had talked about for months! It reminds me to be humble. And that motivation to change can come from anywhere.

What would be the one thing you would change in our community if you had the power to do so? I wish that social workers would stop thinking and acting from a "one down" position and step up to claim our power, expertise, and leadership.

This chapter will make a brief foray into social welfare history. Others have undertaken comprehensive examinations of social welfare history (Axinn & Levin, 1982; Chambers, 1967; Jansson, 2004; Katz, 1986; Lubove, 1965; Trattner, 1989), and this area is well worth the effort of further investigation. We will briefly examine significant events and trends that influenced the emergence of our current American social welfare system.

THE ELIZABETHAN POOR LAW OF 1601

Most social work historians would agree that the watershed year for social welfare was 1601, when English **poor laws** were *codified* or brought together under one law. This codification is commonly called the Elizabethan Poor Law of 1601. Colonial America adopted the central tenets of this law, and many of its principles continue to underpin the design and implementation of our current social services.

As an important note of caution, welfare did not begin with the Elizabethan Poor Law of 1601. Karger and Stoesz (2010, pp. 41–42) tracked the development of the English poor laws back through a series of events to the mid-fourteenth century. Gilbert and Specht (1981, p. 17) noted that modern-day social welfare has roots in the Reformation period and the Middle Ages. And Trattner (1989), in his classic work *From Poor Law to Welfare State*, traced the roots of American welfare efforts to the ancient Greeks and Romans. In advanced social policy courses, you'll learn more about the rise of social welfare as a system, but for our purposes, we will begin with the Elizabethan Poor Law.

Before 1601 in Europe, welfare attempts to assist people in need were generally viewed as the province of the church. With the advent of the industrial era, great changes occurred in society. Many new and better paying jobs were created, and men and women of all ages were encouraged to apply. Rural communities began to decrease in population as people left the limited and shrinking opportunities of farm life for what the industrialized cities offered. Unfortunately, the promise of more jobs and a better way of life was not fulfilled for everyone, and many became unemployed and homeless. The newly destitute turned to the churches, the traditional providers of assistance to the poor. With the ranks of the poor growing to unprecedented levels, however, these urban churches did not have the resources or the expertise to cope with the swelling numbers of rural migrants and their assorted needs.

Faced with a growing population of urban poor, the English government implemented a series of sweeping reforms in an attempt to gain control of this problem. The result, the 1601 Poor Law, radically changed the form, function, and scope of welfare assistance. First, it redefined welfare as a public responsibility rather than a private affair. Second, it identified local government as the public entity responsible for the poor. Last, it denied relief if family resources were available (Katz, 1986, pp. 13–14).

In addition to setting the parameters for public aid, the 1601 Poor Law divided potential recipients into two groups, the **worthy poor** and the **unworthy poor**. The worthy poor included the ill, the disabled, orphans, and elders. These people were viewed as having no control over their life circumstances. A second group of the worthy poor consisted of people who were involuntarily unemployed.

Although they were seen as bearing some responsibility for their own situations, due consideration was given to the fact that their misfortunes were beyond their control. The unworthy poor, on the other hand, included the vagrant or able-bodied who, although able to work, did not seek employment (Cole, 1973, p. 5).

Overall, assistance was first given to the worthy poor, who were considered helpless to control their situations. Some assistance was provided to those who were involuntarily unemployed. No assistance was given to the unworthy poor, who were treated with public disdain.

COLONIAL AMERICA

The provision of public assistance in colonial America was tenuous at best. Influenced by strong Puritan and Calvinist views, most citizens regarded both the worthy and the unworthy poor as morally flawed. They believed that the poverty-stricken had somehow caused their own distress. This belief released society from any obligation to lend assistance and implied that it was the impoverished individual who was responsible for finding and providing a remedy. Aid or **charity assistance**, in any form, was thought to lead to an "erosion of independence and self-respect; the spread of idleness and the loss of the will to work; the promotion of immorality in all its ugly forms; and the increase in public costs through the growth of poorhouses and jails" (Katz, 1986, p. 40). Benjamin Franklin, for example, strongly opposed public aid: "[The] 'natural state' of working persons was one of sloth, wastefulness, and dissipation. The Common people do not work for pleasure, but for necessity" (Williams, 1944, p. 83). Relief, Franklin felt, simply provided an opportunity for people to return to their natural state of laziness at the expense of others.

> *Did You Know...In 1931, Jane Addams, social worker and founder of Hull House, was the first American woman to win the Nobel Peace Prize. The Jane Addams Hull-House Museum in Chicago is an excellent source for more information; www.hullhouse museum.org.*

Based on a weak commitment to a public welfare system, American colonists developed a dual system of relief that was modeled on the English Poor Law of 1601. The resulting programs provided aid to the worthy poor, who in this case comprised the ill, seniors, orphans, widows, and veteran soldiers. The unworthy or able-bodied poor, who included the involuntarily unemployed, were provided little if any assistance.

Support to the worthy poor was given primarily in the form of **outdoor relief**, which was aid to a person or a family in the home; the assistance may have been cash but generally was in-kind provisions such as food and clothing. Conversely, the unworthy poor were not provided aid in their homes but were typically moved to the local poor house, commonly referred to as **indoor relief**. It was also commonplace for a community to encourage the unworthy poor to move on to another county. Further, an individual deemed as unworthy would be required to return to his/her county/town of origin to receive any help.

Funds to support the worthy and unworthy poor were collected at the town or county level through a special tax assessed by the local **overseer of the poor**. In many ways this overseer was a colonial version of a social worker. The overseer's responsibilities included identifying the local poor, determining if they in fact were residents of the particular jurisdiction, determining what their specific needs were, classifying the individual or family as worthy or unworthy poor, and determining how the community would respond to this particular individual or family (see Figure 1).

In general, the availability and accessibility of colonial public services reflected Franklin's negative view of relief. These programs were often designed with a punitive intent in an effort to shame people out of their poverty (see box 1). Typical of this approach was the practice of forcing the poor into apprenticeships and indentured service offered by the lowest bidder—that is, the person who would charge the community least for taking a pauper off its hands. Another example of this reluctant attitude toward helping the poor is the treatment of a widow in Hadley, Massachusetts. In 1687, this woman, who had no resources of her own, was forced to live for two-week periods with those families who were "able to receive her" (Trattner, 1989, p. 18). Further, in Pennsylvania those receiving aid were required to wear a scarlet letter *P* sewn on their right sleeves "with the first letter of the county, city, or place of his or her residence underneath" (Heffner, 1913, p. 11). Even more extreme was a 1754 North Carolina law that allowed vagrants (in 2015 they would be called homeless) to be whipped in the public square simply because of their impoverished state (Rothman, 1971, p. 25).

Not all potential recipients of social welfare services were viewed negatively in colonial America. For example, veteran soldiers who had fought for the colonies and later became impoverished were given a more honored status because they were generally considered to be among the worthy poor (Axinn & Levin, 1982, p. 31). As early as 1624, veterans could expect to receive social welfare benefits as a right earned by the service they had provided. It was believed that, because veteran soldiers had shown their willingness to risk life and limb in defense of their nation, they deserved public aid if they needed it. Providing relief to veterans was not considered the responsibility of the town; rather it was the obligation of the colony. In addition, veterans did not have to satisfy residency requirements in order to receive aid (Axinn & Levin, 1982, p. 31). In summary, two of the primary components of colonial poor relief legislation—local responsibility and residency—did not apply to veterans because they enjoyed the status of the worthy poor.

Figure 1: A United Charities of Chicago caseworker or visiting housekeeper calling on a family about 1909. Formed when the Relief and Aid Society merged with the Bureau of Charities, United Charities of Chicago was the city's oldest private welfare organization. It was the best known of the family service agencies and worked on prevention, easing desperate social situations, and creating better living environments.

Box 1. Selected Dates in American Social Welfare History

1601	Elizabethan Poor Law enacted by the English parliament.
1642	Plymouth Colony enacts first poor law in the colonies.
1657	Scots Charitable Society, first nonprofit organization focused on the provision of welfare, founded in Boston.
1773	First public mental asylum opens in Williamsburg, Virginia.
1790	First public orphanage opens in Charleston, South Carolina.
1798	U.S. Public Health Department established.
1817	Gallaudet School, a school for the deaf, founded in Hartford, Connecticut.
1822	Kentucky opens first public asylum for deaf people.
1829	First asylum for the blind opens in Massachusetts.
1841	Dorothea Dix begins investigations into mental institutions in the United States.
1851	The YMCA is founded in North America (Montreal).
1853	The Reverend Charles Loring Brace organizes Children's Aid Society.
1854	President Pierce vetoes federal legislation designed to use federal land for state asylums.
1865	Freedmen's Bureau is organized.
1869	The first permanent state board of health and vital statistics is founded in Massachusetts.
1880	The Salvation Army is organized in the United States although it was founded in London in 1878.
1889	Hull House is opened in Chicago, Illinois, by Jane Addams and Ellen Gates Starr.
1905	Medical social work is initiated at Massachusetts General Hospital in Boston.
1912	The Children's Bureau is organized by the federal government.
1917	*Social Diagnosis*, the first textbook on social casework, is written by Mary Richmond.
1923	The first course on group work is offered at Western Reserve University in Cleveland, Ohio.
1934	The first social work licensing law is passed in Puerto Rico and becomes the precursor for other state licensing and registration laws.

For other dates and events, see *Distinctive Dates in Social Welfare History* by Chauncey Alexander (http://www-personal.umich.edu/~mdover/website/Social%20Welfare%20Policy%20Main%20Folder/DistinctiveDates.pdf). What events in social welfare history strike you or surprise you? What do you think is the most important social welfare event on the list? Why?

Did You Know...Jeannette Rankin, a social worker, was the first woman elected to the U.S. Congress, representing Montana, in 1916. And she was elected prior to the passage of the Nineteenth Amendment, which granted women the right to vote.

NINETEENTH CENTURY REFORM EFFORTS

Throughout American history, immorality and pauperism have been tightly linked by the idea that poverty is a direct result of an individual's flawed character. Nineteenth-century programs intended to help the poor sought to do so by changing their behavior and making them overcome their personal failings. At the same time public opinion turned hostile toward all those living in poverty. As Benjamin Disraeli lamented following passage of the punitive 1834 British poor law reform, it was "a crime to be poor" (Trattner, 1989, p. 49).

Despite the strong resistance to helping the poor, poverty was widespread enough that some form of relief was necessary. Welfare organizations became more formalized and commonplace, particularly in large urban areas. The most prominent agencies for the delivery of social welfare services and programs for the poor were **almshouses** and asylums, charity organization societies, and settlement houses.

Almshouses and Asylums

The roots of service provision for the poor and disabled can be traced back as far as the 1700s to the first almshouses. Almshouses, also called poorhouses, were intended to be places of refuge for the poor, medically ill, and mentally ill of all ages. In colonial times, however, caring for the family and its members was considered a private matter, and people who had any kind of family support were kept at home. Therefore, the almshouse was an option of last resort, providing shelter and relief for society's outcasts—those who were poor, incapacitated, or suffered from contagious disease. Severely underfunded, almshouses were dirty and disease filled, and the workers who staffed them, who can be regarded among the earliest practical social workers and health care providers, often became ill (Dziegielewski, 2013).

> *Did You Know…In 1713 William Penn founded the first almshouse in Philadelphia. In 1736 a second almshouse was founded at Bellevue Hospital in New York. The almshouse in Bellevue usually housed the mentally ill and later became one of the most famous mental health hospitals in the country.*

At one point, almshouses housed all of the poor. However, children were eventually removed from almshouses by the efforts of the Children's Aid Society and later placed in orphanages. In 1851 the mentally ill were also removed and sent to improved facilities and asylums primarily through the crusading efforts of Dorothea Lynde Dix. Basically, the almshouse as *holding tank* was replaced with more segregated forms of institutionalized care such as orphanages and other residential facilities, referred to as asylums.

Asylums, the most common human service organizations in the 1800s, became the homes for the blind, deaf and dumb, and insane and developed regimented programs formed by a guiding trinity of work, religion, and education. Tightly regulating an inmate's life with scheduled activities throughout each day, according to Rothman (1971, p. 145), reflected belief in the "therapeutic value of a rigid schedule." For example, in the Pennsylvania Hospital, patients were awakened at 5:00 a.m. They "received their medicines at six, and breakfast at 6:30; at eight o'clock, they went for a physical examination, and then to work or to some other form of exercise. At 12:30 they ate their main meal and then resumed work or other activities until six, when everyone joined for tea" (Rothman, 1971, p. 145).

As can been seen from this cumbersome schedule, labor was a central component of asylum life. Inmates, as they were being taught jobs, learned the value and importance of work. This training, coupled with the regimented schedule, in theory imparted "habits . . . necessary for patients' recovery" (Rothman, 1971, p. 146). A poem allegedly written by a young woman in the Texas Asylum for the Blind reveals the negative side of work as the cornerstone of welfare programming:

Work, work, work
till the brain begins to swim;
work, work, work
till the eyes are heavy and dim;
seam, gusset, and bond,
bond, gusset, and seam
till over the buttons I fall asleep
and sew them on in dream.

Did You Know... The first American charity organization society was established in Buffalo, New York, in 1877.

Charity Organization Societies

A second innovative approach to combating poverty was the **charity organization society (COS)**, founded in London, England, in the mid-1800s. Besides its significance as a social welfare development, the COS is important to the history of social work because some social work historians view its founding as the profession's birth event. The first American COS, modeled after the British program, was founded in Buffalo, New York, in 1877 by the Reverend Humphrey Gurteen.

In the mid-1800s, private charitable efforts proliferated in American cities, resulting in many duplicated and uncoordinated programs. Following the British model of coordination, the COS movement made its way to the United States, first in Buffalo, New York, to organize the various charities within a city to reduce program duplication and to certify the needs and claims of clients in a systematic investigative fashion. Only those individuals or families certified as eligible by the COS were able to receive services from the various charities. Finally, the COS sought to change the lives of the poor through home visits by volunteers; these so-called **friendly visitors** are generally considered to be the forerunners to the American social worker. The friendly visitors by and large were females from middle to upper middle class families; the local COS was characteristically headed by a male, who was the only paid staff person in the organization.

Charity organization societies subscribed to the philosophy that poverty was a consequence of moral decay, and the eradication of the slum depended on the poor recognizing and correcting their personal deficiencies (Boyer, 1978, p. 144). The friendly visitor, a key volunteer in the COS movement, was to establish a personal relation with each client through home visits and by serving as a role model to help the poor change their behavior. The 1889 *Buffalo Charity Organization Society Handbook* declared that the friendly visitor soon would be a power in the home:

> In a very short time the houses would be clean and kept clean for her reception. Her advice would be sought. . . . In a word, all avoidable pauperism would soon be a thing of the past when the poor would regard the rich as their natural friends (Gurteen, 1882, p. 117).

Women volunteers, particularly those from middle- and upper-class families, were preferred for the role of friendly visitor. These women would be able to demonstrate and foster the values of the successful family to less fortunate individuals and families. In essence, by psychological and social osmosis, poverty and its companion evils would be uprooted through the kind works of middle class ladies. Specifically, Gurteen wrote,

> [All that is] needed to make our work a grand success . . . is hundreds of women from the educated and well-to-do classes, especially women of our city, who as mothers and daughters, coming from bright and happy homes—homes adorned by virtue and radiant with love, can impart to the cheerless tenement or the wretched hovel, a little of their own happiness (1882, p. 116).

The COS movement also relied on female volunteers to staff the various organizations. As these societies became more accepted and formalized, the role of women changed. For example, the COS women, by the end of the nineteenth century, were paid for their work, and charity organization societies became a primary employment arena for women. It is interesting to note, however, that the first COS administrators were men and the first female administrator, Mary Richmond, was not appointed until late 1891.

Did You Know...Frances Perkins, a social worker, was the first woman appointed to the U.S. cabinet when she was named secretary of labor in 1933.

In summary, the charity organization societies were an important development in the history of social work because they provided the basis for the modern social service agencies of today. The workers they employed were some of the first to deliver social services in the home setting to poor and disenfranchised people. Charity organization societies provided an opportunity for systematic investigation of those in poverty and need. Home visitation, which today remains a highly valued social work intervention technique, allowed volunteers to learn more about individuals and their environments.

Did You Know...The first social work educational program started in 1898 as a summer training course at the New York Charity Organization Society. It later became Columbia University School of Social Work.

Settlement House Movement

Another major British innovation also crossed the Atlantic during the mid-1800s and made a significant impact in the American social service arena. Known as the settlement house movement, its philosophy was remarkably different from that of the charity organization societies. The settlement house movement sought the causes of poverty in macrosystems rather than microsystems. For example, poor education, lack of health care, and inadequate housing were considered the primary reasons for poverty. The settlement house was an actual house in a neighborhood where the workers lived year-round coordinating and providing programs, activities, and services directed to the needs of their neighbors.

The most famous nineteenth century settlement house was Hull House, founded by Jane Addams and Ellen Gates Starr in 1889. Located in a poor West Side Chicago neighborhood, Hull House forged a strong bond between neighborhood immigrants and social workers with its efforts to bridge the gulf between rich and poor (Leighninger, 2008). By the beginning of the twentieth century there were more than one hundred settlement houses located in the United States.

The settlement house movement initiated the macro model for social work practice, more commonly referred today as *community organization* and *group practice*. Problems were seen as resting not with the individual, but at the larger organizational or community level. Poverty was the result not of an individual's lack of morality, but of a system that kept wages low, did not enforce housing or health codes, and maintained a marginalized working class. Through client empowerment, problems could be confronted and social resources redistributed.

Did You Know...The Scots Charitable Society, organized in Boston in 1657, was the first voluntary society (i.e., nonprofit agency) in the colonies to focus on welfare needs.

THE TWENTIETH CENTURY

At the dawn of the twentieth century, the United States was poised to become a world economic leader. By the 1920s, economic prosperity seemed within reach of a growing number of Americans. Yet for Blacks and immigrants, economic gains were elusive. Blacks continued to suffer racism and discrimination, especially under nineteenth century Jim Crow laws that were commonplace in the South. As immigration increased, laws inspired by xenophobia (fear of foreigners) framed social policy initiatives.

The prosperity of the first quarter-century quickly unraveled in the worldwide depression of the 1930s. By 1929, 1.6 million people were unemployed, and by the mid-1930s, nearly one in four Americans was unemployed.

Everyone knew someone—a brother, sister, father, mother, aunt, uncle, grandparent, or friend—who was out of work. Poverty was no longer a distant concept reserved for Blacks, immigrants, and other minorities. Very quickly, the philosophy that the poor were morally depraved and had no work ethic became unacceptable because more people had become poor who were never poor before. The new poor were everyone's friends and family and didn't fit the image of the lazy, immoral poor.

With the presidential election of Franklin Roosevelt, relief measures were immediately put in place, followed by the ambitious New Deal programs. These programs were funded and coordinated at the federal level and dramatically changed government's ambivalent role in social welfare (see the activity below).

The most important New Deal initiative was the Economic Security Act of 1935, which established the Social Security System to provide cash assistance to retired workers. This act—which also established the precursors of today's Temporary Assistance to Needy Families (TANF) program and unemployment insurance—became the organizing framework for the federal social service system. By the end of the twentieth century, the 1935 Act had been amended on numerous occasions to include cash assistance, health benefits, and services for the disabled, the blind, families, children, and seniors.

The New Deal, which was the nation's first national welfare program, included initiatives directed toward a variety of people. The Federal Emergency Relief Act, the Civilian Conservation Corps, and the Works Progress Administration formed the backbone of the New Deal. All of these programs were unprecedented in that they were developed and coordinated by the federal government, but like local relief efforts of the nineteenth century, they made work a condition of relief.

Activity...Go to a library or online and read newspapers from the 1930s. Try to get a feel for life during the Depression. Then visit a local nursing home or senior center to meet people who lived during the Depression. Ask them how the Depression affected their families and neighbors and how it influenced the rest of their lives.

The New Deal essentially affirmed the federal government's role in social welfare. The national effort was unparalleled in American history until the massive social movement of the 1960s.

Social Reform in the 1960s

By 1960, slightly more than one in five Americans lived in poverty. In 1962, Michael Harrington's classic work *The Other America: Poverty in the United States* (1962) helped the nation to rediscover the poverty in its backyard. This short book had a profound impact within the halls of Congress and reawakened nationwide debate on the role of government in combating poverty.

In the early part of his administration, President Lyndon Johnson declared a *War on Poverty* that would make full use of the nation's resources. The resulting initiative—later referred to as the Great Society programs—brought a new federal presence into local communities far different from previous welfare program efforts. Guided by the phrase "maximum feasible participation" of the poor, welfare programs involved the poor in local decision making in their neighborhoods and communities.

The coordinating agency for the Great Society was the Office of Economic Opportunity (OEO). Typical new welfare strategies included assistance to newborn babies and their mothers (Women, Infants, and Children or WIC), preschool education (Head Start), health care for seniors (Medicare) and the poor (Medicaid), employment programs for young adults (Job Corps), community action programs that encouraged neighbors to marshal resources, legal services for the poor, food stamps, and model city projects that were designed to provide assistance to the poorest neighborhoods.

Did You Know...Social worker and civil rights trailblazer Whitney M. Young, Jr. became the executive director of the National Urban League while serving as dean for the Atlanta School of Social Work. He also served as president of the NASW in the late 1960s.

The Great Society was spurred by a newfound belief that the nation could fight and win any battle it chose, and the War on Poverty had no borders. The Peace Corps, developed in 1965, sent volunteers to nations around the world to work in poor communities. Volunteers in Service to America (VISTA) was a domestic version of the Peace Corps with volunteers working in low-income American neighborhoods.

By the end of the 1960s, the Great Society was under growing attack for being too costly with too few benefits to the larger society. During the presidential administration of Richard Nixon, the influence of the OEO was minimized, and numerous programs were scrapped. In their place Nixon proposed an innovative guaranteed annual income for the poor—a *negative income tax*. Known as the Family Assistance Program (FAP), Nixon's plan would have subsidized a poor family by $2,400 a year. This plan required work or job training, with the states eventually having full responsibility for program operation. This controversial proposal was ultimately rejected by Congress, but it was nevertheless a dramatic attempt to establish a minimum income based on work requirements.

The 1980s and 1990s: A Return to the Work Ethic

With the election of Ronald Reagan to the presidency and a more conservative Congress, the attacks on public service relief programs became more numerous and boisterous. Numerous federal public assistance programs were eliminated whereas others had their funding cut and their eligibility requirements tightened to weed out the unworthy poor. The results of this realignment were dramatic. Palmer and Sawhill (1984, pp. 363–379) found that 500,000 families were removed from **Aid to Families with Dependent Children (AFDC)** and an additional 300,000 families received reduced benefits. One million people were eliminated from food stamp rolls. In 1985, the National Anti-Hunger Coalition charged that the federal government was not spending allocated funds for the WIC nutrition program, depriving thousands of pregnant women and newborn infants of health and nutrition services.

Children, women, seniors, and minorities were the primary victims of the Reagan welfare reforms. The message of the 1980s was clear: First, public assistance was contributing to the national debt. Second, only the truly needy, the poorest of the poor, would be helped with a safety net to ensure survival. Third, welfare was a state and a local, not a federal, concern.

The safety net approach places responsibility for helping the poor and **disadvantaged** at the doorstep of local government and private sources; the federal government becomes a resource of last resort. To achieve this purpose the Reagan administration adopted three overriding goals with regard to income security programs: (1) reduce short-term spending by implementing changes in entitlement programs, (2) turn over welfare responsibility to the states, and (3) promote reliance on individual resources rather than create and maintain dependence on governmental benefits (Storey, 1982). According to the American Assembly at Columbia University, the result was

> a patchwork of programs at the federal, state, and local level that results in gross inadequacies in education. . . . We have developed too few resources to prevention and maintenance, and too many to picking up pieces after the damage is done. On the other hand, the United States has established a broad welfare system for the non-poor while the middle and upper classes and corporate America are able to

take advantage of many benefits and, to a large extent, have become dependent on government support (American Assembly, 1989, p. 34).

Welfare reform continued in the 1990s with the 1992 presidential election of Bill Clinton, who promised to "end welfare as we know it." His ambition came within reach with later developments in Congress. The mid-term congressional election in 1994 brought a Republican sweep, and in their "Contract with America," conservative congressional Republicans made welfare reform a top priority.

In 1996 Congress essentially ended federal relief programs with the passage of the Personal Responsibility and Work Opportunity Reconciliation Act. In other words, Clinton's pledge "to end welfare as we know it" became reality. The new law abolished specific categorical programs and provided federal block grants to the states. Today, the federal government is no longer responsible for operating public welfare programs. No longer does the country have a national welfare program. Rather each state operates its own set of public welfare services, each with its own set of eligibility criteria, program rules, and benefits. Another way of looking at public welfare is to recognize that the nation has fifty different welfare programs, each operating under a different set of rules. Commonalities come from conditions placed on federal block grants: a lifetime limit of five years of relief, a work requirement, and participation in job-training programs.

According to the Federal Welfare Reform Act of 1996, all adult welfare recipients are required to work, be registered for work, or be participating in job-training or educational programs. The Food Stamp Program—now run by the states—has similar eligibility criteria; failure to follow these work guidelines results in program disqualification. This welfare reform act also ended the AFDC program, in place since the New Deal. It was replaced by Temporary Assistance for Needy Families (TANF), a short-term program that incorporates lifetime limitations and work requirements.

The Clinton administration can claim a number of achievements: lowest number of people receiving public welfare; an 80-percent increase in child support payments; increased availability of housing vouchers; the creation of incentives to save, such as the Individual Development Acccounts; increased minimum wage; protected Medicare and modest health care reform; immunization rates raised to an all-time high; and the enactment of the largest health care act for children (Children's Health Insurance Program [CHIP]).

COMPASSIONATE CONSERVATISM AND THE NEW MILLENIUM

Moving into the twenty-first century, President George W. Bush pledged a new approach to social welfare, which he referred to as *compassionate conservatism.*

Essentially this philosophy relies on the private, voluntary sector to provide assistance. Through volunteerism and private, nonprofit, and faith-based organizations, people in need of help are provided with locally developed programs. At the same time, the compassionate conservative philosophy seeks out programs and policies that support the traditional two-parent family; strategies that encourage a rewards-based public education system; public assistance programs that are temporary in nature and support individual responsibility; and, when appropriate, assistance, both monetary and humanitarian aid, to Third and Fourth World nations. What emerged was a federal welfare program that was almost 180 degrees from the 1930s New Deal program or the 1960s War on Poverty. President Reagan's stance that "government is not the solution but the problem" was almost completely realized under compassionate conservatism.

Yet, when looking at the Bush years, one must recognize that slightly less than eight months after Bush took office, the United States was attacked. Eighteen months after 9/11, in March 2003, the United States invaded Iraq, and this war became the singular focus of the Bush administration, resulting in becoming the nation's longest war. Some might argue that the Bush presidency was not preoccupied with Iraq, but we will leave that analysis to the historians.

Allard (2007, p. 305) notes that the Bush presidency significantly changed public welfare from direct cash benefits to "a system that provides most assistance through social services program supporting work activity." The Bush years also saw a further reliance on faith-based charities, blurring what had been a distinct line between church and state. Other significant changes revolved around increasing the TANF work requirement from twenty to thirty hours per week. At the same time, TANF moved away from direct cash payments to providing more services, such as day care, job search, mental health services, and substance abuse programs. By the mid-2000s, the Earned Income Tax Credit (EITC) program became the largest means-tested program with work as the key criterion for entry, thus reinforcing the Bush administration goal of independence with less reliance on the government (Allard, 2007).

By the time President Obama took office in 2009, the nation's economy was in dire straits—unemployment was rising, along with home foreclosures, and businesses were collapsing. The pressures felt in the United States were reverberating around the world. People understood that Main Street and Wall Street were connected.

The first term of the Obama Administration was filled with congressional gridlock. Little got done as the art of political compromise seemed to be a memory of the distant past. The most significant act passed during Obama's first term dealt with health care. A Democratically controlled Congress passed the Patient Protection and Affordable Care Act, also referred to as the Affordable Care Act

(ACA) and sarcastically referred to as Obama Care, which was signed into law on March 23, 2010. From the first day the law was passed and then signed into law, the Republican Party and many state governments challenged the legality of this new law. More than half of the states, as well as a number of faith-based organizations and nonprofit agencies, challenged the legality of the law while the U.S. House of Representatives voted more than fifty times to defund ACA. The U.S. Supreme Court, somewhat surprisingly, upheld the key parts of the law on two separate occasions, first in 2012 and once again in 2015. The latter Supreme Court decision basically ended the major legal tests to the veracity of the ACA. No doubt legal challenges will continue to plague the ACA, just as there were ongoing legal battles over the Social Security Act following its passage in 1936 and the Medicare Act in 1965. In the end, just as with Social Security and Medicare, the ACA will remain a major frontline social welfare program.

This health insurance law created important access to the health care system for many who, prior to its enactment, were unable to receive health services. Other important features include provisions that individuals with preexisting conditions could not be denied health insurance, younger adults could remain on their parent's insurance program, and states were to create exchanges whereby insurance companies competed, by offering lower prices, to enroll individuals.

In 2012, as Obama headed into his second term as president, he set forth a progressive agenda that clearly addressed social justice issues including women's rights, African American rights, and gay rights. As the Twitter verse noted the day following his inaugural address, "no other president has even mentioned gay rights in an inaugural speech, let alone mentioned it alongside other movements that forged a more equal America." And on June 26, 2015, the U.S. Supreme Court legalized same sex marriage; that night the White House was lit up in rainbow colors to celebrate the broadening of rights to all people.

Issues regarding immigration and so-called border control came to the forefront by 2014 and became central to the national discussion around citizenship. The political right called for tightening border security by building walls on the country's southern border with Mexico while sending National Guard and federal troops to guard the border. It is interesting to juxtapose the current conservative call for building a wall to keep people out of the United States with conservative President Ronald Regan's 1987 speech in Berlin, demanding of Russian leader Mikhail Gorbachev that he "tear down this wall." How is it that over thirty years the United States changed its position from tearing down barriers to freedom to building both legal and physical hurdles to citizenship?

The political world of the twenty-first century is fraught with emotion and gridlock. The idea to seek common ground and negotiate on differences seems lost in today's bitter political discourse. Social issues are complex and interwoven with the ever-changing global environment. We do not know how social media will continue to affect or change how we work with and on behalf of others. We do know, however, that as social workers we must stay informed of the present while recognizing and understanding the successes and failures of the past. The social work profession has much to offer, but without a doubt you must watch to see what unfolds over these next critical years, and most importantly, to become an engaged partner in the process of change. And as you participate in the molding of our collective future, be sure that your debate is fair and accurate, no matter what your position.

SUMMARY

American social welfare history is marked by a deep mistrust of the poor. Persistent beliefs that the poor are immoral and lacking either the ability or the desire to work have inspired repeated attempts to condition relief on work and improved behavior—and, above all, to make relief as difficult to obtain as possible. Social welfare and ensuring social justice are much bigger than programs to support the poor and disadvantaged such as Section 8 housing and the Supplemental Nutritional Assistance Program. The federal government provides support to a variety of groups; banks requiring bailouts, farmers needing subsidies, and cities requiring federal loans to make payrolls are just some of the many acceptable forms of welfare. In these circumstances, however, bankers, farmers, and mayors do not consider themselves welfare recipients; rather, these federal supports are viewed as necessary subsidies that benefit the community.

Workfare, training programs, and stringent program eligibility requirements, coupled with ongoing recertification required to continue receiving even minimal assistance, are the punitive features of today's federal and state welfare systems. When it comes to poverty, Americans are inclined to continue to blame the victim. Rather than maintaining a dignified helping system accessible to the poor, American welfare policy is designed to exclude people and to discourage clients by constantly setting hurdles to eligibility.

The philosophy that undergirds today's welfare system for the poor reflects some of Benjamin Franklin's admonitions. The reluctance to acknowledge government responsibility continues, and with a lifetime limit on years of eligibility for welfare, so do deep concerns about dependence. Recipients are to be forced into a totally independent and self-reliant mode of existence.

Throughout its history, finding the appropriate balance between public and private responsibility has plagued American social welfare. There is a clear record of national ambivalence and resistance toward welfare services and the poor. The current debate on welfare is an extension of a discussion that extends back to colonial times. The lack of national consensus on who is to receive what type of social provisions for what period of time and on how these services will be funded means that the debate will continue well into the twenty-first century. Therefore, social workers are among the leaders promoting social justice by advocating for increased and improved services for all groups. This challenge supports the notion that social justice is a human issue and much more than just a legal or moral issue (Monroe, 2003). Primary emphasis needs to be placed on: (1) understanding the current social, political, and economic environment; and (2) using this knowledge to educate and mobilize the community and other stakeholders to work together to identify and address social problems and to develop effective programs designed to address these needs.

MOVIES

Movies on social welfare history rarely receive Academy Award consideration or excite producers. The following movies, while not specifically detailing social welfare history, help us to better understand people and their conditions in the past. Many of these films can be found on Netflix.

Across the Sea of Time: 1920s New York City through the eyes of Russian immigrants.

All Mine to Give: Orphaned children in nineteenth century Wisconsin are put in different homes in order to survive.

America, America: In the 1890s, a Greek youth immigrates to New York City; emotional presentation of an immigrant's challenges.

April Morning: A solid portrayal of a teenager's life in the American colonies immediately before the American Revolution.

Attacks on Culture: A brief (forty-nine minute) examination of the U.S. government's legislative attacks on Native Americans.

Autobiography of Miss Jane Pittman: An examination of life from the Civil War through the 1950s as remembered by a one-hundred-ten-year-old former slave.

Avalon: A Russian Jewish immigrant family moves to New York City.

Black West: An examination of African American cowboys, the unsung heroes of the West.

Cyberbully: A teenager finds herself the target of bullying on a popular social media website.

Freedom Writers: A young teacher has her students keep journals about their troubled lives, hoping they will apply history's lesson from *The Diary of Ann Frank* to break the cycle of violence and despair.

Ghandi: 1982 film about a young attorney who leads change in India and becomes a global symbol of nonviolence and understanding.

Grapes of Wrath: Classic John Steinbeck story of a family's search for a better life than in 1930s Depression Oklahoma.

I am Sam: After fathering a child with a homeless women, Sam—who is developmentally delayed—raises the baby until Child Protective Services steps in.

Jasper, Texas: Film on the horrific 1998 murder of African American James Byrd in Jasper, Texas.

Lean on Me: A tough-talking high school principal uses everything in his power to turn around an inner city, drug-infested, violence-ridden school.

The Molly Maguires: Interesting film set in the 1870s Pennsylvania coal country, as the Irish try to organize a union.

Philadelphia: An attorney sues his law firm after being fired because he is gay and HIV-positive.

Precious: Viciously abused by her mother and impregnated by her father, a Harlem teen has an unexpected chance at a different life when she enrolls in an alternative school while continuing to face barriers and struggles.

Roll of Thunder Hear My Cry: A Black teen copes with depression, poverty, and racism in 1930s Mississippi.

Separate but Equal: An examination of Thurgood Marshall as the NAACP attorney whose U.S. Supreme Court case led to the end of segregation.

Sounder: A sharecropper is forced to steal to feed his family while the family deals with poverty and racism in the 1930s.

To Kill a Mockingbird: A White southern attorney defends an innocent Black man against rape charges and ends up in a maelstrom of hate and prejudice.

We Were Here: The AIDS health crisis changed the culture in San Francisco; this documentary explores the lives of five individuals affected by this disease.

Wild Women of the Old West: The stereotype of the quiet housewife is broken with this analysis of women in the 1800s.

A Woman Called Moses: An examination of the life of Harriet Ross Tubman, a fugitive slave, founder of the Underground Railroad, and leader in the abolitionist movement.

Quiz Answers

1. In October 1492 Christopher Columbus reached the Bahamas, marking Europe's first documented contact with the Americas.

2. The New Deal was the name given to a set of social and economic programs established under the leadership of President Franklin D. Roosevelt in the 1930s to combat the Depression.

3. The Emancipation Proclamation freed slaves in areas (rebellion states) no longer loyal to the union.

4. In Seneca Falls, New York, in 1848 women's rights advocate Elizabeth Cady Stanton organized a convention that generated a declaration of women's rights.

5 Earlier immigrants arrived from northern and western Europe. By 1900, there was a significant rise in people from eastern and southern Europe.

6. In the late seventeenth century nineteen people were executed for witchcraft in Salem, Massachusetts.

7. In 1845 the United States annexed most of what is now Texas. Mexico ceded the remaining land in 1848 following the Mexican-American War.

8. The Articles of Confederation, adopted in 1777, united the colonies; it created a one-house congress.

9. In 1867, William Seward negotiated the purchase of land, now Alaska, from Russia for $7.2 million. This transaction was called Seward's Folly because, until the discovery of gold, people saw little value in this distant purchase.

10. Dred Scott, a Missouri slave, sued for his freedom in 1847. The 1857 Supreme Court decision held that slaves were property and had no claim to the rights of citizenship.

REFERENCES

Alexander, C. (1995). Distinctive dates in social welfare history. In R. Edwards et al. (Eds.), *Encyclopedia of social work* (19th ed., pp. 2631–2647). Washington, DC: NASW Press.

Allard, S. (2007). The changing face of welfare during the Bush administration. *Publius: The Journal of Federalism, 37,* 304–332.

American Assembly. (1989, November). *The future of social welfare in America.* Columbia University. Harriman, NY: Arden House.

Axinn, J., & Levin, H. (1982). *Social welfare: A history of the American response to need* (2nd ed.). New York: Harper and Row.

Boyer, P. (1978). *Urban classes and moral order in America, 1820–1990.* Cambridge, MA: Harvard University Press.

Chambers, C. A. (1967). *Seedtime of reform: American social service and social action, 1918–1933.* Ann Arbor, MI: University of Michigan Press.

Cole, B. (1973). *Perspectives in public welfare: A history* (3rd ed.). Washington, DC: Government Printing Office.

Dziegielewski, S. F. (2013). *The changing face of health care social work: Opportunities and challenges for professional practice* (3rd ed.). New York: Springer.

Gilbert, N., & Specht, H. (1981). *The emergence of social welfare and social work* (2nd ed.). Itasca, IL: Peacock.

Gurteen, H. (1882). *A handbook of charity organization.* Buffalo, NY: Charity Organization Society.

Harrington, M. (1962). *The other America: Poverty in the United States.* New York: Macmillan.

Heffner, W. (1913). *History of poor relief legislation in Pennsylvania, 1682–1913.* Cleona, PA: Holzapfel.

Jansson, B. S. (2004). *The reluctant welfare state: American social welfare policies past, present, and future* (5th ed.). Pacific Grove, CA: Brooks/Cole.

Karger, H. J., & Stoesz, D. (2010). *American social welfare policy: A pluralist approach* (6th ed.). Boston, MA: Pearson Education, Inc./Allyn Bacon.

Katz, M. B. (1986). *In the shadow of the poorhouse: A social history of welfare in America.* New York: Basic Books.

Leighninger, L. (2008). The history of social work and social welfare. In K. M. Sowers & C. N. Dulmus (Series Eds.) & B. W. White (Vol. Ed.), *Comprehensive handbook of social work and social welfare: The profession of social work* (vol. 1, pp. 1–24). Hoboken, NJ: Wiley.

Lubove, C. (1965). *The professional altruist.* Cambridge, MA: Harvard University Press.

Monroe, I. (2003). Becoming what we ought to be: We cannot separate our efforts to heal the world from the difficult work of healing ourselves. *The Other Side, 39,* 43–45.

Palmer, J., & Sawhill, I. (1984). *The Reagan record.* Cambridge, MA: Ballinger.

Rothman, D. (1971). *The discovery of the asylum social order and disorder in the new republic.* Boston: Little, Brown.

Storey, J. R. (1982). Income security. In J. Palmer & I. Sawhill (Eds.), *The Reagan experiment* (vol. 5, pp. 361–392). Washington, DC: Urban Institute Press.

Trattner, W. (1989). *From poor law to welfare state: A history of social welfare in America* (4th ed.). New York: Free Press.

Williams, H. (1944). Benjamin Franklin and poor laws. *Social Service Review, 18,* 77–84.

CHAPTER 4
SO YOU WANT TO BE A SOCIAL WORKER!

THERE ARE NUMEROUS JOBS FOR SOCIAL WORKERS THROUGHOUT the country in cities, suburbs, and rural communities. Through 2020 employment opportunities for social workers will be "faster than average" with a 19-percent projected increase in opportunities (U.S. Department of Labor [DOL], 2014a). The growth in positions will be in both public and private agencies, large and small alike. Gerontology, long-term care services, health care (particularly in hospitals), substance abuse, school social work, and private practice are cited in the DOL's *Occupational Outlook Handbook* as having the greatest opportunities for social workers.

On any given day social work job opportunities across the country are listed by a variety of sources, including the national and state offices of the National Association of Social Work (NASW), schools of social work, university career placement offices, and national magazines such as *Social Work Today*. For example from August 14, through September 15, 2014, seventy-five different social work openings were posted on the University of Houston Graduate College of Social Work website (http://www.uh.edu/socialwork/alumni/career-services/job-board/). Not surprisingly, positions were in a variety of public and private nonprofit settings working with different population groups on a wide range of issues. Just as interesting is the number of international opportunities for social workers with nongovernmental organizations (NGOs) such as Amigos de las Américas; CARE; the Association of Women's Rights in Development; the American Refugee Committee; Counterpart International, Inc.; and Doctors of the World.

Suffice it to say, there is an array of employment opportunities for BSW, MSW, and DSW or PhD practitioners in every state and throughout the world. What is probably most exciting to the job seeker is that social work positions offer a variety of challenges working with individuals, groups, families, organizations, and communities.

This chapter will explore the nature of employment opportunities in the field of social work. We will first discuss the educational requirements to become a social worker and the role that accreditation standards play. Then we will look at an overview of prospects for social workers today, presenting salary and employment projections into the twenty-first century. We will conclude with tips on finding that first social work job.

THE EDUCATION OF A SOCIAL WORKER

What educational criteria are needed to make a person a social worker? The answer is simple: a baccalaureate or master's degree in social work—that is, a BSW, BSSW, or BA or BS in social work or an MSW, MSSW, or MA or MS in social work— from a program accredited by the Council of Social Work Education, more commonly referred to as the CSWE. When students graduate from these kinds of degree programs in social work, they are considered to have professional practice degrees.

A degree in sociology, psychology, anthropology, or any other *ology* does not make a person a social worker. The major difference between a degree in social work and these other degrees is that sociology, psychology, and anthropology are science-based. People who major in these fields may specialize in practice or complete practice-based courses, but they are not based in practice as social work graduates are.

It is also important to note that working in a social agency for ten years, even under the tutelage of a degreed social worker, does not alone make a person a qualified social worker. Further, a doctoral degree or PhD in social work is not recognized as a practice degree. Since the early 2000s, a number of graduate social work programs began to offer the DSW or doctorate in social work as a practice doctorate, and a number of states will license an individual with a DSW for practice even if he or she does not have a BSW or MSW degree. These programs are not regulated by the CSWE, and their graduates are considered researchers, administrators, educators, or scientific practitioners. As a result, entry into the social work profession is limited, and those interested in becoming social workers must pass through at least one of the two doors.

Not to muddy the waters, but in some states, it is possible to be licensed to practice social work without having a degree in social work. For example, some states may choose to *grandfather in*—or make exceptions for—certain individuals to practice or sit for a qualifying exam. Generally, each state sets its own criteria and deadlines for this type of exception so it is best to contact the state licensing board directly to find out if and how these exemptions are made. For example, in Alabama certain client protection workers for the state have been grandfathered in and are therefore eligible to be licensed as baccalaureate level social workers; these individuals do not have BSWs, a standard requirement in most states. West Virginia has also used a similar practice. Caution should be exercised, however, because people who use this nontraditional door into social work may be disappointed if they move from the granting state. Other states may not honor their designated status, and no appeal based on reciprocity is possible.

Remember that the best way to ensure entry into the field of social work is the traditional way: by earning a baccalaureate or master's degree in social work from a program accredited by the CSWE. As of June 2015, the CSWE had accredited 734 BSW and MSW social work programs across the country (Council on Social Work Education, 2015a).

The difference between someone who simply wants to help and someone who is professionally educated in the knowledge and skills to give help is pronounced. Nevertheless, some professionals from other disciplines feel that the demanding requirements that must be satisfied to qualify as a social worker are unfair. That most states require a professional social worker to have either a bachelor's or a graduate college degree in social work strikes them as elitist. In fact, they may say, a lot of good people carry out important activities on behalf of individuals in need, and these helping workers should also be considered social workers. Most professional social workers would disagree because they believe that social work is indeed a profession and, as such, must have clear rules and requirements for entry. Social workers believe that within the field, professionals are expected to confront the full range of human problems and to do so in multiple practice settings (Burger & Youkeles, 2004); this requires professional education as a generalist.

To support this position, let's look at the entry requirements for several professions:

- ◆ *Law*: Completion of a baccalaureate degree in any discipline, graduation from a law program accredited by the American Bar Association, and successful completion of a state bar examination. At one time, a person could sit for the bar exam without graduating from a law program. In such cases, individuals were required to have worked in a law office under the mentorship of a board-certified lawyer, that is, one who had passed the bar exam, for a number of years. This practice is no longer allowed. In January 2013 the American Bar Association accredited 202 programs (http://www.americanbar.org/groups/legal_education/resources/aba_approved_law_schools.html).
- ◆ *Medicine*: Completion of a baccalaureate degree, preferably in the hard sciences (which include the natural or physical sciences, such as chemistry, biology, physics, or astronomy); graduation from a medical school accredited by the American Medical Association; and successful completion of a state medical examination. In the past, as with law school graduation, medical school graduation was not a requirement for practice, but that is no longer the case. The accreditation standards of the Accreditation

Commission on Colleges of Medicine (2014) require both "didactic and practical" educational experiences.

◆ *Nursing*: Education in the scientific basis of nursing under defined standards of education and concern with the **diagnosis** and treatment of human responses to actual or potential health problems (*PDR Medical Dictionary*, 2005). Most nurses have completed their education in accredited programs and can practice at the level appropriate to their educational qualifications. Degrees include associate degree in nursing, bachelor of science in nursing, master of science in nursing, and doctorate of nursing practice. In addition, there are several specializations such as midwifery and nurse practitioner (http://www.allnursingschools.com/nursing-careers/entry-to-nursing/nursing-school-accreditation). For example, a licensed practical nurse has graduated from an accredited school of practical (vocational) nursing (one year of training) and passed the state exam for licensure, and is licensed to practice by the state authority. Similar requirements with varying education exist at the associate, baccalaureate, and graduate levels. An individual without a degree in nursing may assist a nurse in daily routines; often this individual is called a nurse's aide. Regardless of education, nurse's aides are not nurses and cannot perform the traditional duties of nurses licensed at different levels of skill acquisition.

◆ *Physical therapy*: Completion of a baccalaureate degree, with emphasis in biology, chemistry, physics, and social sciences or graduation from a graduate physical therapy program accredited by the Commission on Accreditation in Physical Therapy Education. In October 2014, there were 218 accredited physical therapist programs and an additional 309 physical therapist assistant programs were accredited nationwide (http://www.capteonline.org/home.aspx).

Law, medicine, nursing, and physical therapy are only a few of the professions that require professional education regulated by a professional accrediting body and usually successful completion of a state examination to practice. Until the nineteenth century, people were not required to complete any formal education in order to enter particular professions. Instead, someone hoping to enter a profession studied and worked as an apprentice under a practicing member of that profession who was recognized as experienced. This mentoring model was acceptable for three main reasons. First, at that time the relatively few colleges and universities were geographically inaccessible to many. Second, because there were fewer schools, the number of people who could participate in higher education was limited by the availability of educators and seats. Third, few families could afford the costs of a college education. Higher education was reserved for the elite and, for the most part, White males. With these limits on access to formal education, most aspiring professionals found it productive to learn under the watchful eye and guidance of a successful practitioner.

With the spread of the public state college system and the democratization of all higher education, the historical barriers were slowly chipped away. As formal education became more accessible, many professionals moved their courses of study from the practical to the academic setting. Social work was no exception.

Did You Know…In 2014, New York had more accredited BSW and MSW programs (48) than any other state. Following New York were Pennsylvania (44) and Texas (44), whereas Wyoming (2) had the fewest BSW and MSW programs; go to CSWE.org for more information about accreditation and updated statistics.

The first documented educational training program in social work was a six-week-long summer institute offered in 1898. Sponsored by the New York Charity Organization Society, this program is credited with helping to found the Columbia University School of Social Work. Before this summer institute was held, almost all social work training took place within agencies and was provided by agency staff.

In the years that followed, social work education became a fixture of higher education. Following the June 2014 meeting of the CSWE's Commission on Accreditation (CSWE, 2015b), there were a total of 500 accredited baccalaureate level and 233 master's level programs; there were also 27 BSW and MSW programs in candidacy (that is, working to meet the CSWE accreditation standards). Table 1 shows the increasing numbers of degreed programs in social work from 2000 until 2015.

Table 1. Number of Accredited BSW and MSW Programs and Number of PhD/DSW Programs

Year	BSW	MSW	PhD/DSW*
2015	504	235	76
2013	482	219	73
2011	472	213	71
2009	470	195	NA
2007	462	186	NA
2005	450	174	NA
2003	437	159	NA
2000	420	139	67

*Note: These numbers include only U.S.-based doctoral programs.
Source: Council on Social Work Education, *Social Work Program Data*, 2015. Retrieved from http://www.cswe.org/CentersInitiatives/DataStatistics/ProgramData.aspx

Social work education also prepares individuals in doctoral education. The national organization for social work doctoral education is called the Advancement of Doctoral Education in Social Work (GADE) with a membership in 2014 totaling eighty-one colleges and universities.

There are thousands of social work educational programs found in all regions of the world. There is no reliable estimate of the total number of social work programs worldwide, but the conservative consensus of the International Association of Schools of Social Work is that there are a minimum of 2,500 programs.

Did You Know...In 2012, the Association of Social Work Boards reported that the national pass rate for the bachelor's licensing exam was 77.1% and 83.6% for the master's exam.

The twentieth century was critical for the developing field of social work. During this time social work was transformed from a volunteer activity into an established profession requiring a clearly designed education. When apprenticeship occurs now, it is intertwined with or follows a competency-based education provided within the rigorous setting of baccalaureate or graduate study.

ACCREDITATION AND WHY IT MATTERS

As an aspiring social work professional, you should be aware of the accreditation standards your social work program must meet. By meeting these standards your program assures you and others that when you complete its requirements you will be well prepared for your future career. Because of the importance of this information, we will present an overview of accreditation and explain how it relates directly to your development as a professional in the field of social work.

Council on Social Work Education

The CSWE is the primary national organization that oversees and provides guidelines for social work education in the United States. The council was organized in 1952 with the merger of the National Association of Schools of Social Administration (NASSA), which had coordinated baccalaureate education, and the American Association of Schools of Social Work (AASSW), the membership body for graduate programs (Beless, 1995). Today, social work education is a big enterprise with programs found on more than 500 different colleges and universities nationwide. There are 116,340 full-time and part-time students enrolled in BSW, MSW, and doctoral programs (see Table 2), supported by 10,929 full- and part-time faculty. In total, 38,694 social work degrees were awarded in 2013.

Table 2. Number of BSW, MSW, and PhD/DSW Students and Graduates of Accredited Programs

	2013	2011	2006	2000
BSW students*	58,087	40,369	32,457	35,255
BSW degrees awarded	17,221	14,662	12,845	11,773
MSW students	54,188	49,236	39,566	33,815
MSW degrees awarded	22,677	20,573	17,209	15,016
MSW applications made, first year	57,454	51,700	36,715	30,262
PhD/DSW students	2,545	2,575	2,554	1,953
PhD/DSW degrees awarded	339	321	293	229

*Includes both full and part-time students.
Source: Council on Social Work Education, *Social Work Program Data*, 2015. Retrieved from http://www.cswe.org/CentersInitiatives/DataStatistics/ProgramData.aspx

Activity... Visit the CSWE webpage at www.cswe.org and look for the listing of schools, colleges, departments, and programs of social work under the Accreditation link. Compare and contrast programs from around the country, urban and rural programs, and large and small colleges/universities. What differences, if any, do you find? What kinds of electives do programs offer? How do BSW and MSW programs differ? What patterns of interesting educational activities do you find?

Although the CSWE was formed by the merger of two organizations that concentrated on baccalaureate and graduate education, respectively, undergraduate education over time appeared to take a back seat to graduate studies (Leighninger, 1987). It wasn't until 1974 that the CSWE implemented accreditation standards for baccalaureate programs. As Gardellia (1997) noted, BSW and MSW educational programs have never been fully integrated—that is, they have never viewed each other as equal partners—which has created tension between the groups. Moreover, the CSWE board of directors initially included ten seats for BSW educators and twenty seats for MSW educators (Gardellia, 1997, p. 39). But over time, the disproportional number of board seats changed to increase the number of BSW educators on the board. In 2009, the CSWE board undertook significant structural revisions that included equal representation of baccalaureate and graduate educators. Even so, there are some social work faculty, both undergraduate and graduate educators alike, who continue to foster unnecessary tensions between the program levels.

For social work students, knowing how CSWE business is conducted can be helpful in understanding why its educational programs are organized as they are. The CSWE is governed by six commissions: Accreditation, Curriculum and

Educational Innovation, Diversity and Social and Economic Justice, Professional Development, Research, and Global Social Work Education. Working with the commissions are councils that focus on specific interest areas. For example, three councils work with the Commission on Diversity and Social and Economic Justice: (1) the Council on Disabilities and Persons with Disabilities; (2) the Council on Sexual Orientation and Gender Expression; and (3) the Council on Racial, Ethnic, and Cultural Diversity. Explore the various councils and commissions at the CSWE website (http://www.cswe.org/CSWE/about/governance). Look at the important work each is doing to promote, enhance, and strengthen social work education. You will discover that social work educators are tackling a variety of issues and that they do this for free! That's right, social work educators volunteer countless hours serving on the board of directors, commissions, and councils. They do this because as social workers they understand the importance of working on behalf of the entire professional community.

Did You Know... The U.S. Department of Labor reported that in 2012 social workers' most frequent employment setting was state and local government (41%) followed by health care (36%); educational settings (15%); and faith-based, grant-making, civic, and professional organizations (5%).

Now let's explore two of these commissions in detail to learn more about their work and significance to you: the CSWE Commission on Accreditation and the CSWE Commission on Educational Policy.

Commission on Accreditation

One of the most important functions of the CSWE is the accreditation of baccalaureate and master's degree programs. Why is accreditation important? States require an individual to graduate from a CSWE accredited program in order to be eligible for licensure/registration to practice social work. This in general is a hard and fast requirement (e.g., state rule) that is in place throughout the United States.

Social work accreditation is coordinated by the Commission on Accreditation, a twenty-five-member committee that includes social work educators representing both BSW and MSW faculties, BSW and MSW students, and social work practitioners. Referred to as commissioners, these individuals are volunteers who are appointed by the president of the CSWE for three-year terms; a commissioner may serve no more than two consecutive terms or a total of six years. A professional CSWE staff supports the commission. The commission influences the direction of social work education through such activities as maintaining and updating accreditation standards; conducting commissioner **site visits** to programs in candidacy; voting on candidacy status, initial accreditation, and **reaffirmation**; and ensuring the quality of social work education and of the commission's functions.

Commission on Educational Policy

This commission sets CSWE's educational direction through its work around educational policy and accreditation standards. The commission is responsible for thinking through current and future practice needs while considering differing ways to build social work educational programs. This commission includes approximately sixteen volunteers who represent all levels and sectors of social work education.

Educational Policy and Accreditation Standards

The Educational Policy (EP) and Accreditation Standards (AS) are written by the CSWE's Commission on Educational Policy and are the central and critical document to social work educators and program developers. As part of its compliance with the CSWE's Bylaws, which require that EP and AS be reviewed at least once every seven years, the board of directors approved the current EP in 2015 (CSWE, Commission on Educational Policy and Commission on Accreditation, 2015, p. 4). The CSWE Commission on Educational Policy is responsible for drafting the EP whereas the CSWE Commission on Accreditation establishes the AS.

The EP serves a threefold purpose. First, it describes in broad terms the essence of social work education at the bachelors and master levels of education. Second, the EP sets forth core practice competencies, that is, measureable practice skills expected for the beginning BSW and MSW practitioner. And third, the EP establishes the basic educational principles from which the AS are developed.

The document is critical to social work education and your program. You may wonder why certain courses are required whereas others are electives; you just need to read the EP and AS to gain a beginning understanding of your program's structure (see CSWE, Commission on Educational Policy and Commission on Accreditation, 2015). Your faculty crafted the curriculum based on the EP in what they believe meets the program's mission and broader practice community needs. You should also know that students are expected to be familiar with the EP and AS. Just as important to remember is that, if your program is being accredited or reviewed for reaccreditation, you may be asked by the site visit team to share your reactions to and observations of the policy.

Did You Know...Social workers spend the majority of their time providing direct client services (96%), followed by consultation (73%) and administration/management (69%).

As you read through the EPAS, you will find that it addresses a number of different subjects, including curricular design and educational context to prepare students for professional social work practice. The focus of the EP and resulting AS is on nine specific practice competencies and related demonstrable behaviors that a social work student must demonstrate in his or her course of study. All students, BSW and MSW alike, must master and demonstrate these nine competencies and their related practice behaviors, but more on that later. According to the EP, the BSW is the entry-level degree, and a BSW practitioner's interventions are developed within a *generalist practice* framework (CSWE, Commission on Educational Policy and Commission on Accreditation, 2015, p. 11). The MSW is the advanced practice degree, and an MSW practitioner's interventions are developed within a **specialist practice** framework (CSWE, Commission on Educational Policy and Commission on Accreditation, 2015, p. 12).

Generalist and specialist social workers can be characterized as follows:

- *Generalist*: A social work practitioner whose knowledge and skills encompass a broad spectrum and who assesses problems and their solutions comprehensively. The generalist often coordinates the efforts of specialists by facilitating communication between them, thereby fostering continuity of care.
- *Specialist*: A social work practitioner whose orientation and knowledge are focused on a specific problem or goal or whose technical expertise and skill in specific activities are highly developed and refined (Barker, 2003).

Accreditation Standards for Social Work Programs

The EPAS requires all social work educational programs to be grounded in the liberal arts from which the professional education grows (CSWE, Commission on Educational Policy and Commission on Accreditation, 2015, p. 11.). According to the Commission on Accreditation, the liberal arts perspective

> enriches understanding of the person-environment context of professional social work practice and is integrally related to the mastery of social work content. . . . It provides an understanding of one's cultural heritage in the context of other cultures; the methods and limitations of systems of inquiry; and the knowledge, attitudes, ways of thinking, and means of communication that are characteristic of a broadly educated person (CSWE, 1994, pp. 99–100, 138).

That is why you were required to complete several courses in liberal arts before you were allowed to enroll in social work classes. The completion of these courses satisfies part of the social work program's liberal arts educational requirement. Content areas most often completed are English, additional electives in the arts and humanities, science, history, political science, sociology, anthropology, and psychology. A point to remember is that accreditation standards do not specify liberal arts courses that must be completed; instead, your program faculty identifies courses that they feel will prepare you for the social work program's course of study.

Did You Know...The average salary for a social work was $44,200 nationwide in 2012.

According to the 2015 EPAS,

The explicit curriculum constitutes the program's formal educational structure and includes the courses and field education used for each of its program options. Social work education is grounded in the liberal arts, which provide the intellectual basis for the professional curriculum and inform its design. Using a competency-based education framework, the explicit curriculum prepares students for professional practice at the baccalaureate and master's levels. Baccalaureate programs prepare students for generalist practice. Master's programs prepare students for generalist practice and specialized practice. The explicit curriculum, including field education, may include forms of technology as a component of the curriculum (CSWE, Commission on Educational Policy and Commission on Accreditation, 2015, p. 11).

The key requirement according to the 2015 EPAS is the mastery of the nine core competencies (see Table 3) though a program may add additional competencies. Again, the actual number of core competencies may change with the current revisions. With that caveat, all programs, BSW and MSW alike, must ensure that students address and are able to demonstrate the ten competencies. As a result of this mandate, a BSW student in New York addresses the same core competencies as a BSW student in Missoula, Montana. This results in a common ground for all social workers whatever their individual agency settings, client populations, practice functions, or practice methods. This common educational content is a real asset. In particular, this competency model helps supervisors and coworkers know what new social workers are able to do as a result of their formal professional education. No such uniformity in educational content exists for some related disciplines such as the various counseling specialties.

Activity...Meet with a social work advisor to discuss your program's admission process. Is the program a limited access program? What is the application process? Are all applicants accepted into the program? What are some of the reasons why people are denied admission to the program? Explore with the advisor the program's liberal arts requirements. Why are these specific courses required? Are you surprised by some of the required courses?

Table 3. 2015 Educational Policy and Accreditation Standards: Nine Core Competencies for Social Work Education

Specific competency	Educational policy explanation of competency	Examples of competencies
Competency 1: Demonstrate ethical and professional behavior	Social workers understand the value base of the profession and its ethical standards, as well as relevant laws and regulations that may impact practice at the micro, mezzo, and macro levels. Social workers understand frameworks of ethical decision-making and how to apply principles of critical thinking to those frameworks in practice, research, and policy arenas. Social workers recognize personal values and the distinction between personal and professional values. They also understand how their personal experiences and affective reactions influence their professional judgment and behavior. Social workers understand the profession's history, its mission, and the roles and responsibilities of the profession. Social Workers also understand the role of other professions when engaged in interprofessional teams. Social workers recognize the importance of life-long learning and are committed to continually updating their skills to ensure they are relevant and effective. Social workers also understand emerging forms of technology and the ethical use of technology in social work practice.	◆ Make ethical decisions by applying the standards of the NASW Code of Ethics, relevant laws and regulations, models for ethical decision-making, ethical conduct of research, and additional codes of ethics as appropriate to context. ◆ Use reflection and self-regulation to manage personal values and maintain professionalism in practice situations. ◆ Demonstrate professional demeanor in behavior; appearance; and oral, written, and electronic communication. ◆ Use technology ethically and appropriately to facilitate practice outcomes. ◆ Use supervision and consultation to guide professional judgment and behavior.

Competency 2: Engage diversity and difference in practice	Social workers understand how diversity and difference characterize and shape the human experience and are critical to the formation of identity. The dimensions of diversity are understood as the intersectionality of multiple factors including but not limited to age, class, color, culture, disability and ability, ethnicity, gender, gender identity and expression, immigration status, marital status, political ideology, race, religion/spirituality, sex, sexual orientation, and tribal sovereign status. Social workers understand that, as a consequence of difference, a person's life experiences may include oppression, poverty, marginalization, and alienation as well as privilege, power, and acclaim. Social workers also understand the forms and mechanisms of oppression and discrimination and recognize the extent to which a culture's structures and values, including social, economic, political, and cultural exclusions, may oppress, marginalize, alienate, or create privilege and power.	◆ Apply and communicate understanding of the importance of diversity and difference in shaping life experiences in practice at the micro, mezzo, and macro levels. ◆ Present themselves as learners and engage clients and constituencies as experts of their own experiences; and ◆ Apply self-awareness and self-regulation to manage the influence of personal biases and values in working with diverse clients and constituencies.
Competency 3: Advance human rights and social, economic, and environmental justice	Social workers understand that every person regardless of position in society has fundamental human rights such as freedom, safety, privacy, an adequate standard of living, health care, and education. Social workers understand the global interconnections of oppression and human rights violations, and are knowledgeable about theories of human need and social justice and strategies to promote social and economic justice and human rights. Social workers understand strategies designed to eliminate oppressive structural barriers to ensure that social goods, rights, and responsibilities are distributed equitably and that civil, political, environmental, economic, social, and cultural human rights are protected.	◆ Apply their understanding of social, economic, and environmental justice to advocate for human rights at the individual and system levels. ◆ Engage in practices that advance social, economic, and environmental justice.

Table 3. 2015 Educational Policy and Accreditation Standards: Nine Core Competencies for Social Work Education—(*Continued*)

Competency	Description	Behaviors
Competency 4: Engage in practice-informed research and research-informed practice	Social workers understand quantitative and qualitative research methods and their respective roles in advancing a science of social work and in evaluating their practice. Social workers know the principles of logic, scientific inquiry, and culturally informed and ethical approaches to building knowledge. Social workers understand that evidence that informs practice derives from multi-disciplinary sources and multiple ways of knowing. They also understand the processes for translating research findings into effective practice.	◆ Use practice experience and theory to inform scientific inquiry and research; ◆ Apply critical thinking to engage in analysis of quantitative and qualitative research methods and research findings. ◆ Use and translate research evidence to inform and improve practice, policy, and service delivery.
Competency 5: Engage in policy practice	Social workers understand that human rights and social justice, as well as social welfare and services, are mediated by policy and its implementation at the federal, state, and local levels. Social workers understand the history and current structures of social policies and services, the role of policy in service delivery, and the role of practice in policy development. Social workers understand their role in policy development and implementation within their practice settings at the micro, mezzo, and macro levels and they actively engage in policy practice to effect change within those settings. Social workers recognize and understand the historical, social, cultural, economic, organizational, environmental, and global influences that affect social policy. They are also knowledgeable about policy formulation, analysis, implementation, and evaluation.	◆ Identify social policy at the local, state, and federal level that impacts well-being, service delivery, and access to social services. ◆ Assess how social welfare and economic policies impact the delivery of and access to social services. ◆ Apply critical thinking to analyze, formulate, and advocate for policies that advance human rights and social, economic, and environmental justice.

Competency 6: Engage with individuals, families, groups, organizations, and communities	Social workers understand that engagement is an ongoing component of the dynamic and interactive process of social work practice with, and on behalf of, diverse individuals, families, groups, organizations, and communities. Social workers value the importance of human relationships. Social workers understand theories of human behavior and the social environment, and critically evaluate and apply this knowledge to facilitate engagement with clients and constituencies, including individuals, families, groups, organizations, and communities. Social workers understand strategies to engage diverse clients and constituencies to advance practice effectiveness. Social workers understand how their personal experiences and affective reactions may impact their ability to effectively engage with diverse clients and constituencies. Social workers value principles of relationship-building and interprofessional collaboration to facilitate engagement with clients, constituencies, and other professionals as appropriate.	◆ Apply knowledge of human behavior and the social environment, person-in-environment, and other multidisciplinary theoretical frameworks to engage with clients and constituencies. ◆ Use empathy, reflection, and interpersonal skills to effectively engage diverse clients and constituencies.
Competency 7: Assess individuals, families, groups, organizations, and communities	Social workers understand that assessment is an ongoing component of the dynamic and interactive process of social work practice with, and on behalf of, diverse individuals, families, groups, organizations, and communities. Social workers understand theories of human behavior and the social environment, and critically evaluate and apply this knowledge in the assessment of diverse clients and constituencies, including individuals, families, groups, organizations, and communities. Social workers understand methods of assessment with diverse clients and constituencies to advance practice effectiveness. Social workers recognize the implications of the larger practice context in the assessment process and value the importance of interprofessional collaboration in this process. Social workers understand how their personal experiences and affective reactions may affect their assessment and decision making.	◆ Collect and organize data and apply critical thinking to interpret information from clients and constituencies. ◆ Apply knowledge of human behavior and the social environment, person-in-environment, and other multidisciplinary theoretical frameworks in the analysis of assessment data from clients and constituencies. ◆ Develop mutually agreed-on intervention goals and objectives based on the critical assessment of strengths, needs, and challenges within clients and constituencies. ◆ Select appropriate intervention strategies based on the assessment, research knowledge, and values and preferences of clients and constituencies.

Table 3. 2015 Educational Policy and Accreditation Standards: Nine Core Competencies for Social Work Education—(*Continued*)

Competency 8: Intervene with Individuals, Families, Groups, Organizations, and Communities	Social workers understand that intervention is an ongoing component of the dynamic and interactive process of social work practice with, and on behalf of, diverse individuals, families, groups, organizations, and communities. Social workers are knowledgeable about evidence-informed interventions to achieve the goals of clients and constituencies, including individuals, families, groups, organizations, and communities. Social workers understand theories of human behavior and the social environment, and critically evaluate and apply this knowledge to effectively intervene with clients and constituencies. Social workers understand methods of identifying, analyzing and implementing evidence-informed interventions to achieve client and constituency goals. Social workers value the importance of interprofessional teamwork and communication in interventions, recognizing that beneficial outcomes may require interdisciplinary, interprofessional, and interorganizational collaboration.	◆ Critically choose and implement interventions to achieve practice goals and enhance capacities of clients and constituencies; ◆ Apply knowledge of human behavior and the social environment, person-in-environment, and other multidisciplinary theoretical frameworks in interventions with clients and constituencies; ◆ Use interprofessional collaboration as appropriate to achieve beneficial practice outcomes; ◆ Negotiate, mediate, and advocate with and on behalf of diverse clients and constituencies; and ◆ Facilitate effective transitions and endings that advance mutually agreed-on goals.
Competency 9: Evaluate practice with individuals, families, groups, organizations, and communities	Social workers understand that evaluation is an ongoing component of the dynamic and interactive process of social work practice with, and on behalf of, diverse individuals, families, groups, organizations and communities. Social workers recognize the importance of evaluating processes and outcomes to advance practice, policy, and service delivery effectiveness. Social workers understand theories of human behavior and the social environment, and critically evaluate and apply this knowledge in evaluating outcomes. Social workers understand qualitative and quantitative methods for evaluating outcomes and practice effectiveness.	◆ Select and use appropriate methods for evaluation of outcomes; ◆ Apply knowledge of human behavior and the social environment, person-in-environment, and other multidisciplinary theoretical frameworks in the evaluation of outcomes; ◆ Critically analyze, monitor, and evaluate intervention and program processes and outcomes; and apply evaluation findings to improve practice effectiveness at the micro, mezzo, and macro levels.

Source: CSWE, Commission on Educational Policy and Commission on Accreditation (2015), pp. 7–9.

Baccalaureate in Social Work (Educational Model). The typical baccalaureate social work program begins in the sophomore year of college and requires four to five semesters of study. Accreditation standards require some form of admission process into the BSW program and these standards are established by the program's faculty. Limited access programs require a formal application and review process for admission. There are no set national admission standards for a program; faculty determines the admission criteria for their program, set within the policies of the home college or university. Admission may depend on such criteria as cumulative grade point average (GPA), successful completion of the liberal arts requirements, reference letters, and a narrative statement. In programs that are not limited access, admission depends on successful completion of the liberal arts requirements. Whether access to a program is limited or not depends on school policy.

Accreditation standards require that, while enrolled in the program as a major, the student receive at least 400 hours of field education, although a particular program may demand more than this minimum. Programs currently use a number of models to address the field placement requirement. One option is *block placement,* in which the student is assigned to an agency full time, forty hours a week, for an entire semester. A second approach, *concurrent placement,* assigns the student to an agency one to three days a week while the student takes courses, usually for two semesters. A third approach combines concurrent and block placements; concurrent placement is used in the student's junior year of study and block placement in the senior year. This approach allows the student to be assigned to different agencies. What's more important to remember is that, whatever field model your program uses, you must complete at least 400 hours in the field practicum. This is nonnegotiable, and previous work experience cannot be substituted for your practicum requirement. Because this requirement is set forth in the accreditation standards, your program is very unlikely to allow modifications or exceptions.

Master of Social Work (Educational Model). Professional education at the master's level requires the equivalent of two academic years of full-time study and combines two components, foundation and specialization in a particular area of study.

The professional foundation content is the same as for baccalaureate programs. Traditionally, the foundation content was most often studied in the first year with specialization taking place during the equivalent of the second year of full-time study. A number of graduate programs are moving away from this so-called 50-50 model by emphasizing specialization with the advanced studies beginning during the first year of study (Colby, 2013). According to the social work educational model, specialization must be firmly rooted in the foundation content. A specialization can be designed around different areas of social work practice (see box 1);

Box 1. Specialization Models

Methodology: Specialization by intervention, such as critical social work, community organization, or group work.

Setting: Specialization by agency setting or type, such as **child welfare**, mental health, criminal justice, rural practice, or gerontology.

Population group: Specialization by a specific client population, such as children, families, women, and seniors.

Problem area: Specialization by a focused problem, such as alcohol, tobacco, and other substances; mental illness; family violence; and poverty.

Combination: A combination of specializations, such as methodology and population growth, for example, or clinical social work with children.

---

second-year courses and field education should reflect this specialization area. Accreditation standards require that MSW students complete at least 900 field hours. Students complete two placements, one in the foundation year and another in the specialization year, and together these must total a minimum of 900 hours.

A common complaint among newly enrolled graduate students is that their field placements are not in their intended areas of specialization. Students need to remember, however, that first field placement is intended to be generalist in nature and to allow them to demonstrate the acquisition of the core competencies. Competencies for specializations are developed in the equivalent of the specialization or advanced study; it is at this point that specialization placements occur.

Did You Know... The Department of Veterans Affairs—the largest employer of social workers in the country—employs more than 6,000 social workers to assist veterans and their families with individual and family counseling, client education, end of life planning, substance abuse treatment, crisis intervention, and other services.

Students choosing a graduate program should know that not all programs offer the same choices of specialization and some limit the advanced study to one specialization. A colleague has remarked that, when she reviews admission folders for her graduate program, she finds that students seem to know little about the program to which they are applying. One student, for example, wanted to study administration, but the school offers only a clinical specialization. The student had a GPA of 3.8 and a Graduate Record Exam (GRE) score of 1,175. Nevertheless, the admission committee rejected the student's application because his career interests did not match the school's mission and curriculum. The applicant was very angry and complained about his rejection. Even when the committee's rationale was explained to him, he did not accept the decision, saying "What I want to do professionally has nothing to do with the type of program I want to apply to." The moral of this story: Be sure that your career goals match the school's mission and educational program.

Did You Know…Forty percent of mental health professionals working with the Red Cross Disaster Services Human Resources system are social workers.

Advanced Standing (Educational Program). Some graduate programs offer advanced standing. Advanced standing, which is limited to graduates of CSWE baccalaureate programs, allows these students to have certain graduate courses waived because they mastered the content in their baccalaureate studies. Advanced standing reflects the long-standing accreditation standard that a graduate program does not require course work to be repeated once it has been mastered; this is detailed in the EPAS under the student admission protocols (CSWE, Commission on Educational Policy and Commission on Accreditation, 2015, p. 15.).

Social work is the only profession that offers an advanced standing option in its educational model. Even within social work, advanced standing is very controversial in both theory and practice. The profession's ambivalence toward advanced standing is seen in its inconsistent application. Some programs waive the entire foundation year of study whereas others limit the exemption to one or two courses. Some require successful completion of content-specific examinations, and some programs do not offer an advanced standing option at all. Some programs require BSW practitioners to enroll in the graduate program within a specific time period from the time of their BSW graduation, typically ranging from four to seven years; otherwise, they are not eligible for advanced standing and are required to complete the regular two-year curriculum.

PhD/DSW (Educational Program). The CSWE does not regulate doctoral study. As a result, doctoral programs differ in required courses, program structure, and specialization. Generally, a doctorate is required for people who teach in BSW or MSW programs. Although it is not required for agency practice, there is a small but growing trend in agencies to hire upper level administrators who hold doctoral degrees.

Two types of doctoral degrees are associated with social work, the PhD and the DSW. The PhD is the familiar research-directed doctorate of philosophy; the DSW designates a practice doctoral course of study. Basically, the two degrees are more similar than different. When doctoral programs first originated in the field of social work, the DSW was awarded. As time passed and social workers were hired as educators, schools changed the doctorate to a PhD, and today that is the more common designation in academia. Both degrees require approximately the equivalent of two years of full-time study, successful completion of a comprehensive qualifying examination, and successful completion of a written dissertation. It is important to remember, however, that, because doctoral level programs, unlike master's and bachelor's level programs, are not accredited by the CSWE, careful exploration to find the right match between student and program is essential.

SOCIAL WORKERS TODAY

Here is some good news for you. According to the DOL, social work through the year 2022 is expected to be among the fastest growing professions with lower unemployment and steady pay. The DOL identified 607,300 social work jobs in 2014, with the majority of positions in children and family settings, health care, and schools (U.S. Department of Labor, 2014b). The DOL also noted that gerontological and hospice and palliative care social work are growth specializations (U.S. Department of Labor, 2014a). A much earlier study (Gibelman and Schervish 1997, p. 5) estimated that the number of people employed in social work and holding social work degrees ranged from 645,000 to 693,000.

The bottom line is that no single information source provides a detailed overview of social work employment. We know that social workers are employed in a variety of settings, both public and private, and employment prospects continue to be sound.

Activity…Contact your state's department of labor. The agency is usually located in the state capital and may have an 800 number. Find out the department's employment projections for social workers in your state. Do the data match national trends?

What Are Social Workers Paid?

Probably of most interest to people considering social work as a career is salary: how much can I make? Well, you won't be poor, and you'll be able to live a comfortable life. Current information on salaries is not available, but in the recent past the average income, although modest, was comfortable. Trying to identify average salaries or answer the question "what can I expect to earn" is difficult. A social worker in New York City will, on average, earn more than a social worker in Reno, NV. The point is not that there is salary discrimination in Reno, but that the cost of living is much less. So be careful when comparing salaries.

The best source on salaries is right in your own city or town. Go to a local NASW unit meeting and ask the social workers what the salaries are in your community. Some social work programs have their own career services office and collect salary information. Check around and see what you find. You can also get a feel for salaries by reading your local newspaper's classified advertisements. (Sunday classifieds are your best bet for finding the most advertisements.)

But let's at least create some parameters on general national average social work salaries. Remember that salary is a function of degree (MSW or BSW), agency setting, and location. The DOL 2014 *Occupational Outlook Handbook* (DOL, 2014c) reported that the median wage for all social workers in 2012 was $44,200; in other words, 50 percent of social workers made a salary higher and 50 percent had a salary lower than $44,200. The median salary for health care social workers was $49,830; that for child, family, and school social workers was $41,530, and that for behavioral health practitioners was $39,980. Remember that these figures combine all salaries and do not take into account the differences based on degree (e.g., BSW or MSW).

Activity...Check out The New Social Worker *online at http://www.socialworker.com. You'll find a number of discussion boards and chat rooms dealing with a variety of topics, including careers, ethics, student forums, general items, announcements, and resource recommendations. Questions about jobs and salaries are hot topics on this website.*

Where Do Social Workers Work?

To better understand where job opportunities might be, let's look at social work practice from four interrelated perspectives: job function, auspices, setting, and practice area (see Table 4).

Any set of choices, one from each list, defines a social work position. For example, you can be a supervisor (function) in a private nonprofit sectarian (auspices) nursing home (setting), providing services to the aged (practice area). Or you may provide direct service (function) in a public local (auspices) outpatient facility (setting) as an alcohol and substance abuse counselor (practice area). The thousands of potential combinations demonstrate the versatility of social work employment opportunities.

Did You Know...There are hundreds of social workers in national, state, and local elected office, including two U.S. Senators and seven U.S. Representatives in 2012.

Another way to discover the breadth of the social work profession is to examine CSWE studies of social work education programs. Each year the council collects

Table 4. Social Work Positions by Common Work Roles, Auspices, Setting, and Practice Area

Common Work Roles: What do I do?

Direct service	Supervision
Management/administration	Policy development/analysis
Consultant	Research
Planning	Education/training

Auspices: Where do I work?

Public, local	Private nonprofit, sectarian
Public, state	Private nonprofit, nonsectarian
Public, federal	Private for profit, proprietary
Public, military	

Setting: What type of agency do I work in?

Social services agency	Nursing home
Private practice, self-employed	Criminal justice system
Private practice, partnership	College/university
Membership organization	Elementary/secondary schools
Hospital	Non–social-service organization
Outpatient facility	Group home

Practice area: What is my practice area?

Children and youth	School social work
Community organization/planning	Services to the aged
Family services	Alcohol and other substance abuse
Criminal justice	Developmental disabilities
Group services	Occupational social work
Mental health	Public assistance

these data in order to track the state of the profession and to detect possible trends in education. In the council's annual program statistics, sixteen different practice area concentrations are offered in graduate social work schools, although the offerings in each program are generally limited to three or four concentrations (see Table 5). The data in Table 5 reinforce the diversity of social work, although mental health,

Table 5. Social Work Annual Income 2014

Average salary range	$29,450–$60,536
Average annual bonus range	$0.0–$1,912
Profit sharing range	$4.00–$16,750
Total average pay range	$28,815–$60,846

Source: Payscale, *Social worker salary (United States)*. (n.d.). Retrieved from www.payscale.com/research/US/Job=Social_Worker/Salary

child welfare, and family services stand out as the three most popular concentrations among students.

GETTING A SOCIAL WORK JOB AFTER GRADUATION

There's no secret to finding a job, whether in social work, law, nursing, or any other profession. It takes a great deal of hard work and a lot of patience on the part of the job seeker. Although jobs in general are available, it takes time to find the one that is right for you. A rule of thumb is that it takes three to four months to find a job from the time you begin your search in earnest. So if you want to have a job by June, you'll need to have your résumé prepared and your search strategy developed and implemented no later than the preceding February.

A note of caution: Be prepared not to get the one job you've always wanted. Even for the most experienced social worker, a job rejection letter hurts. Great jobs are waiting for competent social workers—the key is finding a position in which you can make full use of your knowledge, skills, and potential (see Table 6).**

Prepare Your Résumé Carefully

Be sure your résumé is up to date. You can get an easy-to-use résumé software program at the college bookstore or computer store. There are also any number of books on résumé writing that you can review. Ask your academic advisor or some other social worker for tips and ideas about what to highlight. (Your field internship supervisor is always a good person to talk to about what to put on a résumé.) Consider taking advantage of your school's job placement office by attending a résumé-writing workshop. But recognize that most helpers in the résumé-writing process are not well versed in social work; their work is geared to a general audience and does not reflect the nuances of social work. The key is to ask social workers in the field what they did and what they listed on their résumés.

Table 6. A Salary of $45,000 in Houston, Texas, in October 2014 Is the Same as . . .

City	Salary
Hartford, CT	$ 62,122
New York City (Manhattan)	$110,362
Orlando, FL	$ 49,957
Fairbanks, AK	$ 68,108
Burlington, VT	$ 59,456
Chicago, IL	$ 58,802
Los Angeles, CA	$ 66,398
Portland, OR	$ 60,915

Source: CNN Money, How far will my salary go in another city? (2015). Retrieved from http://money.cnn.com/calculator/pf/cost-of-living

Be sure your résumé is clean and as error free as possible—no spelling errors, no photocopies with wrinkled edges, and so on. Your résumé is your introduction to a potential employer, and you want to make the best impression possible. Consider writing an initial goal or objective for the type of work you want to do in the field. Be sure to link the contents of this statement with the job you are applying for. You may not have much paid clinical or administrative experience, so be sure to highlight volunteer experiences and start with your most recent field placement. For other tips and suggestions present a draft of your résumé to a favorite social work instructor or a social worker in the field. Listen to their suggestions carefully because they have been through the employment process; hearing their words of wisdom first may save you a great deal of time and effort later.

Licensing Requirements

All states have some sort of regulation on social work practice; some regulate BSW and MSW practice whereas others regulate only advanced (e.g., MSW/DSW/PhD) practice. As you begin your job search, you must become familiar with the state's requirements as well as the agency's expectations. Check to see if your state provides a temporary license; this license allows you to be licensed for a short period of time, generally six months, without having to take an exam. Some states allow you to sit for the exam in your last semester of study. The bottom line: become familiar with your state's licensing/registration requirements. Go to the website for your state, get a recent application, and look at the requirements carefully. You can learn a great deal and you can be linked to other states' licensing/registration information through the national organization Association for Social Work Boards (ASWB); go to http://www.aswb.org for information related to licensing. Because rules and regulations can vary from state to state, be sure to stay aware of the latest changes and check the website regularly for updated information. Getting a license in your profession is your responsibility, so take a proactive role in learning what is needed and stay aware of the state's licensing/registration requirements.

Attend Local NASW Meetings or Meetings of Other Professional Groups

To facilitate your job search, attend local NASW meetings as often as you can. You can begin to network by attending meetings and becoming active with this group as soon as you declare your major. Dues for a student are a real bargain! Simply contact your state NASW office for information about your local unit and for the name of a contact person. You should be able to get an NASW membership application from your school's social work office or through the state NASW office.

While attending local NASW unit meetings you'll make new friends, begin to develop a professional network, and keep abreast of issues within your new social work community. Moreover, the monthly or bimonthly meetings often include time for members to announce job opportunities. Most people would be surprised at how much information about job openings and availability is spread by word of mouth and through these types of informal networks. For example, you may even get firsthand information on a position that has just become available from the contact person within the agency.

Activity...Attend a local NASW meeting. Talk to members about finding jobs and see what hints they can give you.

Get on the Internet and see what kind of jobs you can find in at least five different states. Try looking in large cities as well as small towns. A first step is to see if a social work program offers a career services program/web page. Read a number of job announcements and look for qualifications that are minimum requirements versus those that are preferences.

Visit your school's job placement office. See what the staff recommends about putting together a job search packet. Remember, it's never too early to begin collecting material for your résumé.

Put together a draft résumé and pass it around asking for suggestions on how to make it better.

Use Your Field Placement Experience

Each student must complete a field placement. Don't be surprised if your field agency offers you a position following graduation. The field site has the luxury of assessing your work; if you do an excellent job, the agency may ask you to consider moving into a regular position. An agency benefits from hiring a field placement student who has already worked in the agency because this new employee can be moved into a regular position more quickly and with less orientation time. Furthermore, there is little need for an initial skill and knowledge assessment period because the agency, through the internship experience, is well aware of the student's practice abilities and thus the level of supervision needed.

Employment in a field placement agency also has advantages for the student accepting the job. The student already knows the agency and how she will fit into the overall organization. Based on direct experience the student knows that it is the setting in which she wants to start a social work career.

Read Local and National Newspaper Advertisements

Local newspapers, *NASW News*, and your state NASW chapter newsletter publish countless employment announcements. Familiarize yourself with the range of

Name: Suzanne L. Cross, LMSW, ACSW, LLC (Bneshinh kwe translation Bird Woman)

Place of residence: Williamston, MI

College/university degrees: BS, Michigan State University; MSW, University of Michigan; PhD, Michigan State University

Present position: Associate professor emeritus, School of Social Work; tribal consultant, National Child Welfare Workforce Institute (NCWWI)

What do you do in your spare time? I attend American Indian cultural events (i.e., pow-wows, feasts, and talking circles). Also, I spend time with children and elders, create art through beadwork, and design traditional shawls for dance regalia. I consult with former students who are now social work professionals, and I attend and present at social work and American Indian conferences.

Why did you choose social work as a career? During adolescence and young adulthood, I was often consulted by my peers in regard to personal and social issues. I did not offer directive advice, but *listened* and held their concerns in *confidence*; two important skills of clinical social work. In addition, I enjoy working with children; including foster parenting. Also, I find dialogue with elders to be gratifying and for whatever I provide for them, I learn much more in return from their traditional teachings (i.e. humility, truth, honesty, love, respect, wisdom, and bravery), which are congruent with social work ethics. Thus, my career path includes clinical work and research with multiple generations in American Indian communities. My research topics include Indian child welfare, grand families, Indian boarding school historical trauma, cultural and behavioral response to pain, and student recruitment and retention.

What is your favorite social work story? One day as I was walking to my office after lunch with two colleagues, I noticed a young man dressed in a suit and tie walking toward me. I stepped to the side, but he continued to walk directly in my path. He then stopped in front of me and said, "Thank you so much. I have had three interviews with major corporations and they have all made me an offer." His face was familiar, and I recognized his voice. At that moment, I realized he was a former client. When he first came to the agency as a freshman, he indicated he was unable to complete his degree because of his preoccupation with and flooding of memories from several years of parental physical and psychological abuse. At that time he questioned his academic abilities and self-worth and his right to a future as a professional. I was so pleased to learn he had attained his goal and was able to heal his spirit.

What would be the one thing you would change in our community if you had the power to do so? If I had the power, I would change the internal pain of many American Indian people who are suffering from historical trauma, which for some has led to present-day trauma.

American Indians are a strong and resilient people, but for some, there continues to be the feeling of despair. The historical dehumanization of this population is unknown to most, even those in the profession of social work. I strongly believe the history of a planned destruction of a people which included war, removal from their land, removal of their children into government boarding schools and adoptions, imprisonment of warriors, testing of medications on segments of the population, misuse of medical research information, sterilization of women, and marginalization due to racism and stereotypes affects the lives of American Indians today. Often when these historic atrocities come to the attention of others, the response is "They just need to get over it; it was a long time ago." My response is, "How do you just get over being dehumanized, especially in front of your children?"

---

jobs that are available as well as the jobs that interest you the most. Read each advertisement carefully. When you apply for a job, be sure to follow the instructions; if it asks for a résumé and the names of three references, provide just that— no more and no less.

Look closely at the words used in the announcement. Words such as *must have* or *minimum* or *required* signal baseline qualifications that the successful candidate must possess. For example, if the announcement requires an MSW degree and five years of post-MSW experience, don't apply if you are a newly graduated BSW or an MSW with three years of experience. On the other hand, words such as *should have* or *preferred* signal not minimum criteria but preferences. These words introduce the agency's wish list for the desired candidate, and employers understand that they often don't get everything on their wish lists. If you find an interesting job for which you meet the minimum requirements but not the preferences, go ahead and apply.

Use the Internet

If you'd like a job outside of your local area, the Internet is your best friend. Through the web you can locate newspapers, state NASW offices, career service web pages on various social work educational programs sites, and employment services across the country. Look for websites that allow you to post your résumé. Social media are a growing source of help in finding a job. People can post information on their Facebook page (https://www.facebook.com) and other similar sites; of course Linkedin (http://www.linkedin.com) is an excellent avenue for creating a professional pathway to employment.

Don't be surprised if you are asked to Skype an interview. This has become a common, easy-to-use, and cost-effective technique for employers to screen in and screen out applications. Be careful if you are Skyping an interview. Be sure that your background is clean, there are no distracting noises, and that what you wear is appropriate. A colleague reported that a job candidate in one Skype interview had clothes dangling over the chair in the background with a beer can on the window sill. Another colleague noted that a dog kept on running in and out of the interviewee's room and barking while the candidate kept on saying "shush!" Suffice it to say, neither candidate was asked to interview at the agency.

A word of caution about the web. Be careful about what pictures and comments you post. Employers typically search an applicant's background on social media. The old saying that a picture is worth a 1,000 words is so true; one college picture of a what seemed to be a fun time may stop your application dead in its tracks.

Get to Know Your Social Work Faculty Advisors and Instructors

One of your best sources of employment information and strategies is your program faculty. They are very interested in your success, they have years of experience, and they know people in the field in the surrounding community who can help you. Your social work teachers have probably had contact with most local agencies. A good word, phone call, or reference letter from a faculty member can be one of your greatest aids in getting your first job.

Don't forget that many programs use adjunct or part-time faculty to supplement their full-time faculty. Adjunct faculty members who are employed full time in the community can help you in your job search because they are tied into the local informal social work network.

Did You Know…All states have some form of licensing or regulation of social work practice, but in many states such regulation is limited to MSW or advanced practice and does not apply to BSW practice. Be sure to check with your academic advisor to learn more about your state's particular licensing requirements.

The NASW also credentials social workers for specific practice specializations. These specializations include leadership, military, clinical, gerontology, hospice and palliative care, youth and families, health care, addictions, case management, and education. Go to socialworkers.org/credentials/list.asp for additional information.

Explore Your Social Work Student Association or Club

Your program's social work student association or club can help in your job search. The association can invite area agency directors to provide workshops or panels on finding a job. The club can also sponsor a job fair on campus at which area agencies set up booths, distribute agency information, and recruit potential employees. The fair can be coordinated with the program's field office and the local NASW unit. Probably the best time to hold a job fair is in the spring, when most potential graduates are looking for jobs.

A job fair is a win-win-win situation. Students win because they have imme-diate access to potential employers. Agencies win because the fair is a cost-effective recruiting mechanism that reaches a large pool of potential job applicants. The social work program and university win because the job fair is a positive public relations tool that strengthens ties between the university and the community.

Last Thoughts about Your Job Search

We often get caught up in salary and look for the best paying jobs. Yes, salary is important, but consider other aspects of the job as well. Who works at the agency? What kind of colleagues will you have, and can you learn from them? Your first job will be a major source of knowledge and experience. Will the job be excit-ing and offer you a variety of learning opportunities? What kinds of benefits are in place? These can range from health care and vacation time to time with pets— one organization allows staff members to bring their pets to work each Friday. (Now what does that say about the organization?)

A few years ago, a student came into the office very excited about a job offer she had received in New York City as a child care worker. She said, "I'm getting a great salary. They're going to pay me $65,000!"

But what does $65,000 mean to a new twenty-one-year-old social worker? It sounds like a great deal, but it's not really. Use the web to find salaries for com-parison purposes; the easiest way is to search for *salary converters*. For example, as you can see in Table 6, $ 45,000 in one city means something quite different some-where else.

Remember that you need to be happy with what you find. Be sure the setting offers you an opportunity for continued professional growth and self-fulfillment. Don't focus only on the salary—there is much more to a job than money!

SUMMARY

Students entering social work will find the field rich in opportunities. The profes-sion's future is bright.

When you embark on a professional career in social work, the selection of an educational program is important. A social work career should begin with either a baccalaureate or a master's degree, and this degree must come from a CSWE-accredited program. Request admission information directly from the programs you are interested in attending. Programs are located in every state in the United States and throughout the world. Be sure to gather information early so you have plenty of time to prepare what is required. Some baccalaureate programs have open admission, whereas others use a formal admission process. Admission to graduate programs, on the other hand, is usually competitive, and about 40 per-cent of applicants are turned down.

Employment possibilities for social workers can be found in both public and private settings. They involve a wide range of activities and tasks and a variety of practice areas. Simply stated, practice opportunities for social work professionals are open and diverse.

The key to a successful work experience in social work is planning your education carefully—whether BSW or MSW—and making the most of it. Take advantage of your educational opportunities to develop new knowledge, theories, and skills that will make you more competent. Remember, before you can help the individuals, groups, families, and communities that you will serve, you must first help yourself to be the best equipped professional, with the best foundation of education and training possible.

REFERENCES

Accreditation Commission of Colleges of Medicine. (2014). *Standards-elements of accreditation.* Retrieved from http://accredmed.org/standards.html

Barker, R. L. (2003). *The social work dictionary* (5th ed.). Washington, DC: NASW Press.

Beless, D. W. (1995). Council on social work education. In R. L. Edwards (Ed.), *Encyclopedia of social work* (19th ed., vol. 1, pp. 632–636). Washington, DC: NASW Press.

Burger, W. R., & Youkeles, M. (2004). *Human services in contemporary America.* Belmont, CA: Brooks Cole.

Colby, I. (2013). Rethinking the MSW curriculum. *Journal of Social Work Education, 49,* 4–15.

Council on Social Work Education. (1994). *Handbook of accreditation standards and procedures.* Alexandria, VA: Author.

Council on Social Work Education (2015a). *Accreditation.* Retrieved from: http://www.cswe.org/Accreditation.aspx

Council on Social Work Education. (2015b). *Commission on accreditation.* Retrieved from: http://www.cswe.org/About/governance/CommissionsCouncils/Commissionon Accreditation.aspx

Council on Social Work Education, Commission on Educational Policy and Commission on Accreditation. (2015). *2015 educational policy and accreditation standards for baccalaureate and master's social work programs.* Alexandria, VA: Author.

Gardellia, L. G. (1997). Baccalaureate social workers. In R. Edwards (Ed.), *Encyclopedia of social work, 1997 supplement* (19th ed., pp. 37–46). Washington, DC: NASW Press.

Gibelman, M., & Schervish, P. H. (1997). *Who we are: A second look.* Washington, DC: NASW Press.

Leighninger, L. (1987). *Social work: Search for identity.* Westport, CT: Greenwood.

PDR Medical Dictionary (3rd ed.). (2005). Montvale, NJ: Physician's Desk Reference.

U.S. Department of Labor (2014a). Job outlook. *Occupational outlook handbook,* Retrieved from http://www.bls.gov/ooh/community-and-social-service/social-workers.htm#tab-6

U.S. Department of Labor (2014b). Social workers. *Occupational outlook handbook.* Retrieved from http://www.bls.gov/ooh/community-and-social-service/social-workers.htm

U.S. Department of Labor. (2014c). Social workers pay. *Occupational outlook handbook.* Retrieved from http://www.bls.gov/ooh/community-and-social-service/social-workers.htm#tab-5

PART TWO

THE PRACTICE OF
SOCIAL WORK

CHAPTER 5
SOCIAL WORK PRACTICE

STEVE, AN UNDERGRADUATE SOCIAL WORK STUDENT, STOPPED BY HIS professor's office. Steve wanted to tell his professor that he was enjoying his introduction to social work class and that he was learning so much that he had not missed a session. He told the professor that he believed his final grade would be high. Steve was a conscientious student who often asked questions and it was obvious that he enjoyed taking part in class discussions. The professor was surprised, however, when he asked, "So, how do you do it?" The professor, who was not quite sure what he meant by "it," asked Steve to clarify what he was asking. Very seriously, Steve said, "You know social work. How do you do social work?" Today, some twenty plus years after this visit, Steve remembers that day and laughs. He now has both a BSW and an MSW and is employed in a public mental health facility. Thinking back on his earlier days he laughs about that question. He says, "I guess I was looking for that magical pill you give a client to make it better or that one specific task we could complete to help a person in pain. I just believed that social workers had a bag of tricks, and when they were applied, something magical would happen and the person's problem would be solved. It certainly is more complicated than that and how wrong I was."

When they enter the field, social workers often expect specific answers with concrete steps for achieving a desired outcome. Yet, the longer you are in the field the more you realize there are no simple answers, and as personal and environmental circumstances change so do the answers and the strategies. So even for seasoned practitioners, the quest never ends.

Steve, like so many beginning social workers, was unsure of what to do in social work practice and hoped for a simple answer. Wouldn't it be wonderful if the unique and ambiguous challenges of human life could be easily addressed by giving a pat answer, prescribing a simple pill, or using a clearly outlined standard procedure? It's tempting, but wholly unrealistic. If social work practice required nothing more than simple prescriptions, and the answers were easily derived, there would be limited need for formal education beyond the basics.

In fact, the practice of social work stems directly from the mission of the profession, which is neither simple nor standardized. Furthermore, market forces, whether academic, governmental, or private in origin, can also affect and transform practice (Reardon, 2011; Witkin & Iversen, 2008). If you look at the definition of social work set forth in chapter 1, you'll be looking in the right direction for practice guidance. Social workers seek to enhance social functioning, promote social justice, and help people to obtain resources. They also support ethical decision making and empower their clients to make their own choices while respecting self-determination, worth, and dignity (International Federation of Social Workers [IFSW], 2012).

Did You Know... The number of social work jobs doubled in the 1930s from 40,000 to 80,000, as public sector income maintenance, health and welfare programs were created in response to the Great Depression (NASW, 1993).

Changes in the detailed definition of social work have occurred over time, yet the basis for social work practice has not changed. Today there are several definitions that outline the profession of social work, but all follow a similar theme highlighting the importance of addressing the person in situation or the person in environment. According to the National Association of Social Workers (NASW, 1993), social work is the professional activity of helping individuals, groups, or communities enhance or restore their capacity for social functioning and create societal conditions favorable for achieving their goals.

Furthermore, as outlined in the preamble of the NASW Code of Ethics, social work is engaged in promoting and empowering the individual well-being of all human beings within the context and environmental forces that influence problems related to their condition (NASW, 2008). Barker (2003) further elaborates that "social work is the applied science of helping people achieve an effective level of psychosocial functioning and effecting societal changes to enhance the well-being of all people" (p. 408).

These different interpretations of the profession make it easy to see how the definition has evolved but remains relevant to the early definition written by Boehm (1959), which defines the profession this way:

Social work seeks to enhance the social functioning of individuals, singly and in groups, by activities focused on their social relationships which constitute the interaction between man [individuals] and his [or her] environment. These activities can be grouped into three functions: restoration of impaired capacity, provision of individual and social resources, and prevention of social dysfunction (p. 54).

Reflective of the revised NASW Code of Ethics (2008), all of these definitions highlight the tasks that social workers undertake, the agencies in which they work, and the social policies they support. These helping efforts are all aimed toward

Name: Paul A. Gildersleeve

Place of residence: Oyster Bay, Long Island, NY

College/university degrees: Adelphi University, BSW, MSW

Present position and title: Currently retired from Nassau County Department of Behavioral Health as a psychiatric social worker who handled crisis situations at Nassau County Department of Social Services.

Previous work/volunteer experience: My volunteer work began with my interest in helping others in the 1960s when I volunteered at the Oyster Bay East Norwich Youth Association. I then volunteered at the Long Island Association for AIDS Care (LIAAC) and for the Long Island Gay Lesbian Switchboard where I was a hotline operator. Because of my volunteer work at LIAAC, I was able to secure part-time work with Nassau County Department of Drug and Alcohol Addiction as an HIV/AIDS counselor/educator/phlebotomist (the county trained me as a phlebotomist). Realizing that I had a lot to learn about addictions, I enrolled at Professional Alcoholism Counseling Education (PACE) and eventually became a credentialed and substance abuse counselor (CASAC). I worked in two methadone clinics and at two inpatient drug and alcohol settings, one with ninety-day treatment and the other a long-term treatment program (twelve months or more). I also worked in a day treatment drug and alcohol setting and set up a new program at a day treatment facility as well as a program with the Nassau County Department of Probation. I gave an educational presentation at Nassau County Correctional Center and was subsequently asked to work at the correctional center as a drug and alcohol counselor.

I worked in the STOP DWI Program and had a caseload of nine to twelve clients and also conducted educational lectures in a sixty-man open dorm. I did an internship in an Alzheimer's facility where I learned that you may only be able to help someone enjoy a brief moment in their life, and I interned in GAMPRO, where I learned how to work with and treat gamblers. Once I earned my MSW, I was transferred as a psychiatric social worker to build a program called Behavioral Health where I would assess and refer clients who had mental health issues and who were not taking medications or diagnosed as having a disorder. I also sat in on the case of the week, where individuals from all parts of DSS as well as outside agencies worked on difficult cases to help the client receive needed treatment or assistance.

Why did you choose social work as a career? My interest in becoming a social worker began when I entered therapy with a local therapist after a friend tried to commit suicide. This was my first experience with anyone trying to kill himself or herself. I lost complete control of my life and needed help.

A friend recommended a book about suicide, the title of which I have since forgotten. I purchased the book and began to read. I was totally amazed to find the book recounted every feeling and stage I had gone through. It also talked about my friend's feelings about death and his suicide attempt. The author did not know me nor did he know my friend, so how could he know what was going on inside either of us? This was my first clue that there was more to therapy than I had previously believed. This caused me to think carefully about the impact this book and therapy had on me. It knew my feelings. It knew the emotions I went through from the beginning to end. Because of this experience I had, I knew that, with training and education, I could help others.

What is your favorite social work story? I remember that a colleague, a person of color with whom I frequently was at odds, said to me at a staff meeting, "You are the only person I know who has no color." I don't think there could ever be a better achievement.

What is one thing you would change in the community if you had the power to do so? To provide treatment and therapy to everyone regardless of ability to pay, but only because of their need for assistance, and to be able to extend the hand of help to those who would never be able to enter an office for treatment.

---

three overarching goals: to enhance client social functioning, to remedy client dysfunction, and to promote social justice (Hepworth, Rooney, Rooney, Strom-Gottfried, & Larsen, 2010). Professional education, whether at the BSW or the MSW level, through academic classes and course work as well as through experiences gained from the field practicum, helps the new social worker to develop the necessary value-driven knowledge and skills to support social work practice.

UNDERSTANDING DIVERSITY

Although today's definition of social work may seem simple, recognizing the diversity, uniqueness, and complexity in individuals, groups, or communities needs further exploration. As a professor of social work and a practicing clinician, one of the authors was asked by a student, "In class, why do you rarely give case examples of what might be considered the traditional family?" The response was simple: "If you mean the traditional family as constituting the biological parents with 2.4 children who have never been divorced or separated, I rarely see them in my practice." At first, this statement may seem shocking, but these changes reflect our current society. In fact, today's traditional family may be better characterized as yesterday's nontraditional family. Diversity within the family system includes blended or stepfamilies and those units headed by a single parent, by gay or lesbian partners, or by a grandparent or other relatives. Today in practice, it has become evident that the basics of what traditionally constituted social structure and societal expectations for individuals, family groups, and communities have changed.

When seeking to understand individuals and families, social workers must consider the uniqueness of each situation as well as the worth and dignity of each individual and family system. Social workers are expected to recognize these differences through a nonjudgmental lens or perspective that embraces rather than discourages diversity. This requires that social workers become familiar with what is considered ethical practice and implement practice strategy that highlights client self-determination in the most nonjudgmental way possible. From this perspective, individual dignity and worth stand at the forefront of all helping activities. Social workers will be actively engaging with many individuals of different social classes, genders, races, ethnicities, and sexual orientations as well as differing belief systems and spiritual views.

Furthermore, awareness of this type of diversity will be coupled with varying personal problems, including individual health and mental health problems and family issues as well as various social problems such as racism, sexism, and violence. When this is coupled with the need for evidence-based practice (EBP) and the push for more clinical trials that highlight teamwork and the connections between health and mental health, the profession will continue to grow more responsive to the needs of those it serves (Ell, Lee, & Xie, 2010). Therefore, effective individual practice must be transactional. In transactional practice, each event is viewed in multiple dimensions, and case-specific factors, practice models, ethical principles, and issues of power must all be considered (Mattaini, 2001).

As the funding for agencies responsible for assisting clients in need has become more competitive, the emphasis on client outcomes has grown. From this perspective agencies and thus the services they provide will become increasingly more accountable, with success being measured by helping clients to move forward and gain their desired outcomes (Poertner & Rapp, 2007). Measurement of client outcomes is shaped by contextual factors such as agency competition for funding, agency practices, natural networks, and social institutions. Social workers must not only be aware of what is changing in the current climate, but they must also learn how to prepare for what could happen. Being prepared for current and future trends in the surrounding environment enables social workers to help individuals, families, groups, and communities enhance or restore their capability for social functioning.

So often, under the guise of diversity, we lump individual or group behavior together and focus on only the similarities while ignoring differences. From this limited perspective broad and sweeping assumptions can be made. For example, consider the term *Hispanic*. From the perspective of the U.S. Census, Hispanic includes people of Latin or Mexican descent or origin. As a result, people from Cuba, Mexico, Argentina, Brazil, and Spain would be Hispanic. Yet, would you say that the culture with its traditions, mores, and folkways is the same for each of these nations? Do you think that a person from Cuba is different from an Argentinean? Of course, Cubans are very different from Argentineans as they are from Mexicans, Brazilians, and Spaniards. Consideration of human diversity in social work practice requires reflection on and consideration of how such diversity affects our worker-client relationship and ensuing problem-solving process.

There are numerous potential examples highlighting the need for the recognition of diversity that expands beyond traditional definitions of family and race. Children learn to use their cultural experiences to interpret their immediate surroundings and interact with others. From this growth and development perspective the interpersonal patterns that will shape the child's life are developed. Similarly, culture and family are the first two powerful determinants of how children understand, internalize, and act on the expectations of their family, community, and larger society (Morales, Sheafor & Scott, 2012),

In the case of African American children, frequent discriminatory experiences provide them with additional information and feelings to decipher and understand. During times of emotional or psychological turmoil, human nature requires that all children strive for meaning in their lives, and the basis of this derived meaning starts with using their cultural lens, which includes learned values, beliefs, and experiences. In social work practice, these children present a rich and complex biopsychosocial picture requiring examination of the biological, psychological, and social factors within a historical and cultural framework (Austrian, 2009). In order to address issues of individual diversity and to carry out this task efficiently, culturally sensitive social workers must be aware of their own values, the African American child's values, and how both relate and integrate with the larger society in which all must coexist. Ridley (1995, p. 10) noted that even the most sincere, caring, and ethical practitioner can be guilty of "unintentional racism." Therefore, all helping professionals providing services to African American children need to be sensitive to the culture of these children. Avoiding bias in mental health assessment and intervention is essential to the provision of culturally sensitive services (Snowden, 2003).

The concepts outlined back in 1990 by Gonzalez-Ramos are still applicable today. Specifically, in order to address diversity, develop cultural sensitivity, and provide effective services, social work practitioners need to recognize, understand, and appreciate geographic and regional differences among children of color (Gonzalez-Ramos, 1990). Regardless of the child's race or creed, social workers must also learn to look critically and carefully at their own feelings while confronting their own expectations and cultural biases (Sue & Sue, 2008). Although the primary experience of the African American child today may reflect the influence of American society, the impact of the family's place of origin and sense of connectedness and belonging should not be minimized. The African American family today may have values and traditions from northern states, southern states, or Caribbean areas. Similarly, family values may reflect differences in urban versus rural expectations and traditions. The first step in combating racism could be as simple as acknowledging that these differences exist and learning more about them (Miller & Garran, 2009).

Congress (2009) and Congress and Gonzalez (2013) recommend that social workers identify appropriate tools to conduct culturally sensitive assessments. One such tool is the *culturagram*, which takes into account different cultural aspects and empowers families to perceive their specific culture as important within the larger society (Congress & Kung, 2013). Congress (2009) believes that creating a culturagram can help the clinician to get a better understanding of the family by examining the following areas: reasons for relocation; legal status; time in community; language spoken at home and in the community; health beliefs; impact of trauma and crisis events; contact with cultural and religious institutions, holidays, food, and clothing; oppression, discrimination, bias, and racism; values about education and work; and values about family structure, power, myths, and rules (p. 970). Once these factors can be identified and understood, families can become empowered to examine their problems and potential solutions as well as the role of their culture and that of mainstream society (Parker & Bradley, 2010).

THE BASICS OF PRACTICE

It is important to recognize that parts II and III of this book will introduce the reader to practice only in general terms. You will not be qualified to *do* social work after reading these chapters. Remember that your career in social work is just beginning and numerous courses and field experiences are before you. These studies combined with your professional learning experiences will provide you with the foundation for social work practice. This chapter will give you a basic overview of the central concepts related to the delivery of social work services and examine the helping process as it can be applied to the practice of social work.

Before we begin to explore the *doing* of social work, however, we need to remind ourselves that the practice of social work is a professional activity intended to achieve the profession's purpose of helping clients. In examining your own motivation for entering this profession, you must ask yourself why you have decided that this is the profession for you. Be honest with yourself as you explore the areas of social work practice, examining and confronting your own biases and using this knowledge to decide which area of practice holds the most interest for you. Don't be surprised if you find that, like many helping professionals, you are initially motivated by wanting to learn more about yourself and your own family. This is not unusual nor is it particularly problematic. However, when this is your motivation for choosing this field, you must be aware that the professional helping services you provide are not designed to help you—they are for the client. Other typical reasons for choosing a helping profession include the desire to be needed, the desire to give something back to society and humankind, the need to care for others, and the desire for prestige and professional status. As you embark on a helping career, it is essential first to examine what motivated you to select this career and what you want to accomplish. As you explore this motivation, do not be shy about asking for feedback from other professionals who know you, particularly your social work teachers and professionals experienced in the field (see the activity below).

Remember that choosing a career path is not simple or quick. Also, staying in the field and flourishing will require work because the pressures that develop from this kind of work require constant self-examination throughout your educational and professional career. Some students decide relatively early that this is not the career for them. This realization should never be considered a personal or professional failure, because a career in the helping professions is not for everyone. It is a good idea to establish and reaffirm this decision as early as possible, especially before investing a great deal of time, effort, and expense into pursuing it.

> *Activity...Is Social Work Practice Really for Me? On a piece of paper write the following questions and answer them individually. For this exercise you may at first feel more comfortable answering them by yourself. Later you may choose to discuss your answers with your instructor or academic advisor. Feel free to add questions to this list. You might also want to save your answers and revisit them later in your professional career.*
>
> 1. *What first attracted you to the profession of social work?*
> 2. *What needs of your own are likely to be met by serving as a social worker?*
> 3. *Who in your life has been instrumental in helping you choose this career?*
> 4. *Have you ever received help from a social worker? What did you like most about this person? What did you like least?*
> 5. *What do you believe you can contribute to the field of social work?*
> 6. *In what ways do you believe this profession can help to make you feel like a better person?*
> 7. *What is evidence-based social work, and how will this trend affect the services you provide?*

CONCEPTS ESSENTIAL TO SOCIAL WORK PRACTICE

We have described social work practice as an art and a science. The art of social work involves the sensitive coordination of complex activities to help clients. The science entails selecting, merging, and understanding potentially voluminous amounts of information and applying the conclusions to a specific case situation. Although many are successful in learning the science of the profession, the art is always more difficult to acquire. The interplay of art and science means that effective social work practice grows from the relation among knowledge, skills, values, and ethics (see box 1). Social work practice requires unique skills, either specialized or generalist, derived from specific knowledge areas and guided by a clear, fundamental set of values and ethics.

Skills

Doing social work implies that a social worker has a set of specific skills used in practice. These skills, which are inseparable from the helping process, include the ability to perform critical tasks in working with clients: basic communication, exploration, assessment and planning, implementation, goal attainment, termination, and evaluation of the services rendered (Hepworth et al., 2010).

Skill building and the acquisition of knowledge form the bridge between values and all subsequent social service (Trevithick, 2012). Unless knowledge and values underlie skills, the practice of social work is undefined and vague. Social workers must have basic competencies in the following skill areas:

◆ Cognitive skills related to conducting evidence-based research and practice.
◆ Administrative skills, including record keeping and report writing.
◆ Solid assessment and interpersonal skills.

Box 1. Dynamic Interplay of Knowledge, Values and Ethics, and Skills

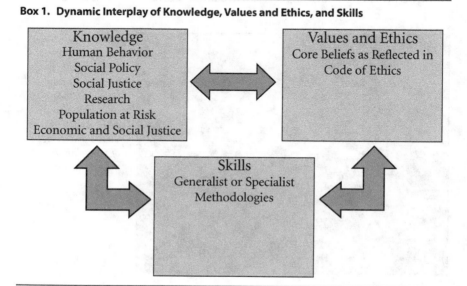

Did You Know…Often you will hear social workers discuss an empathetic relationship or read in the social work literature about the importance of empathy in the social work process. What is the difference between empathy and sympathy? It was once described as follows:

Sympathy is what you feel when you begin actually to feel the pain of the client. In a sympathetic relationship the helping professional cannot be objective or render the nonjudgmental intervention required. Say, for example, you wear a size 8 shoe and your client wears a size 7. If you actually put the client's shoes on your own feet, your feet will be so squeezed that you cannot concentrate on the issues the client is facing.

Empathy, on the other hand, is what you feel when you remain in your own shoes while imagining what it is like for the client in his or her situation. The client's situation is assessed based on direct observation and information provided by the client or people from the client's environment. In an empathetic relationship the helping professional uses objective and subjective information and professional helping skills to truly understand the client's situation and the pain that the client is experiencing.

A social worker must be able to balance many critical aspects of the practice relationship with each client. For example, whether in the home or a health care facility, the worker must first establish and then maintain a worker-client environment of trust (see Figure 1).

In this environment, the client can feel safe revealing emotions and thoughts that might disturb an untrained practitioner; for the skilled worker, the ethical values of client worth, dignity, and self-determination are paramount. When a social worker is providing counseling services to culturally diverse individuals, an aware-

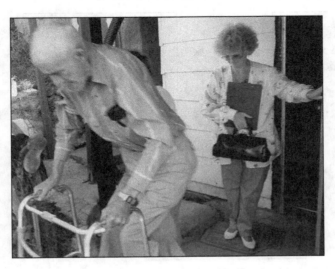

Figure 1: An elderly man leaves a rural West Virginia home after a visit from a home healthcare worker. In many such rural areas there is a shortage of physicians and medical facilities.

ness and respect for the clients' beliefs, values, and lifestyles is central to creating an atmosphere of sensitivity and trust (Sue & Sue, 2008). The worker also must know how and when to approach those of the client's problems that need further explanation and exploration. The skilled social worker is well versed in empathetic communication and helps the client to clarify and confront what may be difficult issues to address. In short, whether in the home or a health-related facility, the skilled professional social worker is an expert at establishing a positive worker-client relationship in which problem identification, helping, addressing, and subsequent healing can take place.

Knowledge Base

The practice of social work is based on a specific body of scientifically tested knowledge. Practice evolves from the knowledge base as social work skills first developed in the academic curriculum later mature through field experiences and continuing education. Without the appropriate knowledge base and awareness of the theoretical constructs that undergird professional practice, skills would be nothing more than a series of unrelated actions that cannot address the total person in situation who is at the heart of professional social work practice. Conversely, knowledge evolves from current practice through practice-based research and evaluation of social work interventions. Without such research and evaluation, social work knowledge would quickly become static, outdated, and unfounded.

In many ways, knowledge drives a professional's daily actions with and on behalf of clients. Knowledge supports practice in its efforts to be client centered and directed to the unique situation of each client. The knowledge base of professional practice premises, skills, and techniques allows social workers to choose the specific set of skills clearly embedded in a theoretical framework best applied to a particular client situation. In other words, to achieve client-centered practice, the professional knowledge base must come first. Once this is established, the development of critical thinking skills will help the new social worker address situations that otherwise might be considered challenging or filled with multiple problems. Utilizing evidence-based practice the social worker is taught to use skills that clearly identify problem areas and express the probabilities of addressing them (Shlonsky, 2009).

Therefore, to create a consistent and comprehensive knowledge base of professional practice, the Council on Social Work Education (2001/2004), which accredits social work programs, requires that all social work educational programs strive for mastery of foundation content in ten areas: social work practice, human behavior and the social environment, social welfare policy and services, social policy, field practicum, research, diversity, social work values and ethics, populations at risk, and promotion of social and economic justice (see Table 3 in chapter 4). Be prepared because the courses you take and the social work program you complete will most assuredly include this information (Jani, Pierce, Ortiz, & Sowbel, 2011). It is clear that all the courses derived will need to be integrated into competency-based social work practice.

Values and Ethics

Values and ethics are the third critical component of social work practice. These humanistic concerns, based on human well-being and justice, help to solidify and provide unification for the field (Hopps & Lowe, 2008, 2012). At the start of your social work education, perhaps during the application procedure itself, you were probably introduced to our professional code of ethics. This document can be called an *ought to guide*: it specifies how social workers ought to conduct themselves and their helping activities in the professional setting (see the activity below). We cannot emphasize enough the importance of becoming familiar with this code from the very start of your career and learning its applicability to your practice activities (Reamer, 2009; Strom-Gottfried, 2007).

Activity...As part of a group, or by yourself, look at the NASW Code of Ethics in appendix A and think about how it will shape your practice experiences. Which parts of the code do you find comforting and compatible with your beliefs? Which parts are more difficult for you to understand or support? List the commonalities and differences and note whether at the end of the educational program whether your views change.

All professionals embrace specific values. All clients embrace specific values. An individual's values, however, may not always be consistent with how he or she behaves (Twohig & Crosby, 2009). Personal values belong to the individual, but professional values are governed by the profession and constitute a professional promise that governs professional conduct and behavior. Although social work values are spelled out in a number of documents, the primary reference for the profession's value base is the NASW Code of Ethics (reproduced in appendix A). This code establishes a set of clear beliefs that define ethical social work practice and thus act as a unifying force among all social workers (Reamer, 2001, 2009). The activities we perform on behalf of others—relationship building and maintenance of professional boundaries—as well as our view of social issues and the remedies we consider for individual, group, or community ills—are all firmly rooted in our value base. All social workers need to be versed in the code and aware of key duties and obligations (Reamer, 2009). Using awareness and knowledge makes ethical decision making a planned and objective process. Reamer (2001, 2009) identified the following core values for the social work profession:

◆ Individual worth and dignity of people
◆ Respect for people
◆ A belief in an individual's capacity for change
◆ A client's right to self-determination
◆ A client's right to confidentiality and privacy
◆ A client's right to opportunities that will enable them to realize their own potential
◆ Belief in social change
◆ A client's right to adequate resources and services to meet basic needs
◆ Client empowerment
◆ Equal opportunity
◆ Antidiscrimination
◆ Diversity
◆ Willingness to transmit professional knowledge and skills to others

As you read the code and consider Reamer's points, several common themes emerge, but let's examine three in particular. First, all people, no matter who they are or what their circumstances, should be treated with respect, dignity, and civility. Respect and civility are cornerstones of a just society. We show respect in any number of ways: being on time for appointments and apologizing to clients when tardy, calling people Mr. or Ms. until asked to do otherwise, and listening without interruption and without looking at our watches during interviews. In these sessions, maintaining client confidentiality and privileged communication should always be at the forefront of all helping efforts (Reamer, 2009). When the term *confidentiality* is used, it generally relates directly to the information shared in the counseling session. When the term *privileged communication* is used, it generally relates to information that will be released only in the context of legal proceedings. Be sure that, as a beginning professional, you discuss this with your supervisor to help make you keenly aware of what information can be shared and how best to do it. Also, as a general rule you should be sure that you have tried to secure written client permission to release information even if you are ordered to do so by a court.

When given the opportunity, people may be able to participate in solving their own problems in a way of their own choosing. We understand that not all people can participate fully in such processes, but we recognize that everyone should be encouraged to participate as much as possible. We support client self-determination when we help them to figure out ways to identify and deal with their problems; we do not say, "If I were you, I would do this." Clients have strengths, and we must help them to discover and use these as energy sources for change. The only exception to this practice principle involves what has been referred to historically as a *danger to self or others*. In these situations, if a client's action poses an imminent threat or danger to self or others, the social worker may be forced to take action to protect the client or those in danger. To interfere with self-determination when a client is not in imminent danger can block self-determination. Therefore, not allowing clients to make their own decisions and doing so deliberately with the intention to stop them and protect them from self-harm is referred to as *paternalism*. According to Reamer (2009), paternalism refers to a situation in which a social worker decides to withhold information from clients or misleads them. It can also involve lying or coercing clients to do what the social worker rather than the client feels is best.

Before you begin your professional practice, topics such as this need to be discussed. It is always best to address a situation before you encounter it. When situations such as this arise and prior to such a discussion, the new social worker should immediately seek guidance on how best to continue and address this type of situation with the intent of protecting all involved.

Although it is not stated explicitly in the code or among Reamer's points, we can infer the basic principle that we do no harm to people. Our work is to help, not harm. We cannot hold back any professional efforts or strategies if we believe they will help our clients. However, we should never work beyond our scope of practice and dabble in areas that we are not yet trained to address. This makes it essential for every social worker to know the intent, limits, and changes in the scope of practice.

As you become more familiar with the NASW Code of Ethics, compare it with other value statements such as that of the International Federation of Social Workers (appendix B). What similarities do you find? The words and phrases may be different, but the respect for the human condition and the goal of social change are the same.

As professionals, social workers must pursue the art of helping within a context shaped by values and ethics. Practice that is not guided by values or ethics has no meaning because it fails to recognize the unique circumstances of our clients, their individual needs, and appropriate change strategies. Unless we operate within an ethical framework, our clients may as well be telling their problems to a computer!

DIFFERENTIATING BETWEEN GENERALIST AND SPECIALIST PRACTICE

Social work practice is organized around two principal service delivery conceptual models: the generalist and the specialist. Generalist social work is more broadly defined and targeted toward a wider variety of clients and problem areas. Specialist social work is more narrowly defined with a sharper focus on specific issues or a particular client population.

Generalist Practice

To date, as a profession we continue to struggle with defining what constitutes true generalist practice. First, most professional social workers agree that generalist social work practice is primarily reserved for social workers at the baccalaureate level, although this view has changed as some graduate programs now offer a specialization reflective of additional course work in the area of advanced generalist practice. The advanced generalist at the master's level will go into more depth in certain areas of practice. Second, generalist social workers are prepared for entry-level social work practice. Although some programs may have their unique spin on the curriculum, for the most part generalist practice social workers take into account the environment as the primary focus utilizing some type of systems approach to professional practice and subsequent intervention. According to the *Social Work Dictionary*, a social work generalist is a practitioner "whose knowledge and skill encompasses a broad spectrum and who assesses problems and their solutions comprehensively" (Barker, 2003, p.176).

The broad-based generalist approach to social work practice integrates clients' needs with those of the environment. In accepting the importance of the person-in-situation, social workers are leaders in understanding and interpreting the interaction among the behavioral, psychological, and social factors in the client's condition and the environmental factors that the client faces daily.

Generalist social work follows an integrated approach designed to assist the client on multiple levels, including individuals, families, societies, communities, neighborhoods, and complex organizations. Generalist practice requires understanding how human behavior can affect the environment and make focused change efforts designed to improve system interactions at all levels. Therefore, it is highly possible that the generalist level social worker may be working directly in a nonclinical setting and that he or she is expected to have developed skills reflective of this type of practice environment (DeAngelis, 2009).

Specialist Practice

The specialist social worker provides a more focused, higher level of intervention. A specialist possesses an MSW degree and is also prepared for advanced social work practice. According to the *Social Work Dictionary*, a specialization is "a profession's focus of knowledge and skill on a specific type of problem, target population, or objective" (Barker, 2003, p. 415). Social work specializations have developed in a number of ways over the years. Although each social work program may offer different concentrations of specialist practice, popular specialization areas include health, mental health, substance abuse, corrections, gerontology, children's services, policy, administration, and community-based practice. Alternatively, programs may focus on geographic areas (urban or rural neighborhoods) or social systems (the individual or microsystem, family group or mezzosystem, or the community or macrosystem). After an extended period of MSW practice, the specialist worker is eligible for independent practice. Through state licensing laws (see chapter 15 for a more complete discussion of licensing and regulation of social work practice) and professional practice certifications, the master's level practitioner can move into private practice or practice independently within the agency context.

Social work remains one of the most diverse fields of practice imaginable. Specialist and generalist level social workers are found in numerous settings: public and private agencies, public and private hospitals, clinics, schools, extended care facilities, private practice, private business, police departments, courts, and countless other workplaces too numerous to name. This diversity of practice can be considered both a blessing and a curse. In one way, it increases visibility and functionality and diversifies the profession. Yet, the diversity of the profession makes it difficult for the broader community to understand what social workers do. It also makes it easier for other disciplines to assume partial roles and specialize in just one or two areas.

In summary, generalist and specialist social workers share similarities as they share a core foundation, although the specialist delves more deeply into a particular concentration. Specializations in social work practice occur as a result of taking advanced graduate courses. Specialist social workers are first trained in the generalist approach to practice and later embark on more specialized career tracks by choosing more concentrated areas in which to apply their skills. It is also in specialization that many professional educators believe *real* training as counseling professionals and therapists occurs. Master's level social workers, with supervised experience (and certification or licensure), are usually free to engage in full non-clinically supervised counseling activities or work privately in practice. In the field of social work, the master's degree is generally considered the terminal practice degree. For those studying at the doctorate (DSW or PhD) level, the focus is on research or science rather than clinical practice.

THE EMERGENCE OF EVIDENCE-BASED SOCIAL WORK PRACTICE

As technology evolves so do the expectations of the clients who are served (Dziegielewski, 2013). Whether they pay for services directly through out-of-pocket costs or indirectly with our tax dollars, people want to receive the best services possible. These expectations extend to social workers, and indeed, the profession itself expects all services and activities performed on behalf of clients to be of the highest quality. Yet, how do we demonstrate to the public that our activities are effective?

Social workers have historically been accused of avoiding the use of empirical techniques to establish practice efficiency and effectiveness. According to Rubin and Babbie (2008), this gap still exists today; the gap between research and the practice community is so large that the lack of connection extends into the classroom as well. As we move into an era of professional accountability and client rights, however, the impetus remains high for continued progress toward change, highlighting the importance of assessment, intervention, and evaluation in all activities completed (O'Hare, 2009). The profession continues to be challenged to prove service effectiveness and ensure that interventions are germane to client issues.

The challenge to tie evidence-based research and evaluation to practice is not new. For example, in 1978, Fischer wrote,

> It seems to be difficult to avoid the conclusion that, unless major changes are made in the practice methods—and hence, the effectiveness—of casework, our field, if not the entire profession of social work, cannot long survive. Indeed, unless such changes are made, it is not clear that as a field, we deserve to survive. On one hand, we have the option of choosing—and building—a new revitalized future for social casework, one rooted in the superordinate principle that our primary if not our sole allegiance is to serve our clients with demonstrable effectiveness. On the other hand, we can continue our outmoded practices, denigrate and resist new approaches to practice, and bury our collective heads in the sand when confronted with the vaguest hint of a threat that we may not be doing all in our power to provide effective services (p. 310).

The new revitalized casework that Fischer envisioned is today called evidence-based social work practice. All social workers, generalist and specialist alike, are expected to apply its principles to their activities. *The Social Work Dictionary* defines **empirically based social work practice** as: "a type of intervention in which the professional social worker uses research as a practice and problem-solving tool; collects data systematically to monitor the intervention; specifies problems, techniques, and outcomes in measurable terms; and systematically evaluates the effectiveness of the intervention used" (Barker, 2003, p. 141).

Furthermore, Barker defines evidence-based practice as "the use of the best available scientific knowledge, derived from randomized controlled outcome studies and meta-analyses of existing outcome studies, as one basis for guiding professional interventions and effective therapies, combined with professional ethical standards, clinical judgments, and practice wisdom" (2003, p. 149).

For the beginning social work professional, it is important to understand that in evidence-based social work practice, the application of clear-cut research and evaluation models is guided by four broad ideas. First, research findings must be shown to be relevant to practice by assessing the change in a client's level of effectiveness after a specific intervention directed at a specific problem. Second, applications, practice and evaluation models, and findings are to be drawn from research reports. Third, research findings are to be disseminated so that the results are known in the practice community. Finally, other social work professionals should be able to interpret, understand, and apply what they read to what they do. Evidence-based practice mandates that, in developing a practice intervention with a client, the practitioner include systematic research activities that provide feedback on the intervention's effectiveness, controlling for bias while being potentially replicable (Bronson, 2009; Shlonsky, 2009; Thyer, 2001, 2004; Thyer & Meyers, 2007). In addition, the practice intervention may provide additional information on how the client's ability to resolve the problem can be strengthened.

THE STEPS IN PROFESSIONAL HELPING

Work with clients in social work practice has five steps. These are illustrated in box 2. Note that evaluation is not a distinct step but rather takes place throughout all steps of the social work process.

Box 2. Social Work Process

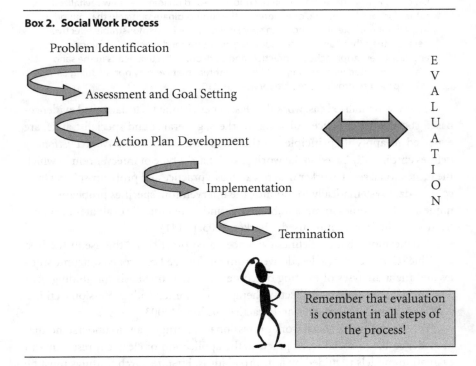

Problem Identification

Assessment and Goal Setting

Action Plan Development

Implementation

Termination

E V A L U A T I O N

Remember that evaluation is constant in all steps of the process!

Step 1: Problem Identification

The first step involves problem identification. The social worker helps the client to identify and concretely define the problem(s) to be addressed by the intervention process. This requires a careful examination of the problem behaviors while establishing a relationship with the client that will foster continued support. Involvement by the client in identifying problem behaviors is crucial to continued engagement.

Once clear mutually negotiated goals and objectives are identified the treatment plan can be formed (Dziegielewski, 2015). The role of the worker is clear: to apply logical thinking to identify the beginning, end, and dynamics of the problem. Engage the client in the problem identification process because it is central to the developing practice strategy. The client's problems are discussed thoroughly, and the client is made aware of the social worker's serious and dedicated efforts to help. It is in this initial step of the helping process that the **rapport** is established that will characterize the remainder of the practice experience. A working alliance is developed, allowing the client to begin to feel comfortable yet eager to embark on change. The social worker avoids simply giving advice to the client. Utilizing empathy helps the client to see that the social worker understands the client's situation and can relate to the client within the context of the other person's perspective (Koerner & Linehan, 2009).

As the sessions progress, the social worker will remain objective when educating, advocating, facilitating, and intervening on behalf of the client. In establishing rapport and giving feedback validation, the worker often uses active communication that the client's perspective makes sense (Koerner & Linehan, 2009). Moreover, as ironic as it may sound, the social worker always begins early in the encounter to plan for what will happen when the session ends. In fact, as explained in chapter 6, plans for what will happen after termination are often outlined in the first session. The client is thus well aware of what is coming and what needs to be accomplished by the end of the therapeutic term.

At the end of the first session and each session thereafter, the technique of *summarization* is used. In this technique the client is asked to state what was most relevant for him or her in the session and whether progress was made in regard to the identified goals and objectives. This helps to focus the client on what was covered while it helps the social worker to know if the session is following the identified goals and objectives. To ensure that the client is understanding and relating directly to what is covered, the social worker should never summarize the session content for the client. Let the client do it in his or her own words. Letting the client state what he or she has gotten from the session helps the social worker to determine what really was accomplished and whether both client and social worker are aiming toward the same intervention outcomes. When relevant, the social worker should acknowledge what a client is feeling and validate emotions and change efforts that support the changes desired (Koerner & Linehan, 2009). Clients often need this feedback and reassurance that understanding has occurred and progress is being made.

It is also during this initial step that the social worker decides how accountability or practice effectiveness will be evaluated after the intervention is completed. Exactly what will be measured and how it will be measured vary from case to case. No magic pill ensures evidence-based practice. We hope, however, that knowing its importance piques your interest in the research course you have yet to take.

Step 2: Assessment and Goal Setting

The second step involves helping the client to set goals and objectives that can be accomplished (Dziegielewski, 2015). Worker and client assess the client's need for assistance and determine how specifically the problem can be addressed. The *goal* is the overall end that the client wants to accomplish and the *objectives* are the concrete steps that the client will take to get there and that allow for measurement of the outcome (Dziegielewski, 2008a, 2008b) When done adequately, setting goals and objectives has the following valuable consequences:

- ◆ It ensures agreement between worker and client on intervention focus and purpose.
- ◆ It provides to the client knowledge about how to address the problem while establishing a basis for continuity of session content across the intervention process.
- ◆ It provides a basis for selecting appropriate treatment strategies.
- ◆ It assists the social worker to structure session content and monitor progress of the intervention.
- ◆ It yields outcome criteria (the objectives) for measurement of intervention effectiveness.

The following guidelines always apply to setting goals and objectives. First, the goals and objectives must relate to what the client wants to achieve at the end of the intervention. Second, the goals and objectives must be defined in explicit terms so that the client knows what is expected of him or her. Third, the objectives must be feasible. Clients must believe that they can succeed; otherwise, they may become disheartened and drop out of the intervention process. Fourth, the goals and objectives must be consistent with the skills and abilities of the helping professional. Social workers should never try to address medical problems they know little about. For example, if the social worker becomes unsure of his or her abilities, he or she should explore supervision, consultation, and continuing education options before proceeding with the intervention process. Ensuring quality of services in this manner is important for both the client and the social worker. Fifth, whenever possible, goals and objectives should be stated positively rather than negatively. Sixth, although all goals should be mutually negotiated with the client, the social worker must express his or her reservations about these goals. Clients desire input in their decision making. However, the social worker must be sure that any hesitation reflects concern for the client's good rather than his or her personal bias.

Step 3: Action Plan Development

Once goals and objectives have been clearly identified, the social worker helps the client to develop a plan of action. The role of the social worker is paramount in identifying strategies for action and change. The worker may be able to provide the direct supervision or consultation necessary to implement the plan. Often, however, the social worker does not have the required expertise—he or she may be a generalist when a specialist is needed—and will contract with another provider or use work strategies to assist the client in meeting the objectives.

The action plan may include a task or a series of tasks. Each task is specific, clear, and supported by a time frame monitored by both worker and client. Each task builds on previous efforts, which together lead to the goals and objectives identified. As with goal setting, each task must be understood by both client and worker and, most importantly, must be within the client's ability to achieve.

Every action plan must have clearly established contingency plans. These plans specify the rewards for completion of the practice strategy agreement and the consequences for noncompliance. Clients participate in this part of the change process because they will accept the consequences of their actions or inactions.

Step 4: Implementation

Implementation takes place when the client is ready to put the plan into action. During implementation, the worker and client together monitor the progress and determine whether any measureable improvement has occurred. Therefore, practice evaluation is basically a determination as to whether there has been useful improvement with the problem situation. Assessing and evaluating the problem behaviors that have been modified assist both the client and the social worker to measure progress. Through monitoring, worker and client are able to assess progress toward the goal and measure the effectiveness of the intervention. Once the goals and tasks have been assessed, the client's reaction to the progress or lack thereof is evaluated. Ongoing monitoring allows worker and client to identify barriers as well as strengths in the process. New strategies can be built to overcome or cope with the barriers. And most importantly, monitoring provides the client with feedback on positive experiences that in turn reinforce the change efforts.

Implementing an action plan can be intimidating for a beginning social worker. Social work practice knowledge is essential because the social worker will be expected to use multiple practice strategies to assist the client. These can involve the application of strategies such as modeling, behavior rehearsal, role playing, or simply paper-and-pencil exercises in which the client writes down feelings experienced as well as steps to be completed in the action plan. Referrals for additional help and assistance should also be considered and discussed at this time—for example, additional individual therapy, group therapy, couples therapy, or family therapy.

Step 5: Termination

The last step in the social work process involves termination. Client and social worker end their working relationship and describe how any change strategy developed will be continued. Many clients realize at termination that they want additional help. If this happens, the social worker informs the client of options for continued intervention and emotional growth by giving appropriate referrals. Referrals for group therapy, individual growth-directed therapy, couples therapy, and family therapy can be considered.

Evaluation and Follow-up

Successful practice intervention results in significant changes in a client's levels of functioning and coping. Measures that can substantiate these changes are essential to evidence-based practice. Measuring intervention effectiveness can be as simple as making a follow-up phone call to discuss how things are going, or it can be as structured as scoring the client's behavior on a standardized scale at the beginning and end of treatment and then comparing the two. Scales that measure depression, trauma, and so forth are readily available. If more advanced methods of measuring practice effectiveness are expected, more advanced training and planning are warranted.

Planned practice evaluation and follow-up at the termination of intervention are essential, but these are steps that are often forgotten. As a matter of fact, when you consider the five steps in the social work process, you will see that research and evaluation seem to be missing. And if these are missing, how does the process we've outlined lead to empirically based social work practice? In fact, they're not missing—they're simply not a separate step because research and evaluation should be included at each step of the helping process.

PRACTICE APPLICATION: THE ROLE OF THE MEDICAL SOCIAL WORKER

Ms. Martha Edda had been living with her family for approximately a year. Before then she had lived independently in her own apartment. Ms. Edda had to leave her apartment after a neighbor found her unconscious. The apartment was unsafe, with rotted food, urine, and feces throughout. Upon discovery, Ms. Edda was immediately admitted to the hospital. Originally, she was believed to have suffered a stroke; later she was formally diagnosed with a neurological condition called vascular dementia. Doctors believed that she was in the moderate to advanced stage of this condition because, at age 62, she had pronounced movement and memory difficulties.

After discussion with the hospital social worker, it became obvious that Ms. Edda needed a supervised living arrangement. Ms. Edda had a daughter, Joan, who said she would try to help. Once in Joan's home, Ms. Edda received home health care services. However, much to Joan's surprise, all services stopped after just two months because Ms. Edda's physical therapy was discontinued. Joan relied heavily on these services, particularly the nurse's aide who helped to give Ms. Edda a bath. Ms. Edda weighed 170 pounds and could not help herself in or out of the tub. Joan recruited the help of her husband, who reluctantly agreed. Unfortunately, Ms. Edda could not get into the adult day care center in the area because no spaces were available, and she was placed on a waiting list. She required help with all of her activities of daily living, and her daughter was afraid to leave her at home alone during the day. Therefore, Joan quit her job to help care for her.

On the morning of January 12, Joan found her mother lying face down in her bed. She had become incontinent of bowel and bladder and unable to speak, and the features on the left side of her face appeared distorted. When Joan could not rouse her mother, she panicked and called an ambulance. Ms. Edda was immediately transported to the emergency room.

In the emergency room, the staff began to administer numerous tests to see if Ms. Edda had suffered a stroke. Plans were made to admit her to the hospital, but no beds were available. Because Ms. Edda needed supervised monitoring and a hospital bed could become available in the morning, an agreement was made to keep her overnight. In the morning, she was admitted to the inpatient hospital where she remained incontinent and refused to eat. She was so confused that the nurses feared she would get out of bed and hurt herself; she was placed in restraints periodically throughout the day.

After two days, most of the medical tests had been performed and determined negative; Ms. Edda's vital signs remained stable. The physician felt that her admission to the hospital could no longer be justified, and the social worker was notified of the pending discharge. On placing the call to prepare Ms. Edda's family for her return home, the social worker was told that the family would not accept her and wanted her placed in a nursing home. The social worker was concerned about this decision because Ms. Edda did not have private insurance to cover a nursing home stay and was too young to be eligible for Medicare. This meant that an application for Medicaid would have to be made. This state-funded program had a lower reimbursement rate, and most privately run nursing homes drastically limited the number of Medicaid clients they accepted. After searching for nursing home services, the social worker was told of the lack of available beds.

When the social worker explained the problems with the discharge plans to the physician, he simply responded, "I am under pressure to get her out, and there is no medical reason for her to be here. Discharge her home today." Since it was after 4:00 p.m. and the administrative offices were closed, the social worker next attempted to secure an out-of-area placement for the following day.

When the physician returned at 6:00 p.m., he wanted to know why the client had not been discharged. The nurse on duty explained that a nursing home bed could not be found; the physician, who was angry, wrote an order for immediate discharge. The nurse called Ms. Edda's family at 6:30 p.m. and notified them of the discharge. Ms. Edda's family was angry and asked why she had not being placed in a home. The nurse explained to the family that discharge orders had been written and that she was only trying to do her job.

Ms. Edda's daughter, Joan, insisted on speaking to the discharge physician prior to picking up her mother. A message was left for him, and at 8:00 p.m, he returned her call. The physician, sounding frustrated, told Joan that all medical emergencies had been addressed and Ms. Edda would have to leave the hospital immediately. Furious, Joan yelled, "If she is still incontinent and in restraints, how do you expect me to handle her?" Listening to Joan's distress, the physician softened his voice and said, "I will put the nurse on the phone to update you on her condition. In addition, the social worker will call you in the morning to arrange home health care services."

Upon arriving at the hospital, Joan found her mother hooked to an IV, wearing a diaper, and still in restraints. Pleased to see a member of Ms. Edda's family, the nurse sent for a wheelchair, unhooked the intravenous tubing, removed the restraints, and placed Ms. Edda in the wheelchair for transport to the family's car.

Discussion

Unfortunately, situations like this occur all too often. The social worker was responsible for **discharge planning**, but many other issues needed to be addressed to best serve the client and her family. With perseverance and the help of the hospital social worker, Joan eventually (several months later) placed her mother in a nursing home. However, the strain on Joan was so severe that she requested medication to combat her depression. Joan also began to fight with her husband and children over numerous issues related to the time and care devoted to her mother and the loss of their second family income. Joan's earnings helped to cover basic necessities such as rent and food as well as family luxuries (such as movies and eating out).

Clearly, in this situation, the price of the *cost-effective* **managed care** strategy far exceeded the dollar value placed on it, and the client and her family became silent victims. The role of the social worker—officially labeled a discharge planner—involved considerably more than just finding a place for the client to go. Referrals, counseling, and openness to service flexibility make the social work professional an invaluable member of any **interdisciplinary team**. (The case scenario is adopted from Dziegielewski, 2013).

SUMMARY

Social work practice evolved from mid-eighteenth and nineteenth century efforts to assist the poor. In those early years activities were carried out by volunteers, with few organizational supports and limited training. Today the profession has a well-established knowledge base, a clearly articulated value orientation, and diverse practice methodologies and interventions, which are transmitted to the new practitioner through formal educational processes.

The practice of social work is generally conducted in one of two major forms: the generalist and the specialist. The generalist works with a wide range of clients and services, whereas the specialist can complete the same duties but can also focus more distinctly on particular groups of clients and provide more individualized therapeutic services. The great variability of what can be done to assist clients and the level at which this can be accomplished are the reasons why social workers are able to practice in a variety of different types of social agencies and organizational settings.

Social work practice has never been static. It has evolved dramatically since its conception and will continue to change in the future. To grow and adapt, practice must be conducted within a systematic, well-thought-out process that allows the use and production of scientifically tested knowledge and skills and it must be founded on a clear and coherent set of professional values.

REFERENCES

Austrian, S. G. (2009). Guidelines for conducting a biopsychosocial assessment. In A. R. Roberts. *Social workers' desk reference* (2nd ed., pp. 376–380). New York: Oxford University Press.

Barker, R. L. (2003). *The social work dictionary* (5th ed.). Washington, DC: NASW Press.

Boehm W. (Ed.). (1959). *Social work curriculum study* (vol. 1). Washington, DC: Council on Social Work Education.

Bronson, D. E. (2009). Critically appraising studies for evidence-based practice. In A. Roberts (Ed.), *Social workers' desk reference* (2nd ed., pp. 1137–1141). New York: Oxford University Press.

Congress, E. P. (2009). The culturagram. In A. Roberts (Ed.), *Social workers desk reference* (2nd ed., pp. 969–975). New York: Oxford University Press.

Congress, E. P., & Gonzalez, M. J. (Eds.). (2013). *Multicultural perspectives in social work practice with families* (3rd ed.). New York: Springer.

Congress, E. P., & Kung, W. W. (2013). Using the culturagram to assess and empower culturally diverse families. In E. P. Congress & M. J. Gonzalez (Eds.), *Multicultural perspectives in social work practice with families* (3rd ed., pp. 1–20). New York: Springer.

DeAngelis, D. (2009). Social work licensing examinations in the United States and Canada. In A. Roberts (Ed.), *Social workers desk reference* (2nd ed., pp. 136–147). New York: Oxford University Press.

Dziegielewski, S. F. (2008a). Brief and intermittent approaches to practice: The state of practice. *Journal of Brief Treatment and Crisis Intervention*, Advance, 8, 147–163. Advance online publication. doi:10.1093/brief-treatment/mhn005

Dziegielewski, S. F. (2008b). Problem identification, contracting, and case planning. In K. M. Sowers & C. N. Dulmus (Series Eds.) & W. Rowe & L. A. Rapp-Paglicci (Vol. Eds.), *Comprehensive handbook of social work and social welfare: Social work practice* (vol. 3, pp. 78–97). Hoboken, NJ: Wiley.

Dziegielewski, S.F. (2013). *The changing face of health care social work: Opportunities and challenges for professional practice* (3rd ed.). New York: Springer.

Dziegielewski, S.F. (2015). *DSM-5™ in action* (3rd ed.) Hoboken, NJ: Wiley.

Ell, K., Lee, P., & Xie, B. (2010). Depression care for low-income, minority, safety net clinic populations with comorbid illness. *Research on Social Work Practice*, 20, 467–475. doi:10.1177/1049731510361962

Fischer, J. (1998). *Effective casework practice: An eclectic approach.* New York: McGraw Hill.

Gonzalez-Ramos, G. (1990). Examining the myth of Hispanic families' resistance to treatment: Using the school as a site for services. *Social Work in Education*, 12, 261–274.

Hepworth, D. H., Rooney, R. H., Rooney, G. D., Strom-Gottfried, K., & Larsen, J. (2010). *Direct social work practice: Theory and skills* (8th ed.). Belmonte, CA: Brooks/Cole Cengage Learning.

Hopps, J. G., & Lowe, T. B. (2008). The scope of social work practice. In K. M. Sowers & C. N. Dulmus (Series Eds.) & B. W. White (Vol. Ed.), *Comprehensive handbook of social work and social welfare: The profession of social work* (vol. 1, pp. 37–64). Hoboken, NJ: Wiley.

Hopps, J. G., & Lowe, T. B. (2012). Social work practice in the new millennium. In C. N Dulmus & K. M. Sowers (Eds.), *The profession of social work: Guided by history, led by evidence* (pp. 51–81). Hoboken, NJ: Wiley.

International Federation of Social Workers. (August, 2012). *Effective and ethical working environments for social work: The responsibilities of employers of social workers.* Retrieved from http://ifsw.org/policies/effective-and-ethical-working-environments-for-social-work-the-responsibilities-of-employers-of-social-workers-3

Jani, J. S., Pierce, D., Ortiz, L., & Sowbel, L. (2011). Access to intersectionality, content to competence: Deconstructing social work education diversity standards. *Journal of Social Work Education, 47*, 283–301. doi:10.5175/JSWE.2011.200900118

Koerner, K., & Linehan, M. M. (2009). Validation principles and strategies. In W. T. O'Donohue & J. E. Fisher (Eds.), *General principles and empirically supported techniques of cognitive behavior therapy* (pp. 674–680). Hoboken, NJ: Wiley.

Mattaini, M. A. (2001). The foundation of social work practice. In Briggs & Corcoran (Eds.), *Social work practice: Treating common client problems* (pp. 15–35). Chicago: Lyceum Books.

Miller, J., & Garran, A. M. (2009). The legacy of racism for social work practice today and what to do about it. In A. Roberts (Ed.), *Social workers' desk reference* (2nd ed., pp. 928–923). New York: Oxford University Press.

Morales, A. T., Sheafor, B. W., & Scott, M. E. (2012). *Social work: A profession of many faces* (updated 12th ed.). New Jersey: Pearson Education, Allyn and Bacon.

National Association of Social Workers. (1993). *Choices: Careers in social work.* Washington, DC: Author.

National Association of Social Workers. (2008). *Code of ethics of the National Association of Social Workers.* Washington, DC: Retrieved from http://www.socialworkers.org/pubs/code/code.asp

O'Hare, T. (2009). *Essential skills of social work practice: Assessment, intervention, and education.* Chicago: Lyceum Books.

Parker, J., & Bradley, G. (2010). *Social work practice: Assessment, planning, intervention and review* (3rd ed.).Great Britain: Learning Matters.

Poertner, J., & Rapp, C. A. (2007). *The textbook of social administration: The consumer centered approach.* Binghamton, NY: Haworth Press.

Reamer, F. G. (2001). Ethics and values in clinical and community social work practice. In H. E. Briggs & K. Corcoran (Eds.), *Social work practice: Treating common client problems* (pp. 85–106). Chicago: Lyceum Books.

Reamer, F. G. (2009). Ethical issues in social work. In A. Roberts (Ed.), *Social workers' desk reference* (2nd ed., pp. 115–120). New York: Oxford University Press.

Reardon, C. (2011, July/August). A decade of *Social Work Today*: 10 trends that transformed social work. *Social Work Today, 11*(4), 10. Retrieved from http://www.socialworktoday .com/archive/071211p10.shtml

Ridley, C. R. (1995). *Overcoming unintentional racism in counseling and therapy.* Thousand Oaks, CA: Sage.

Rubin, A., & Babbie, E. (2008). *Research methods for social work* (6th ed.). Belmont, CA: Brooks/Cole.

Shlonsky, A. (2009). Evidence-based practice in social work education. In A. Roberts (Ed.), *Social workers desk reference* (2nd ed., pp. 1169–1176). New York: Oxford University Press.

Snowden, L. R. (2003). Bias in mental health assessment and intervention: Theory and evidence. *Journal of Public Health, 93*, 239–243. doi: 10.2105/AJPH.93.3.239. Retrieved from: http://ajph.aphapublications.org/doi/full/10.2105/AJPH.93.2.239

Strom-Gottfried, K. (2009). Enacting the educator role: Principles for practice. In A. R. Roberts (Ed.), *Social workers' desk reference* (2nd ed., pp. 720–725). New York: Oxford University Press.

Sue, D. W., & Sue, D. (2008). *Counseling the culturally diverse: Theory and practice.* Hoboken, NJ: Wiley.

Thyer, B. (2001). Evidence-based approaches to community practice. In H. E. Briggs & K. Corcoran (Eds.) *Social work practice: Treating common client problems* (pp. 54–65). Chicago: Lyceum Books.

Thyer, B. A. (2004). What is evidence-based practice? *Brief Treatment and Crisis Intervention, 4,* 167–176.

Thyer, B. A., & Meyers, L. L. (2007). *The social worker's guide to evaluating practice outcomes.* Alexandria, VA: CSWE Press.

Trevithick, P. (2012). *Social work skills and knowledge: A practice handbook* (3rd ed.). England: Open University Press/McGraw-Hill Education.

Twohig, M. P., & Crosby, J. M. (2009). Values clarification. In W. T. O'Donohue & J. E. Fisher (Eds.), *General principles and empirically supported techniques of cognitive behavior therapy* (pp. 681–686). Hoboken, NJ: Wiley.

Witkin, S. L., & Iversen, R. R. (2008). Issues in social work. In K. M. Sowers & C. N. Dulmus (Series Eds.) & B. W. White (Vol. Ed.), *Comprehensive handbook of social work and social welfare: The profession of social work* (vol. 1, pp. 467–496). Hoboken, NJ: Wiley.

CHAPTER 6
RECOGNIZING DIVERSITY AND APPLYING IT TO GENERALIST PRACTICE

IN HIS FIRST FIELD PLACEMENT JUAN, A SOCIAL WORKER WORKING with older adults, often found himself struggling. He joked that he was waiting for the single-problem client to come in so that he could carefully choose the best method of helping. Although he sincerely wanted to help his clients address their problems, remembering what had been taught to him in school, the thought of applying this knowledge was frightening. In school Juan learned numerous intervention methods that supported his generalist approach to practice, and similar to most beginning professionals, he was concerned that he would not interpret the client's problems correctly and would make the wrong decisions when he began helping activities. Important expectations such as always remembering to respect the individual worth and dignity of each client and maximizing self-determination were strong in his memory. He knew that he should never show a lack of respect for the client's culture, values, or beliefs. For Juan, as for many beginning social work professionals, it is never easy to discover the best way to recognize, respect, and utilize client empowerment to help the client.

Furthermore, Juan found himself questioning who his client was. Was it the person suffering from the problem? Was it the family? Was it the group the person associated with or the community in which the person lived? Was it the policy or legislation leading to the client's problem that required change? Or was it all of the above?

Juan's experience is quite normal for a beginning social worker. As we've noted before, social work is not purely a science. Many aspects of comprehensive helping may need to move beyond the science and require individualistic helping activities that create the best fit for the client in his/her situation. The skills required to practice the art and science in social work take time and experience to develop. In fact, the science of social work will always require continual updating as we continue to prove that what we do does indeed make a difference. In this way, we can show that the client situation improves with the intervention and this is measured through clear goals and guidelines within the practice structure.

For Juan, and all beginning as well as seasoned social workers, deciding how best to handle a client's situation is never easy—nor should it be. The best practice interventions require constant assessment, reassessment, evaluation, and collaboration with other professionals (Dziegielewski, 2013; O'Hare. 2009). Furthermore, on any professional team, options will vary as to how to interpret, select, and apply best helping strategies. Remember, applying helping skills to problem situations is an art; situations vary and options are diverse. From an ecological systems perspective, practice strategy and intervention must occur on multiple levels to achieve treatment goals and objectives (Franklin, Jordan, & Hopson, 2008). This diversity is a strength within the social work profession, and an important part of the helping process is identifying and supporting alternatives and innovative strategies. Therefore the goal will never be chaotic improvisation. The general practice consensus is that all client-based interventions must take place within a practice framework with clear theoretical foundations. In the practice environment it remains clear that the expectation is to have good problem identification, contracting, and case planning skills (Dziegielewski, 2008a; 2008b, 2013). This is further highlighted by using a strengths-based approach (Poulin, 2010).

This chapter will explore the concept of diversity and how it relates to generalist social work practice. From this orientation all clients (individuals, families, and groups) are viewed through a culturally sensitive lens, and client strengths are recognized and supported at each step of the helping process (Diller, 2011). We will also discuss the three most common approaches to social work practice: micropractice, mezzopractice, and macropractice. Social workers must be well versed in all three, although their efforts to assist clients may be concentrated in only one or two of these.

DIVERSITY AND SOCIAL WORK PRACTICE

A hallmark of the social work profession is its insistence on viewing practice within a specific context, commonly referred to as *contextual practice*. As a client-centered approach, contextual practice suggests that all practice methods consider a variety of unique attributes or characteristics, which in turn influence what we do with and on behalf of clients. One type of intervention may work for one person or group, but not necessarily for another. It should come as no surprise that two significant groups in the social work profession, the Council on Social Work Education (CSWE) and the National Association of Social Workers (NASW), have been active in defining and infusing cultural awareness and competence into curriculum and content. As early as the 1960s, the CSWE noted the importance of diversity and encouraged the social work profession to infuse this information into the curriculum as well as to encourage diversity in hiring faculty and recruiting students (NASW, 2012). This was further reinforced by the NASW Code of Ethics (2008), which stated that social workers must honor the ethical responsibility to serve clients in culturally competent ways.

It is clear that throughout its history the profession of social work has placed great emphasis on understanding culture as inclusive of an integrated system linked to human behavior. Therefore, promoting cultural competence should be reflected in education, research, and practice (NASW, 2012). This inclusiveness makes understanding diversity somewhat complicated if is defined simply by the race of a client. When a simplified definition of race is coupled with the historical definition that is related to an individual's genetics and color, the recognition of diversity is limited. When diversity is defined from a social work perspective, it is much broader. From a social work perspective the concept of culture is not viewed as static and it embodies the beliefs, customs, norms, and other realisms identified within a particular society. Therefore, cultural sensitivity is not achieved by recognizing distinctions of gender, age, race, or creed alone, but rather by allowing inclusive explanations that are never static. In social work recognizing diversity involves recognizing groups not traditionally seen as diverse and also being sensitive to differences within groups, thereby creating subgroupings or recognizing individual responses that may or may not be shared by the group. This requires being vigilant in recognizing cultural differences and using acquired information to adapt helping services to meet the culturally unique needs of the client (NASW, 2001). In social work the basic premise "start where the client is" allows for increased understanding and awareness that improve the effectiveness and the fit of the helping strategy. As you continue to read this chapter, keep that premise in mind because it is the foundation for what is to come.

The characteristics that an individual, family, group, or community bring to the helping relationship are powerful influences shaping and molding the client-centered intervention. Why? The key to understanding is found in recognizing differences in backgrounds, experiences, ideas, philosophies, and traditions that make all individuals unique. A simple way to start to understand basic differences in thinking and responding is to read John Gray's classic book *Men Are from Mars, Women Are from Venus* (1992), which details gender differences. Think back to your introductory sociology course in which you learned that norms, mores, and folkways create our individual skeletal system from which our character and behaviors take shape.

It is not easy to define gender-specific roles and what constitutes male and female behavior. Spade and Valentine (2014) define gender simply as ". . . the meanings, practices and relations of masculinities and femininities that people create as we go about our lives in different settings" (p. xiii). The authors warn, however, that this simplistic definition can limit the potential for understanding what is and what could be, referring to defining gender as more like looking through a kaleidoscope where all views are possible and numerous interpretations can flourish.

Regardless, of gender, race, age, or the more inclusive culture of the individual, the first step toward understanding differences is recognizing the life experiences of each individual. For example, a person with a disability may not experience an event in the same way as someone who does not have these same life or health issues. The person with a disability may have to contend with socially marginalzing beliefs. Mackelprang and Salsgiver (2009) use the term *ableism* (often interchangeably with the term *disableism*) to describe the belief that people with disabilities are inferior to people without disabilities because of their differences (p. 9). Furthermore, people with disabilities may be left vulnerable, requiring the help and assistance of others simply to meet their daily needs (Fitzsimons, 2009). The author will never forget discussing planning a trip with a client who was paralyzed. The client said that you have no idea what it is like to fly on an airplane and wonder if your "chariot of fire" (another name for his wheelchair) would arrive and be ready when it was time to leave the airport.

What makes understanding diversity more complicated is that there are differences within differences. Ryle (2012) reminds us that a cross-cultural perspective can be further complicated by a person's age, especially when related to sexuality and expression. Another example is related directly to race and ethnicity and labeling diverse peoples as all acting alike. Labeling diverse peoples as Hispanic ignores the fact that there are cultural differences among those who are Mexican, Cuban, Puerto Rican, or Spanish, just as there are differences among Asian Americans who are Chinese, Filipino, Japanese, Korean, Vietnamese, or Samoan. And, to further complicate matters, is it fair to say that all Mexicans will act one way and all Puerto Ricans another way? Saying that all Native Americans fall into one group or act the same can be equally inaccurate. Defining who and what constitutes these indigenous people is difficult. Generally the term Native American (indigenous people of North America) is preferable to American Indian, which refers to the indigenous people of North and South America (not including Aleuts, who inhabit aouthwest Alaska, and Eskimos). According to the 2010 U.S. Census (2011a), the U.S. population included approximately 2.871 million Native Americans and approximately 124,000 Alaska Natives. When Native Americans and Alaska Natives are connected with more than one tribal association or if they are considered mul-

Name: Jason Cross

Place of residence: Manistee, Michigan

College/university degrees: Michigan State University, BSW, MSW student (graduating May 2015)

Present position: Family services case manager, Little River Band of Ottawa, Indiana.

What do you do in your spare time? In my spare time I enjoy spending time with my wife and three children. In addition to several Tribal events we attend in the area every year, we also enjoy spending time outdoors including an annual trip down one of our local rivers. Living less than one mile from Lake Michigan and the Manistee National Forest, I remind my children to take advantage of the natural opportunities many people must travel hundreds of miles to see.

Why did you choose social work as a career? I compare my journey to the social work field to that of a calling to help others. I have held many other positions in my life, but always felt something missing. Having the opportunity to guide others along the path to their purpose in life is truly a blessing. Every day I have the chance to assist an individual or family through difficult times. The social work field comes with great responsibility, but the rewards are just as great.

What is your favorite social work story? In my position as a tribal social worker I work with many cases related to the Indian Child Welfare Act (ICWA). One case in particular involved a single mother of three children. She was in an abusive relationship with the father of one of the children. Even after she ended the relationship, the private foster care agency and county court sought to terminate her parental rights, claiming that she failed to protect her children. Having spent significant time with the mother and the children both individually and during visitation, it was clear that there was a strong bond built on a foundation of love and trust between them. Because of the ICWA I was able to hold off the termination proceedings to allow the mother to prove her ability to parent the children safely. Eventually the children were returned to her and the case was closed. I still receive e-mails thanking me for the work on the case and they are doing great.

What would be the one thing you would change in our community if you had the power to do so? As a tribal member and through my work with the Native American population I have seen the damage caused by historical trauma and its manifestation in self-destructive behaviors such as substance abuse, domestic violence, and shame. These behaviors coupled with generational poverty provide a perfect breeding ground for hopelessness and misery. Reducing poverty while helping individuals find their purpose and worth is my long-term vision of change for my community. As part of a collaborative project I have been working on a culturally competent anti-poverty program that considers all aspects of the individual to allow for a holistic service plan. Instead of focusing on one area at a time, we look at all systems collectively and bring a myriad of community resources to the table. The use of existing resources in a coordinated effort improves outcomes without increasing expenses. Because of the use of volunteerism and peer mentors, we have discovered that a stronger community has emerged as a secondary outcome.

---

tiracial, they constitute approximately 5,366,625 people. Native Americans constitute 562 independent tribes that exist as sovereign nations and speak more than 200 unique languages (Thompson, Johnson-Jennings, & Nitzarim, 2013). This makes communicating between the tribes as well as understanding government-to-government treaties outside of the tribal setting a unique cultural challenge not experienced with other cultural groups in the United States. The term balancing or *walking between two worlds* is often applied to Native American students and youth (Thompson, et al., 2013).

Identifying different cultural groups will always be insufficient if it does not include the awareness of variation in ethnic communities and the impact of these communities on the lives of those involved (Hiller & Barrow, 2011). Also, it is important not to assume, for example, that one Muslim student in a group represents all Muslims (Nadir & Dziegielewski, 2001; Rehman & Dziegielewski, 2003). Nothing could be further from the truth, and this type of attitude can be frustrating for all involved. Yet at times this unfortunate mistake continues to be made, and all individuals in certain groupings are assumed to be alike. It is critical to remember in all attempts at grouping that individual differences and ethnic variations will always exist.

Did You Know... The term homophyly *acknowledges that people derive comfort and support from people who are like themselves. Culturally sensitive social work practice recognizes this phenomenon. It is one reason why social workers are always encouraged to use a client's own naturally occurring support network whenever possible. Clients are more likely to achieve needed changes when they can work within a system that is familiar to them.*

The second step in understanding and recognizing diversity involves factoring individual differences and life experiences as part of the intervention strategy. In this way, we recognize the uniqueness of the individual and understand the influence and power of these unique dimensions on the human experience. Therefore, before we talk about the types of practice utilized in social work, it is crucial to understand diversity—what are the similarities and differences—by taking an individualized approach and recognizing how shared perceptions of differences influence practice. And, once it has been identified, we must understand how this information can be integrated into generalist practice strategy.

Understanding, recognizing, and integrating diversity into practice strategy is so important in the field that often social work programs, undergraduate and graduate alike, require students to complete one or more courses on this topic. In addition, elements of diversity are generally included in almost every course in your undergraduate or graduate program. So don't be surprised if this topic in one form or another continually resurfaces in this book. Sue and Sue (2013) discuss a concept called cultural universality and how it relates to cultural relativism. The term *etic* relates to what is culturally universal whereas the term *emic* relates to what is culturally specific. From an etic perspective the social worker emphasizes an outsider view and what he or she considers important. From an emic perspective, the social worker looks carefully at the customs and beliefs of the local community. After these values and beliefs are recognized, this information is applied to any future helping activities. The new social worker should always operate from the emic position where everything is examined in regard to the relevant culture and later challenged and explored. From this perspective, it is important to outline how cultural values, lifestyles, and worldviews can affect how a client thinks and responds. Space limits our discussion and focus. Therefore, although not all groups can be included in our discussion, the authors expect that by the end of this chapter you will understand three key points: (1) it is important to understand your own cultural perceptions and potential biases; (2) cultural, racial, or ethnic dimensions are critical elements of successful professional helping; and (3), not ALL people who constitute certain similar groups are the same.

MEASUREMENT OF DIVERSE PEOPLE—THE U.S. CENSUS

Since 1790, the United States census has been taken every ten years. This count gives the government direction in a variety of matters, such as the number of U.S. Representatives assigned to a state or the amount of funding a state receives from the federal government for certain programs. Census data are used by public and private agencies to chart population trends and shifting mobility patterns. These planners then interpret data and project need and response to changing demographic patterns. For example, at the turn of the twentieth century, census data revealed significant migration streams of people from rural communities to the nation's urban areas, and within a few short years the majority of the nation's population lived in urban areas. In 2006 the census reported an increase of no-employee businesses or small businesses that do not hire employees. This included family-run businesses or husband and wife teams and definitely showed the changing demographic (see the activity below).

Activity… Try this. Go to http://www.census.gov/popclock, look up the U.S. and World Population Clocks, and see how fast the numbers change.

According to the 2000 census, the United States population was 281,421,906. For the 2007 census, the population had increased to 305,931,227, and as of 2010 it was 308.7 million, an increase of 9.7 percent (retrieved from http://www.census .gov/prod/cen2010/briefs/c2010br-01.pdf). The most recent number from the U.S. and World Population Clock on October 5, 2014 (U.S. Census Bureau, 2014), is 318,024,945 individuals. This website is updated regularly and by the time you read this number, it will already be out of date!

After trying the activity above, you may find that the published numbers may vary because the actual survey was conducted several years ago and may no longer be accurate. The population continues to grow and therefore the growth-related changes that occurred after the numbers were published are not reflected. In addition, regardless of when the information is collected, it remains difficult to count every person in the United States.

Questions to consider are: How would you count the homeless population, in particular those who do not live in shelters but stay on the street? How do you count the migrant worker population (see Figures 1a and 1b)? And how do we locate every house, home, or shelter in the United States? Although numerous controls are in place to help with this, the basic problem in recording the total picture can affect

Figures 1a, b: Scenes in a migrant farm worker camp in Michigan. Workers come to Michigan in June to pick strawberries and leave in late fall after the apple harvest. The workers travel in vans and trucks as they move from one region of the country to another, following the harvest cycles.

many aspects of the numbers being reported. For example, as of 2007, people living in poverty totaled 29,869,900, with 7,399,600 of these individuals under the age of eighteen and 3,679,000 of age sixty-five or older (U.S. Census Bureau, 2008). In 2011, however, the U.S. poverty rate was not statistically different from that in 2010, while the real median income of households during this same time period declined (DeNavas-Walt, Proctor, & Smith, 2012). Although you may find these numbers helpful, caution should always be used. Dated census information and undercounting of the poor and underserved in the population are just two reasons why the numbers generated by the census data are not an absolute measure.

DIVERSITY BY RACE AND ETHNICITY IN THE UNITED STATES

The United States is a patchwork quilt of people—including males, females, old, young, people of multiple or single races, an array of ethnic groups, and rural and urban dwellers. These are just a few ways to identify diversity. However, the most common denominator of diversity seems to be race and/or ethnicity. This understanding is further complicated by couples and families with multiple heritages or multiple races (Kelley & Kelley, 2012).

The U.S. Census contributes to a better understanding of diversity by breaking down race into separate categories. As updated in July of 2014, of the reported population of 316,128,839 people, 13.2 percent were identified as Black or African American alone and 77.7 percent were identified as White alone, not Hispanic. Additionally, 2 percent were identified as Native Hawaiian and other Pacific Islander alone and 1.2 percent as American Indian or Alaska Native (U.S. Census Bureau, 2014b). Tables such as this help to break down categories by race; however, it is essential to remember that numbers like this can be limiting because race is often determined by self-identification, which may be sociopolitical rather than anthropological (Mulroy, 2004; Wallerstein, 2002).

In 1997, the federal government's Office of Management and Budget identified five racial categories that remained the key organizing groups to identify diversity for the ten-year census categories starting with the 2000 census: American Indian and Alaska Native, Asian, Black or African American, Native Hawaiian and other Pacific Islander, and White. The term Hispanic was denoted as ethnicity. This category on the 2000 survey was different from those on previous surveys because individuals were given the choice of using one or more racial categories to identify their racial identity. This major change in categorization that occurred in 2000 has strongly affected our ability to compare the 2000 and later surveys with those that came from the 1990s and before. In addition, for those who could not fit into any of the above categories, an additional category, "some other race," was added; in this category, a respondent can simply check the box and write in a more specific racial group. This type of reporting continues in the 2010 survey as well, in which racial and ethnic data showed that the Hispanic and Asian populations had increased significantly during the past ten years, which is attributed to the high number of immigrations. Nevertheless, the non-Hispanic White population remained the largest race and ethnic group in the United States (U.S. Census Bureau, 2011b).

Within each of these racial groupings are subgroups. For example, Asian includes Asian Indian, Chinese, Filipino, Japanese, Korean, Vietnamese, Cambodian, Hmong, Laotian, Thai, and other Asian. Each of these subgroups has additional identifiers: Hmong, for example, includes people who categorize themselves as Hmong, Laohmong, or Mong. For Hispanic individuals, a self-identification question was used. These individuals were asked if they were persons of Spanish/Hispanic/Latino origin. Further classification of this group included Mexican, Puerto Rican, and Cuban, as well as others who indicated that they were from Spain or the Spanish-speaking countries of Central or South America, or that they were other Hispanic or from other Spanish or Latino origins (U.S. Census Bureau, 2011c). As you can see in Table 1, in 2009 the majority of the population clearly

Table 1. United States Selected Languages Spoken at Home, 2009

Total population 5 years old and over	285,797,349
Speak only English	228,699,523
Spanish or Spanish Creole	35,469,501
French (incl. Patois, Cajun)	1,305,503
French Creole	659,053
Portuguese or Portuguese Creole	731,282
Serbo-Croatian	269,333
Chinese	2,600,150
Japanese	45,471
Korean	1,039,021
Mon-Khmer, Cambodian	202,033
Hmong	193,179
Thai	152,679
Laotian	146,297
Vietnamese	1,251,468
Other Asian languages	783,140
Tagalog	1,513,734
Navajo	169,009
Other Native North American languages	196,372
African languages	777,553
Other and unspecified languages	134,670

Source: U.S. Census Bureau, *The Statistical Abstract of the United States* (2012), American Community Survey, Table 53: Languages Spoken at Home. Retrieved from http://www.census.gov/compendia/statab/cats/population/ancestry_language_spoken_at_home.html

spoke only English at home; the second largest number spoke Spanish or Spanish Creole. The American Community Survey, on which this table is based, included the household population and the population living in institutions, college dormitories, and other group quarters.

When diversity is applied in generalist practice, it is crucial to remember that diversity is not limited to racial identity, but also includes a variety of other attributes. Differences may be obvious, such as those in the spoken language, or more subtle, as in cultural expectations and mores. Unless the social worker is aware of potential differences, misunderstandings can easily impair communication. Knowledge and recognition of ethnic differences and variation can help the social worker better understand the client and improve practice strategy.

THE GENERALIST SOCIAL WORKER AND DIVERSITY

Generalist social workers are employed in a variety of agencies, both public and private, and must develop helping relationships with all kinds of clients. Generalist work therefore, as articulated in the CSWE Curriculum Policy Statement, requires a broad range of knowledge and skills, allowing problems and their solutions to be assessed comprehensively (Barker, 2003). Furthermore, the definition that we as a profession use to represent diversity goes beyond that outlined in the U.S. Census. In social work, we are very concerned about enunciating a commitment to improving practices and policies, whether intentional or unintentional, related to racism, immigrants, and refugees as well as lesbians, gays, bisexuals, and transgendered people. Moreover, generalist social workers often extend beyond what would be considered clinical services, bridging the person-in-situation/person-in-environment stance and allowing for the coordination and expansion on the work of other professionals. In such cases the generalist is an invaluable member of the helping team, not only bridging the person and the environment, but also facilitating communication and fostering continuity of care (Dziegielewski, 2013).

Did You Know…In 1998 the field of social work in the United States celebrated a century of professional social work education and recognized more than 100 years of contributions to the well-being of individuals, groups, families, communities, and the natural environment. This was such an important event that volume 43, number 6, of the NASW journal Social Work *was dedicated to accomplishments in social work practice.*

Taking an Empowering Approach to Practice

In today's social work practice environment, the idea of empowerment and using client-oriented resources and support systems should not be underestimated (Turner, 2011). It is the uniqueness of the individual, group, or community that we must emphasize in each step of the helping process, whatever the method of practice selected. Further, intervention efforts need to be tied to self-empowerment whereby the changes made are fostered for continuance within the system. To put it simply, when the formal intervention ends, the effects and changes always need to be self-sustaining. These changes need to be fostered in such a way that they continue long after the social worker is gone. Almost all clients respond favorably when they are acknowledged for their strengths and challenged to achieve their full potential. Also, when they feel there is a plan that will allow the changes to continue, they can feel secure in what can and will continue to be accomplished.

Empowerment, as a central theme of social work practice, reflects the profession's emphasis on strengths and suggests that the client has the ability to make decisions and pursue change. So often in looking at a problem we focus on the pathology rather than on the strengths that the client brings to the situation. For example, when addressing the needs of a disabled client, we may focus on accommodations needed to participate fully at the workplace. This narrow view, however, can ignore valuable information. The client experiencing trouble functioning may have been unsuccessful in some ways, but what about the ways in which he or she has been successful? Individuals with disabilities often overcome barriers that those without disabilities may not notice. Social workers must always assess the strengths a client has and how the client has overcome obstacles in his/her life. The emphasis is placed on the client's strengths, resiliency, and coping style, with a clear focus on the client's ability to succeed. What makes more sense if you want to motivate and support someone—focusing on strengths and successes or on problems and failures?

Empowerment also requires providing access to the resources and information necessary for success (Fitzsimons, 2009). We cannot expect clients to succeed if they do not have the resources or know how to get them. When resources are provided without the knowledge of how to make changes self-sustaining, the results will be limited.

Trust, respect, and treating the client with civility are all part and parcel of empowerment. Without these core ingredients, we cannot foster the client's sense of self-worth and ability to look realistically at resolving a problem. People often say that "social workers empower their clients"—and wouldn't it be nice if we had a bag of magic dust that we sprinkle on clients? However, empowerment comes from within. Therefore, social workers help clients to find and sharpen the skills and tools they already possess and add support, encouragement, and in some cases direct intervention to help them get the additional resources they need to be successful. Social workers facilitate the empowerment process, but it is the individual client who makes it happen. In addition, the cornerstone of all intervention efforts rests in the social worker's ability to understand his or her own values without imposing those values and beliefs on others (Sue & Sue, 2013). Therefore, cultural confidence rests on self-awareness. From this perspective the social worker recognizes the importance of not encouraging the client to change his or her views to reflect those of the social worker and thus achieves client-centered empowerment.

Did You Know...The Hollis-Taylor report, a study conducted in 1951, showed that the social work profession was becoming increasingly specialized and fragmented in the delivery of services. Many social workers were treating client problems on a case-by-case basis. The report emphasized a more generic orientation to social work practice, with greater concern for social issues and social action. Many objectives set in this report were accepted by the profession and now form the basis of what is taught in many schools of social work today (Barker, 2003).

The Systems Perspective

Social work's mission is to engage in a helping activity that enhances opportunities for all people in an increasingly complex environment. From a systems perspective, the essential realization is that human systems are different from other types of systems (Forder, 2008). Social work professionals deal with a variety of human systems—individuals, couples, families, groups, organizations, and communities. In its simplest form a *system* consists of parts that interact so that a change in one part affects all others and the relations among them.

In future social work classes and texts, you'll come across the term *client system*. The addition of the word *system* indicates that an individual, her family, her group, and her community are all interrelated; all are part of the individual's galaxy of relations, each influencing the others. In considering the client system we focus on the individual within his/her relations with and to other parts of his/her system and seek to understand the extent to which these influence the client (see the activity below).

Activity...Visit the U.S. Census Bureau web page (http://www.census.gov) and download a copy of the short and long forms for the census. Which do you think provides information that gives a better picture of the United States? Why?

Although a client may initially seek individual help, the social worker may determine that expanding and including a spouse or a significant other may increase the chances of positive change (see the case of Don in box 1).

Box 1. The Case of Don: The Systems Perspective

Don, a fifty-four-year-old Hispanic male, was not following his diabetic diet and was referred to a social worker for discharge planning. Don's medical condition was worsening and his physician had become very frustrated with Don's noncompliance with his assigned treatment. According to the physician, Don was well aware that he was causing himself harm and might lose his eyesight if he did not change his behavior. In the interview with the social worker, Don appeared resistant and stated he was trying but found it hard to stick to his diet. He was too busy and tired when he got home from work to worry about the food he ate. He said his wife worked hard to cook what he liked, and he did not want to disappoint her.

During the interview the social worker explored Don's situation by asking questions about his lifestyle, his job, and whether he lived alone. Don stated that he had been married for thirty years and had no children. Don's wife was a homemaker who prepared most of the meals, which included packing his lunch that he took to work each day. In an attempt to find out more about Don's support system, the social worker asked Don if his wife had participated in the dietetic counseling he was provided. Don seemed surprised and said, "no, she did not." When asked why his wife had not participated in any of the educational sessions about his condition, Don replied that she had not been invited. Also, since she was such an excellent cook he was not sure this type of class would interest her anyway.

With Don's permission, the social worker called his wife to talk about meeting with both of them. The social worker set up a meeting with both of them to discuss Don's diabetic condition with the dietitian and his physician. At Don's request the social worker joined them in these meetings, helping Don and his wife to explore what they needed to do to safeguard his health. In discussions it became apparent to the social worker that Don's wife felt that she might have caused his condition because her mother-in-law told her that her cooking was what caused his health to get worse. Information about the probable causes of the condition was explained and the social worker provided Don's wife with written materials about the condition to take to her mother-in-law. A meeting with the dietician was also arranged and copies of meal plans were provided for sharing with relatives if needed to assure them that they were working together on his health issues. The counseling the social worker provided helped the couple feel more secure with immediate needs as well as how to address the concerns of other family members. After this intervention and at a six-week follow-up, Don continued to follow his diet regime. He even joked that his wife was enjoying the cooking classes that she had attended and now he never knew what he was going to eat for lunch or supper. He also stated that he wished he could get his mother to attend as well.

Consider the case described in box 1 in which the social worker was given a referral to see one client, Don, but after meeting and talking with him, realized the importance of including Don's wife and his dietitian. A basic assessment, intervention plan, and referral process initiated by the social worker with Don's permission and participation helped to harness the strengths of the client system, thereby helping Don to promote his own physical health.

In addition to addressing Don's particular needs, the social worker believed that advocacy might be needed in order to help other clients like Don. The social worker talked with other professionals in the hospital to inquire about similar prior occurrences. It soon became apparent that Don's situation wasn't unusual. The discussions initiated by the social worker led to the issue being brought before the hospital's quality care management team and the development of a new protocol that required interviewing and assessing all diabetic clients regarding their living situations. This advocacy did not benefit Don directly, but it benefited others who could be prevented from landing in a similar situation.

For the generalist social worker using a systems perspective, the helping activity assumes four roles: education, advocacy, facilitation, and intervention. Through this perspective the social worker serves as enabler, broker, mediator, advocate, resource person, gatekeeper, educator, and trainer (Chan & Law, 2008). While performing these functions that often overlap the helping activities, social workers often go beyond working with the originally identified client.

In client advocacy, the first step in the helping process involves education related to factors in the client's situation. Problem-focused education is intended to increase awareness of the services needed and to empower clients to address problems that previously seemed insurmountable. The social worker's practice activities often involve helping clients to secure the information they need and fostering connections that link clients to services and resource systems that contribute to resolving their problems.

Social workers can educate clients in many different areas. In Don's case the social worker provided education in the meeting with Don and his wife while focusing on the wife's concerns about the family blaming her for making him ill. The couple needed to be educated in an atmosphere where they were comfortable asking questions about the causes of diabetes. The social worker can work with the couple to facilitate communication by exploring questions or having them write down the questions to ask the physician at the next visit. The social worker also saw the wife's frustration with the family and suggested that she take home written information to show them that she was taking care of her husband as expected and, as she put it, "following orders." Facilitating the meeting with the dietitian was important to discuss the medical need for Don to continue on the proposed diet and the consequences if he did not. Getting copies of the meal plans helped to formalize what the wife was trying to do in terms of cooking differently. The worker facilitated the dialogue between the dietitian and the family and helped to support both in asking questions and clarifying discussion. After the meeting,

Don's wife understood what was needed from her, and Don's diet compliance improved dramatically. This case demonstrates how a social worker can assist by educating the entire client system—the client, his family, and other members of the delivery team.

Education is important in all practice settings. Child abuse, domestic violence and incest dynamics, parent-child relations, caregiving, homemaker services, and health care, just to name a few, are areas in which education commonly takes place. Social workers understand the importance of going beyond the traditional bounds of just providing supportive counseling. They can assist in educating clients to better maintain not only their own safety, security, and wellness, but also those of their families. Indeed, social workers are uniquely placed to participate in education, particularly in the areas of prevention and continued health and wellness.

> *Activity...Look at yourself as a system. Identify the components of your galaxy— family, friends, associations, workplace, and other aspects of your life. Imagine arranging these items with "me" in the middle and drawing a circle around each one to indicate the portion of your environment that it makes up. Do any of the circles overlap? For example, do you work with any members of your family? Is one circle more influential than the others? Why? Do any of the circles influence the others?*

Advocacy also helps clients to identify their own strengths and use individual and community resources to support their efforts to change. Advocacy does not always mean doing something for the client; it often means helping or teaching the client how to do things for herself or himself. Issues of individual worth and dignity must always be considered. Therefore, every social worker must know how to maintain cultural integrity while fostering change, allowing diversity to flourish.

Facilitation consists of making connections among different resource systems that enhance responsiveness and usefulness. The social worker may contact agencies to support and mobilize the client and others in the client system. It is here that direct intervention is found, whereby the social worker actually makes the connections needed to help the client (e.g., arranging transportation services to a medical appointment or registration with programs such as Meals on Wheels). Direct intervention occurs when the client is unable to intervene on his/her own behalf or simply needs assistance to do so successfully.

PERSON-IN-SITUATION: GUIDING THE PRACTICE FRAMEWORK

Generalist practice is more than simply combining methods of practice such as casework, group work, and community organizing. It requires a theoretical practice framework involving structured ideas and beliefs that provide a foundation for helping. Within this framework, the applied knowledge and theory are consistent with social work values and ethics from a person-in-situation context. This person-in-situation or person-in-environment context differentiates social work from other helping professions. Additionally, most professional social workers feel strongly that practice should be guided by theory. Therefore, engaging in a theory absent from practice is deficient, helping efforts are decreased, and the client system is deprived of needed professional helping activities.

Did You Know...Lee Frankel (1867–1931) was an early social work educator and developer of family casework theories and practice. He established the Training School for Jewish Social Work in New York and became a national leader in early health and welfare organizations (Barker, 2003).

The systems perspective is part of the conceptual framework used to understand and assess human relations in context in social work. It reflects the person-in-situation or person-in-environment stance that has always reinforced social work practice, focusing attention on an individual, a collective, a policy, a program, a practice, or any concrete or abstract unit in dynamic interaction with an environment.

A practice framework always addresses issues of human diversity. As we have stated throughout this book, social workers always recognize and respect human diversity when forming and maintaining professional relations. Furthermore, social workers are committed to promoting social justice and professional ethical conduct. Social work has historically been concerned with oppressed and disadvantaged populations. The profession's focus on human diversity and social justice reinforces its ethically driven commitment to serving people who do not receive an equitable share of social resources. The commitment and adherence to a professional code of conduct is essential for any type of professional practice, be it generalist or specialist.

For beginning social work professionals, deciding where and how best to engage the client can be difficult because this choice must be linked to the theoretical principles that underlie certain types of helping activity. To accomplish this goal, the social worker reviews the client's situation and based on the client's needs decides what theoretical perspective to use. In other words, it is the client's, not the worker's, comfort with or allegiance to a particular practice theory that drives the choice of perspective. The theoretical practice approach and helping strategy are firmly based in the reality of the client's environment.

At times making this link may seem too difficult or time consuming, but acknowledging the relation between environment and the selected practice method is critical. For example, one of the authors worked with an elderly male client with a history of alcohol abuse who received treatment only to be discharged back into an environment that encouraged him to relapse. The return to his previous environment negated much of the influence of the intervention and started a pattern of repeated rehabilitation attempts with numerous admissions to treatment centers. He always seemed to respond well while in the program, but on discharge he quickly relapsed into alcohol abuse. After numerous failed interventions, he was referred to a social worker. The social worker assessed his situation thoroughly and examined the type of home environment to which he was returning. The social worker discovered that because of his instability and troubles with alcohol, the client was unable to maintain a bank account. Therefore, when it was time to cash his social security check, he used the local bar as his bank. His check arrived each month, he picked it up, and he went to the one place he knew was willing to cash it—that local bar. To complicate matters, the bar would cash checks only upon purchase. It's clear what the consequences were. Assessing the client's discharge environment was critical to applying a helping strategy. To assist the client, the social worker initiated a supervised living arrangement and helped the client to acquire his own bank account where his social security check was directly deposited.

The helping strategy must be congruent with the needs and desires of the client system being served as well as reflective of the values and ethics of the social work profession. Beginning social workers often feel trapped within a system driven by social, political, cultural, and economic factors so powerful that they influence the practice techniques and skills that are utilized. In addressing the needs of the poor, the disadvantaged, and those who are different from the majority culture, recognizing the diversity of problems and how they relate to the people who experience them makes social work practice an art. How can social workers constantly evaluate what is happening to the client and whether societal factors—race, sexual orientation, and so forth—affect the way a problem is viewed? How can the beginning professional take into account all system variables that affect the helping relationship? How does a social worker maintain the dignity and worth of each client served and ensure that her own feelings and prejudices never enter the helping relationship?

The social work profession celebrates all forms of diversity and recognizes that differences among people provide valuable opportunities and tools in the helping relationship. At the same time, there is another side to diversity that we must address—fear of others and their differences. Sociology refers to this as *xenophobia*, a fear or hatred of foreigners or strangers. Hate crimes are a direct by-product of xenophobia and are directed at people who are *different*—differences are based on characteristics such as race, gender, sexual orientation, religious affiliation, or political views. Simply stated, there is no logic to a hate crime other than fear. Social workers recognize that clients are often victims, or at risk of being victims, of hate crimes. If a client has values or beliefs that could lead to hate crimes and actions, the social worker must be able to identify them and help the client address them before a potential hate crime erupts (see box 2). Extreme difficulty accepting and

---

Box 2. Hate Crimes

Examples of hate crimes in the United States are listed below. Using intimidation through emotional, physical, or psychological means, hate crimes are a mechanism to oppress individuals and groups.

JOHNSTON COUNTY, NC

After getting a tip about a plot to blow up the local sheriff's office, the county jail and the sheriff himself, federal and local law enforcement officers arrested Xxxx, fiery leader of the Nation's Knights of the Ku Klux Klan, on July 19. After the arrest, a search of Xxxx's home uncovered an Uzi and an AK-47, two homemade bombs and bomb-making materials. In January, Xxxx pleaded guilty to weapons charges. While he awaited sentencing, his wife and three other local Klan members were charged with the murder of an unidentified man. The victim was allegedly killed because he knew about threats against law enforcement officers supposedly made by xxx, grand dragon (or state leader) of a Klan faction based in nearby Robeson County.

SEMINOLE, FL

When police answered a domestic dispute call on Aug. 22, they ended up searching the townhome of podiatrist Xxxx, uncovering plans and ammunition for a series of attacks on Islamic targets in Florida. Xxxx, who was reportedly seeking to retaliate for the Sept. 11 attacks and the Palestinian intifada, faces up to 30 years in prison. His wife, xxxi, charged in October with being his accomplice, agreed to cooperate with prosecutors in a plea bargain.

PHOENIX, AZ

When an Oct. 16 brawl spilled out of the River City Pockets pool hall, police say three white supremacists viciously attacked 20-year-old Xxxx., who was standing nearby waiting for a taxi after applying for a job at the club. The three allegedly chased, tackled and stomped Bailey to death while yelling "white power."

REDDING, CA

Xxxx, a devotee of the anti-Semitic Christian Identity religion who teamed with his little brother to firebomb three California synagogues and an abortion clinic, killed himself in Shasta County Jail on Nov. 17. His trial for murdering a gay couple—a crime he said was "God's will" in a confession to newspaper reporters—had been scheduled to start this January.

Source: Southern Plenty Law Center, *Hate and extremism*. http://www.splcenter.org/ intelligenceproject/ip-index.html

Additional references and information are available at http://www.splcenter.org/ get-informed/hate-incidents?year=&state=All

adjusting to differences can lead to hate crimes, and this unfounded fear and hostility are directed at the victim as a member of a group, based on color, creed, gender, or sexual orientation. This makes self-awareness and self-knowledge central to the helping process (Morgaine & Capous-Desyllas, 2015). Understanding our own values and beliefs is the starting point for recognizing the importance of honoring differences in others.

There are no easy answers as to how best to address the client in his/her environment. Addressing each of the questions posed in this section of the chapter and giving it the attention it deserves would require several books. Yet it is critical that each client system be treated individually, no matter how similar a case may be to one the social worker has already encountered.

Did You Know...The Southern Poverty Law Center (http://www.splcenter.org/) is a nationally recognized organization that tracks and combats hate crimes in the United States. According to the Center, in 2012 the United States had 1,007 active hate groups and 1,360 patriot groups, that is, organizations that define themselves as opposed to the "New World Order" or advocate or adhere to extreme antigovernment doctrines. More information is available at http://www.splcenter.org/get-informed/hate-map, http://www.spl center.org/get-informed/intelligence-report/browse-all-issues/2013/spring/active-patriot-groups-in-the-united-s, and http://www.splcenter.org/intelligenceproject/ip-index.html

---

SELECTING A PRACTICE METHOD

A multitude of factors must be considered in selecting the most appropriate practice method. Who makes up the client system? What is the target of change? What resources are available to the client system? What is the probability of success given the many elements that can affect the situation? This already sounds complicated, and in fact, it is only a small part of what needs to be considered when choosing a practice method. You'll learn more about these factors and others in future social work practice classes.

Although it is beyond the scope of this book to explain the many theoretical and practice frameworks available to social workers and how to use them, we will explain the most common practice methods: micropractice, mezzopractice, and macropractice.

Micropractice, more commonly called direct or clinical practice, with target populations including individuals, families, and groups, primarily uses face-to-face interaction with clients. Because people deliver services, not programs, emphasis is placed on the highly trained case manager or clinical social worker. It is at the micro level where the emphasis remains on ensuring ongoing supervision, training, and continuing education designed to improve individual skills and strategy (Walsh & Holton, 2008). From this perspective it is often assumed that the greatest interest lies in the for-profit sector and private practice (Segal-Engelchin & Kaufman, 2008).

Mezzopractice involves environmental system variables and agency administration with minimal client contact; it examines agency effectiveness and policy implementation. It can also evaluate the quality of programming, systematic organizational barriers, and organizational management functions, including trends with respect to market stabilization of human capital stressing employee maintenance and well-being (Cabrera & Raju, 2001; Everhart & Wandersman, 2000). When agencies offer adequate material supports such as compensation packages, agreeable working conditions, and adequate agency material supports, workers are more likely to stay and support the programs offered (Walsh & Holton, 2008).

Macropractice defines the client more extensively to include the community or organizations; it often deals with broader social problems that affect the community (Hepworth, Rooney, Rooney, Strom-Gottfried, & Larsen, 2010). Here the greatest emphasis is often on working in social change agencies and the application of skills designed to change social programs and policies for the betterment of all involved (Segal-Engelchin & Kaufman, 2008).

In the broadest of terms, micropractice is undertaken with individuals, families, and groups; mezzopractice is directed at organizational administration; and macropractice involves change within larger systems, such as communities and organizations. You might be thinking that we're playing semantic games, that micro, mezzo, and macro are just new names for casework, group work, and community practice. This is not really true because all three perspectives—micro, mezzo, and macro—apply a systems perspective to analyzing the presenting problem. For example, there are not multiple foci in micropractice; the individual's system is the focus—note the use of singular versus plural. Micropractice involves an individual client with a presenting problem, and our work includes assessment of the system's role in creating, sustaining, or solving the problem—in fact, the system may play all three roles.

As we have discussed in a number of places in this book, social work has two significant professional goals. The first is to help people to achieve their potential and to adjust more effectively to the demands of their environment. The second is to make social resources more responsive to people's needs, particularly for poor and disadvantaged people who often are avoided or neglected. Incorporating these goals into the helping process reinforces social work's dual focus on personal and social problems and emphasizes the importance of linking micro, mezzo, and macro change efforts.

Micropractice

In micropractice the focus is on the individual and his/her system. When individuals are helped directly on the micro level, strengths are highlighted. From the strengths-based approach the individual is the hero and change agent (Jones-Smith, 2014; see box 3, for the example of Maria).

Maria is a client who survived a horrible ordeal after being raped. After the event Maria was so traumatized that she feared leaving her apartment. A social worker serving as a victim's advocate proved instrumental in helping Maria to overcome many of her initial fears. The social worker provided a supportive role with a constant reassuring presence for Maria during the difficult times following the rape. The advocate explored issues from Maria's childhood and identified unresolved feelings that resurfaced following the rape. Rather than trying to provide in-depth clinical help to Maria, the advocate referred her to a more advanced MSW social worker who had expertise in violence against women. The skilled worker was able to help Maria by using a variety of strategies including both education and

---

Box 3. The Case of Maria: Micropractice

Maria, at age twenty-two, was a victim of rape at her workplace. At the outset of the criminal investigation, she met a victim's advocate, who was a BSW social worker employed by the police department. The advocate brought Maria to the hospital and became a major support person for her in the following days. During one of their conversations, the advocate learned that Maria had been a victim of sexual abuse during her childhood. The rape, compounded with her childhood experiences, now had put Maria in a very vulnerable emotional and psychological state: she was unable to go to work or meet family or friends, saying that she would rather just stay at home. Maria blamed herself for the rape, stating, "I deserved it. Look at my whole life. I deserve it all." The social worker quickly recognized that Maria needed more in-depth help. She referred Maria to a family service agency, where Maria first took part in individual sessions with an MSW social worker.

After a month, the social worker asked Maria how she felt about joining a group of women who had been raped. At first Maria refused, but with gentle, persistent encouragement from the social worker, she reluctantly joined the weekly group. Maria's group included seven other women aged eighteen to fifty-two. All of the participants reached out to Maria and welcomed her. The social worker, who facilitated the group, told Maria that she did not need to talk unless she wanted to. Discussion at Maria's first group meeting focused on the court hearing. Women shared their fears about the hearings, and some who had been through the courts shared their experiences. Subsequent sessions looked at anger control, relationship building, and becoming a survivor. Maria became an active member of the group and after one year joined the police department as a volunteer victim's advocate.

supportive therapeutic techniques. Group sessions helped to validate Maria's experiences and allowed her to share with other group members.

In micropractice, as in all social work methods, social worker and client work together to establish goals and objectives and to develop the steps that must be taken to reach these goals. A typical micro approach has social workers dealing with clients, family members and significant others, and at times other groups of people. In this micro approach, the first step is always deciding what the client wants and taking the action needed to help make it happen (Lanci & Spreng, 2008). Thyer (2008) warns, however, that all information gathered in addressing the needs of the client should be based on empirical data that clearly outline what has been done and the treatment gains that have been made. Maria, for example, was first seen as an individual and later referred to the group setting to continue the intervention process. Had Maria's family lived in the same geographic area, they too might have become directly involved in the healing process.

Mezzopractice

Mezzopractice involves minimal face-to-face client contact, focusing rather on administrative intervention within the agency organization. Typical administrative titles include supervisor, unit director, director, executive director, chief executive officer, and president. When the social service agency has a more positive work and service environment, staff turnover will be less and the delivery of higher quality services can result (Glisson, 2008).

It is important to recognize that micro workers do engage in mezzo activities, however. In fact, any competent social worker will be knowledgeable and possess basic abilities in mezzo level tasks. Organizing the workload, preparing monthly reports, conducting policy analysis, supervising staff, and making public presentations to service groups are all mezzo tasks that micro workers will find themselves undertaking.

Individuals in mezzo roles develop expertise in a number of areas, but particularly the following (Hepworth, Rooney, & Larsen, 2002):

- ◆ Policy formulation and implementation
- ◆ Program development
- ◆ Funding, budgeting, and resource allocation
- ◆ Management of internal structures
- ◆ Staff and professional supervision
- ◆ Organizational and professional representation with internal and external groups
- ◆ Community presentations
- ◆ Ongoing evaluation of agency effectiveness

Generally, you will find MSW workers assigned to mezzo positions in agencies, whereas BSW workers are limited to direct service lines. This may not be the case in rural and small communities, however, where fewer MSW professionals are available and the BSW worker is more likely to find an administrative assignment. Although their knowledge and skills may not be as broad and as deep of those of master's level practitioners, baccalaureate practitioners do possess beginning knowledge and skills in mezzo work.

Macropractice

Macropractice directs the worker's attention to change in the larger community, organizational, and policy arenas (Burghardt, 2014). Similar to community organization, macro work involves helping individuals, groups, and communities with common interests to deal with "social problems and to enhance well-being through planned collective action" (Barker, 2003, p. 84). Typically, micropractice or mezzopractice identifies problems, needs, concerns, or issues needing to be addressed that require intervention or change strategy at a much higher level (Jansson, 2004; Mulroy, 2004; Sakamoto & Pitner, 2005). Just as micro practitioners and mezzo practitioners have specialized knowledge and skills, so too does the macro worker.

Did You Know...Mother Jones was Mary Harris Jones (1830–1930), a community organizer and labor union advocate who led many strikes against inhumane treatment of children and adults. She advocated better child labor laws and less dangerous working conditions in the mining and steel industries (Barker, 2003).

The macro worker has expertise in the following areas:
- Communities, their composition and type—for example, geographic or professional
- Power structures within communities and their influence within communities
- Policy-making procedures
- Human service organizations, their purposes, functions, and constituencies
- Dynamics and nuances of social problems
- Macro-specific tasks such as collaboration and capacity building, negotiation, task group dynamics, marketing, research and analysis, and teaching

Macropractice builds on private issues that become public matters. Substance abuse, for example, involves individuals. Yet the abuse quickly becomes a public matter when it leads to increased crime related to the selling of drugs, lack of workforce participation or missed work due to drug abuse, poor school grades and eventual dropout, and family dysfunction. In the example described in box 4, the macro approach involved a not-so-subtle nonviolent confrontation with a local storeowner.

As outlined in box 4, the owner wasn't sure which would be worse: the wrath of the drug dealers or the lack of neighbors who would purchase items from his store. He decided the latter, and with help from the local police department, drug sales disappeared from the area. As an interesting note, when the group's organizer was told that the dealers were only going to another neighborhood, he responded, "Then that's their problem and they will have to organize them out of the community like we did."

Did You Know...Hull House is the most famous of all settlement houses, founded in Chicago in 1889 by Jane Addams. Settlement houses were community centers where poor and disadvantaged residents of the area could go for help. These centers were major innovators in social reform.

Box 4. The Case of a Drug-Free Community: Macropractice

A drug-related shooting took place in the middle of the day in a poor area of town. A few people gathered that evening in a local church and decided that they had had enough, but they didn't know what to do. One of the participants was a social worker from the local neighborhood center. She suggested that the group in fact knew what it wanted—a drug-free community—but now needed to figure out where to begin in order to make this happen. The group expanded and created a neighborhood drug-free task force to act as a conduit for the community. Neighbors were invited to share their frustrations at meetings held in churches, school halls, and the neighborhood center. Local social service agencies and elected and appointed officials were asked to come and listen to the neighbor's concerns.

Out of these meetings came a plan for a march through the neighborhood, with the police leading the parade and marching with citizens. The group decided to include a social action activity by marching to the primary spot where drugs were sold, a mom-and-pop convenience store one block from the public elementary school. Once at the store, the marchers, about two hundred people, formed a long single-file line, and each walked in without saying a word and left one dollar on the counter. The police stood in front of the store and within minutes the drug pushers had disappeared! Over the following weeks, the storeowner worked with the local task force and police; the drug pushers stopped selling in the neighborhood and moved out of the community. The storeowner joined the task force when it took on other substance abuse issues in the community.

In this application of macropractice the social worker helped the group to develop a plan of action and supported the group as it organized itself. The worker facilitated the process, helped to mobilize significant agencies and local leaders, and provided background research—essentially equipping the neighborhood group with the tools it needed to become successful. What began as an individual problem ended up as a community macro issue whose resolution brought about significant changes in the daily lives of individuals, families, and organizations in the neighborhood (see the activity below).

Activity...Go to the library and find the journal Social Work, *volume 43, number 6. Think about what the articles in this special issue tell you about the following questions:*

1. What types of contributions did social workers make in micropractice, mezzopractice, and macropractice?

2. How do social workers feel about the NASW Code of Ethics and what does it mean to each area of social work practice discussed in this chapter?

3. What issues in the history of social work do you believe helped to make the profession what it is today?

4. What issues in the field of social work need the attention of today's workers?

In Brief: Short-Term Intervention Approaches

Having looked at micropractice, mezzopractice, and macropractice, we would be remiss if we didn't touch on one major issue facing social workers who practice at the micro level. Whether we like it or not, current social work practice is now dominated by brief, or short-term, practice models. There are many different approaches that could fall into this category, but regardless of the methods that are used there are two requirements that seem to overlap. The first is that the helping process needs to occur quickly (short duration) and the second is to prove that it works. This means clearly identifying what the client wants to accomplish and working out a system to measure the accomplishments of the goals and objectives outlined. Practice reality dictates that the duration of most practice sessions, regardless of the methodology used or the orientation of the mental health practitioner, remain relatively brief. For many practitioners, seeing a client only once is becoming commonplace with the realization that most practice encounters are going to be brief and self-contained (Sommers-Flanagan & Sommers-Flanagan, 2009). There are many reasons for this trend, but the major influence is money: getting the "biggest bang for the buck." Our current environment is limited in terms of financial and human resources, and there is little chance that this will ever change (Ligon, 2009). Insurance companies, as third-party payers (those who pay a provider for services to another person, thus third party), and health care organizations limit the time during which a client system may receive a service. Simply stated, third-party payers will not underwrite long-term intervention if a short-term model will help, even if the end is less desirable than what a longer-term approach may yield. Social workers therefore employ time-limited approaches as a major practice model.

In other cases clients simply don't have the time, desire, or money for long-term micro-level social work services. People today are working more hours, sometimes two jobs, and have less time to devote to the self. With less time available, they are unwilling to commit extra time and energy to go beyond simply addressing the cause of the problem. Practitioners can become frustrated when the presenting problem and the underlying issues clearly require a long-term model but the client system, for any number of reasons, is willing or able to look only at the surface issue.

So often, new social workers aren't interested in social welfare policy. Students taking policy courses often complain, "Why do I need this course? It has nothing to do with social work!" The ongoing national debate about health insurance and resulting services outlines clearly why we need to understand policy and how to influence its scope and design. Our practice grows out of policy: Change policy and you can change practice. Change the ways that third-party payers reimburse for service and you can change your practice. These days insurance rarely covers long-term encounters, and short-term time-limited practice is the norm.

We must realize that social work practice encounters are going to be brief. Planning for this short duration in implementing a helping strategy is critical; lack of planning can result in numerous unexpected endings for the client and feelings of failure and decreased job satisfaction or even exit from the job market for the social work professional (Cabrera & Raju, 2001). Limited time and service provision can result in increased job complexity and fewer defined procedures for achievable successful outcomes.

WE WILL NEVER HAVE ALL THE ANSWERS!

A number of years ago a t-shirt frequently seen at social work gatherings had a Superman logo on the front and yellow and red lettering that spelled out "Super Social Worker." The apparent exaggeration was ironic because at times the efforts of social workers really did seem Herculean. No one can dispute, however, that social workers are human beings and therefore, unlike Superman, they are vulnerable and may not always have the ideal solution to a problem. Systems are limited and most helping strategies can only go so far. Social workers are only human!

Therefore, all social workers must be aware of the services available and try their best to mitigate any potential harm that may come to the clients served. Moreover, when a social worker does not have an answer to a problematic situation, it should be viewed as a *learning moment*. A natural reaction may be to act defensively and to try to blame the system or the lack of services; however, professionals take responsibility for what they do and for knowing the services that are available. When in supervision with a trained professional, the beginning social worker has the opportunity to explore previous helping strategies, as if watching them on videotape. It is important to evaluate what actually happened and what might have happened had some other strategy been implemented. Social workers use professional supervision as a forum for these detailed discussions so that the same or similar mistakes can be avoided in the future. The most powerful resource that a social worker has is the ability to seek supervisory help or peer consultation in order to better define a problem.

CULTURALLY SENSITIVE PRACTICE

Social workers must help clients to maintain cultural integrity and must respect diversity. The term *ethnic identity* is generally defined as common heritage, customs, and values unique to a group of people (Fong, 2009). Social science researchers often gather information on race and ethnicity, yet the difference between these two concepts is pronounced. Historically, race is partly based on physical characteristics of genetic origin (Helms, 1990). Ethnicity embraces a much broader range of commonalities, such as religion, customs, geography, and history. These commonalities between individuals and within a community define and bond members, thereby giving an ethnic backdrop to everyday life. Ethnicity can thus influence thinking and feeling and can pattern behavior in both obvious and subtle ways (Sakamoto & Pitner, 2005). It is easy to overlook the deeper influence of ethnicity because it often appears to be natural and to consist simply of daily behavior—for example, what individuals eat or how they react.

The development of ethnic identity occurs on a continuum determined by acceptance of one's ethnicity (Sakamoto & Pitner, 2005). A client may either embrace or reject his or her own ethnicity, as he or she can be influenced by a particular reference group that is influential in dictating behavior and decision-making practices. Personal identity is how an individual sees herself/himself, whereas ascribed identity is how society values or perceives her/him. Crucial to understanding the concept of ethnicity is realizing that, although it is a potent factor in the professional helping relationship, it is not easy to identify, and the degree to which it influences life decisions and behavior is not the same for every client.

To provide culturally sensitive practice, social workers must avoid applying a narrow cultural lens that can interpret client system traditions and problem-solving processes as abnormal or dysfunctional. In mental health, for example, social workers must thoroughly understand, appreciate, and assess cultural differences in order to enable providers to develop culturally compatible services. For example, the social worker who works with an Asian client needs to be aware of Asian customs and expectations. In Asian cultures, there may be resistance to outside intervention because family matters are viewed as private. In the mental health area in particular, there is shame and stigma attached to needing these types of services (Ofahengaue-Vakalahi & Fong, 2009). Social workers need to be aware of and to respect this cultural tradition and to know how it can affect the helping relationship. Culturally sensitive services must extend beyond the general task of making services more accessible and include specifically relevant therapeutic interpretations to guide the framework used.

One last issue in providing culturally sensitive practice from a systems perspective is that the beliefs and values of social workers and other helping professionals generally reflect those of the greater society. These workers may view client systems differently through their own cultural lens, consequently overlooking the need to help the client and his system to maintain cultural and ethnic heritage as well as feelings of integrity throughout the intervention process. It is therefore the role of the social worker to acknowledge and facilitate family adjustment and acculturation whether working with Asians, Latinos, African Americans, or any other diverse groups (Earner & Garcia, 2009; Logan, 2009; Ofahengaue-Vakalahi & Fong, 2009).

Professional helpers must be aware of the probable tendency to assess clients based on the helper's own values, beliefs, biases, and stereotypes (Sakamoto & Pitner, 2005; Sousa & Eusebio, 2005). Lack of awareness of ethnicity and culture may distort perceptions of clients and of their family dynamics. The potential danger here is that the client's right to self-determination may be violated (Reamer, 2009). Providing ethnically sensitive practice requires social workers to assess clients and client systems very clearly in regard to the effects that culture, environment, and family can have on behaviors and responses. Being aware of ethnicity and culture and accepting diversity are essential in culturally sensitive practice (Morgaine & Capous-Desyllas, 2015).

In closing, culturally sensitive practice requires that the social worker:

- ◆ Be aware of the family's identity, values, and norms and note problems related to acculturation or immigration.
- ◆ Identify and discuss the impact of psychological problems than can result from adaptation to a new situation or environment.
- ◆ Encourage the development of positive and supportive peer relations.
- ◆ Encourage relations outside of the client system that can help to reduce feelings of isolation and facilitate transition.
- ◆ Help the client to develop new coping skills with which to negotiate the new environment.

◆ Explore ways in which culturally sensitive measurements can be conducted and ways that these standardized measures can take into account multi-cultural differences.

Today, in our global society so much of what is considered learned is measured through testing for competence. Testing is used now from the earliest grades to later in life. For a complete list of articles and discussion related to measurement instruments and providing relevant and accurate psychoeducational assessments, see *Multicultural Psychoeducational Assessment*, edited by Grigorenko (2009). Because it is beyond the scope of this book to address the specifics of how these types of measurements are used, the reader is urged to refer to the chapters in Grigorenko's book. This book can help to break down this complex area and link multicultural assessment across multiple languages as well as multiple domains of functioning.

SUMMARY

To understand the practice of social work within a culturally sensitive framework you must appreciate the broad range of activities and areas that practice involves. Choosing from among the varied roles and tasks that social workers perform, as well as identifying what constitutes the client system, is not easy within the dynamic social work practice environment. Therefore, it is not uncommon for beginning professionals to struggle with basic practice principles and how best to help the client they serve. Our advice is simple: Do the best you can and do not be afraid to ask for help! Even the most experienced MSW practitioner can feel frustrated. Deciding what helping approach to use and when to apply it requires a delicate balancing act among the needs of the client, the demands of the environment, the skills and helping knowledge available to the social worker, and the sanction of the social welfare agency.

Social workers assist a variety of people, groups, and communities whose issues, concerns, and needs more often than not are unique to their particular status. The information gleaned from diversity and differences strengthens the social worker's ability to be an effective practitioner and helps develop a specialized intervention reflecting the client system's specific needs.

So where does the social worker begin with matters of diversity? The social worker should begin with the basic premise "start where the client is," never forgetting that each client can have individual concerns that may or may not be relevant to his or her primary reference group. From a social work perspective, diversity must first be recognized; second it must be understood; and third, this knowledge needs to be applied to provide culturally sensitive practice. Once we take hold of diversity from these three venues, always starting where the client is, we integrate this information into practice strategy. Recognizing the importance of diversity with the populations we serve, incorporating this knowledge and awareness into our practice skills, and supporting the provision of a diversity of services and programs stands at the forefront of all professional helping (Carlton-LaNey, 2008). Also, with the increasing number of multiple heritage couples, balancing how to best help these individuals in the micro and mezzo environments becomes essential. Furthermore, balancing individual needs with societal and political initiatives provides fertile ground for macro interventions.

In closing, realize that recognition, understanding, and acceptance of another person, in this case a client, will never require the social worker to abandon his or her personal values and beliefs. In the professional helping relationship, our personal beliefs are set aside as we embrace those of the client system. The new and experienced professional social worker both struggle with difference and diversity: Such reactions as "Why do they do that?" or "That lifestyle is not for me" or "Their views are very different from mine" are human and natural. As a professional, however, the client is always our primary concern, and this should never require that the client match the worker's individual value and belief system. At the same time, our personal values and beliefs may be in such conflict with those of a particular client that we are not able to help that client. At that time, the most important thing to do is to recognize this and transfer the case to a supervisor or another worker who can effectively work with the client—this is in the client's best interests and reflects the professional's ability to determine his or her own level of effectiveness.

When confronted with a new culture or experience, it is essential that the social workers take into account diversity and learn about the culture. Pieces of the human experience cannot be disregarded simply because the social worker is not familiar with them. Discovery comes through many venues—including talking with your supervisor and other colleagues who may be better versed with the culture. Always allow clients to help you learn and develop sensitivity to those matters with which you are unfamiliar. Remember, helping is a two-way street and reciprocity is commonplace in a just society.

The numbers from the Census Bureau provide important information regarding the breadth of diversity. These numbers, however, do not illustrate the latent issues such as racism, prejudice, and discrimination. Disproportionate levels of poverty, individual and family incomes, and high school and college graduation rates are just some of the indicators that demonstrate that diverse people may be treated differently from others.

Recognizing and understanding diversity can help the social worker understand how clients can develop anger, hostility, passivity, low self-esteem, poor self-worth, and a sense of hopelessness. The social work relationship should consider and take underlying factors into account, especially those that might not be considered obvious to the untrained eye.

Acknowledging the strength in client system diversity can assist in the helping process. For example, the strong family and, in particular the extended family, is a hallmark in the African American community. For cognitively mature Native American children, identifying closely with similar peer groups may help to improve self-esteem (Corenblum, 2014). Acknowledging peer group influences and utilizing this strength will allow the social worker working with an African American client to consider the possible role of the family or extended family in the helping process. Recognizing and understanding diversity is the essence of *contextual practice*—seeing each client as an individual who is set within a specific culture, and whose decisions and actions result from his or her life experiences.

Today's society suffers from a multitude of complicated problems that need to be addressed, and social workers, like other helping professionals, are being pressured to assess and address them as quickly and as effectively as possible. Varied social work roles and fluctuating environmental influences reinforce the ongoing need for educational preparation and training in practice. Even after receiving a degree, every social worker needs to enhance his or her knowledge and skill bases while developing new areas for more effective practice. We must all continue learning and growing in order to anticipate the needs of our clients.

Social workers believe that competent ethical practice is more than simply helping clients by using what is known. It also involves knowing the client, respecting cultural diversity and the uniqueness of the individual, assessing the environmental situations and resources available, and recognizing the strengths and limitations of the intervention strategy employed. The social worker must decide what method of change to use and at what level—micro, mezzo, or macro—the client will best be served.

Micro approaches to social work practice help clients, whether individuals, families, or groups, to feel better about themselves and to address previous relationship experiences affecting new or current relationships. Mezzopractice strengthens an agency's ability to respond more congruently with worker practice needs and client issues. And macropractice confronts larger issues affecting individuals, families, groups, or communities.

In this chapter and in chapter 5, we have tried to explain as briefly as possible the basics of social work practice. We have presented a few case scenarios that exemplify how different social workers have tried to help their clients. These cases offer a glimpse of the exciting, challenging, and often frustrating world of the practicing social work professional.

Social workers are needed in the practice arena to address the wide array of social problems. And yes, although social workers face numerous external pressures from funding groups, we cannot allow these to limit our practice strategies. Clients need and continue to want supportive services; as the number of people suffering from anxiety and depressive disorders, self-destructive behavior, and life-threatening illnesses continues to grow, so too does the need for social workers who engage in professional practice.

REFERENCES

Barker, R. L. (2003). *The social work dictionary* (5th ed.). Washington, DC: NASW Press.

Burghardt, S. (2014). *Macro practice in social work for the 21st century: Bridging the macro-micro divide* (2nd ed.). Thousand Oaks, CA: Sage.

Cabrera, E., & Raju, N. (2001). Utility analysis: Current trends and future directions. *International Journal of Selection and Assessment, 9*, 92–102.

Carlton-LaNey, I. B. (2008). Diversity. In K. M. Sowers & C. N. Dulmus (Series Eds.) & B. W. White (Vol. Ed.), *Comprehensive handbook of social work and social welfare: The profession of social work* (vol. 1, pp. 395–417). Hoboken, NJ: Wiley.

Chan, C. L. W., & Law, C. K. (2008). Advocacy. In K. M. Sowers & C. N. Dulmus (Series Eds.) & W. Rowe, & L. A. Rapp-Paglicci (Vol. Eds.), *Comprehensive handbook of social work and social welfare: Social work practice* (vol. 3, pp. 161–178). Hoboken, NJ: Wiley.

Corenblum, B. (2014). Relationships between racial-ethnic identity, self-esteem and in-group attitudes among First Nation children. *Journal of Youth Adolescence, 42*, 387–404.

DeNavas-Walt, C., Proctor, B. D., & Smith, J. C. (2012, September). *Income, poverty, and health insurance coverage in the United States: 2011* (U.S. Census Bureau, Current Population Reports, P60-243). Washington, D. C.: U.S. Government Printing Office. Retrieved from: http://www.census.gov/prod/2012pubs/p60-243.pdf

Diller, J. V. (2011). *Cultural diversity: A primer for human services* (4th ed.). Belmont, CA: Brooks/Cole.

Dziegielewski, S. F. (2008a). Brief and intermittent approaches to practice: The state of practice. *Journal of Brief Treatment and Crisis Intervention, 8*, 147–163.

Dziegielewski, S. F. (2008b). Problem identification, contracting, and case planning. In K. M. Sowers & C. N. Dulmus (Series Eds.) & W. Rowe, & L. A. Rapp-Paglicci (Vol. Eds.), *Comprehensive handbook of social work and social welfare: Social work practice* (vol. 3, pp. 78–97). Hoboken, NJ: Wiley.

Dziegielewski, S. F. (2013). *The changing face of health care social work: Opportunities and challenges for professional practice* (3rd ed.). New York: Springer.

Earner, I. A., & Garcia, G. (2009). Social work practice with Latinos. In A. Roberts (Ed.), *Social workers' desk reference* (2nd ed., pp. 959–962). New York: Oxford University Press.

Everhart, K., & Wandersman, A. (2000). Applying comprehensive quality programming and empowerment evaluation to reduce implementation barriers. *Journal of Educational and Psychological Consultation, 11*, 177–191.

Fitzsimons, N. M. (2009). *Combating violence & abuse of people with disabilities: A call to action.* Baltimore, MD: Brooks Publishing.

Fong, R. (2009). Overview of working with vulnerable populations and persons at risk. In A. R. Roberts (Ed.), *Social workers' desk reference* (2nd ed., pp. 925–927). New York: Oxford University Press.

Forder, A. (2008). Social work and system theory. *British Journal of Social Work, 6,* 23–42.

Franklin, C., Jordan, C., & Hopson, L. (2008). Intervention with families. In K. M. Sowers & C. N. Dulmus (Series Eds.) & W. Rowe & L. A. Rapp-Paglicci (Vol. Eds.), *Comprehensive handbook of social work and social welfare: Social work practice* (vol. 3, pp. 423–446). Hoboken, NJ: Wiley.

Glisson, C. (2008). Interventions with organizations. In K. M. Sowers, & C. N. Dulmus (Series Eds.) & W. Rowe & L. A. Rapp-Paglicci (Vol. Eds.), *Comprehensive handbook of social work and social welfare: Social work practice* (vol. 3, pp. 556–581). Hoboken, NJ: Wiley.

Gray, J. (1992). *Men are from Mars, women are from Venus.* New York: HarperCollins.

Grigorenko, E. L. (Ed.). (2009). *Multicultural psychoeducational assessment.* New York: Springer.

Helms, J. E. (Ed). (1990). *Black and white racial identity: Theory, research, and practice.* Westport, CT: Praeger.

Hepworth, D. H., Rooney, R. H., & Larsen, J. (2002). *Direct social work practice: Theory and skills.* Pacific Grove, CA: Brooks/Cole.

Hepworth, D. H., Rooney, R. H., Rooney, G. D., Strom-Gottfried, K., & Larsen, J. (2010). *Direct social work practice: Theory and skills* (8th ed.). Belmonte, CA: Brooks/Cole Cengage Learning.

Hiller, S. M., & Barrow, G. M. (2011). *Aging, the individual and society.* Belmont, CA: Wadsworth.

Jansson, B. S. (2004). *The reluctant welfare state: American social welfare policies past, present, and future* (5th ed.). Pacific Grove, CA: Brooks/Cole.

Jones-Smith, E. (2014). *Strengths-based therapy: Connecting theory, practice, and skills.* Thousand Oaks, CA: Sage.

Kelley, K. R., & Kelley, M.E. (2012). Contemporary US multiple heritage couples, individuals, and families: Issues, concerns and counseling implications. *Counseling Psychology Quarterly, 25,* 99–112.

Lanci, M., & Spreng, A. (2008). *The therapist's starter guide: Setting up and building your practice, working with clients and managing personal growth.* Hoboken, NJ: Wiley.

Ligon, J. (2009). Fundamentals of brief treatment. In A. Roberts (Ed.), *Social workers' desk reference* (2nd ed., pp. 215–220). New York: Oxford University Press.

Logan, M. L. (2009). Social work with African Americans. In A. Roberts (Ed.), *Social workers' desk reference* (2nd ed., pp. 962–969). New York: Oxford University Press.

Mackelprang, R. W., & Salsgiver, R. O. (2009). *Disability: A diversity model approach in human service practice* (2nd ed.). Chicago: Lyceum Books.

Morgaine, K., & Capous-Desyllas, M. (2015). *Anti-oppressive social work practice: Putting theory into action.* Los Angeles, CA: Sage.

Mulroy, E. (2004). Theoretical perspectives on the social environment to guide management and community practice: An organizational-in-environment approach. *Administration in Social Work, 28,* 77–96.

Nadir, A., & Dziegielewski, S. F. (2001). Called to Islam: Issues and challenges in providing ethnically sensitive social work practice with Muslim people. In M. Hook, B. Hugen, & M. Aguilar (Eds.), *Spirituality within religious traditions in social work practice* (pp. 144–166). Pacific Grove, CA: Brooks/Cole.

National Association of Social Workers. (2012). *Social work speaks* (9th ed.). Washington, DC: Author.

National Association of Social Workers. (2001). *NASW Standards for cultural competence in social work practice.* Washington, DC: Author.

National Association of Social Workers. (2008). *Code of ethics.* Washington, DC: Author.

Ofahengaue-Vakalahi, H. F., & Fong, R. (2009). Social work practice with Asian and Pacific Island Americans. In A. Roberts (Ed.), *Social workers' desk reference* (2nd ed., pp. 954–958). New York: Oxford University Press.

O'Hare, T. (2009). *Essential skills of social work practice: Assessment, intervention, and education.* Chicago: Lyceum Books.

Poulin, J. (2010). *Strengths-based generalist practice: A collaborative approach* (3rd ed.). Belmont, CA: Wadsworth, Cengage Learning.

Reamer, F. G. (2009). Ethical issues in social work. In A. Roberts (Ed.), *Social workers' desk reference* (2nd ed., pp. 115–120). New York: Oxford University Press.

Rehman, T. F., & Dziegielewski, S. F. (2003). Women who choose Islam: Issues, changes and challenges in providing ethnically diverse practice. *International Journal of Mental Health, 32*(3), 31–50.

Ryle, R. (2012). *Questioning gender: A sociological exploration.* Thousand Oaks, CA: Sage.

Sakamoto, I., & Pitner, R. (2005). Use of critical consciousness in anti-oppressive social work practice: Disentangling power dynamics at personal and structural levels. *British Journal of Social Work, 35*, 435–452.

Segal-Engelchin, D., & Kaufman, R. (2008). Micro and macro orientation: Israeli students' career choices in an antisocial era. *Journal of Social Work Education, 44*(3), 139–157.

Sommers-Flanagan, J., & Sommers-Flanagan, R. (2009). *Clinical interviewing* (4th ed.). Hoboken, NJ: Wiley.

Sousa, L., & Eusebio, C. (2005). When multi-problem poor individuals' values meet practitioners' values! *Journal of Community & Applied Social Psychology, 15*, 353–367.

Spade, J. Z., & Valentine, C. G. (2014). Introduction. In J. Z. Spade & C. G. Valentine (Eds.), *The kaleidoscope of gender: Prisms, patterns and possibilities* (4th ed., pp. xiii–xxiv). Thousand, Oaks, CA: Sage.

Sue, D. W., & Sue, D. (2013). *Counseling the culturally diverse: Theory and practice* (6th ed.). Hoboken, NJ: Wiley.

Thompson, M. N., Johnson-Jennings, M., & Nitzarim, R. S. (2013). Native Americans under-graduate students' persistence intentions: A psychosociocultural perspective. *Cultural Diversity and Ethnic Minority Psychology, 19*, 218–228.

Thyer, B. A. (2008). Practice evaluation. In K. M. Sowers & C. N. Dulmus (Series Eds.) & W. Rowe & L. A. Rapp-Paglicci (Vol. Eds.), *Comprehensive handbook of social work and social welfare: Social work practice* (vol. 3, pp. 98–119). Hoboken, NJ: Wiley.

Turner, F. J. (Ed.). (2011). *Social work treatment: Interlocking theoretical approaches* (5th ed.). New York. NY: Oxford University Press.

U.S. Census Bureau. (2008). *Current population survey [CPS]: A joint effort between the Bureau of Labor Statistics and the Census Bureau.* Retrieved from https://www.census.gov/hhes/www/cpstables/032009/pov/toc.htm

U.S. Census Bureau. (2011a). *American Indian and Alaska Native population by tribe for the United states 2010* [Table 1]. Retrieved from: http://www.census.gov/prod/cen2010/briefs/c2010br-01.pdf

U.S. Census Bureau. (2011b). *The Black alone population. Population by sex and age, for Black alone and White alone, not Hispanic* [Table 1]. Retrieved from: http://www.census.gov/population/race/data/ppl-ba11.html

U.S. Census Bureau. (2011c). *Overview of race and Hispanic origin: 2010* (2010 Census Briefs). Retrieved from http://www.census.gov/prod/cen2010/briefs/c2010br-02.pdf

U.S. Census Bureau. (2012). *The Statistical Abstract of the United States.* Population: Ancestry, Language Spoken At Home. Retrieved from http://www.census.gov/compendia/statab/cats/population/ancestry_language_spoken_at_home.html

U.S. Census Bureau. (2014a). *State and county quick facts.* Retrieved from: http://quickfacts.census.gov/qfd/states/00000.html

U.S. Census Bureau. (2014b). *U.S. and world population clock.* Retrieved from http://www.census.gov/popclock

Wallerstein, N. (2002). Empowerment to reduce health disparities. *Scandinavian Journal of Public Health, 30,* 72–77.

Walsh, J., & Holton, V. (2008). Case management. In K. M. Sowers & C. N. Dulmus (Series Eds.) & W. Rowe & L. A. Rapp-Paglicci (Vol. Eds.), *Comprehensive handbook of social work and social welfare: Social work practice* (vol. 3, pp. 139–160). Hoboken, NJ: Wiley.

Wells, R. A. (2010). *Planned short-term treatment* (2nd ed.). New York: Simon and Schuster.

PART THREE

SETTINGS FOR SOCIAL WORK PRACTICE

CHAPTER 7
POVERTY AND INCOME MAINTENANCE

THROUGHOUT ITS HISTORY, THE CORE FUNCTION OF THE SOCIAL work profession has been service on behalf of those who are economically, socially, or politically disadvantaged. From the earliest efforts of the charity organization societies (COS) and settlement houses of the nineteenth century, social workers have always tried to help people to achieve their potential and participate in the development of their communities.

As we entered the new millennium, the United States experienced unparalleled economic growth. There were more millionaires and billionaires than at any time in U.S. history. The stock market boomed to new and unexpected heights. Unemployment and inflation reached their lowest levels in decades, and new job opportunities abounded. The United Nations, in September 2000, passed the Millennium Declaration that included among its eight goals the eradication of extreme poverty and hunger worldwide by 2015 (*see* United Nations, 2000). Optimism was evident in research think tanks and institutes, such as the Carter Center, which reported the possibility of reducing poverty for all (Carter, 2000). All of these developments showed signs of a growing, prospering global economy. And then the worldwide economic walls came tumbling down in 2008 and 2009. Banks collapsed, people lost their homes due to foreclosures, and business and companies closed. Everyone knew someone who was affected by this economic crisis. The pain was shared and felt by many, yet one group of people sustained the hardest hit, and those were people in poverty.

What do we mean by poverty? Poverty can be considered in a number of different ways, but most use *income* as the most common variable. Why income? Because money gives a person the ability and opportunity to purchase goods and services. Money allows you to purchase or access quality health care, decent and safe housing, and an adequately nutritious diet. Income affects who you are and what you are able to do. As Darby wrote, "Being poor hurts. By itself, poverty diminishes the quality of life" (1996, p. 3). Certainly, there are many heroic examples of people and families who have risen above the limitations of poverty by taking full advantage of public welfare programs and services. For the vast majority of people in poverty, this is not possible. Living in poverty is far more often associated with negative life experiences that can leave deep scars. Crime, low educational attainment, inadequate health care, substandard housing, and minimum-wage employment with little opportunity for promotion are among the many debilitating experiences faced by the poor. For the economically disadvantaged—that is, people who cannot financially support themselves and their families—life is not easy.

Imagine what it would be like not to have enough money to feed, clothe, or house yourself and your family. Now imagine what it would be like if, in addition to these troubles, you were viewed negatively and treated differently simply because your income is low.

Poor people are often regarded as contributing less than their share to society. Indeed, society emphasizes rugged individualism (e.g., you take care of yourself and your family, and you "pull yourself up by the bootstraps.") Well-educated people who we believe should know better sometimes make statements such as "poor people are disadvantaged because they don't work or try hard enough to better themselves." Reflecting this sentiment, John Boehner (R-Ohio), Speaker of the House, said in a talk to the American Enterprise Institute in September 2014,

> We've got a record number of Americans not working. We've got a record number of Americans . . . stuck, if you will. And I think it's our obligation to help provide the tools for them to use to bring them into the mainstream of American society. I think this idea that's been born out the last—maybe out of the economy last couple of years that, "you know, I really don't have to work. I don't really want to do this, I think I'd just rather sit around." This is a very sick idea for our country (Malloy, 2014).

Further reflecting the notion that those who are poor or near poverty do so through their own choices, U.S. Senate Minority Leader Mitch McConnell (R-Kentucky) said in July 2014 that the federal government should not support student loan forgiveness programs: "I think the best short-term solution is for parents to be very cost-conscious in shopping around for higher education alternatives. Not everybody needs to go to Yale. I don't know about you guys, but I went to a regular ol' Kentucky college. And some people would say I've done okay" (Terkel, 2014).

In spring 2015, the Kansas senate proposed significant revisions to its existing Temporary Assistance for Needy Families (TANF) law including the following:

> No TANF cash aid could be spent out-of-state or anywhere for expenditures in a liquor store, casino, jewelry store, tattoo or body piercing parlor, spa, massage parlor, nail salon, lingerie shop, tobacco paraphernalia store, psychic or fortune telling business, bail bond company, video arcade, movie theater, swimming pool, cruise ship, theme park, dog or horse racing facility or sexually oriented retail business (Carpenter, 2015).

The bill also limited ATM withdrawals under TANF to $25.00 per day. Can you find an ATM machine that dispenses $25.00? And consider that the ATM fee, which ranges from $2.00 to $2.50 at most places, is nearly a 10-percent tax on the withdrawal.

Think about it. Can you remember any discussions you've had with friends or family about people who are poor? How were these people characterized? How often have discussions of this type become emotionally charged? Now think about pronouncements you've heard politicians make in the heat of political campaigns. How did these politicians present the issue of poverty, and what kinds of plans were proposed to address it? Why do you think people who want to hold office seem to constantly attack poverty-related social programs? We believe that most of the time politicians wish to please their constituents, so they pander to widespread beliefs and attack these programs as costly and wasteful.

Regardless of your opinion about people who live in poverty, it is clear that the poor and disadvantaged inspire strong emotions. Views and expectations about those living in poverty are founded on myths and stereotypes that unfortunately are assumed to be fact. We actually know quite a lot about poverty, particularly that the state of poverty is persistent. Poverty affects all races and ages. Poverty affects both men and women. Poverty is found in urban, suburban, and rural communities. Those who live in poverty are often disadvantaged or disenfranchised by the greater society. Finally, poverty cannot be isolated within a particular segment of society. Through its effects on educational performance and crime, poverty affects everyone in society—the young, old, Anglos/Whites, African Americans, Hispanics, Asians, people who live in the city, and people who live in rural America (see Table 1).

Did you know… The means test is the process by which an individual or family's eligibility for governmental assistance is determined; the test assesses whether the individual or family possesses the means to do without that help.

In this chapter, we will cut through many of the myths that surround the poor and impart critical information to make you a more informed helper. We will then look at several important social programs and assess their effectiveness within a framework of facts rather than mythology. Do not become overwhelmed by the numbers and do recognize that the numbers are constantly changing. A good exercise for you is to search the Internet to find updated data regarding poverty rates for 2014 and 2015 as well as for other years.

Did You Know…In 2013, in the United States 45.3 million people, 14.5% of the population, were living in poverty.

Table 1. Profile of Persons in Poverty, 2013

	Number in poverty (thousands)	Percent of population
Total	45,318	14.5
White	29,926	12.3
Black	11,041	27.2
Asian and Pacific Islander	1,785	10.5
Hispanic	12,744	23.5
Under 18 years	14,659	19.9
18 to 64 years	26,429	13.6
65 years and older	4,231	9.5
In families	31,530	12.4
Northeast	7,046	12.7
Midwest	8,590	12.9
South	18,870	16.1
West	10,812	14.7
Lives in metropolitan area	37,746	14.2
Lives outside metropolitan area	7,572	16.1

POVERTY DEFINED

According to the *Social Work Dictionary* poverty is "the state of being poor or deficient in money or means of subsistence" (Barker, 2003, p. 333). Other definitions similarly stress the link between resources and livelihood: Poverty is a "condition of being without basic resources" (Segal & Brzuzy, 1998, p. 78).

Two ideas further refine the concept of poverty: **absolute poverty** and relative poverty. *Absolute poverty* is determined by comparison with a fixed numerical standard that is applied in all situations and usually reflects bare subsistence. *Relative poverty* is determined by comparison with some normative standard that may reflect a living standard far higher than subsistence.

Absolute measures are usually income based. For example, if a person's annual income is below a certain figure, then the individual is regarded as poor. On the other hand, a relative measure—though still income based—would compare the individual with someone else. A single person with a $45,000 annual income is not absolutely poor, but is poor relative to Bill Gates, one of the richest people in the world. Absolute measures make it easy to count people and minimize the array of subjective variables.

A relative measure is based on the ability, or inability, to meet a standard that is set and approved by the community. For example, if immunizations are expected but a family cannot afford them for its children, then that family is considered poor by this measure. The key is identifying a threshold below which people are counted as poor. Relative measures are much more difficult to formulate or to reach consensus about. They are also difficult to use. For example, a common criticism of the poor in the United States is they have it easy compared to the poor elsewhere, in India or the Sudan, for example. But this is like trying to compare apples with oranges. Different countries have different beliefs, values, and economic and social systems, all of which affect the standards by which people are judged to be poor. The bottom line is that poverty affects more than 40 million people in the United States.

Measuring Poverty

The U.S. government measures poverty using a standard called the *poverty threshold*. The measure is based on a formula established in 1963, more than fifty years ago, by Mollie Orshansky, director of the Social Security Administration. She conceptualized the poverty threshold as an absolute measure so that statistical processes could be used to simply count the number of poor. Orshansky's formula is based on the amount of money that a family must spend on food and on the portion of overall income that this expense constitutes. Orshansky assumed that a family spends one-third of its total income on food. After calculating the cost of a minimum, or economy, food plan as determined by the Department of Agriculture, she multiplied that amount by three to establish the poverty threshold. This value, which is essential in determining benefits, is updated annually and adjusted to reflect inflation, family size, age, and the increased cost of living in Hawaii and Alaska. Its application is simple: a person or family whose gross income falls below the poverty threshold is counted as being in poverty.

Did You Know…In 2013, 19.9% of children under age 18, 14.7 million young people, lived in poverty.

Now that we've explained the poverty threshold calculation, let's complicate matters a bit. The poverty threshold was the government's original attempt to establish a poverty measure under the oversight of the Social Security Administration. Its purpose was to establish a basis for counting retrospectively the number of people who live in poverty. Each year, however, another branch of the federal government, the Department of Health and Human Services (HHS), is responsible for issuing poverty guidelines (see Table 2). These prospective guidelines, which closely approximate the poverty threshold, are used in determining financial eligibility for certain federal programs.

Table 2. 2014 HHS Poverty Guidelines

No. of persons in household	Poverty guideline
1	$11,670
2	$15,730
3	$19,790
4	$23,850
5	$27,910
6	$31,970
7	$36,030
8*	$40,090

Source: U.S. Department of Health and Human Services. (2014).
*For families/households with more than eight persons, add $4,060 for each additional person. Note that there are separate guidelines for Alaska and Hawaii, which are published on the Health and Human Services website.

An important point to remember is that the HHS poverty guidelines are used for determining eligibility for many federal programs, but not for all of them. Examples of federal programs that use the HHS guidelines are Head Start, the Low-Income Energy Assistance Program, the Supplemental Nutritional Assistance Program, the National School Lunch and School Breakfast Programs, Legal Services for the Poor, the Job Training Partnership Act, the Special Supplemental Nutrition Program for Women, Infants, and Children (WIC), and Job Corps. Some of these programs base eligibility on a multiple of the guideline percentage, such as 125, 150, or 180 percent. For example, a program may use 125 percent of the HHS guidelines to determine eligibility. In 2014 this eligibility standard for a four-person family was $23,850 x 125 percent, or $29,813. In other words, a family of four was eligible for the program if its income was below $29,813. The percentages of the HHS guidelines used by different programs are established by congressional committees and, predictably, can create a great deal of confusion between programs. Moreover, several well-known programs—Supplemental Security Income, Social Services Block Grant, Section 8 housing, the Earned Income Credit, and Temporary Assistance for Needy Families—are not tied to the HHS guidelines (see the activity below).

One last point about counting people in poverty is that not all people are actually counted. The Census Bureau does not include or attempt to estimate the poverty status of individuals who fall into the following groups:

♦ Unrelated individuals under age fifteen, such as foster children (income questions are asked of people of age fifteen and older)

♦ Individuals under age fifteen who are not living with a family member (maybe a runaway, throwaway, or push-out teen)

Activity…Using the 2014 poverty guideline (see Table 1) for a family of four, $23,850, imagine what life is like. You'd have $1,987.50 (before taxes) each month for expenses. Based on Orshansky formula's assumption, one-third of your income, $656, would go for food, leaving you $1,311 for other expenses including housing, transportation, health care, clothing, recreation, and so on.

Put together a monthly food menu with the $656. Find a place to live and set up other expenses with the remaining $1,311. The two children are five and thirteen years old, and the two adults are the biological parents.

Now, how realistic are the poverty guidelines? What does this exercise tell you about the level at which poverty guidelines are set? If this were your family of four and these were the resources you had available, could you make ends meet?

◆ Those who live in institutional group quarters (such as prisons or nursing homes, college dormitories, military barracks, and living situations without conventional housing) and those who are not in shelters—the homeless

Therefore, when you are looking at the poverty numbers and related rates, recognize that these are underestimates of the real numbers. The extent of the undercount is not known; it may be small—less than 100,000 persons—or it may be large—more than 1,000,000 persons. So what we do know is that the official federal numbers are at best a low number and do not accurately reflect the true number of persons in poverty.

Did You Know…A single parent with two children making the minimum wage and working forty hours a week in 2014 would not make enough money to raise this family above the poverty threshold, which was $17,970. This parent would need to make $8.90 per hour to be above the poverty threshold; the federal mandated minimum wage in 2014 was $7.25 per hour.

Other Considerations in Measuring Poverty

Setting poverty thresholds and thus establishing exactly who will be counted as poor is very controversial. Orshansky's definition, when examined closely, has all sorts of limitations. First, it doesn't consider geographical differences in cost of living, other than for Alaska and Hawaii—and this is an important consideration in the United States. What do you think: Is it cheaper to live in Los Angeles, California, or in Tallahassee, Florida? Second, the threshold is based on food costs but does not adjust for the different nutritional needs among children, women, women of child-bearing age, and men. Last, assuming that one-third of a family's income is spent on food purchases is itself problematic. Over the years this has not proved to be a well-founded assumption (see the activity below).

> *Did You Know...In statistics the mean, median, and mode are indicators of how a set of numbers tends to focus around central values. Applied to income, the mean income is the average income of a population—50% of the population has income above median income and 50% below—and the mode income is the most frequently occurring income.*

Beyond problems with the formula used to determine poverty is the question of what should or should not be counted as income. For example, should federal cash subsidies such as Social Security retirement payments or monthly checks from Supplemental Security Income be counted as income? Should income be established as the pretax or the posttax (e.g., what you take home after taxes) amount? Should the cash value of in-kind benefits from federal subsidy programs such as the SNAP (Supplemental Nutritional Assistance Program, aka, Food Stamps) and Section 8 housing be counted as part of a family's income?

> *Activity...Determine what the minimum wage in 2014 would need to be for a family to be above the 2014 Health and Human Services Guidelines (see Table 1). A full-time job is generally calculated to total 2,087 hours per year.*

How income is defined affects actual poverty estimates. Critics of the federal government's income maintenance programs argue that the poor are receiving numerous supports and that these should be counted as income, which in effect raises a number of individuals above the poverty threshold and lowers the number of people in poverty. What do you think would happen to the number of people in poverty based on a combined count that includes Earned Income Credit (EIC), means-tested cash transfers, SNAP benefits, Medicaid subsidies, and rent subsidies? Would the number of people in poverty increase or decrease? If you think decrease, you are correct—but will this net number portray a realistic picture of the nation's poverty level?

So, will we have an accurate picture of U.S. poverty if we count the various poverty-related subsidies? Does it really matter if the subsidies are counted? If they are and the poverty rate actually declined from the 2013 rate shown in Table 2, would it be a safe bet that the lower rates would be used to justify reductions in welfare programs? And, if welfare programs were reduced, wouldn't the poverty rate rise again?

Nevertheless, agency administrators and welfare advocates often argue that data produced by a standardized process applied consistently from year to year are essential, even if that process is rife with potential measurement flaws. Such numerical measures allow a community to follow trends in poverty and to assess the effects of different attempts to reduce poverty among its citizens. In other words, even though the poverty rate itself may have little intrinsic meaning, it is nonetheless important because its fluctuations over time serve as a barometer of economic well-being.

Number in Poverty versus Poverty Rate

Note that our discussion of measuring poverty started with counting the number of people in poverty but is now framed in terms of the poverty rate. The poverty rate is a more illuminating way to quantify poverty because it provides context by expressing the number of people in poverty as a percentage of the total population. This context is important for two reasons. First, the scale of poverty is difficult to judge if we know only the number of poor people: One thousand people in poverty is a far more serious problem if the total population is 2,000 than if it is 100,000. The poverty rates, 50 percent and 1 percent, show how different the two situations are. Second, trends in poverty cannot be judged by changes in the number of poor people alone. Suppose that over a decade the number of people in poverty rises from 1,000 to 2,000. If the total population remains stable at 100,000, the poverty rate has doubled from 1 to 2 percent; if, however, the population grows from 100,000 to 200,000, the poverty rate is unchanged at 1 percent—the rate distinguishes between worsening poverty and population growth. As a result, it is more accurate to use the rate (i.e., percentage) than the actual number. As the population increases in number over time, so too will all related indices, including the number of people in poverty. Those who ignore the rate or percentage and solely use the actual number are biasing their arguments.

Table 3 shows the different eras in the recent history of poverty. Remember that the U.S. population has grown every year since the nation's founding. You can now "read" different eras in the recent history of poverty. In the 1960s the number of people in poverty actually declined, a dramatic development, as evidenced by the sharp drop in the poverty rate from 22 to 12.1 percent. This decrease was achieved primarily through the federal government's activist War on Poverty. Over the following years the poverty rate fluctuated, but has remained in the low to mid teens since 1990. Indeed, although poverty rates are well below the 1960s' level prior to the War on Poverty, the numbers in poverty were not far different and most troubling, poverty continues.

WHO ARE THE POOR?

Poverty cuts across all races, ethnic groups, and ages and darkens the lives of both men and women. In this country there has always been a myth that the poor are almost all non-White. Yet this is far from true (see Table 4). Numerically there are more Whites in poverty than any other single race. However, poverty rates for Blacks and those of Hispanic origin are much higher than that for Whites. In 2013, 45.3 million people were in poverty, down from the previous year (2012), by 1.2 million; note that this is the first time since 2006 that the U.S. poverty rate declined.

Table 3. Poverty Status, 1990–2013

Year	Poverty (in thousands)	Rate (%)
2013	45,318	14.5
2012	46,496	15.0
2011	46,247	15.0
2010	46,343	15.1
2009	43,569	14.3
2008	39,829	13.2
2007	36,460	12.3
2006	36,460	12.3
2005	36,950	12.6
2004	37,040	12.7
2003	35,861	12.5
2002	34,570	12.1
2001	32,907	11.7
2000	31,054	11.3
1999	32,258	11.8
1998	34,476	12.7
1997	35,574	13.3
1996	36,529	13.7
1995	36,425	13.8
1994	38,059	14.5
1993	39,265	15.1
1992	38,014	14.8
1991	35,708	14.2
1990	33,585	13.5

Source: DeNavas-Walt & Proctor (2014).

Poverty rates in 2013 were disproportionately higher for minority groups compared to the Anglo/White population: The Anglo/White poverty rate was 9.6 percent compared to 27.2 percent, 23.5 percent, and 10.5 percent for African Americans, Hispanics, and Asian Americans, respectively. The poverty rate in 2013 was lower than in 1959, the first year for which poverty estimates are available.

Did You Know...In 2014, the number of people living below the poverty threshold totaled 45.3 million Americans. To think about how large this number is, consider that the total population of Maine, New Hampshire, Vermont, Massachusetts, Connecticut, Rhode Island, New York, Pennsylvania, and New Jersey is smaller. The total combined population of some of the Midwestern states—Wisconsin, Michigan, Illinois, Ohio, Iowa, and Missouri—is also smaller than the total number of people in poverty.

Table 4. Poverty Rates (%) for All People by Race and Hispanic Origin, 1990–2013

Year	All Persons	White	Black	Hispanic	Asian
2013	14.5	12.3	27.2	23.5	10.5
2012	15.0	12.7	27.2	25.6	11.7
2011	15.0	12.8	27.6	25.3	12.3
2010	15.1	13.0	27.4	26.5	12.2
2009	14.3	12.3	25.8	25.3	12.5
2008	13.2	11.2	24.7	23.2	11.8
2007	12.5	10.5	24.5	21.5	10.2
2006	12.3	10.3	24.3	20.6	10.3
2005	12.6	10.6	21.9	21.8	11.1
2004	12.7	10.8	24.7	24.9	9.8
2003	12.5	10.6	24.3	22.5	11.8
2002	12.1	10.2	24.1	21.8	10.1
2001	11.7	9.9	22.7	21.4	10.2
2000	11.3	9.5	22.5	21.5	9.9
1999	11.6	9.7	23.1	22.1	10.7
1998	12.7	10.5	26.5	27.1	12.5
1997	13.3	11.0	29.3	30.3	14.0
1996	13.7	11.2	28.4	29.4	14.5
1995	13.8	11.2	29.3	30.3	14.6
1994	14.5	11.7	30.6	30.7	14.6
1993	15.1	12.2	33.1	30.6	15.3
1992	14.8	11.9	33.4	29.6	12.7
1991	14.2	11.3	32.7	28.7	13.8
1990	13.5	10.7	31.9	28.1	12.2

Source: DeNavas-Walt & Proctor (2014).

The data to be presented in Table 6 will also challenge the idea that most poor people should be supporting themselves. Using simple mathematics, we can see that children, those under age eighteen, account for almost 32 percent of all poor, and seniors, those of age sixty-five and over, account for more than 9 percent. We also see that people in families account for 69.6 percent of all poor; this statistic alone challenges the common myth that the poor are mainly single middle-aged persons.

Poverty and Location

In 2014, the U.S. Census Bureau reported that the number of people in poverty living in metropolitan areas totaled 37.8 million (14.2%) compared to 7.6 million (16.1%) of those living outside of metropolitan areas (DeNavas-Walt &

Proctor, 2014, p. 12.). Few Americans think of the poor as living in rural areas or small communities, which are generally associated as tranquil places for vacation or weekend escapes. Creating successful programs for the rural poor is a significant challenge; certainly what works in New York City may not work in rural northwest Wyoming.

Poverty and Race

As Table 4 clearly shows, poverty rates for Blacks and Hispanics have been about twice that for Whites for years. Averages by decade show that over time the differences have lessened, but they remain extreme. In 2013, 12.3 percent of Anglos/Whites were in poverty compared to 27.2 for African Americans and 23.5 percent for Hispanics. The poverty rate for Asians is also disproportionately lower than that of African Americans and Asians.

Did You Know... The term Hispanic *is unique to the United States? No other nation uses this word in the same manner as the U.S. government. "Pertaining to the culture of Spanish- and Portuguese-speaking people ... this term is often applied to people of Latin American ethnic background. .... Some people prefer the term Latino" (Barker, 2003, p. 216). According to the U.S. Bureau of the Census, which first used the word in 1980, a person of Hispanic origin can be of any race. This means that people who describe themselves as Hispanic can have diverse backgrounds and very different mores and cultural expectations.*

Poverty and Gender

Gender historically and today plays an important role in income distribution. Simply stated, women are more susceptible to poverty than men. Even social workers, members of a profession that proudly advocates for social and economic justice, work in organizations and agencies that discriminate against women. Gibelman and Schervish (1997) found that in 1995 the median income for female social workers was $34,135 compared with $37,503 for their male counterparts. And a 2003 salary study provides evidence that the more a service profession is dominated by women, the lower the workers' average weekly salary (Gibelman, 2003). The ongoing gender-based salary differentials for social work are the same for society in general. For example, in 2013 the median salary for men was $50,116 compared to $38,340 for women; the female-to-male earnings ratio (.78) was basically the same as in 2012 (DeNavas-Walt & Proctor, 2014, pp. 6–7).

During the twentieth century, American family structure underwent significant changes. Two-parent families declined while single-parent families increased, birth rates declined for the general population but rose dramatically among teenagers, and women entered the workforce in great numbers. The United States now has many single-parent families that depend on the wages of a female head of household for their income.

Census Bureau data for 2013 show that families headed by females are 2.7 times more likely to be in poverty than all families—33.2 percent compared to 12.4 percent (DeNavas-Walt & Proctor, 2014, p. 44). Even more disturbing are the data for households headed by African American and Hispanic females. The three-year average, 2011 to 2013, found that 42 percent of African American families headed by females and 42.8 percent of Hispanic families headed by females were in poverty—that is, more than two in five African American and Hispanic families were in poverty (DeNavas-Walt & Proctor, 2014, pp. 44, 47, 49).

This hierarchy of poverty faithfully reflects income inequalities. The nation's median income for all households in 2013 was $51,939. For married couple families it was $76,509 compared to $35,154 for families with a female head of household (DeNavas-Walt & Proctor, 2014, p. 6). And as you can probably guess, correctly by the way, race and ethnicity make a difference; this is not a new finding but reflects a long-term pattern. The median income in 2013 for Anglo/White families was $55,257 compared to $34,598 for African American families and $40,963 for Hispanic families (DeNavas-Walt & Proctor, 2014, p. 6). As Landrine and Klonoff wrote in 1997, ethnic and gender discrimination together generate extremely low salaries for minority women and "impair women's ability to support themselves and their children" (p. 8):

If a job paid Anglo/White men $20,000, then Anglo/White women received $15,000, African American women $12,200, and Latinas $11,000 for the same work. If a job paid Anglo/White men $35,000, then Anglo/White women received $26,250, African American women $21,350, and Latinas $19,250 for the same work. If a job paid Anglo/White men $50,000, then Anglo/White women received $37,500, African American women $30,500, and Latinas $27,500 for the same work (p. 8).

The group with perhaps the greatest risk of poverty consists of teenage parents and their children. The National Center for Health Statistics reports a consistent decline in teen childbearing since 1940 with a few exceptions; the rate dropped to 26.6 births per 1,000 in 2013 (Ventura, Hamilton, & Matthews, 2014, p. 2). The Center also reports that the number of births to unwed teenagers has significantly increased over time; 89 percent of teen births in 2013 were to unmarried individuals, with only 2 percent of teens giving birth being married (Ventura et al., 2014, p. 3). The report goes on to note that babies born to teen mothers ". . . are more likely to have low birth weight . . . at greater risk of serious and long-term illness, developmental delays, and of dying in the first year of life" (Ventura et al,, 2014, p. 5).

Poverty and Age

The younger the person, the more likely he or she is to live in poverty. In 2013, 19.9 percent of children were in poverty and the age cohort with the next largest poverty rate was young adults, aged eighteen to twenty-four (Table 5). In the primary work years, ages twenty-five to fifty-four, poverty rates decreased. Finally, for people in retirement and relying on fixed incomes, poverty rates fluctuated slightly but remained slightly below 10 percent between 1990 and 2013 (see Table 6).

The percentage of older Americans in poverty was lower than the rate for the whole population—9.5 percent compared to 14.5 percent in 2013. This was not always the case. In 1959, 35.2 percent of seniors lived in poverty compared with 22.4 percent of all people; between 1967 and 1970, the senior poverty rate ranged from 21.6 to 29.5 percent compared with a range of 12.6 to 14.2 percent for the whole population. For the most recent decade, 2000 to 2010, the rate ranged from a low of 8.9 percent (2010) to a high of 10.4 percent in 2002 (DeNavas-Walt & Proctor, 2014, p. 51). The average poverty rate among elders between 1990 and 2013 was 10.3 percent (see Table 6).

The sharp decline in the poverty rate for older Americans over time was a clear result of specific federal legislation (Jansson, 1993, p. 306). The Older Americans Act of 1965, the Supplemental Security Act, and the indexing of social security retirement checks in the early 1970s all helped to raise seniors' fixed incomes above the poverty threshold. Social insurance programs, as DiNitto and Johnson wrote, ". . . are a primary strategy for preventing poverty among workers and retirees and their dependents or survivors" (2012, p. 120). It's important to recognize that the reductions in senior poverty are primarily due to federal support that pushes income levels slightly above the poverty threshold.

Of all the figures we have discussed so far, those that probably disturb people the most are the ones that involve our nation's children. For the better part of twenty years, poverty rates for children hovered around 20 percent—that is, one in five

Table 5. Poverty Rates by Age, Group, and Ethnicity, 2013

	Percentage below poverty level		
Group	18 and younger	18–64	65 and over
All	19.9	13.6	9.5
White	16.4	11.8	8.4
Black	36.9	36.7	23.8
Asian	9.6	9.4	10.2
Hispanic	30.4	20.2	19.8

Source: DeNavas-Walt & Proctor (2014).

Table 6. Poverty Rates Based on Age, 1990–2013

Year	Children under 18 Number	Percent	People 18 to 64 years Number	Percent	People 65 and older Number	Percent
2013	14,142	19.5	26,429	13.6	4,231	9.5
2012	15,437	21.3	26,497	13.7	3,926	9.1
2011	15,539	21.4	26,492	13.7	41,507	8.7
2010	15,598	21.5	26,499	13.8	3,558	8.9
2009	14,774	20.1	24,684	12.9	3,433	8.9
2008	13,507	18.5	22,105	11.7	3,656	9.7
2007	13,324	18.0	20,396	10.9	3,556	9.7
2006	12,827	17.4	20,239	10.8	3,394	9.4
2005	12,896	17.6	20,450	11.1	3,603	10.1
2004	13,041	17.8	20,545	11.3	3,453	9.8
2003	12,866	17.6	19,443	10.8	3,552	10.2
2002	12,133	16.7	18,861	10.6	3,576	10.4
2001	11,733	16.3	17,760	10.1	3,414	10.1
2000	11,587	16.2	16,671	9.6	3,323	9.9
1999	12,280	17.1	17,289	10.1	3,222	9.7
1998	13,467	18.9	17,623	10.5	3,386	10.5
1997	14,113	19.9	18,085	10.9	3,376	10.5
1996	14,463	20.5	18,638	11.4	3,428	10.8
1995	14,665	20.8	18,442	11.4	3,318	10.5
1994	15,289	21.8	19,107	11.9	3,663	11.7
1993	15,727	22.7	19,783	12.4	3,755	12.2
1992	15,294	22.3	18,793	11.9	3,928	12.9
1991	14,341	21.8	17,586	11.4	3,781	12.4
1990	13,431	20.6	16,496	10.7	3,658	12.2

Source: DeNavas-Walt & Proctor (2014).
*Numbers in thousands.

children was poor. In 1990, the poverty rate among children was 20.6 percent, and ten years later in 2000, it had dropped to 16.2 percent, its lowest point between 1990 and 2013 (see Table 6). Although trends have been negative since 2000, the recent minimal decline in numbers of children in poverty can be attributed to the nation's economic strength and growth. The Children's Defense Fund (CDF), a national advocacy organization for children, notes that, although child poverty decreased in general rates, it rose in working-class families. According to the CDF,

> Every child deserves a safe, permanent and loving family and all parents and caregivers aspire to support and prepare their children for a better life than the previous generation. Children do not choose their families. The structure and financial status of the family into which a child is born impacts their development and ability to reach their full potential" (2014, p. 24).

We know that poverty has negative consequences for those who live in it, but what specific effects does it have on children? What exactly does it mean to be a child raised in an impoverished home? Again, according to the Children's Defense Fund (2015),

> They [poor children] are less healthy, trail in emotional and intellectual develop-
> ment, and are less likely to graduate from high school. Poor children also are
> more likely to become the poor parents of the future. Every year that we keep
> children in poverty costs our nation half a trillion dollars in lost productivity,
> poorer health and increased costs of the criminal justice system.

We've seen that race and ethnicity affect poverty rates for women and for the general population, so we shouldn't be surprised to learn that race and ethnicity also affect age-specific poverty rates. In 2013, the poverty rates were 30.2 percent for Black youths, 10.1 percent for Asian youths, and 30.4 percent for Hispanic youths, compared with 16.4 percent for Anglo/White youths; poverty rates were 21.9 percent for Black seniors, 13.6 percent for Asian seniors, and 19.8 percent for Hispanic seniors, compared to 8.4 percent of Anglo/White seniors (DeNavas-Walt &Proctor 2014, pp. 51–55). These disproportional rates represent long-standing inequalities.

WHY IS THERE POVERTY IN A WEALTHY NATION?

Entire university courses are devoted to studying how poverty can exist in the midst of great wealth. Countless books and articles also attempt to answer this question. The breadth of this topic allows us only to review some theories put forth to explain why poverty continues to exist.

Theories vary as to what causes poverty. In fact, if we knew and agreed to the cause or causes for poverty, we would have long ago ended this very debilitating life experience. But there has not been agreement as to the causes nor a long-term commitment to find its foundations and create the necessary opportunities and protections for all people.

Bruening (2014) writes that there are essentially two conflicting theories as to the cause of poverty. One perspective is that poverty is individually caused; that is, the individual is the cause of his/her poverty. Proponents of this school of thought use a variety of data to substantiate their thesis. For example, low educational attainment, unemployment, and low rates of marriage are common characteristics among the poor.

The alternative theory that Bruening cites is structurally based. The under-lying cause of poverty rests with larger, macro issues such as low-paying jobs, schools that are inadequate in teaching, lack of access to health care, and an abun-dance of crime-filled neighborhoods. Again, specific statistics are used to support this perspective.

Another perspective on poverty (and yes, it is dated) was proposed by Darby (1996, p. 20), who listed four factors that result in poverty:

1. *Decline in low-wage jobs*: Fewer jobs are available for the labor pool.

2. *Immigration*: New immigrants take low-paying jobs away from unemployed residents.

3. *Decline in labor force participation and work effort*: Work effort among men is down over the long term.

4. *Breakdown of traditional family structures*: The number of single-parent families has increased, particularly among Blacks.

Darby believes that these four conditions are intertwined and that one is no more or less important than the others. As a result, programs that address poverty but are narrow in scope, function, and funding will result in minimal changes, if any at all. Rather, Darby argues that antipoverty efforts must be coordinated to target all of these areas.

Bradshaw (2007) argued that five different and competing theories shape social welfare antipoverty programs: (1) individual deficiencies, (2) cultural beliefs (i.e., traditions), (3) political and economic distortions, (4) geographic differences (e.g., rural-urban and north-south), and (5) cumulative and circumstantial situations.

Another perspective on the causes of poverty was set forth by Johnson and Schwartz (1988), who divided the causes of poverty into three broad areas: economic, social, and political:

◆ Economic causes relate to unequal distribution of income across society and inadequate income supports in public assistance programs and unemployment programs.

◆ Social causes of poverty refer to the public's negative views of the poor; the strong belief in self-reliance; and discrimination against people based on race, ethnicity, and gender.

◆ Political causes include lack of participation in the political process by the poor and unjust social policies. Poverty and welfare programs are not popular in political circles and seem to be more vulnerable to public scrutiny and cutbacks than other public programs.

Representing a very strong conservative view of poverty is the so-called Tea Party Nation. The website notes that poverty

... is a condition that stems from a multiplicity of sources. ... In America poverty stems from a culture that celebrates drugs, crime, and disdains work as some sort of selling out. Education–which is free and available–is frowned upon in America's ghetto. A sense of entitlement reigns in these places, a sense that "The Man" cheated them out of what was theirs by right of birth. This IS poverty, but it is not the result of a lack of stuff, but rather a lack of virtues (Birdnow, 2013).

So what is the cause of poverty in the wealthiest nation in the world? There is no agreement or consensus as to one specific cause. Statistics are used to support each theory. As a result, the theory you currently subscribe to or may endorse in the future is one that matches your political ideology. There is no way to escape the relationship between the theories of poverty and ideology. Just remember that, whichever theory you subscribe to, you must be sure that it supports the tenets of social justice.

PROGRAMS TO AID THE POOR

It is time to examine current programmatic responses to poverty in the United States and to consider how these programs are viewed and how their recipients are treated. This section will present a brief overview of major public assistance programs. We approach this section with great hesitancy and caution. Programs come and go, eligibility rules change each year, and dollar supports frequently change. As a result we encourage you to web search the various programs for the most current, up-to-date information.

In chapter 3, we learned that the modern welfare system has its roots firmly planted in the Great Depression of the 1930s and the passage of the Economic Security Act of 1935. A second major federal welfare initiative occurred in the 1960s with the advent of President Johnson's War on Poverty. Finally, a third, dramatic shift in federal social welfare programs for the poor took shape with the passage and implementation of the Personal Responsibility and Work Opportunity Reconciliation Act of 1996. This act was a sweeping reform of the role of the federal government in welfare provision. It dramatically restructured programs to aid the poor and ended the nation's six-decade-old guarantee (i.e., entitlement) of cash assistance to poor families.

Temporary Assistance for Needy Families

In 1996, the primary public assistance program was totally changed under the guise of *welfare reform*. Officially known as the Personal Responsibility and Work Opportunity Reconciliation Act (PRWORA), the new federal program, Temporary Assistance for Needy Families (TANF), replaced Aid to Families with Dependent Children (AFDC), the AFDC Emergency Assistance program, and the Job Opportunities and Basic Skills Training (JOBS) programs. More commonly referred to as welfare, TANF is the monthly cash assistance program for poor families with children under age eighteen. The program itself is state-based; that is, each state receives funding as a block grant from the federal government and is given broad discretion in determining how TANF funds are spent. The differences among the states are represented in the various TANF program names across the country (see Table 7).

Table 7. Names of State TANF Programs*

State	Name
Alabama	FA (Family Assistance Program)
Alaska	ATAP (Alaska Temporary Assistance Program)
Arizona	EMPOWER (Employing and Moving People Off Welfare and Encouraging Responsibility)
Arkansas	TEA (Transitional Employment Assistance)
California	CALWORKS (California Work Opportunity and Responsibility to Kids)
Colorado	Colorado Works
Connecticut	JOBS FIRST
Delaware	ABC (A Better Chance)
D.C.	TANF
Florida	Welfare Transition Program
Georgia	TANF
Guam	TANF
Hawaii	TANF
Idaho	Temporary Assistance for Families in Idaho
Illinois	TANF
Indiana	TANF, cash assistance; IMPACT (Indiana Manpower Placement and Comprehensive Training), TANF work program
Iowa	FIP (Family Investment Program)
Kansas	Kansas Works
Kentucky	K-TAP (Kentucky Transitional Assistance Program)
Louisiana	FITAP (Family Independence Temporary Assistance Program), cash assistance; FIND Work (Family Independence Work Program), TANF work program
Maine	TANF, cash assistance; ASPIRE (Additional Support for People in Retraining and Employment), TANF work program
Maryland	FIP (Family Investment Program)
Massachusetts	TAFDC (Transitional Aid to Families with Dependent Children), cash assistance; ESP (Employment Services Program), TANF work program
Michigan	FIP (Family Independence Program)
Minnesota	MFIP (Minnesota Family Investment Program)
Mississippi	TANF
Missouri	Beyond Welfare
Montana	FAIM (Families Achieving Independence in Montana)
Nebraska	Employment First
Nevada	TANF
New Hampshire	FAP (Family Assistance Program), financial aid for work-exempt families; NHEP (New Hampshire Employment Program), financial aid for work-mandated families
New Jersey	WFNJ (Work First New Jersey)
New Mexico	NM Works
New York	FA (Family Assistance Program)
North Carolina	Work First

Table 7. Names of State TANF Programs*—(Continued)

State	Name
North Dakota	TEEM (Training, Employment, Education Management)
Ohio	OWF (Ohio Works First)
Oklahoma	TANF
Oregon	JOBS (Job Opportunities and Basic Skills Program)
Pennsylvania	Pennsylvania TANF
Puerto Rico	TANF
Rhode Island	FIP (Family Independence Program)
South Carolina	Family Independence
South Dakota	TANF
Tennessee	Families First
Texas	Texas Works (Department of Human Services), cash assistance; Choices Texas Workforce Commission), TANF work program
Utah	FEP (Family Employment Program)
Vermont	ANFC (Aid to Needy Families with Children), cash assistance; Reach Up, TANF work program
Virgin Islands	(FIP) Family Improvement Program
Virginia	VIEW (Virginia Initiative for Employment, Not Welfare)
Washington	WorkFirst
West Virginia	West Virginia Works
Wisconsin	W-2 (Wisconsin Works)
Wyoming	POWER (Personal Opportunities With Employment Responsibility)

*The Federal Office for the Administration of Children and Families (ACF), which is responsible for TANF nationwide, no longer posts the states' TANF program names; this table is the last ACF listing.

Obviously, a federally mandated program that is developed and implemented differently in each state can and does become very confusing.

The federal government's 2013 fiscal year TANF budget request was $17.35 billion; in 2004, the actual appropriation was slightly more than $17 billion (Department of Health and Human Services, n.d., p. 300). The TANF benefits differ by state and the grant awards are not that large. For example, in 2013 in Alabama, the cash benefit ranged from $165 to $605, the average benefit in Oklahoma in 2010 was $434 per month, and the maximum benefit in Texas for one parent and two children was $260 per month. The U.S. Department of Health and Human Services Office of Family Assistance reported that the national average monthly TANF benefit for 2010 was $392 (Office of Family Assistance, 2012). For additional information on all the states go to the TANF website (http://www.tanfprogram.com/tanf-eligibility).

Did You Know...To qualify for the federal assistance program for the poor, TANF, a teen-age parent must live at home with parent(s) or in a home supervised by an adult. Also a teen mother must attend school or a training program once her baby is twelve weeks old.

At the time this book was written (2014–2015), the most current TANF data from the U.S. Department of Health and Human Services, Office of Family Assistance, which has oversight for TANF, was for fiscal year 2010 (i.e., 2009–10). Some of the key points included the following:

◆ The average number of TANF families was 1.8 million per month.

◆ The average size of a TANF family was 2.4 persons.

◆ Almost half the TANF families had no adult recipients.

◆ 82 percent of TANF families received SNAP benefits.

◆ 16.6 percent of the TANF cases were closed due to a family member finding full-time employment.

◆ TANF included 31.8 percent Anglo/White families, 31.9 percent African American families, and 30.0 percent Hispanic families.

◆ 59.2 percent of TANF recipients were under age twenty-nine.

◆ 42 percent of children receiving TANF were under age five.

Temporary Assistance to Needy Families does have some minimal requirements that all states must include in their programs, although a state can add to these requirements as well (U.S. Department of Health and Human Services, n.d.):

◆ Although, as with all programs, there are exceptions, the participant must work as soon as he or she is *job ready* or no later than two years after coming on assistance.

◆ Single parents are required to participate in work activities for at least thirty hours per week.

◆ Two-parent families must participate in work activities for thirty-five or fifty-five hours a week, depending upon circumstance.

◆ Failure to participate in work requirements can result in a reduction or termination of benefits to the family.

◆ There is a maximum lifetime of five years (sixty months) during which a person may receive benefits.

Temporary Assistance to Needy Families provides all states the flexibility to structure its programs within broad and flexible guidelines set by the U.S. Congress. As a result, states have different names for the programs, as well as different time limits, program requirements, and cash benefits. Essentially, a person living in Florida is treated differently from a person living in Wisconsin. Even with this flexibility, the lifetime limit of sixty months is a national limit. If a person receives TANF aid for fifty months in one state and then moves to a state with a lower time limit, such as Florida, the second state's limit has already been exceeded and the person receives no further TANF aid there. Even if the person moves to a state that has not lowered its time limit, only ten more months of TANF assistance will be available.

TANF and Native Americans

There is a different set of protocols that govern public programs for Native Americans. The federal office of the Division of Tribal Management, which is part of the HHS Administration of Children and Families, is a central point for assisting in implementation and coordination of ongoing consultation with tribal governments relating to TANF. Essentially these regulations recognize the unique cultural attributes and needs of tribal communities and allow for tribes to develop and administer TANF programs. In 2012, there were sixty-eight approved Tribal TANF programs that worked with 299 federally recognized Tribes and Alaska Native Villages (Administration for Children and Families, n.d.).

Food Programs

The primary federal food support program is called the Supplemental Nutritional Assistance Program or SNAP (U.S. Department of Agriculture, 2014b) and is operated through the U.S. Department of Agriculture. More commonly and incorrectly referred to as Food Stamps, the federal SNAP is designed to offset hunger and malnutrition. The program's name was changed from the Food Stamp Program in 2008 to reflect a new focus on nutrition. Note, however, that states have the option of not using the federal name and can call the program by another name. Another significant change is that the program no longer uses paper coupons, which were previously known as stamps. In 2009, SNAP benefits were available only on an Electronic Benefit Transfer (EBT) card; this significant change was made to reduce costs and fraud.

Prior to the Great Depression, no national coordinated effort addressed these fundamental issues. The problem was largely left to the states and local communities. For the most part, anti-hunger programs distributed actual food items. This practice moved to the national level when, in 1933, the Federal Surplus Relief Corporation was created to distribute surplus food.

Did You Know…In 2014 the average SNAP allotment for a three-person family was $497 per month or about $5.46 per meal.

The first Food Stamp Program project, which ran from 1939 to 1943, used two types of stamps: blue and orange. Blue stamps could be used only for surplus commodities, whereas orange stamps allowed the purchase of any type of food.

In 1961, a demonstration Food Stamp Program was started. It led in 1964 to the passage of the Food Stamp Act. Under the auspices of the Department of Agriculture, clients received stamps that allowed them to purchase certain American-grown or American-produced food at certain supermarkets. The current program structure was implemented in 1977 with the goal of alleviating hunger and malnutrition by permitting low-income households to obtain a more nutritious diet through normal channels of trade.

Participation in the SNAP in 2012 totaled 46.6 million persons with an average monthly benefit of $274 (Gray, 2014, p. xvii). The average size of a SNAP family was 3.2 people with the majority led by a single parent; 86 percent of families were in poverty and 13 percent of them would not be counted as being poor if the value of the SNAP benefit were calculated into the poverty measure (Gray, 2014, p. xvii).

Eligibility for the SNAP is based on financial and nonfinancial factors. The application process includes completing and filing an application form, being interviewed, and verifying facts to determine eligibility. With certain exceptions, a household that meets the eligibility requirements is qualified to receive benefits.

The basic SNAP income eligibility requirements for 2014 include the following, but these are subject to change (for current information (http://www.fns.usda.gov/snap/facts-about-snap):

◆ Households may have $2,000 in countable resources, such as a bank account, or $3,250 in countable resources if at least one person is age sixty or older or is disabled. However, certain resources are NOT counted, such as a home and lot, the resources of people who receive Supplemental Security Income (SSI), the resources of people who receive TANF (formerly AFDC), and most retirement (pension) plans.

◆ The values of licensed vehicles (e.g., cars, trucks, or motorcycles) are generally not counted.

◆ Almost all types of income are counted to determine if a household is eligible. Most households must have income at or below certain dollar limits before and after deductions are allowed. However, households in which all members are getting public assistance or SSI (or, in some locations, general assistance) do not have to meet the income eligibility tests.

For 2014, the monthly income limit for a three-person family was $2,116 (gross income) or $1,628 (net income); note that income ceilings for all family sizes may be found at http://www.fns.usda.gov/snap/eligibility. An hourly wage below $12.57 meets the gross income limit for a three-person family.

Contrary to the myth, people cannot use SNAP benefits to purchase any items they want. In fact, the SNAP has stringent limits on what may be purchased. Eligible items include breads and cereals, fruits and vegetables, meats, fish and poultry, and dairy products. Additionally, seeds and plants that produce food for the household to eat may be purchased with the SNAP benefit. Conversely, one cannot purchase beer, wine, liquor, cigarettes, or tobacco; pet foods; soaps, paper products, and household supplies such as toothpaste and grooming items; vitamins and medicines; food that can be eaten in the store; and hot foods, (Additional information is available at http://www.fns.usda.gov/snap/facts-about-snap)

School Lunch and Breakfast and Other Food Programs

Other federal food programs we need to consider include the National School Lunch and Breakfast Program, WIC, and Meals on Wheels. Targeted toward the poor, these programs were developed as supplements for specific vulnerable population groups, particularly children. According to the Children's Defense Fund, in 2012, more than 1 in 9 children lived in households where children were food insecure, meaning that they lacked consistent access to adequate food (Children's Defense Fund, 2014). This report also noted that children who were food insecure in kindergarten saw a significant drop in their reading and math test scores by third grade compared to their food-secure peers.

The National School Lunch Program (NSLP), which provides school children in the United States a lunch every school day, was created by Congress following World War II. At that time, the military draft showed a strong correlation between physical deficiencies and childhood malnutrition. In 2014 there were more than 100,000 public and private schools participating in the program providing meals to more than 31 million children (http://www.fns.usda.gov/nslp/national-school-lunch-program-nslp).

Children from families with incomes at or below 130 percent of the poverty level are eligible for free meals. Those with incomes between 130 percent and 185 percent of the poverty level are eligible for reduced-price meals, for which they can be charged no more than 40 cents. For the period July 1, 2013, through June 30, 2014, 130 percent of the poverty level was $30,615 for a family of four; 185 percent of the poverty level was $43,568 (http://www.fns.usda.gov/nslp/national-school-lunch-program-nslp).

The National School Breakfast Program (SBP), which operates similarly to the National School Lunch Program, was established by Congress as a pilot program in 1966 in areas where children had long bus rides to school and in areas where many mothers were in the workforce. The program was standardized as a

Name: Ian M. Danielsen, L.C.S.W

Place of residence: Powhatan, Virginia

College/university degrees: Virginia Commonwealth University: MSW, 1992; Radford University: BA, Sociology, 1989

Present position: Program coordinator, Greater Richmond SCAN (Stop Child Abuse Now) Child Advocacy Center; adjunct instructor, Virginia Commonwealth University School of Social Work

What do you do in your spare time? I am married and the father of two kids, a daughter named Rachel who is eighteen years old and has Down syndrome and a son named Rowan, age 4. I am a musician who plays guitar and sings, specializing in Irish and American folk music and singer/songwriter genres. I am also an outdoorsman who enjoys hiking, canoeing, and cycling.

Why did you choose social work as a career? I chose social work as a career because of the freedom it allows to be a change agent at micro, mezzo, and macro levels. In my present position I am able to provide direct clinical and advocacy services to children and care- givers experiencing trauma, coordinate the general activities of a child advocacy center as part of a nonprofit agency mission, and engage in legislative and other policy initiatives designed to improve the safety and well-being of children. So our profession's values around providing needed direct services for clients but also supporting system reform were values I embraced as a young social work student and continue to embrace today.

What is your favorite social work story? The mother of a teen-aged daughter who had been sexually abused by an extended family relative attended a caregiver support group I facilitated. As the group was nearing the end of its cycle of sessions, "Patricia" inquired if I knew of opportunities for her to engage in legislative advocacy to reform laws around sexual abuse or to support model programs that assist children and families experiencing abuse. When we learned in 2012 that state funding for sixteen child advocacy centers was in jeopardy of being eliminated, Patricia testified at the VA General Assembly about her personal experience as part of advocating for the restoration of these critically important funds. And in April of 2012 funds were indeed fully restored owing to collaborative efforts by her and others. So this experience just illuminates for me how helpees can become helpers and how there can be a brilliant interweaving of the micro and macro efforts for the good of children and families.

What would be the one thing you would change in our community if you had the power to do so? I would change the mindset of many in the community-at-large that advocacy for the underserved is only for "those special professionals over there." The truth is, every- one has an essential part to play in helping those in need, whether as a social worker, nurse, volunteer, legislator, police officer, or student. Humans are meant to collaborate, and part of why social problems continue is that human systems become fragmented or *other-ized*. The good news is that models of collaboration are emerging everywhere—in child abuse **multidisciplinary teams**, in collaborative law, in legislative working groups—society is slowly catching on that we are not effective in silos. Humans with problems don't exist in silos. So why should human helpers? So the truth is, we need expertise, experience, and action to be carried out in team fashion. And that idea, reflected in our code of ethics, if truly realized, will set the stage for real and lasting change for those we endeavor to serve.

---

permanent entitlement in 1976 to assist schools in providing nutritious morning meals to the nation's children. Research clearly shows that beginning each day with a nutritious breakfast results in better and stronger learning outcomes. Studies conclude that students who eat school breakfast increase their math and reading scores as well as improve their speed and memory in cognitive tests. Research also shows that children who eat breakfast at school, especially closer to class and test-taking time, perform better on standardized tests than those who skip breakfast or eat breakfast at home.

Any child at a participating school may purchase a meal through the School Breakfast Program. As with the School Lunch Program, children from families with incomes at or below 130 percent of the Federal poverty level are eligible for free meals. The number of children participating in the breakfast program has grown slowly but steadily over the years: 0.5 million in 1970, 3.6 million in 1980, 4.1 million in 1990, 6.3 million in 1995, 8.2 million in 2002, 8.9 million in 2004, and 10.6 million in 2008. In fiscal year 2011, more than 12.1 million children participated every day. Of those, more than 10.1 million received their meals free or at a reduced price (U.S. Department of Agriculture, 2014a).

The Special Supplemental Nutrition Program for Women, Infants, and Children (WIC) was enacted in 1972 to provide nutritional counseling and basic food supplements to prenatal and postpartum low-income women and their children. Target populations for WIC are low-income, nutritionally at risk (U.S. Department of Agriculture, 2015b) including

- ◆ Pregnant women (through pregnancy and up to six weeks after birth or after pregnancy ends).
- ◆ Breastfeeding women (up to the infant's first birthday).
- ◆ Non-breastfeeding postpartum women (up to six months after the birth of an infant or after pregnancy ends).
- ◆ Infants (up to the first birthday). Note that WIC serves 53 percent of all infants born in the United States.
- ◆ Children up to their fifth birthday.

Coordinated by the U.S. Department of Agriculture's Food and Nutrition Service, WIC is not an entitlement program. It is administered by ninety WIC state agencies. As with TANF and other state-based programs, eligibility requirements and benefits differ by state. According to the Food and Nutrition Service, in 2014, WIC operated through 1,900 local agencies in 10,000 clinic sites and in 50 state health departments, 34 Indian tribal organizations, the District of Columbia, and five territories including the Northern Mariana Islands, American Samoa, Guam, Puerto Rico, and the Virgin Islands. During fiscal year 2013, the number of women, infants, and children receiving WIC benefits each month averaged over 8.6 million per month (U.S. Department of Agriculture, 2014c).

Eligibility for WIC requires participants to receive an income at or below a level or standard set by the state agency or to be determined automatically income eligible based on participation in certain programs. In 2014–15, the maximum annual income level for a three-person family was $29,901 (U.S. Department of Agriculture, 2015a) and, as with other means-tested programs, the maximum allowable income is varies by family size. A state's income standard must be between 100 and 185 percent of the federal poverty guidelines. Some individuals are eligible for WIC due their eligibility for certain federal programs including

◆ Eligibility to receive SNAP benefits, Medicaid, or TANF
◆ Eligibility of certain family members to receive Medicaid or TANF

At the state's option, individuals may be eligible if they participate in certain state-specific programs (U.S. Department of Agriculture, 2015b).

According to the Department of Agriculture, WIC supplements participants' diets with specific nutrients. Different foods are provided to each category of participant. These foods include infant cereal, iron-fortified adult cereal, fruit or vegetable juice rich in vitamin C, eggs, milk, cheese, peanut butter, dried and canned beans/peas, and canned fish. Soy-based beverages, tofu, fruits and vegetables, baby foods, whole wheat bread, and other whole-grain options were recently added to better meet the nutritional needs of WIC participants. In recent years, WIC has strongly supported breastfeeding. Pregnant women and new WIC mothers are provided educational materials and support for breastfeeding through counseling and guidance. Further, WIC mothers who breastfeed receive a higher level of priority for program certification, a greater quantity and variety of foods than mothers who do not breastfeed, a longer certification period than non-breastfeeding mothers, one-to-one support through peer counselors and breastfeeding experts, and breast pumps and other aids to help support the initiation and continuation of breastfeeding (U.S. Department of Agriculture, 2014c).

Targeted to supplement and improve the nutritional needs of seniors in poverty, the current Meals on Wheels program began in 1972 as part of the federal Older Americans Act. The very first U.S.-based Meals on Wheels program, however, began in Philadelphia, PA, in 1954. Coordinated through the Meals on Wheels Association of America, in 2014 there were more than 5,000 senior nutrition programs in the United States providing in excess of one million meals every day and supported by nearly two million volunteers (*see* http://www.mowaa.org).

In some instances, meals are provided in the senior's home, whereas in other cases, meals are provided at a central location such as a senior center. An important and unintended benefit of the program is that seniors, many of whom are isolated, are provided daily contact with others. Volunteers who deliver meals to seniors are able to check on the elderly and ensure that all is fine with them.

Supplemental Security Income

Supplemental Security Income (SSI) was enacted in 1972 by combining three categorical programs that had been part of the Economic Security Act: Old Age Assistance, Aid to the Blind, and Aid to the Totally and Permanently Disabled. Prior to 1972, these three programs had been run by the states. With the creation of SSI, operations were transferred to the federal government. Recipients of SSI are also eligible for other social services including SNAP, Medicaid, assistance paying Medicare, and other social services.

Supplemental security income is a means-tested public assistance program; age is not an eligibility requirement. Potential clients include individuals over age sixty-five who have little or no income, those who are legally blind, those who with disability due to physical or mental impairment (including an emotional or learning problem), some people with visual impairment who do not meet the requirements for blindness, addicts and alcoholics in treatment, and children under age eighteen who have an impairment comparable to those that determine eligibility for adults. The 2014 resource limits (e.g., monthly income) were $2,000 for an individual/child and $3,000 for a couple (see http://www.ssa.gov/ssi/text-eligibility-ussi.htm).

In January 2014, there were 8.15 million SSI recipients who received an average benefit of $516 (Social Security Administration, 2014). Note that each benefit is different depending on the individual's circumstances. In 2014, the maximum federal SSI benefit rate was $721 for an individual and $1,082 for a couple (*see* http://www.ssa.gov/OACT/COLA/SSIamts.html). Note that SSI benefits do increase on an annual basis as a result of a cost of living adjustment (COLA). For example, in 2009, the SSI COLA was 5.8 percent (as a direct result of the 2008 economic crisis) and most recently in 2014, the COLA was 1.5 percent (*see* http://www.ssa.gov/OACT/COLA/SSIamts.html). Some states supplement the Federal SSI benefit with additional payments.

Legal Immigrants

One of the most significant changes introduced by the 1996 Welfare Reform Act was the sweeping elimination of legal immigrants from all public programs. Legal immigrants become eligible for public assistance only when they become citizens or have worked for forty calendar quarters (ten years). A public outcry led to the amendment to allow legal immigrants receiving SSI on or before August 26, 1996, to continue to receive payments. Yet this wasn't the case for all programs. The National Immigration Law Center (NILC) reports that the 1996 welfare reforms, ". . . cut most lawfully residing immigrant children from food stamp eligibility" (NILC, 2013). For example, approximately 300,000 legal immigrant children were removed from SNAP shortly after the 1996 welfare reforms. By 2002, persistent lobbying efforts opened the doors for some immigrant children to receive SNAP yet the NILC reported in 2013 that only 50 percent of eligible immigrant children were enrolled in the SNAP program (NILC, 2013). Ginsberg (1998, p. 192) suggests that the rationale behind this decisive move against immigrants is to force legal immigrants to seek and obtain citizenship. Until they are citizens, new immigrants are expected to support themselves or find assistance from private sources, including family or sponsors. As the current 2014 immigration reform debates continue, their ability to access federal programs remains fragile at best.

Earned Income Tax Credit

The Earned Income Tax Credit (EITC) is a tax credit for working families with low incomes. One of the Clinton Administration's major welfare initiatives, it was developed to stimulate work among the poor. The EITC is a federal income tax credit for low-income workers who are eligible for and claim the credit. The credit reduces the amount of tax an individual owes, and the tax may be returned in the form of a refund. The EITC is viewed as one of the most important antipoverty policies implemented over the past twenty-five years. In most cases, the EITC benefit does not affect other program benefits such as housing supplements, TANF, SNAP, Medicaid, and SSI.

Eligible working families, either with or without children, pay less federal income tax or receive a larger tax refund. To claim the EITC, families must meet certain rules. Income and family size determine the amount of the EITC. Prior to the June 2015 Supreme Court decision legalizing same sex marriage, same-sex couples in those states that recognized such marriages were treated as married for federal tax purposes and eligible for the EITC. Qualifying for the credit requires both the earned income and the adjusted gross income for 2014 to be less than the following amounts (Internal Revenue Service, 2015):

- ◆ $46,997 ($52,427 married filing jointly) with three or more qualifying children
- ◆ $43,756 ($49,186 married filing jointly) with two qualifying children
- ◆ $38,511 ($43,941 married filing jointly) with one qualifying child
- ◆ $14,590 ($20,020 married filing jointly) with no qualifying children

The maximum allowable tax credit for 2014 was set at

- ◆ $6,143 with three or more qualifying children
- ◆ $5,460 with two qualifying children
- ◆ $3,305 with one qualifying child
- ◆ $496 with no qualifying children

SUMMARY

This chapter has looked at poverty and provided information on just a few of the antipoverty and public assistance programs. Entire courses and books are devoted to this subject. Our purpose is to help you understand the nature of poverty in the United States in 2014 as well as to review some of the programs that are in place.

We can agree that poverty cuts across all races and ethnic groups, both genders, and all age groups. Indeed, more Whites are poor than members of any other group. Nevertheless, poverty rates reveal that some groups are especially vulnerable (Carter, 2000). Women, minorities, and children suffer disproportionately from poverty. One in six of all children are in poverty and one in four of children under age six.

No consensus exists about causes of poverty, and theories to explain it are diverse and controversial (O'Gorman, 2000). Proposed causes of poverty range from an individual's genetic makeup to deep, complicated structures of society. Also, considering the popularity of terms such as family empowerment, it is time to do more than use these terms and to address the long-term effects of such concepts and how they can be measured (Bartle, Counchonnal, Canda, & Staker, 2002). And as we stated, theories of poverty, while each is supported by its proponents' statistics, are clearly rooted in political and ideological beliefs.

We also recognize that 1996 was a pivotal year in redirecting the nation's 1960s War on Poverty as well as the role of the federal government in promoting antipoverty programs. Today, public programs are time limited with greater state discretion in imposing additional program limits and adding more stringent criteria. In general, a family is left to its own devices once it has exhausted its TANF sixty-month lifetime limit. Temporary Assistance for Needy Families represents a new direction in welfare programming that stresses employment and penalizes clients who do not work or are unable to meet program requirements on a consistent basis.

As social work professionals, what does this mean for us? The social worker's role in public assistance programs is not as clear as it once was. A visit to your local SNAP or TANF office reveals that few if any of the workers are professional social workers. The public may believe that social workers run these programs, but the reality is that we do not. The staff are generally called *eligibility workers*, not social workers; their educational degrees may require a bachelor's degree at the most, but often a two-year associate degree meets the educational requirement.

One of the ongoing historical parts of the social work profession's mission has been its work with and on behalf of the poor. Although they may not work directly in specific antipoverty programs, social workers do work in agencies and programs that engage the poor and those at risk of becoming poor. To that end, McPhee and Bronstein (2003) outline four critical implications for social workers:

1. Social workers are encouraged to find ways to include the opinions and wishes of program recipients in future changes and continued implementation of the program.

2. The common myths about the poor and women on governmental and state subsidy need to be identified and addressed based on evidence, not opinion.

3. Adequate resources need to be provided to frontline workers to assist them to do their jobs.

4. If TANF proponents are going to claim that it supports families, then the disproportionate concentration on work needs to be addressed, as in many ways this can be counterproductive to basic family reunification.

Poverty and its ravages can't be washed away by finding people jobs and wishing them well. Nor will it be eliminated by providing minimum wage jobs for women and children living in poverty because unfortunately, no matter how much effort is made to raise a family out of poverty, these types of efforts will never work (O'Gorman, 2002). Clients need to be linked with appropriate resources—they need professionals who understand the emotional and psychological toll that poverty takes and who can suggest how best to respond to this personal turmoil. Someone with a personal problem expects the best possible professional service from the social worker at the local mental health center. A patient in the hospital expects high-quality care from the hospital's social worker (Dziegielewski, 2013). Why should a poor person expect and receive anything less than quality services provided by experts who are compassionate and advocates?

An important question concerns the sixty-month limit set by TANF. What happens at the end of five years? Do we really believe that people without proper education who are forced into low-paying jobs will be self-sufficient within sixty months? And remember, a number of states have shorter time limits, some as short as twenty-four months. Where will these people go? Will they simply disappear? Of course not. They will remain in our communities—some more visible than others. Some people will say that they were given a chance and we shouldn't do anything else. But what will happen when the first child dies on the streets because a parent's TANF time expired? This question is extremely relevant because, for TANF, positive effects depend on improved income, not just the ability to increase employment (O'Gorman, 2002). What will happen when our country experiences an economic recession and jobs are not available?

The poor will always be part of our society, and we must have public policies in place that protect them rather than cause them harm. Social workers can and should take the lead in promoting just social policies that create opportunities for all people to achieve their full potential and gain economic independence.

FURTHER READINGS ON THEORIES ABOUT POVERTY
Culture of Poverty

Banfield, E. C., & Lewis, O. (1966). *The unheavenly city.* Boston: Little, Brown.

Moynihan, D. P. (1965). *The negro family: The case for national action.* Washington, DC: Office of Policy Planning and Research.

Eugenics

Jensen, A. R. (1969). How much can we boost IQ and scholastic achievement? *Harvard Educational Review, 39,* 1–23.

Shockley, W. (1976). Sterilization: A thinking exercise. In C. Bahema (Ed.), *Eugenics: Then and now.* Stroudsburg, PA: Doidon, Hutchinson and Ross.

Radical School

Gil, D. (1981). *Unraveling social policy.* Boston: Schenkman.

Piven, F., & Cloward, R. (1971). *Regulating the poor.* New York: Vintage.

Underclass

Auletta, K. (1982). *The underclass.* New York: Vintage.

Ricketts, E., & Sawhill, I. (1988). Defining and measuring the underclass. *Journal of Policy Analysis and Management, 7,* 316–325.

Wilson, W. J. (1987). *The truly disadvantaged.* Chicago: University of Chicago Press.

REFERENCES

Administration for Children and Families, Office of Family Assistance. (n.d.). *Tribal TANF.* Retrieved from http://www.acf.hhs.gov/programs/ofa/programs/tribal/tribal-tanf

Barker, R. L. (2003). *The social work dictionary* (5th ed.). Washington, DC: NASW Press.

Bartle, E. E., Couchonnal, G., Canda, E. R., & Staker, M.D. (2002). Empowerment as a dynamically developing concept for practice: Lessons learned from organizational ethnography. *Social Work, 47,* 32–44.

Birdnow, T. (2013, December 10). The antithesis of poverty. *Tea party nation* [Web log post]. Retrieved from: http://www.teapartynation.com/profiles/blog/show?id=3355873%3 ABlogPost%3A2726424

Bradshaw, T. (2007). Theories of poverty and anti-poverty programs in community development. *Community Development, 38.* 7–25.

Bruening, M. (July 28, 2014). Two theories of poverty. *Policy shop* [Web log post]. Received from http://www.demos.org/blog/7/28/14/two-theories-poverty

Carpenter, T. (2015, April 1). Senate moves bill containing GOP-backed welfare reforms. *Hutchnews.com.* Retrieved from http://www.hutchnews.com/news/local_state_news/ senate-moves-bill-containing-gop-backed-welfare-reforms/article_830f1a8d-a577- 559a-9e44-87e40a638270.html

Carter, J. (2000). Reducing poverty: It can be done. *New Perspectives Quarterly, 17,* 41–44.

Children's Defense Fund. (2014). *The state of America's children 2014 report.* Washington, DC: Author. Retrieved from: http://www.childrensdefense.org/child-research-data- publications/state-of-americas-children

Children's Defense Fund. (2015). *Ending child poverty now.* Retrieved from http://www.childrens defense.org/library/PovertyReport/EndingChildPovertyNow.html

Darby, M. R. (1996). Facing and reducing poverty. In M. R. Darby (Ed.), *Reducing poverty in America: Views and approaches* (pp. 3–12). Thousand Oaks, CA: Sage.

DeNavas-Walt, C., & Proctor, B. (2014). *Income and poverty in the United States: 2013* (Current Population Reports, P60-249, p. 44).Washington, D.C: U.S. Government Printing Office.

DiNitto, D. M., & Johnson, D. H. (2012). *Essentials of social welfare, politics and public policy.* Upper Saddle, NJ: Pearson Education, Inc.

Dziegielewski, S. F. (2013). *The changing face of health care social work: Opportunities and challenges for professional practice* (3rd ed.). New York: Springer.

Gibelman, M., & Schervish, P. H. (1997). *Who we are: A second look.* Washington, DC: NASW Press.

Gibelman, M. (2003). So how far have we come? Pestilent and persistent gender gap in pay. *Social Work, 48,* 22–32.

Ginsberg, L. (1998). *Conservatives social welfare policy: A description and analysis.* Chicago: Nelson-Hall.

Gray, K. F. (2014) *Characteristics of Supplemental Nutrition Assistance Program households: Fiscal year 2013.* Prepared by Mathematica Policy Research for the Food and Nutrition Service. Retrieved from http://www.fns.usda.gov/characteristics-supplemental-nutrition- assistance-program-households-fiscal-year-2013

Internal Revenue Service (2015). *2014 EITC income limits, maximum credit amounts and tax law updates.* Retrieved from http://www.irs.gov/Credits-%26-Deductions/Individuals/ Earned-Income-Tax-Credit/EITC-Income-Limits-Maximum-Credit-Amounts

Jansson, B. S. (1993). *The reluctant welfare state: A history of American social welfare policies* (2nd ed.). Pacific Grove, CA: Brooks/Cole.

Johnson, L. C., & Schwartz, C. L. (1988). *Social welfare: A response to human need.* Boston: Allyn and Bacon.

Landrine, H., & Klonoff, E. A. (1997). *Discrimination against women: Prevalence, consequences, remedies.* Thousand Oaks, CA: Sage.

Malloy, S. (2014, September 19). Boehner messes up Paul Ryan's image rehab: Attacks unemployed as lazy and unmotivated. *Salon.* Retrieved from http://www.salon.com/2014/09/19/boehner_messes_up_paul_ryans_image_rehab_attacks_unemployed_as_lazy_and_unmotivated

McPhee, D. M., & Bronstein, L. R. (2003). The journey from welfare to work: Learning from women living in poverty. *Affilia, 18*, 34–38.

National Immigration Law Center. (2013). *Nutrition assistance for immigrant children.* Retrieved from http://www. nilc.org/nutritionassistancechildren.html

Office of Family Assistance. (2012). *Characteristics and financial circumstances of TANF recipients, fiscal year 2010.* Retrieved from http://www.acf.hhs.gov/programs/ofa/resource/character/fy2010/fy2010-chap10-ys-final

O'Gorman, A. (2002). Playing by the rules and losing ground. *America, 187*(3), 12–16.

Segal, W., & Brzuzy, S. (1998). *Social welfare policy, programs, and practice.* Itasca, IL: Peacock.

Social Security Administration. (2014). *2014 annual report of the SSI program.* Retrieved from http://www.ssa.gov/OACT/ssir/SSI14/C_exec_sum.html

Terkel, A. (2014, July 14). Mitch McConnell's solution to soaring student debt: Less Yale, more for-profit schools. *Huff Post Politics.* Retrieved from http://www.huffingtonpost.com/2014/07/14/mitch-mcconnell-student-debt_n_5585521.html?1405371686

United Nations. (2000). *Millennium summit.* Retrieved from https://www.un.org/millennium goals/bkgd.shtml

U.S. Department of Agriculture. (2014a). *School breakfast program (SBP).* Retrieved from http://www.fns.usda.gov/sbp/school-breakfast-program-sbp

U.S. Department of Agriculture. (2014b). *Supplemental nutrition assistance program (SNAP).* Retrieved from http://www.fns.usda.gov/snap/facts-about-snap

U.S. Department of Agriculture. (2014c). WIC–The Special Supplemental Nutrition Program for Women, Infants and Children. Retrieved from http://www.fns.usda.gov/sites/default/files/WIC-Fact-Sheet.pdf

U.S. Department of Agriculture. (2015a). WIC income eligibility guidelines. Retrieved from http://www.fns.usda.gov/wic/wic-income-eligibility-guidelines

U.S. Department of Agriculture. (2015b). Women, infants, and children (WIC). Retrieved from http://www.fns.usda.gov/wic/about-wic-wic-glance

U.S. Department of Health and Human Services. Administration for Children and Families (n.d.). *Temporary assistance for needy families.* Retrieved from http://www.acf.hhs.gov/sites/default/files/assets/TANF%20final.pdf

U.S. Department of Health and Human Services. (2014). *2014 poverty guidelines.* Retrieved from http://aspe.hhs.gov/poverty/14poverty.cfm

Ventura, S., Hamilton, B., & Matthews, T. J. (2014). National and state patterns of teen births in the United States, 1940–2013. *National Vital Statistics Report, 63*(4). Hyattsville, MD: National Center for Health Statistics.

CHAPTER 8
CHILD WELFARE SERVICES

WITH A 50-PERCENT INCREASE SINCE 1950, CHILDREN CONSTITUTE A growing portion of the U.S. population. In 1995, over 70 million children under age eighteen made up 26.8 percent of the U.S. population (Baugher & Lamison-White, 1996, p. C-5); in 2002, this number rose to 72 million (Fields, 2003). In 2006, the number continued to rise to 73.7 million, and in 2013 it is estimated that 23.3 percent out of a population of 316,128,839 were under age eighteen (U.S. Census Bureau, 2013). In terms of population numbers, according to the U.S. and World Population Clock (updated October 5, 2014, at 18:57), this number is already outdated. The new total U.S. population was 319,025,352, and the number of children under age eighteen in 2014 reached 14.6 million (DeNavas-Walt & Proctor, 2014).

Births in the United States are declining. In 2011 there were 3,953,590 births, a 1-percent decrease from 2010. This is the lowest fertility rate ever reported. Furthermore, the fertility rate for teenagers aged fifteen to eighteen dropped by 8 percent from 2010 to 2011 (Martin et al., 2013). The number of births outside of marriage also declined in 2011, falling 3 percent from 2010 (Martin et al., 2013). In addition, the birth rate for teenage mothers reached a historic low in 2011, and this decrease remained consistent for all cultural and ethnic groups (Hamilton, & Ventura, 2012). This is very different from 2006, where for the first time in fourteen years the numbers of teen births actually rose (Reinberg, 2007).

What is very clear from these evolving birth patterns is that the traditional family structure is changing rapidly. When the population shift is superimposed on the changing family structure in U.S. households, it's apparent that the traditional family structure of two biological parents is dwindling. Also, the role of the father as both a single parent and primary caretaker is gaining increased attention (Coady, Hoy, & Cameron, 2014). In addition, there is an increased diversity in children's living arrangements that can be related to family structure (e.g., single parents, stepparents, adoptive parents, grandparents, or other caretakers such as relatives, friends, or significant others; Kreider & Ellis, 2011). As a result, supporting and caring for these millions of children, taking into account the limited resources and incomes that many caretakers have, is the single most important investment we can make in the future of our society. As the baby boomers continue to age, it should come as no surprise that over the next ten years, people now in their sixties will rely heavily on the children of today to keep the United States prosperous.

We cannot overestimate the importance of today's children to tomorrow's society. We can all agree that we need the best and brightest people leading our country. Don't you want competent and self-assured people in the labor force who can take over and move us beyond what has been accomplished? In 2012, the number of childhood deaths resulting from abuse and neglect totaled 1,640, which is about 100 fewer deaths than in 2008 (Children's Bureau, 2014, p. 2). The Children's Bureau is quick to note that these numbers are seen as underreporting because not all states submitted their data. But the bottom line remains: children are needlessly dying as a result of abuse and neglect. Certainly an appropriate and just goal is to end this type of injustice and plan for the future by helping to protect children from abuse through education and advocacy.

The importance of nurturing children is not a new idea. Indeed, a complex child welfare system exists to give children the opportunity to grow and reach their full potential. Karger and Stoesz (2010) have asserted, however, that child welfare programs and services are controversial because many people see them as an intrusion: "they sanction the intervention of human service professionals in family affairs that are ordinarily assumed to be private matters related to parental rights" (2010, p. 338). Furthermore, although these programs are designed to provide assistance to this vulnerable population, the lack of resources severely limits service assistance (National Association of Social Workers [NASW], 2012).

Most of us can remember being told that being a child should be fun. Many adults long to return to a simpler time in their lives when cares and responsibilities were few and far between. For many, Norman Rockwell's images of small-town America capture the ideal childhood. Television too has actively promoted the idea of families as caring groups always having fun, even during hard times. Older shows such as *Father Knows Best, Good Times, The Brady Bunch*, and *The Cosby Show* illustrated life in suburbia and the city within a happy and caring family. When outside help was required, it often came from extended family members, friends, neighbors, religious organizations, and even membership associations.

In this society we expect, and the media encourages us to expect, that no child will face the horrors of poverty, homelessness, abuse and neglect, and inadequate health care or live in an environment where crime, alcohol, tobacco, and drug abuse are the norm. This is a worthy goal, but we have to be careful because such an ambitious goal can sometimes be satisfied by simply denying that such problems exist. Few sponsors, if any, would want to be the ones to tell America that all is not well with its children. It is critical to know how many children do not have their needs adequately met (Southwell, 2009). But the simple fact is that all is not well with America's children. Even in the United States, considered one of the most advanced of the developed countries, for millions of children life is filled with turmoil. These children are repeatedly forced to face crises that may eventually lead to chaos and tragedy. In this chapter, we will look in depth at America's children. We will examine what life is like for many of them and explore the laws, programs, and services geared toward helping them. In addition, we will discuss how the public and voluntary child welfare systems work together. The role of the social worker in protecting and advocating for the child will be highlighted and concepts such as mandatory reporting explained.

CHILD WELFARE DEFINED

Let's begin by looking at how child welfare has been defined. *The Social Work Dictionary* defines child welfare as

> . . . programs and policies oriented toward the protection, care and healthy development of children. Within a national, state and local policy and funding framework, child welfare services are provided to vulnerable children and their families by public and non-profit agencies with the goals of ameliorating conditions that put children and families at risk; strengthening and supporting families so that they can successfully care for their children; protecting children from future abuse and neglect; addressing the emotional, behavioral, or health problems of children; and when necessary providing permanent families for children through adoption or guardianship (Barker, 2003, p. 69).

The child welfare system can be complex as it works to ensure child safety and well-being (Bearman, Garland, & Schoenwald, 2014). It encompasses a wide array of programs and policies that address the needs of children, youth, and families. Berzin, Thomas, and Cohen (2007) go so far as to say that involving the family and community in decision making for the best practices related to child welfare services is not just innovative—it is our standard for practice. Furthermore, fathers are often ignored in the current child welfare system even though research supports the active involvement that often is part of the family system (Coady et al., 2013). This type of inclusive definition was reflected in the writings of Linderman (1995), who emphasized that the formal organizational aspects of child welfare need to remain inclusive of the interrelated aspects of family and community action. His definition of child welfare characterizes it as both a public and a voluntary effort to coordinate seven interrelated objectives:

1. To protect and promote the well-being of children
2. To support families and seek to prevent problems that may result in neglect, abuse, and exploitation

3. To promote family stability by assessing and building on family strengths while addressing needs

4. To support the full array of out-of-home care services for children who require them

5. To take responsibility for addressing social conditions that negatively affect children and families, such as inadequate housing, poverty, chemical dependence, and lack of access to health care

6. To support the strengths of families whenever possible

7. To intervene when necessary to ensure the safety and well-being of children

When discussing child welfare organizations, Dobelstein (2002) omitted the voluntary sector and concluded that child welfare involved a broad range of public activities undertaken on behalf of children. Within child welfare these services can be viewed as supplementing and supporting family life and in some cases substituting for it (Crosson-Tower, 2012). Services provided involve a multitude of policy sectors including areas such as health, nutrition, education, and income maintenance. This is further supported by the need for programs to measure effectiveness and track the outcomes that support continued well-being from childhood through adolescence and into adulthood (Hook & Courtney, 2010).

The work of Kadushin and Martin (1988), who wrote a seminal textbook on child welfare, is important because they were among the first to clearly examine these services from a social work perspective. For them, "child welfare is concerned with the general well-being of all children. It encompasses any and all measures designed to protect and promote the bio-psycho-social development of children" (p. 1). Gil (1985) gave another historic and straightforward definition of child welfare: "In the simplest terms, as well as in a most profound sense, child welfare means conditions of living in which children can 'fare well,' conditions in which their bodies, minds, and souls are free to develop spontaneously through all stages of maturation" (p. 12).

Over the years, the definitions have changed slightly; some include public and private responsibilities and others do not, but all of these definitions of child welfare have several points in common. First, the child welfare system is firmly established within the public sector; whether or not private sector involvement occurs, it clearly will have a less prominent role. Second, child welfare policy is closely tied to and directly influenced by family policy. The importance of the family and community connectedness is always a central part of the integration. Third and probably most important is that all policies, services, and programs included in child welfare cover a broad range of interventions and services, but all efforts aim to improve child well-being. In this way the child's resilience and ability to cope are maximized and the child is provided with as safe a nurturing environment as possible, one that fosters positive growth and full development. Taking into account all of these commonalities, we define the child welfare system as the system of services and programs that protects, promotes, and encourages the growth and development of all children in order that they can achieve their full potential and function at their optimal level in their communities.

As child welfare services continue to develop, the expectation of clear outcomes and the use of performance measures continue to increase. This can be particularly problematic given the variety of programs and services available—all having the common goals of safety, permanency, and well-being, but with each program having numerous variations in how this is accomplished. Samples, Carnochan, and Austin (2013) recognized these differences and called for the implementation of flexibility in federal performance requirements that remain sensitive to local values and priorities as well as keeping in tune with all stakeholders involved in the delivery of child welfare services. It should come as no surprise that, similar to other areas of social service, this area of study struggles to bridge the practice/policy gap (Wulcyzn & Landsverk, 2014). This is particularly difficult in this field because of the variety of agencies, standards, and procedures.

AMERICA'S DIVERSE CHILDREN AND THEIR FAMILIES

The abuse and neglect of children cross all cultural and ethnic groups (Washington State Department of Health and Human Services, 2012). In the United States, minority children are now the majority, surpassing White children; immigrant children in particular are surpassing the other groups and have become the fastest growing population (U.S. Census Bureau, 2012). Although there are more White children than children of any other racial or ethnic group, population increases for Blacks and Hispanics have been far greater than for Whites (see chapter 7). The Hispanic population in the United States has grown quite dramatically, but it is important to note that these rates may be inflated. The term Hispanic is difficult to define. In the U.S. census Latinos can classify themselves as Hispanic, Black, or White; in other cases, they may be listed as both Hispanic and Black. Part of the growth in the Hispanic population may actually reflect resolution of this confusion as individuals switch affiliations.

In addition, according to Tyser, Scott, Readdy, and McCrea (2014), promoting resiliency in American Indian youth has never been more important. Because of the collective nature of their culture, developing and maintaining self-esteem are deeply embedded in their cultural system (Smokowski, Evans, Cotter, & Webber, 2014). For Native Americans, this places the probability of therapeutic success squarely in utilizing culturally based interventions (Garrett et al., 2014). With this assumption, it should come as no surprise that the Indian Child Welfare Act (ICWA) passed into Federal Law in 1978 remains central to the protection of Indian (Native American and Alaska Native) children and, in suspected cases of maltreatment, prohibits the removal of children or adoption of these children by public or private agencies without direct consultation and direction of the child's tribe and family (National Indian Child Welfare Association [NICWA], 2014).

Did You Know...More information related to the Indian Child Welfare Act is provided by the National Indian Child Welfare Association (NICWA). The NICWA is an excellent resource for clear, easy-to-read information related to Native American and Alaska Native children. Its section on frequently asked questions about ICWA will be an interesting and informative read for those wanting to know more about protecting the rights of Native American and Alaska Native children. Retrieved from http://www.nicwa .org/indian_child_welfare_act/faq/

Just as American children have become more diverse, so too have their families. The family is a critical institution in shaping and transmitting from generation to generation the values and rich traditions of culturally and ethnically diverse Americans. The kaleidoscope of families includes those whose roots are Anglo-European, Native Indian, African, Latino, Asian, and Middle Eastern, to mention a few. American families, whatever their ethnic heritage, are expected to respond to the expectations and norms of this society, even though many have very different cultural traditions, values, beliefs, norms, folkways, and mores. Some families hold their distinctive beliefs so strongly that they refuse to change; instead, they pass the same set of rigid expectations from one generation to the next. The key challenge for families is to balance the rich traditions and customs of their cultural heritage with the values and beliefs of the dominant society. If cultural competency is to truly be assessed, oppression and perceptions of inferiority need to be addressed to avoid systematic biases applied to certain groups (Sawrikar & Katz, 2014). For example, recognition of systemic biases is especially important for immigrant children who may have increased difficulty obtaining food or health care based on negative perceptions related to the immigrant status of their parents (Johnson-Motoyama, 2014).

Family structures are also becoming more diverse. No longer do families mirror the traditional stereotype of a two-parent household in which the father works and the mother maintains the home. Nontraditional families are growing in number, and it is no longer uncommon for children to be raised in a single-parent household or by lesbian, gay, or transgendered parenting couples. And, as stated earlier, although the number of births is decreasing, increased divorce rates have fueled an increase in the number of single-parent households. Regardless of the type of family or whether the parents are heterosexual, research does appear to suggest that two-parent families appear to be more successful in child rearing (Mallon, 2008). For many couples raising children, however, one parent staying at home with the child has clearly become a luxury because both parents often work outside of the home. For so many of these parents, working outside the home, and in some cases having a second job, is not a choice—it is a necessity.

Divorce rates are increasing; in particular, more children of first marriages are seeing their parents split up than ever before (Copen, Daniels, Vespa, & Mosher, 2012). In the thirty-two years between 1960 and 1992, the number of divorces tripled from 400,000 to 1,200,000 annually, with nearly 50 percent of all marriages ending in divorce (Lindsey, 1994, p. 73). In 2013, the United States was listed as number 6 of the top ten countries with the highest divorce rates. Although these numbers have been challenged, the rate appears to remain at 50 percent for first marriages ending in divorce, 67 percent for second marriages, and 74 percent for third marriages (DivorceRate, 2014). What is of most concern about these high rates of divorce is the effect they can have on children under the age of eighteen (see the activity below). Robbins (2008) reports that, although some children do just fine and adapt to the divorce, some of the problems that become more likely include abuse and neglect, health problems, behavioral health and emotional problems, crime and drug abuse, suicide, poor school performance, less success in school-related goals and activities, and growing up in poverty.

Activity...Discussion of factors. Following is a complete list of the circumstances Robbins (2008) cites as affecting children after their parents' divorce. Do you agree with these and are there any others that you believe should be added? Be sure to say why you agree or why you don't and what supporting information you have on which to base your opinions.
According to research, children of divorced parents:
* *Are more often involved in abuse or neglect*
* *Have more health, behavioral, and emotional problems*
* *Are more involved in crime and drug abuse*
* *Have more incidents of suicide*
* *Perform poorly in reading, spelling, and math*
* *Are more likely to repeat a grade, drop out, and be unsuccessful at completing college degrees*
* *Will likely earn less as adults than children of intact families*
* *Lose their virginity at a younger age*
* *Are less likely to have children of their own*
* *Are more likely to divorce as adults*
* *Are more likely to grow up in a level of poverty*

Have you ever wondered why so many people worry about the growing number of single-parent households? Why does it matter whether a family has a single parent or two parents? The primary reason is that two-parent families usually have a greater income and therefore greater resources with which to carry out their parenting obligations and responsibilities. Simply stated, by pooling their income, two parents have more money for the family to spend on goods and services. Underlying this concept is the fact that most single parents are women, who have income levels much lower than average. Although fathers are taking a more active role in families, the parent primarily responsible for the care of the child generally remains the mother. Involving fathers and helping them to understand the importance of their influence on the child can be central to increasing interactions and relationships (Storhaug, 2013), thereby reducing the pressure on the mother as a single parent. Further, when a child lives in a two-partner family or, in the case of a divorced or missing father, when the other partner is more involved, this supportive relationship allows for more flexibility in child care and supervision. With two adults available, one parent can take a break when the relationship gets too stressful, and whether taking turns or caring for children jointly, more nurturing parent-child time is available. The single parent often has no one to help ease the child-care burden. Facing daily problems alone and having to live on one income can be frustrating.

A third significant development in the changing family structure is the rise in blended families. A **blended family** is one in which the primary caretakers did not give birth to one or more of the children who live in the household. Such families are most often the result of divorce and remarriage. With the high rate of American divorce and lifestyle adjustment, blended families are becoming more common. These families often face a difficult task because supportive relationships may need to be developed before they can be nurtured. Becoming a blended family requires adjustment because members may enter and leave the family at various times throughout their lives. These adjustments intensify the need to establish and maintain family unison and support. Although all family systems need constant negotiation to maintain equilibrium, blended families face the added struggle of keeping their balance as family members come and go.

The kind of family situation regarded as ideal is often shaped by a **political lens**. Think about political candidates and their campaign rhetoric and advertisements. How often have you seen the family play a starring role in a local, state, or national election? Why have children and families become such hot political items? Two reasons come to mind immediately:

1. Every human being was once a child: Having been a child and had experiences that influenced the way you think and feel about things as you grew up helps raise your consciousness in this area. Most of us identify with

children's issues simply because of our own experiences. All of us had positive and negative childhood experiences. Most of us cherish the good times and wish we could have avoided the bad ones. Few, if any, adults believe it is in a child's best interest to suffer physical or emotional pain. Therefore, social workers and other professionals will continue to support and encourage programs and services that prevent and alleviate unfair treatment of all vulnerable groups (Eamon, 2008). Because children are considered a vulnerable population, most adults agree that all children should be protected and have a safe environment in which to grow. Adults are responsible for ensuring that children are shielded from various risks.

2. Everyone has a family: Just as all of us were children once, we were all raised in some kind of family. Our families probably differed vastly. Some people had two parents; others came from single-parent homes. Some people were raised with siblings and others without. Some were raised in foster homes or were adopted; others had aunts, uncles, or other relatives as their primary caretakers; and for some, institutions played the family role. No matter what our family background, our experiences mean we have strong feelings about what families should be like.

THE RIGHTS OF CHILDREN

Children are dependent on their parent(s) and as minors their rights are connected to those of their parent(s). From this perspective there are two counterbalancing forces at play. On one hand, we recognize that children generally are not able to make mature decisions. This is not a negative statement about young people, but rather refers to their inexperience. For this reason, children's rights are limited and critical decisions about and responsibility for their lives rests, not with them, but with their caregivers. On the other hand, we also recognize that children need protection—sometimes from their own caretakers. As a result, we have established a complex system of child protective services (see box 1).

Thus, the interesting history of children's rights for the most part reflects ambivalence. From a legal standpoint children are treated differently from adults. Children can face *status offenses*, that is, crimes based on status—in this case, age. For example, a child can be arrested or detained for drinking alcohol, smoking cigarettes, being truant, or being a runaway. An adult cannot be arrested merely for

---

Did You Know...The terms runaway, throwaway, and push-out describe youths (under age 18), who no longer live at home with their legal guardians. A runaway is a person running away from home. A throwaway is a person forced or thrown out of home by the caretaker. A push-out is a person who with the agreement of the caretaker decides it is in everyone's best interest that he or she leaves the home.

Box 1. Child Fact Sheet

Child Welfare in the United States
Number of children who are victims of abuse and neglect: 666,298
Number of children in foster care: 396,177
Number of children adopted from foster care: 50,460
Number of grandparents raising grandchildren: 2,732,099

Youth at Risk in the United States
Averaged freshman high school graduation rate: 78.2%
Percent of 16- to 19-year-olds unemployed: 23.3%
Number of juvenile arrests: 1,216,481
Number of children and teens in juvenile residential facilities: 81,015
Ratio of cost per prisoner to cost per public school pupil: 2.4 to 1
Number of children and teens killed by firearms: 2,694

smoking or drinking (unless doing so causes a public disturbance) or for running away from home or being truant.

The overriding principle of **parens patriae** (which is Latin for father of the people)—under which children can become wards of the state—guided interpretations of children's rights. This principle supported creation of a broad range of juvenile services including parent-child relationships (Crosson-Tower, 1998, p. 270). Taking this basic position, child advocates were able to argue that children should be viewed in a different light from adults and offered rehabilitation rather than punishment (see Figures 1a, 1b, and 1c).

In 1899, the first juvenile court was established in Chicago based on the principle of parens patriae and the belief that children could be rehabilitated, which required a legal system far different from the punishment-based adult system. By 1925, all but two states—Maine and Wyoming—had juvenile courts; by 1945 all states had such courts. Prosecution took a back seat to treatment as the primary focus of the juvenile justice system. Hearings were closed to the public to protect the child's right to confidentiality, and all juvenile legal records were sealed once the child reached the legal age of maturity, generally age eighteen. The juvenile court operated very informally. Attorneys were rarely provided for child offenders, and trial by jury and the right to appeal a decision were not available options. In these courtrooms hearsay evidence was admitted. Remember, the court's purpose was twofold: (1) to identify the problem and (2) to develop and implement an appropriate treatment plan.

Figures 1a, b, c: These photographs were developed in an Arts Outreach project for teenage mothers. The program, "My Life, My Lens, My Child," was part of an effort to help the mothers to finish high school. The program, staffed by social workers and teachers, taught photography skills, provided enrichment, and offered a positive school experience. The mothers photographed their children in various settings and created collages.

The juvenile court changed dramatically as a result of U.S. Supreme Court decisions in the 1960s. Juveniles were given many of the legal protections enjoyed by adults. Courts were required to allow attorneys to be present, witnesses could be cross-examined, defendants had the right to refuse to incriminate themselves, and guilty decisions (or, in some states, *not innocent* decisions) had to meet the legal standard of reasonable doubt.

In recent years, as violent juvenile crime has worsened, people have begun to ask whether children should face some of the same penalties as adults. Horrific crimes committed by children have left many people in shock. Two young boys, eight and nine years old, in Chicago, Illinois, murdered a young girl in order to ride her bicycle; two teenagers in Arkansas shot and killed schoolmates; another teenager walked into a school hallway and indiscriminately murdered his junior high school peers. The Chicago youth were released to their parents because state law forbade the incarceration of a child under age ten. These cases sparked a national debate over whether teens should be tried in adult courts and, if found guilty, should serve their sentences in adult prisons or even be subjected to the death penalty. Is there an answer? At what age do we stop trying to rehabilitate young people? As you have probably guessed there are no clear-cut answers to these questions.

In a nutshell, children historically have had few rights, and there has been little agreement on what further rights, if any, they should be granted. In the past, the courts primarily defined children's rights with regard to criminal proceedings against them. In addition, children have the right to financial support and education (Gustavsson & Segal, 1994, p. 4, 6). Today, the United Nations continues to bring the rights of children to the forefront. The United Nations Convention on the Rights of the Child adopted in 1989 a declaration of children's rights. By 2003, 192 countries had formally ratified this act, and the two remaining countries, the United States and Somalia, had announced agreement to do so (Convention on the Rights of the Child, 2003).This important declaration is very specific in identifying the issues facing children (United Nations, 1989):

- ◆ Preamble: . . . Childhood is entitled to special care and assistance. . . . The child . . . should grow up in a family environment, in an atmosphere of happiness, love, and understanding. . . . The child, by reason of his physical and mental immaturity, needs special safeguards and care, including appropriate legal protection.
- ◆ Article 3(1): In all actions concerning children . . . the best interests of the child shall be a primary consideration.
- ◆ Article 18(1): . . . Both parents have common responsibilities for the upbringing and development of the child. Parents or, as the case may be, legal guardians, have the primary responsibility for the upbringing and development of the child.
- ◆ Article 19(1): State parties (government) shall take appropriate legislative, administrative, social, and educational measures to protect the child from all forms of physical or mental violence, injury or abuse, neglect or negligent treatment, maltreatment or exploitation, including sexual abuse, while in the care of parent(s), legal guardian(s) or any other person who has the care of the child.

THE DESIGN OF THE AMERICAN CHILD WELFARE SYSTEM

Formal child welfare programs and services are found in both public and private settings. Government programs—local, state, and federal—are augmented by both for-profit and nonprofit agencies. In addition, privatization or contracting with nongovernmental agencies for the provision of services continues to grow as these programs are either state or federally funded (Hubel, Schreier, Hansen, & Wilcox, 2013). Together, these programs form a complex system that starts with prenatal care and ranges to opportunities for teenagers. As we start this section, look carefully at Table 1, which provides a snapshot of children most at risk of needing services from our welfare system. Programs are varied, but they can generally be categorized as child protective services, family preservation, out-of-home services, and other services.

Child Protective Services

Child protective services (CPS) is probably the best known as well as the most controversial children's program. The intent of CPS is to protect children from abusive situations in order that they can grow and develop (see box 2). We've all heard stories about abusive CPS workers responding to unfounded charges, taking children from their parents, breaking up families, and ruining the lives of countless people. In fact, the CPS worker investigates each allegation of abuse or neglect and determines whether the charges are founded or unfounded. A case is opened if the investigation demonstrates that abuse or neglect is indeed occurring. A child is removed from the home only if his or her life is in immediate danger. Neglect, however, when it occurs during critical periods in a child's life can have long-term effects on normative development that may extend across the life span (Boyce & Maholmes, 2013).

Table 1. America's Most Vulnerable Children: A Snapshot

Numbers (2011)	
Estimated referrals of possible child abuse and neglect	3,426,000
Children substantiated/indicated as abused or neglected	676,569
Children who died as a result of abuse or neglect	1,570
Children living in out-of-home care	400,540
Children adopted from the public foster care system	50,516
Children waiting to be adopted	104,236
Children living in poverty	16,134,000
Children living in low-income families	32,678,000
Percentages (2011)	
National poverty rate children in low-income families	200%
National poverty rate	15%
National poverty rate for children under age 18	21.98%
National poverty rate for children under age 6	24.5%

Source: Child Welfare League of America. (2013). *National Fact Sheet 2013*. Retrieved from http://www.cwla.org/advocacy/2013Factsheets.htm

Name: Angelo McClain, PhD, LICSW

Place of residence: Washington, DC, and Boston, Massachusetts

College/university degrees: West Texas A&M University, BSW; University of Texas Arlington, MSW; Boston College School of Social Work, PhD

Present position: Chief executive officer, National Association of Social Workers

Previous work experience:

Commissioner, Massachusetts Department of Children and Families

VP and executive director, Value Options New Jersey

VP, Network Management and Regional Operations, Massachusetts Behavioral Health Partnership

What do you do in your spare time? I enjoy time with my family and friends, playing board games, and reading for pleasure. I also like biking on the weekend with my wife.

Why did you choose social work as a career? I was always interested in helping people. My mom said that we should make time to help others. I was often the kid in school and on sports teams who helped my classmates and teammates deal with their personal issues. At my final football game in high school (20 tackles and 3 touchdowns), a scout offered me a college scholarship on the spot. When he asked me what I might like to major in, I asked if there was a degree for helping people. He said that social work would be a good thing for me to study.

What is your favorite social work story? Belinda, a parent I was working with in Boston in 1988, had three children and an addiction problem. Although she tried her best, her personal problems forced me one day to give her a final warning about finding a different home for her children. On my next visit, I was greeted by an angry crowd from the neighborhood and found Belinda sitting alone. She knew that I needed to take her children into custody that day and said that she "hid them." Fortunately, she eventually brought her children out of hiding and the crowd dispersed. That weekend Belinda suffered through a cold turkey detox and I was able to get her into a substance abuse recovery program the next week. A year later, her children were back at home and we were able to close her case. When I made one last home visit, she asked to videotape that session and wanted to discuss how our relationship had evolved from distrust to trust during our working together. Three years later I bumped into Belinda and found out that she had a job, her kids were doing well, and that she had been clean since she regained custody. I also learned that she was a volunteer at a health clinic where she showed the video of our final meeting to all of the mothers she was trying to help, encouraging them to trust their social worker (if they had one).

What would be the one thing you would change in our community if you had the power to do so? Raise expectations for vulnerable young people. In my many jobs, I have tried to encourage youth to think beyond their current circumstances. When I was leaving my job as child welfare commissioner, during a farewell party the youth held in my honor, a young graduate reintroduced herself. She told me that, when she was in the child welfare system, I met her briefly and said "we expect that you are going to make something of yourself and have a good life." She told me that knowing that we believed in her made a huge difference. Today, she's a second year MSW student and a BSW social worker, making a difference for others like her. We need to tell our youth who don't have advantages that they matter in this world, and then do what we can to help them see themselves fulfilling their dreams.

Neglect, although chronic in nature, can also end in death and similar to physical abuse should be included in prevention efforts (Damashek, Nelson, & Bonner, 2013). An open case may receive direct services from the agency or from other contract agencies, such as a family service agency. The case is reviewed by CPS staff and is closed once all goals are achieved. All states provide some form of CPS. In 1962, a study of battered children in hospitals recommended that suspected cases be

---

Box 2. The Beginning of CPS: The Case of Mary Ellen

In 1873, Mrs. Etta Angell Wheeler, a church visitor in New York City, learned from people in a neighborhood about a nine-year-old girl, Mary Ellen Wilson, who had been whipped and left alone for hours on end. Neighbors in her apartment building heard the child's cries time and again. The New York City Department of Charities had placed Mary Ellen in this home when she was eighteen months old. There had been no follow-up by the agency to assess the placement. Mrs. Wheeler sought help from a number of charitable organizations and the police to protect Mary Ellen, but no agency was willing to intervene and no CPS organization existed. She turned for help to Mr. Henry Bergh, president of the New York Society for the Prevention of Cruelty to Animals. The society intervened with court action and Mary Ellen was removed from the home.

The court found the home to be abusive. The foster mother, Mrs. Mary Connolly, was arrested and found guilty of assault. The court decided that Mary Ellen was to move to a group home, but Mrs. Wheeler asked that the child be placed in her care. Mary Ellen moved in with Mrs. Wheeler's mother and stayed with her until her death. Within a few months of the reported abuse, the New York Society for the Prevention of Cruelty to Children was founded, the first such organization in the world (Watkins, 1990).

reported so that protective measures could be taken. By 1966 all states had passed legislation concerning abuse (Lindsey, 1994, p. 92).

As of 2012, approximately 3.4 million referrals of child abuse and neglect were received, involving approximately 6.3 million children (U.S. Department of Health and Human Services, 2013a). For the forty-six states considered in the report, 62 percent of the received reports of child abuse and neglect were screened in and the remaining 38 percent were screened out because they did not meet the state's standards for investigation. More than half of these reports (58.7%) were submitted by professionals who are termed *mandatory reporters,* such as teachers, police officers, legal staff, and social service staff workers. Nonprofessional reporting, which made up approximately 18 percent of the reports, came from sources including parents, family and other relatives, friends, neighbors, and other interested individuals. There was also a percentage (23.3%) of the reports listed as other or non-classified because the sources of the reports were anonymous. Children in the first year of life had the highest rate of victimization. Boys accounted for nearly 49 percent of the victims and girls were at 51 percent (U.S. Department of Health and Human Services, 2013a). Based on reporting strategy and other factors, the numbers are not an exact match. A second set of estimates included in the Adoption and Foster Care Analysis and Reporting System (AFCARS) report as of September 30, 2012, changed somewhat; boys were reported slightly higher at 52 percent (207,947) and girls slightly lower at 48 percent (189,113) (U.S. Department of Health and Human Services, 2013c).

According to the Children's Defense Fund, infants and toddlers are the age group most vulnerable to child abuse and constitute the largest group entering foster care. In 2013 alone the Children's Defense Fund advocacy centers served more than 290,000 children; of these, 62 percent were involved in sexual abuse cases and 90 percent knew their perpetrator (National Children's Alliance, 2014). Maltreatment categories typically included neglect, medical neglect, physical abuse, sexual abuse, and psychological maltreatment.

> *Did You Know...Neglect is maltreatment through the failure to provide needed, age-appropriate care. There are numerous types of neglect including: Physical neglect, emotional neglect, medical and dental neglect, educational neglect, inadequate supervision and exposure to violent environments (Centers for Disease Control and Prevention, 2015).*

Family Preservation Services

Family preservation services (FPS) are short-term family-focused social services that are designed to stabilize troubled families. Family preservation services can vary, but what all programs share is the focus on keeping children in the home and providing family-based intensive social services. The goal of family preservation is to prevent child removal from the parental home with the expectation that direct services may avoid the need for out-of-home placement, allowing the family to stay together and strengthen family bonds (Tracy, 2008). One type of intensive family preservation that includes smaller caseloads, shorter duration of services, and twenty-four-hour availability of staff is referred to as intensive family preservation services (IFPS; Department of Children and Families, 2012). The IFPS is a special type of family preservation programming that provides these intensive services on a time-limited basis.

Gaining in popularity in the 1970s and 1980s, these services received a boost in 1980 with the passage of the Adoption Assistance and Child Welfare Act (P.L. 96–272). The 1980 act called for reasonable efforts to be made to keep children within their families and to minimize family disorder. The Convention on the Rights of the Child (2003) identified important issues for children. This convention ensured that the rights of children are protected in the areas of health care, education, legal and civil services, and provision of social services. In FPS/IFPS, the support services work is intensive, and although programs can vary in content and delivery, it is not unusual for the child serviced to receive anywhere from six to ten hours of direct worker-family contact each week. The typical case requires four to twelve weeks of contact, and with IFPS, a worker's caseload can range from two to six families, providing twenty-four-hour-a-day accessibility.

Did You Know…The Department of Health and Human Services has a 2013 resource guide titled **Preventing Child Maltreatment and Promoting Well-being: A Network for Action** *(https://www.childwelfare.gov/pubpdfs/2013guide.pdf). There are numerous other resources that can be retrieved from the Child Welfare Information Gateway, https://www.childwelfare.gov/preventing*

Out-of-Home Services

Out-of-home services are programs for children no longer living with their biological or legal guardians, whose parental rights have been or may be terminated. Typical out-of-home programs are foster care, residential care, and adoption.

Foster Care

Children enter into the foster care system because they are unable to get the care they need in their parent's or guardian's home. Removal can be based on numerous factors stemming from abuse and neglectful living conditions or state-of-care (Zill & Bramlett, 2014).

The Social Work Dictionary defines foster care as physical care for children "who are unable to live with their natural parents or legal guardians" (Barker, 2003). The goals of foster care include (1) maximum protection for the child, (2) permanency, and (3) family preservation. Foster care is generally organized through state or county social services and services may be provided within foster family homes, residential group homes, or institutions (Everett, 2008).

In 1997 the Adoption and Safe Families Act (ASFA; Public Law 105-89, 1997) was passed with the intention of addressing some of the preexisting problems in the foster care system related to the adoption of special needs children, and later its interpretation emphasized the importance of keeping families together. Thereafter states were expected to implement ASFA with emphasis on safety, permanency, and well-being of children who are found to be abused and neglected. In doing this, ASFA outlined the need for evaluation of the safety of children in foster care and the need for the measurement of child well-being. From this perspective, well-being is a multidimensional construct involving the child's overall functioning levels in terms of health, mental health, and education (Jacobs, Bruhn, & Graf, 2008). Therefore, if protection is needed to ensure the child's safety, a child may need to be placed in a foster home temporarily.

Immediate placement decisions may be needed if at the start of a CPS investigation the worker assesses that the child's life is in imminent danger. This decision is never made lightly as every effort is made to keep families together whenever possible. If the child is to be removed, however, the family is entitled to a court hearing, in most states within twenty-four to seventy-two hours of the time of removal if the child was removed without a court order. In other cases, placement may occur after a court hearing if a CPS investigation finds that this action is in the best interests of the child. Any placement must be in the least restrictive setting (see box 3). For example, a foster home is less restrictive than a residential treatment center; placement with a relative is less restrictive than removal to a nonbiological foster home.

Children in foster care are provided with certain protections including the following:

◆ A detailed written plan that describes the appropriateness of the placement, the services to be provided to the child, and a plan for achieving permanence.

◆ Periodic case review at least once every six months, although a jurisdiction may review a case more often.

◆ A state inventory of children who have been in care for more than six months in order to track these children and the goals related to their placement.

Box 3. Myths and Facts about Out-of-Home Placements

Myth: Foster care is in the best interests of children who have known the hurt of abuse and neglect.

Fact: In some cases, when the child is at great risk, removal from the home is necessary, but it is not necessarily the solution. The devastating norm for foster children is multiple moves, extended stays, and the lack of stable permanent family ties.

Myth: Foster care is principally a problem of poor and minority families.

Fact: Problems leading to abuse and neglect know no race or class boundaries.

Myth: Most children in foster care are placed there because of physical or sexual abuse.

Fact: More than half of child removals are for neglect.

Myth: Child abuse is on the rise.

Fact: Although the number of reports has increased, the evidence does not clearly substantiate that the actual incidence is on the rise. The growing number of reports may be a result of the public's growing awareness of child abuse and of resources to contact.

Myth: Parents whose children are removed from the home do not want their children, do not deserve their children, and cannot or will not change their behavior.

Fact: Experts working with troubled families find that their problems are more extreme versions of similar issues confronting any family. Troubled families often lack resources, knowledge, and skills that most take for granted. Most parents want their children and really want to be good parents. Proper help can benefit many families, but it must be timely.

Myth: Child protective service workers are well-trained professionals but have little authority to protect children.

Fact: The child protective service worker position is an entry-level job requiring minimal education. Most states do not require education in social work and allow a person to work in this position with a degree in music, math, or other non-human-service disciplines. Caseloads are usually high, pay and morale low, and employee turnover high. Child protective service workers have a wide range of authority, including the power to remove a child from a home, in some instances without supervisor or court approval (Edna McConnell Clark Foundation, n.d.).

- ◆ Procedural safeguards that involve parental input in the development of case plans.
- ◆ Reunification or permanency planning services, programs that include day care, homemaker services, counseling, parent education, adoption services, and follow-up (Everett, 2008).

For the most part, all states are similar in that most children in foster care are placed in foster family homes (Everett, 2008). As of July 2003, the Department of Children and Families in the State of Illinois estimated that 20,508 children were in substitute care. In 2012, this number decreased and only an estimated 15,000 children were in substitute care in the state of Illinois (Voices for Illinois Children, 2013). This decreasing number has been credited to early intervention efforts and permanency services such as adoption. According to the National Child Abuse and Neglect Data System, approximately 794,000 children were found to be victims of child abuse and neglect in 2007, and this resulted in about 3.8 million children needing preventive services. Furthermore, an estimated 271,000 children received foster care services and, as a result of assessment and intervention, preventive services were provided (U.S. Department of Health and Human Services, 2009).

How are foster parents selected? What is their motivation—money? What about reports that children in foster homes are often subjected to more abuse? Despite the few cases and problems that make the press, for many foster parents there is a calling and a true desire to help the children they serve. Most people choose to be foster parents because of their love for children. Taking in children for the money does not sound like a lucrative proposition because this twenty-four-hour commitment can take extreme time and energy.

We need to keep in mind that children in foster care are coming from terrible home situations. Because permanency planning interventions are preferred, only those children in the most unbearable situations are removed. Most foster children are burdened by a unique set of complex problems that requires understanding and compassion. Being a foster parent is not easy, and it does require a special person. At times foster parents choose to adopt the children placed in their homes. Recent evidence suggests that adoption of children in foster care provides socioeconomic advantages for the child as well as less cost to the public for children without the possibility of being reunited with their biological families (Zill & Bramlett, 2014).

Residential Care

Residential group care may also be termed institutional care and generally takes place in a facility setting apart from the natural parents or legal guardians. Residential settings can include residential treatment centers, state hospitals, detention centers, runaway shelters, and halfway houses. All of these facilities provide highly supervised or specialized twenty-four-hour residential care.

Did You Know…The first residential program for children was established in 1729 in New Orleans. The program was developed by Ursuline nuns to care for children orphaned as a result of the battle with Native Americans at Natchez.

A number of trends in residential care have been consistent over time:

- The number of residential facilities is increasing although the actual number of youth in care has declined.
- The two main types of new facilities are juvenile delinquent centers and mental health centers.
- The average number of children in facilities has declined to fewer than thirty per facility.

Residential programs are also available for children who no longer live with their legal caretakers. Typically such programs are shelters that provide temporary housing and counseling. The purpose of the runaway shelter is to get youths off the streets, provide protection, and attempt to reunite children with their families. Social service providers recognize the importance of getting runaways off the streets and into services as quickly as possible to avoid problems related to theft, drugs, prostitution, or pornography (see the activity below).

Activity...Contact your local runaway shelter and ask about the rules of admission and length of stay. Ask what happens to youths who leave the shelter but do not return home.

A state-established limit on the length of time that young people may reside in shelters generally restricts these settings to homeless youths. Some programs require parental consent for children to remain in shelters. What happens to youths whose parents do not grant permission for them to remain in the program? And some programs do not allow disruptive youths or youths with mental health problems to enter shelters. What types of community programs, if any, are available for these youths?

Adoption

The Social Work Dictionary defines adoption as "accepting and treating a child legally as though born into the family." (Barker, 2003). Adoption creates a "legal family for children when the birth family is unable or unwilling to parent" (Barth, 1995, p. 48). For example, in 2011 there were 61,000 children waiting to be adopted (U.S Department of Health and Human Services, 2012).

Massachusetts is credited with being the first state to enact an adoption law in 1851 (Cole, 1985, p. 639), although some cite Mississippi, in 1846, and Texas, in 1850, as having earlier adoption statutes (Crosson-Tower, 1998, p. 356). Whichever state was first, there is consensus that the Massachusetts legislation served as the model for other states (Crosson-Tower, 1998, p. 639; Kadushin & Martin, 1988, p. 535). By 1929 all states had enacted some form of adoption law.

During the nineteenth and much of the twentieth century most children in need of homes lived in orphanages. Young people were placed in orphanages for any number of reasons, including having poor parents who couldn't afford to raise them, having been born to unwed mothers, or having no parents because of death or abandonment (Crosson-Tower, 1998, p. 357).

Charles Loring Brace, a minister and organizer of the Children's Aid Society in New York City, led one of the more compelling child welfare efforts of the nineteenth century. Brace developed what became known as the Orphan's Train, through which some 50,000 to 100,000 urban orphans were placed on Midwestern and Western farms (Quam, 1995, p. 2575). The children, picked up on the streets of New York City, were put on a wagon train heading west. In town after town, city after city, the train would stop and put the youths up for adoption. Brace (1872) believed that moving waifs off city streets, away from the temptations of urban life, to more rural, tranquil lives of work and family, would allow them to be prosperous and productive.

The Orphan's Train was a manifestation of the nation's prevailing belief, no less strong today, that children should live in wholesome environments where caretakers can provide for their needs. Remember the basic child welfare principle: in the best interests of the child. Brace's program and other child-saving programs, including orphanages, were built on this ideal.

Today, adoption takes place in many different ways. These include placing children through child placement agencies and through direct agreements between two parties sanctioned by the courts.

Agency-based adoption occurs in government, nonprofit, and for-profit family welfare settings. It entails a rigorous and time-consuming process, which generally includes the following steps:

- ◆ Identification of suitable children ensures that all children in need of adoptive homes are included.
- ◆ Freeing for placement is the legal process by which custody of the child is removed from one set of parents in order that it can be assigned to the adoptive parents.
- ◆ Preparation for adoption involves working with the child before adoption to prepare him for his new family. Potential adoptive parents are closely scrutinized by the agency to ensure they have the resources needed to raise a child in a loving, caring environment.
- ◆ Selection of adoptive parents is conducted by the agency after close review of applications and supporting materials. The agency's goal is to match a child with the adoptive parents who can best meet his or her unique needs.

♦ Placement with an adoptive family is characterized by many social workers as one of the most exciting days for worker, family, and child. It is a time
of joy as the new family begins its life together. Everyone involved often
sheds tears!

Post-placement services include a variety of agency-based supports to the family as it makes the transition to a new system of relations. By placing a child with
a specific family, the agency is affirming that the placement is in the best interests
of the child. To increase the likelihood of success, the agency offers the family continuing supports ranging from individual and family counseling and support
groups to social worker home visits. Although the exact types of intervention may
differ, within the home visit the target of intervention is generally characterized as
child and family focused (Cook & Sparks, 2008). These home visits can support the
parent by providing education, training, and information that help the adjustment
process. Again, although the agency wants as few disruptions as possible with the
adoption, sometimes the child is removed from the adoptive family's home. When
this happens, the social worker does not blame anyone or refer to the original
placement as a failure, but instead looks again at what supports are needed for the
child and what type of child is best suited for that particular family.

Legal finalization of the adoption takes place after a period of time following
initial placement. There is a popular myth that adoption is final when the child is
placed with the family. This is not so for agency-based adoptions. The final legal
assignment of custody is made after an extended period of time. The period varies
among agencies; the norm seems to be six months to one year following placement. The court is the final authority in legally assigning custody of the child to the
adoptive parent. The court's decision is reached after review of the agency's reports
and recommendations.

Post-adoption services provide children with any needed supports such as
counseling, and parents with educational or ongoing counseling sessions. Agencies
recognize that it may be in the best interests of the child for support services to be
provided for extended periods beyond the legal adoption phase (Cole, 1985).

Have you seen advertisements in your college or local newspaper that read
something like this: Loving couple with a great deal to give looking to adopt a newborn. Will pay all fees, including prenatal, delivery, hospitalization, legal, and
follow-up costs. Please call . . .

Some families resort to private sources, also called independent adoption,
rather than using agency-based adoption services. Agreements are reached between
the two families involved, and the courts, assisted by attorneys, finalize the legal

arrangements. These adoptions can take place much faster and with less red tape than the agency-based process. The prospective adoptive parents usually provide financial support for the pregnant mother and her family, cover all related health costs, and often add a financial stipend—that is, a salary.

Independent adoption is costly, running to tens of thousands of dollars. For-profit adoptions are against the law. Recognize that with independent adoptions there is less scrutiny and follow-up than with agency-based services. Cole (1985) suggested that problems with independent adoptions can be reduced if the following steps are taken:

◆ Courts require a detailed statement of all monies that change hands relating to the adoption.

◆ Violators are vigorously prosecuted and subjected to severe sanctions.

◆ Communities provide enough financial support to adoption agencies that they can offer the same level of health and maintenance care as independent adoption (Cole, 1985).

There are three potential pools for adoption: healthy infants, children with special needs, and children from foreign countries (Kadushin & Martin, 1988). Fewer healthy infants are available for adoption because of the increased availability of birth control and abortion (Crosson-Tower, 1998). Unfortunately, it is not uncommon for a couple to be told the waiting period for a healthy infant may be up to ten years!

A special needs child has unique characteristics that can include "race and ethnicity, medical problems, older age (over age 3), attachment to a sibling group, developmental disabilities, and emotional difficulties" (Crosson-Tower, 1998, p. 374). Such children are much harder to place because of their special needs and are more available than healthy infants for adoption.

In recent years, more and more people are looking to the international community for children to adopt. Children born in areas of civil strife or extreme poverty are the main subjects of such adoptions. Latin America, Vietnam, Korea, the Philippines, India, and other Asian countries have been the principal nations and regions sending children to the United States (Crosson-Tower, 1998).

CHILDREN WITH SPECIAL NEEDS

According to the AFCARS report in 2012 there were approximately 397,122 youth in foster care (U.S. Department of Health and Human Services, 2013b). This number is down from 2005 when there were approximately 513,000 children in the foster care system (U.S. Department of Health and Human Services, 2007). In terms of exiting and entering the foster care system in 2012, the numbers are compara-

Name: Xan Boone

Place of residence: Cincinnati Ohio

College/university: University of Cincinnati, B.S., political science, 1998; MSW, 1995

Present position: Field service instructor at the School of Social Work, University of Cincinnati, and trainer for the Ohio Child Welfare Training Program, conducting caseworker and foster parent training that is required by the state.

Previous work experience:

1989–2007: Child Welfare Professional. Two years as a dependency investigator for Lucas County Juvenile Court, two years as an ongoing caseworker for Hamilton County Children's Services, one year as a Family Preservation caseworker, four years as a family conference facilitator, and nine years as a new caseworker trainer for Hamilton County Children's Services.

Volunteer experience:

Mission trip to rebuild homes for Hurricane Katrina victims; traveled to Ukraine to assist the government in development of an updated child welfare system; Sunday school teacher, fellowship committee vice president and president, and pastoral liaison committee at Lutheran Church of the Resurrection.

Why did you choose social work as a career? Like many career child welfare professionals before me, I did not choose child welfare as my career initially. I planned to be a juvenile probation officer. However, although I did not get the job that I had hoped to get, the Lucas County Court offered me another position. This would be to work in conjunction with the local child welfare agency to place children in safe family homes. I conducted the investigation of those families for the court and testified regarding their appropriateness to raise a child. I never looked back. Twenty-one years later I am still in child welfare. I feel that social work is a calling and that social work really comes from the heart as much as it does from the head. I was inspired to get my master's degree and am very proud to call myself a career social worker.

What is your favorite social work story? I remember running into a family on the streets of downtown Cincinnati on a sunny Saturday. There was something familiar about them. As they approached, I realized that this was a family with whom I had worked when I was doing family preservation several years back. They stopped and looked at me. I know that the mother recognized me immediately. She ran over to give me a hug. The daughter just kept staring at me. Finally she recognized me. She said, "I remember you; you helped me make my mom a birthday cake when we didn't have any money." It had been several years, but, yes, I had helped her brother and her make her mom a birthday cake. This family was being torn apart by anger, poverty, and mental health issues. When I saw them again, the mother was working and the kids were in school and they appeared to be doing well. There are few times we see the results of what we do to help us in the field of social work. This was a rare but wonderful glimpse of both the formal and the informal work we do to help others. When successes happen we might not even know it! I still smile when I think of baking that cake.

What would be the one thing you would change in our community if you had the power to do so? I wish people in the world could spend a day walking in the shoes of another. It might be a first step to truly eradicating racism as well as addressing issues related to poverty and other environmental factors.

---

ble to 251,764 entering foster care in 2012 and 240,923 leaving it. In terms of adoptions, in 1998, 36,000 of the approximately 120,000 children adopted in the United States were adopted from the public foster care system. In 1999, the number of children adopted from foster care was 47,000; in 2000 and 2001 it was up to 51,000; in 2002 it was 52,000, and in 2003 it went down to 50,000; in 2004 it went up to 51,993; and in 2005 it was 51,323 (Child Welfare League, 2006).

As of 2011 the number of adoptions actually decreased, from 54,000 in 2010 to 51,000 in 2011 (U.S. Department of Health and Human Services, 2013c). In 2012, according to the AFCARS report there were 101,666 children waiting to be adopted and of these 58,625 were waiting to be adopted after parental rights for all living parents were terminated (U.S. Department of Health and Human Services, 2013c).

As of September 30, 2012, there were 397,122 children in foster care. Many of these children had suffered abuse, abandonment, and/or neglect (U.S. Department of Health and Human Services, 2013c). Due to a history of trauma, these children were considered *special needs* and required special parenting once placed into either temporary or permanent homes. The term special needs is often associated with children within the U.S. welfare system. Each state's specific criteria may vary slightly, but in general, these children meet special criteria and are either emotionally or physically handicapped. Due to their trauma histories, special needs children require special attention and can be difficult to parent.

Adoption is the permanent legal transfer of full parental rights from one parent or set of parents to another parent or set of parents (Henry & Pollack, 2009, p.1). The social stigma attached to adoption has a long history in our society and can be fueled by disparaging community attitudes toward adoptive kinship. Many couples would prefer to have their own biological children rather than adopt. When a couple adopts a special needs child, in particular, they do not start with a clean slate. Many of these children have had difficult lives and after suffering either physical or emotional abuse they may have difficulty overcoming past experiences and memories. The negative experiences imbedded in these children can make trusting difficult. This fear of social connections can create a distance between the new parent and the new extended family system. Given the extensive needs of these children, adjustment for the adoptive parents can also be difficult. These new parents may go through their own grieving process, experiencing feelings of shock, denial, anger, depression, and physical symptoms of distress and guilt as the dreams of the child they wished for or expected are replaced by the realities of the actual child.

After a brief honeymoon period, the adoptive parents of a special needs child may experience a shocking realization that the new child is unhealthy, either physically or emotionally. Despite the information provided prior to the adoptive placement, many adoptive parents cannot comprehend the full realm of the behaviors and difficulties of the child prior to placement. Consequently, the parents, especially the mother, may experience shock and bewilderment and may start making excuses for the child's behavior. After living with a child who is unresponsive to them, parents may experience anger and rage. The adoptive mother may discover feelings of guilt for not truly loving her adoptive child and for feeling ambivalent or angry toward her child (Forbes & Dziegielewski, 2003).

Many times the biases of society are as strong, if not stronger, within the nucleus of the immediate family and extended family. Adoption of a special needs child involves integrating adopted children into the entire family social system. Therefore, Henry and Pallack (2009) outline the importance of pre-placement training that involves education about adoption issues and feelings that may surface and includes the extended family as part of the pre-adoptive process. Lack of support from the extended family can undermine the legitimacy of the adoptive placement for the adoptive mothers. Therefore, professionals should encourage participation in post-placement services as a necessary part of practice (Henry and Pollack, 2009).

In summary, a final but controversial point about adoption is the notion of placement in the best interests of the child. One practice in adoption may run counter to this central tenet of child welfare—strong pressure to place children with adoptive families of the same race or ethnicity. Among the many types of adoption, transracial adoptions, also referred to as interracial, biracial, multicultural, or multiracial adoption, have gained increased attention (Henry & Pollack, 2009). The justification is that the cultural needs of a child far outweigh other placement considerations. For example, the National Association of Black Social Workers does not support the placement of African American children in non-Black homes. Similarly, the 1978 Indian Child Welfare Act places responsibility for adoption of Native American children within tribes rather than with traditional public child welfare agencies. The 1978 law requires Native American children to be placed with extended family members as a first option and then with other tribal families, regardless of the wishes of the parents.

Should adoption be constrained by race and ethnicity and other cultural factors? Does the compelling need for permanency override the cultural needs of a child? Can a child develop cultural competence and identity in a home of different racial or ethnic origin? What about religion? In Judaism, for example, the religion's law is that a child born to a Jewish mother is always Jewish. Should a Jewish child always be placed in a Jewish home? Should Catholic children always be placed with Catholic families? Is it best to keep a child in a temporary foster home if no culturally similar family can be found? There are no easy answers to these questions and they may require individual evaluation that clearly takes into account the best interests of the child.

Other Services

A number of other child welfare services meet additional needs of children. It is impossible to discuss all of them, but we will touch briefly on two important program areas.

Youth Programs

Most of us at one time or another have participated in youth programs sponsored by such groups as the YMCA, YWCA, Boys Clubs, Girls Clubs, Blue Birds, Girls Scouts, Boys Scouts, Brownies, or Little League baseball. Many agencies in our communities work with young people through an array of programs ranging from gym-and-swim to therapeutic prevention.

The YMCA, for example, offers parent-child programs called Y-Indian Guide and Y-Indian Princess. The parent and child meet with other parents and children one evening each week. Ostensibly providing recreational opportunities, these programs also ensure that the parent and child have at least one evening each week of quality interaction. In addition, the parent and child carry out tasks and activities in the home between group meetings. These activities strengthen relations when time is limited.

Youth programs have four important functions in our communities:

♦ Youths have positive peer experiences in a formal supervised atmosphere.
♦ Youths learn to interact with others in groups.
♦ Youths are able to develop their own extended networks outside of the family.

◆ Youths find a safe haven, particularly with after-school, weekend, or evening activities that take place when caretakers may be at work and unable to supervise their children.

CHILD SEXUAL ABUSE AND TRAUMA

According to the U.S. Department of Health and Human Services, sexual abuse is a type of maltreatment involving a child in sexual activity that provides sexual gratification or financial benefit to the perpetrator. This includes ". . . intentional touching, either directly or through clothing, of the sexual or other intimate parts of the child, or allowing, permitting, compelling, encouraging, aiding, or otherwise causing a child to engage in touching the intimate parts of another for the purpose of gratifying the sexual desire of the person touching the child, the child or a third party" (Washington State Department of Social & Health Services, 2012, p. 2).

Due to the secrecy that surrounds this activity, the abuse of power—often by someone close and trusted by the child—and the emotional reactions it causes, this can be a difficult subject for most people to talk about. As society's awareness of children's issues has grown, so has awareness about child sexual abuse. It is estimated that by the time children reach age eighteen, one out of every four females and one out of every six males has been confronted with sexual abuse (Townsend & Reinhold, 2013). This means that by the time many children reach adulthood their lives have been affected by some type of sexual abuse.

Social work programs often offer courses in assessment where the presence and subsequent signs of child sexual abuse are identified. This area of practice can be particularly disturbing for social workers. Children represent such a vulnerable population and the desire to protect them will affect even the most seasoned social worker. This means that all intervention must start with a self-awareness that will result in a greater understanding of others (Morgaine & Capous-Desyllas, 2015). To start the process, most social workers will interview the child, careful to build rapport and use techniques such as play therapy that make the child feel as comfortable as possible when discussing such a disturbing and confusing topic. Once rapport is built, the physical indicators of sexual abuse will be identified and documented accordingly. Careful discussion of emotional and physical concerns is the focus, and information shared will later be given to medical staff who will conduct a physical exam on the child. Physical indicators medical staff will examine for are bruises or bleeding in the external genital or anal areas, and medical tests will be run for possible venereal diseases, and if relevant, pregnancy. Other symptoms include difficulty walking or sitting, reports of nightmares and bed wetting, demonstration of bizarre or unusual sexual knowledge or behavior, pregnancy or a venereal disease, and reports of sexual abuse by a parent or another caregiver (Washington State Department of Social and Health services, 2012). Such children may also withdraw from social contacts and exhibit poor interpersonal skills. With the secretiveness and shame that often surrounds sexual abuse, social workers need to be skilled at assessing children who are survivors to help them to move past the abuse.

Mandatory Reporting: Who Is Expected to Report?

Social workers, similar to other professionals, are considered mandatory reporters. There are numerous professionals who are responsible for mandatory reporting, including all licensed or registered professionals of the healing arts and any health-related occupation who examine, attend, treat, or provide other professional or specialized services including, but not limited to, physicians (including physicians in training), psychologists, social workers, dentists, nurses, osteopathic physicians and surgeons, optometrists, chiropractors, podiatrists, pharmacists, and other health-related professionals. This also generally includes

- Employees and officers in both public and private schools
- Employees or officers of any public or private agency or institution or other individuals providing social, medical, hospital, or mental health services, including financial assistance
- Law enforcement agency officials including courts, police departments, correctional institutions, and parole or probation offices
- Individual providers of child care, or employees or officers of any licensed or registered child care facility, foster home, or similar institution
- Medical examiners or coroners
- In some states, employees of any public or private agency providing recreational or sports activities.

As you can see there is a diverse group of professionals expected to care for and ensure the safety of our children (Department of Human Services, 2007; U.S. Department of Health and Human Services, 2009).

As a professional social worker, we are mandatory reporters, and therefore we are expected to report any situations in which it is believed that child abuse or neglect will occur in the reasonably foreseeable future. All social workers regardless of where they work need to be aware of what is considered reportable and how to make a report. When a report is indicated, it must be made to the child welfare services office or the police department. If a social worker, similar to other professionals, fails to make a report of an incident involving child abuse or neglect, or knowingly fails to provide additional information, or prevents another person from reporting such an incident, he or she can be found guilty of criminal charges.

The following types of incidents need to be reported (Department of Human Services, 2007):

◆ Substantial or multiple skin bruising or any other internal bleeding.
◆ Any injury to skin causing substantial bleeding.
◆ Malnutrition.
◆ Failure to thrive.
◆ Burn(s).
◆ Poisoning.
◆ Fracture of any bone.
◆ Subdural hematoma.
◆ Soft tissue swelling.
◆ Extreme pain.
◆ Extreme mental distress.
◆ Gross degradation.
◆ Death, and when such injury is not justifiably explained, or when the history given concerning such condition or death is at variance with the degree or type of such condition or death, or when circumstances indicate that such condition or death may not be the product of an accidental occurrence.
◆ Sexual contact or conduct, including, but not limited to, rape, sodomy, molestation, sexual fondling, incest, or prostitution; obscene or porno-graphic photographing, filming, or depiction; or other similar forms of sex-ual exploitation.
◆ Injury to the psychological capacity of a child as evidenced by an observ-able and substantial impairment in the child's ability to function.
◆ Lack of timely provision of adequate food, clothing, shelter, psychological care, physical care, medical care, or supervision.
◆ Exposure to dangerous, harmful, or detrimental drugs (this does not apply to drugs that are provided to the child pursuant to the direction or pre-scription of a practitioner).

Before you call the child welfare services office in your state to make a report of abuse or neglect, you will need to gather certain information. If you are con-cerned that the report is not needed or if you are not sure if you should make the report, call anyway and confer with the intake worker. It is not your responsibility to prove that abuse or neglect has occurred, but only that you suspect it. If you make a report and it is found that the report was made in good faith, you will be immune from liability. In the best-case scenario, the family will not find out who made the report, but this can never be guaranteed. If you do not want your name released, be sure to tell the intake worker that this is your preference. Also, many experienced social workers question whether they should tell the child or the child's parents that they are making a report. For the most part, it is best to tell them, but never tell them if you feel it could put you in danger. Your safety is an important priority that should not be underestimated. Whether or not you tell the child's parents about the report, you still need to make the report. As you prepare to make the report, be sure that you gather information about the details related to the situation and refer the case as soon as possible. Time is always of the essence, and the sooner you report the case, the less likely it is that the child will be subjected to any further abuse or neglect or to numerous interviews in which the information will have to be repeated numerous times if the case is accepted.

Every state in the United States may vary slightly in procedure, but for the most part the social worker will want to obtain as much of the following information as possible before referring the matter for investigation (Department of Human Services, 2007):

◆ Name and address of the child victim and his/her parents or other persons responsible for his/her care
◆ Child's birth date or age
◆ Names and ages of other persons who live with the child and their relationship to the child if known
◆ Nature and extent of the child's abuse or neglect (including any evidence or indication of previous abuse or neglect)
◆ Date, time, and location of incident
◆ Child's current location and condition
◆ Identity of the alleged perpetrator
◆ Whereabouts of the alleged perpetrator and any history if available
◆ Any other information that may be helpful in determining the cause of abuse or neglect and whether or not there is a family member who can protect the child

Once the report is filed, the social worker may be called on to provide any information relating to the incident of abuse or neglect that needs clarification or was not contained in the original report. When the intake worker arrives, the social worker should facilitate the assessment as much as possible by providing a private place for him or her to meet with the child. The intake worker will almost always want to meet with the child alone without the parents present. He or she will decide whether police intervention is needed. If it is not an emergency situation and the child is in a protected environment, the police may not need to be called. This decision will depend on the time and the circumstances of the situation, but the social worker should be prepared for what could happen. The social worker may also be asked to testify in court; again this will depend on the individual situation.

The families and the child involved will be assessed and offered services to assist in addressing and remedying the problem. The ultimate goal is to protect the safety and integrity of the child. There are varied services that can be provided; those that are offered will be directly related to the needs determined on the intake and follow-up interviews. Services that can be offered can include diversion services; counseling services; child care/day care; chore services; emergency help such as food, clothing, or rent; and referrals for other services not offered by the department as well as foster care and foster-care-related cost (e.g., clothing for the child).

If it is determined that the potential for harm does exist, a case plan will be developed and implemented. The case plan will outline the safety issues, the goals and objectives to be accomplished to ensure the protection of the child, and the desired outcomes. Indicators and consequences related to success or nonsuccess of the plan will be clearly identified. It is important to find out the reporting procedures for your state before an issue occurs. Hence, you will be well aware of what is expected and what needs to be done to facilitate the situation and protect the child.

SUMMARY

Children are an essential part of our country's future development. What we do with and for them benefits all of us. Homer Folks, in 1940, wrote, "The safety of our democracy depends in large measure upon the welfare of our children" (White House Conference, 1942). Our nation's history shows an open sense of caring and responsibility for children and although we want to protect them—even from themselves—we also want to ensure they are provided as many opportunities as possible. For certain minority groups, especially Native Americans, cultural integrity remains at the heart of successful intervention and building resilience when serving these youth (Corenblum, 2014). How we care for our children tells us a great deal about our society's beliefs, hopes, and aspirations. Involving the family and community support systems as well as understanding spiritual ways and customs provides the foundation for successful integration back into the family and support systems (Garrett, et al., 2014).

We do a great deal to care for our nation's children, but we need to do more. We need to find ways to guarantee every child a healthy, caring home. A stimulating environment that encourages growth and development should be the norm for all children. We can accept nothing less. We also need to become aware of our own feelings and how this can affect the helping relationship (Morgaine &

Capous-Desyllas, 2015). The desire to protect children is strong and this must be balanced with a professional intervention that is always best for the child.

Child welfare is an exciting field. Exploring possibilities for maximizing a highly organized system of care and commitment will remain the challenge (Hubel et al., 2013). Programs still have a long way to go but more interest in evidence-based outcomes measures is expected. To further these goals, agencies will need to support professional staff by providing in-services and continuing education on the topic to ensure buy-in from existing employees. When education is combined with connected and well-informed social networks, the fabric to support evidence-based practices will come to the forefront (Horwitz et al., 2014). When this is paired with a well-trained professional workforce, we will have the best recipe for success.

Child welfare is an exciting and rewarding field with one of the noblest purposes—to preserve the well-being of our nation's children. Agency and professional efforts in this area will always be in constant flux, although always under the watchful eyes of the public and of policy makers. Social workers have been, are, and will continue to be significant players in child welfare.

REFERENCES

Adoption and Safe Families Act of 1997. Pub. L. No. 105-89, 111 Stat 2115 (1997).

Adoption Assistance and Child Welfare Act of 1980. Pub. L. No. 96-272, 94 Stat 500 (1980).

Barker, R. L. (2003). *The social work dictionary* (5th ed.). Washington, DC: NASW Press.

Barth, R. P. (1995). Adoption. In R. Edwards & J. G. Hopps (Eds.), *Encyclopedia of social work* (19th ed., vol. 1, pp. 48–59). Washington, DC: NASW Press.

Baugher, E., & Lamison-White, L. (1996). *Poverty in the United States, 1995* (Current Population Reports, Series pp. 60–194). Washington, DC: U.S. Department of Commerce, Bureau of the Census.

Bearman, S. K., Garland, A. F., & Schoenwald, S. K. (2014). From practice to evidence in child welfare: Model specification and fidelity measurement of team decision making. *Children and Youth Services Review, 39*, 153–159.

Berzin, S. C., Thomas, K. L., & Cohen, E. (2007). Assessing model fidelity in two family group decision-making programs: Is this child welfare intervention being implemented as intended? *Journal of Social Service Research, 34*(2), 55–71.

Boyce, C. A., & Maholmes, V. (2013). Attention to the neglected: prospects for research on child neglect for the next decade. *Child Maltreatment, 18*, 65–68.

Brace, C. L. (1872). *The dangerous classes of New York and twenty years' work among them*. New York: Wynkoop and Hallenbeck.

Centers for Disease Control and Prevention. (2015). *Child maltreatment definitions*. Retrieved from http://www.cdc.gov/ViolencePrevention/childmaltreatment/definitions.html

Child Welfare Information Gateway. (2015). *Child abuse and neglect fatalities 2013: Statistics and interventions*. Washington, DC: U.S. Department of Health and Human Services, Children's Bureau.

Child Welfare League of America. (2006). *CWLA survey of post-adoption services*. Washington, DC: Author. Retrieved from http://www.cwla.org/programs/adoption/adoptionsurvey.htm

Child Welfare League of America. (2013). *National fact sheet 2013*. Retrieved from http://www.cwla.org/advocacy/2013Factsheets.htm

Coady, N., Hoy, S. L., & Cameron, G. (2013). Fathers' experiences with child welfare services. *Child and Family Social Work, 18*, 275–284. doi:10.1111/j.1365-2206.2012.00842.x

Cole, E. S. (1985). Adoption: History, policy, and program. In J. Laird & A. Hartman (Eds.), *A handbook of child welfare: Context, knowledge, and practice* (pp. 638–666). New York: Free Press.

Convention on the Rights of the Child. (2003). *Chapter IV: Human rights*. United Nations Treaty Collection. Retrieved from https://treaties.un.org/Pages/ViewDetails.aspx?src=TREATY&mtdsg_no=IV-11&chapter=4&lang=en

Cook, R. E., & Sparks, S. N. (2008). *The art and practice of home visiting: Early intervention for children with special needs & their families*. Baltimore, MD: Brooks Publishing.

Copen, C. E., Daniels, K., Vespa, J., & Mosher, W. D. (2012). First marriages in the United States: Data from the 2006–2010 national survey of family growth. *National Health Statistics Reports,* (No. 49). Hyattsville, MD: National Center for Health Statistics, Retrieved from http://www.cdc.gov/nchs/data/nhsr/nhsr049.pdf

Corenblum, B. (2014). Relationships between racial-ethnic identity, self-esteem and in-group attitudes among First Nation children. *Journal of Youth Adolescence, 42*, 387–404.

Crosson-Tower, C. (1998). *Exploring child welfare: A practice perspective*. Boston: Allyn and Bacon.

Crosson-Tower, C. (2012). *Exploring child welfare: A practice perspective* (6th ed.). Saddle River, NJ: Pearson Prentice Hall.

Damashek, A., Nelson, M. M., & Bonner, B. L. (2013). Fatal child maltreatment: Characteristics of deaths from physical abuse versus neglect. *Child Abuse & Neglect, 37*, 735–744.

DeNavas-Walt, C., & Proctor, B. (2014). *Income and poverty in the United States: 2013* (Current Population Reports P60-249, p. 13). Washington, DC: U.S. Government Printing Office.

Department of Children and Families. (2012). *Family Preservation Services, program report, fiscal year 2012*. Retrieved from http://www.state.nj.us/dcf/news/reportsnewsletters/dcfreportsnewsletters/FPSAnnualRpt_2012.pdf

Department of Human Services. (2007). *A guide for mandatory reporters*. Social Services Division, Child Welfare Services Branch. Retrieved from http://humanservices.hawaii.gov/ssd/files/2013/01/MANDATED-REPORTER-HANDBOOK.pdf

DivorceRate. (2014). *Divorce rate*. Retrieved from http://www.divorcerate.org

Dobelstein, A. W. (2002). *Social welfare: Policy and analysis* (3rd ed.). Pacific Grove, CA: Cengage Learning.

Eamon, M. K. (2008). *Empowering vulnerable populations*. Chicago: Lyceum Books.

Edna McConnell Clark Foundation. (n.d.). *Keeping families together: Facts on family preservation services*. New York: Author.

Everett, J. E. (2008). Child foster care. In T. Mizrahi & L. E. Davis (Eds।)., *Encyclopedia of social work* (20th ed., vol. 2, pp. 375–389). Washington, DC: NASW Press.

Fields, J. (2003). *Children's living arrangements and characteristics: March 2002.* (Current Population Reports, P20-547). U.S. Department of Commerce, Economics and Statistics Administration. Washington, DC: U.S. Census Bureau. Retrieved from http://www.census.gov/prod/2003pubs/p20-547.pdf

Forbes, H. T., & Dziegielewski, S. F. (2003). Issues facing adoptive mothers of children with special needs. *Journal of Social Work, 3,* 301–320.

Garrett, M. T., Parrish, M., Williams, C., Grayshield, L., Portman, T. A., Rivera, E. T., & Maynard, E. (2014). Invited commentary: Fostering resilience among Native American youth through therapeutic intervention. *Journal of Youth Adolescence, 43,* 470–490.

Gil, D. (1985). The ideological context of child welfare. In J. Laird & A. Hartman (Eds.), *A handbook of child welfare: Context, knowledge, and practice* (pp. 11–33). New York: Free Press.

Gustavsson, N. S., & Segal, E. A. (1994). *Critical issues in child welfare.* Thousand Oaks, CA: Sage.

Hamilton, B. E., & Ventura, S. J. (2012). Birth rates for U.S. teenagers reach historic lows for all age and ethnic groups. *NCHS Data Brief* (no. 89), pp.1–8. Hyattsville, MD: National Center for Health Statistics. Retrieved from http://www.cdc.gov/nchs/data/databriefs/db89.pdf

Henry, M. J., & Pollack, D. (2009). *Adoption in the United States: A reference for families, professionals, and students.* Chicago: Lyceum Books.

Hook, J. L., & Courtney, M. E. (2010). *Employment of former foster youth as young adults: Evidence from the midwest study.* Chicago: Chapin Hall at the University of Chicago.

Horwitz, S. M., Hurlburt, M. S., Goldhaber-Fiebert, J. D., Palinkas, L. A., Rolls-Reutz, J., Zhang, J., . . . Landsver, J. (2014). Exploration and adoption of evidence-based practice by US child welfare agencies. *Children and Youth Services Review, 39,* 147–152.

Hubel, G. S., Schreier, A., Hansen, D. J., & Wilcox, B. L. (2013). A case study of the effects of privatization of child welfare on services for children and families: The Nebraska experience. *Children and Youth Services Review, 35,* 2049–2958.

Jacobs, M. A., Bruhn, C., & Graf, I. (2008). Methodological and validity issues involved in collection of sensitive information from children in foster care. *Journal of Social Service Research, 34*(4), 71–83.

Johnson-Motoyama, M. (2014). Does a paradox exist in child well-being risks among foreign born Latinos, US-born Latinos and Whites? Findings from 50 California cities. *Child Abuse & Neglect, 38,* 1061–1072.

Kadushin, A., & Martin, J. A. (1988). *Child welfare services* (4th ed.). New York: Macmillan.

Karger, H. J., & Stoesz, D. (2010). *American social welfare policy: A pluralist approach* (6th ed.). Boston, MA: Pearson Education/Allyn Bacon.

Kreider, R. M., & Ellis, R., (2011). *Living arrangements of children: 2009* (Current Population Reports P70-126), Washington, D.C.: U.S. Census Bureau. Retrieved from http://www.census.gov/prod/2011pubs/p70-126.pdf

Linderman, D. S. (1995). Child welfare overview. In R. Edwards & J. G. Hopps (Eds.), *Encyclopedia of social work* (19th ed., vol. 1, pp. 424–433). Washington, DC: NASW Press.

Lindsey, D. (1994). *The welfare of children.* New York: Oxford University Press.

Mallon, G. P. (2008). Social work practice with LGBT parents. In G. P. Mallon (Ed.), *Social work practice with lesbian, gay, bisexual, and transgender people* (2nd ed., pp. 269–312). New York: Taylor & Francis Group/Routledge.

Martin, J. A., Hamilton, B. E., Ventura, S. J., Osterman, M. J. K., Kirmeyer, S., Mathews, T. J., & Division of Vital Statistics. (2013). Births: Final Data from 2011. *National Vital Statistics Reports, 62*(1). Retrieved from http://www.cdc.gov/nchs/data/nvsr/nvsr62/nvsr62_01.pdf

Morgaine, K., & Capous-Desyllas, M. (2015). *Anti-oppressive social work practice: Putting theory into action.* Los Angeles, CA: Sage.

National Association of Social Workers. (2012). Foster care and adoption. In *Social work speaks* (9th ed., pp. 148–153). Washington, DC: Author.

National Children's Alliance. (2014). *NCA statistics–Statistical report 2014*. Retrieved from http://www.nationalchildrensalliance.org/sites/default/files/download-files/2014 NationalAnnual_0.pdf

National Indian Child Welfare Association. (2014). *Frequently asked questions about ICWA*. Retrieved from http://www.nicwa.org/indian_child_welfare_act/faq

Quam, J. (1995). Charles Loring Brace (1826–1890). In R. Edwards & J. G. Hopps (Eds.), *Encyclopedia of social work* (19th ed., vol. 2, p. 2575). Washington, DC: NASW Press.

Reinberg, S. (2007, December 5). Teen birth rates up for the first time in 14 years, U.S. reports. *Healthday News*. Retrieved from http://consumer.healthday.com/mental-health-information-25/behavior-health-news-56/teen-birth-rates-up-for-first-time-in-14-years-u-s-reports-610651.html

Robbins, J. M. (2008, February 22). *The costs of rising divorce rates across the US*. Retrieved from http://ezinearticles.com/?The-Costs-of-Rising-Divorce-Rates-Across-The-US&id=1003126

Samples, M., Carnochan, S., & Austin, M. (2013). Using performance measures to manage child welfare outcomes: Local strategies for decision making. *Journal of Evidence-Based Social Work, 10*, 254–264. doi: 10.1080/15433714.2013.788954

Sawrikar, P., & Katz, H. B. (2014). Recommendations for improving cultural competency when working with ethnic minority families in child protection systems in Australia. *Child Adolescent Social Work, 31*, 393–417.

Smokowski, P. R., Evans, C. B., Cotter, K. L., & Webber, K. C. (2014). Ethnic identity and mental health in American Indian youth: Examining mediation pathways through self-esteem, and future optimism. *Journal of Youth Adolescence, 43*, 343–355.

Southwell, P. (2009). The measurement of child poverty in the United States. *Journal of Human Behavior in the Social Environment, 19*, 317–329.

Storhaug, A. (2013). Fathers' involvement with the child welfare service. *Children and Youth Services Review, 35*, 1751–1759.

Townsend, C., & Rheingold, A. A. (2013). *Estimating a child sexual abuse prevalence rate for practitioners: A review of child sexual abuse prevalence studies*. Charleston, SC: Darkness to Light. Retrieved from http://www.d2l.org/site/c.4dICIJOkGcISE/b.8766307/k.A6B6/Prevalence_1_in_10.htm

Tracy, E. M. (2008). Family preservation and home-based services. In T. Mizrahi & L. E. Davis (Eds.), *Encyclopedia of social work* (20th ed., vol. 1, pp. 973–983). New York: Oxford University Press/NASW Press.

Tyser, J., Scott, W. D., Readdy, T., & McCrea, S. M. (2014). The role of goal representations, cultural identity, and dispositional optimism in the depressive experiences of American Indian Youth from a Northern Plains tribe. *Journal of Youth Adolescence, 43*, 329–342.

U.S. Census Bureau. (2012). *Most children younger than age 1 are minorities, Census Bureau reports*. Retrieved from http://www.census.gov/newsroom/releases/archives/population/cb12-90.html

U.S. Census Bureau. (2013). *State and county quick facts*. Retrieved from http://quickfacts.census.gov/qfd/states/00000.html

U.S. Census Bureau. (2014). *U.S. and world population clock*. Retrieved from http://www.census.gov/popclock

U.S. Department of Health and Human Services. (2007). *AFCARS report #13: Preliminary FY2005 estimates as of September 2006*. Retrieved from http://www.acf.hhs.gov/sites/default/files/cb/afcarsreport13.pdf

U.S. Department of Health and Human Services. (2009). *Child maltreatment 2007*. Washington, DC: U.S. Government Printing Office. Retrieved from http://www.acf.hhs.gov/programs/cb/pubs/cm07/chapter3.htm#child

U.S. Department of Health and Human Services. (2010). *Child maltreatment 2010—Data tables*. Washington, DC: Department of Health and Human Services. Retrieved from http://www.acf.hhs.gov/programs/cb/resource/child-maltreatment-2010-data-tables

U.S. Department of Health and Human Services. (2012). *Trends in foster care and adoptions-FY2002–FY2011*. Retrieved from http://www.acf.hhs.gov/sites/default/files/cb/trends_fostercare_adoption2012.pdf

U.S. Department of Health and Human Services. (2013a). *Child maltreatment 2012*. Washington, DC: Author. Retrieved from http://www.acf.hhs.gov/programs/cb/resource/child-maltreatment-2012

U.S. Department of Health and Human Services. (2013b). *Trends in foster care and adoption: FY2002–2012*. Retrieved from http://www.acf.hhs.gov/sites/default/files/cb/trends_fostercare_adoption.pdf

U.S. Department of Health and Human Services. (2013c). *The AFCARS report*. (no. 20, pp. 1–6). Retrieved from http://www.acf.hhs.gov/sites/default/files/cb/afcarsreport20.pdf

United Nations. (1989). *United Nations convention on the rights of children*. Retrieved from http://www.ohchr.org/EN/ProfessionalInterest/Pages/CRC.aspx

Voices for Illinois Children. (2013). Illinois kids count 2013: "Moving policy, making progress." Retrieved from http://www.voices4kids.org/wp-content/uploads/2013/02/Key-Highlights-Illinois-Kids-Count-20131.pdf

Washington State Department of Health and Human Services. (2012). *Protecting the abused and neglected child: A guide for recognizing & reporting child abuse & neglect* (DSHS 22-163). Olympia, WA: Author.

Watkins, S.A. (1990). The Mary Ellen myth: Correcting child welfare history. *Social Work*, *35*, 500–503.

White House Conference on Children in a Democracy. (1942). *Final report*. Washington, D.C., January 18–20, 1940 (Publication No. 272). Washington, DC: U.S. Government Printing Office. (Reprinted in *Children and youth: Social problems and social policy* (1974), New York: Arno Press.)

Wulcyzn, F., & Landsverk, J. (2014). Research to practice in child welfare systems: Moving forward with implementation research. *Children and Youth Services*, *39*, 145–146.

Zill, N., & Bramlett, M. D. (2014). Health and well-being of children adopted from foster care. *Children and Youth Services Review*, *40*, 29–40. doi:10.1016/j.childyouth.2014.02.008

CHAPTER 9
HEALTH CARE

FOR MANY OF US, STARTING ONE CAREER IN THE HELPING PROFESSIONS and changing to another is not that unusual. This was Liz's experience. She began her professional career as a nurse but after several years decided to switch to social work. Liz felt that her knowledge of the medical aspects of a client's condition blended beautifully with mental health considerations. Collaboration in the delivery of health care between nursing and social work is just one way that can lead to improved services promoting health and well-being (Lam, Chan & Yeung, 2013). Liz's belief is not unique; most health care social workers quickly agree that successful intervention requires interprofessional collaborations that stress the link between the mind and body (Dziegielewski, 2013). From this perspective, interprofessional collaborations can benefit both policy and practice.

Therefore, the contention is made that mind and body cannot be separated, and each client must be treated individually with a focus on continued wellness and prevention (Zechner & Kirchner, 2013). The health care social worker, who often works as part of an interdisciplinary team, brings knowledge and understanding of the importance of focusing on more than just the medical condition a client is suffering from. Each client is part of a system; the social worker uses his or her knowledge and skills to link the client to the environment. This emphasis is central to treatment as well as discharge planning and case management.

Health care social workers face great challenges in the new century. Issues of behaviorally based coordinated care, downsizing and reorganization of hospital social work staffs, limited availability of services to insured and uninsured populations, and increased demand for brief interventions make health care a formidable setting for creative social work practice (Dziegielewski, 2013). For many of the nonprofit organizations, the mere struggle for survival has caused social workers serving as administrators to explore sound fiscal management strategy (Burke, 2008). Many Americans have simply come to accept rising prices and limited and often stagnating services in health care, but Rugy (2014) and other key social policy advocates ask, does it really have to be that way? There are many other questions:

- ◆ Is there a way to cut costs in the system we currently have while maintaining essential services?

- Do all Americans truly need and deserve the same level of health care availability and affordability?
- Do we provide health care to groups such as the homeless—and if so, to what extent?
- What about people in prison? Do we provide health care to those serving life sentences with no possibility of parole?
- How do we ensure that people in rural and sparsely populated areas have access to high-quality health care?
- Should we continue to move efforts toward a national health insurance model rather than the present coordinated care perspective?
- Should we finance alternative, nontraditional health interventions?

These questions are very thought provoking and there will be no easy answers. At the center of this and any future discussion is acceptance of the premise that health care is costly and access is limited. How can the best compromises be made so that all get the greatest benefit?

Given the increasing rise in health care costs, the Affordable Health Care Act (ACA), often referred to as *Obama Care*, provides a major example of the effort to ensure that Americans have access to health care (U.S. Department of Health and Human Services, 2012). This law reached its full implementation as planned in 2014 and seeks to hold insurance companies accountable by setting standards for reform that allow for lower health care costs as well as the guarantee of more choices that enhance quality of care. The ACA supports health care changes as well as improvements in health care access, quality, and service. The expectation was that this program would support the coverage of 32 million Americans who currently do not have health care coverage while opening doors for accessible health care (Ofosu, 2011). New programs such as this continue to evolve and require that all health care professionals be open to change while balancing quality of care and utilizing evidence-based practices that are effective and cost efficient (Dziegielewski, 2010).

From your own experiences buying medication or paying for medical treatment you know that, even with the advent of Obama Care, the appropriate covered services remain costly. Social workers have an important role in helping clients identify and get the services they need. One reason why so many Americans have no form of health insurance and are willing to risk paying a fine for not adopting provider coverage under the ACA is the expense! Even with programs such as the ACA, large deductibles and copayments can be a problem. This, in combination with states that have not accepted the Medicaid waivers, can place our poorest at the greatest risk. Even with the increased access afforded by the ACA there is no reason to expect that health care delivery costs will ever go down. It is common to hear social workers in the health care field discuss the complexity of the system and the frustration they experience when they try to connect clients to the services they need.

Did You Know…In current health care practice the term patient *is returning to the vocabulary of social workers, especially those in the health care area. In this setting titles such as patient, consumer, and client are often used depending on the setting. To best talk-the-talk and/or walk-the-walk, social workers are keenly aware that to use accepted ter-minology helps to bring them to the table as part of an interdisciplinary collaborative team that uses similar terminology when referring to the individual being served.*

Miller (2008) rated our health care system as "complex, under-funded, dis-parate, inconsistent, state of the art, miraculous, successful, unjust, illogical and more" (p. 219). With the numerous system changes and the implementation of the ACA, this complexity in trying to help an individual meet his/her own needs is a central issue.

HEALTH CARE SOCIAL WORK DEFINED

Health care social work, historically called *medical social work* and today called *clinical social work* (not to be confused with the work of the private practitioner, also referred to as a clinical social worker), is one of the oldest, best-established fields of professional social work practice.

Did You Know…In 1918, the National Conference of Social Work in Kansas City helped to form the American Association of Hospital Social Workers. This was the first professional social work organization in the United States.

Simply stated, health care social work practice deals with all aspects of general health and strives to promote and restore social functioning for clients, families, and small groups. This type of integrated care requires taking into account all aspects of people's physical health as well as their mental well-being (Dziegielewski, 2013).

Did You Know…In 1928, the American College of Surgeons developed and included a minimum standard of service provision for social service—that is, social work—departments.

In health care practice, as in other areas of social work, the tasks performed are collaborative yet diverse and unique. Social workers serving in health care settings must be well trained in providing services to clients because they are competing in a service provision environment that is overcrowded with health care professionals. Moreover, today's health care social workers are exposed to all the turbulence and change of managed health care (Dziegielewski, 2013). In this environment, the insurance company dictates the level of service; no longer are recommendations from physicians or other professionals treated as sacrosanct. Pressures to cut costs mean that health care service must be provided in the briefest, most effective manner possible (Dziegielewski, 2008a; 2008b).

There is also a movement to provide what has been termed *wrap-around services*. This involves a collaborative process for the implementation of individualized care plans capable of addressing the needs of each individual (generally children) and/or families in need (Walker, Bruns, & Penn, 2008). This system of care highlights the importance of the client-in-situation or the client-in-environment. From this perspective, addressing clients' problems includes taking into account the supports that are available upon their return home, such as family and friends and other resources in the community (Summers, 2012). As a result of interdisciplinary approaches, all health care providers including social workers must work in a versatile, flexible manner to complete tasks with limited resources. The varied tasks coupled with the dynamic environment and limited fiscal resources complicate our simple definition of health care practice.

Tom Carlton, a major social work thinker and advocate in health care social work during the 1970s and 1980s, defined health care social work in its broadest sense as "all social work in the health field" (1984, p. 5). Carlton felt that social workers interested in this area must be prepared to do more than engage solely in direct clinical practice. His vision of health care practice includes program planning and administration; preparation, supervision, and continued training for social workers and other health care professionals; and social research. It is not surprising that the term health care social work has historically been used interchangeably with the term medical social work. Using these two terms interchangeably, however, can obscure a subtle difference in meaning.

In *The Social Work Dictionary*, medical social work is defined as a form of practice that occurs in hospitals and other health care settings. This type of practice facilitates good health and prevention of illness, and it aids physically ill clients and their families in resolving the social and psychological problems related to disease and illness (Barker, 2003). Health care social work is more encompassing, indicating a type of practice that can take place in more than one setting.

Health care social workers often serve as members of professional multidisciplinary and interdisciplinary teams. As part of a multidisciplinary team, the social worker can help link the services provided by each of the helping disciplines. In the interdisciplinary team, the shared roles and responsibilities allow the social worker to share his/her expertise as part of the team. Regardless of the type of team effort utilized to help the client, the role of the social worker is essential in sensitizing the other team members to the social-psychological aspects of illness (Barker, 2003). Health care social workers are expected to address the psychosocial aspects of client problems. They are also expected to alert other team members to these psychosocial needs and to ensure adequate service provision within the discharge environment. In performing these functions, social work professionals not only represent the interests of clients, but they often become the moral conscience of the health care delivery team. According to Leipzig et al. (2002), although provider satisfaction with interdisciplinary teamwork was often high, client satisfaction was low. Information such as this further reinforces the role of the social worker as one of the primary providers responsible for increasing communication and understanding for all involved.

Did You Know...In the early days, hospital nurses generally performed medical social work services. These nurses were convenient choices for this employment because they were easily accessible, already knew agency procedure, and were aware of community resources. Later, however, when it was established that more specialized training in understanding social conditions was needed, the employment of social work professionals began.

The struggle to define exactly what health care social workers are expected to do reflects the changing nature of the health care system. Part of the struggle involves trying to establish concrete cost-containing goals and objectives that clearly represent the diverse and often unique service provided. This inability to document a concrete service strategy has long been a thorn in the side of health care administrators, who need this information to justify and compete for continued funding. Nevertheless, simple descriptions of service provision vary, depending on the client population served and the services needed.

Health care social workers practice in a setting where doctors are expected to fix what's broken and do so with incredible speed and competence. This has resulted in the push for quick and not always complete solutions such as a pill to address a situation rather than behavioral types of treatment interventions (Dziegielewski, 2006, 2010). As a result these workers are often expected to do the same. Given the complexity of the human situation, however, this task is not at all straightforward. In adapting to their diverse clients while anticipating changes in the health service environment, social work professionals must employ flexible and constantly updated skills.

Name: Dodie M. Stein

Place of residence: Indianapolis, IN

College/university degrees: PhD, The University of Iowa; MSW, Indiana University; MA, University of Southern California; BS, Syracuse University; LCSW Indiana (pending)

Present Position and Title: Medical social worker, Clarian Home Dialysis, ClarianHealth Partners

Previous Work/Volunteer Experience:

Medical social worker, in-center hemodialysis, hospice social worker

Fellow, Fairbanks Center for Medical Ethics, Clarian Health

Clinical and educational audiologist in private practice and university, special education, community speech and hearing center, and medical practices

Grant reviewer, U.S. Department of Education

Editor and reviewer, Sertoma, various professional journals and publishers in communication disorders

Committee and board activities in audiological organizations, Kentucky technology assistance projects, National Governors Association

Why did you choose social work as a career? I was in an allied health field working with babies, young children, and older adults ("womb to tomb" as they say) for many years. After leaving the field and doing other things, I found I missed health care. This was about the time I spent a last year with a friend dying from breast cancer, and I volunteered for hospice at a local hospital. That's what inspired me to go into social work—working with hospice patients and folks with life-threatening chronic diseases, having the honor of helping them manage their illnesses, whether they are in a transition in their lives (starting dialysis) or at the end of their lives (hospice).

What is your favorite social work story? The series of events that I see every day as a renal social worker are inspiring: Patients waiting for years, then finally getting a transplant; patients feeling better and feeling like they have more control over their lives with home dialysis; patients who are depressed and not coping well getting better with appropriate meds and counseling and feeling more sense of control and contentment. These are patients who have to constantly deal with dialysis as their lifeline, their many comorbidities, and the many meds they take to manage the renal disease . . . not to mention the financial aspects of insurances, high monthly copayments, or having to pay full price for very expensive meds, juggling work and dialysis if they are well enough; multiple physicians' appointments, family demands; transportation difficulties; other activities. I have enormous respect for them and all they cope with and juggle. I always wonder if I could do it if I were faced with all of it. At least I know I can help them learn to manage, "stay steady," and get back to enjoying what they used to enjoy before renal disease changed their lives.

What is one thing you would change in the community if you had the power to do so?
Universal health care (as in health care for all living in this country), preferably single-payer health care, to provide "health," not "sick" care, including preventative care at all ages. This also assumes physicians and other health care providers are making decisions with their patients, not insurance or government bureaucrats "practicing medicine without a license!"

A BRIEF HISTORY OF HEALTH CARE SOCIAL WORK

Medical social work can be traced back to the nineteenth century public health movement. With urban growth, a result of industrialization, came overcrowding and the spread of disease. In Trattner's (1989) graphic words:

> American cities were disorderly, filthy, foul-smelling, disease-ridden places. Narrow, unpaved streets became transformed into quagmires when it rained. Rickety tenements, swarming with unwashed humanity, leaned upon one another for support. Inadequate drainage systems failed to carry away sewage. Pigs roamed streets that were cluttered with manure, years of accumulating garbage, and other litter. Slaughterhouses and fertilizing plants contaminated the air with an indescribable stench. Ancient plagues like smallpox, cholera, and typhus threw the population into a state of terror from time to time while less sensational but equally deadly killers like tuberculosis, diphtheria, and scarlet fever were ceaselessly at work (p.57).

All in all, this was not a great place or time to live. It soon was evident that public sanitation programs were needed. The resulting laws and health care efforts helped doctors and related medical professionals to gain in stature (Segal & Brzuzy, 1998, p. 108). Hospitals too changed dramatically during this era. Once a haven for the poor, the hospital became a "scientific center for the treatment of illness" where physicians provided oversight and subsequent control of the helping activities and services provided (Popple & Leighninger, 1990, p. 436). Medical social work was first practiced in 1900 in Cleveland City Hospital, when the workers helped to discharge from overcrowded wards patients with chronic conditions and homeless Civil War veterans (Poole, 1995). It subsequently developed as a specialization through the efforts of Richard Cabot and shortly thereafter Ida Cannon, a new graduate from Simmons College. Cabot in 1905 set up the first social service (work) department in a hospital. Though trained as a physician, Cabot recognized the unique and important contributions of social workers when he served as director of the Boston Children's Aid Society. The social worker's skill in linking social environment to disease, thought Cabot, would be extremely helpful in medical diagnosis. The social work department established at Boston's Massachusetts General Hospital is regarded as the debut of medical social work.

> *Did You Know…Johns Hopkins Hospital established its first social work program in 1907. The first social worker to be employed there was Helen B. Pendleton (Nacman, 1977).*

Health care social work today, as in Cabot's time, takes place in a *host* setting—that is, an organization whose primary purpose is something other than providing social work services. You'll find social workers in hospitals (a hospital accreditation requirement), neighborhood health centers, health maintenance organizations (HMOs), city public health departments, veterans' hospitals and clinics, military hospitals and clinics, and nonprofit and for-profit health-related organizations.

> *Did You Know…The U.S. Veterans' Bureau, now the Department of Veterans' Affairs, began hiring social workers to work in its hospitals in 1926.*

One new aspect of today's health care social work is that it is team based and interdisciplinary in nature. Health care social workers need to be invested in both the process and the structure of the services that are to be performed (see the activity below). Each discipline needs to be competent in the practice and approach utilized. Competency involves being able to link the knowledge, values, and skills the professional has to help the client directly to the practice approach selected and the outcome that results (Damron-Rodriquez, 2008).

> *Did You Know…In the 1920s and 1930s the U.S. military started to add social workers to its ranks. Military social workers usually work in mental health, health, and protective service settings.*

In interdisciplinary collaborations social workers can help the team of professionals communicate with one another and the client to be served. The social worker can also help members of the team become aware of their own values, behaviors, habits, and emotions that can affect the helping process. Creating an atmosphere of self-knowledge yields a deeper awareness that results in a more culturally sensitive approach for the client (Morgaine & Capous-Desyllas, 2015). In addition, the social worker can help to connect those clients entering the system with the supports that are needed while in the system and upon discharge. This

Activity…Have you ever been admitted to a hospital? While you were there did you see a social worker? If you didn't, would you have liked to? If you did, what services did he or she provide? Make a brief list of the services that you believe social workers can provide in the hospital setting.

intervention from start to finish builds continuity of care and links the client to helping networks that can continue long after the service has ended. Social workers are part of a professional team that may include physicians, nurses, vocational rehabilitation workers, psychologists, and psychiatrists. Today's social worker must therefore understand and value the contributions that other professionals offer. For our clients and ourselves, we can no longer see matters solely through our individual professional lens.

UNDERSTANDING THE CURRENT HEALTH CARE ENVIRONMENT

Throughout the last quarter of the twentieth century, spiraling costs and growing numbers of uninsured people challenged the American health care system. And the crisis is hardly abating. According to Dziegielewski (2013) several reasons of direct interest to social workers have been cited:

1. The aging population needs more costly health care services.
2. Americans are resistant to paying additional fees for medical services.
3. The insurance industry is highly fragmented, with managers trained under different environmental conditions.
4. There is excessive pressure to fill an oversupply of hospital inpatient beds.
5. There is a focus on treating acute illness rather than a more holistic, wellness, or preventive perspective that can lead to more costly treatment.
6. Insufficient medical outcome data impair decision making.
7. Too many heroic attempts are made to implement expensive procedures without regard to quality of continued life.
8. Professionals try to be cautious and can order unnecessary tests and procedures to avoid malpractice suits.

Even though many of the underlying factors are difficult to change, predictions of vastly increased health care urgently require a response of one type or another. During the early 1990s, politicians were responsive to the American public's demand for health care reform. During his first term as president, Bill Clinton, who had made a campaign promise to address this issue, formed a major task force chaired by his wife, Hillary Clinton, which began to develop a national health care policy (Mizrahi, 1995). The task force considered numerous proposals for health care reform from single-payer systems to limited forms of universal coverage. The eventual proposal was not a single-payer approach, but rather a type of *managed competition* in which purchasing alliances were formed that would have the power to certify health plans and negotiate premiums for certain benefit packages (The President's Health Security Plan, 1993). Payment for these plans was financed by employer-employee premiums. The actual consumer out-of-pocket cost would vary based on the benefit package chosen. The Clinton proposal eventually failed after concerted attacks by the health care industry and conservative members of the Congress. As you begin to read the information on the ACA below, this new plan will sound similar to this original failed proposal. Some political commentators felt this was the last chance to change the health care system, yet during the 2000 presidential campaign, health care resurfaced as a hot topic, with arguments over insurance coverage and a patient's bill of rights. This led to renewed interest in finding something, possibly not as ambitious, that would take us closer to universal health care.

Today, health care affordability continues to remain a significant problem. In March of 2010, after continuous vigorous debate, Congress enacted the ACA (U.S. Department of Health and Human Services, 2012). The purpose of the ACA is to give the American people back some degree of control related to their health care by providing coverage options that provide stability, flexibility, and informed choice (U.S. Department of Health & Human Services, 2014). Box 1 below provides basic coverage, costs, and care information. To read more about the law and learn more about the ten titles that outline the premises for inclusion within the ACA outlined in 2009, see the activity below.

Activity... The Affordable Care Act (ACA) has ten titles that outline the purpose of the law and what it is designed to accomplish. The ten titles of the Affordable Care Act are listed with the amendments to the law called for by the reconciliation process.

Go to http://www.hhs.gov/healthcare/rights/law/index.html and read each section. Do you believe that this law will be able to meet what it has outlined to do in terms of the factors (cost, care, and coverage) outlined in box 1? Why or why not?

The Affordable Care Act, Section by Section

Title I. Quality, Affordable Health Care for All Americans
Title II. The Role of Public Programs
Title III. Improving the Quality and Efficiency of Health Care
Title IV. Prevention of Chronic Disease and Improving Public Health
Title V. Health Care Workforce
Title VI. Transparency and Program Integrity
Title VII. Improving Access to Innovative Medical Therapies
Title VIII. Community Living Assistance Services and Supports Act (CLASS Act)
Title IX. Revenue Provisions
Title X. Reauthorization of the Indian Health Care Improvement Act

---

Box 1. Affordable Care Act (Patient's Bill of Rights)
Coverage Highlights:

- *Ends preexisting condition exclusions for children*: Health plans can no longer limit or deny benefits to children under 19 due to a pre-existing condition.
- *Keeps young adults covered*: Those under age 26 are covered under the parent's health plan.
- *Ends arbitrary withdrawals of insurance coverage*: Limits cancelling coverage for mistakes.
- *Guarantees the right to appeal*: Can further the right to appeal denial of payment decisions.

Cost Highlights:

- *Ends lifetime limits on coverage*: Lifetime limits on most benefits are banned for all new health insurance plans.
- *Reviews premium increases*: Insurance companies must now publicly justify any unreasonable rate hikes.
- *Maximizes health care expenditure premiums*: Premiums relate more directly to health care benefits rather than administrative costs.

Care Highlights:

- *Covers preventive care at no cost to the covered person*: May also have preventative health services with no copayment.
- *Protects consumer choice of doctors*: Choose primary care doctor from plan's network.
- *Removes insurance company barriers to emergency services*: Can seek emergency care at a hospital outside of the health plan's network.

Source: U.S. Department of Health and Human Services (2014).

Through the ACA, "... [Americans'] health insurance options were provided through a disconnected, patchwork of programs including employment-based insurance, Medicare, Medicaid, S-CHIP, the Veterans Health Administration, the Indian Health Service, the Public Health Service and community mental health centers" (Moniz & Gorin, 2014, p. 10). Although it is beyond the scope of this chapter to describe the ACA in detail, establishing and agreeing upon a unified definition of health care social work remains critical for survival in today's service delivery environment. What seems to have remained consistent over the years is that service reimbursement is clearly linked to performance indicators. This means that there must be a clear linkage to consumer outcomes, service events, resource acquisition, and efficiency (Poertner & Rapp, 2007). We don't want to paint a bleak picture, but rather a realistic one. The continual changes and swirling controversies contribute to a turbulent health care environment. Declining hospital admissions, reduced lengths of stay, and numerous other restrictions and methods of cost containment are common threats that unite all health care social workers.

In summary, it is beyond the scope of this chapter to identify all issues central to health care reform. The most salient one in need of reform for the overall health care system is the refined use of enhanced state-of-the-art information technology to be shared across health care settings. For the most part, the health care sector has languished behind almost all other industries in adopting a shared system of information technology. For example, many caregivers still record client data on paper documents that cannot be easily accessed by other providers in different settings—or sometimes even the same setting; this can result in errors and costly duplication of effort. Other agencies provide electronic access to patients but do not teach patients how to use the system or access the data. Electronic service delivery options can be increased and improved by providing online education to consumers and providers alike as well as online group participation and networking (Nicholas et al., 2007). With all the electronic technology available, it is surprising how little is understood and shared as part of standard care and delivery of services.

A second issue and probably the most daunting of health care challenges is providing care to the remaining uninsured and underinsured Americans. Some ways of increasing inclusion for the uninsured involve extending health coverage to all residents through the provision of tax credits designed to offset the costs of eligible participants' insurance premiums and monitoring and coordinating the patchwork availability of current plans and high deductibles and co-pays. Another way to confront this issue may be to consider expanding Medicaid in states that currently have not adopted the Medicaid waiver under the ACA and the State Children's Health Insurance Program to cover a broader range of participants. Among the anticipated benefits is coverage of families under a single plan and access to a personal clinician, both of which increase the likelihood that patients will receive appropriate, timely care in the right setting.

Measuring the number of underinsured and improving access to care are much more complicated concepts. The term *underinsured* refers to people who have medical insurance but whose employers try to save dollars by cutting back policy coverage or benefits. These employers, in an effort to reduce costs, can eliminate benefits, reduce benefits for family members, or increase employees' contributions to insurance benefits. This is also complicated by the fact that health insurance coverage is relative to the number of hours a person works; many part-time or temporary workers may still not be able to afford health insurance and may continue to go uninsured regardless of the potential fines imposed.

A third area is malpractice reform. It has become commonplace to see debates over malpractice insurance and refusal by some physicians to provide care because of what they perceive to be unreasonable rates for this insurance. This debate and subsequent refusal to provide services has resulted in limited access to care for patients in some communities. This professional fear of liability has also impeded efforts to identify sources of error so that they can be prevented. Moreover, the tort system frequently does not result in compensation of injured patients; those who are compensated often experience long delays. One way to address this issue might be to have states create injury compensation systems outside of the court-room that are client centered and focused on safety. These systems would set rea-sonable payments for avoidable injuries and provide fair, timely compensation to a greater number of clients while stabilizing the malpractice insurance market by limiting health care providers' financial exposure.

Another area of growing concern that needs attention relates to the recogni-tion of the quality and appropriateness of patient care, given the rising prevalence of chronic conditions such as diabetes and heart disease. Roughly 120 million Americans have one or more chronic conditions, many of which could have been prevented or delayed through education or other interventions that promote healthy behaviors. Improving lifestyle behaviors can help to reduce the risks of diabetes and other chronic conditions. Interventions that recognize the impor-tance of lifestyle on behavior include behaviorally based changes as a crucial com-ponent designed to assist individuals suffering from chronic disease (Gross et al., 2007). The physical and psychological implications are that living with a chronic condition can disrupt every area of a client's life. From the moment a client is diag-nosed with the condition, the social and psychological factors will become a key area for the health care social worker to recognize and help the health care deliv-ery team to access (Zabora, 2009).

As stated earlier, all too often health care practices focus on the physical symp-toms. When these symptoms are acute and reflective of episodic problems, this type of focus cannot effectively provide the ongoing treatment and coordination among multiple care providers and settings needed by those with chronic ailments. Moreover, health care still focuses largely on treatment of the physical symptoms rather than the psychological ones. In addition, a focus on treatment that lacks an emphasis on prevention can be equally problematic. For example, many people with diabetes still do not receive foot examinations to check for nerve damage, and smokers fail to receive counseling about quitting smoking and the health benefits that quitting can bring.

Last, the need remains to enhance primary care facilities, because this is where the majority of clients enter the health care system and where most of their health care needs are met. The reliance on the primary care facility and receiving care in this way is critical to achieving goals related to treatment of acute and chronic conditions, prevention, and health promotion. For example, in order to improve delivery, community health centers need to undertake initiatives to reinvent and substantially enhance primary care through new models of care delivery, support for patient self-management, and other strategies. These centers as access and transition points need to build on their existing innovations in electronic record keeping and management of chronic diseases. New incentives should be considered, such as enabling centers and their staffs to share in the rewards of the cost savings they generate by eliminating waste.

For the most part, when we are confronted with challenges, it is easy to unequivocally state that "we are at a crossroads" or "we are facing a crisis." Yet social work is full of challenges, no matter what the setting—health care or some other area of practice. And even the most experienced health care social workers have felt that, no matter how hard they try, health care organizations represent large bureaucracies that seem impossible to change. As a result, we can become mired down at the crossroad, never moving and feeling that others control our destiny—or we can begin to understand and identify the problems and explore potential solutions for change.

ROLES AND TASKS OF THE HEALTH CARE SOCIAL WORKER

According to *The Social Work Dictionary*, health care workers can be defined in a generic sense as all "professional, paraprofessional, technical and general employees of a system or facility that provides for the diagnosis, treatment and overall wellbeing of patients" (Barker, 2003, p. 192). Nevertheless, a clear distinction must be made between health care workers and allied health care professionals. Health care workers are nonprofessional service support personnel such as home health aides, medical record personnel, nurse's aides, orderlies, and attendants (Barker, 2003). Allied health care providers, by contrast, are generally professionals such as social workers, psychologists, audiologists, dietitians, occupational therapists, optometrists, pharmacists, physical therapists, and speech pathologists.

It is as allied health care professionals that you will find social workers practicing in health care settings. Health care social workers appear to serve this area well because of their broad-based training in evaluating, based on behavior, the biological, psychological, and social factors that can affect a client's environmental situation—that is, the behavioral **biopsychosocial approach**. The beginning generalist (BSW) and advanced specialist (MSW) levels of education help to make the social work professional an invaluable member of the health care delivery team. The services that health care social workers provide can be divided into two major areas: direct practice and support or ancillary services.

Where do physicians and nurses, the most recognizable health care providers, fit in? Physicians and nurses are not considered allied service providers. Because their services are necessary to any type of medical care, they are called *essential health care providers*—they are the major players in the host environment (Dziegielewski, 2013).

DIRECT PRACTICE

Today, social workers can be found in every area of our health care delivery system. Providing culturally sensitive practice is at the core of what social workers do. Therefore, don't be surprised if you find yourself in a situation in which providing culturally sensitive practice can become a balancing act between client self-determination and respect for cultural expectations. For most social workers, realizing the need to start from where the client is provides a firm basis for any intervention to follow (see the activity below).

> *Activity...* **Cultural Diversity in the Medical Setting**
>
> *Read and process the following case. Consider getting the opinions of other classmates in terms of their perception of this case and how to best address the needs of the client. Based on the input and ideas you receive, as well as class discussion, prepare a plan on how to best assist the client situation described.*
>
> *When the social worker arrives in a client's hospital room to gather some routine admission information, she walks in on a couple having a very heated discussion. Jon is a forty-year-old Hispanic male who is in the hospital for routine same-day exploratory surgery. Jon's wife is visibly upset and crying. The social worker feels a bit awkward for intruding and asks if the couple would like her to leave. Jon motions that he would like her to stay and begins to tell her that he is furious that his wife has decided to go on a trip alone to see her mother. When questioned as to whether he is disappointed because he wants to go with her, he quickly says no. He is angry because she made plans without getting his permission first. His wife states that she is sorry for not asking him first, but she felt that the decision had to be made quickly. The couple asks the social worker for her opinion.*
>
> *In view of her need to respect cultural diversity and maintain professional integrity, what types of responses and/or assistance could the social worker provide? What types of responses should be avoided?*

Dziegielewski (2013) identified several areas in which practitioners typically provide a wide variety of services to clients and their families:

- ◆ *Case finding and outreach*: Assist client to identify and secure the services they need.
- ◆ *Preservice or preadmission planning*: Identify barriers to accessing health care services.
- ◆ *Assessment*: Identify service needs and screen to identify health and wellness concerns.
- ◆ *Direct provision*: Secure concrete services such as admission, discharge, and aftercare planning.

◆ *Psychosocial evaluation*: Gather information on client's biopsychosocial, cultural, financial, and situational factors for completion of the psychosocial assessment or social history.

◆ *Goal identification*: Establish mutually negotiated goals and objectives that address client's health and wellness issues.

◆ *Counseling*: Help client and family to deal with their situation and problems related to health interventions needed or received.

◆ *Short- and long-term planning*: Help the client and family to anticipate and plan for the services needed based on the client's current or expected health status.

◆ *Service access assistance*: Identify preventive, remedial, and rehabilitative service needs and assist the client and family to overcome potential barriers to service access.

◆ *Education*: Instruct the client and family on areas of concern in regard to their health and wellness.

◆ *Wellness training*: Help the client to establish a plan to secure continued or improved health based on a holistic prevention model.

◆ *Referral services*: Provide information about services available and make direct connection when warranted.

◆ *Continuity of care*: Ensure that proper connections are made among all services needed, taking into account the issue of multiple health care providers.

◆ *Advocacy*: Teach and assist clients to obtain needed resources or on a larger scale advocate for changes in policy or procedure that directly or indirectly benefit the client.

◆ *Case management and discharge planning*: Ensure that clients are connected to the services they need after leaving general health care facility.

The clinical services that health care social workers provide have clearly expanded far beyond the traditional core of discharge planning. Health care is a changing environment in which even the classic definition of discharge planning has been altered. Social workers not only coordinate discharges, but they also oversee the multidisciplinary or interdisciplinary teams of which they are members to be sure that clients are getting the services they need. Because discharges can involve numerous individual, family, and community factors, counseling services for the client that facilitate placement are often needed (Summers, 2012). Social workers are often called upon to provide more than just concrete services, and counseling designed to prepare the person for discharge is often needed. Furthermore, once the team agrees that a client is ready for discharge, it is often the social worker who is responsible for ensuring that the transfer is complete and goes smoothly. Often this involves the connection of services to ensure continuity of care and any client and family education needed.

SUPPORT SERVICES

Social workers can also provide health-related services that are not considered direct practice. These support or ancillary services include staff supervision, administration, and community-based services:

- *Direct supervision*: Provide direct professional social work supervision through direction, guidance, and education on case services and counseling.
- *Consultation*: Provide consultation services to other social workers and multidisciplinary and interdisciplinary teams.
- *Agency consultation*: Provide consultation to agency administrators on how to enhance service delivery to clients and organizations.
- *Community consultation*: Provide consultation services to communities to assist with the development of community-based services.
- *Policy and program planning*: Assist in formulation and implementation of health care policies and programs that will help to meet client needs.
- *Program development*: Assist the agency to refine and develop new and improved programs.
- *Quality improvement*: Assist the agency to ensure that continuous quality services are provided that meet standards of professionalism and efficiency.
- *Service advocacy*: Assist the agency to recognize the needs of clients.
- *Service outreach*: Identify unmet needs and services that are not available to clients; advocate for improved programs and services, provide home visits.
- *At-risk service outreach*: Identify clients at risk of decreased health or illness and advocate securing services for them.
- *Health education*: Participate and instruct communities on developing and implementing health education programs.
- *Agency liaison*: Serve as liaison to the agency on behalf of the client, ensuring that connections are made among client, supervisor, and community.
- *Community liaison*: Serve as a contact or connection among the client, family, and community.

Support services often go beyond what we generally consider to be the core of health care social work, and social workers often extend beyond the agency setting and when needed go directly into the home of the client and visit with caregivers and families (see Figure 1). We must recognize the importance of all practitioners who do this type of work day in, day out. These tasks and functions cannot be overemphasized, particularly in this era of coordinated care.

Figure 1: Home healthcare worker examining a developmentally disabled senior who lives with his sister.

Direct Supervision

Staff supervision is a major support activity with a long and rich history in health care social work. The National Association of Social Workers (NASW, 2013) maintains that supervision and continuing education are essential for competent practice and the skillful development of professional practice. Supervision requires specialized knowledge that builds on years of practice. It also requires updated information as the environment and the practice setting are constantly in flux. To support the requirements for advanced knowledge and oversight experience, most social workers performing supervision, whether it is clinical or administrative oversight, have an MSW degree. On occasion, you may find a BSW worker in a supervisory role, but this is the exception.

Supervision is a complicated activity, but it is necessary for the professional growth of all social workers. Supervisors are mentors, or teachers if you will, who can be sounding boards, share practice frustrations, and look at different ways of working with a particular client or group. When the social worker is working as part of a collaborative team, individual and/or team-related supervision efforts should always emphasize client skill building and strength enhancement. A team approach helps to build satisfaction among members and provides leadership that enhances satisfaction among all team members (Baran, Shanock, Rogelberg, & Scott, 2012).

The supervisor has many roles in health care, but generally he or she oversees the services provided and can help to coordinate, develop, and evaluate those he or she supervises as well as perform administrative, educational, and supportive functions (NASW, 2013). In health care, repeated policy changes and consequent organizational instability, which leads to rapid changes, reorganization, and cutbacks, can make supervision a challenging role to assume. For the social worker, whether a new or experienced practitioner, such uncertainty can be difficult to handle. Let's be honest—no one likes to be in an uncertain work environment where the rules may change from one day to the next. In health care, social workers must continually modify details of their practice.

In social work, supervision is viewed as a tool to help the new social worker develop and refine skills with the help of a more senior professional knowledgeable and skilled in the area (Gelman, 2009). In mediating between supervisees and clients, coworkers, or the larger community, the supervisor should always try not to adopt the opinion of any side. Supervisors must be sensitive to their staff's ongoing struggles to create proactive client-directed services within the constraints set by payers. Supervisors too must balance the demands of their jobs with those of third-party payers. To say the least, the supervisor's role is difficult. Flexibility and the time to provide proper oversight, then, are central to competent supervision as well as good practice skills. The need to be flexible, however, and the environment that creates this need are a major source of stress. Stress and its management are therefore important issues for both supervisor and staff.

Supportive supervision addresses such issues as stress, staff morale, and work-related anxiety and worry, which if left unattended, can lower job satisfaction and commitment to the agency. Supportive supervision builds worker self-esteem and emotional well-being. In the long run, it can reduce stress levels and thus the dissatisfaction that ultimately results in employee burnout (Sheafor & Horejsi, 2014).

As if system uncertainty were not enough of a problem for the health care supervisor, let's add another challenge to the job: lack of clarity in staff roles and responsibilities. In particular, what are the differences in the work carried out by BSWs and by MSWs in the practice setting? You may find that what BSWs do in one setting is done only by MSWs in another. Or in today's competitive environment, it may be done by another professional altogether with very different training and background. This lack of clarity about functions means that supervisors must be careful in assigning cases and tasks. In social work, supervisors must ensure that tasks assigned to BSWs are within their scope of practice. That another organization assigns a particular task to BSWs is no guarantee that the activity is appropriate for an entry level practitioner. Rather, that organization may not be able to assign or even hire an MSW, but the task must be done, so it must be given to a BSW. Although professionally unsound, this task assignment can be made less daunting by discussing it with the supervisor.

In active supervision, advice and direction are given on the best way to handle client care for the supervisee, the multidisciplinary or interdisciplinary team, the agency, and the community. Mediation requires the supervisor to recognize that conflicts are not intentional and to help supervisees to address them in the most ethical, moral, and professional way possible. In advocacy the supervisor empowers the supervisee to assist with the development of needed services for clients, their families, and significant others; this requires keeping current on the services available and keeping in mind changes that occur rapidly and without warning.

As brokers, social workers must establish a link for clients with community services and other agencies. Remember, when most people come into a medical setting, such as a hospital, their stay is limited. The social worker must elicit a great deal of information on the client's environment and do this quickly and concisely. Information on social, emotional, and physical factors and their relation to the illness is a critical factor in understanding the person in his/her situation. From the early days of medical social work Richard Cabot saw this as the most important role of social work practice in health care. The social worker may discover that a client needs a variety of follow-up support services to sustain his or her family through the recovery period or through ongoing illness. Brokering is how the social worker seeks out these community-based services and develops a case plan that is tailored to the client.

Health Education and Health Counseling

Social workers were part of the nineteenth century public health education movement, also called the *Sanitation Movement*. Therefore, providing education and instruction is not new to social work—although recognition and emphasis of the importance of health care counseling were limited. Attention wasn't directed toward counseling until training became institutionalized in colleges and moved to an educational model.

Psychoeducation involves a wide array of services, but in health care, similar to other areas of practice, this type of supportive intervention involves helping clients identify the challenges they are facing and develop social support and coping skills to address them (Walsh, 2009). Health care counseling is especially important with the increased participation of social work professionals as educators in new health care areas such as weight reduction and smoking cessation that we might call *nontraditional social work*. The worker continues to teach new patterns of behavior but then employs counseling theory and skills to help the client negotiate the period of change. The worker calls on a variety of skills and strategies ranging from support to confrontation. According to Strom-Gottfried (2009, p. 721), effective educational practice relies on six essential components:

1. The development of clear and appropriate objectives
2. An understanding of the learner's needs and abilities
3. An atmosphere that is conducive to learning
4. Knowledge of the material to be conveyed
5. The skill to select and use teaching methods appropriately
6. The ability to evaluate one's performance and the learner's acquisition of the educational outcomes

Administration

Administration and related tasks have not been considered core practice areas of health care social work. In fact, most prospective social workers shy away from studying administration, focusing instead on client-related courses. If you don't believe us, ask your classmates how many of them plan to major in or develop a specialization in administration. You'll probably find that everyone agrees that someone should study administration—"but not me." Yet administration, particularly in health care, directly affects the types of services that are offered in a setting. The role that administration plays in strengthening direct practice cannot be overstated. For the social worker serving as an administrator, training in time management, organizational management and operations, and sound fiscal awareness are only the start of what is needed.

Social work administrators, like other health care administrators, must respond to often competing management philosophies. These conflicting styles can affect the provision of client care. For example, the social work administrator may receive a directive from the hospital central administration to increase the participation of professional staff members in the organization's decision-making processes. The idea behind this directive is that greater involvement will strengthen commitment to the hospital. The social work administrator decides that quality circles and total quality management (TQM) will best achieve the culture that central administration is seeking. While the social work administrator is attempting to put TQM in place with quality circles among staff members, central administration announces that reimbursement from third-party payers and census data (e.g., patient bed days) are down. These announcements are an unmistakable signal of financial pressure (always remember that a hospital is a business and, like all businesses, needs to make a profit). Therefore, the social work administrator must now be concerned with generating significant patient numbers to justify and sustain the department. The new goal is to maximize reimbursement potential. If numbers are not increased, then the department will be forced to cut back on staff while raising workloads for those who stay. A *do more with less resources and support* mentality takes hold while the edict to develop staff loyalty remains in place.

Does this sound frustrating? Does stressing a profit motive seem unfair, or does it simply not make sense? This example may help you to understand why so many health care social work administrators become frustrated and feel trapped. Double-edged and conflicting messages sent by central administration, fueled by the pressure for reimbursement, can make social work administration one of the most difficult, frustrating, and challenging jobs in our field. However, the situation is not as dismal as it seems. Health care social work administrators do have some individual power in that they can assume a leadership role in balancing these pressures while influencing the agency's policy decisions. Miller (2008) reminds us that all policy drives practice so that being a part of the policy making can help to bring about needed changes. Therefore, serving on agency committees or boards allows the administrator to help construct new policy directions and provides an opportunity to meet funding bodies in order to explain practice realities and discuss ways to enhance service delivery. This strategy is called *practice policy*. It reflects the understanding that social work activities are born of policy decisions. As social workers, we must be informed about and involved in the development of organizational policy—our clients are stakeholders in the policy-making process. Our practice knowledge, advocacy skills, and ability to mediate between conflicting parties are all contributions that we as social workers can make to the health care policy-making process.

Acute and Long-Term Care Settings

Social work has long been at the forefront in providing health care services to clients in acute care and long-term care settings (Beder, 2006; Chapman & Toseland, 2007). In a national survey of licensed social workers, Whitaker, Weismiller, Clark, and Wilson (2006) reported that general and acute care medical facilities are the most common employment settings for health care social workers. Therefore, as the number of practicing health care professionals continues to rise (Jansson, 2011), the role and influences of the health care social worker in the acute practice setting will remain pronounced (Dziegielewski, 2013). The health care social worker's roles and responsibilities in the acute care setting are clear:

- ◆ To provide assistance with treatment plans and compliance issues
- ◆ To assist clients and families with discharge planning and referral
- ◆ To provide counseling and support for clients and significant others in the areas of health, wellness, mental health, bereavement, and so forth
- ◆ To ethically assist clients and their families to make difficult decisions that can affect physical health and mental health
- ◆ To educate clients, their families, and significant others about psychosocial issues and adjusting to illness and to assist in resolving behavioral problems
- ◆ To assist in identifying and obtaining entitlement benefits
- ◆ To secure nonmedical benefits and assist with risk management and quality assurance activities
- ◆ To advocate for enhanced and continued services to ensure client well-being

Long-term and transitional care restorative settings may not be that familiar to you. Let's try some other names that you're more likely to recognize: rehabilitative hospitals and clinics, nursing homes, intermediate care facilities, supervised boarding homes, home health care agencies, hospices, and hospital home care units. These settings require careful attention to ensuring continuity of care from one transitional facility to another, taking into account an assessment that will need to change accordingly as the patient's condition and situation also change (Diwan, Balaswamy, & Lee, 2012). These settings are usually multidisciplinary, and social workers provide services within the areas of assessment, treatment, rehabilitation, supportive care, and prevention of increased disability of people with chronic physical, emotional, or developmental impairments. The use of transitional care options continues to gain in popularity because transitional facilities such as long-term and community-based **home care** can help to save money for hospitals by reducing acute care services such as those provided in the emergency department (Dziegielewski, 2013).

Due to the variability of tasks to be performed in these settings, the Murray Alzheimer Research and Education Program (MAREP; 2007) outlined the importance of staff participation. The role of the social worker is essential in helping to create a welcoming environment, act as a resource for the family, and facilitate communication about the resident with all care providers including those in the facility (Dziegielewski, 2013). Creating a climate of *re-enablement* allows the patient to be viewed as a person with abilities who is once again empowered to regain what was lost as a result of illness or injury (Nursing Times.net, 2012).

Empowering clients to reach their maximum level of independence reflects the core values and ethics set out in the code of ethics. Our code reminds us of how important it is to maintain sensitivity and respect for people served, to be aware of the individual's right and ability to make decisions for himself or herself (in most situations), and to focus on client strengths and resources that can be maximized. In building self-awareness for the social worker the helping activity becomes more client sensitive and maximizes self-determination (Morgaine & Capous-Desyllas, 2015).

The phrase *long term* indicates that the client has a chronic condition that may affect his or her abilities. Unfortunately, many chronic conditions are unlikely to improve. The sheer utility of placement in a long-term care facility is the provision of twenty-four-hour care and support. Therefore, the majority of the individuals served in these facilities will be older adults, and providers will often be specialists in geriatric care and focus their care provision services in this area (Temkin, 2009). This may be a particular problem for the younger adult in need of these services; therefore, it is essential to be aware of the services a facility provides as well as the age group it serves. Other populations served in these settings can also include persons with disabilities and children with serious medical illnesses that require twenty-four-hour care. Care needs may be intensive and long term, but that doesn't mean that the social worker and other team members give up hope or stop trying to ensure that the client receives the highest quality of professional treatment. We must be realistic, but optimistic. We should not hide information from clients or discount their feelings. Remember, we are all people who think, feel, and care.

Health care social workers employed in long-term care must develop specialized knowledge of various chronic conditions and learn to identify and assess signs and symptoms of the expected progression of various diseases (Dziegielewski, 2013). Such information is critical to being an effective practitioner with the client, family, and friends. Family, friends, and significant others often need assistance to participate in the care of their loved ones (see, for example, Figure 2). Many people don't know what to say or how to say it and, as a result, feel overwhelmed and even useless. We should never underestimate the importance of *others* in the healing or sustaining process. Emerging evidence exists that the involvement and support of family and friends and teaching about the importance of incorporating the whole person contribute greatly to the overall wellness and satisfaction of all involved (Zechner & Kirchner, 2013). One last thought: When addressing the needs of a client who suffers from a chronic condition, the beginning professional should strive not to be afraid. Rely on what you have learned in school, and always be a compassionate person who uses skills and theory grounded in values and ethics that allow for the celebration of the entire human experience.

Figure 2: A daughter is about to give her father a haircut. The father and an adult son who was injured in an auto accident live together. Neither is able to drive and the other adult children take turns dropping by and helping out. Both the father and the son gain a sense of responsibility and accomplishment by taking care of each other.

Hospital Emergency Room Social Work

Social work services are offered in many hospital emergency rooms across the country, yet, in this fast-paced environment the actual services provided can differ greatly. For the social worker assigned to the emergency room, this employment setting is generally perceived as fast paced. Crises, deaths, and severe client problems need to be assessed and addressed as quickly and efficiently as possible. Once the emergency medical crisis is stabilized, the social worker needs to assist with the psychosocial protocol (Boes & McDermott, 2005).The social worker can provide psychosocial services such as education and support to the client being admitted to the hospital as well as to the client's family and friends (Beder, 2006).

In cases of disaster, terrorism, and other trauma-based occurrences, clients experiencing these events often present in the emergency room. Having a strong skill set relating to immediately addressing the needs of the client is essential; this needs to be combined with clear clinical standards on how to provide the best psychosocial care (Brake & Duckers, 2013). The pressure for immediate action in this setting is intense, and the social worker must remain in a constant state of readiness, prepared for whatever might come through the door next. According to Van Wormer and Boes (1997), working in emergency room settings is different from working in other settings in the hospital because of the speed and intensity with which services must be assessed and provided. There are numerous types of cases that can be seen in the emergency room; among the most common are (1) trauma-related events, which are often complex problems stemming from individual events to more global ones; (2) acute or chronic mental health and chronic medically related conditions; (3) substance-related conditions; (4) family-related events such as domestic violence or rape; and (5) family-related events such as child abuse and neglect. This can be further complicated by working with vulnerable populations such as the homeless or those who do not have the resources to help themselves. Continuity services are needed so that once the acute crisis is addressed, the client will be provided ongoing support and referral that maintains the level of care and avoids readmission and more extended hospital stays.

For many social workers in the emergency room setting, it is not uncommon to work as part of a collaborative interprofessional team (Dziegielewski, 2013). Teamwork in this setting often involves a variety of professionals including physicians, nurses, respiratory technicians, health unit coordinators, x-ray technicians, nurse case managers, social workers, and other health care professionals. One especially helpful team approach is the nurse-social worker collaboration (Lam, Chan & Yeung, 2013). Some emergency departments divide this team further into what is often termed a case management subteam or dyad that utilizes the combined services of a nurse and a social worker (Bristow & Herrick, 2002). In this setting, the case management subteam members work together to provide social services and discharge planning, and to ensure that continuum of care needs are met for each client served.

Historically, the presence of a social worker in the emergency room setting has been important from a supportive/clinical perspective as well as to provide direct case management and discharge planning services (Beder, 2006). Supportive services for helping clients include discharge planning or counseling services for the family support system of the client. In the emergency room, the problems for which clients seek treatment are multifaceted and complex. The types of problems addressed are diverse, ranging from auto accidents to other types of accidental and non-accidental injuries. Many individuals may have acute or chronic episodes of an illness, first or repeated episodes of a physical or mental illness, or suicide attempts related to health and/or emotional issues. Treatment of these individuals by health care professionals, especially for vulnerable populations who are subject to stigma, has never been more important (Schroeder, 2013).

According to Bristow and Herrick (2002), the services that social workers provide in this setting include psychosocial assessments, bereavement counseling and support, substance abuse assessment and referral, discharge planning, referrals for community resources, emotional support, and educating and advocating for patients. In addition, the emergency room social worker can assist with case management by gathering contact information for family and friends as well as finding additional means for meeting the client's health needs. Unfortunately, some believe that the emergency room has become a dumping ground for those who lack insurance or are homeless. This group of individuals has a unique set of circumstances requiring short-term intensive support designed to facilitate the discharge process and decrease the chance of recidivism (Dziegielewski, 2013). Because many individuals who seek care in the emergency room lack or have inadequate health care coverage, the hope is that the ACA will help to assist with the catastrophic costs that result from non-coverage.

Social work in the emergency department plays an important role in providing for the psychosocial needs of the patients in a time of crisis. Although this role is important, emergency room social workers warn that medical staff may overlook social work services because of their focus on the medical needs and not the psychosocial needs of the client being served. Thus, to utilize the services of social workers in the emergency department better, emergency room staff as well as hospital administrators must be educated about the role of the social worker in their department.

Home Care Services

Home care agencies have been providing high-quality in-home services to Americans and have remained an integral part of the provision of health services since 1905. Health care social workers help patients and their families cope with chronic, acute, or terminal illnesses and handle problems that may stand in the way of recovery or rehabilitation.

Home care refers to health care and the social services that are provided to individuals and families in their home or in community and other homelike settings (Dziegielewski, 2013). Home care includes a wide array of services such as nursing, rehabilitation, social work, home health aides, and other services. This rapidly expanding area of health care social work can be traced back as far as the early nineteenth century (Cowles, 2003; National Association for Home Care, 2010). In 1955, the United States Public Health Services endorsed a physician-oriented and organized home health care team designed to provide medical and social services to patients within their homes. The team consisted of a physician, nurse, and social worker (Goode, 2000). Since that time social workers have continued to provide social services in the home care setting, and this area of health care social work remains a diverse and dynamic service industry. The demand for home care services is increasing as hospital stays are decreasing.

For the most part, the majority of home care services are considered third party and reimbursable by Medicare, Medicaid, private insurance policies, health maintenance organizations (HMOs), and group health plans. Payments are determined by several factors, including client diagnosis and types of services required. Medicare recipients are the largest group of clients needing home health care services. Furthermore, Medicare beneficiaries, referred to as the *duals* because they are also eligible for Medicaid, are often considered a vulnerable population and one of the largest high-risk groups (Frank, 2013). More frequently than not, the services they need involve social as well as medical supports, making the role of social work crucial in the field of home care. Unplanned discharges where an individual's psychosocial needs go unmet puts the client at risk for readmission.

Cowles (2003) identified six categories of home care client problems: (1) barriers to service admissions; (2) service adjustments; (3) diagnosis, prognosis, or treatment/care plan adjustments; (4) lack of information to make informed decisions; (5) lack of needed resources; and (6) service barriers related to discharge. Rossi (1999) described home care social workers' duties as the following:

> (1) helping the health care team to understand the social and emotional factors related to the patient's health and care; (2) assessing the social and emotional factors to estimate the caregiver's capacity and potential, including but not limited to coping with the problems of daily living, acceptance of the illness or injury or its impact, role reversal, sexual problems, stress, anger or frustration, and making the necessary referrals to ensure that the patient receives the appropriate treatments; (3) helping the caregiver to secure or utilize other community agencies as needs are identified; and (4) helping the patient or caregiver to submit paperwork for alternative funding (p. 335).

McLeod and Bywaters (2000) validate the need for social workers in health care and report that there is substantial scope for social work involvement by working toward greater equality of access to existing health and social services. Equally important is to participate in shaping how social workers are viewed, establishing their role as a knowledgeable, positive, and supportive resource to support staff, coworkers, and administration (Neuman, 2000).

One additional concern relates directly to older adults. Maust, Oslin, and Marcus (2014) found in a recent study that oftentimes older adults were prescribed mental health medications without an existing mental health condition to support it. This makes the role of the social worker essential in protecting the rights of older adults in this setting and avoiding stigma as well as overprescribing of dangerous medications that may not be relevant to the care needed.

Hospice Social Work

Hospice care is a special way of caring for people who are terminally ill and their families. The goal of a hospice is to care for the client and the family with open acknowledgment that no cure is expected for the client's illness. Hospice care includes physical, emotional, social, and spiritual care; usually a public agency or private company that may or not be Medicare-approved provides this service. All age groups are serviced including children, adults, and the elderly during their final stages of life, and the majority of this care occurs at the client's home. In 2012, approximately 1.5 to 1.6 million patients received hospice services (National Hospice and Palliative Care Organization, 2013). In the hospice setting, both in-patient and in-home services can be provided. In this setting the individual is prepared for a dignified death that is satisfactory to him or her and to those who participate in his or her care (McSkimming, Myrick, & Wasinger, 2000).

In hospice the role of the social worker is crucial to the family planning process, and efforts are made to help family members deal with the client's illness and impending death in the most effective way possible. The social worker tries to facilitate open communication between patient and family and assess levels of stress—especially the ones that affect coping and prognosis. In addition, special attention is given to assessing the spiritual needs of the client and his/her family and helping them to adjust and accept. In the hospice setting there is a strong interdisciplinary focus with a team approach that will continually assess environmental safety concerns. One of the first tasks of the social worker is to address grieving with an initial bereavement risk assessment for the caregiver, thereby assisting the patient and family to identify strengths that help cope with loss (Dziegielewski, 2013). Families are supported as time is allowed for the patient and family to progress through stages of grieving. Other duties of the hospice social worker involve updating bereavement care plans and assessing the type of bereavement program to be initiated upon the death of the patient. Referrals are also provided for bereavement support services.

WHY DO IT?

By now you may be wondering why anyone would want to work in the changing, often unsettling, health care system. This is a fair question, so let's try to find an answer.

Social workers are among the many allied health professional groups that make up the health care army. Given the interdisciplinary nature of today's work, it is incumbent on the social work profession to promote a clear understanding of its purpose and role in order to maintain a place in health care delivery. What we bring to the health care arena is vital. History shows this. Nevertheless, we must always define our role and be players in this process. Social workers cannot afford to let others decide what they can do with and on behalf of clients and their families. The roots of health care social work, as part of the social work profession, lie in serving the poor and disenfranchised. As the medical arena has changed over the years, so too has the role of the health care social worker.

And now, as the social environment changes, expectations for health care are becoming clouded. Is health care a right or a privilege? Should the government guarantee a minimum standard of health care for all people? Who would establish such a standard? What role should the insurance industry have in such deliberations? Should a patient's bill of rights be developed as a new initiative? (FYI: In New York City taxicabs you will find a rider's bill of rights. It is interesting that taxicab riders are provided certain guarantees, but not people in the health care system!) While the public debates these issues, the day-to-day work of the social worker in health care is daunting. Flexibility is a prerequisite for helping our clients and for adjusting to the constantly renegotiated health care environment.

All health care social workers—whether in the role of clinical practitioner, supervisor, or administrator—face the challenge of understanding and anticipating health care trends. Social workers need to know how society operates as well as having an appreciation for the causes of diseases and an understanding of psychological processes (Rosenberg, 2008). Each worker's skills must therefore be current, flexible to change, and proactive with clients. And yes, all health care social workers must also understand macroeconomics, and its influence on health care delivery. The current economic environment is characterized by a shifting tension between quality of care and cost containment. Although the goal of the social work profession is to provide high-quality care, these services are shadowed and ultimately influenced by cost containment strategies. Health care social workers are expected to include cost containment among their practice principles whether they serve as direct practitioners, professional supervisors, administrators, or community organizers (Dziegielewski, 2013).

The viability of health care social work rests on two points. First, medical settings must place greater emphasis on the macro perspective in health care. Policy and practice are clearly linked (Miller, 2008). The social work profession must work actively to help the larger community understand its responsibility to create a cradle-to-grave health care system similar to those in other countries. Believing that the health care system will eventually solve its own problems is ludicrous. Health care social workers, whatever roles they choose for practice delivery, must take the lead in developing a more humane health care system that meets the needs of all people, regardless of their financial capabilities.

The second point that must be ingrained into all areas of health care social work practice is that advocacy leads to client empowerment. Health care social workers must change the mindset that coordinated care and the policies dictated by it are all bad. Social workers must recognize that there are benefits in a coordinated care system for both clients and providers. Probably the greatest strength of the ACA and coordinated care is coverage in a catastrophic situation. Advocating for systems of care that help provide a comprehensive approach to care stands at the forefront of providing comprehensive efforts, and advocacy in this area remains central.

We must recognize, however, that coordinated care also has many pitfalls, starting with large monthly premiums, extensive co-pays, and large deductibles. In these areas, health care social workers are therefore needed to advocate for clients. Workers must always stress development of new and needed services within the managed care framework. They must also teach clients how to obtain needed resources and help them to do so. On a larger scale, social workers are required—by their code of ethics—to advocate changes in policies or procedures that will directly or indirectly benefit clients.

Working as a health care social worker is far from easy. If you decide, nonetheless, that it's the area for you, the question is how do you best respond to the challenge? You will often be tempted to switch areas and collect a paycheck in a less volatile setting. Health care social work is suited to people who will relish the changing environment, want to maximize resources for clients, look to serve on boards and committees to influence policy and practice, and enjoy the idea that every day will be different. If that's you, the health care setting is worth considering.

SUMMARY

Health care social work is a dynamic, exciting, constantly changing field of practice. The past twenty years have brought things never seen before. Experienced social workers are forced to address specific issues in an environment where the rules are evolving. Health care social work's history is an extensive one, deeply rooted in the activities of pioneers such as Ida Cannon and Richard Cabot. These early practitioners directly linked social work practice to the medical model considered the core of health care practice.

Today health care social workers continue to strive to restore the highest level of functioning for each client, family, small group, and community served. The struggle with integrating practice and theory continues, for which translating academic practice into successful helping activities is the key (Brake & Duckers, 2013). Health care social work remains central to building the profession. Starting long ago and continuing to this day, health care social work remains an important and vital force, both in the profession and in communities across the country and around the world. People with medical illnesses often have other related problems and may need help reestablishing their routines once they arrive home from the hospital, or they may have trouble paying their bills. Families who lose a loved one may need counseling to process their grief, and those with hereditary conditions may need help sorting through their fears and concerns about the future. Health care social workers use a wide range of skills in all of these settings, employing both a family- and a systems-oriented approach to psychosocial care. The incorporation of health and wellness strategy goes beyond just addressing emergent health care needs and takes us one step closer to achieving what some could term a balanced life (Zechner & Kirchner, 2013). Social workers, similar to other helping professionals, provide counseling, help families develop strengths and resources, and run programs for patients who have diseases such as AIDS and heart disease (Centers for Disease Control and Prevention,2014; NASW, 2008). The settings these workers occupy vary from acute short-term settings to extended care long-term settings. Regardless of the type of clientele served, or the area of practice, health care social work is a challenging and essential area of practice.

Today's health care system is imbued with knowledge, expertise, equipment, and technologies never before even dreamed of or thought possible. Within our lifetime we have seen transplants go from headline news to no news, diseases eradicated, and life expectancy dramatically increased. Yet we all know that the health care system is challenged. Costs have risen, and continue to rise, to levels that require health insurance to help make care affordable. Even so, more than 40 million people are without health insurance. Scores of individuals and families are often forced to weigh the importance of simple decisions such as "Do I put food on the table tonight or buy the prescription for my child?"

Let's for a moment consider what the health care system might be like—reflecting on Ida Maude Cannon's ideals and imagining how they would translate to a health care system at the outset of the twenty-first century. One way to consider *what might be* is to identify core principles that you feel are central to your organization's purpose. These principles are integrated without bias or consideration of who is favored or not favored, and we need to begin to think about what is in the best interest of the whole. Some areas for future thought include

1. Given the most recent strides with the ACA, health care modification efforts need to be affordable to individuals and families, businesses, and taxpayers, and consistency among the states in providing these benefits is the key.

2. Health care needs to be as cost efficient as possible, spending the maximum amount of dollars on direct patient care.

3. Health care needs to provide comprehensive benefits, including benefits for mental health and long-term care services.

4. Health care needs to promote prevention and early intervention.

5. Health care provisions and services need to eliminate disparities in access to quality health care.

6. Health care needs to address the needs of people with special health care requirements, particularly those within underserved populations in both rural and urban areas.

7. Health care needs to promote quality and better health outcomes.

8. Health care services need to be inclusive by having adequate numbers of qualified health care caregivers, practitioners, and providers to guarantee timely access to quality care.

9. Health care needs to ensure adequate and timely payments in order to guarantee access to providers.

10. Health care services need to be comprehensive, fostering a strong network of health care facilities, including safety net providers.

11. Health care services need to maximize consumer choice in terms of health care providers and practitioners.

12. Health care services need to ensure continuity of coverage and care.

REFERENCES

Barker, R. L. (2003). *The social work dictionary* (5th ed.). Washington, DC: NASW Press.

Baran, B. E., Shanock, L. R., Rogelberg, S. G., & Scott, C. W. (2012). Leading group meetings: Supervisors' actions, employee behaviors, and upward perceptions. *Small Group Research, 43*, 330–335.

Beder, J. (2006). *Hospital social work: The interface of medicine and caring.* New York: Routledge/ Taylor and Francis.

Boes, M., & McDermott, V. (2005). Crisis intervention in the hospital emergency room. In A. R. Roberts (Ed.), *Crisis intervention handbook* (3rd ed., pp. 543–565). New York: Oxford University Press.

Brake, H. T., & Duckers, M. (2013). Early psychosocial interventions after disasters, terrorism and other shocking events: Is there a gap between norms and practice in Europe? *European Journal of Psychotraumatology, 4*, 1–10.

Bristow, D., & Herrick, C. (2002). Emergency department: The roles of the nurse case manager and the social worker. *Continuing Care, 21*(2), 28–29.

Burke, T. N. (2008). Nonprofit service organizations: Fidelity with strategic plans for financial survival. *Journal of Human Behavior in the Social Environment, 18*, 204–221.

Carlton, T. O. (1984). *Clinical social work in health care settings: A guide to professional practice with exemplars.* New York: Springer.

Centers for Disease Control and Prevention. (2014). *Recommendations for HIV prevention with adults and adolescents with HIV in the United States.* Retrieved from http://stacks.cdc.gov/ view/cdc/26065

Chapman, D. G., & Toseland, R. W. (2007). Effectiveness of advanced illness care teams for nursing home residents with dementia. *Social Work, 52*, 321–329.

Cowles, L. A., (2003). *Social work in the health field: a care perspective* (2nd ed.). Florence, KY: Routledge.

Damron-Rodriquez, J. (2008). Developing a competence for nurses and social workers. *Journal of Social Work Education, 44*(3), 27–37.

Diwan, S., Balaswamy, S., & Lee, S. E. (2012) Social work with older adults in health-care settings. In S. Gehlert, & T. Browne (Eds.), *Handbook of health social work* (2nd ed., pp. 392–425). Hoboken, NJ: Wiley.

Dziegielewski, S. F. (2006). *Psychopharmacology for the non-medically trained.* New York: Norton.

Dziegielewski, S. F. (2008a). Brief and intermittent approaches to practice: The state of practice. *Journal of Brief Treatment and Crisis Intervention, 8,*147–163.

Dziegielewski, S. F. (2008b). Problem identification, contracting, and case planning. In K. M. Sowers & C. N. Dulmus (Series Eds.) & W. Rowe & L. A. Rapp-Paglicci (Vol. Eds.), *Comprehensive handbook of social work and social welfare: Social work practice* (vol. 3, pp. 78–97). Hoboken, NJ: Wiley.

Dziegielewski, S. F. (2010). *Psychopharmacology and social work practice: A person-in-environment approach* (2nd ed.). NY: Springer.

Dziegielewski, S. F. (2013). *The changing face of health care social work: Opportunities and challenges for professional practice.* (3rd ed.). New York: Springer.

Frank, R. G. (2013). Mental illness and a dual dilemma. *Journal of the American Society of Aging, 37*(2), 47–53.

Gelman, S. R. (2009). On being an accountable profession: The code of ethics, oversight by boards of directors, and whistle-blowers as a last resort. In A. R. Roberts, *Social workers' desk reference* (2nd ed., pp. 156–162). New York: Oxford University Press.

Goode, R. A. (2000). *Social work practice in home health care.* Binghamton, NY: Haworth Press.

Gross, R., Tabenkin, H., Heymann, A., Greenstein, M., Matzliach, R., Portah, A., & Porter, B. (2007). Physician's ability to influence the life-style behaviors of diabetic patients: Implications for social work. In S. Dumont & M. St. Onge (Eds.), *Social work health and international development: Compassion in social policy and practice* (pp. 191–204). Binghamton, NY: Haworth Press.

Jansson, B. S. (2011). *Improving healthcare through advocacy: A guide for health and helping professionals.* Hoboken, NJ: Wiley.

Lam, W., Chan, E. A., & Yeung, K.S. (2013). Implications for school nursing through inter-professional education and practice. *Journal of Clinical Nursing, 22*(13/14), 1988–2001.

Leipzig, R. M., Hyer, K., Ek, K., Wallenstein, S., Vezina, M. L., Fairchild, S., . . . Howe, J. L. (2002). Attitudes toward working on interdisciplinary healthcare teams: A comparison by discipline. *Journal of the American Geriatric Society, 50,* 1141–1148.

Maust, D., Oslin, D. W., & Marcus, S. (2014). Effect of age on the profile of psychotropic users: Results from the 2010 National Ambulatory Medical Care Survey. *Journal of the American Geriatrics Society, 62,* 358–364.

McLeod, E., & Bywaters, P. (2000). *Social work, health and equality.* New York: Routledge.

McSkimming, S., Myrick, M., & Wasinger, M. (2000). Supportive care of the dying: A coalition for compassionate care—conducting an organizational assessment. *American Journal of Hospice & Palliative Care, 17,* 245–252.

Miller, P. J. (2008). Health-care policy: Should change be small or large? In K. M. Sowers & C. N. Dulmus (Series Eds.) & I. C. Colby (Vol. Ed.), *Comprehensive handbook of social work and social welfare: Social policy and policy practice* (vol. 4. pp. 219–236). Hoboken, NJ: Wiley.

Mizrahi, T. (1995). Health care: Reform initiatives. In R. Edwards. (Ed.), *Encyclopedia of social work* (19th ed., vol. 2, pp. 1185–1198). Silver Spring, MD: NASW Press.

Moniz, C., & Gorin, S. (2014). *Health care policy and practice: A biopsychosocial perspective* (4th ed.). New York: Routledge.

Morgaine, K., & Capous-Desyllas, M. (2015). *Anti-oppressive social work practice: Putting theory into action.* Los Angeles, CA: Sage.

Murray Alzheimer Research and Education Program. (2007). *Perceptions of the transition process to long-term care.* Ontario: University of Waterloo. Retrieved from https://uwaterloo.ca/murray-alzheimer-research-and-education-program/research/projects/family-transition-research-program/staff-perceptions

Nacman, M. (1977). Social work in health setting: A historical review. *Social Work in Health Care, 2,* 407–418.

National Association for Home Care & Hospice. (2010). Basic statistics about home care (p. 1–14). Retrieved from http://www.nahc.org/assets/1/7/10HC_Stats.pdf

National Association of Social Workers. (2008). *HIV/AIDS: General overview.* Retrieved from http://www.socialworkers.org/practice/hiv_aids/aidsday.asp

National Association of Social Workers. (2013). *Best practice standards in social work supervision.* Washington, DC: Author.

National Hospice and Palliative Care Organization. (2013). *NHPCO's facts and figures: Hospice care in America.* Alexandria, VA: National Hospice and Palliative Care Organization. Retrieved from http://www.nhpco.org/sites/default/files/public/Statistics_Research/2013_Facts_Figures.pdf

Neuman, K. (2000). Understanding organizational reengineering in health care: Strategies for social work's survival. *Social Work in Health Care, 31,* 19–32.

Nicholas, D. B., Darch, J., McNeill, T., Brister, L., O'Leary, K., Berlin, D., & Koller, D. (2007). Perceptions of online support for hospitalized children and adolescents. In S. Dumont & M. St.-Onge (Eds.), *Social work health and international development: Compassion in social policy and practice* (pp. 205–224). Binghamton, NY: Haworth Press.

NursingTimes.net. (Practice Comment). (2012). *Expand HCA role to focus on older people's rehabilitation.* Retrieved from http://www.nursingtimes.net/nursing-practice/clinical-zones/older-people/expand-hca-role-to-focus-on-older-peoples-rehabilitation/5048850.article?blocktitle=Practice-comment&contentID=6854

Ofosu, A. (2011). Implications for health care reform. *Health & Social Work, 36,* 229–231.

Poertner, J., & Rapp, C. A. (2007). *The textbook of social administration: The consumer centered approach.* Binghamton, NY: Haworth Press.

Poole, D. (1995). Health care: Direct practice. In R. Edwards & J. G. Hopps (Eds.), *Encyclopedia of social work* (19th ed., vol. 2, pp. 1156–1167). Washington, DC: NASW Press.

Popple, P., & Leighninger, L. (1990). *Social work, social welfare and American society.* Needham, MA: Allyn and Bacon.

Rosenberg, G. (2008). Social determinants of health: Twenty-first-century social work priorities. In K. M. Sowers & C. N. Dulmus (Series Eds.) & I. C. Colby (Vol. Ed.), *Comprehensive handbook of social work and social welfare: Vol. 4. Social policy and policy practice* (pp. 237–247). Hoboken, NJ: Wiley.

Rossi, P. (1999). *Case management in healthcare.* Philadelphia: W. B. Saunders.

Rugy, V. D. (2014). Where is the innovation in health care? *Washington Examiner.* Retrieved from: http://mercatus.org/expert_commentary/where-innovation-health-care

Schroeder, R. (2013). The seriously mentally ill older adult: Perceptions of the patient-provider relationship. *Perspectives in Psychiatric Care, 49,* 30–40.

Segal, W., & Brzuzy, S. (1998). *Social welfare policy, programs, and practice.* Itasca, IL: Peacock.

Sheafor, B. W., & Horejsi, C. R. (2014). *Techniques and guidelines for social work practice* (10th ed.). Boston: Allyn & Bacon/Pearson.

Strom-Gottfried, K. (2009). Enacting the educator role: Principles for practice. In A. R. Roberts (Ed.), *Social workers' desk reference* (2nd ed., pp. 720–725). New York: Oxford University Press.

Summers, N. (2012). *Fundamentals of case management practice: Skills for the human services* (4th. ed.). Belmont, CA: Brooks/Cole.

Temkin, M. (2009). *Aging and developmental disabilities strategic issues for service agencies. Garth Homer Society*. Retrieved from http://www.garthhomersociety.org/sites/default/files/imce/FinalAgingReport_GarthHomer_2009.pdf

The President's health security plan: The Clinton blueprint. (1993). New York: Times Books/Random House.

Trattner, W. (1989). *From poor law to welfare state: A history of social welfare in America* (4th ed.). New York: Free Press.

U.S. Department of Health and Human Services. (2003). *The AIDS epidemic and the Ryan White CARE Act: Past progress, future challenges 2002–2003*. Retrieved from http://hab.hrsa.gov/data/files/progressrpt200203.pdf

U.S. Department of Health and Human Services. (2012). *Fact Sheet: The Affordable Care Act's new patient's bill of rights*. Retrieved from http://healthreform.gov/newsroom/new_patients_bill_of_rights.html

U.S. Department of Health and Human Services (2014). *About the law*. Retrieved from http://www.hhs.gov/healthcare/rights

Van Wormer, K., & Boes, M. (1997). Humor in the emergency room: A social work perspective. *Health and Social Work, 22*(2), 87–92.

Walker, J. S., Bruns, E. J., & Penn, M. (2008). Individualized services in systems of care: The wrap-around process. In B. A. Stroul & G. M. Blau (Eds.), *The system of care handbook: Transforming mental health services for children, youth and families* (pp. 127–155). Baltimore, MD: Brookes.

Walsh, J. (2009). Psychoeducation. In A. R. Roberts (Ed.), *Social workers' desk reference* (2nd ed., pp. 474–478). New York: Oxford University Press.

Whitaker, T., Weismiller, T., Clark, E., & Wilson, M. (2006). *Assuring the sufficiency of a front line workforce: A national study of licensed social workers* (Special Report: Social Work Services in Health Care Settings). Washington, DC: NASW Press.

Zabora, J. R. (2009). Development of a proactive model of health care versus a reactive system of referrals. In A. R. Roberts (Ed.), *Social workers' desk reference* (2nd ed., pp. 826–832). New York: Oxford University Press.

Zechner, M. & Kirchner, M. P. (2013). Balanced Life: A pilot wellness program for older adults in psychiatric hospitals. *Psychiatric Rehabilitation Journal, 36*, 42–44.

CHAPTER 10
MENTAL HEALTH

THERE ARE 607,300 DOCUMENTED JOBS HELD BY SOCIAL WORKERS IN the United States and more than 57 percent of them are in the area of health, mental health, substance abuse, medical social work, and public health, where many are directly involved in the diagnostic process (U.S. Department of Labor, 2014b). Social workers are the nation's largest providers of mental health services. In the United States in 2006, it is estimated that there were 166,000 psychologists, 25,000 marriage and family therapists, and approximately 595,000 social workers (U.S. Department of Labor, 2014a). There is also a fast growing body of mental health counselors estimated at 120,000 (American Counseling Association, 2011). When compared to psychiatrists, psychologists, and psychiatric nurses, social workers continue to be the largest group of mental health providers having a significant effect on diagnostic impressions related to the current and continued mental health of all clients served. If simply for no other reason, social workers clearly outnumber the other counseling disciplines working in the field of mental health.

According to the *Occupational Outlook Handbook* (U.S. Department of Labor, 2014a) there are now 607,300 social work positions. Social workers are employed in a variety of settings including health care and mental health and substance abuse settings. Furthermore, from the years 2012 to2022 social work positions in general are expected to grow by 19 percent, which is faster than the average (11-percent) growth rate for other professions. It is clear that health and mental health are two areas in the field that are expected to grow. Social workers have a long history of leadership in this area, advocating at multiple levels with targeted interventions for individuals, families, groups, and communities and at the macro level with larger provider systems (National Association of Social Workers [NASW], 2012b). For social workers, ensuring that clients have access to mental health services remains an important aspect of client advocacy. The profession clearly supports mental health parity. In 2012, as in previous versions of *Social Work Speaks*, the NASW supported the policy of mental health parity, requiring both public and private insurance plans to provide comparable coverage for physical and mental health conditions. Supporting efforts toward mental health parity would give numerous individuals suffering from a mental illness equal access to health-related treatments and services. In addition, achieving mental health parity could help to dispel the widespread fears and stigma associated with suffering from a mental illness. It could also give consumers equal access to health care in a system that often limits mental health and substance-related treatments. Although some states have adopted laws to ensure mental health parity, we still have a long way to go.

In mental health practice, social workers are essential service providers, helping individuals meet their daily needs. Services provided include treating individuals with mental illness and other mental-health and substance-abuse–related problems. Social workers in the area of substance abuse treat many individuals suffering from abuse of alcohol, tobacco, and numerous other legal and illegal substances. Social workers practicing in this area engage in numerous services and functions, including mental health counseling in community mental health centers, private practice, psychiatric hospitals and psychiatric units, long-term care facilities, mental health courts, and prisons; case management; discharge planning, intake, or admission evaluation; high social risk case identification and patient education, support, and advocacy; crisis intervention; and interdisciplinary collaboration (Dziegielewski, 2013). Assessment and diagnostic services are considered an essential part of social work education and practice (Munson, 2009; Williams, 2009). Services are provided to all clients and their families, and all major psychiatric disorders are addressed, including schizophrenia, affective and mood disorders such as depression, neuropsychiatric disorders, eating disorders, personality disorders, phobias, substance abuse, childhood disorders, and organic psychoses (Dziegielewski, 2014; Munson, 2009).

Social workers serving in the area of mental health usually have either a baccalaureate or a master's degree from an accredited school of social work. Social work in general is not a highly paid profession, but of all the practice areas, those who work in the hospital setting seem to fare the best. For example, in May of 2012, the U.S. Department of Labor (2014a) placed the median annual income for positions in the field at $44,200.00 with a median annual income for hospital social workers of $56,290. Lower salaries are noted for social workers in residential care facilities, with a median wage of $34, 950 a year. Unfortunately, the labor statistics do not break down income by degree; however, according to the NASW (2012a), social workers at the baccalaureate level earned a median income of $40,599 to $54,132 (amounts vary based on experience) whereas those at the master's level earned approximately $50,753 to $69,999.

Did You Know…Massachusetts General Hospital in Boston pioneered hospital and psychiatric social work, starting a social service department in 1905, and hiring social workers to work with patients who suffered from mental illness in 1907 (NASW, 1998).

When a social worker employed in a local mental health clinic outside of Orlando, Florida, was asked how she felt about her job, she said she could describe it best as "challenging, rewarding, and most of the time quite frustrating." She believed that the role of the mental health social worker is complicated because allegiances must be divided, and always placing the needs of the client first forced her to maintain a delicate balance between the needs of the family, the society, and the agency. Because clients with mental impairment often cannot handle their own affairs, the social worker must ensure that the rights of these clients in terms of respect for individual dignity, worth, and self-determination are not violated, thereby finding a balance between encouraging autonomy and minimizing risk (Scheyett et al., 2009). Working to get clients access to mental health treatment and whenever possible working to keep families together in the home are emphasized (Barth, Kolivoski, Lindsey, Lee, & Collins, 2014).

The mental health social worker must also be well aware of *duty to warn*. If a client is perceived as a *danger to self or others*, action is taken to protect any person or persons who may be at risk (Fox, 2009). Duty to warn may force a social worker to violate the confidence of the client in order to protect others in the immediate environment or, if the client is threatening suicide, to protect the client. Therefore, mental health social work practitioners must always strive for balance between the rights of the client and the needs of the client and family. Social workers must be advocates for clients with mental impairment; these clients will often be provided services through facilitation and referral, especially when they are not capable of representing themselves.

Many beginning social work professionals are attracted to the area of mental health because they aspire to do therapy with the clients they serve. The NASW (2011, p. 1) described several essential components of psychosocial psychiatric services as:

1. Determining client eligibility for services
2. Conducting timely biopsychosocial assessments and social histories
3. Assessing clients for substance use, support systems, physical and emotional functioning, financial stability, safety, suicidal and homicidal ideation, etc.
4. Developing and implementing treatment and discharge plans that adhere to client self-determination
5. Providing direct therapeutic services to clients such as individuals, families, and groups, related to specific mental health issues
6. Performing crisis management and other types of administrative, supportive, and management functions all designed to aid in providing ethical client care

This early stance by NASW is used today and highlights how important it is for the social worker to understand diagnosis and assessment, particularly because most social workers serve as advocates, facilitating and ensuring as part of the interdisciplinary team that the client gets the services needed.

In this chapter we will introduce the role of social worker in mental health. In particular, we will introduce a multidimensional psychosocial assessment that allows the social worker to gather information needed to understand the client and his or her environment. In closing we will examine several potential areas of practice for the social worker interested in working in the area of mental health.

MULTIDIMENSIONAL PSYCHOSOCIAL ASSESSMENT

In the area of mental health, the profession of social work did not develop in isolation. Therefore, in order to survive and compete in the mental health practice environment, many social workers have adapted to the dominant culture. This means that the practice approaches and methodologies employed by social workers at all levels may be influenced by the expectations delineated by a team approach or agency designation. Furthermore, expectations that outline the connection between service provision and reimbursement become significant contenders in the delivery of care. For example, outcome measures, which dictate service reimbursement, have become mandatory (Dziegielewski, 2013); the more client focused these measures can become, the better (Pike, 2009). Moreover, it is not uncommon for social workers to feel forced to reduce services to some clients, focusing their efforts instead on those covered by insurance or able to pay privately. Clients who cannot pay privately or afford the co-payments required by many insurance plans may self-terminate services if they are viewed as too costly (Dziegielewski, 2013). This problem can be further complicated for older adults, whom Frank (2013) terms the *duals*. These individuals, who qualify for both Medicare and Medicaid services, tend to be a highly heterogeneous, vulnerable, high-cost group requiring a multitude of services. Accurate psychosocial assessment is therefore a critical tool for all mental health and health care social workers because it documents a client's needs and can support not only the efficiency but also the continued necessity of a chosen intervention. Such assessments not only open the door for services, but they can also help to justify the need for the service, ultimately determining who will receive initial and continued services as well as what will be provided.

Currently, many social workers work with clients who suffer from mental illness. These social workers range from the baccalaureate level practitioner, who is active in case management, initial assessment, and discharge planning, to the master's level social worker, who is an active participant in completing assessments and diagnoses (see box 1 for application of a case). Regardless of the social worker's

Box 1. Mental Illness Can Strike Anyone and the Consequences Can Be Devastating: A True Case Story

Fort Worth—Jane fell so far so fast. A woman of education with a soft spot for the underdog, Jane combined a master's degree in social work with a compassion for the homeless that propelled her into Austin's power circles. She drove an expensive car, lived a full life, and was devoted to a loving family.

And she lost it all as a victim of mental illness.

The petite, blue-eyed blonde who once turned heads was beaten to death Saturday, left alone on a dirty sidewalk among those she once helped. At age 43, she died penniless and homeless, all her worldly goods in two plastic grocery bags.

For those who knew Jane, the tragic end was no surprise. Jane suffered from bipolar and personality disorders that left her without a family, unable to work, and on the street. "It is sad to say, but we feared something like this would happen," said her friend for 12 years. "She was so out of control, and no matter how hard we tried to help, she wouldn't take it."

Early Saturday, Jane was found slumped over in front of Mental Health–Mental Retardation Services day resource building. An autopsy showed she died from blunt force injuries to her head. Her killer remains a mystery, and there are no new leads in the case. Witnesses told police they saw Jane talking to an unidentified man about an hour before she was found dead, said the homicide detective.

A composite of the man has been posted on fliers and tacked up around the shelters and known hangouts for local indigents. "He could be a witness or a suspect, and right now we just want him for questioning."

Jane's daughter said the fact that her mother wouldn't accept help from loved ones adds to her sadness. "A lot of people ask me, 'Why didn't you help? Why didn't you do anything?' Well, what they don't know is that it is harder than that," her daughter said.

Jane's former social work professor, who taught and served as a mentor, said Jane is proof that mental illness can tear apart lives. "I don't think the general public knows just how vicious mental illness is. It can destroy you. . . It destroyed her to the end."

Her daughter stated that most of her family hadn't seen Jane for two years. Her mother had avoided seeing loved ones but managed to keep in touch through phone calls and letters. She described her mother as someone who had inner and outer beauty, a person with a great sense of humor who was articulate and who made sure the family went to church. "During the summer she used to make me volunteer. She was just that way. She really cared about others. But the mental illness tore our relationship apart," her daughter said.

"I had a real good conversation with her, a week ago," her daughter continued. "It was the best we had in a long time. I was beaming for days afterward. . . . I think, since it was the last time we talked that is was a gift from God."

News about Jane's slaying unnerved the night shelter residents, who expressed fear that the killer might be among them.

"Women who are street-wise know how to protect themselves," said the executive director of the shelter. "Unfortunately, Jane didn't. Jane did not fit the stereotypes of a homeless person. She was educated and not addicted to drugs or alcohol. But the mental illness left her destitute. Jane didn't say anything to anybody. She kept to herself and roamed all over the city. I was really crushed when I heard what happened to her. She didn't deserve this."

"About 60 percent of the homeless in this country suffer from some form of mental illness, and about 40 percent have a substance abuse problem," said the chief of mental health and addiction services. Jane was first diagnosed with depression when she was about 18, relatives and friends said. She was in and out of treatment facilities much of her life, beating the illness long enough to fall in love, get married, and raise a family.

At some point, Jane, who was adopted, sought out her birth mother. The reunion proved devastating when her mother rejected her, friends said. The illness resurfaced and her marriage failed. She divorced her husband and lost custody of her daughter.

She remarried and enrolled in college while in her 30s. Her friend remembered the days when they went to the state capitol to lobby for welfare reform and how easily Jane fit into the social work community and the jobs that followed.

But Jane left the work she loved in 1993, when she learned she was pregnant with her second child. After the birth, manic depression took its toll, relatives and friends said. The marriage failed and her second husband took custody of her son, who is now 4.

Those close to her said those events may have triggered her depression and mood swings. And by the spring of 1996, Jane found comfort living on the streets, traveling between Fort Worth, Las Vegas, and San Diego.

Her friend tracked her down at a psychiatric facility in Fort Worth and found Jane staring blankly at daytime television through a fog of medication. She said, "Hi, what are you doing here?" And I said, "To see you. What are you doing here?" And she said, "Well, this is where I belong." This memory left her friend feeling helpless and frustrated.

"Jane used to work hard to help people who had fallen through the cracks and were unemployed or near homeless," her friend said. "She was a good person who took everything to heart. . . . To me, this is proof that if it can happen to Jane, it can happen to the rest of us." (Modified from Craig, 1998; names were either deleted or changed and text was abridged.)

---

degree and subsequent level of practice, he or she must be aware of the tools and expectations characteristic of the field. The importance of the initial psychosocial assessment should not be underestimated because it provides the foundation and the framework for any current and future intervention.

Assessment is defined as "the process of determining the nature, cause, progression and prognosis of a problem and the personalities and situations involved therein; the social work function of acquiring an understanding of a problem, what causes it, and what can be changed to minimize or resolve it" (Barker, 2003, p. 30). Social workers assume that assessment is a key component to the start of any intervention and always begins with the first client-worker interaction (Austrian, 2009). The information that the social worker obtains determines the requirements and direction of the helping process. The mental health social worker gathers information about the present situation, elicits history about the past, and anticipates service expectations for the future. This assessment should always include creative interpretations of alternatives to best assist the client to get the services needed (Dziegielewski, 2014).

In mental health assessment, as in all social work assessments, the client is regarded as the primary source of data. In most cases, the client is questioned directly, either verbally or in writing. Information about the client is also derived from direct observation of verbal and physical behavior and interaction patterns between the client and other interdisciplinary team members, family members, significant others, or friends. Viewing and recording these patterns of communication can be extremely helpful in later identifying and developing strength and resource considerations (see Figure 1). In addition, background sheets, psychological tests, and tests to measure health status or level of daily functioning may be used. Furthermore, in keeping with social work's traditional emphasis on including information about other areas, the worker talks with family members and significant others to estimate planning support and assistance. It may also be important to access secondary sources such as the client's medical record and other health care providers.

To facilitate assessment, the social worker must be able to understand the client's medical situation or at least know where to go for information and help. Knowledge of certain mental health conditions, as well as common accompanying medical conditions, can help the social worker to understand the breadth of what is affecting the client's behavior. Referrals for a complete medical checkup should always be considered (Dziegielewski, 2014). Social workers should not hesitate to ask for clarification of medical problems and the complications they can present in regard to a client's care, especially when they are unsure about how the information may enhance their understanding of the client's situation.

Five expectations guide the start of the assessment process in the health and mental health setting (Dziegielewski, 2013):

1. *Clients must be active and motivated in the treatment process.* As in almost all forms of intervention, the client is expected to be active. The client must often expend serious energy in attempting to make behavioral changes. Clients therefore must not only agree to participate in the assessment process, but they must also be willing to embark on the intervention plan that will produce behavioral change. Social workers usually practice verbal therapy; however, clients who are unmotivated or unwilling to talk or discuss change strategies may require more concrete goals and objectives to bring about specific behavior change.

2. *The problem must guide the approach or method of intervention used.* Social workers need to be aware of different methods and approaches to practice. It is crucial to ensure that the approach favored by the social worker is not what guides the intervention that follows. The approach that best addresses the client's circumstance should be what guides the choice of the intervention. The social worker must always be careful to avoid becoming over-involved and wasting valuable time in trying to match a particular problem to a particular theoretical model or approach. Health and mental health social workers must never lose sight of the ultimate purpose of the assessment process, that is, to complete an assessment that helps to establish a concrete service plan that addresses the client's needs (see the activity below and the definition of assessment).

Activity...Review the definition of assessment, and look at the reasons given for social workers to participate in this function. Discuss these issues with your classmates and decide whether you believe it is essential for social workers in health care and mental health to participate in assessment. Explain both what you see as reason for participation and what you see as problems that might be caused by taking this active stance as a member of an interdisciplinary team.

3. *The influence of values and beliefs needs to be made apparent in the process.* Each one of us, professional or not, is influenced by our own values and beliefs. These beliefs are the foundation of who we are. In the professional practice of social work, however, it is essential that these personal beliefs and values do not override the outcome of the assessment and subsequent intervention process. This requires taking into account the social worker's personal values and beliefs and being aware of how these beliefs can influence practice strategy. Professional helping strategy should always be guided toward what is best for the client and not founded on preset personal assumptions or beliefs that the client does not hold.

For example, what if an unmarried client in a psychiatric hospital has tested positive for pregnancy? The social worker will realize that, due to the client's mental health condition, life circumstances, and other factors, she may have limited capability to parent the child. The social worker personally believes that abortion is wrong. This personal value is so strong that the social worker feels that she cannot in good conscience or objectively discuss abortion as an option. The client is unsure about what to do, although she realizes she cannot stop taking her medications to address the **hallucinations** and delusions. The social worker also knows that, if the client continues to take these medications in the formative stages of the pregnancy (the first three months in particular), the baby could be placed at risk. The client realizes her current limitations and states that she would not be a good parent and cannot take care of herself without help. She asks the social worker for help in deciding what to do and what her options are.

From a personal perspective this can be a difficult case; yet from a professional perspective the answer becomes clearer. From the professional perspective, the ultimate assessment and intervention strategy must be based on the client's needs and desires, not those of the social worker. Therefore, guided by the profession's code of ethics, the social worker will not tell the client of her personal feelings and will explore all options. If the personal perspective is so pronounced that the social worker feels she cannot fully empower the client to make the best decision and explore all potential options available, he/she must refer the client to another social work professional who can be more objective.

Most social work professionals agree that clients have the right to make their own decisions. Clients exercise this right especially when they are aware of their situation and want to participate in their own individualized health care plans. Whatever their own feelings, social workers must do everything possible to protect this right and to keep their personal opinions from preventing a proper assessment.

The beliefs and values of the members of the interdisciplinary team must also be considered. Social workers need to recognize value conflicts that arise among the other team members and to make team members aware of how their personal feelings and opinions may keep them from exploring all possible options for a client. This is not to suggest that social workers are more qualified to address this issue or that they always have an answer. It means that social workers should strive to assist these professionals and should always keep the goal—how to best serve the client in a nonjudgmental way—at the forefront. Furthermore, social work has a very comprehensive code of ethics, and at times this may be different or have a different emphasis from that used by other professionals on the team. Good sound ethical decision making is expected, and educating other professionals about ethical conduct in social work may be warranted (Strom-Gottfried, 2008).

4. *Issues of culture and race should be addressed openly in the assessment and treatment.* The understanding of racial identity and the effect it can have on psychological well-being should not be underestimated (Woods & Kurtz-Cotes, 2007). In addition, social workers need to be aware of their own cultural heritage as well as the client's to create the most open and receptive environment possible. To facilitate the assessment the following basic guidelines are suggested:

- ◆ Note cultural factors and remain open to cultural differences (Locke & Bailey, 2014).
- ◆ Recognize the integrity and the uniqueness of the client, respect self-determination, and provide services within a nonjudgmental framework (Dziegielewski, 2014).
- ◆ Empower the client using his/her own learning style, including use of his/her own resources and supports (Dziegielewski, 2013).

Did You Know...The fifth edition of the **Diagnostic and Statistical Manual of Mental Disorders (DSM-5),** *which was released in May of 2013 and is considered the major reference for the diagnosis of mental disorders and related mental health conditions, stresses that cultural factors must be considered before establishing a diagnosis. To assist with this, cultural concepts of distress that can mimic a mental disorder but are related to an individual's culture are outlined and an interview format, called the Cultural Formulation Interview (CFI), is provided to identify and measure cultural factors. All social workers must know how cultural and ethnic factors can affect assessment.*

---

5. *Assessment must focus on client strengths and highlight the client's own resources.* Identifying how to use the client's own strengths and resources is

central to creating sustained change (Corcoran, 2010). Many times clients can have enormous difficulty identifying and planning to use their own strengths. Clients are no different from the general population in this regard; people in general tend to focus on the negative and rarely praise themselves for the good they do. Also, admitting to a mental health problem may carry stigma the client may not want to accept. This stigma may be carried over to family and friends as *courtesy stigma* and that may disturb the supportive helping networks the client needs (Rosenzweig & Brennan, 2008). The client's perceptions are important to the helping relationship, especially whether he or she believes that the provider is listening and understands what is being said (Schroeder, 2013).

Empowering the client's use of a **strengths-based assessment** is considered critical (Corcoran, 2010; Morales & Sheafor, 2006). For so many clients, especially those with mental health problems, their opinions of the world around them can become distorted. Also, it is always important for the social worker to avoid confusing the boundaries between normal human behavior and pathology because this can cause false diagnoses and a medicalization of what might actually be considered adaptive behavior (Frances & Jones, 2013). The way clients see and think of themselves and the tasks that need to be accomplished can become clouded. An all-or-nothing approach may cause them to feel lost, alone, and ineffective in what they have done or tried to do. Therefore, it is the role of the social worker to assist the client in identifying positive behaviors and accomplishments. Some social workers also feel strongly about the importance of teaching life skills and expanding upon this area to increase psychosocial functioning (Reddon, Hoglin, & Woodman, 2008).

In today's high-pressure health and mental health environments, social workers cannot spend time exploring issues and the related behaviors that don't contribute to the client's well-being. They must quickly utilize a strengths-based assessment by helping the client to identify her own strengths and thereby maximize skill-building potential. Because most treatment is time limited these days, individual resources are essential for continued growth and maintenance of wellness after the formal treatment period has ended. Although there are many different time-limited approaches to practice, most social workers agree that their first task is to clearly identify the client's strengths to use them as part of the treatment planning process. Focusing on a client's strengths can help the client to become empowered and make changes that otherwise may have seemed impossible (Corcoran, 2010).

Figure 1: This woman was previously hospitalized for schizophrenia. With family support she was able to live outside of an institution, enjoy her grandniece, and live a fuller life.

Person-in-Environment: A Systematic Approach to Assessment

In mental health practice today many forms of formal assessment can assist in the development of a treatment plan. One system of assessment that favors the person-in-situation approach is the **Person-in-Environment Classification System**, also known as the PIE. Designed primarily for advanced master's level practice, the PIE was underwritten by an award given to the California chapter of NASW from the NASW Program Advancement Fund (Whiting, 1996). Knowledge of the PIE is relevant for all mental health social workers regardless of educational level because of its emphasis on situational factors (Karls & O'Keefe, 2008. 2009). This assessment is built around two major premises that are basic to all social work practice: recognition of social considerations in every identified problem and relating these factors back to the person-in-situation stance. The PIE responds to the need to identify the problems of clients relative to what is being experienced around them, creating a comprehensive perspective that mental health and health professionals can easily understand (Karls & Wandrei, 1996a, 1996b):

[It] calls first for a social work assessment that is translated into a description of coding of the client's problems in social functioning. Social functioning is the client's ability to accomplish the activities necessary for daily living (for example, obtaining food, shelter, and transportation) and to fulfill major social roles as required by the client's subculture or community (Karls & Wandrei, 1996a, p. vii).

The PIE provides the following (Karls & Wandrei, 1996a):

◆ A common language with which social workers in all settings can describe their client's problems in social functioning

◆ A common capsule description of social phenomena that can facilitate treatment or ameliorate problems presented by clients

◆ A basis for gathering data to be used to measure the need for services and to design human service programs to evaluate effectiveness

◆ A mechanism for clearer communication among social work practitioners and between practitioners, administrators, and researchers

◆ A basis for clarifying the domain of social work in human service fields

The PIE is an excellent tool for advanced social workers; beginning professionals are not ready nor will they be expected to use this complex assessment tool. As you progress through human behavior and practice courses you will become more familiar with this technique, its advantages, and its uses in mental health practice. It's enough now to observe that the PIE provides an important vehicle to understanding the many factors that affect a client's behavior, which is an important part of the assessment process.

The PIE system is user friendly because it classifies clients' problems into four distinct categories, or *factors*. For the purpose of this chapter we have presented an abbreviated version of this assessment system. This information is not meant to be all-inclusive; rather it is intended to help introduce beginning social work professionals to the knowledge base underlying the use of the PIE and to its relevance to formalized mental health assessment (Karls & O'Keefe, 2008). For tips on documentation, see box 2.

Diagnostic and Statistical Manual of Mental Disorders, DSM-5

Another important tool for social workers in the mental health arena is the *Diagnostic and Statistical Manual of Mental Disorders*; the latest version is the *DSM-5* (American Psychiatric Association, 2013). The *DSM* is considered an advanced tool to assess mental health disorders and supporting conditions. Its use is generally covered in graduate courses, and in some schools, entire courses are devoted to the study and application of the *DSM* and its relationship to social work practice. In the beginning of the *DSM-5*, the list of professionals who are expected

---

Box 2. Tips on Information Recording and Documentation

Social workers must document their assessment plans clearly. Although it is beyond the scope of this book to discuss electronic and paper documentation techniques in detail, the following tips introduce the most important aspects of accurate and timely record keeping.

   1. Always document justification for the "service necessity" of what you do.

   2. Be sure to clearly document purpose, content, and outcome in every note you write—regardless of the type of note or reason for making the entry.

   3. Always sign your name, include credentials, and so forth, at the end of every note you write. Be sure to include the date and time the service was provided in every note. Don't forget to put in the record the amount of time spent with the client.

   4. All those who review records for billing say that the biggest problems are lack of information and inaccurate information in the record.

   5. Always document problem behaviors in terms of frequency, intensity, and duration.

   6. Always be able to benchmark progress.

   7. When you complete paper records, always use a black or blue pen (whose ink does not run) and never reproduce notes for others.

   8. If you do not document it, it did not happen. If you did document it, it did happen.

   9. When you use assessment systems such as the PIE, be sure to identify the factors related to the individual's psychological and social situation.

---

to use the book includes social workers. Based on the number of different professionals that use the book, and given that the *DSM-5* is written and revised by the American Psychiatric Association (APA) with limited input from other professional disciplines, it should come as no surprise that controversy continues to surround its usage (Frances & Jones, 2013). One major reason social workers can be conflicted is the fear that diagnosing a mental disorder can result in a **label** for a client that will be carried indefinitely. For a more detailed explanation of the *DSM-5* and its relation to treatment planning and practice see Dziegielewski (2015) or for a more detailed explanation of the PIE see Karls and O'Keefe (2008).

   In professional practice, tools such as the PIE can facilitate the identification and assessment of clients from a person-in-environment perspective that is easy for social workers to accept as comprehensive (Dziegielewski, 2014). When compared to the **DSM-IV-TR** and *DSM-5*, the PIE provides mental health professionals with a classification system that enables them to codify the numerous environmental factors considered when looking at an individual's situation. In summary, regardless of what type of mental health assessment is conducted, classification systems such as the PIE and *DSM-5* allow mental health professionals to first recognize and later systematically address mental health problems and behavioral difficulties. The PIE, in particular, can help professionals to obtain a clearer sense of the relationship between the problem and the environment in a friendly and adaptable way.

THE BEHAVIORAL BIOPSYCHOSOCIAL APPROACH TO SOCIAL WORK PRACTICE

Social work practice in assessment and intervention today (Dziegielewski, 2013), as in the past (Carlton, 1984), should recognize three factors: the biomedical, the psychological, and the social. A social worker who understands the biopsychosocial approach to health and mental health practice strives to ascertain for each client the appropriate balance among biomedical, psychological, and social considerations (Austrian, 2009). Balance, however, doesn't mean that these factors are treated as equal for every client. The particular situation experienced by the client determines where emphasis must be placed and what area must be addressed first. In today's practice environment, with its insistence on an observable, measurable outcome, the mental health social worker addresses the biopsychosocial factors in the client's life through the behavioral aspects of the client's condition. One of the first aspects to address is a careful risk assessment. Because the most significant risk factors for suicide include suffering from a severe mental disorder or a mood disorder combined with substance abuse, this type of assessment should always come first (Yeager, Roberts, & Saveanu, 2009). This involves creating a culture of safety for assessing the client as well as the physical environment. Yeager, Roberts, and Saveanu (2009) stress that to assess for suicidality the social worker needs to identify psychiatric signs and symptoms, as well as past and current suicidal ideation, past attempts, and current plans (see the activity below for a sample treatment plan with a client who is suicidal).

For example, if a client is newly assessed as having schizophrenia while also being HIV positive, many issues must be addressed. At first the emphasis may be placed on the biomedical or biological area. The client needs to be told immediately that the medical test for HIV is positive and to be given information about what a positive test means. The task can be complicated by the client's mental condition. The schizophrenia may produce periodic breaks from reality, such as hallucinations and delusions that keep him or her from accurately interpreting

Activity...Here is a sample treatment plan for a client who is suicidal. Taking a behavioral biopsychosocial approach, what do you think of this plan? What are its strengths and its limitations for the client being served?

Sample Treatment Plan for Suicidal Ideation/Behavior

Definition: Suicide is a human act of self-inflicted, self-intentional cessation. Simply stated, it is the wish to be dead with the act that carries out the wish.
Suicide ideation: Thinking about suicide.
Suicide verbalization: Talking about suicide.
Parasuicide: Attempting suicide.

Signs and Symptoms to note in the record (be sure to document any of these signs in the record):
Changes in eating and sleeping,
Changes in friends and social programs.
Changes in grades, job status, or love relationships.
Changes in usual daily activities.
Constant restlessness or unshakable depression.
Neglected appearance or hygiene.
Increase in drug or alcohol use.
Giving away of material possessions.
Recurrent thoughts or preoccupation with death.
Recent suicide attempt.
Ongoing suicidal ideation and any previous or present plans.
history of suicide attempts in the family.
Sudden change in mood that is not consistent with life events.
Past suicide attempts and what was done.
History of drug abuse.

Goals:
1. Stabilize suicidal crisis
2. Place client at appropriate level of care to address suicidal crisis
3. Reestablish a sense of hope to deal with the current life situations
4. Alleviate suicidal impulses and intent and return to higher (safer) level of functioning

Objective	Intervention	Time frame*
Client will no longer feel the need to harm self	Assess for suicidal ideation and concrete plan of execution. Then make appropriate disposition/referral.	
Client will discuss suicidal feelings and thoughts	Complete no-suicide contract. Address suicidal thoughts or impulses. Determine level of depression or suicide precaution. Assess and monitor suicide intervention.	
Identify positives in current life situation	Assist client to develop awareness of negative self-talk patterns and encourage positive images and self-talk.	

Help client to identify consistent eating and sleeping patterns	Educate client in deep-breathing and relaxation techniques. Assist client in developing coping strategies.
Take medications as prescribed and report any inconsistencies or side effects	Monitor for medication use and misuse and confer with treatment team on a regular basis.
Complete assessment of functioning.	Arrange or complete Activities of Daily Living (ADLs) assessment. Determine services needed for community placement

*Time frame is to be individualized to the client.

medical information. The client may have difficulty understanding how far the disease has progressed and what can be expected medically, for example. Nevertheless, every attempt must be made to help the client to understand the medical aspects of his or her condition and what being infected with this virus actually means. It is critical to ensure that the client understands terms such as t-cell count and future self-protection from illness and opportunistic infectious diseases. While information such as this about the medical condition is shared, a constant vigil is needed to maintain client safety, with assessment and reassessment as needed for continued safety (Yeager, Roberts, & Saveanu, 2009).

Once the biomedical situation and support for what the client is experiencing emotionally are addressed, emphasis may shift to the social and psychological aspects of the client's condition. Because HIV is clearly communicable, the client must realize quickly that his or her behavior can have significant effects on people in his or her support system. Early education about how the virus is transmitted can be critical. Because HIV is most often sexually transmitted, the client's past and present sexual partners must be considered. Alone or with help, the client must face telling loved ones about what has happened and what it will mean for future social relations.

The client may also be frightened by the changes in his or her mental status and unsure of how to control the symptoms related to schizophrenia. First, the client must understand what is happening. Second, the client must be helped to realize what schizophrenia means for him or her and for those he or she comes in contact with. Important information must be shared with family and friends. The social perspective of the biopsychosocial approach focuses on the individual client together with the family, significant others, and friends—on how best to protect them but also to involve them in problem solving. The psychological perspective focuses directly on the fears and concerns of the individual, on how to help him to understand his mental health and the emotions he exhibits.

As you can see, if a client has a dual diagnosis, helping can become very complicated. In our example, the dual diagnosis of HIV and schizophrenia means that the client may be losing touch with reality and how his or her behaviors can harm others at a time when this knowledge is especially important. Once the immediate needs of the client and his or her family have been addressed and a risk assessment has been completed, the focus of intervention should shift to the functional/situational factors affecting the individual client. A functional assessment allows the social worker to determine the level at which the client is capable of responding to a concrete intervention-based plan.

It is essential that assessment and intervention be related to the needs and abilities of the client. The social worker begins with exploration to examine and organize the unique aspects of the client (Austrian, 2009). A complete assessment is designed to help the client better understand himself or herself, and the factors identified during the procedure are shared with the client to assist in self-help or continued skill building (Eamon, 2008). Boxes 3 and 4 list factors to be considered in the mental health assessment. The assessment process is initially used to examine the situation and initiate the helping process; later it contributes to an intervention plan.

MENTAL HEALTH AND WORKING WITH THE FAMILY IN ACUTE CARE SETTINGS

As early as 1903 at Massachusetts General Hospital, Richard C. Cabot realized the importance of addressing psychosocial factors in medical illness. From this early perspective the assigned duties of the medical social worker included focusing on the economic, emotional, social, and situational needs of patients and their families (Cabot, 1913). To accomplish the assigned tasks in the late 1800s and early

---

Box 3. Biomedical or Biological Factors to Be Considered in Mental Health Assessment

Area	Explanation
General medical condition	Describe the physical illness or disability from which the client is suffering.
Overall health status	Client is to evaluate her self-reported health status and level of functional ability.
Overall level of functioning	Describe what the client is able to do to meet her daily needs. Concrete tasks are assessed and documented for focus on future change effort.
Maintenance of continued health and wellness	Measure the client's functional ability and interest in preventive medical intervention.

Box 4. Social Factors to Be Considered in Mental Health Assessment

Area	Explanation
Social/societal help-seeking behavior	Is the client open to outside help? Is the client willing to accept help from those outside his/her immediate family or the community?
Occupational participation	How does the client's illness or disability impair or prohibit functioning in the work environment? Is the client in a supportive work environment?
Social support system	Does the client have support from neighbors, friends, or community organizations (church membership, membership in professional clubs, etc.)?
Family support	What support or help can be expected from relatives of the client?
Support from significant other	Does the significant other understand and show willingness to help and support the needs of the client?
Ethnic or cultural affiliation	If the client is a member of a certain cultural or religious group, will affiliation affect medical treatment and compliance issues?

1900s, health care social workers were required to have adequate medical knowledge, an understanding of disease and factors that affected mental health, and a firm comprehension of public health. With the medical advances of the late 1950s the social worker was expected to bridge "... the gap between the hospital bed, the patient's home and the world of medical science" (Risley, 1961, p. 83).

In health and mental health today the role of the social worker continues much along the same path, with extensive focus also on meeting the needs of the client and his or her family members. Although the family members are not the actual client being served, it is not uncommon for services to be provided to them that include education, supportive interventions, and referrals, as well as reporting of problematic social conditions, assisting and ensuring treatment compliance with the established medical regime, and providing linkages between the acute care setting and the appropriate community agencies. Box 5 lists psychosocial factors to be considered in the mental health assessment. Often it is the family who first recognizes the problem and seeks help for the client (Brennan,

Box 5. Psychological Factors to Be Considered in Mental Health Assessment

Area	Explanation
Life stage	Describe the development stage in life at which the individual appears to be functioning.
Mental functioning	Describe the client's mental functioning. Complete a mental status measurement. Can the client participate knowledgeably in the intervention experience?
Cognitive functioning	Does the client have the ability to think and reason about what is happening to him/her? Is the client able to participate and make decisions in regard to her own best interest?
Level of self-awareness and self-help	Does the client understand what is happening to her? Is the client capable of assisting his/her level of self-care? Is the client capable of understanding the importance of health and wellness information? Is the client open to help and services provided by the health care team?

Evans, & Spencer, 2008). Other areas of service provision in these acute health care settings include case consultation, case finding, case planning, psychosocial assessment and intervention, collaboration, treatment team planning, group therapy, supportive counseling, organ donation coordination, health education, advocacy, case management, discharge planning, information and referral, quality assurance, bereavement, and research (Dziegielewski, 2013; Holliman, Dziegielewski, & Datta, 2001).

In this fast-paced environment, all health care professionals are being forced to deal with numerous issues that include declining hospital admissions, reduced lengths of hospital stay, and numerous other restrictions and methods of cost containment (Dziegielewski, 2013). Struggling to resolve these issues has become necessary because health care spending has far exceeded any hopes of budget negotiations. The concern for reducing expenditures in an environment that also requires maximizing scarce and dwindling resources continues to prevail (Yeager & Latimer, 2009). This is further complicated by expectations of state-of-the-art care in the United States (Anderson & Froger, 2008). Technological advances have clearly increased and changed the way clients and professionals view expected treatment and care (Palmo, 2011). Yet, regardless of these expectations and resources, receiving quick, cost-cutting services can also be linked to increased rates of high-risk patient relapse. Therefore, it should come as no surprise that some researchers question why so many people are dying because they simply do not receive preventive services in one of the most technology advanced countries in the world (Miller, 2008).

When a client is discharged from a facility, an important part of discharge planning is ensuring an appropriate follow-up service plan for return to a lesser level of care. In the past, the role of the social worker was often expected to end once the client was discharged from the facility (Simon, Showers, Blumfield, Holden, & Wu, 1995). Today, however, social workers are finding that these traditional roles have expanded to cover a broader function, linking the client to other systems of care as well as developing specific care plans with a clear focus on continuity of care (Yeager & Latimer, 2009).

A significant issue to consider when dealing with the client's mental health issues is the psychological and social burden that is often placed on the client's family. This burden can either lead to or exacerbate higher rates of mental health problems. From an environmental or situational (mezzo) perspective, the family of the client is left at increased risk for psychological disturbances and should always be included in the treatment process (Mason, 2013). Mental illness and its chronic nature can strain family relationships at a time when clients may not realize they are becoming ill and in need of help (Marshall & Solomon, 2009). Often family members may have different expectations of what they perceive as their role in the inpatient and discharge process (Blumenfield & Epstein, 2001). When dealing with the family of a client with mental illness, the social worker needs to assume a flexible and diverse role. Special challenges when working with families include finding treatment goals and objectives that are effective for the client, but also of interest and importance to the members of the family (Jordan & Franklin, 2009; Mason, 2013). Helping to make all goals and objectives mutually negotiable for all is central because at times different expectations may lead to blurring and overlap of the services provided.

It is crucial for the social worker to examine each family member's sense of personal well-being, ability to self-care, and level of family and environmental support because many times these factors become essential to the discharge of the client. If these personal/social and environmental issues are not addressed, the client with mental instability may be put at risk for harm. When a client is discharged home to a family that does not want him or her, he or she is more at risk of abuse and neglect. Family members can feel that a situation is hopeless, placing them at greater risk for depression or even suicide.

Name: Laura DeAngelo

Place of residence: West Springfield, MA

College/university degrees: MSW, Springfield College, Springfield, MA

Present position: Clinical worker with adults and children

What do you do in your spare time? In my spare time I like to spend time with my husband and children, take walks with my dog, and try to keep up on the latest research in the field of autism, my area of special interest. I also enjoy listening to music, singing and cooking.

Why did you choose social work as a career? Social work is actually my fourth career. My first was insurance, after receiving a degree in economics from Dartmouth College. After five years I decided to get my MBA in health care administration and worked in that field for seven years after receiving my degree. When my third child was diagnosed with autism, I left the workforce and advocated for my son for several years. As I gained knowledge about the disability and available treatments, I found myself helping other parents, and discovered that I loved the feeling of connecting with and helping people. I became certified in a parent-training autism intervention, Relationship Development Intervention; received training in educational advocacy; and opened my own business, Autism Family Services, LLC. After several years of working on my own, I decided to get my MSW in order to gain a broader perspective on the social service field and improve my formal credentials.

What is your favorite social work story? I have many, so it is difficult to choose! I would say my favorite social work story is one that is continuing to unfold as we speak. One of my clients is a young lady who recently graduated from high school. She has been in foster care for many years after being removed from her home by DCF. She currently lives in a group home. In the few months I have treated this women, I can tell she is extraordinarily intelligent. She recently started taking classes at a local community college and told me she is delighted to be back in the academic environment. I commented that I thought she had the intelligence to attend and be successful at a highly competitive four-year college. She was thrilled at that feedback and shared that she had done extremely well on standardized assessments in high school. When I mentioned one prestigious college in particular, she said that it had been her dream to attend that college but she never thought it was possible. So, I am working with my client, one step at a time, to try to help her make her dream a reality. It is a great feeling to help someone realize her full potential!

What would be the one thing you would change in our community if you had the power to do so? In my community, I know of many families who are suffering because a family member is severely affected by autism. These families often do not have the financial means to pay for effective treatments for the individual and training and support for family members. In my community, and in other communities as well, I would increase the funding in order to provide ample financial resources for families to pay providers for effective services and supports for the person and the family. Autism has bankrupted families, and there is limited funding available through insurance companies and government payers. With the numbers of diagnosed individuals with autism continuing to grow, we need a better solution. I would like to be part of that solution.

The social worker must always recognize the importance of culture and environmental factors as paramount to efficient and effective practice. When cultural differences exist, they can clearly influence the therapeutic process (Duckworth, 2009). For example, depression that results in suicide can be viewed differently in some societies and by certain ethnic and racial groups. The importance of culture as a variable in suicide is modest at best, but understanding culture can help the clinician to gain a more robust assessment of suicidal reasoning and purpose (Leach, 2006). Another example of a situation in which cultural and environmental factors play a part in patient care is that in which family members of a sick infant object to a blood transfusion for religious reasons or the family refuses life support because it is viewed as disturbing the natural life progression. The de-emphasis or denial of this consideration can result in the delivery of substandard care.

In today's environment of behaviorally based managed care, capitation, fee for service, and decreased number of hospital inpatient beds, health care social work continues to hold a place in the acute care hospital setting. According to Dziegielewski (2013), the challenge for acute medical hospitals is to combine the humanitarian objective of practice with the hospitals' agenda for cost control and rationing of resources. In addition, recognition that the client is part of a family system places importance on the overall health and wellness of the individual. Often family members need assistance, and the acknowledgment and addressing of family problems can help to improve and maintain quality of life for the mentally ill client and his or her support system (Marshall & Solomon, 2009). The functions of the mental health social worker in this setting include psychosocial evaluations (assessment for the treatment plan), casework (counseling and supportive intervention), group work (education and self-help), information and referral, facilitation of community referrals, team planning and coordination, and client and family education, as well as advocacy for clients within the setting or beyond with local state and federal agencies (NASW, 2008). Social workers provide the backbone for frontline services that create a safety net for all clients served (Hoffler & Clark, 2012). In addition, with the numerous service cutbacks and cost-effectiveness strategies, many social workers are now being required to expand their duties (Yeager & Latimer, 2009). Many are being asked to serve as financial counselors to ensure that the client and the service agency will receive adequate reimbursement for services needed. These services can involve assisting clients to apply for outside insurance carriers to cover additional services not directly covered under current policy.

Dziegielewski (2013) believes that there are several essential skills and practice techniques that social workers in acute care mental health settings need. The social worker remains integral in providing assistance with:

- ◆ Providing comprehensive diagnostic assessments utilizing a strengths-based biopsychosocial approach that assists in resolving behavioral problems.
- ◆ Providing supportive treatment to individuals, families, and groups such as counseling for clients and significant others in the areas of health, wellness, mental health, bereavement, and so on.
- ◆ Providing assistance and guidance to clients and their families in making ethical and morally difficult decisions that can affect health and mental health.
- ◆ Educating clients, their families, and significant others to psychosocial issues and adjusting to illness.
- ◆ In a case management role, assisting clients and families with discharge planning and referral, as well as identifying and obtaining entitlement benefits and securing non-medical benefits.
- ◆ Assisting with risk management and quality assurance activities.
- ◆ Advocating for enhanced and continued services to ensure continued client well-being.

THE MENTALLY ILL IN THE CRIMINAL JUSTICE SYSTEM

The practice of deinstitutionalization, which resulted in the closing of many federal and state mental health facilities, has had devastating effects on the provision of mental health services, including those in the criminal justice system (Byron, 2014). Some were shocked when the sheriff of Los Angeles County told the press he ran the largest mental hospital in the county (Lopez, 2005). As the number of inmates suffering from mental illness in our prisons increases, more and more social workers interested in the area of mental health have begun to accept posi-

Figure 2: Members of the Berrien County Association of Retarded Citizens (ARC) gather for a photo after a Fourth of July field trip with a social worker to a town on Lake Michigan. These citizens live either in group homes or with families.

tions in this area. What is most concerning is that an alarming 16.9 percent of those in state prisons and local jails have diagnoses related to mental illness (Amrhein & Barber-Rioja, 2011). Additionally, these individuals are 53 percent more likely to be incarcerated for a violent offense, and, according to year 2000 population statistics, this would equate to 296,176 incarcerated individuals with a diagnosed mental illness. Furthermore, if this trend is extended into the year 2002, incarcerated individuals may exceed 718,000 who are suffering from a diagnosed mental illness. Beck and Maruschak (2001) also found a large incarcerated population with mental illnesses. Utilizing a survey, these authors found that, in 1,394 of 1,558 U.S. adult correctional facilities, 1 in 8 state prisoners were receiving mental health services, and 1 in 10 were provided with psychotropic medications. The majority of the facilities were able to provide psychiatric assessment (65 percent), therapy, and/or counseling by trained mental health professionals (71 percent) and distribution of psychotropic medications (73 percent). When the care received in correctional facilities was compared to that received in forensic hospitals, where services are provided for treatment offenders who have been found not guilty by reason of insanity, the return rate to crime-related behaviors decreased significantly for those that were treated in a forensic hospital (Byron, 2014).

Name: Ariel Champaloux Heaton

College/university degrees: BSW and MSW, University of Central Florida, Orlando, FL

Employment history:

Emergency Department/trauma social worker

Social worker, psychiatric hospital

Social worker on inpatient unit

Hospital social worker/discharge planner

What do you do in your spare time? I enjoy exercising, running, step aerobics, and lifting weights. I love going to church, shopping, going to the movies, and cooking.

Why did you choose social work as a career? My mother is an LCSW and I have always been fascinated with her job and how she helped people. When I was a little girl she would take me to her office and I would wait in the waiting room. When she finished a session I could see how her clients looked so much more relaxed and relieved compared to when they arrived.

At first, I thought that I wanted to be a nurse and was accepted into University of Florida, School of Nursing. During the first semester of the program my educational experience included "clinicals" where you work to provide direct patient care. As I was on one of my rotations in the hospital and started seeing patients, I found myself talking to the patients and enjoying it more than just physically providing patient care. It was then that I realized I wanted to be a social worker and I left nursing school and was accepted at the University of Central Florida, School of Social Work, where I completed my BSW and later my MSW degree.

What is your favorite social work story? One of my favorite social work stories was when I working working in the hospital emergency room. One night a forty-eight-year-old male was rushed to the emergency room because he was in severe respiratory distress. Sadly, despite the best efforts of the emergency room medical staff, the patient passed away soon after arriving. Soon after his death, his family arrived in the waiting room unaware of what had just transpired. His family included his parents and his fiancée, who said they were to be married that weekend. As the social worker, I took the family to a quiet area. I was able to answer their questions and support them once they were told the news.

His fiancée asked, "What is going on? I will be his wife on Saturday." The physician told the family the horrific news. The family was devastated and we sat and talked for quite some time about what had happened and to support them in terms of what they would do next. I will never forget, how much it meant to this family and that I was able to provide support to this patient's family during one of the most tragic days of their life.

What would be the one thing you would change in our community if you had the power to do so? If I could change something in the community, I would advocate for more resources for mental health. I see so many people who suffer from debilitating mental illness who do not have access to proper treatment because of the limited resources in the community.

For social workers, the greatest challenge is how to help these facilities to recognize and address the medical and mental health needs for those diagnosed as mentally ill. This requires a twofold approach for individuals that includes a helping strategy while incarcerated as well as after release (Slate, Buffington-Vollum, & Johnson, 2013). Attention to current needs may not be enough, and help that extends beyond the release from prison needs to provide supportive services through probation and parole. Prison systems designed purely to house rather than to treat mentally ill inmates will fall short when the mentally ill offender is finally released back into the community.

The implementation of deinstitutionalization provides a perfect example of how a political and economic proposal that is not thoroughly explored prior to implementation can have devastating effects on those caught in the system. Many professionals in mental health firmly believe that deinstitutionalization has put tremendous pressure on families to care for their loved ones as well as to bear the stigma of having done something wrong or, worse yet, causing the problem (Olson, 2006). For some, the inability of the family and community to address the needs of these individuals has resulted in utilizing the prison system as a holding tank for those with serious mental disorders. From this perspective the prisons can be viewed as a replacement for the mental hospitals that have been closed (Butterfield, 1998). Furthermore, the mental health services that are provided within the prison system are limited because of the lack of public concern for rehabilitation of offenders. When an individual with mental illness is incarcerated, the stigma is twofold, first as a prisoner and then as a person suffering from a mental illness (Slate, Buffington-Vollum, & Johnson, 2013). Regardless of the exact reason, the number of offenders with mental illness is growing in our prisons and jails and within the probation and parole system.

Moreover, closing the state mental health facilities and trying to treat chronic offenders in the community has left many of those with mental illness homeless and without care (Slate, Buffington-Vollum, & Johnson, 2013). Individuals with mental illness may also be unfairly arrested and jailed because their behaviors present a danger or risk to those around them. This is further complicated by the fact that the most appropriate placements, such as mental health centers in the community, may be either unwilling or unable to help due to the indigent status of those with chronic mental illness and their subsequent inability to pay for services

(Harrington, 1999). This problem requires a connection between law enforcement officers and mental health professionals.

To help address this issue, social workers have advocated for the development of case management services as a humane, effective, and efficient way of interpersonal connection and information gathering (Frankel & Gelman, 2012). Additionally, this method can be used to help offenders return successfully to the community; assertive case management and collaboration between mental health providers and the criminal justice system encourage joint problem solving. The Council of Social Work Education (CSWE) also supports providing training on trauma-based care, particularly at the graduate level, and believes that stress and trauma are so influential on mental health that educational programs have been incorporated into the curriculum standards (2012). Social workers are taking a more active role in police departments as well as correctional facilities.

In police departments, social workers can assist with multiple types of crimes, assisting trauma victims, survivors, and family members (Knox & Roberts, 2009). Whether it is offered in the police departments or in other types of correctional facilities, this type of professional activity and coordination can lead to reduced hospital stays, improved living situations, and improved social relationships for the mentally ill offender (Calsyn, Morse, Klinkenberg, Trusty, & Allen, 1998). Mechanic and McAlpine (1999) further support this stance by seeking more appropriate placement for those with mental illness through assertive case management with the presumption that this type of service can bring about beneficial results at a low cost (compared with the cost of incarceration) to the community.

Similar to problems occurring in the health care system, recidivism or the readmission of individuals to the penal justice system has presented a serious concern (Hiller & Knight, 1996). Hiller and Knight asserted that the rates of mental illness within the community-based setting were consistent with those within the rest of the correctional system, and that some offenders may be more at risk than others for rearrest (especially those with comorbidity involving depression and substance abuse).

For mental health social workers in this area, a partnership between criminal justice professionals and social workers and other counseling professionals is blossoming (Kirschman, Kamena, & Fay, 2014). This collaboration could result in early identification and treatment of those who end up in the criminal justice system because of the lack of support in diagnosing and assessing mental health symptoms that can lead to criminal behaviors. Without such a partnership, offenders with mental illness will continue to be rotated from mental health centers to jails in a cycle that causes further disease deterioration and increased criminality (Harrington, 1999). Jails are not staffed as mental hospitals, and a short period of incarceration can compound the problems of the offender with mental illness because the jail is not geared toward providing treatment or achieving stabilization. Therefore, planned efforts to achieve better community treatment would result in fewer costly hospital stays and less jail time for the offender with mental illness. Furthermore, encouraging voluntary treatment of the individual is the best way to avoid a crisis that might lead to legal concerns (National Alliance on Mental Illness, 2008). With this in mind, mental health courts have become an emerging strategy designed to avoid placing those with mental illness directly into the criminal justice system. These courts are based on the drug court model and seek to assist clients who suffer from severe mental illness (Hodges & Anderson, 2005).

Another important concept leading to this advocacy for service unification of the disciplines revolves around societal cost, financial and otherwise. Spending for behavioral health care is falling behind that for other types of health care, and the quality of care is suffering (Mechanic & McAlpine, 1999). With deinstitutionalization, many of those with mental illness were diverted into substance abuse programs that the federal government funded because the community programs were unprepared to handle the influx of patients (Slate, Buffington-Vollum, & Johnson, 2013). Those individuals with serious mental illness who were not placed in residential treatment facilities were criminalized because the mental health providers were actively involved with treating societal coping skills (Harrington, 1999). Assessing for functional situational factors in the mental health assessment is paramount to helping clients within the mental health system (see box 6).

This union of the disciplines will never succeed unless both disciplines acknowledge its importance and strongly advocate for collaboration and information sharing between the various professionals as well as the organizations involved in the process (Kirschman, Kamena, & Fay, 2014). Because there is no single system or organization that can meet all of the conditions needed for optimal treatment of those with mental illness (Schnapp & Cannedy, 1998), sharing information is critical. Awareness or familiarity with the police culture and collaboration fosters more supportive and integrated planning as well as policy development and facilitation of the highest degree of complete and accurate information for decision making (Kirschman, Kamena, & Fay, 2014).

SPECIAL CONSIDERATIONS: MENTAL HEALTH AND THE DUAL DIAGNOSIS

With any population or in any field of practice, social workers are increasingly confronted with the dually diagnosed client. These clients have more than one mental health problem and each must be equally addressed in the intervention process. In order for mental health social workers to work successfully with dually diagnosed clients, they must be cognizant of client problems, diagnostic assessments, clinical interventions, and current case studies. For example, clients with

Box 6. Functional/Situational Factors to Be Considered in Mental Health Assessment

Area	Explanation
Financial status	How does the health condition affect the financial status of the client? What income maintenance efforts are being made? Do any need to be initiated? Does the client have savings or resources to draw from?
Entitlements	Does the client have health, accident, disability, or life insurance benefits to cover his/her cost of health service? Has insurance been recorded and filed for the client to assist with paying of expenses? Does the client qualify for additional services to assist with illness and recovery?
Transportation	What transportation is available to the client? Does the client need assistance or arrangements to facilitate transportation?
Placement	Where will the client go after discharge? Is there a plan for continued maintenance when services are terminated? Is alternative placement needed?
Continuity of service	If the client is to be transferred to another health service, have the connections been made to link services and service providers appropriately? Based on the services provided, has the client received the services she needs during and after the treatment period?

psychiatric and comorbid substance use disorders may be best served by utilizing a more holistic strengths-based perspective that avoids placing labels and seeks policy change and advocacy (Reedy & Kobayashi, 2012). This is especially important when noncompliance with treatment occurs upon return to the outpatient setting. Returning to a similar environment without system-level intervention can leave these individuals vulnerable to a variety of negative clinical ramifications, including problems with relapse and rehospitalization.

Although addressing the needs of a client with more than one mental health problem will be covered in more depth in your clinical courses, this client can often be misdiagnosed and/or given inadequate treatment due to the limited time frame allowed for inpatient care. Resources and at times intervention strategy are shaped and influenced by cost containment, with an emphasis placed on time-limited, outcome-oriented interventions (Dziegielewski, 2014; 2015). As health care delivery changes, funding for mental health is limited and the need for programs specializing in integrated treatment is clear.

Daley and Zuckoff (1998) highlight the following adverse effects that can transpire for noncompliant, dually diagnosed clients:

- ◆ Poorly compliant clients are more likely to experience clinical deterioration of their psychiatric condition, relapse to alcohol or other drug use, and return to the hospital as a result of severe depression, thoughts of suicide or homicide, mania, or psychotic decompensation.
- ◆ Missing outpatient appointments often leads to failure to renew medication prescriptions, which in turn contributes to exacerbations of psychiatric and substance use symptoms.
- ◆ Poor treatment compliance causes the loss of supportive relationships and contributes to frustration among professionals and family members, who can end up watching helplessly as their loved one's condition deteriorates.
- ◆ Due to increased risk of hospitalization, poor outpatient compliance leads to increased costs of care as a result of more days spent in expensive inpatient treatment facilities.

Assessing the impact of trauma and other life events that could affect the performance of the individual with mental illness is needed. Although trauma is well recognized and practice recommendations exist for providing early psychosocial care, imbedding these recommendations into assessment guidelines with clear standards could benefit all (Brake & Duckers, 2013). This assessment will identify conditions that can make the current situation worse, such as sexual abuse, medical emergencies, car accidents, overdoses from prescribed medications or illegal drugs, and other events and sudden losses that can complicate the mental health condition (O'Hare & Sherrer, 2009). Furthermore, when dealing with older adults, Maust, Oslin, and Marcus (2014) found that the medications prescribed, which could have dangerous side effects, were often not clearly related to any mental health condition being treated. This makes knowledge of medications essential (Dziegielewski, 2010). In addition, mental health social workers must be educated and trained in the treatment of clients who suffer from more than one mental health problem and/or condition. For the dually diagnosed client, treating one condition without recognition of the comorbid or contributing factors is not considered acceptable (see box 7 for an overview of questions to guide the assessment and intervention process and box 8 for important professional contact information).

Box 7. Mental Health Social Work Practice in the New Millennium

Questions to Guide Assessment and Intervention Success

1. Are you able to complete a diagnostic assessment of the individual, and show the relationship between the mental illness and the behaviors that resulted?

2. Can you show that the identified condition is treatable with a realistic chance of success?

3. Have you developed specific goals and objectives for the treatment of the client?

4. Do you provide a clear rationale for the level of care, modality, types of intervention, and duration of treatment?

5. Is there a process for updating and periodic review of goal and objective attainment?

6. Is the client involved in the treatment development process?

7. If treatment is to be longer than originally expected, is a rationale for extension provided?

8. What specific things will happen to indicate that treatment goals and objectives have been met?

9. Is the intervention plan utilized consistent with social work values and ethics?

Box 8. Professional Contact Information and e-mail Addresses

Professional organization:

National Association of Social Workers, 750 First St. N.E., Suite 700, Washington, DC, 20002-4241. Internet: http://www.socialworkers.org

Accredited social work programs:

To determine whether individual social work programs have either specialized courses or a concentration in mental health, contact: Council on Social Work Education, 1725 Duke St., Suite 500, Alexandria, VA 22314-3457. Internet: http://www.cswe.org

Information on licensing requirements and testing procedures for each state may be obtained from state licensing authorities, or from:

Association of Social Work Boards, 400 South Ridge Pkwy., Suite B, Culpeper, VA 22701. Internet: http://www.aswb.org

SUMMARY

Whatever we call them, diagnosis, assessment, or diagnostic assessment, the psychosocial assessments performed by mental health and health care social workers are essential (Dziegielewski, 2014). Assessment is the critical first step in formulating a plan for intervention. It thus sets the tone and framework for the entire mental health social work process. In order to compete in today's mental health environment, social work professionals must play a twofold role: (1) to ensure that high-quality service is provided to the client and (2) to ensure that the client has access and is given an opportunity to see that her or his mental health needs are addressed. Neither of these tasks is easy, nor will they make a social worker popular in today's environment. Mental and other health services must now be delivered with limited resources, and the pressure to reduce services is intense. There is also the danger of false diagnosis and over-medicalizing or placing a label on what might otherwise be considered adaptive behavior (Frances & Jones, 2013). Social workers must know the assessment and treatment planning tools that are used in the field and be able to use them, always being careful not to falsely support a diagnosis or place a label that may affect the client for the rest of his or her life. Assessment and treatment planning are together the first step in providing services, a step that social work professionals cannot afford to neglect.

Numerous tools and methods exist to assist social workers in the mental health assessment process, and the *DSM-5* and the PIE are only two examples of what is available. These forms of systematic assessment can provide social workers with frameworks for practice. Such tools should always be used cautiously, however. As you will learn in practice courses yet to come, many social workers fear that these methods can place labels on clients that are very difficult to remove. These fears are well founded, but they shouldn't cause social workers to shun assessment. Indeed, the fact that social workers are aware of such dangers makes their participation in assessment essential. In addition, the social worker brings a wealth of information to the interdisciplinary team about a client's environment and family situation. Social workers who focus on building on the skills and strengths of the client are well equipped to help design a treatment plan that is realistic and effective. Although assessments completed today appear to have a more narrow focus, it is essential that utility, relevance, and salience be maintained (Dziegielewski, 2013).

Because social workers practice in numerous health and mental health settings and perform many different duties, it is not surprising that the processes of assessment and treatment planning show great diversity. Assessment and subsequent treatment plan development depend on a multiplicity of factors, including client need, agency function, practice setting, service limitations, and coverage for provision of service. Many times the scope of assessment and intervention must be narrowed in response to reductions in economic support. Therefore, overall practice in the mental health setting must continually be examined to ensure high quality. If the process of helping is rushed, superficial factors may be highlighted and significant ones overlooked. All social workers, regardless of their mental health care setting, must establish services that are quality driven, no matter what the administrative and economic pressures may be.

Questions to Consider

1. Based on the information provided in this chapter, what do you see as the future role for mental health social workers in the assessment process?

2. Do you believe that, when compared to the *DSM-5*, the PIE could gain in popularity, particularly for identifying the supportive factors that surround the mental health disorder in health and mental health settings with practitioners other than social workers? Why or why not?

3. Do you believe that a complete assessment and treatment planning framework is needed to guide social work practice and that it will continue to be required for reimbursement in order for social work services to increase?

REFERENCES

American Counseling Association. (2011). *2011 statistics on mental health professionals.* Retrieved from: http://www.psych.org

American Psychiatric Association. (2013). *Diagnostic and Statistical Manual of Mental Disorders, DSM-5* (5th edition). Washington, DC: Author.

Amrhein, C., & Barber-Rioja, V. (2011). Jail diversion models for people with mental illness. In S. A. Estrine, R. T. Hettenbach, H. Arthur, & M. Messina (Eds.), *Service delivery for vulnerable populations.* New York: Springer.

Anderson, G. F., & Frogner, B. K. (2008). Health spending in OECD Countries: Obtaining value per dollar. *Health Affairs, 24,* 903–914.

Austrian, S. G. (2009). Guidelines for conducting a biopsychosocial assessment. In A. R. Roberts, *Social workers' desk reference* (2nd ed., pp. 376–380). New York: Oxford University Press.

Barker, R. L. (2003). *The social work dictionary* (5th ed.). Washington, DC: NASW Press.

Barth, R. P., Kolivoski. K., Lindsey, M. A., Lee, B. R., & Collins, K. S. (2014). Translating the common elements approach: Social work experiences in education, practice and research. *Journal of Clinical Child and Adolescent Psychology, 42,* 301–311.

Beck, A., & Maruschak, L. (2001). *Mental health treatment in state prisons, 2000.* Washington, DC: U.S. Department of Justice, Office of Justice Programs, Bureau of Justice Statistics.

Blumenfield, S., & Epstein, I. (2001). Introduction: Promoting and maintaining a reflective professional staff in a hospital-based social work department. *Social Work in Health Care, 33*(3/4), 1–13.

Brake, H. T., & Duckers, M. (2013). Early psychosocial interventions after disasters, terrorism and other shocking events: Is there a gap between norms and practice in Europe? *European Journal of Psychotraumatology, 4,* 1–10.

Brennan, E. M., Evans, M. E., & Spencer, S. A. (2008). Mental health services and support for families. In J. M. Rosenzweig & E. M. Brennan (Eds.), *Work, life, and mental health system of care* (pp. 3–26). Baltimore, MD: Brooks Publishing.

Butterfield, F. (1998, March 5). Prisons replace hospitals for the nation's mentally ill. *New York Times*, p. A1, A26.

Byron, R. (2014). Criminals need mental health care: Psychiatric treatment is far better than imprisonment for reducing recidivism. *Mind & Brain, 25*, 2, 1–7.

Cabot, R. C. (1913). Letter. *Journal of the American Medical Association, 60*, 145.

Calsyn, R., Morse, G., Klinkenberg, W., Trusty, M., & Allen, G. (1998). The impact of assertive community based treatment on the social relationships of people who are homeless and mentally ill. *Community Mental Health Journal, 34*, 579.

Carlton, T. O. (1984). *Clinical social work in health care settings: A guide to professional practice with exemplars*. New York: Springer.

Corcoran, J. (2010). *Clinical assessment and diagnosis in social work practice* (2nd ed.). New York: Oxford University Press.

Council on Social Work Education (CSWE). (2012). *Advanced social work practice in trauma*. Alexandria, VA: Author.

Craig, Y. (1998, August 19). Victim dived from La Madeline lunches to homeless. *Star-Telegram*. Retrieved from http://www.star-telegram.com

Daley, D. C., & Zuckoff, A. (1998). Improving compliance with the initial outpatient session among discharged inpatient dual diagnosis clients. *Social Work, 43*, 470–474.

Duckworth, M. P. (2009). Cultural awareness and culturally competent practice. In W. T. O'Donohue & J. E. Fisher (Eds.), *General principles and empirically supported techniques of cognitive behavior therapy* (pp. 63–76). Hoboken, NJ: John Wiley.

Dziegielewski, S. F. (2013). *The changing face of health care social work: Opportunities and challenges for professional practice* (3rd ed.). New York: Springer.

Dziegielewski, S. F. (2014). *DSM-IV-TR™ in action (with DSM-5 updates)*. New York: John Wiley.

Dziegielewski, S. F. (2015). *DSM-5™ in action*. New York: John Wiley.

Eamon, M. K. (2008). *Empowering vulnerable populations*. Chicago: Lyceum Books.

Fox, R. D. (2009). The essential elements of private practice social work. In A. R. Roberts (Ed.), *Social workers' desk reference* (2nd ed., pp. 53–60). New York: Oxford University Press.

Frances, A., & Jones, K. D. (2013). Should social workers use the diagnostic and statistical manual of mental disorders-5? *Research on Social Work Practice, 24*, 11–12.

Frank, R. G. (2013). Mental illness and a dual dilemma. *Journal of the American Society of Aging, 37*(2), 47–53.

Frankel, A. J., & Gelman, S. R. (2012). *Case management: An introduction to concepts and skills* (3rd ed.). Chicago: Lyceum Books.

Harrington, S. (May/June, 1999). New bedlam: Jails not psychological hospitals now care for the indigent mentally ill. *Humanist, 59*, 9–13.

Hiller, M., & Knight, K. (1996). Compulsory community-based substance abuse treatment and the mentally ill criminal offender. *Prison Journal, 76*, 180–185.

Hodges, J. Q., & Anderson, K. M. (2005). What do social workers need to know about mental health courts? *Social Work in Mental Health, 4*(2), 17–30.

Hoffler, E. F., & Clark, E. J. (2012). *Social work matters: The power of linking policy and practice*. Washington, DC: NASW Press.

Holliman, D., Dziegielewski, S. F., & Datta, P. (2001). Discharge planning and social work practice. *Social Work in Health Care, 32*(3), 1–19.

Jordan, C., & Franklin, C. (2009). *Clinical assessment for social workers: Quantitative and qualitative methods* (3rd ed.). Chicago: Lyceum Books.

Karls, J. M., & O'Keefe, M. E. (2008). *The PIE Manual*. Washington, DC: NASW Press.

Karls, J. M., & O'Keefe, M. E. (2009). Person in environment system. In A. R. Roberts (Ed.), *Social workers' desk reference* (2nd ed., pp. 371–376). New York: Oxford University Press.

Karls, J. M., & Wandrei, K. M. (Eds.). (1996a). *Person-in-environment system: The PIE classification system for social functioning problems.* Washington, DC: NASW Press.

Karls, J. M., & Wandrei, K. M. (1996b). *PIE manual: Person-in-environment system: The PIE classification system for social functioning problems.* Washington, DC: NASW Press.

Kirschman, E., Kamena, M., & Fay, J. (2014). *Counseling cops: What clinicians need to know.* New York: Guilford Press.

Knox, K. S., & Roberts A. R. (2009). The social worker in a police department. In A. R. Roberts (Ed.), *Social workers' desk reference* (2nd ed., pp. 85–94). New York: Oxford University Press.

Leach, M. M. (2006). *Cultural diversity and suicide: Ethnic, religious, gender and sexual orientation perspectives.* Binghamton, NY: Haworth Press.

Locke, D. C., & Bailey, D. F. (2014). *Increasing multicultural understanding* (3rd ed.). Thousand Oaks, CA: Sage.

Lopez, S. (2005, December 11). Mentally ill in the jail? It's a crime. *Los Angeles Times.*

Marshall, T. B., & Solomon, P. (2009). Working with families of persons with severe mental illness. In A. R. Roberts (Ed.), *Social workers' desk reference* (2nd ed., pp. 491–494). New York: Oxford University Press.

Mason, S. E. (2013). Best practices for family caregivers of people with mental illness. In V. L. Vandiver (Ed). *Best practices in community mental health* (pp. 211–221). Chicago: Lyceum Books.

Maust, D., Oslin, D. W., & Marcus, S. (2014). Effect of age on the profile of psychotropic users: Results from the 2010 National Ambulatory Medical Care Survey. *Journal of the American Geriatrics Society, 62,* 358–364.

Mechanic, D., & McAlpine, D. (1999). Mission unfulfilled: Potholes on the road to mental health parity. *Health Affairs, 18*(5), 7–21.

Miller, L. (2008). *Counseling crime victims: Practical strategies for mental health professionals.* New York: Springer.

Morales, A. T., & Sheafor, B. W. (2006). *The many faces of social work clients.* Boston: Allyn & Bacon.

Munson, C. E. (2009). Guidelines for the diagnostic and statistical manual of mental disorders (DSM-IV-TR) multiaxial system diagnosis. In A. R. Roberts (Ed.), *Social workers' desk reference* (2nd ed., pp. 334–342). New York: Oxford University Press.

National Alliance on Mental Illness. (2008). *Beyond punishment: Helping individuals with mental illness in Maryland's criminal justice system.* Charleston, SC: BookSurge Publishing.

National Association of Social Workers. (1998). *Centennial information: Celebrating 100 years of social work practice* [pamphlet]. Washington, DC: Author.

National Association of Social Workers. (2008). *Code of ethics.* Washington, DC: NASW Press.

National Association of Social Workers. (2011). *Social workers in mental health clinics & outpatient facilities: Occupational profile.* Washington, DC: Author. Retrieved from http://workforce.socialworkers.org/studies/profiles/Mental%20Health%20Clinics.pdf

National Association of Social Workers. (2012a). *NASW salary guidelines: Social work salaries are highly variable.* Retrieved from http://workforce.socialworkers.org/studies/2012/SalaryGuidelines.pdf

National Association of Social Workers. (2012b). *Social work speaks* (9th ed.). Washington, DC: Author.

O'Hare, T., & Sherrer, M. V. (2009). Impact of the most frequently reported traumatic events on community mental health clients. *Journal of Human Behavior in the Social Environment, 19*, 186–195.

Olson, M. E. (2006). Family and network therapy training for a system of care. In A. Lightburn & P. Sessions (Eds.), *Handbook of community-based practice* (pp. 135–152). New York: Oxford University Press.

Palmo, A. J. (2011). *Foundations of mental health counseling.* Springfield, IL: Charles C. Thomas.

Pike, C. K. (2009). Developing client focused measures. In A. R. Roberts (Ed.), *Social workers' desk reference* (2nd ed., pp. 351–357). New York: Oxford University Press.

Reddon, J. R., Hoglin, B., & Woodman, M. (2008). Immediate effects of a 16-week life skills education program on the mental health of adult psychiatric patients. *Social Work in Mental Health, 6*(3), 21–40.

Reedy, A. R., & Kobayashi, R. (2012). Substance use and mental disorders: Why do some people suffer from both? *Social Work in Mental Health, 10*, 496–517.

Risley, M. (1961). *The house of healing.* London: Hale.

Rosenzweig, J. M., & Brennan, E. M. (2008). The intersection of children's mental health and work-family studies. In J. M. Rosenzweig & E. M. Brennan (Eds.), *Work, life, and mental health system of care* (p. 3–26). Baltimore: Brooks.

Scheyett, A., Kim, M., Swanson, J., Swartz, M., Elbogen, E., Dorn, R. V., & Ferron, J. (2009). Autonomy and the use of directive intervention in the treatment of individuals with serious mental illnesses: A survey of social work practitioners. *Social Work in Mental Health, 7*, 283–306.

Schnapp, W. B., & Cannedy, R. (1998). Offenders with mental illness: Mental health and criminal justice best practices. *Administration and Policy in Mental Health, 25*, 463–466.

Schroeder, R. (2013). The seriously mentally ill older adult: Perceptions of the patient-provider relationship. *Perspectives in Psychiatric Care, 49*, 30–40.

Simon, E. P., Showers, N., Blumfield, S., Holden, G., & Wu, X. (1995). Delivery of home care services after discharge: What really happens. *Health and Social Work, 20*, 5–14.

Slate, R. N., Buffington-Vollum, J. K., & Johnson, W. W. (2013). *Mental illness: Crisis and opportunity for the justice system.* Durham, NC: Carolina Academic Press.

Strom-Gottfried, K. (2008). *The ethics of practice with minors: High stakes, hard choices.* Chicago: Lyceum Books.

U.S. Department of Labor. (2014). Work environment. *Occupational outlook handbook*, Retrieved from: http://www.bls.gov/ooh/community-and-social-service/social-workers.htm#tab-3

U.S. Department of Labor. (2014). Social workers. *Occupational outlook handbook*. Retrieved from http://www.bls.gov/ooh/community-and-social-service/social-workers.htm

Whiting, L. (1996). Foreword. In J. M. Karls & K. M. Wandrei (Eds.), *Person-in-environment system: The PIE classification system for social functioning problems* (pp. xiii–xv). Washington, DC: NASW Press.

Williams, J. B. (2009). Using the diagnostic and statistical manual of mental disorders (4th ed., text revision). In A. R. Roberts (Ed.), *Social workers' desk reference* (2nd ed., pp. 325–334). New York: Oxford University Press.

Woods, T. A., & Kurtz-Cortes, B. (2007). Race identity and race socialization in African American families: Implications for social workers. *Journal of Human Behavior and the Social Environment, 2*(3), 99–116.

Yeager, K. R., & Latimer, T. R. (2009). Quality standards and quality assurance in health settings. In A. R. Roberts (Ed.), *Social workers' desk reference* (2nd ed., pp. 194–203). New York: Oxford University Press.

Yeager, K. R., Roberts, A. R., & Saveanu, R. (2009). Optimizing the use of patient safety standards, procedures, and measures. In A. R. Roberts (Ed.), *Social workers' desk reference* (2nd ed., pp. 174–186). New York: Oxford University Press.

CHAPTER 11
OLDER ADULTS

LET'S BEGIN BY EXPLORING YOUR THOUGHTS ABOUT AGING. TO START, answer these questions about getting older and let us explore your impressions of aging and what this means

1. For me, getting older means . . .
2. Close your eyes and imagine yourself at various ages. What do you see?
   a. At age sixty, I am . . .
   b. At age seventy, I am . . .
   c. At age eighty, I am . . .
   d. At age ninety, I am . . .
   e. At age one hundred, I am . . .
3. Name a person who is sixty-five or older whom you admire or have admired. What is so special about this person? How can this person be a role model for you?

No one escapes the aging process. In fact, from the moment we're born we all begin to age. During the aging process, as in all phases of human growth and development, people must adjust to changes in their life circumstances. Unfortunately, many of these changes are viewed negatively in our society (Algilani et al., 2014). Declines in physical functioning, changes in physical appearance, loss of income, retirement, and loss of partner and social supports are all associated with aging. But not everyone experiences these shifts in quite the same way. Although aging is often thought of as an individual process, it can also include a more metaphorical reference including its potential effects as the numbers of older individuals increase in a society (Moody & Sasser, 2012). Most professionals agree that, to understand aging, we must look at more than just a person's chronological age—that is, how old he is. The study of older adults therefore embraces varied life circumstances and issues and must consider physical and psychosocial factors (Dziegielewski, 2013, Zarit & Zarit, 2007).

Did You Know…One myth about aging is that all older people age in the same way and display predictable patterns of age-related behavior that can easily be studied. Nothing could be further from the truth. As we age, the shifts can differ dramatically based on many individual factors including mental health and social factors as well as physical factors such as diet and health.

Name: Panu Lucier

Place of residence: Anchorage, Alaska

College/university degrees: University of Alaska, Anchorage, BSW

Present position and title: Executive Director, Alaska Children's Trust & Friends of the Alaska Children's Trust

Previous work/volunteer experience: Director, Rose Urban Rural Exchange; youth worker; Court Appointed Special Advocate; member, National Advisory Committee for the National Quality Improvement Center on Early Childhood

What do you do in your spare time? Outside of work, I have continued my role as a volunteer CASA. I enjoy the beauty of Alaska, spending time with my three grandchildren, traveling, gardening, reading and relaxing in my tipi.

Why did you choose social work as a career? Social work offered me a flexible and professional degree guided by a code of ethics, values, and theories that are very compatible with the values of Alaska native cultures, specifically, our relationship with and respect for all living things.

What is your favorite social work story? I helped convince the court to return four little boys to their village after they were taken into state custody while visiting Anchorage with their mother. I escorted them home. From them I learned courage and never to give up hope.

What is one thing you would change in the community if you had the power to do so? I would break down the social and political barriers that contribute to the division of the "haves" and "have-nots" so that all people have access to education, health, and social services, which are essential to the integrity of a healthy community.

Over the years, however, use of a chronological age cutoff has been the most common way to decide who is an older adult. Although this is a popular way to define old age, the number appears to be highly dependent on whom you ask. If you ask people who are forty-five or younger, the answer will probably be sixty-one and older, but if you ask people who are quite a bit older than sixty-one, they may see this age as young (Arnquist, 2009; *Huffington Post*, 2012).

Did You Know…At one time people used to talk about retiring at age sixty-five. Well, retirement age has increased for most people. Can you retire at any age? Sure, but if you retire before full retirement age your monthly social security check will be reduced. An eligible person may begin receiving retirement checks at age sixty-two or delay receiving checks while working past retirement age. Note that the longer you wait to collect your benefits, the larger your monthly checks will be.

You may also know people who began to receive retirement information from various groups shortly after their fiftieth birthdays. You can join the AARP (Association for Retired Persons) at age fifty. A number of major airlines offer *senior discounts* to people who are fifty-five or older. The senior golf tour has a minimum age of fifty, as do senior games and athletic contests in various states. Most political scientists agree that the definition of senior status began with the Economic Security Act of 1935 and was based on the German precedent, which established sixty-five years as the appropriate age for benefits to begin (Brieland, Costin, & Atherton, 1980). And indeed, this simple definition is administratively useful because it establishes clear eligibility standards for programs such as Social Security, which historically began at age sixty-five.

Did You Know…According to the Social Security Administration, the life expectancy for a male in 2014 is 82.8 years of age and 85.4 years of age for a female. See what your life expectancy is according to the Social Security Administration at http://www.socialsecurity .gov/OACT/STATS/table4c6.html

Nothing lasts forever, however, and now those born after 1959 will have to wait until age sixty-seven to collect full benefits (*Huffington Post*, 2012). For others born earlier, the benefit rate can vary depending on age. For example, if you were born in 1955, you will have to wait until you are sixty-six years and two months to collect full benefits from Social Security (see the activity below and visit the official Social Security website (http://www.ssa.gov/retirement/ageincrease.htm) to calculate retirement benefits based on age).

Activity… **When Can I Collect Social Security Benefits?** *Go to the Social Security website at http://www.ssa.gov/retirement/ageincrease.htm and enter your year of birth to determine how old you will need to be to collect 100 percent of your social security benefits. Also, enter your parents' birth years and see how old they will need to be to retire with full, 100-percent Social Security benefits. Review your partner/spouse's benefit eligibility as well.*

The population shift, often referred to as *population aging*, that is occurring as the population of older adults increases is so striking that it is attracting widespread attention (Federal Interagency Forum of Aging-Related Statistics, 2012). In the United States, as in other countries, as the general population continues to increase, the number of older adults is outpacing the number of all younger cohorts; this can have major implications for the overall population. The U.S. Census Bureau (2014) estimates that the number of older adults in the United States (40.3 million in 2013) will more than double to 83.7 million in 2050. Furthermore, the group of adults of age ninety or older is growing more rapidly than expected; this group is expected to quadruple by 2050 (U.S. Census Bureau, 2014). In addition, earlier predictions of life expectancy—approximately 81.1 years for women and 76.2 years for men—remain realistic.

Did You Know...As the population numbers change so do the social support programs. When the Economic Security Act was passed in 1935, age sixty-five marked the 95th percentile of the U.S. age distribution. By 1986, age sixty-five marked the 76th percentile. As the share of the U.S. population of age sixty-five has continued to increase dramatically, the age at which benefits are offered has changed as well.

It is clear that the aging of our population has had far-reaching effects; the sheer number of older adults has attracted significant interest (Zarit & Zarit, 2007). For administrators and policy planners, the simplest way to define what constitutes older adults uses chronological age and population numbers. However, this definition is deficient when used alone because it cannot reflect changes in the composition of the older adult population. As a result of these changes, older adults have become a much less homogeneous group. About sixty years ago there were equal numbers of men and women of age sixty-five or older. As Americans continue to enjoy longer life spans and lower death rates, the numbers of older women who live longer than men has continued to increase. As of 2010, however, although women have a longer life expectancy than men, the number of older men is expected to continue to grow (Ortman, Velkoff, & Hogan, 2014). The exact reason for this increase in older males is not clear, but may be related to the fact that most males are married and do not live alone. This changing demographic may lead to more options for home care and for spouses to take care of each other in the community setting. Social support and connection to family supports including an intimate partner may be a major factor in recovery from illness (Aldwin & Gilmer, 2013).

Because women often outlive men by several years, it is no surprise that 70 percent of nursing home residents are reported to be women and the average admission age is eighty (American Association for Long Term Health Insurance, 2008). After retirement, women often assume the role of primary caregiver within a family unit, taking primary responsibility for helping the partner or other aged family members in need of care. This additional burden for the female can put additional stress on the aging couple. The statistic that 70 percent of women of age seventy-five or older are living alone (widowed, divorced, or never married) may at first seem shocking. However, we all are aware that living on a single income is more likely to result in poverty. Therefore it is not surprising that in 2010 the median income for women older than sixty-five was $15,072 as opposed to $25,704 for males in the same age cohort and $45,763 for households (e.g., families) headed by a male older than sixty-five for married couples (U.S. Department of Health and Human Services, 2011, p. 10).

There are many factors that complicate a simple definition of the term *older adult* and the more inclusive term *baby boomer* such as the wide range of ages that may be included in these groups. Some people live into their nineties and beyond. Richardson (2009) reports that Americans who are eighty-five or older are one of the fastest growing population segments; this astounding statistic alone requires attention. As this oldest age group continues to age, they are more likely to have significant health problems than adults aged fifty-five through sixty-five and even those in their seventies. This makes it very difficult to treat all of these older adults equally and lump them into one category.

To further identify age-related groups, older adults have been divided for purposes of simplicity into the terms older adults and *aged* to refer to all people of age sixty-five or older, and baby boomers to include those born between 1946 and 1964 as defined by the U.S. Census.

During the late 1990s, the John A. Hartford Foundation, a national foundation that supports gerontological efforts, financially supported the development of both master's level and baccalaureate level educational initiatives in aging (http://www.jhartfound.org/). In schools and departments of social work, gerontology field placements, elective courses, and concentrations (at the graduate level) were developed as a direct result of support by the Hartford Foundation. The Council on Social Work Education (CSWE, 2001) has developed a national gerontological project, SAGE-SW (Strengthening Aging and Gerontology Education in Social Work), which in turn has supported national meetings focusing on gerontology and gerontological educational modules. And in 2001, a second major national foundation, the Randolph Hearst Foundation, awarded each of five schools of social work a $500,000 endowment to support scholarships in gerontology. Endorsed by the CSWE and supported by the Hartford and Hearst Foundations, social work programs and their educators have been spurred to embrace gerontology as a key educational area and practice domain.

In this chapter we will introduce you to the topic of aging, a normal and universal stage of human development. As the number of older citizens continues to increase, so does the need for social work services. Fortunately, many services provided to older adults are considered human rights and are not subject to the means testing so common elsewhere in the social service arena. We will highlight issues and trends essential to an understanding of America's aging population.

AGING: WHAT CAN BE EXPECTED

Van Hook (2014), Dziegielewski (2013), Richardson (2009), and others are clear in pointing out the implications of the increasing numbers of older adults for practice in the twenty-first century. One factor contributing to this increase is the very large portion of the population that will fall into the category of older adults; this segment of the population is often referred to as baby boomers (see the activity below).

*Activity...*Using Census Bureau Information: *Explore the concept of aging by visiting the Census Bureau website: http://www.census.gov/population/age*
You can use this website to compare the national levels of older adults in your own home state or county.

Prior to World War II, large numbers of young immigrants came to America. Many immigrants came legally and were therefore reflected and counted in the national statistics, whereas others came illegally and were not counted. Many of these immigrants (legal and illegal) are now reaching retirement age. This group will grow as many of the people born after World War II (between 1945 and 1955), as well as those officially classified as baby boomers, (born between 1946 and 1964), reach retirement age (Barr, 2014).

Another factor underlying the growth in the number of aged individuals is the number of births relative to the number of deaths. The trend in recent years has been fewer births and longer and healthier lives, resulting in lower death rates (U.S. Census Bureau, 2014). It is predicted that death rates will continue to decline, leaving more aged individuals in society, especially the *old-old*, or those older than seventy-five.

As the numbers of older adults continues to rise so will the health care utilization (Tompkins & Rosen, 2014). As older adults retire from the workforce there will be fewer young adults to step up and supplement the financing of our health care system. The aging for the boomers will be pronounced, especially as people develop more chronic conditions that require ongoing treatment. Social workers have become keenly aware of the need for providers to look carefully at the needs of older clients to ensure that quality of life is maximized for both older adults and their caregivers (Gellis, 2009). After all, as Kim, Hayward, and Kang (2013) remind us, the spiritual, physical, and social well-being of older adults and their caregivers are intimately connected.

The aging process and working with older adults as a field of study, known as gerontology, did not become popular until the end of the 1930s (Shock, 1987). This increased attention to older adults was related to three major events: (1) the implementation of the Economic Security Act, (2) the development of a scientific basis for the study of the aged, and (3) the dramatic population trends involving older people.

To track this development, it is important to recognize that, in the 1930s, the United States was experiencing the aftermath of many major social changes. As World War I ended many people were thrust into poverty. The Great Depression made destitute many people who had never been poor before. Faced with these newly and unusually impoverished fellow citizens, American society showed increased willingness to help certain disadvantaged groups, particularly older people and young children (Frank, 1946). At the same time, the country still held a strong work ethic; regardless of age or circumstances every person was expected to be a productive part of society. It was during this period that the public, among whom social workers were active, began to insist that government take the necessary steps to ensure that the older adults and children did not, through their inability to work, become burdens on society (Stern & Axinn, 2011).

The Economic Security Act of 1935 was a societal response to the problem of widespread unemployment caused by the Great Depression. This act mobilized an unprecedented redistribution of income within society. As a result of this legislation, older citizens were provided with a government-assisted income because they were officially designated as unemployable (Stern & Axinn, 2011). This new guaranteed income helped to make this *worthy* group prosperous enough to command additional professional and societal attention. Also in the 1930s, an improved scientific basis for the study of the aged developed. The year 1942 saw the publication of *Problems of Aging* by E. Cowdry, a collection of papers by eminent scientists from many disciplines that represented the first compilation of scientific data on aging (Shock, 1987, p. 34). It is interesting to note that, following Cowdry's publication, the first issue of the *Journal of Gerontology* appeared in January 1946. This journal claimed to be the first in the field of gerontology and was designed "to provide a medium of communication and of interpretation in our efforts to gain a much surer knowledge of human growth and development" (Frank, 1946, p. 3). The journal represented the Gerontological Society, whose primary interest was to assist the elderly "against the present almost brutal neglect of the aged, by which many have been misused" (Frank, 1946, p. 3). These two publications highlighted the point that science and technology could assist in providing preventative health care for this vulnerable population. Now, over a half-century later, a large body of literature reflects the popularity of aging as a subject of study. Numerous books, textbooks, and classes are offered in this area. Furthermore, chemists, physicians, economists, dentists, psychologists, and social workers are among the professionals who have all contributed to existing knowledge about the aging population.

Did You Know...The social work profession has a long-standing interest in aging. This interest was expressed as early as 1947 at the National Conference of Social Work. Issues in aging were also included in the 1949 Social Work Yearbook (as cited in Lowry, 1979).

One last reason for the increased attention focused on the needs of older adults was the growth trend predicted for this population. Data collection had reached such a level of sophistication that it was able to track population trends within the 1930s showing that this population group was sure to grow. The growing numbers of older individuals in the late 1930s were clearly documented (Stern & Axinn, 2011), causing much concern because these people were not always considered capable of contributing to the national economy in terms of work (Frank, 1946). Today, this fear has taken a new direction as many professionals worry that these early attempts at meeting the needs of older individuals and the resulting programs to support them may not be enough. The programs born of good intention under the Economic Security Act to assist this population may no longer suffice. This fear is inspired primarily by expected increases in the numbers of older adults and the extended life spans that older people will enjoy. Given the open advocacy and concern expressed for older adults today as well as the severe financial constraints in our economy, a sense of cautious optimism has developed. However, resistance to providing these services for older adults continues because their problems are often complex and involve an integrated approach to care that highlights the health and mental health as well as the social and cultural dimensions (Dziegielewski, 2013; Richardson, 2009).

THEORETICAL FRAMEWORKS FOR PRACTICE WITH OLDER ADULTS

A cornerstone of all social work programs is the acknowledgment of the influence of human growth and development theory. This theoretical framework became popular in the 1970s because its broad approach takes into account the benefits and challenges that individuals encounter as they mature. The personality of an individual is assumed to be consistent with the way life tasks are developed and managed throughout his or her lifetime (Rhodes, 1988). For older adults there is a great need to be accepted and participate fully within families and communities (Podnieks, 2006). For social workers borrowing from this psychological theory, the most comprehensive and widely used work is that of Erik Erikson (1959). Erikson looked at the psychosocial aspects of human development and outlined eight stages that individuals experience. His model extended beyond childhood and adulthood and recognized the stages that older individuals are most likely to experience (see box 1).

Box 1. Erikson's Stages of Human Development

Basic trust versus mistrust
Autonomy versus shame and doubt
Initiative versus guilt
Industry versus inferiority
Identity versus identity diffusion
Intimacy versus self-absorption
General activity versus stagnation
Integrity versus despair

Erikson believed that, once an individual had successfully completed all eight stages, he or she would accept the self and take responsibility for his or her own life. In the last developmental stage, integrity versus despair, an individual's life goals reach finalization and reflection and contemplation become important tasks. Ryff (1982), among others, expanded on Erikson's last developmental stage for older adults by including such tasks as adjusting to their inability to supplement their sense of identity through work. Therefore, individuals become accepting of the physical limitations imposed by the aging process and learn to cope with death while embracing spirituality. Encouraging the connectedness that is often found through spirituality may be one way of staying engaged (Stinson, 2014).

Human growth and development theories have largely displaced older theories about how older individuals adjust to their changing societal role. Two other theories related to healthy aging that have received attention are disengagement theory and activity theory. Historically, in their quest to understand the aging process and the milestones that older people attain, social workers considered the concepts of disengagement and activity. These theories postulate that both activity and disengagement from traditional life experiences are normal and natural parts of the aging process.

Disengagement theory, introduced by Cumming and Henry (1961), focused on the normal process of withdrawal from the social environment. It was believed that the aging person would initiate withdrawal from usual life events and acknowledge his or her impending death, reduced physical energy, or poor health. The process of acknowledging the life situation and resulting disengagement was considered beneficial to both the individual and society (see box 2, Disengagement Theory).

Box 2. Disengagement Theory

According to proponents of disengagement theory, the role of the social worker is to help the client to disengage from mainstream society. This allows a natural transition by physically separating the individual from mainstream life and fostering an adjustment period. Disengagement is viewed as an inevitable process that every aging individual must undergo. Further, if a person resists this natural process of letting go, then problems in adjustment to the elderly years will develop (Cumming & Henry, 1961).

Disengagement theory can be helpful in understanding the need for changes in roles and life transitions. However, most social workers, although they are aware of this theoretical perspective, do not embrace it wholeheartedly. This is especially true because the research on disengagement theory has been limited, controversial, and contradictory. The extent to which older adults will practice disengagement after leaving mainstream society remains unclear. Furthermore, some individuals do not separate but rather stay engaged by changing the focus of their activities. In closing, more research is needed to determine whether disengagement is a natural part of the aging process, but recognizing that the concepts can be helpful in identifying the transitions that could likely occur.

The roots of activity theory are based in the idea that the older adult has the same social and psychological needs as the middle-aged adult. Early proponents of activity theory believed that professional intervention involved helping the client to continue an active existence. For example, a social worker might encourage an older adult to do volunteer work as a way to replace previously paid employment (See box 3, Activity Theory).

Box 3. Activity Theory

The concepts of activity theory were introduced before disengagement theory, but activity theory was not formalized until 1972 with the work of Lemon, Bengston, and Peterson. These authors were among the first to test activity theory in relation to reported life satisfaction. They hypothesized that, as activity increased, life satisfaction would also increase, and conversely, as role loss increased, life satisfaction would decrease. Basically, getting older is characterized by the desire to remain middle aged. Therefore, in order for aging to be successful, the elderly individual needs to continue activities similar to those that were important in middle age (Lemon, Bengston, & Peterson, 1972).

Today, most social workers working with older people are aware of this theory and of its influence on ideas about the aging process; however, most agree that more research is needed before activity theory can be used as a framework for practice. In particular, there needs to be a direct link between level of activity and life satisfaction (Hoyt, Kaiser, Peters, & Babchuk, 1980; Rhodes, 1988). Taking this perspective into account, the social worker has an important role in highlighting the need for older adults to maximize the positive experiences in their lives while minimizing the negative ones. To assist with this transition social workers help to create an environment where successful aging can occur.

Three theories will be introduced to help the reader focus on ways to better understand normal aging and how to best assist the older adult in identifying the transitions that will need to be addressed. Whatever theoretical practice framework is used, more empirical research is needed to establish the utility of developmental theories in working with all populations including older adults (Dziegielewski & Powers, 2000). Ryff' (1982) argued that, to better understand which model works best, the factors that result in accomplishment of Erikson's developmental stages should be isolated and those that allow older adults to achieve optimal levels of performance should be examined. This argument is still valid. However, it is important to add another caution about these theories, namely that, because of the time when they were written, they could incorporate apparent middle-class and sexist biases. Although research has not proved these theories to be comprehensive enough to explain all life changes experienced by older adults, their influence is deep in the roots of social work practice. Furthermore, although many interventions that were originally developed for younger persons may work well with older adults, there are modifications needed for certain individuals (Richardson, 2009).

Social workers need to be aware of the different treatments that are used, but most of all they need to recognize how societal perspectives on aging can influence all treatment outcomes. Whether or not these theories are valid, the fact that many professionals and lay people believe them may strongly affect their expectations and behavior. Keeping an open mind and avoiding uncritical adherence are central to keeping practitioners thinking about alternative explanations for clients' behavior and trying innovative problem-solving techniques. Furthermore, each older adult is indeed an individual and circumstances can vary. What they share in common, however, is that all will have to face objective losses in the body and the mind, and anything that helps to address these expected changes may lay the foundation for future acceptance. As individuals age it is common for them to become frustrated with what their bodies can and cannot do and to be frustrated with their lack of ability to complete tasks that used to be so much easier. As the older adult continues to age, his or her ability to act and manage independent living activities is sure to be affected; therefore, including the family and recognizing the role of supportive networks are critical to situation betterment and treatment success (Dziegielewski, 2013).

HEALTH, MENTAL HEALTH, AND THE OLDER ADULT

How often have you heard someone describe an aged loved one as "dying of old age?" How often have you heard professionals encourage this notion? How often have you seen or heard of an older person who consulted a physician about a certain ache or pain only to be told that the pain was simply related to old age? Dying of old age is a myth that should not be propagated (see box 4).

Box 4. The Pain in My Elbow

> A ninety-year-old man visits a physician for pain in the elbow joint of his right arm. After the client explains his symptoms to the physician, the physician says, "You are ninety years old. It's possible that the pain is merely related to your age, and there may be no plausible medical explanation for your pain." After hearing this theory, the patient thought for a moment and asked, "If your idea is tenable, why doesn't my other elbow hurt? After all, it's the same age."

Social workers must always give older clients the respect they deserve, allowing them to state their concerns in a nonjudgmental atmosphere. Remember that no one ever died of old age! The aging process is further complicated by the stigma that can be placed on getting older. This focus on the negatives can affect not only older individuals themselves, but also how they are perceived by the community as well as other health professionals. Avoiding stereotyping and actively listening to older individuals, especially those with severe mental illness, can improve patient-provider outcomes (Schroeder, 2013). There are many causes of social isolation in older persons, including such serious conditions as chronic illness and visual, hearing, or cognitive impairment (Eamon, 2008) or decreased physical functioning and medical frailty that may be caused by heart disease, cancer, and stroke (Ald-

---

Helpful Point... When working with clients approaching retirement, social workers should have them contact the Social Security Administration to get a copy of their lifetime earnings report. They should do this each year to verify the amount earned and credited toward their retirement. Any problems can be corrected with documentation of salary, but it's best to catch errors early rather than waiting until retirement.

win & Gilmer, 2013). When death occurs due to a medical condition, it should never be dismissed as dying of old age. This attitude can lead to actual diseases going undetected because symptoms characteristic of disease may be attributed by both client and medical provider as normal and due to the aging process itself (Sadavoy, Jarvik, Grossberg, & Meyers, 2004).

Did You Know...Knowledge that no one dies of old age is not new. For example, Mosher-Ashley (1994) in an archival study of records on 298 clients treated by a mental health center found that issues surrounding death often revolved around life-situation problems such as: (1) family conflicts, (2) poor physical health, and (3) feeling that they were not in control of their lives.

It is actually this recognition of how functional decline is attributable to medical or mental disorders rather than normal aging that has made it easier to diagnose certain disorders and to establish subsequent treatment modalities. Older adults deserve the same professional treatment as any other age group, and social work professionals have a role in educating and helping all clients to secure the specific health services they need.

The increased numbers of older adults have led to increased concern related to health care services utilization. Older individuals are more likely to experience medical concerns and chronic conditions requiring continued care (Aldwin & Gilmer, 2013). Just based on sheer numbers, older adults are important consumers of health care. Tan (2009) warns, however, that with all the research on the subject, there is no clear consensus among studies regarding the measurement of service use. Service use is generally defined by the type of service utilized. For example, hospital use by older individuals received a strong boost in 1965 with the initiation of Title XVIII (Medicare), one of the amendments to the Economic Security Act of 1935, which provided health insurance for the older adults, a high-risk group in terms of vulnerability to illness and poverty (Stern & Axinn, 2011). To date, Medicare remains one of the largest health insurance programs in the world (National Bureau of Economic Research, n.d.; Nesvisky, 2006). Medicare's introduction in 1965 was, and remains to date, the single largest change in health insurance coverage in U.S. history. Medicare is the closest program we have in the United States to universal health insurance, providing services to adults of age sixty-five and older as well as to many with disabilities. It is estimated that Medicare accounts for about 17 percent of U.S. health expenditures, one-eighth of the federal budget, and 2 percent of gross domestic production (Nesvisky, 2006).

Obviously, as people get older they are more likely to need health care services. Since 1965 and the implementation of Title XVIII, however, regardless of problems defining what is meant by services, the increase in health care consumption at age sixty-five has been dramatic. Medicare brought health care benefits to many older people who could not afford them otherwise; physicians and hospitals also benefitted from the greater assurance of payment for providing needed health care services. The benefits to health care recipients and providers, however, came at a particularly high price for the federal government. As the cost of services continued to escalate, the government became determined to control Medicare expenditures (Starr, 1982).

In 1983, Congress mandated a radical change in the payment structure for hospital care to rescue the Hospital Insurance Trust Fund from imminent bankruptcy (Lee, Forthofor, & Taube, 1985). The original system required Medicare to pay whatever hospitals charged for a particular service. Faced with these various and fluctuating costs, the government wanted to achieve uniformity and predictability. To control costs and develop an equitable payment system, Diagnostic Related Groups (DRGs) were developed (Begly, 1985).

The formal DRG system instituted in the past served as the basis for grouping individuals who had similar diagnoses, regardless of age or general health status. Each diagnostic category was assigned a particular standard of care, including the length of stay for which the government was willing to pay—for example, gallbladder removal was allowed seven days of hospital treatment. This system thus had a fixed payment schedule, and hospitals knew how much money they would receive for each individual. Unfortunately, for older people, who are more fragile and often have chronic or complicating conditions, this system and its newer derivatives remain problematic. Today, similar problems exist as little incentive exists for hospitals to accept patients who may require extended stays. When hospitals do accept older patients, many social workers have noted that they are discharged as quickly as possible. Quick discharges are problematic because discharge options may be limited, especially for frail older adults who also have limited incomes and few community supports. Furthermore, extended care facilities may be reluctant to take these recently discharged individuals because their current condition is medically less stable. In addition, facility staff become stressed when these new patients require much more care and observation. Inadequate placement options can lead to readmission, which is costly for the individual and for the hospital.

The Affordable Health Care Act (ACA)

To help address health care financing concerns and out-of-control spending, legislation such as the Affordable Health Care Act (ACA) was passed (Centers for Medicare and Medicaid Services, 2012). This law, enacted in 2010, seeks to hold insurance companies accountable by setting standards for reform that allow for lower health care costs while guaranteeing more choices that enhance quality of care. The ACA supports health care changes as well as improvements in health care access, quality, and service. The basic premise underlying the implementation of the ACA is to help provide coverage for 32 million Americans who currently do not have health care coverage, while opening the doors for affordable care to many more (Ofosu, 2011). Programs such as this continue to evolve and require that all health care professionals be open to change while balancing quality of care and utilizing evidence-based practices that are effective and cost efficient (Dziegielewski, 2014).

Effectiveness in working specifically with older adults involves patient/client/consumer advocacy at the most basic level. In this system of care, health care professionals will ultimately decide, with the input of consumers, who will qualify for and receive services (Dziegielewski, 2013). Therefore, education and awareness of the services offered have never been more important. Social workers are trained to address the psychosocial needs of the patients served and to support an important continuum of care essential for linking the person to the environment (Ofosu, 2011). The time has come for social workers to embrace illness prevention that can help to minimize the effects of chronic illness on individuals, families, and their support systems (Zabora, 2011). These efforts have been hailed as critical to tertiary prevention; when applied properly, they can lead to the detection of psychological distress. When the stresses related to chronic illness are not identified and addressed they can magnify medical symptoms experienced, such as pain and other somatic complaints (Zabora, 2011).

Medicare, Medicaid, and the ACA—and insurance reimbursement in general—are of particular interest to social workers working with older adults because they are the ones who generally handle the discharge and placement of older clients in both nursing home and hospital settings. Social workers must be aware of community supports for discharge back into the community and the availability of special treatment or services. Discharging older people who cannot complete their own activities of daily living (ADLs) may place great stress on the family and home services extended care staff. Few experienced professionals would argue that, with discharges back to the community, family stress can be a factor contributing to long-term care admission. Measures should be taken to allow families to communicate needs, problem solve, and participate in support groups. Social workers provide an excellent entry point for supportive and educational services to both older adult clients and caregivers. Similarly, placing an older client who needs a great deal of individual care into a long-term care facility can create great stress for the staff. Support groups and regular in-service training on how to treat these clients is mandatory. If additional staff is needed to facilitate placement, social workers should recommend such support.

Frank (2013) refers to Medicare beneficiaries who are also eligible for Medicaid as duals. This high-risk group is generally of sufficiently low income to qualify for Medicaid and tends to have more health-related problems than non-dual older adults. The worst fear for so many frail older adults is that of developing a chronic health condition because it can impair activity and hamper independence. The chronic conditions from which older adults often suffer are either physical (biological or physiological) or mental (psychological) in nature. We make this distinction only for simplicity's sake; it is important to note that physical and mental health conditions are often related and interdependent. For example, a physical event such as a stroke may develop into the mental health condition dementia. Also, there are a number of stress-related conditions that can complicate the medical condition an individual is suffering from.

> *Did You Know…A* chronic *condition is generally defined as a condition or disease that lasts a long time. An* acute *condition, however, often starts quickly and affects the individual greatly but generally lasts for only a short duration once treatment has been received. Frail older adults are often affected more by chronic than by acute conditions.*

Physical Health Conditions and the Older Adult

"Probably no factor is of more immediate concern to older people than physical health" (Maldonado, 1987, p. 99). As the numbers of older adults are growing globally so are the physical and mental health-related illnesses (Tiwari et al., 2013). Many older people fear the loss of individual unaided activity or perceived independence. When assessing an older adult, the social worker must first look carefully at the signs and symptoms that occur and whether these symptoms can be explained by medically related factors (Aldwin & Gilmer, 2013; Woo & Keatinge, 2008). For example, has the individual been placed on a new medication? For all individuals, medications should be monitored carefully. In older people, however, for whom slower metabolisms are the norm, metabolizing drugs may not be as simple as for someone younger (Dziegielewski, 2006, 2010). Furthermore, a recent study by Maust, Oslin, and Marcus (2014) found that, although many older adults were less likely to have a psychiatric disorder, they were often prescribed mental health medications. The authors therefore advocate more control of the medications that are being prescribed to this population. To address this issue completely, it is important to ensure that a general medical practitioner has been consulted and a general medical exam has been conducted.

Of all physical health conditions, heart disease remains the leading cause of death among those aged sixty-five or older, followed by cancer, stroke, chronic obstructive lung disease, pneumonia and influenza, and diabetes. For those individuals aged eighty-five or older heart disease was responsible for 40 percent of all deaths (Federal Interagency Forum on Aging-Related Statistics, 2000). Although

Name: Ramsi Wilkes

Place of residence: Birmingham, Alabama

College/university degrees: University of Montevallo, BSW

Present position: Admissions Coordinator, Galleria Oaks Guest Home

Previous work/volunteer experience: Discharge planner in a rehab hospital (Healthsouth) and retirement community

What do you do in your spare time? I participate in church activities, and I like music.

Why did you choose social work as a career? It was a way to act compassionately for others and make a difference. I was drawn to geriatrics from personal experience and I believed service in this area represented my Christian beliefs.

What is your favorite social work story? I will never forget working with a terminally ill client who was receiving hospice services. She lived in the supervised housing facility where I worked. I was with her when she was dying, and she told me what she was seeing and experiencing. She told me she saw angels in her room while she breathed her last breaths. She described everything about them and pointed them out. Spine tingling!

What would be the one thing you would change in our community if you had the power to do so? I would encourage more people to work with seniors and to learn to respect them more.

these conditions (excluding cancer) are considered acute, patients often gradually fall prey to chronic conditions such as paralysis and mental impairment that result in some type of dementia, making dementia the sixth leading cause of death among the elderly (Federal Interagency Forum on Aging-Related Statistics, 2000). Other major chronic conditions that result in the restriction of activity include rheumatism and hearing and vision impairments.

Among vision conditions, cataracts and glaucoma are most common. Social workers should always encourage older clients suffering from vision impairments to receive regular checkups to aid in detecting such conditions before permanent damage results. It is also important for social workers to consider how decreased vision can affect the counseling relationship (Dziegielewski, 2014). For example, an older client may not want to admit that he cannot easily read written material or navigate in a particular setting. Even for the oldest-old adults with vision impairment, encouraging exercises and activities adapted to their capabilities is always encouraged (Hackney, Hall, Echt, & Wolf, 2013).

Special attention should also be paid to possible hearing loss in clients. Some-one who seems withdrawn and unresponsive to conversation may simply be suf-fering from hearing loss and may be hearing only part of what is said and hypoth-esizing the rest (Dziegielewski, 2014). If the client's response is not appropriate, it can seem like confusion. Family members, in particular, may believe that their aged relative is becoming confused or simply ignoring them. Communication problems tend to increase the stress felt by family members (Dziegielewski, 2013).

In closing, social work professionals should always be aware that older adults are often shocked and embarrassed by changes in their health, and that these feel-ings may lead to denial. All of us can understand reluctance to admit individual inadequacy. Counseling and interviewing should include initial assessment to determine whether health concerns are affecting the interview process.

Mental Health and the Older Adult

Older individuals suffer many life circumstances that can affect their mental health. It is virtually impossible to age and not have traumatic life-changing expe-riences (Richardson, 2009). Common stressful life events include loss of a spouse, social and occupational losses, and physical health problems. In addition, criminal victimization is listed as a critical factor in the area of health risks (Federal Inter-agency Forum on Aging-Related Statistics, 2000). Because of the sheer number of life tragedies that older people have faced, it would seem logical that they would seek more mental health services than other population groups; however, this is often not the case. Many older individuals do not openly seek mental health ser-vices. One reason for this is the method of delivery. When living in the community, older psychiatric clients generally go to community mental health centers for checkups and medication; many older adults refuse these services because they don't want to leave their homes (Dziegielewski, 2013).

Depression

For many social work practitioners, clients who report symptoms of depres-sion are commonplace. Nearly 30 million of the U.S. adult population may be affected with major depression and approximately one-third are classified as severely depressed (Nemeroff, 2007). Furthermore, it is reported that approxi-mately 16 percent of the population will suffer from depression at some point in their lifetime (Capriotti, 2006; Hansen, Gartlehner, Lohr, Gaynes, & Carey, 2005). About 25 percent of people older than sixty-five with a chronic medical illness suf-fer from depressive symptoms, and approximately 15 percent suffer from major depressive disorder (Sheikh et al., 2004).

Because they are reported so frequently during routine medical visits and throughout the course of psychological treatment, depressive symptoms can seem like the common cold of mental health. Therefore, it comes as no surprise that depression is a common mental health problem for older adults, one frequently associated with physical symptoms and illness. The symptoms of depressions are considered important indicators for general health and wellness. It is clear that depressive disorders in the older population are prevalent and can be highly associated with medical conditions, particularly those of a chronic nature (Woodward, Taylor, Abelson, & Matusko, 2013). The Federal Interagency Forum on Aging-Related Statistics (2012) stated that older women (16–19%) were more likely to report clinically significant symptoms of depression than older men.

Although it is obvious that depression occurs in older adults, measuring what it means to each individual is not easy. Unfortunately many older adults may deny what they are feeling and avoid seeking treatment for depression or any other mental health condition. Furthermore, depression is believed to be related to the disproportionately high suicide rate among individuals aged eighty-five and older (43 deaths per 100,000 for men and 3 per 100,000 for women; Federal Interagency Forum on Aging-Related Statistics, 2012). As you can see, the suicide rates are higher for males after age eighty-five; this remains consistent because suicide rates are higher for males, even for younger adults.

Common signs and symptoms of depression include feelings of sadness, loneliness, guilt, boredom, marked decrease or increase in appetite, increase or decrease in sleep behavior, and a sense of worthlessness (Dziegielewski, 2014). For older adults, as the circadian rhythms change with advanced age, getting good restful sleep becomes more difficult (Rybarczyk, Lund, Garroway, & Laurin, 2013). Insomnia, characteristic of disturbed sleep, can easily affect mood as well as cognitive and behavioral responses.

When depression occurs in response to life circumstances, it is called *situational*. Situational depression is a particular risk for older adults because they generally endure many tragedies including loss of loved ones, jobs, status, and independence as well as other personal disappointments. Feelings of depression can be triggered by such experiences as bereavement for a deceased loved one or frustration with a medical condition (Dziegielewski, 2013). Of particular concern when working with older adults are the additional problems that can accompany increased mortality and chronic medical conditions. Older individuals who have increased limitations in mobility and the ability to carry out activities of daily living, self-perceived poor health, life dissatisfaction, and cardiac problems are at the highest risk for poor outcomes and recovery (Woo & Keatinge, 2008).

Social work intervention and counseling can help older clients to deal with situational depression and achieve greater life satisfaction. For example, social workers can teach older adults how to control the frequency of their depressive thoughts and to use relaxation techniques, such as imagery and deep muscle relaxation, to calm down during anxious times. Concrete problem solving and behavioral contracting can be used to help the older client change problem behaviors. Whenever possible, family members should be included in treatment contracting because they can provide support and assist in recording and observing behaviors that the older client is seeking to change.

Caution should always be used, however, because not all cases of depression in the older individual are situational. Some cases of depression may arise directly from internal causes; these are called *endogenous* depression. Furthermore, the etiology of depression in older adults is not always distinct; depression may be the result of a combination of situational and endogenous factors. For example, many chronic medical conditions, such as hypothyroidism, Addison's disease, Parkinson's disease, Alzheimer's disease, and congestive heart failure, are often accompanied by depression. It is also possible that symptoms of depression are by-products or side effects of medication taken for another condition (Dziegielewski, 2010) or symptoms of something else. The American Psychiatric Association (2013) has warned that the diagnosis of depression in older adults can be particularly problematic because the symptoms of dementia in its early stages and those of depression are very similar. Symptoms such as loss of interest and pleasure in usual activities, disorientation, and memory loss are common to the two conditions. There is one big difference, however. Although many signs and symptoms are the same, the person in the early stages of dementia will rarely improve as a result of treatment.

For the beginning social work professional, working with clients who are depressed can be frightening. You may feel uncertain about what questions to ask or what to do if they tell you they would like to harm themselves. This makes it a practice necessity to gather a detailed social, medical, and medication history as soon as possible. In addition, older clients with depression should always be referred for medical examination in order to rule out any physical reasons for depressive symptoms. Depression is most dangerous when it is unrecognized. When implemented, treatment for depression in the older adult is as effective as it is with other age groups (Dziegielewski, 2013).

Discharge Options

The current trend is for many older people with mental impairment who cannot be handled at home or in the community to be discharged to long-term care facilities. This practice has increased as a result of the deinstitutionalization that over the past thirty-three years has reduced state mental health hospitals to one-third their former capacity and thus eliminated one important placement option (Dziegielewski, 2013). In response to the consequent need for more constricted placement, many privately run long-term care facilities, including adult congregate living facilities (boarding homes) and nursing homes providing intermediate and skilled care, have been opened. In the past thirty years the number of nursing homes alone has increased dramatically in the United States (Dziegielewski, 2013). These homes provide a discharge option for older clients with mental impairment that other population groups do not have. Most patients admitted to long-term care facilities are older than sixty-five.

Dziegielewski (2013) warns that long-term care facilities, although convenient, are inappropriate placement options for older adults with mental impairment because these facilities generally do not provide mental health services. Furthermore, too many long-term care facilities provide minimal psychosocial interventions, with medication being the primary method of treatment. Beginning social work professionals must exercise caution when placing a client in a long-term care facility, especially if the client needs mental health services. Each facility is different. Social workers need to be aware not only of what long-term facilities exist in an area but also of which services these different facilities offer to the older client with mental impairment. Because many older adults fear functional activity loss, social workers must be aware of this fear, regardless of whether such loss has actually occurred. Such worries have a real foundation. Because many older individuals suffer from chronic conditions, the probability that these conditions will improve is low. It is important to support the individual client as well as his or her caregiver by giving him or her as much freedom of choice as possible when selecting a facility and the treatment to be received (Zegwaard, Aartsen, Grypdonck, & Cuijpers, 2013).

Our society tends to deny that problems may be terminal. Family members and some professionals may tell aged people that they'll get better rather than helping them to develop ways to cope (Dziegielewski, 2013). It is important for social work practitioners to be knowledgeable about common chronic conditions, their signs and symptoms, their expected progression, and when and where to refer clients for additional treatment. Furthermore, there is considerable evidence that the involvement and support of family members is important in creating a general sense of well-being for older adults (Dziegielewski, 2013). Therefore, the role of the social worker is essential in educating aged clients and their family members to cope with and understand changes that will occur. A comprehensive assessment of the individual, including health conditions and environmental factors, is critical.

EMPLOYMENT CHANGES, OLDER ADULTS, AND SOCIAL WORK PRACTICE

Today, problems associated with unemployment in the United States are inspiring social work professionals to look seriously at the social and economic consequences of being without a job (Rife & Belcher, 1994). At the same time, a growing number of low-paying and minimum wage jobs are not being filled. Having to address these problems has made the public aware of the specific experiences of certain groups such as older adults. Currently, the trend toward early retirement, in conjunction with the diminishing number of youths entering the workforce (as a result of lower birth rates), has created interest in older adults as a potential source of labor to help fill this gap. People who are living longer and healthier remain viable employees and constitute an underutilized labor pool that should not be ignored (Federal Interagency Forum on Aging-Related Statistics, 2000). In addition to societal need, many older individuals who enjoy good health see continued employment as desirable. Loss of the work role and the steady income it provides can be a big step for anyone to take. Furthermore, it is not uncommon for an older adult to be called upon to help younger extended family members.

Living Longer, Working Longer

Over the past forty years, older individuals have become better educated and wealthier than previous generations. It is expected that this trend will continue and that future generations will have even more education (Zarit & Zarit, 2007). Many individuals may not want to retire and may see employment as a way to supplement income as well as an opportunity for continued meaningful engagement (Zarit & Zarit, 2007). Sadly, if an older adult decides to return to work there is no guarantee that he or she will get a job. Regardless of protective legislation, age discrimination can and still does exist in the job market. There are many ways to subtly avoid hiring older adults, especially in non-trained positions that require physical agility. In addition, many jobs now require an application and search process that involves use of a computer and access to the Internet. The expectation of online application has increased and now many front-end nonprofessional-level positions also use an Internet application process (Mueller & Overmann, 2008). For older individuals, particularly those with low income, this can be problematic, serving as a block to seeking employment.

Until recently, Social Security rules created an unnecessary barrier for seniors who wished to work. Seniors who worked full or part time and earned income over a certain level were penalized for working by having their social security checks reduced. The U.S. Congress continues to address this issue while proposing strategies that would decrease and/or eliminate this penalty and allow seniors to earn as much as they can while retaining their retirement checks.

Social work professionals assist older clients returning to the workforce in several ways. First, social workers must encourage older clients to update or learn new

Box 5. Social Security Retirement Benefits

At one time people talked about retiring at age sixty-five. Well, retirement age has increased for most people, as seen in the table below. Can you retire at any age? Sure, but if you retire earlier than full retirement age, your monthly Social Security check will be reduced. An eligible person may begin receiving retirement checks at age sixty-two or delay receiving checks while working past retirement age. Note that the longer you wait to collect your benefits, the larger your monthly checks will be.

Year of birth	Full retirement age (years)	Reduction of benefits for retiring early*
1937 or earlier	65	20%
1940	65.6	22.5%
1943–54	66	25%
1960 and later	67	30%

Source: U.S, Social Security Administration (n.d.). *Retirement planner: Benefits by year of birth*. Retrieved from http://www.socialsecurity.gov/retire2/agereduction.htm
*Early retirement is at age sixty-two. An advantage of early retirement is that you collect your benefit for a longer period (if you live). The disadvantage is that your monthly check is permanently reduced by some percentage for the remainder of your life.

skills so that they can remain competitive throughout their careers. This is especially important because of the rapid technological advances occurring today, as well as the use of computer and automation technologies in most occupational settings. For an older client, learning and maintaining these types of skills can be frightening. This apprehension creates the need for the next point of social work intervention.

Second, social workers must work with employers to make job sites more worker friendly while linking older clients to larger support systems. Programs are often needed to accommodate older workers. These may include work schedule modifications such as job sharing between two or more workers, flextime schedules, and reduced work weeks. Furthermore, programs that are designed to build worker skills, motivation, and self-confidence need to be made available, either by the employer through in-house programs or through community-based programs. Assistance programs such as the job club described by Rife and Belcher (1994), which utilized a specialized job assistance strategy, provide an excellent practice environment in which social workers can help older workers to become reemployed.

Caregiving in the Community

Social workers must be aware that caregiving assistance may be needed to allow older adults to leave the home and continue working. Caregiving can be as serious an issue for older couples as for younger couples. In addition, the woman is often the family member identified for this caregiving role (Conway-Giustra, Crowley, & Gorin, 2002). Other studies have found that supportive services are valuable in easing the burden on caregivers (Dziegielewski & Ricks, 2000). Furthermore, working with both the client and the caregiver highlights the connection that fosters well-being for both (Kim, et al., 2013). For all extended families, the need for eldercare services will become a reality (Dziegielewski, 2013). Provision of elder day care services similar to child day care services can help these families. Social workers should advocate for companies to consider adding eldercare as a standard option in employee benefit packages (see Figure 1).

Figure 1: Rosa is an older woman who lives with her daughter and receives help from a visiting social worker.

Name: Ellendeer Berkowitz

Place of residence: Lima, New York

College/university degrees: BS, S.U.C. at Brockport; Collaborative MSW Program of Brockport and Nazareth Colleges, Rochester, NY

Present position: I am a social worker at St. John's Nursing Home in Rochester, NY. My heart's passion is most reflected in my work as a comfort care social worker, and I also work with elders needing rehabilitation, as well as those who have dementia. Monthly, I facilitate a dementia support group for families. I have also done presentations for staff in regard to quality of care and providing compassionate care at the end of life.

Previous work/volunteer experience: I worked for twenty-three years for Hillside Children's Center in Rochester, NY. I supported children and teenagers who had experienced abuse in their lives and who had suffered from different learning impediments. In this position, I learned to measure success not only by the completion of tasks or by improving grades but by the smiles and heart connections I was able to foster.

Why did you choose social work as a career? The difficult challenges that I experienced as a child and as an adolescent transformed into passion, within my heart, and I developed a sincere desire to help others in a meaningful way. Once my own healing journey began, I learned never to underestimate the power of love and compassion. I also learned that true healing occurs when you are able to help someone find their heart's connection or strength, as this helps enhance the healing process in beautiful ways. (Validating feelings and instilling hope are also very important.) I am very grateful to all my teachers for their inspiration, especially Shaman-Brant Secunda, M. Howden, and B. Allardice.

What is your favorite social work story? There have been many special moments. One of them was when my supervisor asked me to assist with an elder who, since admission, had not made eye contact and who hadn't spoken a word. I thought long and hard about how to help her. I remembered my teachings. After I spent some supportive time with her and placed a compassionate hand on her shoulder, she turned her head and her eyes met mine. She then spoke some words to me; the last words she spoke so clearly were "thank you."

What is one thing you would change in the community if you had the power to do so? I would like to continue to empower people and help others to learn to be respectful and accepting of those who are different from us. This includes uniting all people regardless of race, culture, faith, or age. Though idealistic, I believe that the lack of this type of unification has resulted in a lot of pain and suffering in our world, as well as in land, air, and water pollution. In addition, I would alleviate the barriers that prevent elders from having dignity and respect as they approach the end of their lives here on earth.

Older Individuals and Retirement

Retirement from the workforce has been viewed in different ways over the years. Attitudes toward retirement have changed with changes in social, emotional, political, and cultural climates. To illustrate how the view of retirement has changed, we will present a brief history of the role of older adults in the labor force.

Activity…Go to the Social Security Administration web page www.ssa.gov and using the on-line retirement planner estimate your monthly social security benefit check. What do you find? Is this what you thought you would get? Can you live on this amount of money?

The early twentieth century saw a shift from an agrarian to an urban industrial economy in the United States (Stern & Axinn, 2011). In agrarian society, all family members were viewed as contributing members of a cohesive unit. The family was responsible for meeting all the needs of its individual members, including

Figure 2: This couple has just celebrated their 50th wedding anniversary. It is often difficult for them to make Social Security income cover all their expenses and they get help from their children.

older family members. Industrialization, however, changed this perspective, establishing different expectations and roles, and many left the farm community to seek other types of income.

During the age of industrialization (1890–1912), one member's income was not enough to support the entire family, and often work outside of the home by all family members, including women, children, and the aged, became mandatory (Stern &Axinn, 2011). The participation of all these groups in the labor force did not last long, however. Family members left the workforce for two primary reasons: (1) industrialization required fewer workers in the production of output and (2) an influx of new immigrants made far more workers available (Morrison, 1982). Women, children, and the elderly were therefore no longer needed in the workforce. It was in this era that the public became increasingly aware of the growth in the elderly population. Morrison (1982) attributed this increased interest to worries that this large population might compete with younger workers for limited jobs.

The Economic Security Act of 1935 was the first time the government acknowledged responsibility for providing the elderly with an income that did not depend on continuing participation in the labor market. "The Social Security Act . . . set up a national system of old age insurance . . . which legitimized retirement at age 65" (Morrison, 1982, p. 9). This act supported limited, although permanent, economic guarantees to elderly adults. According to Morrison, Social Security helped to ensure that retirement benefits would moderate the reduction in income that workers faced when they left the labor market, and it helped to establish sixty-five years as the encouraged or expected retirement age (see Figure 3).

The lives of older adults have not changed radically over the past fifty years; what has changed, however, is society's view of these individuals and how it acts upon this view. In working with older clients, social workers need to be aware of the following aspects of retirement, and how they can affect the lives of the aged. Over the short span of forty years, retirement has become an important concern of the American people; almost every day, articles and commentaries appear in publications throughout the country on the economic, social, and psychological consequences of retirement (see the activity below). In the past, it was clear that this interest in retirement was heightened by the rising costs of public and private retirement benefits and now fluctuating investment opportunities make confidence in sustained viability almost impossible.

Today, this concern about the viability of the Social Security System continues, but added to it is the fear of many individuals that they will not be able to afford to retire because of the rising cost of living and health care expenses (Iftekhar, 2008).

Figure 3: An 80-year-old at the ecumenical social center after an exercise class. This is a drop-in center that offers seniors lunch and a variety of activities.

As baby boomers approach retirement age, fiscal concerns increase related to whether the Social Security system can handle the inevitable growth in the number of beneficiaries in view of the recent downturns in our economy. Social work intervention can be critical in helping an aged client make a successful transition from the role of worker to the new role of retiree. It is important, however, that the social worker clearly communicate to older clients about their role in the delivery of services because the provision of such services may be poorly understood (Scharlach, Mor-Barak, & Birba, 1994). For example, preretirement planning is one of the services a social worker can provide to assist in the transition process. Through counseling and more specific assistance, the social worker can help aged clients to plan for the role adjustment they will face. It is important to remember that many people gain status or identity through working (Mosher-Ashley, 1994). They enjoy the work they do and don't want to give up the internal and external rewards they derive from it. Some older people can afford to retire, but choose not to because of the value this society places on working for money (Davidson & Kunze, 1979). Ekerdt (1986) concurred that the importance of the work ethic in our society should not be underestimated. He recommended that older adults reaching retirement plan their leisure time as carefully as they planned their work time; otherwise, their self-esteem may suffer. Social workers need to be sensitive to this aspect of work in order to help older individuals to find other activities that they will find fulfilling.

> *Activity…Retirement involves both endings and beginnings. Take a look at your own retirement and think about your beginnings and endings. To assess your endings, consider what your life will be like when you retire. Think about your paycheck, alarm clock, commute . . . .*
>
> **What Will End**   **Will You Miss It?**
>   Yes   No
> 1._____   _____   _____
> 2._____   _____   _____
> 3._____   _____   _____
> 4._____   _____   _____
>
> *When you think about your beginnings, consider what you will miss from your work environment and what can you replace it with. For example, you might miss managing projects, and you might replace this task with volunteering in a program that requires management skills.*
>
> **Miss**   **Replace**
> 1._____   _____
> 2._____   _____
> 3._____   _____
> 4._____   _____
> 5._____   _____
>
> *Source*: **Arnone, Kavouras, & Nissenbau (2001).**

To plan leisure time, the degree and type of activity that a client can perform (and afford) must be considered. Worker and client can together create a list of options and discuss each option in a problem-solving, decision-making manner. Once they have chosen an appropriate leisure activity, they can develop an individual contract. The contracting of leisure time activity can give the client permission to engage in restful activities that can provide structure to an otherwise ambiguous period in life.

Financial concerns, including the fear of not having enough income or of being inundated with medical bills and having difficulty securing health insurance, are another factor that may deter an older individual from entering retirement. Concerns such as this can mount and may cause an individual approaching retirement to delay it as long as possible. There has not been a clear link between suicide and retirement, but the changes in the economic, social, and emotional contexts of a client's life can be severe, causing difficulties in any transitions that are yet to come (Zarit & Zarit, 2007). A social worker must be aware of the resources available to the older client and must help the client to obtain adequate financial counseling. Employers often will provide such counseling on request. Insurance brokers can be consulted about health and life insurance. These brokers are usually able to discuss numerous policy options because they represent several different companies.

When conducting retirement counseling, social workers should always remember that people often resist change and avoid what they cannot predict. Many people approaching retirement have grown comfortable in their careers and established job patterns that are integral parts of their lives. Older adults need to be made aware of the options available to them in retirement, especially in regard to leisure activities.

Planning retirement is an important step in transition, yet many people continue to avoid it. Most social work interventions in this area come after the fact and are supportive in nature. Montana (1985) stated that preretirement counseling is necessary because it can help older people to decrease their anxiety about what retirement will bring. Social workers can take a more active role in pre-retirement counseling by telling clients about its importance, as well as about how to plan for the future and what to expect in the way of benefits and activities. The way an individual approaches retirement and the attitude developed can be very important in determining life satisfaction during retirement.

COMMUNITY CARE AND CASE MANAGEMENT

Case management is a collaborative process that assesses, plans, implements, coordinates, monitors, and evaluates the options and services required to meet an individual's health needs, using communication and available resources to promote high-quality, cost-effective outcomes (Mullahy, 1998). Case management services for older individuals are considered an important and necessary service for the continuity of care (Austin & McClelland, 2009). Case management services with older individuals, similar to those provided to recipients of all ages, seek to ensure that all clients receive the services that they need in a system that sometimes appears fragmented and difficult to navigate. The tasks in case management can vary; for the most part, however, for older adults these services can include the concrete tasks of completing psychosocial assessments, initiating and implementing advanced directives, connecting to resources and obtaining insurance verification for hospital stays, accessing community resources, and obtaining referrals for services and durable medical equipment. They can also include more supportive services such as counseling. All of these services are designed to help the individual maintain his or her current status in the community. After all, social support and connectedness remain an important ingredient in continued well-being and can provide the support needed (Waite, Iveniuk, & Laumann, 2014).

> *Did You Know…Two general terms are often used in the medical community to describe the process of getting older. The first,* aging, *is defined as the condition of growing older regardless of chronological age; the second,* senescence, *is used to characterize the process of deterioration that occurs in the later years in an individual's life.*

For the older adult, community-based care and case management services often begin with assessing the person-in-situation. For example, what type of support system does the older adult have to stay in the community safely? When support systems are severely limited or do not exist, a client can refuse to consider more restrictive care. Therefore, it is a delicate issue when a client who is unable to handle activities of daily living or personal affairs refuses to go to a nursing home.

In the broadest sense, the social work case manager is the person who makes the health care system work, influencing both the quality of the outcome and the cost (Mullahy, 1998). Roles are diverse but perhaps the case manager can facilitate an earlier, more supported and stable discharge when a client has been hospitalized; negotiate a better fee from a medical equipment supplier; or encourage the family to assume responsibility for assisting with the day-to-day care for an older relative. In addition, the social worker can serve as a catalyst for change by seeking solutions that promote improvement or stabilization rather than simply monitoring patient status (Mullahy, 1998). Often the social worker may have to arrange home health care for the patient, nursing home placement, provision of medical equipment, hospice care, transplants, or simply transportation for the patient (Nelson & Powers, 2001). To ensure that individual worth, dignity, and safety are always maintained, the social worker must take into account the wishes of the client and the client's family, the needs of the client, and the potential for future growth in this environment.

ABUSE, NEGLECT, RISK OF EXPLOITATION, AND AGING

Vulnerable older adults can easily become targets for financial, physical, and psychological abuse (U.S. Department of Justice, 2011). Elder abuse and neglect remain a significant concern of practitioners as well as policy makers and program planners (Nerenberg, 2006). The definition of exactly what constitutes abuse in older adults can vary widely. According to Nerenberg these circumstances appear to be the most problematic for treatment, similar to child abuse situations that involve physical abuse, sexual abuse, verbal or psychological abuse, and the violation of basic human rights including abduction and abandonment. In addition to this, elders may be subjected to domestic violence, homicide, homicide-suicide, and financial abuse. The term *elder justice* is used to signify the connection between adult protective services (APS) and the criminal justice system and the assurance that, when victimization rises to a criminal standard, it will be addressed and, if needed, prosecuted to the fullest extent of the law (Dubble, 2006). The process of taking reports of elder abuse, assessing and substantiating the reports, and providing intervention rests with the APS agencies.

Individuals with cognitive impairment disorders such as dementia are at increased risk of elder abuse. These disorders and others that disturb cognitive functioning can be the most difficult for APS workers to assess because of an elder's right to choose. This is very different from working with children, where intervention is expected regardless of choice. Elders who are mentally competent are capable of making their own decisions, and for workers it can be difficult to decide what to do if the older adult does not want intervention. Generally, there is only one reason cited by APS workers for disregarding a client's right to choose, and that is when the client is deemed to be mentally incompetent (Bergeron, 2006). As mandatory reporters, social workers must be sure that every effort has been made to protect the client and to determine whether the client who is refusing services is capable of rational thought. Both violent behaviors between caregivers and care recipients and self-neglect often require the case to be reported to APS.

Bomba (2006) suggests three essential questions to address when elder abuse is suspected:

1. Is the patient/client safe?
2. Does the patient/client accept intervention?
3. Does the patient/client have the capacity to refuse treatment?

Drifthnery (2000) examined abuse, neglect, and exploitation of the elder population and found that factors such as self-imposed neglect, endangering behaviors, financial mismanagement, and environmental dangers as well as physical illness and/or disability, along with mental health conditions such as alcohol or other substance abuse, can increase cases of abuse of older adults. Social workers are in a unique position to recognize and assess on behalf of this vulnerable population throughout the different levels of care.

Choi and Mayer (2000) believe that one way to decrease the problem of elder abuse is to open up more community-based care opportunities such as case management. In the community care setting, social workers are encouraged to provide education to older adults, their families, and the public to prevent elder maltreatment. Also, greater advocacy to increase funding for prevention, detection, support, and intervention in older adult abuse and neglect is needed. This trend is in its infancy because law enforcement agencies have just begun to see the need to develop programs to investigate and identify crimes against older people. According to the U.S. Department of Justice (2011), in 2009, 11 percent of older adults living in the community who responded to a phone survey reported that they had experienced at least one form of mistreatment that involved physical abuse, emotional abuse or neglect, or sexual abuse. Financial exploitation by a family member was reported by 5.2 percent of older people in one year. In 1999, 3.8 of every 1,000 persons sixty-five and older were victims of crime. Unfortunately, many older adult victims, especially those who live alone, worry that reporting crime can bring embarrassment, along with additional harassment. Even worse, victims think that concerned family members may use the incident as leverage to put them in a nursing home. Social workers need to review warning signs, such as withdrawal of large sums of money from the bank accounts of older adults; family members and financial institutions should also watch for these transactions. Because agencies and victim support services are ill prepared to deal with an increase in victims, advocacy to avoid crimes against the vulnerable older adult is necessary and urgent.

ASSESSING SUICIDE RISK AND PLANNING FOR DEATH

In general, people with serious mental illness have a life expectancy that is eight to thirty-two years shorter than that of the general population (Druss, Zhao, Von Esenwein, Morrato, & Marcus, 2011). When this is coupled with rising suicide rates among the aged, suicide risk should always be assessed for in those individuals with a history of mental illness. Perkins and Tice (1994) reported that among the general population, the suicide rate is 12.4 per 100,000 persons; in 1990, the recorded suicide rate for older people was 20 per 100,000. Persons sixty-five and older comprise 12.5 percent of the population and account for 20.9 percent of the suicides annually (Perkins & Tice, 1994, p. 438). As of 2000, the American Association of Suicidology continued to support this contention, reporting that this rate is approximately 18.1 percent. This organization also reports that in 2000 suicide rates ranged from 12.6 percent or 100,000 persons for those aged seventy-five to eighty-four. For older adults, the rate is almost double that for the overall U.S. population. Leach (2006) reported that today European American older adults have the highest suicide rates among all age groups, with the highest rate among people in their eighties. Depression seems to be a key factor leading to these suicides. This statistic alone is hard to believe: Although older Americans constitute 15 percent of the population, those older than sixty-five also constitute 25 percent of all suicides.

Did You Know...Suicide is the tenth leading cause of death in the United States and accounts for over 39,518 deaths reported in 2011. In that year someone died by suicide every 13.3 minutes.

Source: *American Foundation for Suicide Prevention. (2012). Facts and Figures, Retrieved from: https://www.afsp.org/understanding-suicide/facts-and-figures*

Why are the rates so high in this group, and will they continue to grow? There is probably no conclusive reason for these trends, but there is a definite connection between stress levels among older adults and illness (Onose et al., 2013). It makes sense that when stress is high usual methods of coping and problem solving become ineffective. Another factor is that religious organizations and family and friends may be uncomfortable discussing suicide with a loved one because they fear it may make the situation worse (Leach, 2006). Furthermore, dissatisfaction with functional abilities caused by ill health can negatively affect emotions and feelings of resilience. Finally, the tremendous number of life stressors that the older adults may experience in a short amount of time—for example, death of spouse, relatives, or friends and changes in social status and employment status—cannot be overemphasized (Dziegielewski, 2013).

Suicide rates are usually considered indicative of the mental health, satisfaction, and well-being of a population. But society doesn't always view suicide among older adults in the same way as suicide involving young people. For example, the increase in suicide rates among adolescents has raised much alarm and led many to a call for solutions. At the same time, however, suicide with older people may not be treated as seriously. Older individuals at the greatest risk are the ones who report feeling lost, trapped, and alone. Fear of declining physical health coupled with increased health care costs can make older adults feel that options are limited. For the most part, the methods for completion of suicide are similar in the young and old, including inappropriate use of prescription medications or alcohol, delaying medical treatment for a life-threatening condition, or risk-taking behavior such as driving recklessly (Zarit & Zarit, 2007). In older adults, however, the self-destructive behaviors tend to be more subtle and range from taking too much prescription medication to none at all (Zarit & Zarit, 2007).

The death of a partner presents a particular coping problem because it may require the older adult survivor to assume new, unfamiliar duties: balancing a checkbook, driving, shopping for groceries, and so forth. These new tasks and the adjustments they imply, in conjunction with the loss of a life partner, can place unbelievable stress on older people. They may feel isolated from married friends and fear possible dependence on family or friends. These feelings of isolation can be considered a significant risk factor to continued well-being (Cacioppo & Cacioppo, 2014). Widowhood particularly affects older women because they generally outlive their male partners (Federal Interagency Forum on Aging-Related Statistics, 2000). Widowhood may not be directly linked to suicide; however, when the male partner outlives a female spouse, the suicide rates are higher for older males than for older females (Zarit & Zarit, 2007). Nevertheless, Zarit and Zarit

(2007) warned that widowhood is likely to have negative effects, including impairment of physical, psychological, and social well-being. Suicide among older adults is almost always a result of major life stresses and accumulated losses; therefore, widows and widowers have a high probability of committing suicide (see box 6). Research indicates that the first year after the death of a spouse is the hardest time of adjustment (Erlangsen, Jeune, Billie-Brahe, & Vaupel, 2004). During this especially stressful period, social workers should keep aware of a client's abilities or problems in coping with grief.

The social worker plays an essential role with potentially suicidal older clients. First, if a client, young or old, expresses a wish to commit suicide and has a concrete plan, steps to ensure hospitalization must be taken immediately. The person needs to be in a safe place. Unfortunately, criteria for hospital admission are not always clear, and the social worker may not know how likely the client is to turn suicidal verbalizations into actions. In any case, some type of counseling must take place. For dealing with aged clients Perkins and Tice (1994) emphasized a counseling strategy that focuses on client strengths. In this method client and social worker identify the client's preexisting coping and survival skills in order to help him or her to accept the role of survivor. This approach, in conjunction with crisis services and bereavement counseling, can help the older client to regain control of her life.

Box 6. Getting Commitment and Formulating a Safety Plan

Social work professionals often help clients to complete professional agreements even when clients have no actual plans to harm themselves. This is not a legal contract; it is merely done to document clearly what has been said and to help the client clearly articulate a plan that can be monitored. If used, this should always be part of a larger and more comprehensive safety plan and should not stand alone. It can assist as part of the standard of practice and documentation of a plan.

> I _____ agree that I will not kill myself or someone else and that I do not have any plans to do so. If I start to feel as though I might want to try to kill myself or someone else, I have voiced my intent to immediately seek help at [insert the name and address of a 24-hour emergency room that handles indigent clients where the client can report to be seen].

*Helpful Hint: Be sure to get permission from the client to call a family member or notify the support system so they too are aware of the pending situation. Document this clearly in the record (Dziegielewski, 2013).

Much of the confusion in our society regarding death can be linked to the atmosphere of denial, secrecy, and fear that we have created around this inevitable part of life (Leach, 2006). Many people attempt to ignore or avoid it, at least until it affects them indirectly. For example, have you prepared for your own death? Do you have a will? Is your family aware of your wishes? For most of us the answer is no. Our reasons vary from "I'm too young to worry about that now" to "I have plenty of time." Now, if you, the helping professional, said no, what do you think your clients will answer? By the way, if you did say no, you're not alone; but don't take too much comfort in this—it's evidence that you need to address these issues in your own life.

No one rationally desires to be dying or to have a terminal illness. Indeed, most people resist even the idea of being ill. For some people, however, regardless of age, there comes a time when they truly do want to die (High, 1978). Many older people fear the chronic conditions that can make them dependent on family and/or friends. Family members too fear this new independent health-related decision-making and can be daunted by the prospect of making decisions without the input of the loved one, especially in regard to continuing or terminating life. The older person and family members often turn to science and medicine for the answers. Physicians, as representatives of the scientific and healing community, are sought out and expected to supply answers and make decisions. Unfortunately, many physicians, taught from the day they enter medical school to preserve life, may feel unprepared to deal with the psychosocial aspects of dying (Nolan, 1987). Trained to help people avoid death, many health care professionals see their role as avoiding death (Dziegielewski, 2013). It is the social worker, often as part of an interdisciplinary team, who will be asked to help the client or family to cope with death.

Before a social worker can successfully help a client and his or her family to deal with death, several issues should be addressed. First, the social worker must explore his or her own feelings about death and address any uncomfortable feelings he or she may feel. By examining alternative conceptions of death and the legitimization of the role of death, social workers can disperse some of the mysticism that surrounds death in this country. Once the social worker feels comfortable talking about death, these concepts need to be discussed with the client as well as family members.

Second, the social worker must know what community resources and services might assist older clients in preparing for death. One example is the hospice program (National Hospice and Palliative Care Organization, 2008). Hospice, which is funded by Medicare, offers services to people suffering from terminal illnesses who are expected to live six months or less (Dziegielewski, 2013). This and similar programs do not focus on prolonging life beyond its natural end. In providing services through such programs the social worker serves on an interdisciplinary team designed to help the client and family members to prepare for natural death.

Finally, the social worker should learn about living wills and decide whether such a measure is appropriate for the client. Most people are aware of the need for a will and some complete a will that declares who is to receive their money, property, and other possessions. However, the concept of a living will is less familiar (Dziegielewski, 2013). Simply stated, a living will allows a person to document, in advance, his or her preferences relating to the use or avoidance of life-sustaining procedures in the event of a terminal illness. This type of documentation is especially helpful to family members burdened with making such decisions when an older relative is mentally incapacitated. Without it, they may avoid making any decision because they feel that doing so gives them too much control and responsibility.

SUMMARY

We all face the prospect of growing old, yet older people often suffer as the result of societal attitudes that devalue old age. Our society fears aging and promotes any number of attempts to overcome the effects of old age on the human body and the mind. The focus on the losses of functioning that come with aging often dominate expectations, and little attention is given to promoting optimal functionality geared toward the individual's capabilities (Algilani et al., 2014). Such prejudices spring from both rational and irrational fears. Rational fears about worsening health, the loss of loved ones, and declining social status can be intensified by negative stereotypes of older people. And irrational fears about changes in physical appearance, loss of masculinity or femininity, and perceived mental incompetence are not unusual. For older people, misinformation and myth, as well as real biological, psychological, social, and economic challenges, can impede self-help and the pursuit of individual contentedness. The fear of isolation can weigh heavy on the mind of the individual, having a toxic effect on his or her well-being (Cacioppo & Cacioppo, 2014). Advocating for all older clients, particularly those with serious mental illness, to receive adequate medical care should always be a top priority (Bartels et al., 2013).

Aging in today's society creates complexities both in policy and in the human experience. Advances in medicine allow people to live longer. You will find many families that have three generations of seniors: the granddaughter in her late 50s, her father in his early 80s, and her grandmother in her 100s, for example. Talk about perplexing family dynamics! As we age and live longer, we will spend more years in retirement. Retirement now can last forty and even fifty years. Income, health care, socialization, loneliness and happiness, and support are among the many areas that policy makers and senior advocates struggle with today.

The good news is that older people are turning more often to mental health professionals to address the problems they are facing (Zarit & Zarit, 2007). At a minimum, social workers need to examine their own attitudes about aging and how these attitudes can affect their practice with older clients and their families. As mandatory reporters, we should be familiar with our roles and what we need to do to protect those who cannot protect themselves. We should be keenly aware of the types of discrimination that can occur, and we must never contribute, directly or indirectly, to any discriminatory practices based on age. All helping professionals need to recognize that each aged person is a valuable resource in our society. Our role is to provide services and advocacy that will help older people in need of services to maximize their life satisfaction and well-being.

REFERENCES

Aldwin, C. M., & Gilmer, D. F. (2013). *Health, illness, and optimal aging: Biological and psychosocial perspectives* (2nd ed.). New York: Springer.

Algilani, S., Ostlund-Lagerström, L., Kihlgren, A., Blomberg, K., Brummer, R. J., & Schoultz, I. (2014). Exploring the concept of optimal functionality in old age. *Journal of Multidisciplinary Healthcare, 7,* 69–79.

American Association for Long Term Health Insurance. (2008). *Long-term care: important information for women.* Retrieved from http://www.aaltci.org/long-term-care-insurance/learning-center/for-women.php

American Foundation for Suicide Prevention. (2012). *Facts and figures.* Retrieved from https://www.afsp.org/understanding-suicide/facts-and-figures

American Psychiatric Association. (2013). *Diagnostic and Statistical Manual of Mental Disorders, DSM-5* (5th ed.). Washington, DC: Author.

Arnone, W. J., Kavouras, F., & Nissenbaum, M. (2001). *Ernst and Young's retirement planning guide: New tips and strategies for building wealth* (2nd ed.). New York: Wiley.

Arnquist, S. (2009, June 30). How old do you feel? It depends on your age. *Health, The New York Times,* Retrieved from http://www.nytimes.com/2009/06/30/health/30aging.html?_r=0

Austin, C. D., & McClelland, R. W. (2009). Case management with older adults. In A. R. Roberts, *Social workers' desk reference* (2nd ed., pp. 797–801). New York: Oxford University Press.

Barr, P. (2014, January 14). The boomer challenge. *H&HN* (Hospital and Health Networks). Retrieved from http://www.hhnmag.com/display/HHN-news-article.dhtml?dcrPath=/templatedata/HF_Common/NewsArticle/data/HHN/Magazine/2014/Jan/cover-story-baby-boomers

Bartels, S., Aschbrenner, K. A., Rolin, S. A., Cimpean, H. D., Naslund, J. A., & Faber, M. (2013). Activating older adults with serious mental illness for collaborative primary care visits. *Psychiatric Rehabilitation Journal, 36,* 278–288.

Begly, C. (1985). Are DRGs fair? *Journal of Health and Human Resources Administration, 8,* 80–89.

Bergeron, L. R. (2006). Self-determination and elder abuse: Do we know enough? *Journal of Gerontological Social Work, 46*(3/4), 81–102.

Bomba, P. A. (2006). Use of a single page elder abuse assessment tool: A practical clinician's approach to identifying elder mistreatment. *Journal of Gerontological Social Work, 46*(3/4), 103–122.

Brieland, D., Costin, L. B., & Atherton, C. R. (1980). *Contemporary social work* (2nd ed.). New York: McGraw-Hill.

Cacioppo, J. T., & Cacioppo, S. (2014). Social relationships and health: The toxic effects of perceived social isolation. *Social & Personality Psychology Compass, 8*(2), 58–72.

Capriotti, T. (2006). Update on depression and antidepressant medications. *MEDSURG Nursing, 15,* 241–246.

Centers for Medicare and Medicaid Services. (2012). *Affordable Care Act implementation FAQs— set 8.* Retrieved from http://www.cms.gov/CCIIO/Resources/Fact-Sheets-and-FAQs/ aca_implementation_faqs8.html

Choi, N. G., & Mayer, J. (2000). Elder abuse, neglect, and exploitation: Risk factors and prevention strategies. *Journal of Gerontological Social Work, 33*(2), 5–25.

Conway-Giustra, F., Crowley, A., & Gorin, S. H. (2002). Crisis in caregiving: A call to action. *Health and Social Work, 27,* 307–311.

Council on Social Work Education/SAGE SW. (2001). *Strengthening the impact of social work to improve the quality of life for older adults and their families: A blueprint for the new millennium.* Alexandria, VA: Council on Social Work Education.

Cowdry, E. V. (Ed.). (1942). *Problems of aging: Biological and medical aspects.* Baltimore: Williams and Wilkins.

Cumming, E., & Henry, W. (1961). *Growing old: The process of disengagement.* New York: Basic Books.

Davidson, W. R., & Kunze, K. (1979). Psychological, social and economic meanings of work in modern society: Their effects on the worker facing retirement. In W. C. Sze (Ed.), *Human life cycle* (pp. 690–717). New York: Jason Aronson.

Drifthnery, F. (2000). Work history and U.S. elders. Transitions into Poverty, *Gerontologist, 40,* 469–479.

Druss, B. G., Zhao, L., Von Esenwein, S., Morrato, E. H., & Marcus, S. C.(2011). Understanding excess mortality in persons with mental illness: 17-year follow-up of a nationally representative U.S. survey. *Medical Care, 49,* 599–604. doi:10.1097/MLR.0b013e31820bf86

Dubble, C. (2006). A policy perspective on elder justice through APS and law enforcement collaboration. *Journal of Gerontological Social Work, 46*(3/4), 35–55.

Dziegielewski, S. F. (2006). *Psychopharmacology for the non-medically trained.* New York: Norton.

Dziegielewski, S. F. (2010). *Social work practice and psychopharmacology: A person and environment approach.* New York: Springer.

Dziegielewski, S. F. (2013). *The changing face of health care social work: Opportunities and challenges for professional practice* (3rd ed.). New York: Springer.

Dziegielewski, S. F. (2014). *DSM-IV-TR™ in action* (2nd ed., DSM-5 Update). Hoboken, NJ: Wiley.

Dziegielewski, S. F., & Powers, G. T. (2000). Procedures for evaluating time-limited crisis intervention. In A. Roberts (Ed.), *Crisis intervention handbook* (2nd ed.). New York: Oxford University Press.

Dziegielewski, S. F., & Ricks, J. (2000). Adult daycare for mentally impaired elderly and measurement of caregiver satisfaction. Activities, *Adaption and Aging, 24*(4), 51–64.

Eamon, M. K. (2008). *Empowering vulnerable populations.* Chicago: Lyceum Books.

Ekerdt, D. J. (1986). The busy ethic, moral continuity between work and retirement. *Gerontology, 26,* 239–244.

Erikson, E. (1959). Identity and the life cycle: Selected papers. *Psychological Issues, 1,* 1–171. New York: International Universities Press.

Erlangsen, A., Jeune, B., Bille-Brahe, U., & Vaupel, J. W. (2004). Loss of partner and suicide risks among oldest old: A population-based register study. *Age and Ageing, 33,* 378–383.

Hoyt, D. R., Kaiser, M. A., Peters, G. R., & Babcuk, N. (1980). Life-satisfaction and activity theory: A multi-dimensional approach. *Journal of Gerontology, 35,* 935-981.

Federal Interagency Forum on Aging-Related Statistics. (2000). *Older Americans 2000: Key indicators of well-being.* Washington, D.C.: U.S. Government Printing Office.

Federal Interagency Forum on Aging-Related Statistics. (2012). *Older Americans 2012: Key indicators of well-being.* Washington, D.C.: U.S. Government Printing Office. Retrieved from http://www.agingstats.gov/agingstatsdotnet/Main_Site/Data/2012_Documents/Docs/EntireChartbook.pdf

Frank, L. (1946). Gerontology. *Journal of Gerontology, 1,* 1.

Frank, R. G. (2013). Mental illness and a dual dilemma. *Journal of the American Society of Aging, 37*(2), 47–53.

Gellis, Z. D. (2009). Evidence-based practice in older adults with mental health disorders. In A. R. Roberts, *Social workers' desk reference* (2nd ed., pp. 376–380). New York: Oxford University Press.

Hackney, M., Hall, C., Echt, K., & Wolf, S. (2013). Dancing for balance: feasibility and efficacy in oldest-old adults with visual impairment. *Nursing Research, 62*(2), 138–143.

Hansen, R. A., Gartlehner, G., Lohr, K. N., Gaynes, B. N., & Carey, T. S. (2005). Efficacy and safety of second generation antidepressants in the treatment of major depressive disorder. *Annals of Internal Medicine, 143,* 415–426.

High, D. (1978). Quality of life and care of the dying person. In M. Blaes & D. High (Eds.), *Medical treatment and the dying: Moral issues* (pp. 65–84). Salem, MA: Hall.

Huffington Post. (2012, May 2). The elderly vs. the middle age: Who is a senior citizen, who is middle aged and why? Retrieved from http://www.huffingtonpost.com/2012/05/02/elderly-senior-citizens-middle-age-aged_n_1471176.html

Iftekhar, A. (2008). Retirement of U.S. elderly in foreign countries: Social and health care issues. Paper presented at the annual meeting of the American Sociological Association, Boston, MA. Retrieved from http://www.allacademic.com/meta/p242458_index.html

Kim, S., Hayward, R., & Kang, Y. (2013). Psychological, physical, social, and spiritual well-being similarities between Korean older adults and family caregivers. *Geriatric Nursing, 34,* 35–40.

Leach, M. M. (2006). *Cultural diversity and suicide: Ethnic, religious, gender and sexual orientation perspectives.* Binghamton, NY: Haworth Press.

Lee, E., Forthofor, R., & Taube, C. (1985). Does DRG mean disastrous results for psychiatric hospitals? *Journal of Health and Human Services Administration, 8,* 53–78.

Lemon, B. L., Bengston, V. L., & Peterson, J. A. (1972). An exploration of activity of aging: Activity types and life-satisfaction among in-movers to a retirement community. *Journal of Gerontology, 27,* 511–583.

Lowry, L. (1979). *Social work with the aging: The challenge and promise of later years.* New York: Harper and Row.

Maldonado, D. (1987). Aged. In A. Minahan (Ed.), *Encyclopedia of social work* (pp. 95–106). Silver Spring, MD: NASW Press.

Maust, D., Oslin, D. W., & Marcus, S. (2014). Effect of age on the profile of psychotropic users: Results from the 2010 National Ambulatory Medical Care Survey. *Journal of the American Geriatrics Society, 62,* 358–364.

Montana, P. (1985). *Retirement programs: How to develop and implement them.* Englewood Cliffs: NJ: Prentice-Hall.

Moody, H. R., & Sasser, J. R. (2012). *Aging Concepts and Controversies* (7th ed.). Thousand Oaks California: Sage Publications.

Morrison, M. (1982). *Economics of aging: The future of retirement.* New York: Van Nostrand Reinhold.

Mosher-Ashley, P. M. (1994). Diagnoses assigned and issues brought up in therapy by older adults receiving outpatient treatment. *Clinical Gerontologist, 15*(2), 37–64.

Mullahy, C. (1998). *The case manager's handbook.* Gaithersburg, MD: Aspen Publishers.

Mueller, S. L., & Overmann, M. (2008). *Working world: Careers in international education, exchange and development.* Washington, DC: Georgetown University Press.

National Bureau of Economic Research, (n.d.). *Medicare and its impact.* Retrieved from http://www.nber.org/digest/apr06/w11609.html

National Hospice and Palliative Care Organization. (2008). Facts and figures. Retrieved from http://www.nhpco.org/sites/default/files/public/Statistics_Research/2014_Facts_Figures.pdf

Nelson, J., & Powers, P. (2001). Community case management for frail, elderly clients: The nurse case manager's role. *Journal of Nursing Administration, 31,* 444–450.

Nemeroff, C. B. (2007). The burden of severe depression: A review of diagnostic challenges and treatment alternatives. *Journal of Psychiatric Research, 41,* 89–206.

Nerenberg, L. (2006). Communities respond to elder abuse. *Journal of Gerontological Social Work, 46*(3/4), 5–33.

Nesvisky, M. (2006). Medicare and its impact. National Bureau of Economic Research. Retrieved from https://nber15.nber.org/digest/apr06/w11609.html

Nolan, K. (1987). In death's shadow: The meanings of withholding resuscitation. *Hastings Center Report, 17,* 9–14.

Ofosu, A. (2011). Implications for health care reform. *Health & Social Work, 36,* 229–231.

Onose, G., Haras, M. A., Sinescu, C. J., Daia, C. O., Andone, I., Onose, V. L., . . . Blendea, C. D. (2013). Basic wellness features and some related actions propensive for active and healthy ageing. *World Medical Journal, 59*(4), 155–160.

Ortman, J. M., Velkoff, V. A., & Hogan, H. (2014). *An aging nation: The older population in the United States* (Current Population Reports, P25-1140). Washington, DC: U.S. Census Bureau. Retrieved from https://www.census.gov/prod/2014pubs/p25-1140.pdf

Perkins, K., & Tice, C. (1994). Suicide and older adults. The strengths perspective in practice. *Journal of Applied Gerontology, 13,* 438–454.

Peterson, M. (1994). Physical aspects of aging: Is there such a thing as normal? *Geriatrics, 49*(2), 45–49.

Podnieks, E. (2006). Social inclusion: An interplay of health: New insights into elder abuse. *Journal of Gerontological Social Work, 46*(3/4), 57–79.

Rhodes, C. (1988). *An introduction to gerontology: Aging in American society.* Springfield, IL: Thomas.

Richardson, V. E. (2009). Clinical social work with older adults. In A. R. Roberts, *Social workers' desk reference* (2nd ed., pp. 938–954). New York: Oxford University Press.

Rife, J. C., & Belcher, J. R. (1994). Assisting unemployed older workers to become reemployed: An experimental evaluation. *Research of Social Work Practice, 4,* 3–13.

Rybarczyk, B., Lund, H. G., Garroway, A. M., & Mack, L. (2013). Cognitive behavioral therapy for insomnia in older adults: Background, evidence, and overview of treatment protocol. *Clinical Gerontologist. 36,* 70–93.

Ryff, C. D. (1982). Self-perceived personality change in adult-hood and aging. *Journal of Personality and Social Psychology, 42,* 108–115.

Sadavoy, J., Jarvik, L. F., Grossberg, G. T., & Meyers, B. S. (Eds.). (2004). *Comprehensive textbook of geriatric psychiatry* (3rd ed.). New York: Norton.

Scharlach, A. E., Mor-Barak, M. E., & Birba, L. (1994). Evaluation of a corporate sponsored health care program for retired employees. *Health and Social Work, 19,* 192–198.

Schroeder, R. (2013). The seriously mentally ill older adult: Perceptions of the patient-provider relationship. *Perspectives in Psychiatric Care, 49,* 30–40.

Sheikh, J. I., Cassidy, E. L., Doraiswamy, M. P., Salomon, R. M., Hornig, M., Holland, P. J., . . . Burt, T. (2004). Efficacy, safety, and tolerability of sertraline in patients with late-life depression and comorbid medical illness. *Journal of American Geriatrics Society, 52,* 86–92.

Shock, N. W. (1987). The International Association of Gerontology: Its origins and development. In G. L. Maddox & E. W. Busse (Eds.), *Aging: The universal experience* (pp. 21–43). New York: Springer.

Starr, P. (1982). *The social transformation of American medicine.* New York: Basic Books.

Stern, M. J., & Axinn, J. J. (2011). *Social welfare: A history of the American response to need* (8th ed.). New York: Pearson

Stinson, A. M. (2014). Spiritual life review with older adults: Finding meaning in late life development. *Dissertation Abstracts International: Section A, 74* (11-A)(E) 2014.

Talbott, J. (1988). Taking issue. *Hospital and Community Psychiatry, 39,* 115.

Tan, J. (2009). Measurement issues of service use among elders. *Journal of Human Behavior in the Social Environment, 19,* 171–185.

Tiwari, S. C., Srivastava, G,. Tripathi, R. K., Pandey, N. M., Agarwal, G. G., Pandey, S., & Tiwari, S. (2013). Prevalence of psychiatric morbidity amongst the community dwelling rural older adults of northern India. *Indian Journal of Medical Research, 138,* 504–514.

Tompkins, C. J., & Rosen, A. L. (2014). *Fostering social work gerontology competence: A collection of papers from the first national gerontological social work conference.* New York: Routledge.

U.S. Census Bureau. (2014). *65+ in the United States: 2010* (Current Population Reports P23-212). Washington, DC: U.S. Government Printing Office. Retrieved from http://www.census .gov/content/dam/Census/library/publications/2014/demo/p23-212.pdf

U.S. Department of Health and Human Services. (2011). *Profile of older Americans: 2011.* Washington, DC: Author. Retrieved from http://www.aoa.gov/Aging_Statistics/Profile/2011/docs/2011profile.pdf

U.S. Department of Justice. (2011). *OJP Fact Sheet, Elder abuse and mistreatment.* Washington, DC: Office of Justice Programs. Retrieved from http://ojp.gov/newsroom/factsheets/ojpfs_elderabuse.html

U.S. Social Security Administration. (n.d.). *Retirement planner: Benefits by year of birth.* Retrieved from http://www.socialsecurity.gov/retire2/agereduction.htm

Van Hook, M. P. (2014*). Social work practice with families: A resiliency-based approach.* Chicago: Lyceum Books.

Waite, L. J., Iveniuk, J., & Laumann, E. O. (2014). Social connectedness at older ages and implications for health and well-being. In C. R. Agnew, S. C. South (Eds.), *Interpersonal relationships and health: Social and clinical psychological mechanisms* (pp. 202–231). New York: Oxford University Press. doi:10.1093/acprof:oso/9780199936632.003.0010

Wolinsky, F. D., & Arnold, C. L. (1988). A different perspective on health and health services utilization. In G. L. Maddox & M. P. Lawton (Eds.), *Annual review of gerontology and geriatrics* (vol. 8, pp. 77–94). New York: Springer.

Woo, S. M., & Keatinge, C. (2008). *Diagnosis and treatment of mental disorders across the lifespan*. Hoboken, NJ: Wiley.

Woodward, A. T., Taylor, R. J., Abelson, J. M., & Matusko, N. (2013). Major depressive disorder among older African Americans, Caribbean Blacks, and non-Hispanic Whites: Secondary analysis of the national survey of American life. *Depression & Anxiety, 30*, 589–597.

Zabora, J. R. (2011). How can social work affect health care reform? *Health & Social Work, 36*, 231–232.

Zarit, S. H., & Zarit, J. M. (2007). *Mental disorders in older adults: Fundamentals of assessment and treatment* (2nd ed.). New York: Guilford Press.

Zegwaard, M. I., Aartsen, M. J., Grypdonck, M. H., & Cuijpers, P. (2013). Differences in impact of long term caregiving for mentally ill older adults on the daily life of informal caregivers: a qualitative study. *BMC Psychiatry, 13*, 1–9.

CHAPTER 12
DOMESTIC VIOLENCE

CONSIDERABLE ATTENTION HAS BEEN PAID TO THE FACT THAT OUR society is violent and incidents of domestic violence committed against those we are closest to continue to happen. With the advent of technology, things that are believed to occur in private may not be so private after all. For women, violence occurs at alarming rates (McMahon, Postmus, Warrener, Plummer, & Schwarts, 2013). In 2014, an ABC news release story headlined a football player who was caught on video in an elevator deliberately punching his girlfriend (who later became his wife) twice in the face after an argument (Murray, 2014). Knocking her unconscious, he emerged from the elevator dragging her body and initially explained that she had passed out from drinking too much until a video taken in the elevator revealed a very different picture. Cases like this are nothing new. Some may remember the lead story in *Time* magazine that showed a bruised and battered woman; the subsequent article reported that women are as likely to be killed by their partners as by any other kind of assailant (Smolowe, 1994, p. 21). From professional athletes to hometown heroes, as the population continues to increase so do the incidences of domestic violence against women. This is further complicated by the limited research related to women of privilege whose social status and resources could clearly be affected by speaking up (Berg, 2014).

Incidents of domestic violence in the home can have far-reaching consequences, especially when children become the forgotten victims. Isn't it amazing that it is against the law to hit another adult (assault and battery), one's partner or spouse (domestic abuse), and animals (cruelty to animals), but it is okay to hit a child as long as bruises and welts are not evident (see chapter 8 on child welfare).

According to Miller (2008) domestic violence is the leading cause of serious injury to women in the United States and adversely affects 1.7 million women at any given moment. Every nine seconds a woman in the United States is beaten by

Did You Know…Domestic violence and its treatment have been recognized as a public health problem. In a 2003 study of 522 individuals in California, 79.4% of the participants agreed and supported the need for more domestic violence prevention programming (Sorenson, 2003).

her husband or her boyfriend. In their lifetime, 20 percent of women will experience physical violence; more than 7 percent are raped by their intimate partner, and almost 5 percent are stalked (Miller, p. 210).

In the past, domestic violence often excluded incidents that happened within the privacy of the home or within the marital relationship. It was not until the second wave of the feminist movement of the 1960s and 1970s that this type of violence was recognized (Ryle, 2012). As reported by Miller (2008), statistics showed that more than 20 percent of all couples have experienced some form of domestic violence during the previous year. There may be mutual battering, but statistics seem to show that in heterosexual couples the male is more likely to be the abuser. In support of this contention, Ryle (2012), utilizing the National Crime Victimization data, reminds us that males make up over two-thirds of those charged with violent aggressive assaults. Each year it is estimated that 8.7 million women will be abused by an intimate partner, and 2 million will be victims of severe violence (Green & Roberts, 2008).

Domestic violence and the abuse that occurs are not always perpetrated by males, nor are they always extremely violent. It is not uncommon for less severe forms of abuse to be perpetrated by both males and females within intimate relationships (Wilke & Vinton, 2003). Furthermore, there is a growing body of research that has linked threats and coercion by the batterer as a means of keeping the victim from leaving the situation. Threatened actions can include harming children, relatives, or even the individual's pets (Faver & Strand, 2003). Nevertheless, many women who experience abuse by partners remain resistant to pressing charges (Green & Roberts, 2008).

Although domestic violence is not purely a crime against women, millions of women are affected by this cyclic pattern of abuse. The numbers are astounding. Each year at least 2,000 women are beaten to death by a domestic partner, and what is saddest is that women are more likely to killed by a domestic partner than by a stranger or anyone else (Miller, 2008). Studies indicate that in any given year between one-third and one-half of women murdered in the United States were killed by a boyfriend, spouse, or ex-mate (Litsky, 1994; Schneider, 1994), whereas 10 percent of the men murdered in America were killed by a female partner, usually in self-defense (Statman, 1990). Gelles's (1979) prediction that as many as half of the couples living in the United States have experienced violence in their relationship seems to remain true. This does not mean that males cannot be abused, but only that less is known about it and that it is reported less commonly (Cook, 2009).

Domestic violence is not unique to heterosexual couples; it can also affect gay, lesbian, and transgendered couples. For these couples, it is no easier to leave an abusive relationship and the love, caring, and remorse remain a part of all relationships (Shernoff, 2008). Although the violence patterns may be similar, these couples face the additional burden of social stigma; the fear that they will not be believed; or, worse yet, the fear that their concerns will not be given adequate attention by law enforcement or the judicial system (Miller, 2008).

Did You Know 2…In 1883 the state of Maryland outlawed wife abuse after acknowledging that violence against women was assault. In 1910 thirty-five states followed this lead and adopted the view that the battering of women is equivalent to assault (Siegler, 1989).

According to Green and Roberts (2008), statistics recorded on a yearly basis for the past twenty years indicate that approximately 1.5 to 2 million women have needed emergency medical attention as a result of domestic violence. Social workers who work in the emergency room setting are sure to see this type of case. To these social workers, it comes as no surprise that approximately 20 percent of female visits to emergency rooms are the result of battering, and more generally, assault by a partner—domestic violence, date rape, and so forth. Domestic violence can also be directed toward male partners. The actual number of domestic-violence-related injuries is further complicated by the statistic that, when domestic violence incidents result in injury to a male, one-third of males are less likely to report and therefore underreport the violence that was experienced within a domestic relationship (Cook, 2009).

With abuse being addressed more often in hospital emergency rooms, many states now allow the police to arrest a suspected abuser without a warrant when there is evidence of an injury serious enough to require attention and medical care. The problem with recording abuse cases is that different police departments may have different reporting methods (Cook, 2009). Therefore, no comprehensive list or national survey is available to show the actual rates of arrest for domestic violence by incident or by gender. This can be further complicated by the variation in legal treatment for domestic violence across the states or even across municipalities. Over the past fifteen years the problem of domestic violence and legal system intervention, as well as the roles of assessment and social work practice, have gained wide recognition within the social work profession. Walker (2009) warns that many women involved in the legal system, especially those who are incarcerated, may settle as soon as possible simply to return home to care for their children. On the other hand, Walker (2009) describes a recent case in which the client actually preferred jail, viewing it as a relief from the abuse she was forced to sustain at home with her partner.

Domestic violence and its relationship to the concept of female subordination to males have deep roots. Numerous theological teachings, Judeo-Christian as well as Moslem, foster the belief that women must submit and answer to their male counterparts. Roman law defined the status of women as subject to the wishes and desires of their husbands because women were regarded as men's personal possessions (Siegler, 1989). Throughout history, father-to-son transmission of wealth has been common, and after marriage a woman's property has fallen under the control of her husband. Under English common law, a woman had no legal existence apart from the relationship with her spouse. For example, if a woman was raped, only her father or her husband could claim compensation from the perpetrator (Siegler, 1989).

The advent of the feminist movement in the 1960s and 1970s greatly altered the perception of violence perpetrated against women. The prevailing psychoanalytic view, which asserted that battered women were masochistic and gained sexual excitement from beatings, was challenged (Constantino, 1981; Gelles & Harrop, 1989). Other theories of violence toward women take the view that battering is rooted in patriarchal society (Srinivasan & Davis, 1991) and that imbalances in power between men and women leave women vulnerable to abuse. The problem is thus redefined as a social issue rather than an individual pathology. According to Gutierrez (1987), sociological perspectives investigate domestic violence in the context of social stress, learned violent response, and cycles of perpetuated family violence; feminist perspectives identify battering as a means of obtaining social control and maintaining social oppression. Indeed, it wasn't until the feminist movement of the 1970s that the battering of women was recognized as a problem that required attention (Siegler, 1989).

In this chapter we will discuss the problems related to domestic violence and the role of social workers in addressing this problem. Recognizing the signs and symptoms of domestic violence and supporting and protected the survivor are essential. With each assessment and intervention provided, we emphasize that social workers must never blame those involved—and must also teach others to never blame those involved in domestic abuse. It is a nationwide problem that can affect anyone of any age, race, creed, or income. Interventions with survivors of domestic violence must be interdisciplinary in nature. Social workers must cooperate closely with other service providers, including members of the criminal justice system.

DOMESTIC VIOLENCE DEFINED

What exactly is domestic violence? We use the word *violence* because "this is not a question of minor arguments or disputes but, rather, intentional hostile and aggressive physical or psychological acts" (Dwyer, Smokowski, Bricout, & Wodarski, 1996). Definitions of violence range from "the use of physical force by one person against another" (Siegler, 1989) to "pushing, slapping, punching, kicking, knifing, shooting, or the throwing of objects at another person" (Gelles, 1987, p. 20). In its most simple form domestic violence is defined as any physical act of violence directed at one partner or the other (Edleson, 1991). As a broader concept, abuse refers to any behavior that harms the target, including psychological, emotional, and nonviolent sexual abuse (Green & Roberts, 2008; Siegler, 1989).

Some researchers differentiate domestic violence into two main types. The first is known as *intimate terrorism*, in which one partner tries to control the other using a variety of coercive strategies (Miller, 2008). The second is known as *situational couple violence*, which is less coercive and results from certain situations in which physical aggression arises and cannot be controlled. Many victims refer to this as *losing it*, or being unable to control the anger. Although research has come a long way over the years in the area of intimate partner violence (IPV), one common and continuing problem is how to clearly define IPV and how to measure the construct (Lehmann, Simmons, & Pillai, 2013). In addition, although the magnitude and severity of domestic abuse varies, it generally involves violent acts perpetuated against a partner in a relationship, oftentimes in the presumed safety and privacy of the one of the most private places of all—the home.

CHARACTERISTICS OF THE ABUSED AND THEIR ABUSERS

Two points must be emphasized with regard to survivors of abuse. First, social workers must be careful never to blame the victim for domestic violence. Unfortunately, both society at large and the abuser may assert that the violence itself is evidence that the victim must have done something wrong (Walker, 2009). It is important to ensure that both the victim and her family understand that blaming her for what is happening simply reinforces the problem. Second, social workers need to be aware that female abuse survivors may blame themselves for the abuse. They may have illusions of being able to control the abuser's behavior and so feel great shame at allowing themselves to be abused (Walker, 2009).

Several studies—admittedly on small samples—indicate that women who are battered experienced childhood family violence, witnessed parental abuse, and were often abused as children (Gelles & Cornell, 1990; Siegler, 1989; Tolman & Bennett, 1990). There is also the assumption that the abuser has been physically abused by parents, caretakers, or others. As adults, abusers do not know how to control their anger and thus take it out on the intimate partner (Glicken & Sechrest, 2003). Another factor to consider involves recruitment of female children and adolescents into the sex industry, where out of economic need and limited financial and social supports, they can become trapped, creating a pathway to violence-prone situations (Willison & Lutter, 2009).

Characteristics of women who feel trapped in abusive relationships include

1. Low self-esteem
2. Lack of self-confidence
3. A tendency to withdraw from marital disputes and stress
4. Increased feelings of depression, hopelessness, and frustration
5. Tendency toward drug and alcohol abuse and dependency
6. Suicide attempts and possible suicidal and homicidal behavior (Liutkus, 1994).

It is unclear how this feeling of being trapped can affect the children in these homes. Yet violence often occurs in the home, with mothers acting alone being considered responsible for approximately 40 percent of the child abuse and neglect cases (U.S. Department of Health and Human Services, 2007).

No one knows exactly why a victim stays in a violent relationship, but numerous reasons have been postulated (see box 1). Probably one of the most sobering statistics outlines the very real danger that can occur in leaving or escaping the violent relationship. One in five women are severely injured or killed by a partner without warning. Oftentimes the fatal or life-threatening incident was the first of its kind, and in 45 percent of the homicides the partner was trying to leave the relationship (Green & Macaluso, 2009). Therefore, once a decision to leave is made, it should never be done on the spur of a moment or used as a threat. Leaving

---

Box 1. History Continues to Repeat Itself: Do You Remember?

Blaming the Victim and the Case of Hedda Nussbaum

Societal contempt was clear in the case of Hedda Nussbaum, who made the cover of *Newsweek* in 1988. Public reaction was one of shock when her live-in boyfriend, Joel Steinberg, was charged with murdering the couple's adopted 6-year-old daughter, after having beaten her face and body. The abuse in this relationship was documented as beginning in March 1978 and ending November 1987, when Hedda asked Steinberg for permission to get help for their abused child. Unfortunately, the child was already dead from the beating she had received. In the aftermath many people blamed Hedda for her failure to save the child. The *Washington Post* described as sickening that the state and its key witness could collude to use "victimization" as an excuse for Hedda's lack of judgment and inaction (Jones, 1994, p. 175). Many people could not believe that the beatings that Hedda received and the fear she developed as a result of the abuse left her incapable of intervening for the life of her daughter, let alone her own.

requires a well-developed safety plan that allows for the safe exit of the partner and children. Devising a safety and escape plan is often the first order of business in the initial interview (Walker, 2009).

In many cases the victim simply believes that the abusive partner will reform, and promises that it will never happen again can be very seductive. The victim may doubt her ability to manage alone or fear the stigma of divorce and of being left alone. The realization that she will have to live on one income and accept full responsibility for the children can be very frightening. Also, the victim may worry about what will happen to her and her children if she leaves—poor employment options and the possibility of homelessness (half of homeless women in this country are fleeing from domestic violence; Mullins, 1994), as well as difficulty finding and affording adequate daycare for her children (Dziegielewski, Campbell, & Turnage, 2005; Gelles & Cornell, 1990). Family ties may be strained and support networks limited.

Among all these possibilities, it has been speculated that the greatest deterrent for women is the fear of economic hardship and inadequate care for their children. This fear is very well founded. Many women, by accepting primary responsibility for home and children, place themselves at a disadvantage as wage earners. Their economic dependence can preserve abusive situations by reducing opportunities for leaving them. On average for all women, not just abused women, marital separation often leads to a significant drop in standard of living within the first year. To complicate this further, child support payments are often not made regularly, and consistent alimony payments are rare even when they are awarded. Economic disparity alone amply explains why women stay in abusive relationships. Social and economic factors clearly indicate the need for therapeutic intervention that is progressive and addresses protection, prevention, and economic support.

A high correlation exists between substance abuse and domestic violence (Liutkus, 1994; Siegler, 1989; Stith, Williams, & Rosen, 1990; Tolman & Bennett, 1990). Furthermore, it appears that women who abuse substances report a higher level of exposure to trauma and dangerous situations (Cohen, Hien, & Batchelder, 2008). To further complicate this situation, spouse abuse is often mutual. Husbands and wives have both been found to initiate repetitive violent interactions; however, the consequences of male physical violence are usually more profound (Siegler, 1989; Stith et al., 1990). Men who physically abuse their partners expect their partners to be subordinate to them (Stith et al., 1990). Abusive males generally adhere to traditional, stereotypic gender or sex roles. Gender expectations lead to the perception that male power and privilege are normal and natural (Anderson & Umberson, 2014). Furthermore, this perception can result in allowing males to use violence to maintain power and control over the family. For many of the male abusers, their own low self-esteem, low assertiveness, low sense of self-efficacy, and possible exposure to childhood family violence limit their coping skills (Green & Roberts, 2008; Tolman & Bennett, 1990). These men are especially prone to feelings of helplessness, powerlessness, and inadequacy. Abusers are often pathologically jealous; prone to addiction; and passive, dependent, and antisocial (Gelles & Cornell, 1990). Histories of sexual aggressiveness and violence toward others, poor impulse control, isolation, and poor relationship skills are also common (Finkelhor, Hotaling, & Yllo, 1988). Educational level, occupational status, and income are customarily low, and in fact, unemployment or underemployment increases the likelihood of battering (Gelles & Cornell, 1990; Siegler, 1989). Alcohol and other drug-related problems were identified in two-thirds of the offenders who committed or attempted homicide (Green & Macaluso, 2009).

Green and Roberts (2008) identify what they refer to as red flags and outline twenty-three warning signs of a potentially abusive partner. Most prominently, the abuser may exhibit the following behaviors (p. 116):

- Is jealous and possessive
- Intimidates and raises fear in the partner by raising a fist or kicking a pet
- Exhibits poor impulse control and explosive anger; needs immediate attention and responses
- Violates personal boundaries
- Often tells the partner what to wear
- Uses extreme control tactics
- Attacks the self-confidence of his or her partner
- Is emotionally dependent and only wants to spend time together
- Becomes hostile after binge drinking
- Never takes responsibility for his or her role in a problem
- Cannot control anger
- Has poor communication skills
- Has a history of abusing a previous partner
- Threatens to hit, slap, or punch when angry
- Acts in ways that are highly impulsive, self-punitive, moody, resentful, and tense

Research has found that many females subject to IPV and forced sex may also have a child with the abuser (Messing, Thaller, & Bagwell, 2014). It is not clear if the pregnancy has been forced as well. In general, whether planned or not, pregnancy can put a significant strain on a relationship. Therefore, as stresses increase in an abusive relationship, pregnancy may escalate potentially assaultive behavior patterns (Green & Roberts, 2008). If this pregnancy is the product of coerced relations or forced sex, the anger and resentment that results can fester within both partners. Claims by the abuser that "she drove me to it" or by the survivor that this pregnancy "will keep me a prisoner" can result in harsh feelings, neglect, or other types of abusive behavior toward the child. Awareness of this potential situation and knowledge of what questions to ask and when to ask them in the assessment can be beneficial in uncovering such situations while avoiding any future negative consequences to the child (Messing et al., 2014).

Did You Know…Although there is no consensus about the causes of domestic violence, the general characteristics defined by Straus (1980) still remain relevant:

- *Partner unemployed*
- *Two or more children*
- *Spouses from violent families*
- *Spouses under 30 years of age*
- *Spouses verbally aggressive*
- *New residence*

- *Spousal concerns about economic security*
- *Spousal disagreements over children*
- *Couples married less than ten years*
- *High levels of family and individual stress*
- *Frequent alcohol use*
- *Primary bread-winner unemployed*

In the discussion of treatment for domestic violence, it is contended that too little attention is given to working with the perpetrator, especially because violence directed at an intimate partner will often reoccur (Westmarland & Kelly, 2013). There are two primary types of intervention often used with batterers: perpetrator groups and couples counseling. In the groups designed specifically for men who batter, relationship issues and the power and control relationship are clearly defined. For example, Pence and Paymar (1993) use a tool called the power and control wheel, which helps the individual identify methods of coercion such as threats, economic abuse, intimidation, emotional abuse, minimizing, denying and blaming, isolation, male privilege, and threats toward children. In couples counseling, nonviolence and equality are emphasized with a focus on stress negotiation and fairness. Learning to react to stressful situations with nonthreatening behaviors while showing respect, honesty, and accountability are given primary attention. It is hoped that intervention efforts to increase trust and support will ultimately result in responsible parenting and shared responsibilities for the domestic partnership.

HELPING SURVIVORS OF ABUSE

To this point we have stressed that domestic abuse is a societal and a family problem and thus needs attention from social workers trained in both macropractice and micropractice. Walker (2009) states that the best way to understand domestic violence is to listen to the stories of those who have experienced it. However, no practitioner should forget that domestic violence can also involve the commission of a crime; therefore, to best help survivors of abuse social workers must be skilled in cooperating and coordinating with representatives of the criminal justice system, from police officers to prosecutors and judges.

Providing Direct Clinical Services

Social workers often provide direct clinical services for survivors of abuse. Because such experiences can result in upheaval in all aspects of a person's life, providing comprehensive and holistic services should be paramount (Haeseler, 2014). The types of services can vary from direct counseling to outpatient services such as community-based domestic violence fatality review teams (DVFRTs). These teams are designed to coordinate the provision of community services to prevent IPV (Chanmugam, 2014). The pooling of resources among this diverse group of disciplines allows for greater awareness and coordination of services.

To facilitate treatment strategy, oftentimes group sessions are offered, either in a shelter or in a safe house. Providing group as well as individual counseling for the survivor is designed to empower her and help her make a decision about the future and whether to stay or leave. Guiding principles for all intervention with the survivor include first and foremost ensuring her safety and, if children are involved, the children's safety as well. A safety plan will always be part of the intervention process. It is also crucial to respect the survivor's choices and not to judge or blame her (Green & Macaluso, 2009). The social worker needs to accept what the client says is the truth and to help her explore choices and courses of action that will ensure safety for all involved.

Dziegielewski and colleagues (2005) believe that a type of reality-based questioning is needed to provide support. This type of therapy does not place blame for the many occurrences of abuse that may have been endured but rather focuses on the present and what can be done about keeping the client and family safe. From this perspective, the social worker leads the domestic violence survivor through a reality-based process highlighting self-forgiveness, which often starts the healing process. Concentration on the here and now is highlighted, emphasizing future healthy relationships and not dwelling on the negative painful relationships of the past. From this perspective, the social worker helps the survivor to explore five reality-based questions:

1. What do you want?
2. What are you doing to get what you want?
3. How will you keep yourself and your loved ones safe while planning to achieve what you want?
4. How will you know if what you are doing is working?
5. What will you do once you get what you want?

Name: Sharon R. Williamson

Place of residence: Walton, KY

College/university degrees: MSW, University of Cincinnati, Cincinnati OH
BA, Sociology, University of Florida, Gainesville, FL

Present position and title: Substance use and mental health therapist, treatment services provider III

Previous work/volunteer experience: Addictions counseling and mental health therapy, case management for various oppressed populations and supportive employment for individuals with developmental disabilities for more than twenty years; previous work with Special Olympics.

Why did you choose social work as a career? My life partner (we live in a state that doesn't allow same sex marriage) is a social worker and professor along with my dearest friend, Dr. D. Having them as wonderful role models helped me decide that the best way to truly have a positive impact on helping people in all aspects of their lives is by becoming an ethical social worker.

What is your favorite social work story? During my internship I received the best education I have had in the field of addictions by the women who are surviving it. Here is just one example. . . . I arrived on a Saturday in the very early stages for my MSW internship at the treatment agency, where I now work, only to find two inpatient women in a verbal altercation that appeared to be seriously leading to a physical confrontation. The weekend staff seemed to be in another area of the building. I quickly intervened and led the less aggressive client to a quiet office to discuss the situation. I asked what had happened to set her off, and she said the other woman called her a whore. I used what I thought was a good therapeutic intervention and stated that, since she was not a whore, it shouldn't matter what she was called. She quickly informed me that she had been a whore so it did matter. I was unaware, at that time, how many women had been involved in sex trafficking as a resource for their drug use. I was able to conceal my shock and informed her that only she can define who she is and to not allow others, whose opinion she doesn't value, to define her.

What is one thing you would change in the community if you had the power to do so? I would advocate that the women suffering from active addiction be allowed to enter treatment programs so that they can learn survival skills to manage their disease. They should not be placed in overcrowded prisons that will only punish them for doing wrong instead of teaching them how to do better. There are too many women in our society, from all walks of life, dying from severe substance use disorder every day!

A structured safety plan will be developed by answering these questions. The survivor thereby accepts responsibility and does not blame herself for her activity in the relationship. Destructive anger can be addressed and plans for how to create a healthier relationship are highlighted. Through educational and supportive interventions, the role of the social worker is essential in helping the client to understand the physical and psychological challenges and coping strategies needed to overcome the obstacles she must face.

Children: The Forgotten Victims

Probably of greatest concern is how does the repeated violence and domestic abuse occurring in a family affect the child who is watching it? Whether children being raised in such a home are abused or just witnessing the abuse, can this have a lasting effect? The sad fact is that studies seem to support that it does indeed affect the child. Using four waves of longitudinal data in a three- to five-year study, Yoo and Huang (2013) found that, particularly for preschool children, the internalizing and externalizing behavior problems were indicative of intervention and prevention efforts. Children raised in violent homes seem to be more vulnerable and can exhibit a range of problems related to adjustment difficulties and anxiety (Green & Roberts, 2008). However, these same children may be less likely to talk about their experiences even though sharing their experiences could have great therapeutic value (Cater, 2014). Because children get many of their reaction cues from their parents, being in this type of a chaotic environment can leave a deep and lasting impression. There is also the risk that the child who witnesses abuse is more likely to grow up and enter abusive situations or become abusive in his or her own relationships.

There is a myth that children under the age of three are generally not affected by this type of behavior. Yet at this age children develop the capacity to experience, regulate, and express emotions as well as to learn from the environment and develop trusting and secure relationships (Kamradt, Gibertson & Jefferson, 2008). Regardless of the age of the child, the social worker should always explore the possible effects of this experience and ensure that the child too receives intervention and assistance. As much as possible, the parents should be involved in this process because adult pathology may continue to be reflected in the parent-child relationship (Novick & Novick, 2005). In child welfare, taking into account witnessing violence and the impact it can have on the child and his or her current or future behaviors is essential to consider when completing a risk assessment (Forgey, Allen & Hansen, 2014).

The Criminal Justice System

Domestic violence and the legal system are closely entwined, especially because more than one in three U.S. women and one in four U.S. men report having experienced domestic violence in their lives (Black et al., 2011). To understand how the legal system treats intimate partner violence, three major areas merit consideration (Siegler, 1989). The first is the ideology of privacy, whereby an individual's home is viewed as a private place. Acts that happen in the home are considered to have occurred in a sacred place. As long as the couple stays together in the same house, the husband cannot be ordered to change his behavior (Siegler, 1989). Many victims fear that, if their case does go to court, judges will not evict a man from his home. The old adage that "a man's home is his castle" remains, and even the victim may be concerned that, if the abuser is evicted from his home, he will have nowhere to go and will end up homeless (Mullins, 1994; Walker, 2009).

Did You Know...A woman could not legally refuse her spouse conjugal rights until the 1970s, when some states legally recognized the concept of marital rape.

The second area is the gap between written law and contemporary practice. Traditionally, the justice system has been unwilling to intercede or intrude in family matters, and society has preferred it that way. Survivors of abuse can feel helpless trying to persuade police officers and the courts to take action to control their partners if violence has not occurred; police officers, for their part, are often frustrated by the situation and by not knowing how to intervene, and this is often complicated by a victim who refuses to admit that abuse occurred or does not want to see his or her partner arrested. In recognition of this weakness in the law, the federal **Violence Against Women Act** of 1994 (VAWA) was designed to improve the response of the criminal justice system to violent crimes against women (National Resource Center on Domestic Violence and Battered Women's Justice Project, 1994).

The purpose of the VAWA is to create policies to prevent domestic violence. It treats domestic violence as a major law enforcement priority and funds improved services to victims of domestic violence. Title II of the bill, the Safe Homes Act, increases federal funding for battered women's shelters and related programs. It also provides a federal crime statute for spouse abuse committed during interstate travel (Mullins, 1994). By creating emergency and long-term solutions for battered women's housing and survival needs, the VAWA is an important step in the government's commitment to preventing domestic violence. Today, police officers have mandatory arrest policies and must make an arrest if it is believed that either party has committed an assault (Miller, 2008). Therefore, if a domestic assault has occurred, an arrest will be made regardless of whether the victim wants the arrest or not. If the abuse is mutual, both may be arrested. This has led to a new trend.

As of 2009 there were approximately 208 domestic violence courts where these types of cases are handled and scheduled on separate calendars (Center for Court Innovation, 2009).

The third area is the complexity and lack of integration of existing legal remedies. The laws that currently exist are complex, contradictory, and at times unenforceable. The law regards property division, divorce, child custody, financial obligations, and criminal culpability as separate matters. Just as marriages can be deemed successful, so can divorces. Unfortunately, in many of these cases, divorces go badly and children are forced to face parental conflict, aggression, and anger (Johnston, Roseby, & Kuehnle, 2009). In domestic violence cases, however, many of these issues continue to overlap. In terms of domestic violence courts, there are three primary objectives that come to the forefront: (1) victim safety, (2) offender accountability, and (3) a mixture of other related goals (e.g., deterrence, rehabilitation, and administration of justice (Center for Court Innovation, 2009). Domestic violence courts and greater organization along with new domestic violence statutes will continue to help reduce confusion and hopefully integrate the jurisdictions.

The assistance provided by police at the domestic violence scene is critical. As first responders, officers must be aware of mediation, listening to the events as presented by both sides, restating key points, and suggesting possible solutions (Miller, 2008). Once this is done, officers must ensure that there is agreement and follow-through by all parties. If an assault has occurred, charges must be processed. Policies that favor the arrest of abusers may address the immediate situation but do little to stop future incidents of abuse from occurring (Roberts, 1996c). Frisch and Caruso (1996) warn, however, against the opposite extreme: even the most complete legal plan to address an abused woman's needs is useless if those responsible for carrying it out have no enforcement power.

The Role of the Social Worker

Oftentimes it is the social worker who first sees the survivor of intimate partner violence, conducts interviews in hospitals and emergency rooms, and relates information directly to law enforcement. Survivors of domestic violence may not openly state their concerns, and clear assessment questions may be needed to facilitate this process (Messing et al., 2014).

Mullarkey (1988) identified five areas in which social workers can join the criminal justice system and prosecutors to assist domestic violence survivors. Regardless of what legal processes are in place, mandatory arrest policies and warrantless arrests can detain the batterer, but they do not address the entire problem (Roberts, 1996c). First, the social worker can help the system to understand the client by completing a detailed and accurate assessment, thus providing more information about the type of abuse, the history of abuse, and the circumstances and repercussions of the abuse. Factors that seem related to domestic violence include mental health status, low self-esteem, and limited social and family support networks (Haesler, 2014). Recognizing these potential indicators and using this additional information, the social worker can assess and identify the most dangerous cases while screening, evaluating, and subsequently contributing to potential treatment outcomes. The social worker can also help the client to understand the system. Abused women have varied needs for legal services, social services, and psychological services. A well-documented community service awareness approach that utilizes domestic violence response teams, coordinated by the social worker, can help to integrate the efforts of health, mental health, social service, judicial, and law enforcement agencies for the benefit of survivor of IPV (Chanmugam, 2014).

The second type of assistance the social worker can provide is education, support, and psychosocial adaption strategies to help get through the crisis situation (Green & Roberts, 2008). These clients can suffer from self-esteem problems as well as concerns related to their own safety and survival of themselves and their children, and this can affect any action or reaction they can have (Dziegielewski et al., 2005). Working closely and supporting and educating the client each step of the way is essential to helping them request and access the services that they need.

Social workers have an obligation to educate their clients, and in turn to be educated by system participants such as police telephone operators and dispatchers, police officers and staff, prosecutors, judges, and those directly involved such as the survivors, the abusers, and family and support system members. They need to be aware of pro-arrest and mandatory arrest policies and what they involve, as well as the potential of electronic monitoring as part of a coordinated community effort (Roberts, 1996c). In addition to helping the client, social workers also need to educate and train police telephone operators, dispatchers, and police officers. Operators and dispatchers are the first to receive the call for help and the officer is usually the first on the scene. This education and training should include telephone training for screening and assessment, basic techniques of police safety, and dispute management and crisis intervention techniques, as well as the ability to provide referral links with the social service worker (Fusco, 1989). Training sessions in these skills can influence police officers to take seriously their role in protecting the abused woman (Roberts, 1996c).

When conducting training the social worker is responsible for creating an atmosphere for a team intervention that reflects respect, support, cooperation, and feedback. Moreover, the social worker plays a crucial role in advocating for the rights of the client, particularly in ensuring equality of access, discouraging sex-role stereotyping, explaining the social and emotional effects of discrimination, and identifying the dynamics of victimization and other relevant psychosocial factors (Martin, 1988). Working in this area can be very stressful for the social worker, and special care should always be given to recognizing feelings of apathy, frustration, and cynicism, often referred to as compassion fatigue or professional burnout (Knoll, 2009). The social worker must also be aware of his or her own feelings related to the domestic violence situation. This self-awareness will allow the social worker to help others involved in the situation become aware of their own value systems and behaviors and how they might affect any subsequent helping efforts (Morgaine & Capous-Desyllas, 2015).

In addition to frontline workers, court clerks, case managers, legal advocates, and judges should receive education and training (Roberts, 1996a). Professionals in the legal system often focus on conviction as the primary means for accomplishing justice. The pain that the abuser has caused the female survivor, her children, and her family can be minimized or overlooked. The social worker therefore has a twofold task: first, to educate people in the legal system about the dynamics and issues within the abusive situation and, second, to remind everyone to address the psychosocial effects that have occurred regardless of the legal outcome (Green & Roberts, 2008).

From assessment to treatment, the third role that the social worker can assume is as a safe individual whom the survivor can trust and feel comfortable with. It is crucial for the professional helper to communicate clearly to the client the purpose of the therapy and to see the sessions as a safe place that is violence and judgment free (Walker, 2009). One dynamic in abusive relationships is for women to become isolated from their family and friends. They have often been taught to fear and avoid contact with others outside the abusive relationship. This isolation is problematic even when a woman has started to receive relief from the legal system. This woman must face her abuser and others who may threaten retaliation if the abuser faces conviction and possible incarceration. Anticipating this outcome of the legal process may leave the survivor feeling a mixture of relief and guilt, and these contradictory emotions can hamper her testimony and make her look like an unreliable witness. To represent herself in the best possible light, the survivor needs to feel supported. The prosecutor is usually rushed, however, and cannot build the rapport needed to get the survivor to trust him or her; therefore, the social worker can be a critical bridge between the prosecutor and the survivor (see the activity below).

Activity…It is important to understand the difference between physical and psychological abuse and how best to handle the two types of situations. Break into groups and take the two case examples below. Decide whether they involve physical abuse or psychological abuse. As a social worker presented with this situation, how would you best intervene to help? What referrals would you make in each situation and for whom would the referral be made?

Scenario 1: A verbal dispute between two partners had resulted in the husband threatening to get a knife and stab the wife if she tried to leave the house with the children. For fear that her husband might act on the threat, the wife did not leave.

Scenario 2: During an altercation two partners yelled and pushed each other repeatedly. Upon being pushed down the male partner hit his head, cutting it on an end table, and the other partner, who was female, later developed bruises on her shoulder and arms where her husband had grabbed her in anger.

The fourth role the social worker embraces is that of advocate. This role has always been critical for social work professionals, and advocating for the survivor within the legal system through all stages of the criminal process is essential. Social workers have the right to serve as advocates for the survivor even before an arrest is made or while a case is awaiting trial or on appeal (Mullarkey, 1988). The role of the survivor's advocate (or. victim's advocate) is to assist the client in acting as her own representative whenever possible (Martin, 1988). When it is not possible—perhaps because the survivor is too distraught or incapacitated by the fear of retribution—the advocate can speak with the client's permission. Many states now permit the survivor or the survivor's advocate to address the judge at sentencing (Mullarkey, 1988). When situations are highly lethal, the professional helper has a responsibility to share and be honest about concerns for the client's safety, especially when the client is planning to return to the abusive situation (Walker, 2009). (See the activity below to identify the needed services and rank their priority.)

Activity…In the classroom, break into small groups of three or more students. As a group review these potential goals for domestic violence programs and rank order what you consider the top three most important goals. Compare your group's choices with those of the other groups. Was it difficult for your group to agree? Why? Why not?

Goals for Domestic Violence Programs

1. *To ensure safe surroundings for survivors and their children*
2. *To increase access to material resources—income, housing, and food*
3. *To establish and enhance legal supports*
4. *To build social contacts and support networks for survivors and their children*
5. *To change societal beliefs about domestic violence*
6. *To provide one-on-one counseling for both the children and the survivor of domestic violence*

The successful advocate for a domestically abused woman must not only address a safety plan to help keep the client safe, but must also recognize and prepare the client for the potential complexities of the legal system. The social worker needs to be aware of the variety of system components that are involved—in particular, law enforcement, prosecution, and corrections. The social worker must also advocate with family members and the support system to which the client will return. Many myths and beliefs about the survivors of domestic violence are ingrained in our society (Roberts, 1996b), and clients may be forced to confront myths subscribed to by family and friends.

The social worker can assist the survivor by telling people in the support system about the survivor's strengths, her reason for leaving the abusive relationship, and why the survivor should put a formal end to the abuse and request legally sanctioned punishment for the abuser.

The fifth role the social worker plays is expert witness. The social worker can assess the situation and help others to understand the underlying reasoning behind resulting behaviors. Although social workers welcome any opportunity to assist their clients, they may worry that acting as a witness will compromise their duty to protect their client's legal rights. Counseling sessions and written notes may contain information that the social worker does not want to share because its disclosure might harm the survivor's case. For example, many times the survivor is angry with the abuser and voices this anger in an attempt to gain emotional distance from the abuser. Nevertheless, the social worker should always take careful case notes despite full awareness that these notes can be subpoenaed by a court of law. As stated by Mullarkey (1988, p. 49), "the constitutional guarantee to confront accusers provided by the sixth amendment can be interpreted by any competent court to over-ride any privacy statute or shield law."

Without a court order, social workers are not required to speak to defendants, attorneys, or investigators outside of the courtroom. Mullarkey (1988) recommended that when social workers are summoned to court they recognize the importance of (1) appearing and being professional and nonpartisan; (2) answering all questions directly or fully; (3) immediately asking for clarification of unclear questions; (4) going over possible questions with the prosecutor before testifying; and (5) ensuring that every note, professional conversation, and report they have prepared is discoverable by the defendant and his legal representatives.

PRACTICE APPLICATION: THE ROLE OF THE WOMEN'S SHELTER SOCIAL WORKER

Susan and her husband have been together for ten years. During that time she has been beaten severely and treated in the local hospital emergency room. Much of the abuse between the couple is reported to be mutual; however, Susan's husband has never been hospitalized as a result of her return attacks. On several occasions, Susan called the police to intervene, but when they arrived on the domestic violence scene, she usually refused to press charges. Susan stated that she once began to press charges but soon dropped them when her husband called from jail to tell her that he loved her and to beg her forgiveness. The police are dispatched to the scene so often that they refer to Susan and her husband by their first names.

Susan has tried to leave her husband several times but he always tracks her down and persuades her to return. Susan's family is well aware of the abuse. Both Susan's mother and her sister have started to refuse her calls asking for help. Susan often calls them when she and her husband are fighting, asking for an "understanding ear or a safe place to stay." Her family is frustrated because no matter what they do Susan always seems to return to the abusive situation. Also, whenever they do take Susan in, her husband arrives and tries to intimidate her mother. Susan's mother doesn't think her health is strong enough to handle the repeated stress.

On a referral from her employer, Susan called the shelter from a pay phone near her home after an altercation with her husband. Upon arrival at the shelter she confided in a shelter social worker that she felt lost and abandoned. During the second session Susan told the social worker that she wanted to kill her husband. When asked how she would do it, Susan immediately broke down and cried that she would probably be better off killing herself. When questioned further, she said that she had not planned to harm herself, but that ending her life would make it easier for all. The event that precipitated Susan's crisis was a fight with her husband on the previous night. Susan's husband insisted that she climb a ladder and help him paint the house. Susan refused because she is four months pregnant and is afraid of heights. Her husband then hit her across her back with the ladder.

Based on the information Susan provided the social worker is able to make the following assessment. First, Susan is being beaten regularly. Second, she fears for her life, is threatening to take the life of another, and might also take her own life if she could. Third, Susan has alienated her family and has no support system available to her. Because she has made vague threats to hurt herself, this needs to be addressed immediately. The social worker feels that immediate intervention is essential to help Susan to adjust to her current situation without violence to herself or others. First, the social worker explores the possibility of getting her a formal assessment to check for any medical concerns with her unborn child and for her suicidal thoughts. After assessment, the hospital staff determine that she is not in need of admission but should be watched for suicidal thoughts. Because Susan has no medical insurance and no support system, she has nowhere to go, so the social worker helps her formulate a plan.

The social worker helps Susan gain admission to the local shelter for abused women. Shelter personnel are notified of Susan's possible desire to end her life and a suicide watch is implemented. Intensive individual and group counseling resources are made available. With the help and support of the social worker, an order of protection is filed. Susan decides to press charges against her husband and asks the social worker to help her to state her case to an attorney; the social worker agrees. Susan does press charges this time and her husband is sentenced to two years in prison with the possibility of parole in six months. After she regains the recognition and assistance of her family, Susan moves to another city and stays with her aunt. Before leaving, Susan has started making plans to give up her child for adoption.

Clevenger and Roe-Sepowitz (2009) reported that most women utilize shelter services if they have children to care for at the time of an abusive incident, call for assistance from a place other than their home, do not have a current order of protection in place, and have been injured during the domestic violence incident. In the case described above, the social worker played a dual role. First, the social worker found a safe environment where the client received help in dealing with her crisis. The social worker also provided counseling and supportive services. Second, the social worker helped the client to create and carry out a plan of action in her dealings with the legal system. Women who have been abused by their spouses or partners need supportive services. In addition, they need the assistance of this country's legal institutions. These women need to know the following: (1) that legal services are available to them, (2) that supportive services such as those provided by a social worker are available, and (3) that the combined use of these services will alleviate and eventually resolve the situation. The role of the social work professional is crucial. Whether working within the criminal justice system itself or outside the system in an ancillary agency, the social worker can make a true difference for a survivor of domestic abuse (see Figure 1).

SUMMARY

Survivors of domestic violence need all the services and protection that law enforcement can provide (Walker, 2009). They also need to be treated with respect and dignity and to be active in planning a course of action to protect all involved, including the children. In domestic violence, substance abuse is often a problem for males, whereas concerns about child maltreatment exist for both males and females

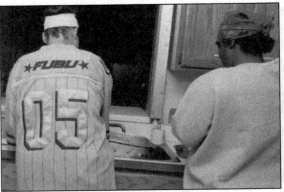

Figures 1a, b, c: These are photographs taken in a shelter for women and children who are victims of domestic abuse. The bedroom with two beds and two bunk beds may be used for one or two families. The women are cleaning up after lunch in the communal kitchen. The child is in a play area. The center is staffed by childcare workers who care for the children while mothers go to work, look for work, or go to counseling.

(Johnston et al., 2009). The children are often the innocent victims. The perpetrators of the violence also need to be treated with respect. When morally objectionable behavior has occurred, it is important not to encourage the view that the abuser is a monster incapable of change (Knoll, 2009).

Social workers play a crucial role by providing multiple services to survivors of abuse. First, they complete detailed assessments that give information about the type of abuse, the history of abuse, and the circumstances and repercussions of the abuse. Second, they actively educate and are educated by law enforcement and justice system participants and people directly involved, such as survivors, abusers, and family and support system members. Third, they act as safe individuals whom survivors can trust. Fourth, they advocate for survivors through all stages of the criminal prosecution (Green & Roberts, 2008). Last, they assist prosecutors and aid survivors by acting as expert witnesses.

Social workers must strive to develop a team approach with the legal professionals involved. Social work programs need to provide curriculum in this area; these specialized courses can help to improve professional attitudes, beliefs, and proficiency when providing services (McMahon et al., 2013). These professionals must be trained to view domestic assault situations as appropriate and routine targets of police intervention. Representatives of the legal system and social workers can work together, each as an integral part of the intervention team. The criminal justice system can be an effective force in decreasing violence against women. Short-term emergency support as well as long-term counseling and supportive services are recommended. When children are involved, especially preschool children, working with the mother and the child together may assist in the adjustment process (Yoo & Haung, 2013). Counseling, social service assistance, and protection must be carefully coordinated and available to the abuse survivor twenty-four hours a day (Green & Roberts, 2008). Morning or next-day referrals are a poor substitute for an immediate response to the crisis. Social work professionals need to be available to work directly with police and to start intervention services at the crisis scene or as soon after the incident as possible. Our current system of referral "after the fact" is not meeting the needs of many survivors of abuse.

The domestic violence shelter can offer an immediate safe place for women who wish to escape an abusive situation. Unfortunately, however, the number of existing shelters is far from adequate (Dziegielewski et al., 2005). There are few shelters convenient for women in rural areas, and attempts to establish emergency shelters for battered women in cities still meet a variety of obstacles. Before a facility is granted approval, many cities require a review of proposed property use by community boards and city planners. However, this requirement may compromise the confidentiality of the women and children who depend on the emergency shelter for services and so risk their safety. In addition, many community residents object to having emergency shelters in their neighborhoods because they believe such facilities are disruptive (Mullins, 1994).

Social workers must participate in and help to establish brief time-limited practice strategies (Dziegielewski, 2008a, 2008b). Also, schools of social work must address this topic and help the beginning social work professional to feel academically prepared (Danis, 2003). The purpose of these programs and policies is to immediately ease the severity of domestic violence as well as to develop long-term solutions to the need for emergency housing and financial support systems. One advance in this direction was the 1994 Violence Against Women Act.

Gender roles are changing, although old patterns of gender-defined ways of behavior keep reemerging (Spade & Valentine, 2014). Until recently, our society and our laws have treated the preservation of the family as paramount. With the many changes in family structure, this too appears to be changing. The traditional definition of the family no longer applies, and with this comes changes in family structure and expectations. We must continue to break from our history of preserving the family at any cost—especially the cost of exposing females to male-dominated roles where violence is considered normal or tolerated (Anderson & Umberson, 2014). Because social workers practice across the public and private sectors, they have enormous potential for influencing approaches to the problem of violence against women (Martin, 1988; National Association of Social Workers, 2003). The profession must demand changes in our laws and legal system that will prevent domestic violence. Social workers clearly recognize the importance of counseling and supportive services. However, to plan for the future, they must never lose sight of the importance of social policy change in assisting the survivors of domestic violence.

REFERENCES

Anderson, K. L., & Umberson, D. (2014). Masculinity and power in men's accounts of domestic violence. In J. Z. Spade, & C. G. Valentine (Eds.), *The kaleidoscope of gender: Prisms, patterns and possibilities* (4th ed., pp. 494–504).

Berg, K. K. (2014). Cultural factors in the treatment of battered women with privilege: Domestic violence in the lives of White European-American, middle-class, heterosexual women. *Affilia, 29,* 141–152.

Black, M. C., Basile, K. C., Breiding, M. J., Smith, S. G., Watters, M. L., Merrick, M. T., . . . Stevens, M. R. (2011). *The National Intimate Partner and Sexual Violence Survey (NISVS): 2010 summary report.* Atlanta: National Center for Injury Prevention and Control, Centers for Disease Control and Prevention. Retrieved from http://www.cdc.gov/violenceprevention/pdf/nisvs_executive_summary-a.pdf

Cater, A. K. (2014). Children's descriptions of participation processes in interventions for children exposed to intimate partner violence. *Child Adolescent Social Work, 31,* 455–473.

Center for Court Innovation. (2009). *A national portrait of domestic violence.* Retrieved from http://www.courtinnovation.org/research/good-courts-case-problem-solving-justice-0

Chanmugam, A. (2014). Social work expertise and domestic violence teams. *Social Work, 59,* 73–79.

Clevenger, B. J., & Roe-Sepowitz, D. (2009). Shelter service utilization of domestic violence victims. *Journal of Human Behavior in the Social Environment, 19*, 359–374.

Cohen, L. R., Hien, D. A., & Batchelder, S. (2008). The impact of cumulative maternal trauma and diagnosis on parenting behavior. *Child Maltreatment, 13*, 27–38.

Constantino, C. (1981). Intervention with battered women: The lawyer social worker team. *Social Work, 26*, 456–460.

Cook, P. W. (2009). *Abused men: The hidden side of domestic violence* (2nd ed.). Westport, CT: Praeger.

Danis, F. S. (2003). Social work response to domestic violence: Encouraging news from a new look. *Affilia, 18*, 177–191.

Dwyer, D. C., Smokowski, P. R., Bricout, J. C., & Wodarski, J. S. (1996). Domestic violence and woman battering: Theories and practice implications. In A. R. Roberts (Ed.), *Helping battered women: New perspectives and remedies* (pp. 67–82). New York: Oxford University Press.

Dziegielewski, S. F. (2008a). Brief and intermittent approaches to practice: The state of practice. *Journal of Brief Treatment and Crisis Intervention*. Advance online publication. doi:10.1093/brief-treatment/mhn005

Dziegielewski, S. F. (2008b). Problem identification, contracting, and case planning. In K. M. Sowers & C. N. Dulmus (Series Eds.) & W. Rowe & L. A. Rapp-Paglicci (Vol. Eds.), *Comprehensive handbook of social work and social welfare: Social work practice* (vol. 3, pp. 78–97). Hoboken, NJ: Wiley.

Dziegielewski, S. F., Campbell, K., & Turnage, B. (2005). Domestic violence: Focus groups from the survivor's perspective. *Journal of Human Behavior in the Social Environment, 11*(2), 9–24.

Edleson, J. L. (1991, June). Note on history: Social worker's intervention in woman abuse, 1907–1945. *Social Service Review, 65*, 304–313.

Faver, C. A., & Strand, E. B. (2003). Domestic violence and animal cruelty: Untangling the web of abuse. *Journal of Social Work Education, 39*, 237–253.

Finkelhor, D., Hotaling, G., & Yllo, K. (1988). *Stopping family violence.* Newbury Park, CA: Sage.

Forgey, M. A., Allen, M., & Hansen, J. (2014). An exploration of the knowledge base used by Irish and U.S. child protection social workers in the assessment of intimate partner violence. *Journal of Evidence-Based Social Work, 11*(1/2), 58–72.

Frisch, L. A., & Caruso, J. M. (1996). In A. R. Roberts (Ed.), *Helping battered women: New perspectives and remedies* (pp. 102–131). New York: Oxford University Press.

Fusco, L. J. (1989). Integrating systems: Police, courts and assaulted women. In B. Pressman, G. Cameron, & M. Rothery (Eds.), *Intervening with assaulted women: Current theory, research and practice* (pp. 125–135). Hillsdale, NJ: Erlbaum.

Gelles, R. J. (1979). Violence in the American family. *Journal of Social Issues, 35*, 15–39.

Gelles, R. J. (1987). *The violent home.* Thousand Oaks, CA: Sage.

Gelles, R. J., & Cornell, C. P. (1990). *Intimate violence in families.* Thousand Oaks, CA: Sage.

Gelles, R. J., & Harrop, J. W. (1989). Violence, battering, and psychological distress among women. *Journal of Interpersonal Violence, 4*, 400–420.

Glicken, M. D., & Sechrest, D. K. (2003). *The role of helping professionals in treating victims and perpetrators of violence.* New York: Pearson Education.

Green, D. L., & Macaluso, B. (2009). The social worker in a domestic violence shelter. In A. R. Roberts, *Social workers' desk reference* (2nd ed., pp. 95–102). New York: Oxford University Press.

Green, D. L., & Roberts, A. R. (2008). *Helping victims of violent crime: Assessment, treatment and evidence-based practice.* New York: Springer.

Gutierrez, L. M. (1987). Social work theories and practice with battered women: A conflict-of-values analysis. *Affilia, 2*(2), 36–52.

Haesler, L. A. (2014). Improving service practices: Collaborative care for women of abuse. *Journal of Evidence-Based Social Work, 10,* 10–18.

Johnston, J., Roseby, V., & Kuehnle, K. (2009). *In the name of the child: A developmental approach to understanding and helping children of conflicted and violent divorce* (2nd ed.). New York: Springer.

Jones, A. (1994). *Next time she will be dead: Battering and how to stop it.* Boston, MA: Beacon.

Kamradt, B., Gilbertson, S. A., & Jefferson, M. (2008). Services for high risk populations in systems of care. In B. A. Stroul & G. M. Blau (Eds.), *The system of care handbook: Transforming mental health services for children, youth and families* (pp. 469–490). Baltimore, MD: Brookes.

Knoll, J. (2009). Treating the morally objectionable. In J. T. Andrade (Ed.), *Handbook of violence risk assessment and treatment: New approaches for mental health professionals* (pp. 311–346). New York: Springer.

Lehmann, P., Simmons, C. A., & Pillai, V. K. (2012). The validation of the checklist of controlling behaviors (CBB): Assessing coercive control in abusive relationships. *Violence Against Women, 18,* 913–933.

Litsky, M. (1994). Reforming the criminal justice system can decrease violence against women. In B. Leone, B. Szumski, K. de Koster, K. Swisher, C. Wekesser, & W. Barbour (Eds.), *Violence against women.* San Diego, CA: Greenhaven.

Liutkus, J. F. (1994, April). Wife assault: An issue for women's health. *Internal Medicine, 7,* 41–53.

Martin, M. (1988). A social worker's response. In N. Hutchings (Ed.), *The violent family: Victimization of women, children, and elders.* New York: Human Science Press.

McMahon, S., Postmus, J. L., Warrener, C., Plummer, S., & Schwarts, R. (2013). Evaluating the effect of a specialized MSW course on violence against women. *Journal of Social Work Education, 49,* 307–320.

Messing, J. T., Thaller, J., & Bagwell, M. (2014). Factors related to sexual abuse and forced sex in a sample of women experiencing police-involved intimate partner violence. *Health & Social Work, 39,* 181–191.

Miller, L. (2008). *Counseling crime victims: Practical strategies for mental health professionals.* New York: Springer.

Morgaine, K., & Capous-Desyllas, M. (2015). *Anti-oppressive social work practice: Putting theory into action.* Los Angeles, CA: Sage.

Mullarkey, E. (1988). The legal system for victims of violence. In N. Hutchings (Ed.), *The violent family: Victimization of women, children, and elders* (pp. 43–52). New York: Human Science Press.

Mullins, G. P. (1994). The battered woman and homelessness. *Journal of Law and Policy, 3,* 237–255.

Murray, R. (2014). *NFL player Ray Rice released after disturbing new video surfaces.* ABC News. Retrieved from http://abcnews.go.com/Sports/ray-rice-cut-ravens-video-elevator-punch/story?id=25347953

National Association of Social Workers. (2003). Family violence policy statement. Social work speaks. Washington, DC: NASW Press.

National Resource Center on Domestic Violence and the Battered Women's Justice Project. (1994). The Violence Against Women Act 1994. Harrisburg, PA: Author. Retrieved from http://legisworks.org/GPO/STATUTE-108-Pg1796.pdf

Novick, K. K., & Novick, J. (2005). *Working with parents makes therapy work.* Lanham, MD: Rowman & Littlefield.

Pence, E., & Paymar, M. (1993). *Education groups for men who batter.* New York: Springer.

Roberts, A. R. (1996a). Court responses to battered women. In A. R. Roberts (Ed.), *Helping battered women: New perspectives and remedies* (pp. 96–101). New York: Oxford University Press.

Roberts, A. R. (1996b). Introduction: Myths and realities regarding battered women. In A. R. Roberts (Ed.), *Helping battered women: New perspectives and remedies* (pp. 3–12). New York: Oxford University Press.

Roberts, A. R. (1996c). Police responses to battered women: Past, present and future. In A. R. Roberts (Ed.), *Helping battered women: New perspectives and remedies* (pp. 85–95). New York: Oxford University Press.

Roche, S. E., & Sadoski, P. J. (1996). Social action for battered women. In A. R. Roberts (Ed.), *Helping battered women: New perspectives and remedies.* New York: Oxford University Press.

Ryle, R. (2012). *Questioning gender: A sociological explanation.* Thousand Oaks, CA: Sage.

Schneider, E. M. (1994). Society's belief in family privacy contributes to domestic violence. In B. Leone, B. Szumski, K. de Koster, K. Swisher, C. Wekesser, & W. Barbour (Eds.), *Violence against women.* San Diego, CA: Greenhaven.

Shernoff, M. (2008). Social work practice with gay individuals. In G. P. Mallon (Ed.), *Social work practice with lesbian, gay, bisexual, and transgender people* (2nd ed., pp. 141–178). New York: Taylor & Francis/Routledge.

Siegler, R. T. (1989). *Domestic violence in context: An assessment of community attitudes.* Lexington, MA: Heath.

Smolowe, J. (1994, July 4). When violence hits home. *Time, 144*(1). Retrieved from http://www.time.com/time/magazine/article/0,9171,981054,00.html

Sorenson, S. B. (2003). Funding public health: The public's willingness to pay for domestic violence prevention programming. *American Journal of Public Health, 93,* 1934–1938.

Spade, J. Z., & Valentine, C. G. (2014). The prism of gender. In J. Z. Spade, & C. G. Valentine (Eds.), *The Kaleidoscope of gender: Prisms, patterns and possibilities.* (4th ed., pp. 3–9).

Srinivasan, M., & Davis, L. V. (1991). A shelter: An organization like any other? *Affilia, 6,* 38–57.

Statman, J. B. (1990). *The battered woman's survival guide: Breaking the cycle.* Dallas, TX: Taylor.

Stith, S. M., Williams, M. B., & Rosen, K. (1990). *Violence hits home: Comprehensive treatment approaches to domestic violence.* New York: Springer.

Tolman, R. M., & Bennett, L. W. (1990). A review of quantitative research on men who batter. *Journal of Interpersonal Violence, 5,* 87–118.

U.S. Department of Health and Human Services. (2007). Child maltreatment, 2005. Administration for Children and Families. Retrieved from http://archive.acf.hhs.gov/programs/cb/pubs/cm05/cm05.pdf

Walker, L. E. A. (2009). *The battered women syndrome* (3rd ed.). New York: Springer.

Westmarland, N., & Kelly, L. (2013). Why extending measurements of success in domestic violence perpetrator programmes matters for social work. *British Journal of Social Work, 43,* 1092–1110.

Wilke, D. J., & Vinton, L. (2003). Domestic violence and aging: Teaching about their intersection. *Journal of Social Work Education, 39,* 225–235.

Willison, J. S., & Lutter, Y. L. (2009). Contextualizing women's violence: Gender-responsive assessment and treatment. In J. T. Andrade (Ed.), *Handbook of violence risk assessment and treatment: New approaches for mental health professionals* (pp. 121–155). New York: Springer.

Yoo, J. A., & Huang, C. (2013), Long-term relationships among domestic violence maternal mental health and parenting and preschool children's behavior problems. *Families in Society, 94,* 1–9.

CHAPTER 13

SOCIAL WORK ADVOCACY IN THE POLITICAL ARENA

THINK FOR A MOMENT ABOUT POLITICS AND THE GLAMOUR OF BEING an elected politician, someone who goes to Washington, DC, and walks the halls and conducts meetings in the Capitol. If you have not seen it, please check out the classic 1939 movie *Mr. Smith Goes to Washington*; you can find it on Netflix by using the search function and keying in "Jimmy Stewart." Ok, the movie is a bit old, and yes, it is in black and white and not high definition, but all in all it still is a fun movie. The venerable actor Jimmy Stewart plays a young idealistic politician who goes to Washington to represent the people and do what is right. He embraces his new job driven by a simple philosophy—government is the friend of all the people, works for all the people, and represents all the people. He believes that elected leaders are simply an extension of our neighbors who act on our behalf and place the community's need above their personal interests. Their overriding purpose is to help achieve what is best for the country. But Mr. Smith finds something else in Washington, DC. He sees a place filled with corruption as people, lobbyists and elected officials alike, solely seek power and money. Mr. Smith is challanged to hold onto his idealism and core principles of doing good for and on behalf of others.

Is Mr. Smith's uncompromising view of politics and government the popular perspective held by most of us today? We suspect not. It's likely that few people today believe that Mr. Smith's principled vision accurately depicts the motivations of politicians as we approach the end of the first quarter of the twenty-first century. Rather, the view of former president Rondald Reagan is probbly more widely held: "Government is not the friend of the people."

For many social workers the political arena is not an enticing place. Politics conjures up ideas of backroom deal making, abuses of rank and power, payoffs, and other unethical activities. Political scandals and allegations of wrongdoing over the past years have reached every level of political office and branch of the government. It's not surprising that you may hold politics in low esteem. In 2014, the national discourse was filled with rancor and partisanship with seemingly little work getting done. Even so, we believe that all social workers should and must be actively engaged in their political envronments, from the local city/county governments to the federal government. And, as we will discuss in this chapter, the so-called political world is not limted to electoral politics and government, but also extends to working in our social service agencies.

But as we begin our exploration of social work in the political arena we recognize a basic belief widely held among social workers: we must continue to ferment our passions and use this energy to directly engage in the political process, no matter if it is at the national, state, or local level of government. We social workers are obligated to work on behalf of our clients and promote social policies that strengthen our communities, our neighborhoods, and our nation.

WHAT IS MEANT BY POLITICS?

We throw around the word *politics* as if we all agree to its meaning. Certainly, politics and the political arena include all elected offices and the officials who fill them at the local, county, state, and federal levels. Yet getting to hold one of these positions involves a process referred to as *electoral politics*. Electoral politics involves getting elected, which by its very nature is incredibly difficult. Electoral politics encompasses a range of activities such as fund-raising, getting out the vote, face-to-face communications, political advertisements, recruiting and sustaining volunteers, and most importantly, communicating a clear message that reflects the candidate's vision.

> *Did You Know... The first women to hold a presidential cabinet position was a social worker, Frances Perkins, who held the postion from 1933 to 1945. She held that post longer than any other person in the department's history.*

Politics, on the other hand, is very different from electoral politics. It incorporates informal and formal interactions that are politically and strategically charged and often not tied to one's ideals. Rather, the "winds of the moment," that is, public opinion, often drives politics and its outcomes. Politics is also alive and well in social welfare organizations, agencies, and even on social work practice teams. How often have you heard someone say "the politics here stink" or "they're just playing politics" or "you have to understand the politics of the situation"? Some of our friends left their jobs primarily due to the agency's politics.

So what is meant by politics? We see politics as being diverse and embracing many of our day-to-day activities. Indeed, Haynes and Mickelson (2009) have gone

> *Did You Know... The first women ever elected to the U.S. Congress was a social worker. Jeannette Pickering Rankin was first elected in 1916 (before women had the right to vote) and again in 1940.*

further, contending that our helping activites make all of social work political. In this chapter we will look at politics and its relation to social work practice. Our discussion will examine political strategies, including electoral, that we hope can serve as a primer for social workers on politics and political activities.

WHY POLITICS AND SOCIAL WORK?

First, let's take a brief look at the political arena and its relation to social service agencies. What guides or directs the activities of social workers in their agencies? We must understand that social workers are not able to take liberties in their practice and provide any type of service they see fit. An organization's policies set forth its programs and services, which in turn direct the social worker to the actual day-to-day work with and on behalf of clients. No one agency offers the comprehensive range of social work activitiers; rather, an agency's programs grow out of its specific function. Let's say, for example, that a practitioner in a child welfare agency wants to offer group therapy to senior citizens in a local housing project. The intervention may be worthy, but the agency in all likelihood will decide that a seniors' group falls outside its purpose and function.

An agency's function is set forth in its mission statement and operationalized by its policies. Policies do not just spring forth; rather they are the result of a political process, be it an agency board of directors or an elected body such as a state legislature. And who are these people? Are they social workers? Are they really expert enough in human services that they should be shaping social work practice? Unfortunately, the majority of people who develop an agency's broad social policies have little, if any, direct social work experience, and even fewer have an educational background in social work or human services. When professional social workers choose to avoid the political aspects of the field, one outcome is inevitable: people who are not social workers will govern social work practice. As a result, social workers need to engage in the political world in order to help shape social policy. This can be done in three ways: (1) by electing individuals who are sympathetic to the profession's interests, (2) by engaging in lobbying and education efforts with those who form social policy, and (3) by encouraging social workers to run for elected office (see the activity below).

Activity…Find out how many social workers there are in your state legislature, both the house and senate. You can do this by checking with your state's secretary of state's office. Then look at the house and senate committees that oversee social problems; they may have titles such as Committee on Health and Human Services. Now, look to see how many committee members are social workers.Look at their staffs to see how many staff members are social workers. What do your findings tell you about the development of social policies in your state?

SOCIAL WORK VALUES AND POLITICAL ACTIVITY

Some social workers allow negative images of politics and political activity to outweigh their responsibility to engage in the political arena. Yet the Code of Ethics of the National Association of Social Workers (NASW, 2008) clearly states our obligations and political responsibilities in two separate places in section 6, "The Social Worker's Ethical Responsibilities to Society":

1. Social workers should facilitate informed participation by the public in shaping social policies and institutions (sec. 6.02).
2. Social workers should . . . advocate for changes in policy and legislation to improve social conditions in order to . . . promote social justice [sec. 6.04(a)].

The 2015 Educational Policy and Accreditation Standards (EPAS) of the Council on Social Work Education (CSWE, Commission on Educational Policy and Commission on Accreditation, 2015) also supports the profession's political involvement and refers to this as "policy practice." Specifically, competency 5 states that "Social workers understand their role in policy development and implementation . . . apply critical thinking to analyze, formulate, and advocate for policies that advance human rights and social, economic, and environmental justice" (p. 8.).

Social work practitioners understand that policy affects service delivery, and they actively engage in policy practice. Social workers know the history and current structures of social policies and services, the role of policy in service delivery, and the role of practice in policy development. Social workers analyze, formulate, and advocate for policies that advance social well-being; and collaborate with colleagues and clients for effective policy action.

Why does the NASW Code of Ethics, as well as similar ethical codes for other professional social welfare organizations and the CSWE's EPAS, emphasize practitioner involvement in the political arena? First and foremost, remember that the definition of social work includes working to bring about a just community built on the tenets of social and economic equality. Second, many of the problems experienced by clients are created by forces external to them and can be remedied only through amended social policy or additional funding for social services. Third, the best advocates for change are those who deal with problems day in and day out. Through direct practice, social workers see firsthand the debilitating effects of problems on clients.

Now this is where it can get a bit messy for social workers. Some groups contend that the social work profession is nothing more then a left wing group of idealogues who want nothing more then socialistic style programs and a big government. So right now let's be clear: there is no accusation that is more unfounded and untrue. Just take a look at where social work educational programs are located; some are in our nation's most conservative faith-based universities whereas others are found in the most liberal universities. In other words, social work crosses the political and ideological spectrum. The social work tent includes conservatives and liberals, Democrats, Republicans, Greens, Independents, Tea Party members, and others from the dozens of political parties that are active in politics. In other words, the social work ideology of justice for all people is not owned by one political party. Our political ideologies and philosophies merely frame different pathways to achieve justice for all.

The political diversity in social work can be difficult to accept, but if we use our critical thinking approaches we can engage in thoughtful debate that will result in answers that benefit the greater good. And that is ultimately what politics is about—doing what is right for the greater good.

A HISTORICAL OVERVIEW OF POLITICAL ACTIVITY BY SOCIAL WORKERS

Social work has had three separate but significant waves of political involvement: the Progressive Era of the nineteenth century, the 1930s New Deal, and the 1960s War on Poverty. In each of these periods, social work's involvement in politics mirrored the profession's growth and internal conflict over mission, scope, and function. In all three periods, leaders disagreed about the causes of social problems and how best to solve them. The Progressive movement was attractive to many social workers and provided a political focus for their philosophical beliefs and commitments. Social workers such as Jane Addams and Florence Kelley used the political system to address social problems. Settlement house workers seemed to be more partisan than other social workers. Weismiller and Rome (1995) noted that settlement workers ran political campaigns, organized neighborhoods to support particular candidates, lobbied, and worked on welfare reform. On the other hand, Mary Richmond, a leader in the charity organization society (COS) movement, believed that social workers should be nonpartisan and confine their efforts to helping clients to resolve their individual issues (Weismiller & Rome, 1995).

The Great Depression of the 1930s created ample opportunity for social workers to venture into the political arena. Schools of social work were more organized than their forerunners during the Progressive Era, and macro content, which focused on political concerns, was included in the curriculum. The federal government's Children's Bureau and Women's Bureau provided social workers with a setting to address significant social issues. In fact, many parts of the Economic Security Act of 1935 were written by social workers (Weismiller & Rome, 1995).

Frances Perkins, a social worker who was President Franklin Delano Roosevelt's secretary of labor in the 1930s and 1940s, was instrumental in bringing about significant social welfare changes such as the forty-hour work week, minimum wage, worker's compensation, child labor laws, unemployment relief, and social security (Downey, 2010, p. 1). Clearly, the profession was beginning to accept political activism as a suitable response to crisis; however, social work remained ambivalent regarding political activity as an appropriate long-term social work methodology (Haynes & Mickelson, 2002).

The third wave of political activism by social workers came in the 1960s. With the emergence of the Peace Corps and VISTA, a domestic version of the Peace Corps program, and the burgeoning civil rights movement, social workers actively promoted a political agenda. Community organization, both as a practice and an educational specialization, took shape in the late 1950s and 1960s. This activity challenged social workers to view systems from the much broader macro prospective. Federal dollars were funneled to initiatives that encouraged neighborhoods and local people to engage in problem solving and community action.

Did You Know... There is a Congressional Social Work Caucus that is bipartisan and bicameral (House and Senate members). The caucus website is http://socialworkcaucus-lee.house.gov

---

Within the profession, debate continued on the role and scope of political activity. Weismiller and Rome (1995) reported in one study that NASW members agreed to pay increased organizational dues if this would bring about greater political activity by members. Yet this somewhat overzealous characterization didn't affect the entire profession, and members continued to debate the merits of efforts at the political level, particularly in light of the massive problems facing individuals and families.

In 1976, the NASW organized its first conference on politics in Washington, DC. Aimed primarily at social work political activists, the meeting gathered NASW members from around the country for a political training institute. The NASW then supplemented this national meeting with regional institutes. By the end of the twentieth century, the NASW discontinued these gatherings and left training to the state chapters and other professional associations.

The 1990s seemed to be a watershed decade for social workers involved in electoral politics. Never before in the profession's history were social workers and their professional organizations as active in political campaigns as in the last decade of the twentieth century. "Lift Up America" was the NASW's 1992 presidential project theme, augmented by numerous national, regional, and state election activities (Landers, 1992), and NASW's political action committee, Political Action for Candidate Election (PACE), endorsed more than one hundred candidates for national office (Hiratsuka, 1992) and contributed approximately $200,000 to national campaigns while state PACE committees dispensed in excess of $160,000 to state and local candidates (D. Dempsey, personal communication, November 30, 1992; Dempsey, 1993).

In 1991, the NASW reported that 113 social workers held elected office (Weismiller & Rome, 1995); by 1992, 165 social workers in forty-three states had won a variety of races (NASW, 1992); and by 1998, there were more than 200 social workers holding political office in the nation! They held elected office at all levels of government from city council to the U.S. Senate. With each succeeding election, individual social workers and their professional associations gained new experiences, built on previous knowledge, and strengthened themselves as active players in the political arena. In 2003, 175 social workers nationwide held a variety of local, state, and federal offices, and as of February 2009, according to the NASW, 177 social workers held elected office. In 2013 the NASW reported that there were nearly 190 individuals elected to various offices (see Table 1), whereas in the 113th Congress (2013–14), social workers held nine postions, two in the U.S. Senate and seven in the U.S. House of Representatives (NASW, 2013).

There are a couple of interesting pieces related to the most recent 113th Congress of 2013–14. First, the so-called dean (e.g., longest serving person) of women in the U.S. Senate is a social worker, Barbara McKulski (D-Maryland), who was first elected in 1986. Senator McKulski is also the longest serving woman in the history of the United States Senate. Furthermore, the individual leading the 2014 Congressional negotaitions around immigration reform was Representative Luis Gutiérrez (D-Illinois), a social worker who was first elected to Congress in 1993. Prior to his election to Congress, Representative Gutiérrez served on Chicago's city council from 1986 to 1993. Representative Gutiérrez is also the dean of the Illinois Congressional delegation, which includes eighteen individuals.

ELECTORAL AND LEGISLATIVE POLITICS

Political social work has two sides that are intricately related; both are important to the social work profession's realization of its goals. First, social workers identify and support candidates who are friends of the profession and support issues that are of direct concern to the profession. By making contributions and working in candidates' campaigns, social workers are able to help pro-human-service candidates to win elections. This is referred to as electoral politics. Second, social workers collaborate with elected officials during the ongoing legislative sessions on policy proposals. This is commonly referred to as lobbying or education

Table 1. Social Workers in Elected Offices, 2013–14

State	Name	Party	Office Level	District	Gender	Credential	Race/ethnicity
AK	Betty Davis	D	State legislature	K	F	BSW	African American
AZ	Paul Cunningham	D	City/municipal	2	M	MSW	Caucasian
AZ	Katie Hobbs	D	State legislature	24	F	BSW, MSW	Caucasian
AZ	Pete Rios	D	County/borough	1	M	MSW	Hispanic/Latino
AZ	Kyrsten Sinema	D	Congress	9	F	BSW, MSW	Caucasian
AZ	Ralph Varela	D	City/municipal		M	MSW	Hispanic/Latino
CA	Fernando Armenta	D	County/borough	1	M	MSW	Hispanic/Latino
CA	Ruth Atkin	D	City/municipal		F	MSW	Caucasian
CA	John Avalos	D	County/borough	11	M	MSW	Hispanic/Latino
CA	Susan Davis	D	Congress	53	F	MSW	Caucasian
CA	Susan Eggman	D	State legislature	13	F	MSW	Hispanic/Latino
CA	Monica Garcia	D	School board	Area 2	F	MSW	Hispanic/Latino
CA	Genoveva Garcia-Calloway	D	City/municipal		F	MSW	Hispanic/Latino
CA	Jorge Gonzalez	D	School board	Area 1	M	MSW	Hispanic/Latino
CA	Cheryl Heitmann	D	City/municipal	Area 2	F	MSW	Caucasian
CA	Barbara Lee	D	Congress	13	F	MSW	African American
CA	Victor Manalo	D	City/municipal	49	M	MSW	Asian/Pacific
CA	David Mineta	D	Other		M	MSW	Asian/Pacific
CA	Nayin Nahabedian	D	School board	43	F	MSW	Other
CA	Bill Rosendahl	D	City/municipal	11	M	MSW	Caucasian
CA	Al Rowlett	D	School board	Area 7	M	MSW	African American
CA	Ann Tanner		School board		F	MSW	Caucasian
CA	Tony Thurmond	D	City/municipal	15	M	MSW	African American
CA	Clark Williams	D	County/borough	6	M	MSW	Caucasian
CA	Mariko Yamada	D	State legislature	8	F	MSW	Asian/Pacific
CO	Tracy Kraft-Tharp	D	State legislature	29	F	MSW	Caucasian
CO	Judy Montero	D	City/municipal	9	F	MSW	Hispanic/Latino
CO	Jonathon Singer	D	State legislature	11	M	MSW, BSW	Caucasian
CT	Julie Cooper Altman	D	School board	5	F	MSW	
CT	Lucille Brown		School board	Windsor	F	MSW	
CT	David Burgess	D	City/municipal	Middlefield	M	MSW	Caucasian
CT	Diane Cady	D	City/municipal	Westport	F	MSW	Caucasian
CT	Steve Cassano	D	State legislature	4	M	MSW	Caucasian
CT	Christopher Donovan	D	State legislature	84	M	MSW	Caucasian
CT	Toni Edmunds-Walker	D	State legislature	93	F	MSW	African American

State	Name	Party	Office Level	District	Gender	Credential	Race/ethnicity
CT	Glen Gemma	D	School board		M	MSW	Caucasian
CT	Rick Lopes	D	State legislature	24	M	MSW	Caucasian
CT	Mary Jane Lundgren	D	City/municipal	New Milford	F	MSW	Caucasian
CT	Christopher Lyddy	D	State legislature	106	M	MSW	Caucasian
CT	Edith Prague	D	State legislature	19	F	MSW	Caucasian
CT	Pedro Segarra	D	City/municipal	Hartford	M	MSW	Hispanic/Latino
CT	Kim Shepardson Watson	D	School board	Groton	F	MSW	
CT	Robert J. Wolf	D	City/municipal		M	MSW	
DC	Tommy Wells	D	City/municipal	6	M	MSW	Caucasian
DE	Ted Blunt	D	City/municipal	Wilmington	M	MSW	African American
FL	Suzanne Gunzburger	D	County/borough	6	F	MSW	Caucasian
FL	Steve Kornell	D	City/municipal	5	M	MSW	Caucasian
FL	John Legg	Re-form	State legislature	46	M	BSW	Caucasian
FL	Diane Scott		School board	1	F	MSW, DSW	Caucasian
GA	Pam Stephenson	D	State legislature	92	F	MSW	African American
GA	Renee Unterman	R	State legislature	45	F	BSW	Caucasian
GA	Evelyn Winn Dixon	D	City/municipal	Riverdale	F	MSW	African American
HI	Haunani Apoliona	I	County/borough		F	MSW	Asian/Pacific
HI	Ryan Yamane	D	State legislature	37	M	MSW	Asian/Pacific
IA	James Anderson	D	Human Rights Commission chair		M	MSW	Caucasian
IA	Martha Anderson	D	State legislature	36	F	MSW	Caucasian
IA	Mark Cowan		School board	Carlisle	M	MSW	
IA	Joni Dittmer	R	School board	North Scott	F	MSW	Caucasian
IA	Joel Fry	R	State Legislature	95	M	MSW	
IA	Susan Kosche Vallem		City/municipal	Waverly	F	MSW	Caucasian
IA	Rebecca Schmitz	D	County/borough	Jefferson County	F	MSW	Caucasian
IA	Mark Smith	D	State legislature	43	M	MSW	Caucasian
ID	Cherie Buckner-Webb	D	State Legislature	19	F	MSW	African American
IL	John Del Genio	I	School Board	#72 & #807	M	MSW	Caucasian
IL	Lori DeYoung	D	County/borough	2-VC	F	PhD	Caucasian
IL	Kenneth Dunkin	D	State legislature	5	M	MSW	African American
IL	Luis Gutierrez	D	Congress	4	M	MSW	Hispanic/Latino
IL	Jane Herron	D	School board	502	F	MSW	Caucasian
IL	Christine Radogno	R	State legislature	41	F	MSW	Caucasian
IL	Susan Rose		City/municipal	Elmhurst	F	MSW, PhD	Caucasian
IL	Edie Sutker	I	City/municipal	Skokie	F	MSW	Caucasian
IN	Oliver Davis	D	City/municipal	South Bend	M	MSW	African American
IN	Joe Micon	I	State legislature	26	M	MSW	Caucasian
IN	Gail Riecken	D	State legislature	77	F	BSW	Caucasian
KS	Robert Byers		School board	Lawrence	M		African American

Table 1. Social Workers in Elected Offices, 2013–14—(*Continued*)

State	Name	Party	Office Level	District	Gender	Credential	Race/ethnicity
KS	Becky Fast		City/municipal	Roeland Park	F	MSW	Caucasian
KS	Vanessa Sanborn		School board	Lawrence	F		Caucasian
KY	Shevawn Akers		City/municipal	2	F	MSW	Caucasian
KY	Diane Lawless		City/municipal	3	F	BSW; MSW	Caucasian
KY	Tina Ward-Pugh	D	City/municipal	9	F	MSW	Caucasian
KY	Jim Wayne	D	State legislature	35	M	MSW	Caucasian
KY	Susan Westrom	D	State legislature	79	F	MSW	Caucasian
LA	Carolyn Hill	D	School board		F	MSW	African American
LA	LaVonya Malveaux	D	City/municipal	Village of Palmetto	F	BSW	African American
MA	Michael Ashe	N/A	County/borough	Hampden	M	MSW	Caucasian
MA	Sally Bleiberg	N/A	City/municipal	Belmont	F	BSW, MSW	Caucasian
MA	Henrietta Davis	D	City/municipal	Cambridge	F	MSW	Caucasian
MA	Susan Falkoff	D	City/municipal	Watertown	F	MSW	Caucasian
MA	Sheila Harrington	R	State legislature	1	F	BSW	Caucasian
MA	Denise Hurst	D	School board	Springfield	F	MSW	African American
MA	Johnathan Lothrop	D	City/municipal	Ward 5	M	MSW	Caucasian
MA	Alison Malkin		City/municipal		F	MSW	Caucasian
MA	Marc McGovern	D	School board	Cambridge	M	MSW	Caucasian
MA	Jennifer McKenna	N/A	City/municipal	8	F	MSW	Caucasian
MA	Sarai Rivera	D	City/municipal	4	F	MSW	Puerto Rican
MA	Karen Spilka	D	State legislature	2	F	BSW	Caucasian
MA	Niki Tsongas	D	Congress	3	F		Caucasian
MA	Judy Zabin	N/A	City/municipal	1	F	MSW	Caucasian
MD	Melony Griffith	D	State legislature	25	F	MSW	African American
MD	Barbara Mikulski	D	Congress	Maryland	F	MSW	Caucasian
ME	Joseph Brannigan	D	State legislature	117	M	MSW	Caucasian
ME	Michael Brennan	D	City/municipal	Portland	M	MSW, BSW	Caucasian
ME	Adam Goode	D	State legislature	15	M	MSW Student	Caucasian
ME	Colleen Lachowicz	D	State legislature	25	F	MSW, BSW	Caucasian
ME	Melanie Sachs	D	City/municipal	Freeport	F	MSW, BSW	Caucasian
MI	Theresa Abed	D	State legislature	71	F	MSW, BSW	Caucasian
MI	Terry Brown	D	State legislature	81	M	MSW, BSW	Caucasian
MI	Marcia Hovey-Wright	D	State legislature	92	F	MSW, BSW	Caucasian
MI	Barbara Levin Bergman	D	County/borough	8	F	MSW, BSW	Caucasian
MI	Debbie Stabenow	D	Congress	Michigan	F	MSW	Caucasian
MI	Jacquelin E. Washington		School board		F	MSW	African American
MN	Lawrence Hosch	D	State legislature	14B	M	MSW	Caucasian
MN	Sheldon Johnson	D	State legislature	67B	M	BSW	Caucasian
MN	Rafael Ortega	D	County/borough	5	M	MSW, BSW	Hispanic/Latino
NC	Alan Beck		School board	Davidson County	M	BSW	
NC	Donna Bell		City/municipal	Chapel Hill	F	MSW	African American
NC	MaryAnn Black		County/borough	Durham	F	MSW	

State	Name	Party	Office Level	District	Gender	Credential	Race/ ethnicity
NC	Jaquelyn Gist	N/A	City/municipal	Carrboro	F	MSW	Caucasian
NC	Michelle Johnson		City/municipal	Carrboro	F	MSW	African American
NC	Graig Meyer	D	State legislature	50	M	MSW	
NC	Paige Sayles		School board	Franklin County	F	MSW	
NC	John I. Steele		City/municipal	Cleveland	M	MSW	Caucasian
NC	Tom Stevens		City/municipal	Hillsborough	M	MSW	Caucasian
ND	Tim Mathern	D	State legislature	11	M	MSW	Caucasian
NE	Kate Bolz	D	State legislature	29	F	MSW	Caucasian
NH	James MacKay	R	State legislature	39	M	DSW	Caucasian
NH	Carol Shea-Porter	D	Congress	1	F	BSW	Caucasian
NJ	Sheila Oliver	D	State legislature	34	F	MSW	African American
NM	Mary Jane Garcia	D	State legislature	36	F		Hispanic/ Latino
NV	Teresa Benitez-Thompson	D	State legislature	27	F	MSW	Hispanic/ Latino
NV	Carolyn Edwards	I	School board	Clark County	F	MSW	Caucasian
NV	David Humke	R	County/borough	Washoe	M	MSW	Caucasian
NV	Annie Wilson	I	School board	2	F	MSW	African American
NY	Patricia Eddington	D	State legislature	3	F	MSW	Caucasian
NY	Earlene Hill Hooper	D	State legislature	18	F	MSW	African American
NY	Fran Knapp	D	County/borough	Dutchess County	F		Caucasian
NY	Henrietta Lodge		School board		F	MSW	
NY	Vito Lopez	D	State legislature	53	M	MSW	Hispanic/ Latino
NY	Katharine O'Connel	D	City/municipal	Syracuse	F	MSW	Caucasian
NY	Angela Petty	D	County/borough	3	F	MSW	Caucasian
NY	Joseph Sanfiliippo	D	City/municipal	4	M	MSW	Caucasian
NY	Ed Towns	D	Congress	10	M	MSW	African American
OH	Jacqueline Bird		City/municipal	Marblehead	F	BSW	Caucasian
OH	Patricia Britt	D	City/municipal	6	F	BSW	African American
OH	Thomas West	D	City/municipal	Canton	M	MSW	African American
OH	Tina Wozniak	D	County/borough	Toledo	F	MSW	Caucasian
OR	William Shields	D	State legislature	43	M	MSW	Caucasian
OR	Carolyn Tomei	D	State legislature	41	F	MSW	Caucasian
PA	William Amesbury	D	County/borough	Luzerne County	M	MSW	Caucasian
PA	John Blake	D	State legislature	22	M	MSW	Caucasian
PA	Diane Ellis-Marsegila	D	County/borough		F	MSW	Caucasian
PA	Allyson Schwartz	D	Congress	13	F	MSW	Caucasian
PA	Maria Weidinger	D	City/municipal	Plymouth Township	F	MSW	Caucasian
RI	Michael Burk	D	School board	Tiverton	M	MSW	Caucasian
RI	Maria Cimini	D	State legislature	7	F	MSW	Caucasian
RI	Gary Cournoyer	D	City/municipal	Jamestown	M	MSW	Caucasian
RI	Stephen Mueller	D	School board		M	MSW	Caucasian
RI	Roger Picard	D	State legislature	20	M	MSW	Caucasian
RI	Michael Reeves	D	School board	5	M	MSW	Caucasian

Table 1. Social Workers in Elected Offices, 2013–14—(Continued)

State	Name	Party	Office Level	District	Gender	Credential	Race/ethnicity
RI	Rita Williams		City/municipal	2	F	MSW	Caucasian
SC	Gilda Cobb-Hunter	D	State legislature	66	F	MSW	African American
SC	Jim Manning	D	County/borough	8	M	MSW	Caucasian
SD	Joni Cutler	R	State legislature	14	F	BSW	Caucasian
TN	Dr. Carol B. Berz		City/municipal	6	F	MSW	Caucasian
TN	Michelle Holt-Horton		School board	McKenzie Special School District	F	MSW	Caucasian
TN	Joe Pitts	D	State legislature	67	M	BSW	Caucasian
TX	Sylvia Garcia	D	County/borough	2	F	BSW	Mexican American
TX	Elliott Naishtat	D	State legislature	49	M	MSW	Caucasian
VA	James Fitzsimmons		School board	4	M	MSW	Caucasian
VT	Janet Ancel	D	State legislature	6	F	MSW	Caucasian
VT	Diane Bugbee	D	School board	South Burlington	F	MSW	Caucasian
VT	Sandra Dooley	D	City/municipal	South Burlington	F	MSW	Caucasian
VT	Michael Fisher	D	State legislature	Addison-4	M	MSW	Caucasian
VT	Ann Denison Pugh	D	State legislature	South Burlington	F	MSW	Caucasian
VT	Sarah Kunz Robinson	D	City/municipal	Winooski	F	MSW	Caucasian
WA	Mary Lou Dickerson	D	State legislature	36	F	MSW	Caucasian
WA	Connie Ladenburg	D	State legislature	29	F	MSW	Caucasian
WA	Tina Orwall	D	State legislature	33	F	MSW	Caucasian
WA	Eric Pettigrew	D	State legislature	37	M	MSW	African American
WI	Tamara Grigsby	D	State legislature	18	F	MSW	African American
WI	Mark Schmitt		County/borough	Rusk County	M	MSW	Caucasian
WI	Nick Smiar	D	County/borough	Eau Claire	M	PhD	Caucasian
WV	Cathy Gatson	D	County/borough	Kanawha County	F	MSW	Caucasian
WV	Becky Jones Jordan		School board	Kanawha	F	MSW	Caucasian
WV	Robert Musick	D	City/municipal	Star City	M	MSW	Caucasian
WV	John David Smith		City/municipal	Athens	M	MSW	Caucasian
WY	Georgia Broyles		City/municipal	III	F	MSW	Caucasian
WY	Floyd Esquibel	D	State legislature	44	M	MSW, BSW	Hispanic/Latino
WY	Jerry Iekel	R	State legislature	29	M	MSW, BSW	Caucasian

Source: National Association of Social Workers (2014). *Social workers in elected office*.
Retrieved from https://www.socialworkers.org/pace/state.asp

Political activity is generally viewed through the lobbying lens. Richman (1991), Haynes and Mickelson (2009), Mahaffey and Hanks (1982), and Wolk (1981), among others, emphasize the lobbying side of politics. Little attention is paid to electing candidates to public office. Deemphasizing electoral politics violates two important legislative lessons, however:

◆ *Lesson 1*: Lobbying is much easier with supporters and friends of social work than with its detractors and antagonists.

◆ *Lesson 2*: Lobbying for prevention proposals is a much better use of energy than lobbying against negative proposals and rectifying previous legislative errors.

You might view the political process as a cycle (see box 1). In a rational logical model, the political life cycle begins with candidate identification and then progresses through participation in electoral politics, educating the candidate on social work issues and advocating certain positions, lobbying the candidate to support the profession's stance, and back to candidate identification and reelection (see box 1). This becomes an ongoing, uninteruppted circle. Not suprisingly, the real life political cycle is not so rational and not so logical; in fact, you can typically enter the process and begin your efforts at any given point.

Suppose, for example, that legislation regarding abortion is up for debate in the state senate. First, you attempt to educate your legislator on the issue from a social work perspective; the representative decides not to support your view. You

Box 1. Political Life Cycle

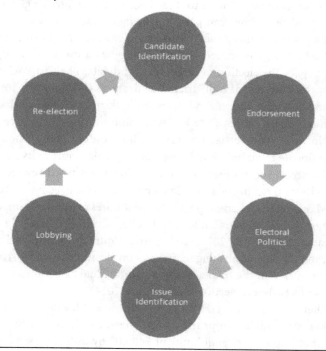

soon realize that a new elected official is needed to better serve the interests of your district and the profession, and you begin to seek an alternative candidate for the next election. And the cycle continues.

Although elected officials are responsible primarily to their constituencies, they are also receiving advice and counsel from their campaign supporters and lobbyists. A long-held political adage, "money buys access," is very true. Even so, active campaign support establishes a relationship between the candidate and possible next officeholder and the social work community. When this is achieved, rather than having to adopt a defensive lobbying posture—protecting what they have from social work antagonists—social workers are able to influence the development and enhancement of social services through public policy. Conversely, when they don't have supporters and advocates in the legislative body, social workers must put most of their efforts into attempting to block of modify coercive public policies.

Social Work Organizations and Electoral Politics

Nonprofit organizations, such as those in which social workers are most typically employed, are not allowed to directly campaign, lobby, or give money to a political candidate. Further, campaign financing laws severely restrict the amount of money a person or group can give to a candidate, campaign, or political party.

Political action committees (PACs) evolved as a mechanism organized to spend money for the election or defeat of a candidate. The first PAC was created in 1944 by the Congress of Industrial Organizations (CIO) so that contributions could be made to pro-union candidates while skirting the federal law that precluded unions giving money to candidates. Political action committees have been and remain very controversial. Federal laws limit the amount of money any one group can donate to an individual. The U.S. Supreme Court in its 2010 decision, Citizens United v. Federal Election Commission, overturned key sections of the Campaign Reform Act of 2002 (also known as the McCain-Feingold Act) that had prohibited corporate and union political expenditures in political campaigns. After this decision, private groups could spend dollars from their general treasuries to finance campaigns. And in 2014, the Supreme Court further opened the door to funding candidates by abolishing limitations on election spending, striking down a decades-old cap on the total amount any individual can contribute to federal candidates in a two-year election cycle (Liptak, 2014).

Another Supreme Court decision, this time in 2012, allowed an individual to give $2,600 per candidate in primary and general elections. The Supreme Court also said that imposing overall limits of $48,600 by individuals every two years for contributions to all federal candidates violated the First Amendment, as did separate aggregate limits on contributions to political party committees, currently $74,600 (Liptak, 2014).

The Center for Responsive Politics (2014b; http://www.opensecrets.org) reports that the top donor PAC for the 2013–14 fiscal cycle was the National Beer Wholesalers Association, which gave $2,511,000. The top donor to Democratic candidates was the International Brotherhood of Electrical Workers with approximately $1.9 million in contributions; the largest donor to Republican candidates for the same time period was the Every Republican Is Crucial PAC with slightly more than $1.8 million in donations (Center for Responsive Politics, 2014).

Social work itself has been actively engaged since the early 1970s in organizing PACs. As with any PAC, the profession's political advocacy group acts as a mechanism to identify candidates who support social work while often providing financial support for their election. And, as shown in Table 2, PACs have their own language.

Table 2. Terms and Definitions Used by PACE, 2014

Contribution—When PACE gives money to a candidate running for office.

Candidate—A person running for election.

Endorsement—A stamp of approval for someone running for office, which means that PACE wants him or her to win the election.

Challenger—A person running for election against an incumbent.

Incumbent—A person who is already elected to the office for which he or she is seeking reelection.

Fund-raiser—An event to raise money for a candidate; takes place at various times of the year; counts as a contribution.

Hard money—A slang term that refers to campaign and PAC funds that are subject to limitations and reporting requirement by the Federal Election Commission. The PACE money is hard money, and is unaffected by the new campaign finance law. Indirectly, it will put more pressure on PACE for its funds.

Open seat—A situation when the incumbent is not running for reelection, or the district was newly created during redistricting and reapportionment.

PACE trustees—The national PACE board of trustees consists of seven NASW members who make decisions about endorsements of and contributions to federal candidates.

Partisan—Relating to a particular political party. (Bipartisan relates to the two major political parties; nonpartisan does not relate to any political parties; multi-partisan relates to more than one political party.)

Political—Relating to government, making or influencing governmental policy, party politics, or the art or science concerned with winning and holding control over a government.

Reapportionment and redistricting—An activity that occurs every ten years after the U.S. Census, during which congressional districts are allocated to states and congressional district lines are redrawn to reflect shifts in population.

Source: National Association of Social Workers (n.d.).

Education Legislative Network

In 1971, the Education Legislative Network (ELAN) was organized by the NASW as a vehicle to bring together divergent and often contentious social work groups, in particular, clinical and macro level social workers. The premise of the ELAN was that a united work community would strive together for the good of the whole and as it did so separate groups would become more friendly toward each other, thus creating broader support for each group's issues.

As a beginning effort, the ELAN was successful in educating NASW members on a number of national policy issues. It used a progressive strategy in which NASW members were (1) informed on issues and (2) encouraged to lobby their elected representatives in Washington. It became obvious, however, that more friendly elected leaders were needed. Concurrent with the association's first organized political efforts, PACs took on greater importance in American politics overall.

Political Action for Candidate Election

In 1976, the NASW organized PACE, which served as the association's national effort to raise money and endorse candidates for national office who supported the profession's agenda. In other words, PACE was the NASW's PAC. Through its bylaws, PACE is a separate organization from NASW, which as a nonprofit organization is not allowed to engage in political activity such as lobbying. However, it is interesting to note that an employee of a nonprofit organization may educate a candidate on an issue. The difference is that to lobby is to get someone to adopt a particular position whereas to educate is to provide an individual with basic facts without endorsing a particular stance.

Political Action for Candidate Election has a threefold purpose. First, it endorses those candidates who are most supportive of social work issues. Second, it sometimes makes campaign contributions to endorsed candidates. And third, it educates NASW members about candidates and encourages electoral participation (see the activity below).

> *Activity…Contact your state PACE unit through the NASW. Find out who serves on the PACE board of trustees. What is the track record of PACE endorsements? Do endorsed candidates get elected? How many Republicans, Democrats, or candidates from other political parties were endorsed in the last election? How much money was contributed to the candidates?*

The national PACE is limited to endorsing and contributing to national candidates, that is, candidates for the presidency, the U.S. House of Representatives, and the U.S. Senate. A board of trustees (seven in total), each appointed by the national NASW president, governs PACE. The board, with consultation from NASW members and state chapters, screens candidates for national elections, endorses candidates, and in some but not all instances makes financial contributions. After a candidate is endorsed, NASW members in the candidate's state or district are encouraged to work in his or her campaign and make additional campaign contributions.

Even as the national PACE effort grew in strength, the NASW recognized the truth of former House speaker Tip O'Neil's (D-Massachusetts) statement, "All politics is local." The NASW therefore encouraged state chapters to organize their own PACE units to endorse local and statewide candidates and raise funds for their campaigns.

By 1998, every state had a PACE unit working to help candidates who support social work positions. The state PACE units are structured in a manner similar to the national PACE: each has a board of trustees, appointed by the state chapter president, and each screens and endorses candidates. The efforts and activities of the state PACE units are separate from each other and from the national PACE; there is no formal mechanism or means for accountability to the national professional association.

In theory, a state PACE unit could work against the interests of the NASW by endorsing candidates who do not support the social work positions outlined at the national level. If this happened there would be no recourse for the NASW or the chapter membership. As trustees, the board members are ultimately responsible for all endorsements and for disbursements of campaign contributions, and they are accountable only to themselves. Nevertheless, the nationwide network of social work PACE units provides an important opportunity to identify, support, and work to elect individuals who can be advocates for social work issues and friends of the profession.

Did You Know…A number of graduate and undergraduate academic programs offer courses focusing on politics and social work. The University of Houston College of Social Work implemented a graduate specialization in politics and social work, and the University of Connecticut sponsors an institute on political social work.

Political Action for Candidate Election Endorsement Process

Each state unit as well as the national PACE develops its own endorsement process and procedures. Remember that the state PACE units are not tied to each other or to the national PACE; they are separate entities, each with its own set of bylaws. A state's PACE unit is separate even from the state's NASW chapter. You can learn more about your own state PACE organization by visiting your NASW state chapter website; look for links directly to PACE or look for a link to *advocacy*. Sometimes you will need to look under the *About Us* link to find the PACE information.

Colby and Buffum (1998) found what seems to be a typical format for state endorsement (but recognize that not all states follow this procedure). The board puts together a survey that is distributed to all candidates (see box 2). Candidates are given a specified period in which to respond; if a survey is not returned, someone calls the candidate's office asking to have the survey completed. If the candidate is seeking reelection, the board will also review his or her voting record. Finally, members of local NASW units will be asked to provide input to the process. Some state PACE units also hire professional lobbyists to help assess candidates. Professional lobbyists work the legislative halls every day, attempting to convince legislators to vote one way or another on specific legislation. As a result they often have a more detailed understanding of candidates than PACE trustees.

Based on the information it accumulates from the survey, the board decides which candidates to endorse. Once endorsements are made, the board then determines whether a financial contribution will be made. The board looks at many issues in deciding whether to make a contribution: Is the candidate opposed in the election? Does the candidate need the money? If unopposed, does the candidate need help in retiring a campaign debt? There are no correct answers to these questions; they simply serve as discussion points to help the trustees to make a final decision.

---

*Did You Know...*Bundling *is a campaign loophole that allows organizations to get around legal financial caps on contributions. For example, a state PACE unit may contribute the maximum amount for a person running for the state house, say $500.00. When the PACE check is presented, additional checks from individual NASW chapter members are given at the same time (thus, the idea of a bundle of checks). So a candidate may receive $500.00 from the organization and perhaps thirty checks for $50.00 each, for a total of $2,000. In effect, the organization, with member support, has increased its level of financial support to the candidate. And the candidate is more likely to remember a $2,000 contribution than individual $50.00 checks.*

Once endorsements are made and the level of contributions determined, NASW members are informed of the PACE decisions. Checks are presented directly to the candidate by social workers from the candidate's district; this provides an opportunity for local social workers to make a direct connection with the candidate and to strengthen the relations for future lobbying efforts.

Social Workers and Political Campaigns

Volunteers and paid campaign staff provide critical support to a candidate's electoral bid. Commitments to a candidate and his or her ideas is the only prerequisite. It doesn't matter where the individual's competence lies: a campaign has

Box 2. Example of a Candidate Survey

Currently, Texas is ranked forty-ninth of the fifty states and the District of Columbia in the delivery of health and human services. At the same time, Texas also ranks near or at the top of all states in terms of the severity of many health and social problems, including teen pregnancy, school dropouts, the number of AIDS cases, infant mortality, and the lack of rural health care.

During the spring Texas legislative session, numerous bills were introduced to address these issues. As with most states, however, the ongoing state deficit forced cuts in social services. Public education to housing and health care were all cut. Nevertheless, the legislature spent three special sessions, at a cost of $1.5 million per session, to redraw congressional district maps in order to eliminate congressional seats held by Democrats and increase the number of Republicans in the U.S. House of Representatives. Obviously the majority of the members in the Texas legislature were more concerned about political self-interest than providing for the public good.

Do you support or oppose the following initiatives?

Support	Oppose	
_____	_____	1. Legislation that would allow parents to take up to three months' leave without pay from their jobs to care for a seriously ill child, spouse, or parent or for the birth or adoption of a child.
_____	_____	2. Increased funding for Aid to Families with Dependent Children (AFDC).
_____	_____	3. Legislation ensuring that all at-risk students have access to pupil services (including school social workers, school psychologists, and counselors).
_____	_____	4. Legislation that would prohibit the use of corporal punishment in Texas public schools.
_____	_____	5. Legislation that would ensure that pregnant women have full access to prenatal care.
_____	_____	6. Legislation that would ensure that children in need receive regular preventive health care and treatment.
_____	_____	7. Include funding in Texas' budget to supplement federal funds for Head Start.
_____	_____	8. Include funding to supplement federal funds for the Supplemental Food Program for Women, Infants and Children (WIC).
_____	_____	9. Legislation increasing the availability of affordable, quality childcare, preschool, and early childhood development programs.

_____ _____ 10. Legislation that opposes mandatory HIV testing of all health care workers who perform invasive procedures.

_____ _____ 11. A state income tax in order to adequately fund state services.

_____ _____ 12. Increased funding for the Texas Department of Human Services Child Protective Services Unit to hire professional social workers in order to provide higher quality services to children at risk and raise the minimum standards of training and qualifications for frontline workers.

_____ _____ 13. In the event the Supreme Court overturns Roe v. Wade, legislation protecting the freedom of choice and access to reproductive health care for women and families.

_____ _____ 14. Legislation that increases the availability of affordable housing in the state.

_____ _____ 15. Legislation amending the Texas Commission on Human Rights Act of 1991 and requiring state agencies to implement affirmative action programs and workforce diversity programs.

_____ _____ 16. Making a substantial investment in initiatives to reform and improve services to children and families involved in protective services, mental health, and the juvenile justice system.

On a separate piece of paper, please answer the following questions:

1. If elected, (a) what would be your main legislative priorities, and (b) what committee assignments would you seek?
2. Are you, any member of your family, or a close personal friend a professional social worker?
3. Many of the health care licensing and certification acts are under Sunset Review, and the legislature will have to re-enact these laws during the next regular session. Social work certification is one of the laws under Sunset Review. NASW/Texas is interested in strengthening this law by refining the definition of social work practice and regulating under the law only those practitioners who hold BSW and MSW degrees. Will you support the continued regulation of social workers? Would you support the narrowing of the law to only regulate social workers who hold professional degrees? Would you support a license for social workers?

_____

Source: National Association of Social Workers/Texas PACE Candidate Questionnaire, 1992.

room for a volunteer to perform an array of tasks—answering phones, preparing bulk mailings, putting up yard signs, conducting social media campaigns, and canvassing neighborhoods.

Social workers, in particular, can contribute many skills typical of their profession to a political campaign. These include planning, decision making, consensus building, group management, research, assessment, relationship building, crisis intervention, and communication. In terms of roles, or functions, that social workers perform, eight are appropriate for political campaigns (see Table 3).

The following are a few simple things that social workers can do to strengthen the presence of the social work profession in a political campaign:

- ◆ *Volunteer at a campaign headquarters.* Traditionally a campaign begins on Labor Day and concludes with the general election in November, generally a ten- to eleven-week period. But now it seems that this traditional election cycle has been thrown away. The day after President Obama was reelected in 2012, political pundits were already prediciting who would be in the running for the Democtraic and Republican nominations in 2014!
- ◆ A campaign relies on volunteers to staff an office, with much of the work taking place during evenings and on weekends. You might organize ten to

Table 3. Beyond Voting—What Can a Social Worker Do in a Political Campaign?

Role	Tasks
Advocate	Speaks on behalf of the candidate and represents his or her position to various constituent groups
Teacher/educator	Instructs staff and volunteers about campaign strategy and issues; in conjunction with advocacy, educates potential supporters about the candidate
Mobilizer	Energizes staff and volunteers; prioritizes and assigns individuals to needed campaign activities
Consultant	Provides expertise in problem solving and strategizing; helps candidate and staff to develop strategies for the campaign
Planner	Identifies key community players and activities; assesses strengths of potential relationships and overall prospects for electoral victory
Caregiver	Provides emotional support to candidate, his family, friends, staff, and supporters (relations can become strained)
Data manager	Develops and implements a data structure that allows for quick and easy access; designs a user friendly system for staff, volunteers, and candidate
Administrator	Develops and implements a well-operating campaign structure that is functional and not overwhelming; keeps the structure simple, efficient, and consistent with the candidate's best interests

fifteen social workers and commit to providing a volunteer for one night each week at the campaign office for the duration of the campaign. Say you select Tuesday evening; this can become known as *Social Work Night* to the candidate and key staff. The potential value to future lobbying efforts of even such a brief commitment is incalculable. The candidate will be much more open and sympathetic to a group that worked throughout the campaign.

◆ *Make your own social work buttons and t-shirts.* Make a modest investment to purchase buttons or t-shirts printed with a simple slogan. Social workers for (candidate's name)—what an effective message! Be sure to wear the buttons or t-shirts on Social Work Night/Day at the campaign office. Let others know who you are and where you stand.

◆ *Host a fund-raiser.* All candidates need money to run a campaign. A bare-bones efficient run for the state house costs at least $100,000, and these costs continue to escalate with each new electoral cycle. Plan a fund-raising event with other social workers. Be sure to coordinate the event with the candidate's campaign staff—there is usually one person who is responsible for scheduling the candidate's time. Make the event brief—the candidate has no extra time during the heat of a campaign and often needs to be in four places at once. Try to make the event fun as well. Be creative. For example, one interesting fund-raiser was a *non-event fund-raiser*; people donated $25.00 not to attend! If you host an event with the candidate present, be sure to wear your buttons or t-shirts.

◆ *Work on election day.* Election day is the longest day in the campaign. With polls opening as early as 6:00 a.m. in some states and closing as late as 8:00 p.m., campaign volunteers work up to eighteen hours! Volunteers are needed to work near the polling places, passing out candidate literature; to put up last-minute candidate yard signs; to provide voters with transportation to the polls (be sure to wear your buttons or t-shirts and to talk about your candidates with those you are driving); and to staff the campaign office, answering phones and dealing with last-minute glitches and crises. When the polls close, go to the candidate's headquarters or wherever the party is being held. You deserve to celebrate after all the energy you've put into the campaign. And be sure to wear your buttons or t-shirts.

◆ *Help with social media.* The power of social media in the political world is only in its infancy in 2014. The 2008 Obama presidential campaign is credited with being the first presidential campaign to effectively use e-mail and other related technologies on a national scale. Political organizers are becoming more savvy about the diverse uses of social media. For example, in September 2014, the Republican National Committee launched a new Voter Challenge Facebook application. Although the traditional door-to-door campaigning, handing out literature, and putting up yard signs will remain a significant part of the electoral process, social media are fast becoming the quickest and most nimble way to communicate with current and prospective supporters.

Lobbying for Social Work Legislation

Lobbying is an act of persuasion in which you educate someone about an issue with the goal of gaining active support. According to the Center for Responsive Politics (2014a), in 2014 there were 11,800 lobbyists registered to persuade and educate the U.S. Congress and the various federal agencies. That's slightly more than 22 lobbyists for each of the 535 members of the U.S. Congress (100 Senators and 435 members of the House of Representatives). You might think that's a lot of people who are paid to influence (e.g., lobby) the U.S. Congress. Yes, it is, but there are far fewer lobbyists (25 percent less) in 2014 than in 2007 when there were 14,837 registered lobbyists. But these numbers are only for the federal government! Every state, county, and city/town government also has its own sets of lobbyists. According to the *Texas Tribune*, 1,706 lobbyists were registered with the state's Ethics Commission in 2013 (Chang & Stiles, 2013). So what is it all these individuals who are paid hundreds of millions of dollars by their clients to lobby have in common? They are the experts with key information and acccess to support, both financial and people. And you too can be a lobbyist with specialized information around a specific social issue.

Lobbying takes many different forms in the attempt to find the best way to communicate a clear and persistent message. Typical activities include writing letters, making telephone calls, making personal visits, and giving public testimony. Each is an effective and important part of the lobbying process. With computer technology, letter writing is not very difficult—a mass mailing to the legislature doesn't take too much longer to compose than a single letter. Telephone calls may be more costly, especially if you don't live in the state capital, but they take far less time. Both e-mails and comments posted on an elected official's web page or Facebook page are quick and easy. Personal visits are expensive if you don't live in or near the state capital, and they also require a great deal of time for what are generally brief meetings, but face-to-face meetings are effective. Remember that elected officals have local offices and you can meet with them there if you are not able to travel to the state capitol. No matter which form of lobbying you select, be sure to be brief, dignified, sincere, and, most important, respectful.

Name: Susan Collins

Place of residence: Washington, DC

College/university degrees: BS, Georgetown University; MSW, University of Houston, Grad College of Social Work

Present position: Chief of Staff to Congressman Luis V. Gutierrez (IL-04)

What do you do in your spare time? I spend most of my spare time with my husband and our eight-year-old daughter. Our weekends are spent over leisurely, full breakfasts and experiencing the city of DC. In the summer we travel some and keep a vegetable garden and in the winter we ski a lot. I'm also a bit of a news junkie and can get lost in a good AMC or Netflix series.

Why did you choose social work as a career? Right after college I spent a year in Nicaragua and another year on the U.S.-Mexico border doing volunteer work, and then worked mentoring other volunteers at the Jesuit Volunteer Corps. Those few years were exceptionally formative for me. After such meaningful experiences with community organizing and human rights and social justice work, I knew a life in public service focused on social change was the life for me. Getting my MSW was a natural next step.

What is your favorite social work story? I could fill a book with humbling and inspiring stories of immigrants who, despite having faced violence, discrimination, and indescribable injustice, are happy and contribute so much to their communities. But my favorite story is still being told; it's the one we are all living in right now, the story of the immigrant civil rights movement. It is hugely rewarding to work with Congressman Luis Gutiérrez and play a role in the struggle for legalization and citizenship for the millions of immigrants contributing to our country, but living in the shadows as second- and third-class individuals. Social workers have an important role to play in this narrative on multiple levels, from community organizing and policy advocacy, to direct services and support. And the work will be with us for decades. Imagine, for example, the kind of support our communities will need now that millions of parents have been deported and hundreds of thousands of U.S. citizens are growing up in the U.S. without their parents, many of them in foster care. And once we finally achieve legalization for millions, imagine the work and advocacy required to ensure them access to U.S. citizenship and full voting rights. This will be an important story to tell our grandchildren.

What would be the one thing you would change in our community if you had the power to do so? I would hope to help people to see their neighbors as they see themselves. The truth is that we rise and fall together as a community, as a city, as a state, as a nation, and as a planet. We must operationalize the Golden Rule of "Do unto others . . ." whether that is in terms of politics, policy, or how we treat each other when stuck in a long line or gridlocked traffic. If we all allow each other the courtesy and consideration we hope others give us and our children, we can solve many problems in our community. Following the Golden Rule, we would better welcome the immigrant stranger, embrace same-sex marriage in every state, provide equal pay for equal work, remove obstacles to full voting rights, etc.

Letter Writing. Write early, before the legislator has made up his/her mind. Write a letter of one page or less; legislators don't have time to read dissertations! Get to the point quickly and be concise. Attach handouts to support the key points. Make sure you educate, educate, and educate the legislator on the issue. If you are writing about a specific bill, be sure to include the bill number. Note how the legislation will affect the legislator's district, mention the names of key supporters of your position from the district or from the legislator's campaign, provide reasons to support the bill, and request an answer to your letter indicating how the legislator plans to vote on the issue. Be sure to say thank you at the beginning and end of the letter, and be sure to use the appropriate salutation (see box 3). Be sure to get your agency's written permission before using its letterhead for a letter. Using letterhead indicates that you are writing on behalf of the agency or, at a minimum, that your views reflect those of the organization.

A typical but not useful letter-writing strategy is the postcard approach. This involves using preaddressed postcards with a prewritten message that requires the person only to sign her or his name. This does not work, nor do duplicated copies of the same letter with a signature line. Politicans know that people have not taken time to share their views and that this is a quick and dirty mail method. The basic lesson is that mass duplicated mailings are a 100-percent waste of time and energy. Write a personal handwritten note; this is your most effective strategy and your best bet to be heard.

E-mail. Now all elected officials have websites that post a variety of information, including a *contact us* section. This is useful if you organize a large group to send a series of e-mails in concert with a letter-writing campaign. But if you plan on writing one e-mail to let off steam, well that's about all that will happen—you'll let off steam but nothing much will happen. Oh, you will probably get two e-mail responses. The first one will come back almost immediately, thanking you for writing the senator or representative. You might get a second e-mail a month or so later, maybe sooner, thanking you "for sharing your views." You might be fortunate enough to get the personal e-mail address of an elected official. If so, use it

Box 3. Salutations for Letter Writing

Governor

1. Writing:
   The Honorable (full name)
   Governor of (State)
   Address: Dear Governor (last name)

2. Speaking: Governor (last name)

Lieutenant Governor

1. Writing:
   The Honorable (full name)
   Lieutenant Governor of (state)
   Address: Dear Lieutenant Governor (last name)

2. Speaking: Lieutenant Governor (last name)

Speaker of the House

1. Writing:
   The Honorable (full name)
   Speaker of the House
   Address: Dear Mr./Madame Speaker:

2. Speaking: Mr./Madame Speaker

State Senator

1. Writing:
   The Honorable (full name)
   The (State) State Senate
   Address: Dear Senator (last name)

2. Speaking: Senator (last name)

State Representative

1. Writing:
   The Honorable (full name)
   The (State) House of Representatives
   Address: Dear Mr./Ms. (last name)

2. Speaking: Representative (last name) or Mr./Ms. (last name)

sparingly unless the elected person tells you otherwise, and certainly do not give it out to others.

As with letter writing, be sure to get your agency approval before sending any e-mails to an elected official.

Telephone Calls. You'll probably talk with a legislative aide, so don't take it personally if you don't speak with the legislator. Also, if there is a phone blitz on the bill you're calling about, the aide may be rather short with you and may cut you off in the middle of your presentation. Again, don't take it personally.

Be brief and to the point; try to take less than three minutes. Make notes before you call and practice what you want to say. Introduce yourself and mention your address, especially if you are from the legislator's home district. Follow the same principles as in letter writing: identify the bill number and describe how it will affect the legislator's district. Ask how the legislator plans to vote on the issue; if the person you speak to doesn't know, ask when you can call back to learn of the decision. End by thanking the legislator or aide for his time and support.

Personal Visits. Personal visits are probably the most time consuming, frustrating, and potentially the most effective form of lobbying. Meetings are as a rule very brief, lasting from a few minutes to no more than fifteen. They usually take place in the legislator's office, but don't be surprised if you find yourself walking down the hall to accompany the representative or senator to a meeting while you lobby for a few short minutes. Most often you'll meet with an aide, but if you have a good relationship with the legislator—in particular, if you were a good campaign volunteer—you'll probably be able to meet with him or her. You'll need to be pleasant, brief, concise, and convincing. Discuss only one legislative issue during your meeting. Be sure to follow up with a phone call and a letter of appreciation.

These meetings may be short, but many social workers have found that they have been able to change a politician's stance on an issue as a result of a face-to-face meeting. Your sincerity, knowledge, and compassion about the issue speak volumes to politicians.

Guest Speakers. Check with your faculty to have them invite elected officials to your school, maybe for a class lecture or a noon presentation. Most elected officials enjoy visiting with college students and try to work in the time if at all possible. Such visits provide a wonderful opportunity to develop a relationship with an elected official as well as for him/her to learn more about social work. There is one basic rule of thumb for such visits—do not get into arguments. Listen, be courteous, and most of all remember that you are representing the social work profession.

Public Testimony. In general, when considering legislation, a committee must allow opportunities for public input. Such testimony usually lasts less than five minutes per speaker. The committee will have rules that govern the testimony's length—check them out beforehand by contacting the committee's staff person in the legislative offices.

Be sure that your testimony is in a typed or word processed format, distribute copies to the committee members, and have a few extra copies available for others who are interested in your comments. Be sure your name, address, and phone numbers are easily found on the cover page of your testimony in case someone wishes to get in touch with you after the hearing. This is important because you may not have time to get all of your ideas across; the written testimoney allows you to do so. In effect, your public testimoney is an abstract or abbreviated version of your wrritten statement.

As with writing letters and sending e-mails, be sure to get your agency's approval. Your agency may ask that you refrain from referencing your employment or they may encourage you to do so. Again, always check with your supervisor or agency executive director prior to giving any testimoney at a hearing.

Don't be surprised if the legislators ask you no questions after your presentation. There may be twenty to thirty people offering testimony, each speaking three to five minutes. Asking questions only prolongs the process. If a question is asked, be sure of your answers. Don't make up an answer; if you aren't sure what the answer is, tell the committee you'll find out and get back to its staff person within twenty-four hours. And be sure you do! Nothing is more damaging to your credibility in the legislature than to give inaccurate or misleading information or to make a promise and not follow up.

Finally, don't argue with the legislators! You are a guest in their workplace. You are there to convince and make friends, not to argue and make enemies. Your legislative opponent today may be your key supporter tomorrow on another issue. Try not to burn your bridges but rather build and strengthen them.

COMMUNITY ORGANIZATION: LINKING THE POLITICAL TO THE COMMUNITY

To best link the political to the needs of the community, a strategy must first be outlined. By strategy we mean the action options that are open to the social worker to help reach the change goals identified. Rothman, Erlich, and Tropman (1995) remind us to start by researching the history and the evolution of strategies that have been applied in the past. After all, the old adage "history can repeat itself" can complicate any type of intervention plan. Second, the social worker must explore the societal climate or environment. What is important to the individuals who live in the community? What are the values, the norms, and the expectations of the constituents to be served? To discover this, the community itself must be examined. The stakeholders must be identified. Small groups, both formal (such as church members) and informal (such as neighborhood support systems), within this community will affect the change efforts to be implemented. These players must be identified and all efforts must be made to ensure that their needs are addressed. In community organizations, the needs and wishes of the community always provide the cornerstone for all helping efforts. Therefore, it is important not to have helping efforts thwarted by individual or institutional agendas that do not operate for the best efforts of the community. To completely describe the fundamentals of this type of practice is beyond the scope of this chapter. Although it is a critical part of social work macropractice, a beginning social worker is encouraged to obtain more specialized training and education before engaging in this type of practice.

SUMMARY

Weismiller and Rome (1995, p. 2312) note that "despite residual skepticism about the appropriateness of political work, there has been a resurgence of political action in recent years" among social workers. Courses in schools of social work, ongoing efforts by national and state PACE units, direct participation in political campaigns, and election of social workers to political office are among the many ways social workers are developing much-needed political savvy.

We have learned through many, often painful, experiences that attempts to influence the development of public policy must begin well before the legislative process. Identifying and working for the election of people who are in favor of human services initiates the lobbying effort; having the right people in place makes lobbying that much easier.

Moreover, elected officials are influenced by groups that "vote regularly and are active in the electoral process" (Parker & Sherraden, 1992, p. 27). Social workers and their membership organizations are making significant contributions to political campaigns. As campaign workers, social workers are able to translate their agency-based practice expertise to the political arena.

The years since 2001 have been tumultuous at best. Wars and economic crisis overshadowed all efforts, no matter the profession or ideological beliefs. Trillions of dollars were spent to reenergize the American economy, pay for the ongoing wars, and fund antiterrorism efforts while, at the same time, the nation's debt grew to unprecedented levels. The continued wars in the Middle East and the ongoing terrorism threats drove much of the political discourse in 2014 and certainly will do so for years to come.

But what of social welfare? How do we solve our most perplexing internal problems? Will funding cuts to the Affordable Health Care Act of 2010 become reality following the fall 2016 national elections and beyond? Will full funding for public education continue to be kept at bay? Will the Congress establish proactive immigration reform that strengthens and extends individual civil liberties to all people? Will new laws expand hate crime statutes? Will Congress create a living wage law rather than continuing to support the minimum wage statutes?

Social work students too will be challenged when they move into the practice world. Current and future social workers must have knowledge and skills in economic and financial literacy, not just around macro policy issues, but in the day-to-day work with those whose homes are in foreclosure, those who have lost their jobs, or retirees whose fixed incomes and pension plans have been devastated.

Even with the daunting global circumstances swirling around us, social workers must pursue legislative agenda for social work education. Social work education must advocate for new ways to increase and broaden access to higher education through new fellowship and scholarship programs; seek ways to strengthen existing loans, create new loan forgiveness programs, advocate for the full and complete funding of Pell Grants, and seek to repair the faulty federal student loan assistance program; and argue for the deepening and expansion of funding streams to our colleges and universities to ensure that the necessary financial support is available for our programs to address their missions in the education of undergraduate and graduate social work students.

Social work practice is directly affected by politics. We cannot ignore this simple reality. Every two years, close to a half million offices are up for election, involving hundreds of thousands of candidates. These individuals represent the broad spectrum of political ideology and views of humankind. Sadly, the vast majority of these individuals are not social workers. Although the number of social workers holding elected office increased significantly over the past quarter of a century, policy decisions are, for the most part, made by non-social-workers and those with little knowledge of the human condition. These uninformed and often misinformed elected individuals will continue to influence the work in our social service agencies.

Social workers face a simple choice: to remain on the sidelines while others make decisions that determine how the social service community operates or to participate aggressively at all levels of political activity in order to open the door for progressive lobbying efforts. Simply put, social workers can sit in the audience watching others or they can be pivotal actors who build on the rich experiences of political campaigns.

REFERENCES

Center for Responsive Politics. (2014a). *Lobbying database.* Retrieved from http://www.open secrets.org/lobby

Center for Responsive Politics. (2014b). *Top PACs.* Retrieved from http://www.opensecrets.org/pacs/toppacs.php?Type=C&cycle=2014&Pty=A

Chang, C., & Stiles, M. (2013, April 1). Texas lobbying spending. *The Texas Tribune.* Retrieved from http://www.texastribune.org/library/data/lobbying

Colby, I., & Buffum, W. (1998). Social work and political action committees. *Journal of Community Practice, 5*(4), 87–103.

Council on Social Work Education. (2008). *Educational policy and accreditation standards.* Alexandria, VA: Author.

Dempsey, D. (1993, March 10). *Letter to chapter presidents.* Washington, DC: NASW Press.

Downey, K. (2010). *The woman behind the new deal, the life and legacy of Frances Perkins, social security, unemployment insurance, and the minimum wage.* New York: Anchor Books.

Haynes, K., & Mickelson, J. S. (2002). *Affecting change, social workers in the political arena* (5th ed.). Boston: Allyn & Bacon.

Haynes, K. S., & Mickelson, J. S. (2009*). Affecting change, social workers in the political arena* (7th ed.). New York: Pearson

Hiratsuka, J. (1992). 114 more races backed. *NASW News, 37*(9), 1, 10.

Landers, S. (1992). NASW steps up efforts to elect Clinton. *NASW News, 37*(9), 1.

Liptak, A. (2014, April 2). Supreme Court strikes down overall political donation cap. *New York Times.* Retrieved from http://www.nytimes.com/2014/04/03/us/politics/supreme-court-ruling-on-campaign-contributions.html?_r=0

Mahaffey, M., & Hanks, J. (Eds.). (1982). *Practical politics and social work and political responsibility.* Silver Spring, MD: NASW Press.

National Association of Social Workers. (n.d.). NASW—PACE Tipsheet. Washington, DC: Author.

National Association of Social Workers. (2008). *Code of ethics of the National Association of Social Workers.* Washington, DC: Author. Retrieved from http://www.socialworkers.org/pubs/code/code.asp

National Association of Social Workers. (2013). *Social workers in Congress, 113th Congress.* Washington, DC: NASW.

National Association of Social Workers. (2014). *Social Workers in elected office.* Retrieved from https://www.socialworkers.org/pace/state.asp

Parker, M., & Sherraden, M. (1992). Electoral participation of social workers. *New England Journal of Human Services, 11*(3), 23–28.

Richman, W. (1991). *Lobbying for social change.* New York: Haworth.

Rothman, J., Erlich, J. L., & Tropman, J. E. (1995). *Strategies for community intervention.* Itasca, IL: Peacock.

Weismiller, T., & Rome, S. H. (1995). Social workers in politics. In R. L. Edwards et al. (Eds.), *Encyclopedia of social work* (19th ed., pp. 2305–2313). Washington, DC: NASW Press.

Wolk, J. (1981). Are social workers politically active? *Social Work, 26,* 283–288.

PART FOUR

EXPANDING HORIZONS FOR SOCIAL WORK

CHAPTER 14
GLOBAL SOCIAL WELFARE

OUR WORLD IS A GLOBAL COMMUNITY. WE NEED TO ALWAYS REMEMber to think of our world on a large scale. Our interests, concerns, influences, and obligation relate to a community that extends far beyond the confines of our geographic neighborhood. As in the past, we continue to call this phenomenon *globalization,* with the creation of an international system that affects domestic economies, politics, and cultures (Midgley, 1997).

Most of us would agree that we live in a global neighborhood. Friedman's (2005) classic work *The World is Flat* vividly describes the shrinking world and shows how our nations' borders have virtually disappeared. Technology has opened the doors to new possibilities for peoples throughout the world. E-mail allows us to communicate in a manner unthought-of at the beginning of the 1990s. Now we can only wonder what the world will look like by 2025.

Twentieth-century history has shown how regional conflicts and disasters can quickly escalate into global issues. The Great Depression of the 1930s, for example, was felt worldwide and not only in the United States where the early effects were concentrated. Later in the 1930s, after the German and Japanese war machines had conquered many of their neighbors, the United States, which had originally assumed an isolationist position, became one of the leading allied nations. The collapse of the Berlin Wall in November 1989 signaled upheavals in many Communist bloc nations that have had significant social and economic consequences around the world. In 2014 the Russian Federation annexed parts of the Ukraine in an attempt to begin the rebuilding of the former Russian empire (Shoichet, 2014). In 1998, weakening in the Asian and Russian economies led to stock market gyrations in the financial centers of the world. And in late 2008 and well into 2009, the weakening global economy reverberated throughout world. The rise of terrorist groups around the world continues to threaten global stability. Boko Haram, which forbids Western style education for women, operates in different parts of Africa and is probably most known for its kidnapping of 276 female students in April 2014. The seemingly sudden rise in 2014 of the Islamic State, more commonly referred to as ISIS or ISIL, in the Middle East threatens people throughout the world as the United States seeks to build a global coalition to counter these threats. Certainly, other examples of global events exist, but the message is clear: what happens across the oceans affects all of us, no matter where we live.

Did You Know...In 2014 nearly 800 women died every day due to complications in pregnancy and childbirth.

We also can learn from other societies and cultures about how to strengthen our own approach to social living. We can study how other countries approach social problems and think about how their successful strategies may work in our communities. Some people believe that the United States has nothing to learn from the rest of the world about technology, education, and other social advancements, but this is not true! As reported by Midgley (1995), "social scientists agree that knowledge can be increased by investigating phenomena in other societies and by testing propositions in different social, economic, and cultural contexts" (p. 1490). The study of international social welfare is an imperative that will move us beyond our many self-imposed barriers and allow all of us to be better off in a cooperative world community.

Did You Know...In 2012, more than 140,000 people in high-income countries had pertussis (whooping cough), a serious disease in infants that is preventable by vaccination.

Despite their awareness of the ever changing world community and their recognition of its importance in our daily lives, American social workers have been ambivalent in their commitment to the international arena. In fact, Midgley (1997, p. 63) contends that the profession is not fully prepared to meet international challenges and opportunities and must be more aggressive in benefiting from international opportunities. In other words, just as the world experiences globalization, so too must the social work profession.

Did You Know...The global population was 2.8 billion in 1955 and was 7.1 billion in 2014. Estimates indicate that the world population will reach 9.6 billion by the year 2050.

In this chapter we will touch on the many international facets of social work. Although we cannot delve into details of cultural differences and economic and demographic trends, we hope to raise your awareness of these issues. By the end of the chapter you'll recognize that social work is a global profession, facing the persistent challenge of promoting social and economic justice.

HOW DO WE COMPARE DIFFERENT NATIONS?

A general question that seems simple enough to answer is how many nations are there in the world? We could look at the United Nations (UN), but not all nations are UN members. We could search the web to see what comes up—why not do that now and see what number you find? For example, when this sentence was being written on September 22, 2014, a web search came up with a number of answers ranging from 192 (UN count) to 243! These numbers include 93 members of the UN (with an additional two so-called *observer states*), 204 eligible Olympic nations, 209 Fédération Internationale de Football Association World Cup soccer nations, and 249 country codes.

What are the numbers now? Look at this website and compare the numbers: http://www.polgeonow.com/2011/04/how-many-countries-are-there-in-world.html (How many countries, 2015).

A second point to consider is that the world's nation states are not static but susceptible to change. A nation emerges in any number of ways, from the spoils of war to a nation giving up its governance over land. Enriquez (2005, pp. 22–23) reminds us that, in 1909, about one hundred years ago, the British Empire included 11.5 million square miles, which was 20 percent of the world's land mass—this led to the saying that the "sun never sets on the British Empire." Yet, within fifty years, the British Empire has shrunk by more than 11.4 million square miles to about 94,248 square miles. And let us not forget that in 1991 the Union of Soviet Socialist Republics splintered into Russia and fourteen other republics. And who is to say that the United States will always consist of fifty states; maybe Puerto Rico and/or Guam will join the country at some point in time. Remember that Hawaii and Alaska joined the United States in 1959. Illustrating the point of changing borders and new countries forming, Enriquez (2005, p.25) notes that there has yet to be a U.S. president who was buried under the same flag under which he was born; in other words, the addition of new states changed the number of stars on the U.S. flag.

To make international comparisons, it is helpful to have a framework for grouping nations based on similarities. Otherwise, comparisons may not be meaningful and can lead to inaccurate conclusions. For example, there is little that can be learned by comparing the economic systems of the United States and Nepal. The vast political, economic, social, historical, and cultural differences between these two nations make such a comparison virtually impossible.

Did You Know...Between 2000 and 2012, measles deaths worldwide have were reduced by almost 80%—from 562,000 to 122,000 deaths.

One framework is based on a nation's technological level, which incorporates three tiers: preindustrial, industrial, and postindustrial (Bell, 1973). This framework can be visualized as a core with circles, or concentric zones, surrounding the core. Core nations include those in Western Europe and North America; a second group of nations surround the core, which then is encircled by the outermost group of nations (Chatterjee, 1996). The second group of nations includes former Communist countries and various nations in Asia and South America; the outermost ring includes the remaining Asian and South American countries and Africa. Chatterjee called these three groups of nations the First World, the Second World, and the Third World (see box 1).

The World Bank, an international organization that promotes economic development and productivity to raise the standard of living in less developed nations, uses a different framework. The World Bank categorizes nations into six regions: South Asia, Middle East and North Africa, Latin America and the Caribbean, Europe and Central Asia, East Asia and the Pacific, and the Africa Region (see box 2).

It is important to be sensitive to our use of words and how they may be interpreted by others. For example, what does it mean to be called *developed* versus *undeveloped*? Even more importantly, what are we implying when we call a nation undeveloped or even underdeveloped? Are we holding that country to our standards or their standards? At best this reference is paternalistic and at worst it suggests cultural elitism.

Box 1. The World System

First World: Also known as the core, includes North America, Western Europe, Australia, and Japan. It is wealthy, capitalist, industrial, and based on the traditions of a market economy and individualism.

Second World: Somewhat outside the core, it consists of Eastern Europe, Central and Northern Asia, and Cuba. It is neither wealthy nor poor and it is socialist, selectively industrial, and based on the traditions of a planned economy and collectivism. A substantial part of the Second World has been attempting to convert to a market economy since 1991.

Third World: It includes nations mostly in Africa, southern and Southeast Asia, and South America. It is mostly poor, often nationalist, selectively industrial to preindustrial, and based on a mixed economy and regional loyalty.

Source: Chatterjee (1996, p. 46).

Box 2. Regions of the World as Defined by the World Bank

South Asia: Afghanistan, Bangladesh, Bhutan, India, Maldives, Nepal, Pakistan, Sri Lanka.

Middle East and North Africa: Algeria, Bahrain, Egypt, Iran, Jordan, Kuwait, Lebanon, Morocco, Oman, Qatar, Saudi Arabia, Syrian Arab Republic, Tunisia, Yemen, United Arab Emirates.

Latin America and the Caribbean: Antigua and Barbuda, Argentina, Belize, Bolivia, Chile, Colombia, Costa Rica, Dominica, Dominican Republic, Ecuador, El Salvador, Grenada, Guatemala, Guyana, Haiti, Honduras, Jamaica, Mexico, Nicaragua, Panama, Paraguay, Peru, St. Kitts and Nevis, St. Lucia, St. Vincent and the Grenadines, Suriname, Trinidad and Tobago, Uruguay, Venezuela.

Europe and Central Asia: Albania, Armenia, Azerbaijan, Belarus, Bosnia and Herzegovina, Bulgaria, Croatia, Czech Republic, Estonia, Georgia, Hungary, Kazakhstan, Kyrgyz Republic, Latvia, Lithuania, Former Yugoslav Republic of Macedonia, Moldova, Poland, Romania, Russian Federation, Slovak Republic, Slovenia, Tajikistan, Turkey, Turkmenistan, Ukraine, Uzbekistan.

East Asia and the Pacific: Cambodia, China, Fiji, Indonesia, Kiribati, Korea, Lao People's Democratic Republic, Malaysia, Marshall Islands, Federated States of Micronesia, Mongolia, Myanmar, Palau, Papua New Guinea, Philippines, Samoa, Solomon Islands, Thailand, Tonga, Vanuatu, Vietnam.

Africa: Angola, Benin, Botswana, Burkina Faso, Burundi, Cameroon, Cape Verde, Central African Republic, Chad, Comoros, Congo, Democratic Republic of Congo, Republic of Côte d'Ivoire, Djibouti, Equatorial Guinea, Eritrea, Ethiopia, Gabon, Gambia, Ghana, Guinea, Guinea-Bissau, Kenya, Lesotho, Liberia, Madagascar, Malawi, Mali, Mauritania, Mauritius, Mozambique, Namibia, Niger, Rwanda, São Tomé and Principe, Senegal, Seychelles, Sierra Leone, Somalia, South Africa, Sudan, Swaziland, Tanzania, Togo, Uganda, Zambia, Zimbabwe.

Question: *What countries are missing from the list and why?* Connect with the World Bank's web page (www.worldbank.org) for additional information and read the organization's purpose for the answer.

Source: The World Bank. (2015). Retrieved from http://www.worldbank.org/en/country

---

We've described two frameworks here, but there are a number of alternative approaches to comparing nations. For example, another model speaks of nations in the north and the south, using the equator as a global dividing line. What we want to accomplish is to organize the world's countries to facilitate discussions that are consistent and appropriate. In other words, we want to compare apples with apples, not apples with peaches!

Let's use Chatterjee's classification to demonstrate how a framework can be applied to make international comparisons. As shown in box 3, Chatterjee identified social issues and then tabulated how the First, Second, and Third Worlds respond to them. Chatterjee (1996, p. 78) also went a step farther by asking the following questions about the three worlds and then compiling responses, listed in box 4:

1. Once a person has been socially defined as unemployable, can he/she ask the state for help?

2. Once a person has been socially defined as employable but is unemployed, can he/she ask the state for support?

3. Once a person has been socially defined as employed but is marginally employed, can he/she ask the state for support?

4. If the state is providing support, is it means tested?

5. If the state is providing support, it is related to past or potential earnings?

6. If the state is providing support, it is a flat rate or with a minimum or maximum or is it linked to an index of fluctuating living costs?

7. Is the state committed to seeing that each citizen receives a basic package of health care, or has it engaged other qualified parties to do so?

8. Is the state committed to seeing that each citizen receives a basic education? If so, has it set up a formal structure to provide such education itself, or has it engaged other qualified parties to do so?

9. Is the state committed to seeing that each citizen receives basic housing? If so, has it set up a formal structure to provide such housing, or has it engaged other parties to do so?

10. Is the state committed to providing protection to various vulnerable groups (children, elderly, developmentally disabled, and mentally ill)? If so, has it set up a formal structure to provide such protection, or has it engaged other qualified parties to do so?

Did you know...In 2014 China's population was estimated to be 1,390,510,630 persons and the Pitcairn Islands had the smallest population of 36 people.

Box 3. Welfare Trends on Selected Issues in the Three Worlds

Issue	First World	Second World	Third World
Housing	Public housing for the poor; some rent control or subsidy	Rationed housing for all	No such concept
Education	Supported; often uneven in various localities and regions of a country	State supported	State efforts do not reach all
Income	Almost all countries	Almost all countries	Minimal with largest number of people living on less than $2 every day
Health care	Almost all countries; rising costs	Almost all countries; supplies and equipment problematic	Crisis-based care to the poor from charitable clinics and hospitals

Box 4. Comparison of Eleven Welfare State Variables

Question	First World	Second World	Third World
1	Yes	Mostly yes	Mostly no
2	Yes	Mostly yes	No
3	Mostly yes	Mostly yes	No
4	Mostly yes	Mostly yes	Does not apply
5	Mostly yes	Mostly yes	Does not apply
6	Mostly yes	Mostly yes	Does not apply
7	Yes except in U.S.	Yes	No
8	Mostly yes	Mostly yes	No
9	Mostly yes	Yes	No
10	Yes	Mostly yes	No
11	Yes	Partly yes	Partly yes

Source: Chatterjee (1996, p. 80).

11. Have one or more occupational groups emerged within the state that are self-appointed advocates for vulnerable groups and are seeking increased professionalization?

> *Did You Know...The World Bank estimates that 900 million adults worldwide are illiterate. Four hundred million 6- to 17-year-olds are not in school and 225 million of them are girls.*

RECENT HAPPENINGS AND THE WORLD TODAY

The September 11, 2001, attacks on the United States marked a watershed moment in American history. The American people have traditionally been expected to adjust to new social environments, maintain good personal and occupational standing, and face pressures related to supporting friends and family. Americans, along with other people around the world, were shocked and stunned as the terrorist attacks of September 11, 2001, unfolded. Following the attacks, debates relating to terrorist activity within the United States and the vulnerabilities inherent within American society began to emerge. Fears that terrorists could cross America's extensive borders, the relative ease with which immigrants could disappear into American society, and the global and open nature of lifestyles Americans had come to depend upon left the society susceptible to terrorist threats and attacks (Dziegielewski & Kirven, in press).

Furthermore, threats of biological warfare proliferated. New measures were put in place ranging from color coding threat levels in U.S. airports to eavesdropping on phone calls of suspected terrorists. As we learned in 2013, the National Security Agency (NSA) had implemented global surveillance including accessing the telephone records of American citizens (Risen & Piotras, 2013).

But the fear of terrorism is not limited to the United States. It is felt in most nations around the world.

> *Did You Know...A baby is born every 8 seconds in the world.*

There are people in the Middle East who live in fear of terrorists threats each day. There are those in Israel who believe that the Hamas, a political group that believes Israel is an illegal nation, will at any moment attack and kill Israelis. The 2014 Israeli-Gaza conflict illustrates the level of fear and hatred felt on both sides. Israel attacked Gaza because Hamas continued to fire rockets into Israel. Hamas said the rockets were fired because Israel closed Gaza's borders to Israel; Israel justified its invasion because of the constant rocket attacks.

Since the astronauts first circled the moon and took one of the most exciting pictures of the planet Earth, there has been a growing awareness of the complexities that exist in our world. Landmark events such as this have helped to connect all people and nations economically and technologically in a way never before experienced.

According to the online world population clock that updates regularly, the earth is a very large home to some 7.1 billion people (U.S. Census Bureau, 2014). There is great diversity among the earth's people, governments, and experiences. And yet within this great diversity, despite the looming threats, there are common social problems that afflict people day in and day out. Poverty, homelessness, mental illness, inadequate housing, hunger, poor health care, physical violence, and neglect are among the many problems that know no geographic borders.

Did You Know...Approximately 35 million people were living with HIV in 2013.

Social problems are enormous from a worldwide perspective. According to the World Bank, 1.4 billion people live on less than $1.25 each day (2014). The World Bank also notes that the impact of the 2008 and 2009 global economic crisis continues to affect every nation. Not surprisingly, it finds that those nations with stronger economic structures will be less affected than those economies that were already weaker. Thus, the underdeveloped and developing nations in the world, those with the largest percentages of people in poverty, will be much more adversely affected.

Consider, for example, that, prior to the economic crisis of 2009, while poverty declined in parts of South Asia, and in the Middle East and North Africa, approximately 3 billion people lived on less than $2 each day. About one-third of the world's developing population is poor. In 2011, 20.3 million people in Africa lived with HIV/AIDS while 2.3 million children were HIV positive in 2009 (http://www.avert.org/africa-hiv-aids-statistics.htm). Earlier in 2002, Fleshman reported that 172 of every 1,000 African children died before reaching age five, 2.4 million African children under age fifteen were HIV positive, and 12.1 million African children were AIDS orphans (Fleshman, 2002); and according to Missionaries of Africa, in 2015 there are more than 34 million African orphans whose parents died from diseases such as AIDS, malaria and tuberculosis (http://www.missionariesofafrica.org/articles/sr/SpRptFall06.html).

Did You Know...Since 1985 the U.S. Congress has refused to authorize payment of the U.S. dues as a member nation of the United Nations.

Infant mortality rate is an indicator of a nation's health care, in particular, of its comprehensiveness and ability to cover the poor and non-poor alike. It counts the number of children under age one who die per 1,000 live births. According to UNICEF, which is sponsored by the UN, the number of children dying before their fifth birthday declined by nearly half between 1990 and 2013. Nevertheless, in 2013, 6.3 million children under age five died and 2.8 million newborn babies died within 28 days of their birth (United Nations Children's Fund, 2014, p. 1). Infant mortality has been and remains a significant global concern. For example, one of the UN's millennium goals was to reduce child mortality by two-thirds by the year 2015 (United Nations Children's Fund, 2014).

The following are some sobering numbers for you to consider. In 2014, the three nations with the highest infant mortality rate were Afghanistan, with an estimated 117 deaths per 1,000 births; Mali, with 104 deaths per 1,000 births; and Somalia, with 71 deaths per 1,000 births. Compare these numbers to those for the three nations with the lowest infant mortality rate: Monaco, with 1.8 deaths per 1,000 births; Japan, with 2.1 deaths per 1,000 births; and Bermuda, with 2.5 deaths per 1,000 births (UN, 2014). And in the United States, which ranked 169th out of 224 nations, the rate was 6.2 deaths per 1,000 births (Central Intelligence Agency, 2014a).

Life expectancy is a second indicator of a nation's well-being. Life expectancy is a numerical estimate of the average age a group of people will reach. Monaco has the longest life expectancy of nearly ninety years, followed by Macau, Japan, and Singapore, with a life expectancy of approximately eighty-four years (Central Intelligence Agency, 2014c). Life expectancy in the United States in 2014 was approaching eighty, with forty-one nations having higher expectancies (see Table 1). On the other extreme, Chad's life expectancy is the lowest in the world at forty-nine years, followed by South Africa and Guinea-Bissau, both with a life expectancy slightly higher than forty-nine years of age.

Death rates, the number of deaths per 1,000 people, also provide an important glimpse into a nation's well-being. In 2013, South Africa and Ukraine led the world in this tragic category with approximately 18 and 16 deaths per 1,000 persons, respectively; on the other hand, United Arab Emirates, Kuwait, Qatar, and Bahrain each report less than 3 deaths per 1,000 persons (Central Intelligence Agency, 2014b).

To be honest, it is sometimes very hard to fully understand and comprehend the meaning of such numbers. For a moment let's say you are in a university with a total of 15,000 students. During one year 91 students die—what do you think will be the public outcry? Clearly this would be a national and probably an international story, with all sorts of investigations taking place. Ninety-one deaths is the same as the U.S. infant mortality rate in 2014. But what if there were 1,755 deaths

Table 1. National Life Expectancies at Birth, Greater than U.S. Life Expectancy, 2014

Rank	Country	Life expectancy at birth* (years)
1	Monaco	89.57
2	Macau	84.48
3	Japan	84.46
4	Singapore	84.38
5	San Marino	83.18
6	Hong Kong	82.78
7	Andorra	82.65
8	Switzerland	82.39
9	Guernsey	82.39
10	Australia	82.07
11	Italy	82.03
12	Sweden	81.89
13	Liechtenstein	81.68
14	Canada	81.67
15	France	81.66
16	Jersey	81.66
17	Norway	81.60
18	Spain	81.47
19	Israel	81.28
20	Iceland	81.22
21	Anguilla	81.20
22	Netherlands	81.12
23	Bermuda	81.04
24	Cayman Islands	81.02
25	Isle of Man]	80.98
26	New Zealand	80.93
27	Ireland	80.56
28	Germany	80.44
29	United Kingdom	80.42
30	Greece	80.30
31	Saint Pierre and Miquelon	80.26
32	Austria	80.17
33	Malta	80.11
34	Faroe Islands	80.11
35	European Union	80.02
36	Luxembourg	80.01
37	Belgium	79.92
38	Taiwan	79.84
39	Korea, South	79.80
40	Virgin Islands	79.75
41	Finland	79.69
42	United States	79.56

Source: Central Intelligence Agency (2014b).

*The *World Factbook* states, "Life expectancy at birth compares the average number of years to be lived by a group of people born in the same year, if mortality at each age remains constant in the future. Life expectancy at birth is also a measure of overall quality of life in a country and summarizes the mortality at all ages."

in the same university of 15,000 students? The outcry would be horrific, with people labeling this a national scandal and calling for immediate safeguards and measures to be put in place so that this never happens again. These 1,755 deaths would be the equivalent of the infant mortality rate for Afghanistan in 2014.

For whatever reason, most Americans and social workers do not consider the world's health as their issue. Why? There are a number of possible reasons, but as a first step, we should recognize the scope and depth of social issues around the world. Once we develop this beginning awareness we can begin to initiate discussions with our global colleagues to determine what we can do together. But the first step rests with each of us to look outside the borders of the United States to gain an understanding of the human condition.

HOW DO WE LOOK AT INTERNATIONAL SOCIAL WELFARE?

The literature detailing international social welfare issues is, to say the least, interesting and stimulating. Consistent themes in international social welfare journals include peace and social justice, human rights, and social development. These areas are critical for all social workers to understand. In fact, the accreditation standards of the Council on Social Work Education (CSWE) require that these topics be included in both baccalaureate and graduate social work programs. Our fascination with international issues transcends our educational mandates, however, and is evident in our day-to-day conversations. How often have we heard people compare the United States with other countries? Typically, the conversation will include a statement such as "The poor in the United States have it easy compared with the poor in India." Statements of this sort form the basis of comparative social welfare discussions.

Midgley's (1995) work continues to be viewed as cutting edge in promoting locality-relevant approaches whose emphasis does not rely solely on Western-based assumptions. He identified five basic types of international social welfare studies:

1. Comparative studies of social need
2. Comparative studies of social policies and human services
3. Typologies of welfare states
4. Studies of the genesis and functions of social policy
5. Studies related to the future of the welfare state

Comparative studies of social need are reports that collect and assess a variety of social and economic data from different countries. These reports are usually quantitative in nature and present tabular data on a variety of topics. Typical studies include data on income, education, birth rates, poverty, and migration.

Comparative studies of social policies and human services are most often qualitative or descriptive presentations of issues. The topics explored are similar to those addressed by comparative studies of social needs, but the discussion includes analysis of political issues, funding patterns, eligibility standards, types of services, and provision or delivery of services.

Typologies of welfare states discuss the ideological and philosophical bases for the welfare systems of different countries. Typology studies, which are generally qualitative or descriptive, can shed light on a nation's view of people and social issues and, at the same time, provide important insight into the direction of its social welfare program. According to Midgley (1995), the most common typology is the Wilensky and Lebeaux conceptual model of residual versus institutional social welfare (see chapter 2 for a discussion of this framework).

Did You Know…More than 125 million girls and women alive in 2014 had suffered female genital mutilation (FGM) in the twenty-nine countries in Africa and the Middle East where FGM is concentrated. Female genital mutilation is viewed as a violation of women's human rights.

Studies of the genesis and functions of social policy are closely related to welfare typology studies. They focus on three areas: how welfare organizations emerged, what forces affect the development of social policy, and what are the functions of social policy in the society (Midgley, 1995). Such studies may be either quantitative or qualitative. They form the theoretical basis for social welfare endeavors.

Studies of the future of the welfare state have become more common recently. Midgley (1995) believed this increased popularity is in response to international criticism of social welfare and worldwide attempts to rethink national social welfare commitments and responsibilities. Such reports integrate the other four types of welfare studies and forecast the future.

INTERNATIONAL SOCIAL WELFARE ASSOCIATIONS

Many social work practitioners and students are surprised to learn that numerous long-standing social welfare associations exist around the world. The number of international social welfare associations greatly increased following World War II, primarily to help rebuild war-torn countries and to assist poor countries in gaining greater economic stability (Healy, 1995). Healy classified international associations into three groups: (1) UN structures, (2) U.S. government agencies, and (3) private voluntary bodies.

United Nations Structures

The UN was originally organized in 1945 by 51 nations to provide a forum to help to stabilize and maintain international relations and to give peace among nations a more secure foundation. By 2014, 193 nations were members plus two observer nations, the Holy See (or the Vatican) and Palestine. The newest member of the UN was Montenegro, which joined in 2006, the same year that it separated from Serbia.

The UN is probably most recognized for its peacekeeping forces, which have been deployed throughout the world to help mediate conflict. In addition to its peacekeeping mission, however, the UN conducts a variety of activities (fifty different areas are listed on its web page), with 80 percent of its work taking place in developing nations. Typical of these services are programs for AIDS, children, women, environmental protection, persons with disabilities, human rights, health and medical research and services, poverty and economic development, agricultural development, family planning, emergency and disaster relief, air and sea travel, use of atomic energy, and labor and workers' rights.

Although the UN is involved in an array of activities, seven specific agencies address social welfare issues:

1. *United Nations Children's Fund*: Probably the best known UN social welfare program, it provides a variety of child-directed services in such areas as health, child abuse, neglect and exploitation, child nutrition, education, and water and sanitation. In 1965 UNICEF received the Nobel Peace Prize for its efforts on behalf of children.

2. *World Health Organization*: This specialized UN agency focuses on worldwide health issues. It works to establish international health standards in a variety of areas, including vaccines, research, and drugs. It monitors and attempts to control communicable diseases, and it has a special focus on primary health care.

3. *UN High Commission for Refugees*: This commission oversees protection, assistance, and resettlement aid. In 1981, it was awarded the Nobel Peace Prize for its work with Asian refugees.

4. *Economic and Social Council*: The council coordinates a number of economic and social activities, with specific commissions for focusing on social development, human rights, population, the status of women, and drugs.

5. *Department of Policy Coordination and Sustainable Development*: Under the auspices of the UN Secretariat, the leading body of the United Nations, this department coordinates the development of welfare policies and activities.

6. *UN Developmental Programme*: This program provides technical assistance grants to developing member nations. Its primary area of support is agriculture, although grants also support health, education, population, employment, and other related human service programs.

7. *UN Population Fund*: This agency collects worldwide population data and implements family programs, including education and contraception.

Did You Know...The United Nations and its organizations have been awarded the Nobel Peace Prize on six separate occasions—1954, 1965, 1969, 1981, 1988, and 2001. In addition, seven people affiliated with the United Nations have received the Nobel Peace Prize—1945, 1949, 1950, 1957, 1961, 1974, and 2001.

The United Nations provides many other social welfare services. Typical activities include scores of annual conferences and conventions, as well *special years* dedicated to a specific issue. Most recent special years included

- 2016 International Year of Pulses, International Year of Camelids
- 2015 International Year of Light and Light-based Technologies, International Year of Soils
- 2014 International Year of Solidarity with the Palestinian People, International Year of Small Island Developing States, International Year of Crystallography, International Year of Family Farming

(See http://www.un.org/en/sections/observances/international-years/index .html for a complete listing of United Nations' special years.) Similarly, conferences focus on very specific themes:

- World Summit for Children (1990)
- Conference on the Environment (1992)
- Fourth World Conference on Women (1995)
- Earth Summit (1997)
- Conference on Fighting Land Mines
- World Food Summit (2002)
- Forum on the Eradication of World Poverty (2006)
- World Conference on Indigenous Peoples (2008)

The UN also sponsors significant special days each year such as the International Women's Day, held on March 8 each year, and World Water Day on March 22.

Of particular interest to social work is the United Nation's sponsorship of Social Work Day at the UN. Typically held in the spring, this annual meeting brings together about 1,000 social workers to discuss and advocate on global human issues. Social work students from around the U.S. participate at the UN event; check with your social work program to see if a student delegation may be attending the next social work UN day.

Did You Know... The headquarters for the IFSW is located in Berne, Switzerland, PO Box 6875, Schwarztorstrasse 22 CH-3001 and can be reached at Fax (41) 22 5181037, or via e-mail: global@ifsw.org

---

U.S. Government Agencies

The United States carries out a variety of international social welfare efforts through federal agencies:

♦ *Administration for Children and Families*: A subsection of the Office of Public Affairs, this agency is the primary conduit for international affairs and social work. Activities include meetings, research, professional exchanges, and cosponsorship of welfare programs (see http://www.acf.dhhs.gov).

♦ *Office of Refugee Resettlement*: This office coordinates resettlement of refugees in the United States. Since 1975 more than 3 million people, of whom nearly 77 percent are either Indochinese or citizens of the former Soviet Union, have been assisted in the United States because of persecution in their homelands due to race, religion, nationality, or political or social group membership (see http://www.acf.hhs.gov/programs/orr/about/history).

♦ *Social Security Administration*: This agency examines social insurance programs worldwide (see http://www.ssa.gov).

♦ *U.S. International Development Corporation*: This corporation has two responsibilities: international private investment and operating the Agency for International Development (AID). The AID provides funding for international projects and is very concerned about AIDS, child welfare, population growth, and basic education. It has given money to welfare groups, including the NASW, to sponsor international programs (see http://www.usaid.gov/what-we-do).

♦ *Peace Corps*: First organized in 1961, the Peace Corps sends American volunteers to different nations to assist in a variety of social, economic, and agricultural projects (see http://www.peacecorps.gov).

♦ *U.S. Information Agency*: This agency sponsors international leaders from around the world to participate with their colleagues in the United States. The agency also sponsors Americans to study abroad. Social work education too has seen an increase of study-abroad programs that include traditional tours, field placement opportunities, and semester study in a social work program in another country. Check with your program director or academic advisor about such opportunities.

Private Voluntary Bodies

Private or nongovernmental groups provide a variety of services and activities throughout the world. Human service organizations such as the YMCA and YWCA sponsor direct services and programs. In addition, nonprofit organizations consult with international agencies and groups about human service issues.

Name: Aida María Hernández Martínez

Place of residence: San Salvador, El Salvador

College/university degrees: Universidad Nacional de El Salvador

Present position: Consultora independiente

¿Qué haces en tu tiempo libre? Realizo actividades como compartir con mi familia, escaparme a un lugar al aire libre como el campo o a la montaña, participar en talleres de fotografía, manualidades, etc., leer un buen libro o artículos en internet.

¿Por qué elegiste trabajo social como una carrera? Nace con la idea de cambiar el mundo, una necesidad personal de hacer algo diferente y contribuir a la transformación de la realidad. Por ello una carrera que permitiría hacer está hermosa y loca idea era Trabajo Social.

¿Cuál es tu historia favorita de trabajo social? Hay tantas historias porque cada experiencia de trabajo con las comunidades, grupos en distintos territorios, deja siempre una historia y a la vez una lección. Una significativa es compartir y aprender con los niños y niñas de las comunidades peninsulares como Chile y Retiro, Isla de Méndez en los Municipios de Puerto El Triunfo y Jiquilisco, Departamento de Usulután, realizando talleres de promoción de derechos, donde la niñez expresaban sus historias daban a conocer sus modos de vida alrededor de la isla y a pesar de sus carencias socioeconómicas miran el mundo con ojos críticos y creativos, sus sueños son en búsqueda de alcanzar un futuro.

¿Cuál sería la única cosa que cambiarías en nuestra comunidad si tuvieras el poder para hacerlo? La dinámica de intervención de las instituciones públicas y privadas, para que propicien verdadera inclusión y participación de las comunidades, así estas desplegaran sin ninguna restricción sus potencialidades, aumentando el nivel de organización y participación.

Name: Jacquelyn Marie Eisenberg-Nelson

Place of residence: Bend, Oregon

College/university degrees: BA, Communication, University of Colorado at Boulder; MSW &graduate certificate in global health, University of Denver

Present position: Sustainable international development consultant

What do you do in your spare time? Anything and everything outdoors (hiking/camping/biking/boating/skiing), listening to live music, photography, and spending time exploring and traveling with my husband, our two dogs, and new baby girl.

Why did you choose social work as a career? As a Peace Corps volunteer in Swaziland, I attended a Baylor weeklong HIV/AIDS workshop and was in awe of the work one of the presenters shared; later on I learned she was a community development social worker. That conversation sent me down the path as a social worker, focusing on women and children's access to basic human rights in the field of international development and public health.

What is your favorite social work story? Make Nonhle lives in a rural community in Swaziland; when we first met she was incredibly sick and bedridden from advance stage HIV/AIDS. She was living in a two-room mud hut with no electricity or running water, caring for her six grandchildren (who also lived with her) and surviving on less than 70 cents per day. Nonhle was determined, caring, and one of the most selfless people I had ever met. With a little support and encouragement, Nonhle applied for a grant to buy a sewing machine, taught herself to sew, and was hired to sew all of the school uniforms for the local primary school. Along the way Nonhle faced countless challenges and setbacks, which she responded to by working harder and getting promoted; she was unflappable and always kept a positive attitude. She learned how to budget and save money, enabling her to put all six children through school (education is not free in Swaziland) and provide them with a safe and dry shelter, nutrition, clothing, and medical care. I visit Nonhle every year and today (10 years later) her health has significantly improved and she's become a vocal advocate and role model for women in her community. Nonhle's hardships never stopped her, they just forced her to get creative and work harder and now, as her grandchildren graduate school and start jobs, her success story has become their opportunity.

What would be the one thing you would change in our community if you had the power to do so? The majority of my social work career has been overseas (Southern Africa, Middle East, Caribbean, Eastern Europe). Coming home to the USA, I'm always humbled at how many systems we have in place to support people in need—they obviously aren't perfect, and as a global superpower I believe we have the resources and knowledge to improve these current systems; however, they still exist in some capacity. One thing I've learned to be true in my career is the old saying "Give a man a fish, you feed him for a day. Teach a man to fish, you feed him for a lifetime." In addition to the tangible resources sometimes needed for some to get back on their feet, I would love to live in a community where the focus isn't on handouts, but on taking the time and energy to train people so they can become self-sufficient. Although this takes more time and isn't a quick quantifiable fix, in my experience, skills training and capacity building are more sustainable in the long run. (That is, a scholarship is offered for someone to attend a trade school, they learn a new skill that makes them marketable to eventually get a stable job, they start earning and saving money, and eventually they begin to support their own nutritional/medical/housing needs, hopefully making them less dependent on someone else and/or in a position to help someone else through a ripple effect. It won't happen overnight, but as Make Nonhle said above, with a little hard work, support, and encouragement almost anything is possible.)

INTERNATIONAL PROFESSIONAL SOCIAL WELFARE ORGANIZATIONS

There are a variety of international social welfare organizations around the world. Some are social work membership associations, similar to the NASW. Others are national and regional educational associations, similar in purpose and function to the CSWE.

Three primary worldwide organizing bodies cross national boundaries and encourage partnerships: the International Federation of Social Workers, the International Association of Schools of Social Work, and the International Council on Social Welfare.

International Federation of Social Workers

The International Federation of Social Workers (IFSW) was founded in 1956 to promote social work on the world stage. The IFSW is divided into five geographical regions: Africa, Asia and the Pacific, Europe, Latin America and the Caribbean, and North America. Membership is open to one professional social work association in each country. In 2014, 116 countries with more than 745,000 members reported belonging to the Federation (see box 5). Individuals and organizations may join the IFSW to take part in the Friends Program. As a friend, a social worker receives the IFSW newsletter, published three times annually, policy papers, and a discount on registration for IFSW international and regional conferences.

Box 5. Members of the International Federation of Social Workers, 2014

Albania	Hong Kong	Norway
Andorra	Hungary	Palestine
Argentina	Iceland	Papua New Guinea
Armenia	India	Peru
Australia	Indonesia	Philippines
Austria	Ireland	Poland
Azerbaijan	Iran	Portugal
Bahrain	Israel	Puerto Rico
Bangladesh	Italy	Republic of Macedonia
Belarus	Japan	Romania
Belgium	Kenya	Russian Federation
Benin	Korea	Rwanda
Bolivia	Kosovo	San Marino
Botswana and Herzegovina	Kuwait	Serbia
Brazil	Kyrgyz Republic	Sierra Leone
Bulgaria	Latvia	Singapore
Canada	Lebanon	Slovakia
Chile	Lesotho	Slovenia
China	Liberia	South Africa
Colombia	Libya	Spain
Costa Rica	Lithuania	Sri Lanka
Croatia	Luxembourg	Sudan
Cuba	Macau	Swaziland
Cyprus	Madagascar	Sweden
Czech Republic	Malaysia	Switzerland/Liechtenstein
Denmark	Malta	Tanzania
Djibitou	Mauritius	Thailand
Dominican Republic	Moldova	Turkey
Estonia	Mongolia	Uganda
F.Y.R.O. Macedonia	Monaco	Ukraine
Faeroe Islands	Montenegro	United Kingdom
Fiji	Morocco	United States of America
Finland	Netherlands	Uruguay
France	Netherlands Antilles	Viet Nam
Georgia	New Zealand-Aotearoa	Yemen
Germany	Nicaragua	Zambia
Ghana	Niger	Zimbabwe
Greece	Nigeria	

The IFSW represents global social work in a variety of international arenas. For example, the IFSW is granted *special consultative status* by the United Nations and United Nations Children's Fund. The IFSW has a long history working with the World Health Organization (WHO) and the United Nations' Office of the High Commissioner for Refugees and the High Commissioner of Human Rights. In addition to these international associations, partner organizations of the IFSW include Amnesty International, The Conference of Non-Governmental Organizations, Commonwealth Organisation for Social Work, Council of Europe, ENSACT, European Union, the International Association of Schools of Social Work, the International Council on Social Welfare, Public Services International, the UN Department of Economic and Social Affairs, and the United Nations Children's Fund.

With the International Association of Schools of Social Work (see below), the IFSW generated a definition of social work that is used around the world. The global definition, which was revised in July 2014, took a number of years to write and gain approval by the various member associations. For a moment think how difficult it is in your class to reach agreement; now transpose this to a worldwide discussion that involves a variety of cultural frameworks and different meanings of words set within historical patterns of mistrust between regions and nations. The idea that people from around the world were able to find common ground speaks volumes about the authenticity and commitment of social workers, no matter where they live and work. Reflecting sensitivity to the diversity of languages and its membership, the IFSW posts the definition in several languages on its website (see box 6).

The IFSW sponsors meetings throughout the world (see box 7). In addition to its biennial international meetings, it sponsors regional meetings that focus on specific area issues; participant costs are much lower for these meetings. Since 1966, there have been more than twenty regional meetings in Europe and in Asia and the Pacific, and approximately fifteen meetings in Africa. Both regional and worldwide gatherings provide social workers from around the world with a chance to share research findings as well as program ideas.

The IFSW also provides critical leadership in the pursuit of human rights for individual social workers, social work students, and social service workers. In 1988, the IFSW established a Human Rights Commission with members representing each region. The commission works with a number of international human rights groups including Amnesty International.

The IFSW is the primary organization to set forth position papers on behalf of the global social work community on a range of social welfare topics. Examples include three 2014 statements regarding the Israeli/Palestinian conflict (see Caissie

Box 6. Global Definition of Social Work as Posted in Various Languages by the International Federation of Social Workers, 2014.

Afrikaans—*Maatskaplike werk is 'n praktyk-gebaseerde professie en 'n akademiese dissipline wat maatskaplike verandering en ontwikkeling, maatskaplike kohesie, en die bemagtiging en bevryding van mense bevorder. Beginsels van maatskaplike geregtigheid, menseregte, kollektiewe verantwoordelikheid en respek vir diversiteit is fundamenteel in maatskaplike werk. Versterk deur teorieë vir maatskaplike werk, sosiale wetenskappe, geesteswetenskappe en inheemse kennis1, betrek maatskaplike werk mense en strukture om lewenseise te hanteer en welsyn te bevorder.*

Die bogenoemde definisie kan verder uitgebou word op nasionale en/of streekvlakke.

Arabic—بالنسبة للعلم العالمي أحناأ فلتخم نم نيييعامتجلاا نيييناصخلاا اوو ءاضعألاا تتامظنملا نم دييدعللا نيذلا

بيهيهسنت يف مههكارتشلا ةقيقشتلا ةمظنملا ةيعامتجلاا ةمدخلا سسررادملا يلوودلا داحتلاا سلجمون نيب راككرراوكلاا يف ةيراجرملا ةعجارملا تامكأ .لامشلاا دداحتلاا لالا هههمم نمبربعر ريبدقة تامك نيييناصخلاا نيييعامتجلاا

ممويوي دعب اموي امويل لمعلا ةسيسيئر ةيمويسيئر امولا ب نيذلا نيييناملاا ةناملاا ءاضعأوأ نيبعو نم رييبكلاا دهجلاب ففرتعن ننأأ اضيئا داددون طلمتلاا امك ةقدقعمت ةمهملا تناك امم للولح دداجيياإ لع لمعلا . دداادعتسا لع امتاادد لمهنولكوو ةيتلمعلا

عامتجلاا نكوكيك ففوسوو .ةنهملاا روطتو لع لللدي امنأأ دقتعذ يذلا حح رتقملا فيير عتلاا للاإ ررووااشتلاا يف ةيلمع تتددددأأ ننأأ ءاادعسا نحذ دييدجلاا وو ةيثيياينفتنلا لجنتللا نع تابياين فيير عتلاا ضوضووو عضوورعتلاا ضض نضرلاا رعتسا يف

نننرروربلم يف . 2014 ويلويوي ةيعامتجلاا نيييناصخل 6 وو 7 يلوودلاا دداحتلاا ةيمومعملاا ةالا بيعمجلاا

English—Social work is a practice–based profession and an academic discipline that promotes social change and development, social cohesion, and the empowerment and liberation of people. Principles of social justice, human rights, collective responsibility, and respect for diversities are central to social work, social sciences, humanities and indigenous knowledge. Social work engages people and structures to address life challenges and embrace well-being.

The above definition may be amplified at national and/or regional levels.

Espanol—El trabajo social es una profesión basada en la práctica y una disciplina académica que promueve el cambio y el desarrollo social, la cohesión social, y el fortalecimiento y la liberación de las personas. Los principios de la justicia social, los derechos humanos, la responsabilidad colectiva y el respeto a la diversidad son fundamentales para el trabajo social. Respaldada por las teorías del trabajo social, las ciencias sociales, las humanidades y los conocimientos indígenas, el trabajo social involucra a las personas y las estructuras para hacer frente a desafíos de la vida y aumentar el bienestar.

La siguiente definición se puede ampliar a nivel nacional y / o regional.

Francaise—Les professionnels du travail social ont pour mission de favoriser le changement et le développement social, la cohésion sociale, le pouvoir d'agir et la libération des personnes. Les principes de justice sociale, de droit de la personne, de responsabilité sociale collective et respect des diversités, sont au cœur du travail social. Etayé par les théories du travail social, des sciences sociales, des sciences humaines et des connaissances autochtones, le travail social encourage les personnes et les structures à relever les défis de la vie et agit pour améliorer le bien-être de tous.

Hebrew—סדקמה ,יעדמ (הנילפיצסיד) תעד םוחתו ימושייו ישעמ עוצקמ איה תילאיצוסה הדובעה
לע שגד תמיש ךות ,סדא ינב לש םתמצעהל לעופו תיתרבח תודיכל ,יתרבח חותיפ ,יתרבח יוניש
,סדא תויוכז ,יתרבח קדצ מה תילאיצוסה הדובעה לש םייזכרמה היתונורקע .םדובכו םתוריח
הדובעב תויוראית לע ססבתהב .ןויוושו ,תונושל דובכ ןתמ ,תודידי ,תיתרבח ללכ תויראחא
לש םהיתוריושב םיערזנה לש תוסנתהה רותמ דמלנ עדי לעו ,חורהו הרבחה יעדמב ,תילאיצוס
תנמ לע ,םישנאל הרבחה לש תודוסמ הליעפמו תמתור תילאיצוסה הדובעה ,םיילאיצוס םידבוע
.הרבחה ללכו תוליהיק ,תוצובק ,החפשמה ,טרפה תחוור תא סדקלו ,םייח ירגתא סע דדומתהל

isiZulu—*Ezenhlalakahle ziwumkhakha ombandakanya ukwenza umsebenzi ophathekayo, uqeqesho lwezemfundo olukhuthaza uguquko lwezenhlalo nokuthuthukiswa komphakathi, ubumbano lomphakathi, ukugqugquzela nokukhululeka kwabantu. Imigomo yobulungiswa, amalungelo esintu, ukubamba iqhaza, nokuhlonipha ukwehlukana kwezinhlanga kuseqhulwini emkhakheni wezenhlalakahle. Ngokusekelwa imibono ehlukahlukene yezenhlalakahle, ubuchwepheshe bezenhlalo, ubuntu, nolwazi loMdabu, ezenhlalakahle zixhumanisa abantu nezakhiwo ezilwisana nezingqinamba zempilo ziphinde zithuthukise nempilo jikelele.*

Lencazelo engenhla ingaguquguqulwa ngokwamazinga ezwe futhi/noma awezifunda.

Italian—Il servizio sociale è una professione basata sulla pratica e una disciplina accademica che promuove il cambiamento sociale e lo sviluppo, la coesione e l'emancipazione sociale, nonchè la liberazione delle persone. Principi di giustizia sociale, diritti umani, responsabilità collettiva e rispetto delle diversità sono fondamentali per il servizio sociale. Sostenuto dalle teorie del servizio sociale, delle scienze sociali, umanistiche e dai saperi indigeni, il servizio sociale coinvolge persone e strutture per affrontare le sfide della vita e per migliorarne il benessere.

La definizione di cui sopra pu essere ampliata a livello nazionale e/o regionale.

Portuguese—O Serviço Social é uma profissão de intervenção e uma disciplina académica que promove o desenvolvimento e a mudança social, a coesão social, o empowerment e a promoção da Pessoa. Os princípios de justiça social, dos direitos humanos, da responsabilidade coletiva e do respeito pela diversidade são centrais ao Serviço Social. Sustentado nas teorias do serviço social, nas ciências sociais, nas humanidades e nos conhecimentos indígenas, o serviço social relaciona as pessoas com as estruturas sociais para responder aos desafios da vida e à melhoria do bem-estar social.

Esta definição de Serviço Social pode ser ampliada ao nível nacional e/ou ao nível regional.

Russian—Социальная работа является практической профессией и академической дисциплиной, которая способствует общественным изменениям и развитию, содействует социальной сплоченности и укреплению способностей к самостоятельному функционированию людей в обществе, их освобождению. Принципы социальной справедливости, прав человека и уважения многообразия являются центральными в социальной работе. Опираясь на теории социальной работы, общественные и гуманитарные науки, специализированные знания, социальная работа вовлекает людей и структуры в решение жизненно важных проблем и повышение благополучия. Данное определение можно расширять на национальном и/или региональном уровнях

Box 7. Meetings Sponsored by the IFSW

1966	Helsinki
1970	Manila
1974	Nairobi
1976	Puerto Rico
1978	Tel Aviv
1980	Hong Kong
1982	Brighton
1984	Montreal
1986	Tokyo
1988	Stockholm
1990	Buenos Aires
1992	Washington, DC
1994	Colombia
1996	Hong Kong
1998	Jerusalem
2000	Montreal
2002	Harare
2004	Australia
2006	Germany
2008	Brazil
2010	Hong Kong–joint meeting with the IASSW and ICSW
2012	Sweden–joint meeting with the IASSW and ICSW
2014	Australia–joint meeting with the IASSW and ICSW
2016	Seoul, Korea–joint meeting with the IASSW and ICSW

& Wheeler, 2014; IFSW, 2014a; Kimura & Henderson, 2014). The IFSW also issued a statement of support for the people of Turkey following the May 2014 mine explosion (IFSW, 2014b).

Another noteworthy activity of IFSW is its research and publication of policy papers that explore social issues that social workers face day in and day out. In addition to the following issues, policy papers are planned to explore indigenous people and international adoptions:

- ◆ Advancement of women
- ◆ Welfare of elderly people
- ◆ Child welfare
- ◆ Health

- ◆ HIV-AIDS
- ◆ Human rights
- ◆ Migration
- ◆ Peace and disarmament
- ◆ Protection of personnel
- ◆ Refugees
- ◆ Rural communities
- ◆ Self-help
- ◆ Youth

International Association of Schools of Social Work

As the name suggests, the International Association of Schools of Social Work (IASSW) is the focal point for social work education around the world. The IASSW does not set international accreditation standards for social work education; rather it promotes social work education and the development of high-quality educational programs around the world. In a 1928 worldwide meeting, attended by more than 3,000 people from forty-two different nations, the participants agreed that social work was a mechanism that could professionalize and achieve better outcomes from charitable activities (Hokenstad & Kendall, 1995). In the following year the IASSW was organized, and today membership is open to national associations, such as the CSWE and its specific educational programs. By 1995 IASSW membership totaled 450 schools from 100 countries (Hokenstad & Kendall, 1995), and in 2009 membership had grown to more than 600 programs in more than 115 nations. Member schools are divided into five regions—Asia-Pacific, Africa, European, Latin American, and North America-Caribbean—which facilitates development of regional educational initiatives.

Did You Know... The journal International Social Work *is sponsored jointly by the International Association of Schools of Social Work, the International Federation of Social Workers, and the International Council on Social Welfare.*

The IASSW sponsors a biennial meeting, the International Conference of Schools of Social Work, and supports a variety of educationally directed projects. In addition, the association publishes a newsletter and texts. Those who are interested in social work education programs around the world might enjoy the joint IASSW-CSWE publication by Rao and Kendall (1984), which provides a useful starting point for understanding social work programs in different countries, their admission standards, and an overview of curricula. Although this publication is out of date, it does provide a fascinating look at the diversity of social work education around the world. For example, in some African countries you'll find a certificate or state diploma awarded after the completion of three years of postsecondary study. In Asia, undergraduate and graduate programs are somewhat similar to those in the United States with comparable course titles and field placements/internships required.

Similar to the IFSW, the IASSW is sensitive to the language barriers in a global community. To that end, the IASSW, as part of its organizational structure, includes a language committee that continually assesses and proposes new ways to communicate across the world::

> The IASSW recognizes that there is and should be no difference in value and importance among any languages, and that all languages on this earth should be treated equally, regardless of the number of users, not to mention to Articles 2 of Universal Declaration of Human Rights and International Covenant on Civil and Political Rights. Based on the nature of social work and the IASSW's mission to promote social work education, as well as its history and membership distribution, the following policy was adopted in July 2005 and revised in July 2007:

The IASSW recognizes four official languages: English, French, Spanish, and Japanese. These are the languages used by the majority of IASSW member schools. However, English is the dominant language (http://www.iassw-aiets.org/language-committee).

International Council on Social Welfare

As stated on its website (http://www.icsw.org/intro/missione.htm), the International Council on Social Welfare (ICSW) is a "global non-governmental organization which represents a wide range of national and international member organizations that seek to advance social welfare, social justice and social development." The primary thrust of the council is to promote social and economic development activities that will reduce poverty, hardship, and vulnerability. The council was founded in Paris in 1928, and today its office is located in London, England. Like the IFSW and IASSW, the council holds a biennial conference as well as regional meetings.

The ICSW is subdivided into five regions—Africa, Asia and Pacific, Latin America and Caribbean, North America, and Europe. In 2014 the ICSW was active in more than seventy countries, nine global regions, and a number of international organizations. Members are limited to organizations and are classified into four categories: national member organizations (programs operating only in one country), international member organizations (programs offered in multiple countries), other member organizations (those that do not meet the preceding two criteria), and associate member organizations (a new classification in 2014 whose specifics have yet to be determined).

Among its important functions, the ICSW publishes a journal, *Global Social Policy*, which includes a creative section titled "Observatory on the Global South." This section highlights social welfare trends in the global south and draws attention to many of the issues that otherwise are left unrecognized.

INTERNATIONAL INITIATIVES OF NASW AND CSWE

National Association of Social Workers

The NASW is active in pursuing and promoting international relations. The association is guided by its International Activities Committee, which was formed in 1986. This committee seeks to adopt a variety of mechanisms to increase the globalization of the NASW.

As part of its international outreach activities, the NASW has sponsored international meetings and travel opportunities. For example, in 1992 the NASW, as part of that year's annual meeting, cohosted the World Assembly, the biannual international conclave of social workers, in Washington, DC. During the 1980s and 1990s, many state NASW chapters forged partnerships with social workers and associations in other countries. In fact, by 1992 twenty-one state chapters had formal relationships with other associations around the world. In addition, the national association and a number of state chapters have sponsored study tours in various countries around the world.

Council on Social Work Education

The CSWE is also extremely active in international circles. It includes the Commission on Global Social Work Education, which works with other international organizations, including the IASSW, to promote international programs and projects and to develop the international dimension of the social work curricula. The commission also is responsible for advising the Foreign Equivalency Determination Service and for maintaining relationships with foreign students and schools. In addition to linking the CSWE with international groups, the commission strongly advocates that schools internationalize curricula and provide students with worldwide opportunities. The Commission also sponsors the Katherine A. Kendall Institute for International Social Work Education, which serves as a conduit for the generation of educational materials for social work educators. For example, the Kendall Institute sponsored a disaster management meeting in the Caribbean with educators and relief workers from around the world. This led to the development of curriculum programs on social workers and disaster relief. The Kendall Institute sponsored similar meetings that were held in South Africa and China. The institute is also leading social work educators in the CSWE-China Collaborative that is promoting the development of MSW education programs in China to reach the government's goal of three million social workers by the year 2020. This collaboration began in 2012, involving seven U.S. social work educational programs (Arizona State University, Case Western Reserve University, Fordham University, University of Alabama, University of Chicago, University of Houston, and University of Southern California) and fifty-two Chinese universities in seven different regions.

The CSWE also sponsors many international study trips. Most recently, social work educators have been developing linkages with colleagues in Cuba through trips that first began in 2012. And in 2014, CSWE organized a social work educators group to Costa Rica.

The CSWE's research and publications around global matters has significantly increased as the profession has become more attuned to the growing global interconnectedness (Finn, Perry, & Karandikar, 2013; Hokenstad, Healy, & Segal, 2013; Lager, Mathiesen, Rodgers, & Cox, 2010). Examples of publications include *Guidebook for International Field Placements and Student Exchanges* (2010), *Teaching Human Rights: Curriculum Resources for Social Work Educators* (2013), and *Gender Oppression and Globalization* (2013). See box 8 for a list of international organizations.

Box 8. Sample of International Social Welfare Organizations and Their Websites

Organization	Contact Information—URLs may change so you may need to do an Internet search on the organization
HelpAge International	www.helpage.org
Inclusion International	www.inclusion-international.org
International Catholic Migration Commission	www.icmc.net
International Council of Jewish Women	www.icjw.org.uk
International Council on Jewish Social and Welfare Services	(no web; phone: 41-22-344-9000)
International Federation of Aging	www.ifa-fiv.org
International Federation of Red Cross and Red Crescent Services	www.ifrc.org/what/health/archi/homepage.htm
International Federation of Settlements and Neighborhood Centers	http://datenbanks.spinnenwerk.de/ifs
International Organization for Migration	www.iom.int
International Planned Parenthood Federation	www.ippf.org
International Social Service	www.iss-ssi.org/index.htm
Salvation Army	www.salvationarmy.org

Other Programs

A number of social work programs offer international student exchanges, field placement opportunities, and study tours. These opportunities are usually open to students and faculty from different colleges/universities; check with your social work faculty to learn more about recent and upcoming international study opportunities either in your program or in other programs. (Remember that you can generally transfer credit back to your home college or university, but you need to check with your academic advisor to see how such study opportunities will affect your degree plan.) The following list is just a small sample of the activities that social work programs have undertaken; check directly with your own social work program about any international opportunities it may offer.

- University of North Carolina–Chapel Hill: study tour of Ireland, Wales, and Scotland
- University of Houston: academic exchange program with City University of Hong Kong and travel courses to Wales, Turkey, South Africa, Mexico, and China
- University of Central Florida: summer course in Mexico
- Florida State University: summer course in England and Spain
- East Carolina State University: summer course in Bristol, England
- University of South Carolina: study tour of Greece

SUMMARY

The events of September 11, 2001, and the fear of terrorism have created a climate never before experienced in this country. These events, however, cannot be used as an excuse to turn away from the issues so germane to the globalization of our society. Problems of substance abuse, child abuse and neglect, spouse battering, poverty, inadequate mental health and health care, and the *isms* of race, age, and gender continue to be found in every region of the world. And social workers too are found throughout the world, helping individuals, families, and communities to confront these and other social issues.

We experience globalization every day. We can cross the oceans in a matter of hours; we can talk to a friend in another nation simply by dialing a telephone. Through e-mail we can send messages around the world to any number of people in mere milliseconds. See box 9 for a list of international acronyms.

Social work and social welfare are part of this fast-paced, ever-changing world. Terry Hokenstad and Katherine Kendall, both recognized as significant leaders in the development of social work on the global level, noted early on that social work

Box 9. International Acronyms

EC	European Community
ECE	Economic Commission of Europe
EFTA	European Free Trade Association
EU	European Union
Eurostat	European Statistical Office
FAO	Food and Agriculture Organization
GATT	General Agreement on Tariffs and Trade; succeeded by WTO
IBRD	International Bank for Reconstruction and Development; usually called the World Bank
IDA	International Development Association
IFAD	International Fund for Agricultural Development
IFC	International Finance Corporation
IMF	International Monetary Fund
NATO	North Atlantic Treaty Organization
OPEC	Organization of Petroleum Exporting Nations
UNDP	United Nations Development Programme
Unesco	United Nations Educational, Scientific, and Cultural Organization
UNICEF	United Nations Children's Fund
UNIDO	United Nations Industrial Development Organization
USAID	United States Agency for International Development
WFP	World Food Programme
WHO	World Health Organization
WTO	World Trade Organization

students had limited exposure to international issues (1995). Certainly social work education, through the EPAS, and the NASW with its ongoing international work with the IFSW, have attempted to broaden the educational experience to include global relevance, but should we be doing more? And if so, what and how?

The social work educational curriculum is already packed with required content. It is easy to say that international content is required in all social curricula, but at what expense? Will existing content need to be dropped or modified? Are social work educators and practitioners willing to decide whether international content, although important in our world today, is necessary for effective social work practice?

Social work practitioners often claim that they are stretched to the limit by work obligations and wonder how they could continue to manage the rigors of work if required to move into the international arena. As one practitioner stated:

> Don't get me wrong, I'm very concerned about poverty in India and the clear mistreatment of people based on a caste system. BUT I just don't have enough time in a day to do what needs to be done for my child welfare clients. What is important for me is that my kids are able to get back with their families and no longer feel the pain of abuse and neglect.

Attending his or her first international meeting is can be an eye-opening experience for the American social worker. It's not uncommon to hear social workers from around the world speak in negative terms about the American social work community. Many believe that American social workers do not value the international experience. Whether this is true or not, they perceive that American social welfare journals discriminate against international authors by declining to publish their manuscripts. They feel that U.S. social work programs do not value international journals and texts, an idea reinforced by the absence of international materials among required readings in social work courses.

There is some truth to allegations that American social workers are ignorant of the international social welfare arena. They are surprised to learn that there are social work organizations similar to the NASW and CSWE throughout the world. Yes, they are surprised to discover that social work extends beyond the borders of North America and some parts of Europe.

Rather than berate the profession and each other, we need to commit ourselves to professional globalization. In the classroom, we need to look at issues and conduct discussions in an international context. That doesn't mean that the focus of all efforts should be global, but it does mean that we should consider topics through an international lens when appropriate.

But what are some specific things we can do? First, we can support the NASW in its organizational efforts on a national level as well as in the state chapters and local units. Dedicating one monthly meeting to an international issue with either a guest speaker or a film will enhance our efforts.

Second, while more ambitious than looking for a guest speaker, a study-travel course organized in conjunction with the NASW or offered by a social work program is a worthwhile activity. Third, we can work to develop a sister program with an international social welfare association or school that can lead to professional exchanges for practitioners and students alike. Such partnerships allow students to meet with students from other countries through social media, and the opportunities for potential collaborations on projects are endless. Fourth, each year most colleges sponsor an international week on their campuses. The local social work student group can sponsor an activity that highlights international social welfare. Alternatively, a program might consider sponsoring an international event during March, National Social Work Month in the United States.

Fifth, social work programs can sponsor global forums by inviting individuals to speak with students and faculty. The list of speakers is endless—members of a foreign consulate, Peace Corp volunteers, and representatives from various international organizations such as UNICEF or CARE. Also, a social work program can easily Skype in a speaker from another country. And finally, a social work program can encourage its students to organize an international student group to become the central organizing home for student global work. Examining hot topics as they are viewed across the globe can result in a fruitful discussion and help to identify commonalities and differences. For women, equality has been placed on the political agenda and this will require widespread support and awareness (Connell, 2014).

International experiences have a way of changing who we are and how we approach our work and daily life circumstances. One of the authors wrote the following to his college's alumni describing a trip he took to Israel in January 2009 during the height of the Gaza war:

> For ten days in early January I travelled around Israel as part of a five-person delegation invited by the Israeli Foreign Ministry. Other delegation members came from Harvard, Georgetown University, Virginia Commonwealth University, and the University of Illinois-Chicago. We met a variety of people including Knesset members, the minister for social welfare, former ambassadors, think tank professionals, educators, lawyers, and leaders of social agencies. The war in Gaza was in its full fury during our visit and framed the majority of our conversations. I was particularly impacted by a meeting with a colleague who teaches at Sapir College, located in S'derot, approximately 4.8 kilometers from Gaza. She described classrooms built like bomb shelters, the air raid sirens going off 15 to 20 times in a typical class; students and faculty know a siren means a rocket will hit within 15 seconds—everyone falls to the floor and waits for the rocket blast. Everyone then gets back in their chairs and resumes class until the next siren goes off. The morning of our discussion she described the college reopening after being closed for three weeks; she described the constant buzz of helicopters flying over the campus while watching smoke rising in the near distance. She said that women do not wear heels—they need to be able to run as fast as possible to a bomb shelter; or people do not use bathrooms all day simply because they are not bomb proof. My colleague noted that approximately 3,000 of the 7,000 students suffer from PTSD.

> I cannot imagine teaching a class in an environment similar to that of my colleague in S'derot. How do you literally pick yourself off the floor and resume teaching as if nothing happened? How different my life would be knowing that at any moment a siren may go off and I will have 15 seconds to find a safe place. As our evening together concluded I said to her that I was having a very difficult time trying to fully understand what she was describing. She interrupted me and said, "I pray you never have to experience what I am in order to understand what our lives are like."

> Most certainly I came away from Israel with a greater understanding of the midEast conflict and all of its complexities. While that is important, I also no longer take for granted the safe and secure environments that many of us enjoy both at

work and at home. I hope that my colleague's wish is realized and that I, we, will never have to experience an air raid siren or dive to the floor for safety.

But even more than that, this one international experience only serves to reinforce my profound respect and admiration for those who teach and work in wartorn and unsafe areas. They are true heroes and remind us all that our mission in social work, the promotion of justice for all, is important and necessary. As the Reverend Dr. Martin Luther King Jr said, the hopes for a livable world rest with those who strive for peace and justice.

What we do is limited only by our creativity and our willingness to grow. But before doing anything, we must first commit to the belief that we live in a global community. We need to embrace the notion that our work influences and is influenced by the global community. Then, and only then, will we be able to confront the social ills that plague the world, and have any chance of achieving social justice for all people no matter where they live or what their social and economic status.

REFERENCES

Bell, D. (1973). *The coming of post-industrial society.* New York: Basic Books.

Caissie, M., & Wheeler, D. (2014). *Statement by the North American region of IFSW on the Israeli/Palestinian conflict.* International Federation of Social Workers. Retrieved from http://ifsw.org/news/statement-by-the-north-american-region-of-ifsw-on-the-israeli palestinian-conflict

Central Intelligence Agency. (2014a). Country comparison: Infant mortality rate. *The world factbook.* Retrieved from https://www.cia.gov/library/publications/the-world-factbook/rankorder/2091rank.html

Central Intelligence Agency. (2014b). Country comparison: Death rate. *The world factbook.* Retrieved from https://www.cia.gov/library/publications/the-world-factbook/rankorder/2066rank.html

Central Intelligence Agency. (2014c). Country comparison: Life expectancy at birth. *The world factbook.* Retrieved from https://www.cia.gov/library/publications/the-world-factbook/rankorder/2102rank.html

Chatterjee, P. (1996). *Approaches to the welfare state.* Washington, DC: NASW Press.

Connell, R. W. (2014). Change among the gatekeepers: Men, masculinities, and gender equality in the global arena. In J. Z. Spade & C. G. Valentine. *The kaleidoscope of gender: Prisms, patterns and possibilities* (4th ed., pp. 564–579). Thousand Oaks, CA: Sage.

Dziegielewski, S. F., & Kirven, J. (in press). An examination of the U.S. Response to Bioterrorism: Handling the threat and aftermath through crisis intervention. In K. Yeager (Ed.), *Albert R. Roberts Crisis intervention handbook* (4th ed.). New York: Oxford University Press.

Enriquez, J. (2005). *The United States of America.* New York: Crown Publishers.

Finn, J. L., Perry, T. E., & Karandikar, S. (2013) *Gender oppression and globalization: Challenges for social work.* Alexandria, VA: Council on Social Work Education.

Fleshman, M. (2002). A troubled decade for Africa's children. *Africa Recovers, 16,* 6.

Friedman, T. L. (2005). *The world is flat: A brief history of the twenty-first century.* New York: Farrar, Straus, & Giroux.

Healy, L. (1995). International social welfare: Organizations and activities. In R. L. Edwards et al. (Eds.), *Encyclopedia of social work* (19th ed., vol. 2, pp. 1499–1510). Washington, DC: NASW Press.

Hokenstad, M. C., & Kendall, K. A. (1995). International social work education. In R. L. Edwards (Ed.), *Encyclopedia of social work* (19th ed., vol. 2, pp. 1511–1520). Washington, DC: NASW Press.

Hokenstad, T., Healy, L., & Segal, U. (Eds.) (2013) *Teaching human rights: Curriculum resources for social work educators.* Alexandria, VA: Council on Social Work Education.

How many countries are there in the world in 2015? (2015). *Political geography now.* Retrieved from http://www.polgeonow.com/2011/04/how-many-countries-are-there-in-world.html

International Federation of Social Workers. (2014a). *Social work for peace and self-determination in Palestine and Israel.* Retrieved from http://ifsw.org/news/social-work-for-peace-and-self-determination-in-palestine-and-israel

International Federation of Social Workers (2014b). *Statement of IFSW Europe e.V. supporting the people of Turkey following the coal mine tragedy,* Retrieved from http://ifsw.org/news/statement-of-ifsw-europe-e-v-supporting-the-people-of-turkey-following-the-coal-mine-tragedy

Kimura, M., & Henderson, R. (2014). *Public statement by IFSW Asia Pacific regional president and member-at-large concerning the humanitarian disaster currently taking place in Gaza.* International Federation of Social Workers. Retrieved from http://ifsw.org/news/public-statement-by-ifsw-asia-pacific-regional-president-and-member-at-large-concerning-the-humanitarian-disaster-currently-taking-place-in-gaza

Lager, P., Mathiesen, S., Rodgers, M., & Cox, S.(2010). *Guidebook for International field placements and student exchanges: Planning, implementation, and sustainability.* Alexandria, VA: Council on Social Work Education.

Midgley, J. (1995). International and comparative social welfare. In R. L. Edwards (Ed.), *Encyclopedia of social work* (19th ed., Vol. 2, pp. 1490–1499). Washington, DC: NASW Press.

Midgley, J. (1997). Social work in international context: Challenges and opportunities for the 21st century. In M. Reisch & E. Gambrill (Eds.), *Social work in the 21st century* (pp. 59–67). Thousand Oaks, CA: Pine Forge Press.

Rao, V., & Kendall, K. (Eds.). (1984). *World guide to social work education.* New York: Council on Social Work Education.

Risen, J., & Poitras, L (2013, September 28). N.S.A. gathers data on social connections of U.S. citizens. *The New York Times.* Retrieved from http://www.nytimes.com/2013/09/29/us/nsa-examines-social-networks-of-us-citizens.html?pagewanted=all&_r=0

Shoichet, C., E. (2014, August 7). What is Putin's endgame in Ukraine? *CNN.* Retrieved from http://www.cnn.com/2014/08/07/world/europe/russia-putin-ukraine-endgame/

United Nations. (2014*). The millennium development goals report 2014.* New York: Author. Retrieved from http://www.worldbank.org/en/news/press-release/2014/10/01/boosting-shared-prosperity-key-tackling-inequality-world-bank-group-president

United Nations Children's Fund. (2014). *Levels and trends in child mortality, report 2014.* New York: Author.

U.S. Census Bureau. (2014). *U.S and world population clock.* Retrieved from http://www.census.gov/popclock

World Bank. (2014). Kim: We aim to reduce global inequality. Retrieved October 5, 2014 from: http://www.worldbank.org/

CHAPTER 15
CONCLUSIONS

THE TITLE OF A BOOK CAN TELL THE READER A GREAT DEAL ABOUT the contents and the views of its authors. Margaret Truman's *Murder at the CIA*, for example, is a murder mystery set within the government. Woodward and Bernstein's *All the President's Men* is a work exploring a president, Nixon in this case, and his staff. On the other hand, titles may mislead you. *Hunt for Red October* is not a story about fall in New England. Salinger's classic *Catcher in the Rye* is not a baseball story about the exploits of Yankee legend Yogi Berra.

In social work, you can also tell a lot from book titles. Look at the following titles from the 1960s to the present and think about what they say to you:

- *The Professional Altruist* (Lubove, 1965)
- *Social Work, the Unloved Profession* (Richan & Mendelsohn, 1973)
- *Introduction to The Drama of Social Work* (Bloom, 1990)
- *Unfaithful Angels* (Specht & Courtney, 1994)
- *Maneuvering the Maze of Managed Care: Skills for mental health practitioners* (Corcoran & Vandiver, 1996)
- *Economics for Social Workers: Social Outcomes of Economic Globalization with Strategies for Community Action* (Prigoff, 2000)
- *Cognitive-Behavioral Interventions: Empowering Vulnerable Populations* (Eamon, 2008)
- *Combating Violence and Abuse of People with Disabilities: A Call to Action* (Fitzsimons, 2009)
- *Taking Charge: A School-Based Life Skills Program for Adolescent Mothers* (Harris & Franklin, 2008)
- *Social Work, a Profession of Many Faces,* 11th edition (Morales, Sheafor, & Scott, 2009)
- *Introduction to Social: The People's Profession,* 3rd ed. (Colby & Dziegielewski, 2010)
- *Service Delivery for Vulnerable Populations: New Directions in Behavioral Health* (Estrine, Hettenbach, Arthur, & Messina, Eds., 2011)
- *The Changing Face of Health Care Social Work: Opportunities and Challenges for Professional Practice,* 3rd ed., (Dziegielewski, 2013).

Each title should tell you something about the author's or authors' view of the profession and the population they seek to serve. Lubove (1965) recognizes social workers as people who want to help others but looks beyond the philanthropic model to someone who is professionally trained in this important art and science. *Social Work, the Unloved Profession* depicts the larger community's somewhat negative view of social work, one in which the profession's activities are not held in high regard. *Introduction to the Drama of Social Work* by Bloom (1990) unfolds the many struggles that social workers face in providing care. *Unfaithful Angels* is a critical look at the social work profession by two social workers who strongly assert that professionals have abandoned advocacy efforts on behalf of the poor in favor of for-profit and private psychotherapeutic services.

As can be seen by the title, *Maneuvering the Maze of Managed Care* by Corcoran and Vandiver (1996) explores social workers' struggles in a fragmented system of delivery that emphasizes time-limited interventions and clearly defined and measured clinical outcomes, with the ultimate responsibility belonging to the funding source. Estrine and Hettenbach (2011) emphasize assisting those in need utilizing a behavioral health concept while avoiding the notion that a "one-size-fits-all" is going to work. In *The Changing Face of Health Care Social Work: Opportunities and Challenges for Professional Practice*, Dziegielewski investigates health care delivery, outlining how managed care has been replaced with coordinated care although many of the same health care premises still remain.

Economics for Social Workers by Prigoff (2000) speaks clearly to the need to recognize economic concerns and the movement toward globalization through community action. *The Changing Face of Health Care Social Work* by Dziegielewski (2013) outlines the many roles that social workers can assume in health care and the flexibility that is needed to embrace what is often termed coordinated care. Eamon (2008), in *Empowering Vulnerable Populations*, highlights the strong focus of many schools of social work on cognitive behavioral therapy and assisting and empowering vulnerable populations. Other books present a call to action for social workers to help vulnerable populations, from combating violence and abuse for people suffering from disabilities (Fitzsimons, 2009) to calling on adolescent mothers to take charge of their lives through empowerment and skill building (Harris & Franklin, 2008).

Consider the work of Morales, Sheafor, and Scott (2009), who see social work as a profession of many faces with numerous varied roles and contributions to society. And, lastly, the authors of this introductory text deliberately chose the title *Social Work: The People's Profession* because the social work practice is an exciting and fascinating, although at times frustrating, way to approach life as a helping professional who works with and on behalf of those in need.

These titles, whether taken individually or viewed as a whole, can inspire an interesting, thought-provoking discussion. And although the main purpose of each of these texts is to educate, advocate, and inform, a text should also get its readers to think about the subject matter in a more critical, insightful manner.

After reading this book, we hope you can see why we chose the title *Social Work: The People's Profession.* Have you learned something new about the social work profession? Do you have a better understanding of the profession, its varied practice methodologies, and the issues faced by today's professionals? For individuals in crisis, do you see the need for providing evidence-based services that meet their diverse needs (Dziegielewski & Jacinto, 2015)?

The primary purpose of this book is to help the reader to develop a better understanding of social work as a profession, including the many intriguing areas of practice and advocacy that social work involves. In providing a reality-based approach to practice, we hope to give the beginning social work professional a tool-kit for examining person-in-environment relations and making this a better place for all.

THE TIME TO DECIDE IS APPROACHING

From the outset, we've made some assumptions about you as the reader of this text and as a beginning social work professional. First, we believe that you are reading this book because it's assigned for a class. We realize this isn't the book of choice for evenings, weekends, or vacations! Second, we think that you are taking a social work course called Introduction to Social Work or something similar because you're interested in learning more about the field. Whatever the title of the course, the class you are taking is probably one of the first, if not the first, social work class in a series of required courses for the degree in social work. Third, we've assumed that, although you or some of your classmates may have had some experience with social work professionals, for the most part you agree that most people do not really have a detailed understanding of the social work profession, including its mission, purpose, and function. Fourth, some of you are seriously exploring social work as a possible career and have registered for this course with that purpose in mind. For others of you, however, this may have been the course that was available at the time or you may have heard that the instructor was really interesting.

Trying to address all of the needs implicit in these assumptions was sometimes daunting, but it was an effort we enjoyed. It feels good to have put together a text that meets the social work accreditation standards, helps people to gain a clear understanding of the social work profession, supports the faculty member's direction, and helps the individual student to make a career decision: is social work for me?

Making a career decision is not easy, nor should it be. We'll be very forthright with our advice to you: Don't make yourself miserable with worry. What you decide today doesn't obligate you for the rest of your life or even through next week! You can change your mind at any time about your career goals. It's not unusual for college students to change majors a number of times before completing their baccalaureate studies.

To be fair, it's true that family, friends, and college teachers and counselors put unnecessary pressure on today's students. Why is it so important to select a major by the end of your sophomore year? When you say that you're going to college, "what's your major?" is often the first question you hear. The reasons for this question vary. Family and friends are probably excited that you're pursuing a college education, and naturally they're interested in what courses you plan to take and what career path you'll follow. Those of us who teach in higher education see the potential major as a means to sustain the field. Academic programs are under constant pressure—intense pressure—to maintain student enrollments. Declining student enrollments jeopardize continuation of a major. Look at what happened to sociology at a number of colleges in the 1980s: it was discontinued as a major, untenured faculty were released from their jobs, and tenured faculty members were moved to other departments.

Only a few years ago, the preference was for a student to get a liberal arts education as an undergraduate. To be considered educated, that is, to develop a broad worldly view of people and their settings, a person must have studied a variety of subjects in the arts, sciences, and humanities. The idea was that a liberal thinker, in the literal rather than the political sense, is better suited to participate in society. For some occupations this broad-based education was sufficient. People could get good jobs without having majored in a specific area. Training for a specific position or workplace happened on the job. People who chose to continue their studies in a specialized field did so in graduate programs.

By contrast, today's undergraduate students are asked to declare their majors early, sometimes even at the time of application. Is it fair to ask someone who is just beginning his or her college education to select a career? Well, we could argue the merits and drawbacks of this practice until we're all blue in the face. The fact is that you must select a major or be cast into the land of the general major (different colleges have different terms for this group; it usually includes all students who haven't chosen a career path).

By this point, most readers of this text have probably made some decisions about social work. We won't take sole credit for influencing the decision-making process. Class lectures and discussions, guest speakers, field trips, and other learning opportunities, in addition to this text, have helped you to make your decision, or at least a partial decision.

The Non-Social-Work Major

We want to offer a few words to those of you who have decided that social work is not for you. First, we're glad you've made a decision that is right for you at this time. Don't be disappointed that you've learned that social work is not your profession of choice. By looking at yourself in the light of information gleaned from this text, you may find yourself challenged on many fronts; the resulting decisions require you to take a very important step in your life. And you can always revisit your decision. When you make career choices, the door never closes for good: you can always reconsider your options.

We hope you have a better understanding and appreciation of social work and the issues that drive our profession. Although you feel that social work is not your career choice, you can nevertheless help to increase other people's understanding. You have learned how to better communicate with them and you know the strengths and weaknesses of our social welfare system so that you can advocate for positive change. You are better informed about a number of social issues and a number of myths that shroud public policy. When you hear others attack social welfare, listen carefully to what is being said and always be sure to take your time and respond with accurate information. Or at least, be slow to judge and be sure to look up or research what others say if it does not sound like what we have discussed thus far. You can be part of the myth-busting squad that dispels misinformation. Let people know the facts about poverty, child welfare, mental health, and the many other areas discussed in this text. Stay informed about the issues: keep up with the e-news or read the daily newspapers and always visit reputable websites for updated information. Information and facts are among the most powerful tools you can have at your disposal.

You can also be invaluable as a social service volunteer. The vast majority of social agencies need people who want to help others. All it takes is one phone call to a specific agency asking if it needs help. Or if you just want to volunteer a few hours a week and the organizational setting doesn't matter, simply call and volunteer at a local service agency. You will most likely be placed in the areas of greatest need where your awareness of the profession and what could help the most will help you to make a meaningful client-empowered contribution.

The Social Work Major

Well, you are about to enter a very structured educational experience. Remember what we learned earlier about the demands of accreditation by the Council on Social Work Education (CSWE). (If you don't remember, you may want to reread chapter 2, especially before your final examination!) With restrictions and expectations related to accreditation and professional practice, you can plan on your academic schedule being outlined for you for the remainder of the program. Because the coursework is so prescribed, be sure to meet with an advisor to discuss the courses you plan to take. This will prevent any surprises as you get ready to graduate. Be sure you are aware of how the courses in your program are sequenced by semester or quarter. You can look at your program's student handbook or ask the course instructor or your academic advisor to review the academic program.

Some aspects of your program are set in granite with little room for modification or negotiation. Additionally, there are some considerations for you to keep in mind:

1. For most students at the graduate or the undergraduate level, the program will take two years of full-time study. Oftentimes courses are sequenced in a certain order. You cannot take these classes out of order and there is generally no way to double up and graduate in one year. We have found over the years that some students spend an inordinate amount of time challenging and trying to change a structured educational program. They often become angry with the faculty and program, calling them inflexible, yet so many of these decisions are beyond the control of the instructor and program. Before you sign on the dotted line and make the decision to become a social work major at either the graduate or the undergraduate level, be sure to check the curriculum model and its specific requirements. This includes mapping out a course of study and accepting the length of time that will be needed to complete the program. Be sure to explore all aspects that may affect your ability to meet these financial and structural requirements. If you are concerned about the requirements, meet with a social work advisor and determine whether your needs can be accommodated.

Don't select this major without planning out the time you will need to complete the degree and explore all possible scenarios. Plan your schedule carefully and make any necessary arrangements, such as those for needed child care or employment, in order to complete all the program requirements (see item 3 below on field placement). Look carefully to see if there are on-line options for some classes and if this will help you to plan your schedule. Keep in mind that the beauty of an online course is flexibility; however, you will still have to plan carefully to meet all program requirements. If you feel you cannot commit to the full-time option, check to see if there is a part-time option. It may take you twice as long to complete the program, but living and working between classes may warrant a slower but steady pace for your course of study.

2. Academic credit will not be given for life experiences, according to CSWE accreditation standards. There are no ifs, ands, or buts on this point. Academic credit is awarded for successful completion of specific college courses and activities only. It doesn't matter if you have lots of experience in the field, worked in the Peace Corps for two years, or worked in a human service agency for five years—no academic credit or course waivers can be awarded for these activities.

3. In social work there is an expectation that each graduate will have supervised work in the field upon graduation. Therefore, you will have a field placement, which is strategically scheduled in your academic program to allow demonstration of specific knowledge and skills learned in the classroom. Your field experience will be sequenced after you have had certain courses. You will not be able to take the field course any earlier in the program, nor can your field course be waived in recognition of previous work experience. Remember that the CSWE does not accept experience in lieu of class work and that this applies to all facets of the educational program, including the field placement.

Be sure to meet the field coordinator in your school; an appointment just to say hello is always a good idea. Meet with the field coordinator as early as possible to discuss your concerns (for example, if you cannot or prefer not to work in any agency or require special considerations in your placement options). Most programs will be as flexible as possible to help meet your needs. You'll also need to be flexible in field placement selection. A program will work with you to find the best site to meet your academic needs, but the final field assignment depends on the social work program and what is available in the community. We've heard students say that, in order for them to get a job, their placement must be in a certain agency. Although programs are concerned about your prospective employment, the primary issue in field assignment is your learning—employment comes later. Be careful to work closely with your field placement director/coordinator and always consider that some programs may have limited resources to meet all or even some of your field placement needs. Remember what we said about planning in advance and making sure that your plan is doable. It is very sad when students cannot receive a BSW or MSW degree simply because they did not complete their field placement hours. Although programs and agency placements try to be flexible, you may not be able to get an evening or weekend placement, and it would be a shame if non-completion of the field hours stopped you from graduating.

4. Remember that your peers in social work courses are in the same place you are. Although everyone's circumstances are different—some are older or younger, some have agency experience whereas others have none—these differences really have minimal importance in the educational setting; all of you are evolving as you begin the process of becoming a professional social worker. No one is better off than anyone else as a result of life experiences. Don't be intimidated by what others say or do or how they come across in class. Try to listen objectively to what others say and process accordingly as you start to question your own assumptions. Allow yourself to expand your previous assumptions as you embrace this professional perspective.

5. The purpose of your baccalaureate educational program is to prepare you for beginning practice. It is not to prepare you for a specialization, which takes place at the graduate level. At this level of your academic career your course instructor and academic advisor care primarily about your development as a beginning social worker.

6. Don't tell an instructor that you need an A in the course for your own personal satisfaction or in order to get into graduate school. There's a saying in Texas that fits this type of situation: "That dog won't hunt!" You certainly have the right to talk with a faculty member about a grade and how it was determined, but it doesn't do any good to be argumentative. The instructor's responsibility is to assess your answers and summarize the quality of your responses with a grade. Grading is not easy—to say the least—and many teachers struggle to ensure that their grades are fair and consistent. Rather than arguing your position, you should use your energy positively, incorporate your social work skills to clarify the situation, and seek a remedy if you feel one is needed. Can you redo the assignment? Is there extra credit work you can do for the course? What changes can you make to do better next time? And so on. If you feel that your grade is incorrect, review the student grievance policy in the program. But, we emphasize, use this only as a last resort

Remember that your faculty members were once students and, like you, they at one time or another felt that an instructor had graded them unfairly. Grading is not an easy task and it is commonplace for a student to be upset or angry when receiving a low grade. Why do we get upset about a grade? The simple reasons is that people don't like getting negative feedback, such as a low grade. Before going to the faculty person's office, we suggest you step back for a moment and look at what the course instructor is saying: What didn't you do on the assignment? What could you have done to get your point across more clearly? What have you learned from this experience that you can apply to future assignments or experiences?

Your goal should be the same as your faculty's goal for you: to develop competence and expertise in entry level generalist social work practice. Your energy should be directed toward developing critical knowledge and skills necessary for effective practice. Learning to be a professional is not easy; it means relooking at your old ways of doing things and applying this new professional strategy. You are a student striving to learn, and if mistakes are made, this is the place where you want to make them.

There are two questions to ask around grades: (1) How will my challenging a grade for a paper, test, or final exam make me a better social work professional? (2) Is there an error in the grading that I can demonstrate to the course instructor and that justifies the assignment of another grade?

THE FUTURE AND YOU

We are now in a new century and the second hundred years of social work practice. As an up-and-coming social worker, you will lay the foundation for the twenty-first century. You represent our future and what you do and say will shape the profession for years to come. As we bring the text to a close, we want to spend our remaining time looking at two premises. First, as you begin your professional career, you should remember always to start each professional activity by applying the knowledge you have learned about social work. Be sure to explore how you can update your knowledge base because environments are not static and all efforts should be relevant to the person-in-situation stance. Finding the best evidence-based practices is essential (Dziegielewski, 2008). Always use this knowledge to guide your helping efforts in the years to come. And second, consider how you can best use these skills to work with clients individually and collectively to provide client-centered care from a micro, mezzo, or macro perspective.

Social Work as a Profession: Future Considerations

You've seen how social work evolved from volunteer effort geared toward the poor to a multifaceted profession working with a variety of client groups. Education was initially limited to on-the-job training, with no oversight of work other than the agency's internal safeguards. Men were the supervisors and women were the caseworkers. Today, social work education is formal (and some say too rigid) because this professional designation must be earned within colleges and universities. There is public regulation in every state for some, but not all, levels of social work practice. Many states are seeking or already have title protection, which means that you simply cannot use the title of social worker unless you have the professional training and qualifications to do so. Social work remains a female-dominated profession. Therefore, it comes as no surprise that, throughout the first

Name: Gary Bailey

Place of residence: Boston, Massachusetts

College/university degrees: Doctor of Humane Letters (honoris causia), University of Connecticut; MSW, Boston University School of Social Work; BA, Eliot Pearson School of Child Study, Tufts University

Present position: Professor of Practice, Simmons College School of Social Work; professor of Practice, Simmons College School of Nursing and Health Sciences

What do you do in your spare time? I am involved in the greater Boston LGBT community serving on the advisory council of the AIDS Action Committee, Inc.; I am a member of the Gay and Lesbian Advocates and Defenders (GLAD) Board of Ambassadors, which focuses on legal issues in the LGBT community; I am a trustee at my church, Union United Methodist Church, which is a 118-year-old congregation . There I am on the internship committee, pastor's advisory committee, and health committee, and I also take care of the grounds and do the planting and beautification of the external church property (mow the grass; cut the shrubs, take care of the flower beds, etc.).

Why did you choose social work as a career? I have always said that social work chose me. I was preparing to go to medical school when I took a winter intercession course at Tufts taught by a social worker. As she described her work with individuals, this just spoke to my heart and my soul; I applied and was accepted at Boson University School of Social Work.

What is your favorite social work story? When I was a student I was an intern in a Montessori elementary school. There I was assigned to work with a young boy whose parents were divorcing, and he was exhibiting certain behaviors that were of concern to his teachers. I remember him as having big blue eyes and red hair. We worked together for the entire year. I often had wondered what had become of him. A few years ago I was walking home from work and I passed this tall handsome man. As I passed I heard him say softly "Mr. Bailey?" I stopped and said hello. He said you probably won't remember me, but I am "Joe Smith" and you were my social worker when I was a little kid. He reminded me of what we use to talk about and the activities we did, and the fact that I sometimes took him to get ice cream after our sessions. He thanked me for making a difference in his life and told me that he often thought about our time together and hoped that one day we might run into one another. He was doing well and now had a son the age he was when I had worked with him. He said thank you for being there for him when he needed someone to talk to. It was a spontaneous and awesome experience.

What would be the one thing you would change in our community if you had the power to do so? Eradicate racism and other forms of intolerance.

hundred years of the profession, it was women's critical contributions to the theory, practice, and politics that make social work what it is today. In the twenty-first century, we find women holding critical positions, leading the profession in academic institutions, professional associations, and social welfare agencies.

The profession's first century required commitment, passion, and vision in order to achieve its current stature. Although we've come a long way, as the poet Robert Frost wrote, "we have miles to go before we sleep." So what are some areas into which the profession should move more aggressively? Let's consider a few ideas:

1. Social work is not designed just to help the individual family or small group. With all the societal upheaval and changes around us, the twenty-first century provides fertile ground for social workers to assume a pivotal position to create positive social change. To empower all individuals, Eamon (2008) identifies four goals: (1) accessing and enhancing social resources, (2) acquiring and increasing economic resources, (3) increasing self-determined behavior, and (4) influencing the social policies and organizational and community practices that affect the lives of vulnerable groups. To achieve these goals, providing services at the micro level only is insufficient; therefore, it is critical to also focus helping efforts at the macro level. Macro level interventions require social change and advocacy that can be most easily accomplished by holding elective office at the local, state, and national levels. We need more of our colleagues to take this chance and run for office and to advocate for policy change.

Richan (2006) reminds us that social problems follow a logical sequence. First the social problem must be recognized and analyzed. Once this is completed, the policy is formalized and later implemented. Once the policy is in effect, expected results and consequences must be evaluated and monitored. This stepwise process creates an interlocking cycle in which one step leads to the next. To create policy, either at the formulation or the evaluation stage, who is better qualified than social workers with their knowledge of and experience with families, children, the poor, the sick, and those at risk? Social workers and lawyers make a great team. Therefore, social workers should never be afraid of being called *bleeding heart liberals*. Instead, they should be proud of it. If assuming the role of a bleeding heart liberal means that we stand for fairness and equity for all people, shelter for the homeless, food for the hungry, and education for all children, then we should stand proudly to acknowledge that role. Wouldn't you love to run against an opponent who claims to oppose care of sick children, to want homeless seniors to live unprotected on the streets, to want people (children in particular) to starve, and to oppose making all of our children the best educated in the world? In other words, the profession must use its assets. If we are a people's profession, our assets start with our attention to human rights striving to protect the rights of all people.

2. The profession of social work needs to recognize the importance of unification and work together, especially on critical issues, presenting a unified front. Social work is a diverse field, and there are those who believe we need special interest groups and membership associations in order to focus on specialized practice matters. But we are fast approaching a crossroad, if we haven't already reached it, where practice membership associations are in conflict with each other and with the overall interests of the profession.

A case in point is public regulation of social work practice. The National Association of Social Workers (NASW) is a staunch advocate of regulation for BSW and MSW levels of practice. The national and state clinical social work membership groups generally oppose licensing of practice other than clinical practice. Why? Could it be that these clinical practitioners feel that, if all social workers could be licensed, this would hurt the clinical practice distinction and therefore decrease their ability to secure fee-paying clients? Some would deny this and point to other factors, but if that is the case, why would they oppose licensing designed to protect all members of the public, not just those who are insured?

How do we bridge the gulf between these two groups? The NASW, nationally and in the states, is an important power than can help clinical social worker membership societies achieve their goals. Tension between members of these two groups is not healthy for the profession or, more importantly, for the public and the clients we serve. Social work membership groups must find common ground if the profession is to become even more effective in its public efforts.

3. The entry degree in the field of social work is the BSW, yet there are far too few at this level who are active in professional membership organizations such as the NASW. Those at the BSW level make important contributions to the field, and their voices need to be heard. We must seek out more BSWs to join the NASW. Because there are too few BSW members in the association, their practice interests are not fully represented at all levels of the association. Annual membership dues certainly are expensive—in particular, for BSWs at lower pay levels—and the NASW has tried to address this by revising the dues structure. But efforts to attract BSWs must go far beyond lower dues. It is essential that MSWs make BSWs feel that they are accepted and important members of the profession. Elitism and professional ethnocentrism will only weaken our efforts.

Social work programs can play a critical role by involving BSW students in the NASW. First, programs can promote membership. Student dues are relatively inexpensive and are far outweighed by the association's benefits. Second, social work programs, together with state chapters and local units, can look at developing student units that hold meetings on campus. Third, social work programs can work with local NASW units to hold meetings on campus—many students are place bound and have no way to get to a meeting. The key is for professional groups and social work programs to be aggressive in recruiting students, to value BSW students as future members, and to involve them in association activities.

4. In chapter 14, we spent time exploring the international social welfare arena. Social work is a worldwide profession that helps people, families, communities, and social systems to deal with issues that cut across national boundaries. Each of these groups comes from a different culture, which requires that a social worker be able to understand and integrate the differences that occur. It is through this understanding that the social worker helps to interpret how all these individuals view the world (Johnson & Grant, 2005). As we grow closer together and the boundaries become more easily crossed, practitioners in the twenty-first century are challenged more than at any other time in the world's history to understand the influence of the international community and be influenced by it. The phrase "think globally, act locally" probably best captures the direction we must go. Yet social workers, for the most part, have little exposure to international social welfare. International course content is sparse in both undergraduate and graduate programs. There are exceptions, of course; some schools sponsor study-abroad programs, offer educationally directed travel programs, or have a greater international emphasis. Yet most social work programs do little more than include brief mentions of international issues as part of a course or courses.

Professional associations also work to promote international issues. Again through study tours and publications, we become more aware of the international community. But is this enough? The authors don't think so. Many in the social work community support the goal of global understanding and activism. Expanding our understanding will help us to be knowledgeable members of the world community. Enhancing global learning and understanding of others will help us to better appreciate the strength and potential of seemingly different people while developing greater awareness of the struggles that will need to be engaged. Global activism builds on knowledge. Once we understand others, we are in a better position to offer effective assistance and support.

There are many mechanisms we can implement to pursue the goal of global understanding and activism. Obviously, the expansion of BSW and MSW curriculum content would help us toward this goal. International content in each course and an additional specific international course would help enhance our knowledge base. We can also become more creative in our approach. Social work educational programs can sponsor annual activities that highlight one or two aspects of international social welfare. Professional associations, both at the national and state level, can sponsor international activities each year. Hosting continuing education workshops, dedicating parts of association newsletters to international issues, and developing dedicated international handouts and brochures will help us to become more global.

The American Social Welfare System: The Future

What a fascinating history we have in social welfare! The overview in chapter 2 was just that, an overview. Even from that brief foray, we can see emerging the long-held myths that underpin the current U.S. social welfare system.

First is the myth that poor people and people in need are different from the rest of us. Some say the poor are morally inferior and lazy; others say they are poorly educated and lack the motivation to change. This negative stereotyping can justify the lack of attention and service provision the system affords. Second, there is a strong belief by the critics of welfare that social services are best left to the local community and private groups. Americans have always been reluctant to support federal involvement in the social welfare system. Social agencies, churches, volunteer associations, and informal networks are more acceptable vehicles for social welfare. Yet, as a society we must be careful not to discriminate against others based on lifestyle or religious preference; this makes suspect service provision provided by those motivated by religious custom and dogma (Blackwell & Dziegielewski, 2005).

Third, social welfare is not an entitlement but rather a temporary support given only to the most worthy. Over time, women, infants, children, the aged, and people with disabilities have fallen into the category of the *worthy poor*. Fourth is the myth that work is the primary way to achieve self-sufficiency. All anyone needs is a job, not even a good-paying job at first, because the early experience will lead to future higher paying jobs.

Now, these views are not necessarily those of most social workers, but they do express the expectations of much of the American public. In chapter 2 we discussed the modern welfare system and, in chapter 7, the 1990s welfare reform package. And we all should remember that in the presidential election of 2000, a new welfare concept came across the national scene: *compassionate conservatism*. These discussions of the late 1990s and early 2000s showed how the four myths described above have become well-ingrained into the American welfare system. This was followed by health care reform of 2010, particularly what is popularly call Obama Care, allowing many more individuals to obtain health care coverage than ever before.

So, where does the American welfare system go? Is the current system working? Here are some underlying assumptions that could support the need for changes to our social welfare programs.

1. The welfare system must be just and treat all people with respect and dignity. How do we explain compassion for the less fortunate when we have in each state a federally mandated and binding welfare program known as Temporary Assistance to Needy Families (TANF)? Although there are some differences among states, this program allows only a maximum of five years of assistance in a lifetime. Some people, no matter what we do, won't be able to care for themselves. Why do we penalize an unborn baby by denying it welfare benefits because the mother was already on assistance? What kind of life are we promising that child? A comprehensive welfare system embraces people and their strengths. We should move away from a punitive system to one based on hope.

2. American welfare carries an enormous stigma. Every day politicians, radio talk show hosts and callers, and newspaper columnists, among others, rail against the poor. With this constant barrage, it would be a wonder if welfare clients didn't hide from the general public. Being poor and receiving public assistance is not the fulfillment of a lifelong ambition. We should work to remove the stigma associated with public aid.

3. The goal of the welfare system should be to help all people with adequate benefits and supports. If the system works, then people who are capable of doing so will move to sustainable work. The purpose of the welfare system's benefits and supports is simple: to help clients to meet their daily needs in order to focus their energies on becoming self-sufficient. The welfare system should concentrate on meeting basic needs: food, shelter, and protection. The ideal social welfare system includes, at a minimum, the following five core pieces: (1) The level of these benefits must be comprehensive. (2) Services include high-quality health care and child care and ongoing supports to adults in their efforts to work. (3) Programs must help people develop the necessary knowledge and skills to become self-sufficient in a technological society. (4) Reliable transportation is needed to ensure that people can get to the training programs, work, or school. (5) Jobs must be permanent (e.g., not seasonal) and offer a living wage, not a minimum wage.

4. A comprehensive welfare system is expensive. But if we truly want to help the poor and less fortunate, the price tag should not matter. Funding decisions for programs are made in a political context. The decision to fund roads and highways at one level and after-school child care at a much lower level is a clear statement about our beliefs. Funds are available to support a comprehensive welfare system, either by changing government spending patterns or by raising taxes. Throughout the text we have referred directly and indirectly to the influence of the political system on social welfare, and in chapter 13 we outlined the role that social workers can assume in politics. As we consider the role of politics in social welfare and questions related to funding, we must first answer two questions: (1) What is the goal of our welfare system? (2) What commitments are we willing to make to achieve that goal?

5. Social welfare and social work should do no harm to any person, group, or community. The *do no harm* philosophy is a fundamental value embraced by the medical community and its ideas should resonate throughout our helping systems. Do we want to create social policies that harm people? Of course we would never want to do this. Yet most agree that the first thrust of TANF is to make it clear that women (particularly unwed teen mothers) do not take personal responsibility for having children. To overcome this and place responsibility for the loss of support on the mother, TANF has a lifetime limit in place on the number of months a person can receive federal assistance (Day & Schiele, 2013). Why do we allow millions of our children not to be fully immunized? Under a "do no harm" philosophy, we would ensure that ALL children would be fully immunized. Do no harm is a core concept that serves as a pivotal girder in the foundation of a just, compassionate society.

SOCIAL WORK PRACTICE

Of all the practice professions, social work has one of the most comprehensive codes of ethics. The profession makes statements such as "once a client, always a client" and "start where the client is" and in every professional encounter holds paramount the individual worth and dignity of each client. Not all social workers are employed as team members or in group practice; in fact, it is common for a social worker to be working on her/his own when confronted with ethical dilemmas (Dolgoff, Harrington, & Lowenberg, 2012). In this situation, a social worker often will contact former colleagues or classmates to discuss the situation and gain advice. When working as a team member, the social worker may note an ethical problem when no one else does. Having such a comprehensive code of ethics can be both a blessing and a curse, especially when other professionals do not view the problem in the same way. This can make ethical practice decisions difficult for the new social worker, especially in an environment of cost containment and behaviorally based coordinated care strategies. To practice in this competitive environment, social workers must either accept this challenge for change or lose the opportunity to be players. Regardless, whether making the decision alone or as part of a team, social workers must be able to show that what they do is necessary and effective while maintaining their own ethical and moral standards for the helping relationship.

As discussed in several chapters of this book, culturally sensitive practice is essential. The nuances of culture can range in subtlety from the differences in meaning of certain nonverbal gestures to the differences in perception of the roles and responsibilities of the practitioner (Arden & Linford, 2009). All groups need to be treated equally, especially groups that have been disenfranchised through preconceived notions and discriminatory practices. Learning more about different groups such as gay, lesbian, bisexual, and transgender individuals is just one way we can provide more culturally sensitive practice (Dziegielewski & Jacinto, 2013).

For social work practice to truly make a difference, all social workers must take a PROACTIVE stance regardless of their practice area. This book is designed to serve as a practical guide for understanding and applying this philosophy in our social work practice environment. Simply stated, all social workers need to embrace the following imperatives at all levels of practice (adapted from Dziegielewski, 2013):

- ◆ *P*: PRESENT and POSITION themselves as competent professionals with POSITIVE attitudes in all service settings, whatever the type of practice.
- ◆ *R*: RECEIVE adequate training and continuing education in the current and future practice area of social work; RESEARCH time-limited treatment approaches that can provide alternatives for social workers struggling to provide high-quality services while cutting costs.
- ◆ *O*: ORGANIZE individuals, groups, and communities to help them to access efficient, effective, evidence-based, safe and affordable services; ORGANIZE other social workers to prepare for the changes that are occurring and develop strategies to continue to provide ethical, cost-effective service.
- ◆ *A*: ADDRESS policies and issues relevant to providing ethical, effective, efficient service.
- ◆ *C*: COLLABORATE with other helping professionals to address client concerns and needs utilizing a client-centered and culturally sensitive approach; COMPLEMENT practices by utilizing holistic practices and alternative strategies that can help clients achieve increased well-being.
- ◆ *T*: TEACH others about the value and the importance of including social work services and techniques; TAKE TIME to help ourselves holistically by preventing professional burnout, thus remaining productive and receptive and serving as good role models for clients and other professionals.

◆ *I*: INVESTIGATE and apply INNOVATIVE approaches to client care problems and issues; INVOLVE all social workers in the change process that
needs to occur in traditional social work.

◆ *V*: VISUALIZE and work toward positive outcomes for all clients and
potential clients; VALUE the roles of all other helping professionals and
support them as they face similar challenges and changes.

◆ *E*: EXPLORE supplemental therapies and strategies that clients can self-
administer at little or no cost to preserve and enhance well-being;
EMPOWER clients and ourselves by stressing the importance of EDU-
CATION for self-betterment as well as individual and societal change.

We will need to face the many changes that continue to challenge social workers as helping professionals, and we need to recognize that social welfare has been
and will remain the primary target for budget cuts, and that in this area of budget
cutting and cost containment we can be viable players. Even so, the NASW Code
of Ethics (NASW, 2008) encourages us to charge reasonable fees and base our
charges on ability to pay. This means that the fees social work professionals charge
are very competitive with those of psychiatrists, psychologists, family therapists,
psychiatric nurses, and mental health counselors, who provide similar services.
This lower cost model may entice health and other service delivery agencies to contract with social workers instead of other professionals to provide services that
have traditionally fallen in the domain of social work practice.

SPECIAL TOPIC: REGULATION OF PROFESSIONAL SOCIAL WORK PRACTICE

In practice we are expected to be accountable professionals, especially because we
work with vulnerable populations (Gelman, 2009). To help ensure accountability,
the government regulates all professions throughout the United States. Regulation
is important to ensure that the public is protected from harm caused by unqualified persons. Credentialing is generally a part of the government's regulatory functions and licensing rules are maintained in the administrative code (Marks & Knox,
2009). Licensing is designed to ensure that the public is protected (DeAngelis, 2009).

Why Do We Regulate Occupations and Why Is Credentialing Important?

A regulated occupation's activities are such that the average citizen may be
harmed physically, emotionally, or financially if he is exposed to the practice of an
unqualified person. Credentialing suggests that a specific educational background
is needed to make a person qualified to carry out the tasks in a regulated occupa-

tion. Through regulation, the public is assured that all regulated persons meet minimum standards of competence as set forth by the state. Additionally, the public is assured that mechanisms are available for the pursuit of grievances against regulated workers. Consider what professions are regulated and how this outlines the scope of practice for the services provided (see the activity below).

Activity...Contact your state's social work licensing board or regulatory body and ask for information about the regulation of social work practice. Are all levels of social work practice licensed? Does the board seem to represent the social work profession's broad range of work, or is its membership restricted to one or two types of practice? Attend a licensing board meeting (they are open to the public) and determine how the board protects the public interest. Finally, how does the local social work community perceive licensing? (Check this out at a local NASW unit meeting.)

Think for a moment about the types of occupations that are regulated by the government. Because decisions about which professions need to be regulated are left to state governments, you'll find that some occupations are licensed in one state but not in another. Even when a profession is regulated by more than one state, the criteria for certification may differ. Types of educational degrees and years of experience required and the use of exams to test competence vary by state and occupation.

The list of occupations that states regulate seems endless. Each state oversees a wide array of occupations that can affect people's lives for good or bad (see box 1, for regulated professions in Florida).

Box 1. Partial List of Occupations Regulated by the State of Florida

Architect	Interior designer	Barber
Public accountant	Pool contractor	Solar contractor
Building contractor	Chiropractor	Nail specialist
Cosmetologist	Hair braider	Dental hygienist
Dentist	Electrical contractor	Alarm system contractor
Embalmer	Talent agency	Physician
Optometrist	Podiatrist	Veterinarian
Nurse	Auctioneer	Athletic trainer
Respiratory therapist	Midwife	Nutrition counselor
Surveyor and mapper	Audiologist	School psychologist
Mental health counselor	Asbestos contractor	Physical therapist
Occupational therapist	Liquor salesperson	Building inspector

The profession of social work is regulated in all fifty states. By that we mean that some form of social work practice is licensed or certified by each state government. For the most part, regulation does not have two levels that mirror the two levels of social work practice, the BSW (generalist practice) and the MSW (specialist practice). For example, some states license both BSW and MSW practitioners together, whereas other states limit licensing to MSW practitioners who specialize in clinical social work. Most, but not all, states require successful completion of a written examination; and most, but not all, states require ongoing continuing education after licensure.

The regulation of social work practice is subject to a number of complications. First, it is tied to the intricacies of the political process. As with any law passed by a state legislature, it reflects political interests. What seems to be a logical, straightforward piece of legislation may end up being defeated for any number of reasons. Some social workers are against formal licensure for the profession, but if we license and regulate hair braiders and surveyors, doesn't it make sense also to regulate a profession that is concerned with the emotional and psychological well-being of people?

Licensing requires social work professionals to overcome their own biases and to act in the best interests of the profession. Unfortunately, this is easier said than done. Many social work special interest groups are most concerned with protecting their own members. A group that feels its interests are enhanced and not compromised will support the legislation. You can imagine what happens to a licensing bill that must satisfy any number of social work interest groups and what can result when ten or more interest groups are actively lobbying at the same time.

Once the profession has pieced together a compromise proposal, the proposal must meet the demands of other human service professions and organizations. Typically, these groups feel that their activities may be affected by the social work licensing legislation. As a result, they work to ensure that the final legislation will not interfere with their day-to-day activities or finances.

Licensing BSW and MSW practice can become very cumbersome and confusing. Although licensing protects the public from nonprofessional practice, state regulation also carves out specific practice areas or *turf* for professions. And turf battles can be hard fought. In Texas, for example, the state legislature in 2003 amended the licensing law to allow BSW degreed individuals to conduct independent practice. For some, this is very confusing—can independent practice be interpreted as being similar to private practice? According to the Texas law, this is not the case. But will the public understand the legal definition?—probably not, given that most social workers themselves are not able to differentiate between independent and private practice.

FINAL THOUGHTS

You should be writing this chapter. As future social workers and members of the global community, you will ultimately be responsible for the social welfare system of the twenty-first century. The types of programs, levels of assistance, and the clients eligible for benefits will all be issues that you will address.

The social work profession will always be part of our community as long as complex human social problems remain. As social workers, our challenge is to remain relevant to our nation's goals and our clients' needs. We can do this by vigorously pursuing competence in practice, by discovering and validating innovative interventions, and by ensuring that our educational and training programs continue to excel.

As you tackle social welfare issues, remain passionate in your convictions, ethical in your actions, knowledgeable about your discipline, and above all, committed to the view that all people have a right to social justice. Our community will be a better place because of people like you. We hope you are excited about the social work profession and what it has to offer people; this excitement can become an incredible source of energy that will strengthen and enhance your passion to work with and on behalf of others for years to come.

REFERENCES

Arden, J. B., & Linford, L. (2009). *Brain-based therapy with adults: Evidence-based treatment for everyday practice*. Hoboken, NJ: Wiley.

Blackwell, C. W., & Dziegielewski, S. F. (2005). The privatization of social services from public to sectarian: Negative consequences for America's gays and lesbians. *Journal of Human Behavior and the Social Environment, 11*(2), 25–43.

Bloom, M. (1990). *Introduction to the drama of social work*. Itasca, IL: Peacock.

Corcoran, K., & Vandiver, V. (1996). *Maneuvering the maze of managed care: Skills for mental health practitioners*. New York: The Free Press.

Colby, I., & Dziegielewski, S. F. (2010). *Introduction to social work: The people's profession* (3rd ed.). Chicago: Lyceum Books.

Day, P. J., & Schiele, J. H. (2013) *A new history of social welfare* (7th ed.). Boston: Pearson.

DeAngelis, D. (2009). Social work licensing examinations in the United States and Canada. In A. Roberts (Ed.), *Social workers desk reference* (2nd ed., pp. 136–147). New York: Oxford University Press.

Dolgoff, R., Harrington, D., & Lowenberg, F. M., (2012). *Ethical decisions for social work practice* (9th ed.), Belmont, CA: Brooks Cole.

Dziegielewski, S. F. (2008). Brief and intermittent approaches to practice: The state of practice. *Brief Treatment and Crisis Intervention, 8,* 147–163.

Dziegielewski, S. F. (2013). *The changing face of health care social work: Opportunities and challenges for professional practice* (3rd ed.). New York: Springer.

Dziegielewski, S. F., & Jacinto, G. (2013). GLBT Cultural sensitivity: Introduction. *Journal of Social Service Research, 39,* 1–2.

Dziegielewski, S. F., & Jacinto, G. A. (2015). Designs and procedures for evaluating crisis intervention. In K. Yeager (Ed.) & A. R. Roberts (Founding Ed.), *Crisis intervention handbook: Assessment, treatment, and research* (4th ed.). New York: Oxford University Press.

Eamon, M. K. (2008). *Empowering vulnerable populations*. Chicago: Lyceum Books.

Estrine, S. A., Hettenbach, R. T., Arthur, H., & Messina, M. (Eds.) (2011). *Service delivery for vulnerable populations: New directions in behavioral health*. New York: Springer.

Fitzsimons, N. M. (2009). *Combating violence & abuse of people with disabilities: A call to action*. Baltimore, MD: Brooks Publishing.

Gelman, S. R. (2009). On being an accountable profession: The code of ethics, oversight by boards of directors, and whistle-blowers as a last resort. In A. R. Roberts, *Social workers' desk reference* (2nd ed., pp. 156–162). New York: Oxford University Press.

Harris, M. B., & Franklin, C. (2008). *Taking charge: A school-based life skills program for adolescent mothers*. New York: Oxford University Press.

Johnson, J. L., & Grant, G. (2005). A multi-systemic approach to practice. In J. L. Johnson & G. Grant (Eds.), *Adoption* (pp. 1–28). New York: Allyn and Bacon.

Lubove, C. (1965). *The professional altruist*. Cambridge, MA: Harvard University Press.

Marks, A. T., & Knox, K. S. (2009). Social work regulation and licensing. In A. R. Roberts, *Social workers' desk reference* (2nd ed., pp. 148–155). New York: Oxford University Press.

Morales, A. T., Sheafor, B. W., & Scott, M. E. (2009). *Social work: A profession of many faces*. Boston: Allyn & Bacon.

National Association of Social Workers. (2008). *Code of ethics of the National Association of Social Workers*. Washington, DC: Author. Retrieved from http://www.socialworkers.org/pubs/code/code.asp

Prigoff, A. (2000). *Economics for social workers: Social outcomes of economic globalization with strategies for community action*. Belmont, CA: Wadsworth/Thomson Learning.

Richan, W., & Mendelsohn, A. R. (1973). *Social work, the unloved profession*. New York: Franklin Watts.

Richan, W. C. (2006). *Lobbying for social change* (3rd ed.). New York: Haworth Press.

Specht, H., & Courtney, M. (1994). *Unfaithful angels*. New York: Free Press.

GLOSSARY

absolute poverty: Qualitative measure of poverty that compares a person's situation with a numerical standard that usually reflects bare subsistence; cf. relative poverty.

abuse: Improper behavior that can result in physical, psychological, or financial harm to an individual, family, group, or community. In social work the term is most often related to acts against children, the elderly, those with mental impairment, or spouses, or used in relation to drug or other substance abuse.

accreditation: Professional recognition that a social work program meets explicit standards; voted on by the Council on Social Work Education's Commission on Accreditation after it reviews the program's self-study documents, the site visitors' written report, and the program's written response to the site visit.

advocacy: Professional activities aimed at educating, informing, or defending and representing the needs and wants of clients through direct intervention or empowerment.

agency: An organization that provides social services and is typically staffed by social service professionals, including social workers. Public, private, and not-for-profit agencies provide an array of services, usually to a target population. Policy is set by a board of directors and is implemented by administrators.

ageism (agism): Stereotyping or generalization based on a person's age. This is considered a form of discrimination that is commonly directed towards older individuals.

agency-based: Occurring in an agency. Agency-based practice can include a few specific practice methodologies or can span the continuum of social work practice, depending on the agency's size, mission, and purpose.

Aid to Families with Dependent Children (AFDC): A means-tested program that provided financial aid to children in need due to parental disability, absence, or death. It was administered nationally through the Administration for Children and Families division of the U.S. Department of Health and Human Services; state and county departments of public welfare provided local administration.

The AFDC ended in 1996 with the creation of Temporary Assistance for Needy Families.

akathisia: A continuous pattern of fidgety movements, for example: swinging of the legs, rocking, pacing, tapping of the feet or hands. Can be associated with anxiety, psychosis, and induced by medication.

akinesia: The loss or reduction of normal motor functioning, resulting in diminished or weakened motor functioning.

almshouse (also known as poorhouse): A place of refuge for those who are poor, medically ill, or mentally ill of all ages; considered the forerunner of the hospital.

assessment: Process of determining the nature, cause, progression, and prognosis of a problem and identifying the personalities and situations involved; process of reasoning from facts to tentative conclusions about their meaning.

at-risk populations (also known as vulnerable populations): Groups with increased exposure to potential harm due to specific characteristics. Examples are infants born to drug-using mothers, who are at risk for birth defects; minorities, who are at risk for oppression; and poor children, who are at risk for malnutrition.

biopsychosocial approach: A perspective to social work practice, especially in health care and mental health, that assesses and places appropriate emphasis on the biological, psychological, and social or environmental aspects of the client's situation.

blended family: A term applied to a family unit when two previously separate families are joined and portray traditional family roles. Often referred to as a step-family.

block grant: A lump sum given to a state by the federal government. The state has authority over expenditure of block grants and may supplement them with state funds.

BSW (baccalaureate in social work): The undergraduate degree in social work from a CSWE-accredited program; the entry level social work qualification. The BSW and BA or BS in social work are equivalent degrees.

candidacy pre-accreditation: Status for a social work program, which generally lasts two years; signifies that an educational program meets general criteria to conduct a self-study for accreditation.

charity assistance: Aid given to the poor in the 1600s; viewed as a mechanism that reinforced dependent lifestyles.

charity organization society (COS): A privately or philanthropically funded agency that delivered social services to the needy in the mid- to late-nineteenth century; considered to be the forerunner of the nonprofit social service agency.

child welfare: A series of human service and social welfare programs designed specifically to promote the protection, care, and health development of children; found at the national, state, and local levels.

client: An individual, couple, family, group, or community that is the focus of intervention.

codependency: A relationship between two or more persons that is based on dependence of the other to meet and provide needs. For the most part this is considered unhealthy because one individual is dependent on the other, making control and manipulation highly probable and difficult to avoid.

Commission on Accreditation: A CSWE committee of twenty-five social work educators and practitioners who oversee the accreditation process. The commission establishes educational standards and reviews programs to ensure that they meet the standards.

continuing education: Training acquired after the completion of a degree program. The NASW and state licensure boards require specified hours of continuing education in order to maintain a license or certification.

Council on Social Work Education (CSWE): The sole national accreditation board for schools of social work; founded in 1952 from the merger of the American Association of Schools of Social Work (founded 1919) and the National Association of Schools of Social Administration (founded 1942).

delirium: A state of mind that often presents itself as a disturbance in one's thinking and attention, often evidenced by hallucinations and anxiety. There can be multiple causes for this, ranging from organic damage to the brain to drug or alcohol use.

diagnosis: The process of identifying a problem—social, mental, or medical—and its underlying causes and formulating a solution.

disadvantaged: A term used to describe individuals, groups, communities, and the like that are unable to access the resources and services needed to maintain a minimal standard of living.

discharge planning: A service provided by health care social workers to assist clients in, for example, securing placement and services to support a timely transition from a health care facility to home or to another less restrictive environment.

discrimination: The prejudgment and negative treatment of someone or a group of people based on known characteristics. Common sources of discrimination include race, gender, ethnicity, religion, or sexual identity.

domestic violence: Violent acts toward another person perpetrated in a domestic situation.

door-knob communication: A term applied when a person in therapy shares something significant just as the therapy session is about to end. This can be something the client felt uncomfortable about that was either mentioned or not mentioned in the session. Often it is considered a stall tactic to prolong the session.

DSM-IV-TR **(Diagnostic and Statistical Manual, 4th edition, Text Revision):** Manual that presents a classification system designed to assist in reaching formal diagnoses. It uses five axes: Axis I, the first level of coding, records such categories as major clinical syndromes, pervasive developmental disorders, learning disorders, motor skills disorders, communication disorders, and other disorders that may be the focus of clinical treatment. Axis II records personality disorders and mental retardation. Axis III records general medical conditions that can affect mental health. Axis IV records psychosocial and environmental problems/stressors. Axis V records level of functioning.

DSW (doctor of social welfare or social work): One of the highest social work degrees; this degree typically requires two years of full-time post-master's course work, successful completion of comprehensive examinations, and successful completion of a dissertation. There is also a PhD in social work or social welfare that often has similar requirements.

educable: Capable of being educated. Professionals often use this term with regard to individuals with mental retardation who have the ability to learn certain social or academic skills.

Educational Policy and Accreditation Standards (EPAS): A written document that outlines the purpose and framework of social work education programs. The CSWE Commission on Accreditation is responsible for oversight of the EPAS.

empirically based social work practice: A type of intervention in which the professional social worker uses research as a practice and problem-solving tool. Data are collected systematically, and problems and outcomes are stated in measurable terms.

entitlement programs: Governmental programs offered to all individuals who meet the predetermined criteria.

ethics: A system of moral principles used in decision making to discern right from wrong or to choose between two or more seemingly equal alternatives.

ethical practice in social work: Adhering to the standards and principles set forth in the profession and acting in a way that highlights the core values and expectations of the profession.

field placement: Work in an agency during the BSW or MSW educational experience, supervised by a social worker. The agency and the educational institution jointly train and monitor the students during placement.

Food Stamp Program: A program that distributes stamps that can be used to purchase basic food items to people in need. It was implemented in 1964 and administered by the U.S. Department of Agriculture until 1996; it is now administered by states under the Personal Responsibility and Work Opportunity Reconciliation Act of 1996.

friendly visitor: A volunteer from a charity organization society who visited poor families to offer aid and to serve as a role model.

generalist practice: Practice underpinned by knowledge and skills across a broad spectrum and by comprehensive assessment of problems and their solutions; includes coordination of activities of specialists.

hallucination: An imagined perception of an object or idea that is not really present. This is often a symptom of psychosis and can include auditory (hearing), visual (seeing), olfactory (smelling), gustatory (tasting), and tactile or haptic (touching) things that are not present. This may most likely be seen in a mental disorder called schizophrenia.

Head Start: A program intended to help preschool children of disadvantaged families to overcome or offset problems related to social deprivation; established in 1965 and administered by Child Youth and Families within the U.S. Department of Health and Human Services.

home care: In this type of health care, social work services are provided to individuals and families in their home or community and/or other home-like settings.

hospice care: This type of care involves providing services to individuals who are considered to be terminally ill and their family members. In this type of care there is open acknowledgment that no cure is expected for client's illness, and the goal is to support the process of dying in a dignified manner; physical, emotional, social, and spiritual care are provided.

hospital social worker: A social worker who practices in hospitals and health care facilities, focusing on assessments, discharge planning, preventive services, interdisciplinary coordination, and individual and family counseling.

human rights: Universal social rights all persons share without distinction as to race, gender, language, or religion. An example of this is civil rights.

indoor relief: Assistance provided during colonial times to the *unworthy* poor in poorhouses.

in kind: A benefit in the form of food, clothing, education, and so forth, in place of, or in addition to, cash.

institutional social welfare: Social programs available to all as a part of well-being in the modern state; cf. residual social welfare.

interdisciplinary team: A variety of health care professionals brought together to provide a client with effective, better coordinated, and improved quality of services.

International Federation of Social Workers (IFSW): An international association of social workers comprising members through their national organizations; founded in 1928 in Paris; promotes social work, establishes standards, and provides a forum for exchange among associations throughout the world.

intervention: Treatment, services, advocacy, mediation, or any other practice action, performed for or with clients, that is intended to ameliorate problems.

label: In mental health it is generally referred to as a clinical diagnosis of a client that stays with the client indefinitely, possibly to the client's detriment.

macrosystem: Community, administrative, and environmental forces that affect the human condition. Political action, community organizing, and administration of large public welfare agencies are examples of macropractice.

managed care: A form of health care delivery within a specific framework with specific rules, requirements, and expectations for the delivery of service.

Meals on Wheels: Delivery of meals to the homes of people unable to meet their own nutritional needs, usually due to physical or mental impairment. The providers of service are usually community agencies, such as senior citizen councils, local human service departments, and private agencies.

means-tested program: A program for which eligibility is determined by the recipient's resources and whether the need is great enough within a predetermined criteria set.

Medicaid: A program established in 1965 that funds hospital and other medical services to people who meet means tests; administered by the federal Health Care Financing Administration.

Medicare: A national health insurance program established in 1965. Eligibility is universal, with attainment of age sixty-five as the criterion for most people; however, there are allied programs for those with disabilities, among others. Medicare is funded through employee and employer contributions and administered by the Social Security Administration and the Health Care Financing Administration.

mezzosystem: A system that connects microsystems and macrosystems.

microsystem: Individual, family, or small group. Direct intervention and case-work are examples of micropractice.

MSW (master of social work): A degree requiring approximately sixty hours of post-baccalaureate education, including 900 hours of field placement, in a CSWE-accredited program. The MSSW and MA or MS in social work are equivalent degrees.

multidisciplinary team: A mix of health and social welfare professionals, with each discipline working, for the most part, on an independent or referral basis.

National Association of Social Workers (NASW): The world's largest social work membership association with approximately 160,000 members in 1999; established in 1955 through the merger of five special interest organizations. Chapters exist in all fifty states and the District of Columbia, New York City, Puerto Rico, and the Virgin Islands, in addition to an international chapter.

nativism: The idea that certain personality factors are present at birth and are not learned.

needs assessments (NA): An assessment made on behalf of the client by agencies to evaluate their clients' needs and establish priorities for service.

New Deal: A set of social welfare programs and legislation implemented during President Franklin D. Roosevelt's administration in response to the Great Depression. Examples include the Economic Security Act of 1935, Works Progress Administration, and Federal Emergency Relief Act.

outdoor relief: Minimal assistance provided during the colonial period to the *worthy poor* in their own homes.

overseer of the poor: An individual responsible during colonial times for identifying the poor, assessing their needs, and coordinating a community response by levying and collecting taxes; considered a colonial version of a social worker.

parens patriae: The principle under which children can become wards of the state. Related to children's rights, this principle has allowed children's advocates to argue that children should be viewed differently from adults and has been used to support the creation of a range of juvenile services.

Person-in-Environment Classification System (PIE): A systematic approach to classifying social functioning. It employs four levels to aid in the systematic collection of data about clients and in planning interventions. Level I is social functioning problems. Level II is environmental problems. Level III is mental disorders—DSM-IV Axes I and II. Level IV is physical health problems.

person-in-situation (also called person-in-environment): A casework concept that focuses on the interrelation among problem, situation, and the interaction between them.

PhD (doctorate in philosophy): The highest social work degree, emphasizing research, knowledge expansion, and advanced clinical practice. It is similar and often identical to the DSW. See DSW for requirements.

policy: The plan that an agency, organization, or governmental institution follows as a framework; includes formal written policies and unwritten (informal) policies.

political lens: The political context—often candidates for public office and their campaigns—that influences how society defines a term such as family.

poor laws: Codified in 1601; redefined welfare as no longer a private affair but rather a public governmental responsibility.

poverty: A general term used to describe a state of deprivation. *See* absolute poverty and relative poverty.

poverty threshold: The level of income below which a person is living in poverty. This level is based on the cost of securing the basic necessities of living.

projection: A defense mechanism one uses when rejecting or attributing unacceptable aspects of one's personality to another person.

psychosocial history: Systematic compilation of information about a client; encompasses family, health, education, spirituality, legal position, interpersonal relations, social supports, economic status, environment, sexual orientation, and culture.

rapport: An important part of the therapeutic relationship that results in harmony, compatibility, and empathy, fostering mutual understanding and a working relationship between the client and social worker.

reaffirmation: Confirmation of CSWE accreditation, for which an accredited program must undergo the self-study and review process every seven years.

relative poverty: Subjective measure of poverty that compares a person's situation with a normative standard (*cf* absolute poverty).

residual social welfare: Social programs activated only when normal structures of family and market are not sufficient (*cf* institutional social welfare).

role: Culturally expected behavior associated with a person or status.

sanction: (1) formal or informal authorization to perform services; (2) penalty imposed for noncompliance with policies and procedures. The NASW sanctions members who have violated the Code of Ethics with membership suspension or removal of certification.

selective eligibility (also called means-tested eligibility): Eligibility based on demonstrating need or inability to provide for one's needs (*cf* universal eligibility{.

site visit: Visit to a social work educational program by a site team composed of social work educators and, for graduate programs, an MSW practitioner. The site team makes a written report to the CSWE Commission on Accreditation that is considered during the commission's deliberations on the program's accreditation.

social justice: A core social work value that involves efforts to confront discrimination, oppression, and other social inequities.

social welfare: (1) society's specific system of programs to help people to meet basic health, economic, and social needs; (2) general state of well-being in society.

specialist practice: Practice focused in approach and knowledge on a specific problem or goal or underpinned by highly developed expertise in specific activities.

strengths-based assessment: This type of assessment relies on the social worker's ability to critically analyze the positive aspects, attributes, or strengths in a client or client system and to utilize these strengths in every aspect of the problem-solving process.

stigma: Negative connotation attached to individuals, or groups of individuals, based on characteristics that may include economic status, health, appearance, education, sexual orientation, and mental health.

Temporary Assistance for Needy Families (TANF): A program established in 1996 to replace AFDC. It is subject to strict eligibility requirements, which mandate employment, and to a lifetime limit on benefits of five years; funded through federal block grants to states, which administer the program.

universal eligibility: Availability to all people regardless of income or social support (*cf* selective eligibility).

unworthy poor: A category of people undeserving of public aid introduced by the 1601 Poor Laws. The unworthy poor consisted of the vagrant or able-bodied who, although able to work, did not seek employment.

victim blaming: A philosophy or orientation that attributes blame and responsibility to the person who is harmed by a social circumstance. An example of this would be a female who is raped but publicly she is accused of dressing seductively and thereby seducing her attacker.

Violence Against Women Act (VAWA): Passed in 1994; a comprehensive federal response to the problems of domestic violence that promotes preventive programs and victim's services.

worthy poor: A category of people deserving of public aid introduced by the 1601 Poor Laws; including the ill, the disabled, orphans, and the elderly—people viewed as having no control over their life circumstances—as well as people who were involuntary unemployed.

APPENDIX A

NATIONAL ASSOCIATION OF SOCIAL WORKERS, CODE OF ETHICS

Approved by the 1996 NASW Delegate Assembly and revised by the 2008 NASW Delegate Assembly

Preamble

The primary mission of the social work profession is to enhance human well-being and help meet the basic human needs of all people, with particular attention to the needs and empowerment of people who are vulnerable, oppressed, and living in poverty. A historic and defining feature of social work is the profession's focus on individual well-being in a social context and the well-being of society. Fundamental to social work is attention to the environmental forces that create, contribute to, and address problems in living.

Social workers promote social justice and social change with and on behalf of clients. "Clients" is used inclusively to refer to individuals, families, groups, organizations, and communities. Social workers are sensitive to cultural and ethnic diversity and strive to end discrimination, oppression, poverty, and other forms of social injustice. These activities may be in the form of direct practice, community organizing, supervision, consultation administration, advocacy, social and political action, policy development and implementation, education, and research

and evaluation. Social workers seek to enhance the capacity of people to address their own needs. Social workers also seek to promote the responsiveness of organizations, communities, and other social institutions to individuals' needs and social problems.

The mission of the social work profession is rooted in a set of core values. These core values, embraced by social workers throughout the profession's history, are the foundation of social work's unique purpose and perspective:

- service
- social justice
- dignity and worth of the person
- importance of human relationships
- integrity
- competence.

This constellation of core values reflects what is unique to the social work profession. Core values, and the principles that flow from them, must be balanced within the context and complexity of the human experience.

PURPOSE OF THE NASW CODE OF ETHICS

Professional ethics are at the core of social work. The profession has an obligation to articulate its basic values, ethical principles, and ethical standards. The *NASW Code of Ethics* sets forth these values, principles, and standards to guide social workers' conduct. The *Code* is relevant to all social workers and social work students, regardless of their professional functions, the settings in which they work, or the populations they serve.

The *NASW Code of Ethics* serves six purposes:

1. The Code identifies core values on which social work's mission is based.
2. The *Code* summarizes broad ethical principles that reflect the profession's core values and establishes a set of specific ethical standards that should be used to guide social work practice.
3. The *Code* is designed to help social workers identify relevant considerations when professional obligations conflict or ethical uncertainties arise.
4. The *Code* provides ethical standards to which the general public can hold the social work profession accountable.
5. The *Code* socializes practitioners new to the field to social work's mission, values, ethical principles, and ethical standards.
6. The *Code* articulates standards that the social work profession itself can use to assess whether social workers have engaged in unethical conduct. NASW has formal procedures to adjudicate ethics complaints filed against its members.* In subscribing to this *Code*, social workers are required to cooperate in its implementation, participate in NASW adjudication proceedings, and abide by any NASW disciplinary rulings or sanctions based on it.

The *Code* offers a set of values, principles, and standards to guide decision making and conduct when ethical issues arise. It does not provide a set of rules that prescribe how social workers should act in all situations. Specific applications of the *Code* must take into account the context in which it is being considered and the possibility of conflicts among the *Code's* values, principles, and standards. Ethical responsibilities flow from all human relationships, from the personal and familial to the social and professional.

Further, the *NASW Code of Ethics* does not specify which values, principles, and standards are most important and ought to outweigh others in instances when they conflict. Reasonable differences of opinion can and do exist among social workers with respect to the ways in which values, ethical principles, and ethical standards should be rank ordered when they conflict. Ethical decision making in a given situation must apply the informed judgment of the individual social worker and should also consider how the issues would be judged in a peer review process where the ethical standards of the profession would be applied.

Ethical decision making is a process. There are many instances in social work where simple answers are not available to resolve complex ethical issues. Social workers should take into consideration all the values, principles, and standards in this *Code* that are relevant to any situation in which ethical judgment is warranted. Social workers' decisions and actions should be consistent with the spirit as well as the letter of this *Code*.

In addition to this *Code*, there are many other sources of information about ethical thinking that may be useful. Social workers should consider ethical theory and principles generally, social work theory and research, laws, regulations, agency policies, and other relevant codes of ethics, recognizing that among codes of ethics social workers should consider the *NASW Code of Ethics* as their primary source. Social workers also should be aware of the impact on ethical decision making of their clients' and their own personal values and cultural and religious beliefs and practices. They should be aware of any conflicts between personal and professional values and deal with them responsibly. For additional guidance social workers should consult the relevant literature on professional ethics and ethical decision making and seek appropriate consultation when faced with ethical dilemmas. This may involve consultation with an agency-based or social work organization's ethics committee, a regulatory body, knowledgeable colleagues, supervisors, or legal counsel.

Instances may arise when social workers' ethical obligations conflict with agency policies or relevant laws or regulations. When such conflicts occur, social workers must make a responsible effort to resolve the conflict in a manner that is consistent with the values, principles, and standards expressed in this Code. If a reasonable resolution of the conflict does not appear possible, social workers should seek proper consultation before making a decision.

The *NASW Code of Ethics* is to be used by NASW and by individuals, agencies, organizations, and bodies (such as licensing and regulatory boards, professional liability insurance providers, courts of law, agency boards of directors, government agencies, and other professional groups) that choose to adopt it or use it as a frame of reference. Violation of standards in this *Code* does not automatically imply legal liability or violation of the law. Such determination can only be made in the context of legal and judicial proceedings. Alleged violations of the *Code* would be subject to a peer review process.

Such processes are generally separate from legal or administrative procedures and insulated from legal review or proceedings to allow the profession to counsel and discipline its own members.

A code of ethics cannot guarantee ethical behavior. Moreover, a code of ethics cannot resolve all ethical issues or disputes or capture the richness and complexity involved in striving to make responsible choices within a moral community. Rather, a code of ethics sets forth values, ethical principles, and ethical standards to which professionals aspire and by which their actions can be judged. Social workers' ethical behavior should result from their personal commitment to engage in ethical practice. The *NASW Code of Ethics* reflects the commitment of all social workers to uphold the profession's values and to act ethically. Principles and standards must be applied by individuals of good character who discern moral questions and, in good faith, seek to make reliable ethical judgments.

Ethical Principles

The following broad ethical principles are based on social work's core values of service, social justice, dignity and worth of the person, importance of human relationships, integrity, and competence. These principles set forth ideals to which all social workers should aspire.

Value: *Service*

Ethical Principle: *Social workers' primary goal is to help people in need and to address social problems.* Social workers elevate service to others above self-interest. Social workers draw on their knowledge, values, and skills to help people in need and to address social problems. Social workers are encouraged to volunteer some portion of their professional skills with no expectation of significant financial return (pro bono service).

Value: *Social Justice*

Ethical Principle: *Social workers challenge social injustice.* Social workers pursue social change, particularly with and on behalf of vulnerable and oppressed individuals and groups of people. Social workers' social change efforts are focused primarily on issues of poverty, unemployment, discrimination, and other forms of social injustice. These activities seek to promote sensitivity to and knowledge about oppression and cultural and ethnic diversity. Social workers strive to ensure access to needed information, services, and resources; equality of opportunity; and meaningful participation in decision making for all people.

Value: *Dignity and Worth of the Person*

Ethical Principle: *Social workers respect the inherent dignity and worth of the person.* Social workers treat each person in a caring and respectful fashion, mindful of individual differences and cultural and ethnic diversity. Social workers promote clients' socially responsible self-determination. Social workers seek to enhance clients' capacity and opportunity to change and to address their own needs. Social workers are cognizant of their dual responsibility to clients and to the broader society. They seek to resolve conflicts between clients' interests and the broader society's interests in a socially responsible manner consistent with the values, ethical principles, and ethical standards of the profession.

Value: *Importance of Human Relationships*

Ethical Principle: *Social workers recognize the central importance of human relationships.*

Social workers understand that relationships between and among people are an important vehicle for change. Social workers engage people as partners in the helping process. Social workers seek to strengthen relationships among people in a purposeful effort to promote, restore, maintain, and enhance the well-being of individuals, families, social groups, organizations, and communities.

Value: *Integrity*

Ethical Principle: *Social workers behave in a trustworthy manner.* Social workers are continually aware of the profession's mission, values, ethical principles, and ethical standards and practice in a manner consistent with them. Social workers act honestly and responsibly and promote ethical practices on the part of the organizations with which they are affiliated.

Value: *Competence*

Ethical Principle: *Social workers practice within their areas of competence and develop and enhance their professional expertise.* Social workers continually strive to increase their professional knowledge and skills and to apply them in practice. Social workers should aspire to contribute to the knowledge base of the profession.

Ethical Standards

The following ethical standards are relevant to the professional activities of all social workers. These standards concern (1) social workers' ethical responsibilities to clients, (2) social workers' ethical responsibilities to colleagues, (3) social workers' ethical responsibilities in practice settings, (4) social workers' ethical responsibilities as professionals, (5) social workers' ethical responsibilities to the social work profession, and (6) social workers' ethical responsibilities to the broader society.

Some of the standards that follow are enforceable guidelines for professional conduct, and some are aspirational. The extent to which each standard is enforceable is a matter of professional judgment to be exercised by those responsible for reviewing alleged violations of ethical standards.

1. Social Workers' Ethical Responsibilities to Clients

1.01 Commitment to Clients

Social workers' primary responsibility is to promote the well-being of clients. In general, clients' interests are primary. However, social workers' responsibility to the larger society or specific legal obligations may on limited occasions supersede the loyalty owed clients, and clients should be so advised. (Examples include when a social worker is required by law to report that a client has abused a child or has threatened to harm self or others.)

1.02 Self-Determination

Social workers respect and promote the right of clients to self-determination and assist clients in their efforts to identify and clarify their goals. Social workers may limit clients' right to self-determination when, in the social workers' professional judgment, clients' actions or potential actions pose a serious, foreseeable, and imminent risk to themselves or others.

1.03 Informed Consent

(a) Social workers should provide services to clients only in the context of a professional relationship based, when appropriate, on valid informed consent. Social workers should use clear and understandable language to inform clients of the purpose of the services, risks related to the services, limits to services because of the requirements of a third-party payer, relevant costs, reasonable alternatives, clients' right to refuse or withdraw consent, and the time frame covered by the consent. Social workers should provide clients with an opportunity to ask questions.

(b) In instances when clients are not literate or have difficulty understanding the primary language used in the practice setting, social workers should take steps to ensure clients' comprehension. This may include providing clients with a detailed verbal explanation or arranging for a qualified interpreter or translator whenever possible.

(c) In instances when clients lack the capacity to provide informed consent, social workers should protect clients' interests by seeking permission from an appropriate third party, informing clients consistent with the clients' level of understanding. In such instances social workers should seek to ensure that the third party acts in a manner consistent with clients' wishes and interests. Social workers should take reasonable steps to enhance such clients' ability to give informed consent.

(d) In instances when clients are receiving services involuntarily, social workers should provide information about the nature and extent of services and about the extent of clients' right to refuse service.

(e) Social workers who provide services via electronic media (such as computer, telephone, radio, and television) should inform recipients of the limitations and risks associated with such services.

(f) Social workers should obtain clients' informed consent before audiotaping or videotaping clients or permitting observation of services to clients by a third party.

1.04   Competence

(a) Social workers should provide services and represent themselves as competent only within the boundaries of their education, training, license, certification, consultation received, supervised experience, or other relevant professional experience.

(b) Social workers should provide services in substantive areas or use intervention techniques or approaches that are new to them only after engaging in appropriate study, training, consultation, and supervision from people who are competent in those interventions or techniques.

(c) When generally recognized standards do not exist with respect to an emerging area of practice, social workers should exercise careful judgment and take responsible steps (including appropriate education, research, training, consultation, and supervision) to ensure the competence of their work and to protect clients from harm.

1.05   Cultural Competence and Social Diversity

(a) Social workers should understand culture and its function in human behavior and society, recognizing the strengths that exist in all cultures.

(b) Social workers should have a knowledge base of their clients' cultures and be able to demonstrate competence in the provision of services that are sensitive to clients' cultures and to differences among people and cultural groups.

(c) Social workers should obtain education about and seek to understand the nature of social diversity and oppression with respect to race, ethnicity, national origin, color, sex, sexual orientation, gender identity or expression, age, marital status, political belief, religion, immigration status, and mental or physical disability.

1.06   Conflicts of Interest

(a) Social workers should be alert to and avoid conflicts of interest that interfere with the exercise of professional discretion and impartial judgment. Social workers should inform clients when a real or potential conflict of interest arises and take reasonable steps to resolve the issue in a manner that makes the clients' interests primary and protects clients' interests to the greatest extent possible. In some cases, protecting clients' interests may require termination of the professional relationship with proper referral of the client.

(b) Social workers should not take unfair advantage of any professional relationship or exploit others to further their personal, religious, political, or business interests.

(c) Social workers should not engage in dual or multiple relationships with clients or former clients in which there is a risk of exploitation or potential harm to the client. In instances when dual or multiple relationships are unavoidable, social workers should take steps to protect clients and are responsible for setting clear, appropriate, and culturally sensitive boundaries. (Dual or multiple relationships occur when social workers relate to clients in more than one relationship, whether professional, social, or business. Dual or multiple relationships can occur simultaneously or consecutively.)

(d) When social workers provide services to two or more people who have a relationship with each other (for example, couples, family members), social workers should clarify with all parties which individuals will be considered clients and the nature of social workers' professional obligations to the various individuals who are receiving services. Social workers who anticipate a conflict of interest among the individuals receiving services or who anticipate having to perform in potentially conflicting roles (for example, when a social worker is asked to testify in a child custody dispute or divorce proceedings involving clients) should clarify their role with the parties involved and take appropriate action to minimize any conflict of interest.

1.07 Privacy and Confidentiality

(a) Social workers should respect clients' right to privacy. Social workers should not solicit private information from clients unless it is essential to providing services or conducting social work evaluation or research. Once private information is shared, standards of confidentiality apply.

(b) Social workers may disclose confidential information when appropriate with valid consent from a client or a person legally authorized to consent on behalf of a client.

(c) Social workers should protect the confidentiality of all information obtained in the course of professional service, except for compelling professional reasons. The general expectation that social workers will keep information confidential does not apply when disclosure is necessary to prevent serious, foreseeable, and imminent harm to a client or other identifiable person. In all instances, social workers should disclose the least amount of confidential information necessary to achieve the desired purpose; only information that is directly

relevant to the purpose for which the disclosure is made should be revealed.

(d) Social workers should inform clients, to the extent possible, about the disclosure of confidential information and the potential consequences, when feasible before the disclosure is made. This applies whether social workers disclose confidential information on the basis of a legal requirement or client consent.

(e) Social workers should discuss with clients and other interested parties the nature of confidentiality and limitations of clients' right to confidentiality. Social workers should review with clients circumstances where confidential information may be requested and where disclosure of confidential information may be legally required. This discussion should occur as soon as possible in the social worker-client relationship and as needed throughout the course of the relationship.

(f) When social workers provide counseling services to families, couples, or groups, social workers should seek agreement among the parties involved concerning each individual's right to confidentiality and obligation to preserve the confidentiality of information shared by others. Social workers should inform participants in family, couples, or group counseling that social workers cannot guarantee that all participants will honor such agreements.

(g) Social workers should inform clients involved in family, couples, marital, or group counseling of the social worker's, employer's, and agency's policy concerning the social worker's disclosure of confidential information among the parties involved in the counseling.

(h) Social workers should not disclose confidential information to third-party payers unless clients have authorized such disclosure.

(i) Social workers should not discuss confidential information in any setting unless privacy can be ensured. Social workers should not discuss confidential information in public or semipublic areas such as hallways, waiting rooms, elevators, and restaurants.

(j) Social workers should protect the confidentiality of clients during legal proceedings to the extent permitted by law. When a court of law or other legally authorized body orders social workers to disclose confidential or privileged information without a client's consent and such disclosure could cause harm to the client, social workers should request that the court withdraw the order or limit the order as narrowly as possible or maintain the records under seal, unavailable for public inspection.

(k) Social workers should protect the confidentiality of clients when responding to requests from members of the media.

(l) Social workers should protect the confidentiality of clients' written and electronic records and other sensitive information. Social workers should take reasonable steps to ensure that clients' records are stored in a secure location and that clients' records are not available to others who are not authorized to have access.

(m) Social workers should take precautions to ensure and maintain the confidentiality of information transmitted to other parties through the use of computers, electronic mail, facsimile machines, telephones and telephone answering machines, and other electronic or computer technology. Disclo-sure of identifying information should be avoided whenever possible.

(n) Social workers should transfer or dispose of clients' records in a manner that protects clients' confidentiality and is consistent with state statutes governing records and social work licensure.

(o) Social workers should take reasonable precautions to protect client confidentiality in the event of the social worker's termination of practice, incapacitation, or death.

(p) Social workers should not disclose identifying information when discussing clients for teaching or training purposes unless the client has consented to disclosure of confidential information.

(q) Social workers should not disclose identifying information when discussing clients with consultants unless the client has consented to disclosure of confidential information or there is a compelling need for such disclosure.

(r) Social workers should protect the confidentiality of deceased clients consistent with the preceding standards.

1.08   Access to Records

(a) Social workers should provide clients with reasonable access to records concerning the clients. Social workers who are concerned that clients' access to their records could cause serious misunderstanding or harm to the client should provide assistance in interpreting the records and consultation with the client regarding the records. Social workers should limit clients' access to their records, or portions of their records, only in exceptional circumstances when there is compelling evidence that such access would cause serious harm to the client. Both clients' requests and the rationale for withholding some or all of the record should be documented in clients' files.

(b) When providing clients with access to their records, social workers should take steps to protect the confidentiality of other individuals identified or discussed in such records.

1.09 Sexual Relationships

(a) Social workers should under no circumstances engage in sexual activities or sexual contact with current clients, whether such contact is consensual or forced.

(b) Social workers should not engage in sexual activities or sexual contact with clients' relatives or other individuals with whom clients maintain a close personal relationship when there is a risk of exploitation or potential harm to the client. Sexual activity or sexual contact with clients' relatives or other individuals with whom clients maintain a personal relationship has the potential to be harmful to the client and may make it difficult for the social worker and client to maintain appropriate professional boundaries. Social workers—not their clients, their clients' relatives, or other individuals with whom the client maintains a personal relationship—assume the full burden for setting clear, appropriate, and culturally sensitive boundaries.

(c) Social workers should not engage in sexual activities or sexual contact with former clients because of the potential for harm to the client. If social workers engage in conduct contrary to this prohibition or claim that an exception to this prohibition is warranted because of extraordinary circumstances, it is social workers—not their clients—who assume the full burden of

demonstrating that the former client has not been exploited, coerced, or manipulated, intentionally or unintentionally.

(d) Social workers should not provide clinical services to individuals with whom they have had a prior sexual relationship. Providing clinical services to a former sexual partner has the potential to be harmful to the individual and is likely to make it difficult for the social worker and individual to maintain appropriate professional boundaries.

1.10 Physical Contact

Social workers should not engage in physical contact with clients when there is a possibility of psychological harm to the client as a result of the contact (such as cradling or caressing clients). Social workers who engage in appropriate physical contact with clients are responsible for setting clear, appropriate, and culturally sensitive boundaries that govern such physical contact.

1.11 Sexual Harassment

Social workers should not sexually harass clients. Sexual harassment includes sexual advances, sexual solicitation, requests for sexual favors, and other verbal or physical conduct of a sexual nature.

1.12 Derogatory Language

Social workers should not use derogatory language in their written or verbal communications to or about clients. Social workers should use accurate and respectful language in all communications to and about clients.

1.13 Payment for Services

(a) When setting fees, social workers should ensure that the fees are fair, reasonable, and commensurate with the services performed. Consideration should be given to clients' ability to pay.

(b) Social workers should avoid accepting goods or services from clients as payment for professional services. Bartering arrangements, particularly involving services, create the potential for conflicts of interest, exploitation, and inappropriate boundaries in social workers' relationships with clients. Social workers should explore and may participate in bartering only in very limited circumstances when it can be demonstrated that such arrangements are an accepted practice among professionals in the local community, considered to be essential for the provision of services, negotiated without coercion, and entered into at the client's initiative and with the client's informed consent. Social workers who accept goods or services from clients as payment for professional services assume the full burden of demonstrating that this arrangement will not be detrimental to the client or the professional relationship.

(c) Social workers should not solicit a private fee or other remuneration for providing services to clients who are entitled to such available services through the social workers' employer or agency.

1.14 Clients Who Lack Decision-Making Capacity

When social workers act on behalf of clients who lack the capacity to make informed decisions, social workers should take reasonable steps to safeguard the interests and rights of those clients.

1.15 Interruption of Services

Social workers should make reasonable efforts to ensure continuity of services in the event that services are interrupted by factors such as unavailability, relocation, illness, disability, or death.

1.16 Termination of Services

(a) Social workers should terminate services to clients and professional relationships with them when such services and relationships are no longer required or no longer serve the clients' needs or interests.

(b) Social workers should take reasonable steps to avoid abandoning clients who are still in need of services. Social workers should withdraw services precipitously only under unusual circumstances, giving careful consideration to all factors in the situation and taking care to minimize possible adverse effects. Social workers should assist in making appropriate arrangements for continuation of services when necessary.

(c) Social workers in fee-for-service settings may terminate services to clients who are not paying an overdue balance if the financial contractual arrangements have been made clear to the client, if the client does not pose an imminent danger to self or others, and if the clinical and other consequences of the current nonpayment have been addressed and discussed with the client.

(d) Social workers should not terminate services to pursue a social, financial, or sexual relationship with a client.

(e) Social workers who anticipate the termination or interruption of services to clients should notify clients promptly and seek the transfer, referral, or continuation of services in relation to the clients' needs and preferences.

(f) Social workers who are leaving an employment setting should inform clients of appropriate options for the continuation of services and of the benefits and risks of the options.

2. Social Workers' Ethical Responsibilities to Colleagues

2.01 Respect

(a) Social workers should treat colleagues with respect and should represent accurately and fairly the qualifications, views, and obligations of colleagues.

(b) Social workers should avoid unwarranted negative criticism of colleagues in communications with clients or with other professionals. Unwarranted negative criticism may include demeaning comments that refer to colleagues' level of competence or to individuals' attributes such as race, ethnicity, national origin, color, sex, sexual orientation, gender identity or expression, age, marital status, political belief, religion, immigration status, and mental or physical disability.

(c) Social workers should cooperate with social work colleagues and with colleagues of other professions when such cooperation serves the well-being of clients.

2.02 Confidentiality

Social workers should respect confidential information shared by colleagues in the course of their professional relationships and transactions. Social workers should ensure that such colleagues understand social workers' obligation to respect confidentiality and any exceptions related to it.

2.03 Interdisciplinary Collaboration

(a) Social workers who are members of an interdisciplinary team should participate in and contribute to decisions that affect the well-being of clients by drawing on the perspectives, values, and experiences of the social work profession. Professional and ethical obligations of the interdisciplinary team as a whole and of its individual members should be clearly established.

(b) Social workers for whom a team decision raises ethical concerns should attempt to resolve the disagreement through appropriate channels. If the disagreement cannot be resolved, social workers should pursue other avenues to address their concerns consistent with client well-being.

2.04 Disputes Involving Colleagues

(a) Social workers should not take advantage of a dispute between a colleague and an employer to obtain a position or otherwise advance the social workers' own interests.

(b) Social workers should not exploit clients in disputes with colleagues or engage clients in any inappropriate discussion of conflicts between social workers and their colleagues.

2.05 Consultation

(a) Social workers should seek the advice and counsel of colleagues whenever such consultation is in the best interests of clients.

(b) Social workers should keep themselves informed about colleagues' areas of expertise and competencies. Social workers should seek consultation only from colleagues who have demonstrated knowledge, expertise, and competence related to the subject of the consultation.

(c) When consulting with colleagues about clients, social workers should disclose the least amount of information necessary to achieve the purposes of the consultation.

2.06 Referral for Services

(a) Social workers should refer clients to other professionals when the other professionals' specialized knowledge or expertise is needed to serve clients fully or when social workers believe that they are not being effective or making reasonable progress with clients and that additional service is required.

(b) Social workers who refer clients to other professionals should take appropriate steps to facilitate an orderly transfer of responsibility. Social workers who refer clients to other professionals should disclose, with clients' consent, all pertinent information to the new service providers.

(c) Social workers are prohibited from giving or receiving payment for a referral when no professional service is provided by the referring social worker.

2.07   Sexual Relationships

(a) Social workers who function as supervisors or educators should not engage in sexual activities or contact with supervisees, students, trainees, or other colleagues over whom they exercise professional authority.

(b) Social workers should avoid engaging in sexual relationships with colleagues when there is potential for a conflict of interest. Social workers who become involved in, or anticipate becoming involved in, a sexual relationship with a colleague have a duty to transfer professional responsibilities, when necessary, to avoid a conflict of interest.

2.08   Sexual Harassment

Social workers should not sexually harass supervisees, students, trainees, or colleagues. Sexual harassment includes sexual advances, sexual solicitation, requests for sexual favors, and other verbal or physical conduct of a sexual nature.

2.09   Impairment of Colleagues

(a) Social workers who have direct knowledge of a social work colleague's impairment that is due to personal problems, psychosocial distress, substance abuse, or mental health difficulties and that interferes with practice effectiveness should consult with that colleague when feasible and assist the colleague in taking remedial action.

(b) Social workers who believe that a social work colleague's impairment interferes with practice effectiveness and that the colleague has not taken adequate steps to address the impairment should take action through appropriate channels established by employers, agencies, NASW, licensing and regulatory bodies, and other professional organizations.

2.10   Incompetence of Colleagues

(a) Social workers who have direct knowledge of a social work colleague's incompetence should consult with that colleague when feasible and assist the colleague in taking remedial action.

(b) Social workers who believe that a social work colleague is incompetent and has not taken adequate steps to address the incompetence should take action through appropriate channels established by employers, agencies, NASW, licensing and regulatory bodies, and other professional organizations.

2.11   Unethical Conduct of Colleagues

(a) Social workers should take adequate measures to discourage, prevent, expose, and correct the unethical conduct of colleagues.

(b) Social workers should be knowledgeable about established policies and procedures for handling concerns about colleagues' unethical behavior. Social workers should be familiar with national, state, and local procedures for handling ethics complaints. These include policies and procedures created by NASW, licensing and regulatory bodies, employers, agencies, and other professional organizations.

(c) Social workers who believe that a colleague has acted unethically should seek resolution by discussing their concerns with the colleague when feasible and when such discussion is likely to be productive.

(d) When necessary, social workers who believe that a colleague has acted unethically should take action through appropriate formal channels (such as contacting a state licensing board or regulatory body, an NASW committee on inquiry, or other professional ethics committees).

(e) Social workers should defend and assist colleagues who are unjustly charged with unethical conduct.

3. Social Workers' Ethical Responsibilities in Practice Settings

3.01 Supervision and Consultation

(a) Social workers who provide supervision or consultation should have the necessary knowledge and skill to supervise or consult appropriately and should do so only within their areas of knowledge and competence.

(b) Social workers who provide supervision or consultation are responsible for setting clear, appropriate, and culturally sensitive boundaries.

(c) Social workers should not engage in any dual or multiple relationships with supervisees in which there is a risk of exploitation of or potential harm to the supervisee.

(d) Social workers who provide supervision should evaluate supervisees' performance in a manner that is fair and respectful.

3.02 Education and Training

(a) Social workers who function as educators, field instructors for students, or trainers should provide instruction only within their areas of knowledge and competence and should provide instruction based on the most current information and knowledge available in the profession.

(b) Social workers who function as educators or field instructors for students should evaluate students' performance in a manner that is fair and respectful.

(c) Social workers who function as educators or field instructors for students should take reasonable steps to ensure that clients are routinely informed when services are being provided by students.

(d) Social workers who function as educators or field instructors for students should not engage in any dual or multiple relationships with students in which there is a risk of exploitation or potential harm to the student. Social work educators and field instructors are responsible for setting clear, appropriate, and culturally sensitive boundaries.

3.03 Performance Evaluation

Social workers who have responsibility for evaluating the performance of others should fulfill such responsibility in a fair and considerate manner and on the basis of clearly stated criteria.

3.04 Client Records

(a) Social workers should take reasonable steps to ensure that documentation in records is accurate and reflects the services provided.

(b) Social workers should include sufficient and timely documentation in records to facilitate the delivery of services and to ensure continuity of services provided to clients in the future.

(c) Social workers' documentation should protect clients' privacy to the extent that is possible and appropriate and should include only information that is directly relevant to the delivery of services.

(d) Social workers should store records following the termination of services to ensure reasonable future access. Records should be maintained for the number of years required by state statutes or relevant contracts.

3.05   Billing

Social workers should establish and maintain billing practices that accurately reflect the nature and extent of services provided and that identify who provided the service in the practice setting.

3.06   Client Transfer

(a) When an individual who is receiving services from another agency or colleague contacts a social worker for services, the social worker should carefully consider the client's needs before agreeing to provide services. To minimize possible confusion and conflict, social workers should discuss with potential clients the nature of the clients' current relationship with other service providers and the implications, including possible benefits or risks, of entering into a relationship with a new service provider.

(b) If a new client has been served by another agency or colleague, social workers should discuss with the client whether consultation with the previous service provider is in the client's best interest.

3.07   Administration

(a) Social work administrators should advocate within and outside their agencies for adequate resources to meet clients' needs.

(b) Social workers should advocate for resource allocation procedures that are open and fair. When not all clients' needs can be met, an allocation procedure should be developed that is nondiscriminatory and

based on appropriate and consistently applied principles.

(c) Social workers who are administrators should take reasonable steps to ensure that adequate agency or organizational resources are available to provide appropriate staff supervision.

(d) Social work administrators should take reasonable steps to ensure that the working environment for which they are responsible is consistent with and encourages compliance with the *NASW Code of Ethics*. Social work administrators should take reasonable steps to eliminate any conditions in their organizations that violate, interfere with, or discourage compliance with the *Code*.

3.08   Continuing Education and Staff Development

Social work administrators and supervisors should take reasonable steps to provide or arrange for continuing education and staff development for all staff for whom they are responsible. Continuing education and staff development should address current knowledge and emerging developments related to social work practice and ethics.

3.09   Commitments to Employers

(a) Social workers generally should adhere to commitments made to employers and employing organizations.

(b) Social workers should work to improve employing agencies' policies and procedures and the efficiency and effectiveness of their services.

(c) Social workers should take reasonable steps to ensure that employers are aware of social workers' ethical obligations as set forth in the *NASW Code of Ethics* and of the implications of those obligations for social work practice.

(d) Social workers should not allow an employing organization's policies, procedures, regulations, or administrative orders to interfere with their ethical practice of social work. Social workers should take reasonable steps to ensure that their employing organizations' practices are consistent with the *NASW Code of Ethics*.

(e) Social workers should act to prevent and eliminate discrimination in the employing organization's work assignments and in its employment policies and practices.

(f) Social workers should accept employment or arrange student field placements only in organizations that exercise fair personnel practices.

(g) Social workers should be diligent stewards of the resources of their employing organizations, wisely conserving funds where appropriate and never misappropriating funds or using them for unintended purposes.

3.10 Labor-Management Disputes

(a) Social workers may engage in organized action, including the formation of and participation in labor unions, to improve services to clients and working conditions.

(b) The actions of social workers who are involved in labor-management disputes, job actions, or labor strikes should be guided by the profession's values, ethical principles, and ethical standards. Reasonable differences of opinion exist among social workers concerning their primary obligation as professionals during an actual or threatened labor strike or job action. Social workers should carefully examine relevant issues and their possible impact on clients before deciding on a course of action.

4. Social Workers' Ethical Responsibilities as Professionals

4.01 Competence

(a) Social workers should accept responsibility or employment only on the basis of existing competence or the intention to acquire the necessary competence.

(b) Social workers should strive to become and remain proficient in professional practice and the performance of professional functions. Social workers should critically examine and keep current with emerging knowledge relevant to social work. Social workers should routinely review the professional literature and participate in continuing education relevant to social work practice and social work ethics.

(c) Social workers should base practice on recognized knowledge, including empirically based knowledge, relevant to social work and social work ethics.

4.02 Discrimination

Social workers should not practice, condone, facilitate, or collaborate with any form of discrimination on the basis of race, ethnicity, national origin, color, sex, sexual orientation, gender identity or expression, age, marital status, political belief, religion, immigration status, or mental or physical disability.

4.03 Private Conduct

Social workers should not permit their private conduct to interfere with their ability to fulfill their professional responsibilities.

4.04   Dishonesty, Fraud, and Deception

Social workers should not participate in, condone, or be associated with dishonesty, fraud, or deception.

4.05   Impairment

(a) Social workers should not allow their own personal problems, psychosocial distress, legal problems, substance abuse, or mental health difficulties to interfere with their professional judgment and performance or to jeopardize the best interests of people for whom they have a professional responsibility.

(b) Social workers whose personal problems, psychosocial distress, legal problems, substance abuse, or mental health difficulties interfere with their professional judgment and performance should immediately seek consultation and take appropriate remedial action by seeking professional help, making adjustments in workload, terminating practice, or taking any other steps necessary to protect clients and others.

4.06   Misrepresentation

(a) Social workers should make clear distinctions between statements made and actions engaged in as a private individual and as a representative of the social work profession, a professional social work organization, or the social worker's employing agency.

(b) Social workers who speak on behalf of professional social work organizations should accurately represent the official and authorized positions of the organizations.

(c) Social workers should ensure that their representations to clients, agencies, and the public of professional qualifications, credentials, education, competence, affiliations, services provided, or results to be achieved are accurate. Social workers should claim only those relevant professional credentials they actually possess and take steps to correct any inaccuracies or misrepresentations of their credentials by others.

4.07   Solicitations

(a) Social workers should not engage in uninvited solicitation of potential clients who, because of their circumstances, are vulnerable to undue influence, manipulation, or coercion.

(b) Social workers should not engage in solicitation of testimonial endorsements (including solicitation of consent to use a client's prior statement as a testimonial endorsement) from current clients or from other people who, because of their particular circumstances, are vulnerable to undue influence.

4.08   Acknowledging Credit

(a) Social workers should take responsibility and credit, including authorship credit, only for work they have actually performed and to which they have contributed.

(b) Social workers should honestly acknowledge the work of and the contributions made by others.

5.   Social Workers' Ethical Responsibilities to the Social Work Profession

5.01   Integrity of the Profession

(a) Social workers should work toward the maintenance and promotion of high standards of practice.

(b) Social workers should uphold and advance the values, ethics, knowledge, and mission of the profession. Social workers should protect, enhance, and improve the integrity of the profession through appropriate study and research, active discussion, and responsible criticism of the profession.

(c) Social workers should contribute time and professional expertise to activities that promote respect for the value, integrity, and competence of the social work profession. These activities may include teaching, research, consultation, service, legislative testimony, presentations in the community, and participation in their professional organizations.

(d) Social workers should contribute to the knowledge base of social work and share with colleagues their knowledge related to practice, research, and ethics. Social workers should seek to contribute to the profession's literature and to share their knowledge at professional meetings and conferences.

(e) Social workers should act to prevent the unauthorized and unqualified practice of social work.

5.02   Evaluation and Research

(a) Social workers should monitor and evaluate policies, the implementation of programs, and practice interventions.

(b) Social workers should promote and facilitate evaluation and research to contribute to the development of knowledge.

(c) Social workers should critically examine and keep current with emerging knowledge relevant to social work and fully use evaluation and research evidence in their professional practice.

(d) Social workers engaged in evaluation or research should carefully consider possible consequences and should follow guidelines developed for the protection of evaluation and research participants. Appropriate institutional review boards should be consulted.

(e) Social workers engaged in evaluation or research should obtain voluntary and written informed consent from participants, when appropriate, without any implied or actual deprivation or penalty for refusal to participate; without undue inducement to participate; and with due regard for participants' well-being, privacy, and dignity. Informed consent should include information about the nature, extent, and duration of the participation requested and disclosure of the risks and benefits of participation in the research.

(f) When evaluation or research participants are incapable of giving informed consent, social workers should provide an appropriate explanation to the participants, obtain the participants' assent to the extent they are able, and obtain written consent from an appropriate proxy.

(g) Social workers should never design or conduct evaluation or research that does not use consent procedures, such as certain forms of naturalistic observation and archival research, unless rigorous and responsible review of the research has found it to be justified because of its prospective scientific, educational, or applied value and unless equally effective alternative procedures that do not involve waiver of consent are not feasible.

(h) Social workers should inform participants of their right to withdraw from evaluation and research at any time without penalty.

(i) Social workers should take appropriate steps to ensure that participants in evaluation and research have access to appropriate supportive services.

(j) Social workers engaged in evaluation or research should protect participants from unwarranted physical or mental distress, harm, danger, or deprivation.

(k) Social workers engaged in the evaluation of services should discuss collected information only for professional purposes and only with people professionally concerned with this information.

(l) Social workers engaged in evaluation or research should ensure the anonymity or confidentiality of participants and of the data obtained from them. Social workers should inform participants of any limits of confidentiality, the measures that will be taken to ensure confidentiality, and when any records containing research data will be destroyed.

(m) Social workers who report evaluation and research results should protect participants' confidentiality by omitting identifying information unless proper consent has been obtained authorizing disclosure.

(n) Social workers should report evaluation and research findings accurately. They should not fabricate or falsify results and should take steps to correct any errors later found in published data using standard publication methods.

(o) Social workers engaged in evaluation or research should be alert to and avoid conflicts of interest and dual relationships with participants, should inform participants when a real or potential conflict of interest arises, and should take steps to resolve the issue in a manner that makes participants' interests primary.

(p) Social workers should educate themselves, their students, and their colleagues about responsible research practices.

6.　Social Workers' Ethical Responsibilities to the Broader Society

6.01　Social Welfare

Social workers should promote the general welfare of society, from local to global lev-els, and the development of people, their communities, and their environments. Social workers should advocate for living conditions conducive to the fulfillment of basic human needs and should promote social, economic, political, and cultural values and institutions that are compatible with the realization of social justice.

6.02　Public Participation

Social workers should facilitate informed participation by the public in shaping social policies and institutions.

6.03　Public Emergencies

Social workers should provide appropriate professional services in public emergencies to the greatest extent possible.

6.04　Social and Political Action

(a) Social workers should engage in social and political action that seeks to ensure that all people have equal access to the resources, employment, services, and opportunities they require to meet their basic human needs and to develop fully. Social workers should be aware of the impact of the political arena on practice and should advocate for changes in policy and legislation to improve social conditions in order to meet basic human needs and promote social justice.

(b) Social workers should act to expand choice and opportunity for all people, with special regard for vulnerable, disadvantaged, oppressed, and exploited people and groups.

(c) Social workers should promote conditions that encourage respect for cultural and social diversity within the United States and globally. Social workers should promote policies and practices that demonstrate respect for difference, support the expansion of cultural knowledge and resources, advocate for programs and institutions that demonstrate cultural competence, and promote policies that safeguard the rights of and confirm equity and social justice for all people.

(d) Social workers should act to prevent and eliminate domination of, exploitation of, and discrimination against any person, group, or class on the basis of race, ethnicity, national origin, color, sex, sexual orientation, gender identity or expression, age, marital status, political belief, religion, immigration status, or mental or physical disability.

For additional information: http://www .naswdc.org/

APPENDIX B

GLOBAL STANDARDS FOR SOCIAL WORK EDUCATION AND TRAINING

The final version of the Global Standards for Social Work Education and Training was adopted by IASSW and IFSW at their General Assemblies in Adelaide, Australia in October 2004.

INTRODUCTION

The process of developing global standards for the education and training of the social work profession[1] is as important as the product; the actual standards that have been developed. In undertaking such an initiative it was also vital that minority opinions were considered and reflected in the development of the document. Thus, Appendix A describes fully the processes that were involved in developing the standards, and it documents the minority views that were expressed. Given the centrality of the process-product dialectic, and the fact that the principles underscoring the standards emerged, to a large extent, out of the processes, it is vital that the standards are read in conjunction with Appendices A and B. Appendix B provides the concluding comments and discusses the kinds of caution that must be exercised in the use of the document. Having duly considered all the concerns expressed in Appendices A and B, and having considered the need to take into account context-specific realities, and the

ambiguities surrounding the education and practice of social work professionals, this document details nine sets of standards in respect of: the school's core purpose or mission statement; programme objectives and outcomes; programme curricula including fieldwork; core curricula; professional staff; social work students; structure, administration, governance and resources; cultural diversity; and social work values and ethics. As a point of departure, the international definition of the social work profession is accepted, and the core purposes and functions of social work are summarised.

INTERNATIONAL DEFINITION OF SOCIAL WORK

In July 2001, both the IASSW and the IFSW reached agreement on adopting the following international definition of social work:

The social work profession promotes social change, problem solving in human relationships and the empowerment and liberation of people to enhance well-being. Utilising theories of human behaviour and social systems, social work intervenes at the points where people interact with their environments. Principles of human rights and social justice are fundamental to social work.[2] Both the definition and the commentaries that follow are set within the parameters of broad ethical principles that cannot be refuted on an ideological level. However, the fact that social work is operationalised differently both within nation states and regional boundaries, and across the world, with its control and status-quo maintaining functions being dominant in some contexts, cannot be disputed. Lorenz (2001) considered the ambiguities, tensions and contradictions of the social work profession, which have to be constantly negotiated and re-negotiated, rather than resolved, to constitute its success and challenge. It is, perhaps, these very tensions that lend to the richness of the local-global dialectic, and provide legitimacy for the development of global standards. According to Lorenz (2001:12): "It is its paradigmatic openness that gives this profession the chance to engage with very specific (and constantly changing) historical and political contexts while at the same time striving for a degree of universality, scientific reliability, professional autonomy and moral accountability."

CORE PURPOSES OF THE SOCIAL WORK PROFESSION

Social work, in various parts of the world, is targeted at interventions for social support and for developmental, protective, preventive and/or therapeutic purposes. Drawing on available literature, the feedback from colleagues during consultations and the commentary on the international definition of social work, the following core purposes of social work have been identified:

• Facilitate the inclusion of marginalised, socially excluded, dispossessed, vulnerable and at-risk groups of people.[3] • Address and challenge barriers, inequalities and injustices that exist in society. • Form short and longer-term working relationships with

and mobilise individuals, families, groups, organisations and communities to enhance their well-being and their problem-solving capacities. • Assist and educate people to obtain services and resources in their communities. • Formulate and implement policies and programmes that enhance people's well-being, promote development and human rights, and promote collective social harmony and social stability, insofar as such stability does not violate human rights. • Encourage people to engage in advocacy with regard to pertinent local, national, regional and/or international concerns. • Act with and/or for people to advocate the formulation and targeted implementation of policies that are consistent with the ethical principles of the profession. • Act with and/or for people to advocate changes in those policies and structural conditions that maintain people in marginalised, dispossessed and vulnerable positions, and those that infringe the collective social harmony and stability of various ethnic groups, insofar as such stability does not violate human rights. • Work towards the protection of people who are not in a position to do so themselves, for example children and youth in need of care and persons experiencing mental illness or mental retardation, within the parameters of accepted and ethically sound legislation. • Engage in social and political action to impact social policy and economic development, and to effect change by critiquing and eliminating inequalities. • Enhance stable, harmonious and mutually respectful societies that do not violate people's human rights. • Promote respect for traditions, cultures, ideologies, beliefs and religions amongst different ethnic groups and societies, insofar as these do not conflict with the fundamental human rights of people. • Plan, organise, administer and manage programmes and organisations dedicated to any of the purposes delineated above.

1. Standards Regarding the School's Core Purpose or Mission Statement

All schools should aspire toward the development of a core purpose statement or a mission statement which:

1.1 Is clearly articulated so those major stakeholders[4] who have an investment in such a core purpose or mission understand it.

1.2 Reflects the values and the ethical principles of social work.

1.3 Reflects aspiration towards equity with regard to the demographic profile of the institution's locality. The core purpose or mission statement should thus incorporate such issues as ethnic and gender representation on the faculty, as well as in recruitment and admission procedures for students.

1.4 Respects the rights and interests of service users and their participation in all aspects of delivery of programmes.

2. Standards Regarding Programme Objectives and Outcomes

In respect of programme objectives and expected outcomes, schools should endeavour to reach the following:

2.1 A specification of its programme objectives and expected higher education outcomes.

2.2 A reflection of the values and ethical principles of the profession in its programme design and implementation.

2.3 Identification of the programme's instructional methods, to ensure they support the achievement of the cognitive and affective development of social work students.

2.4 An indication of how the programme reflects the core knowledge, processes, values and skills of the social work profession, as applied in context-specific realities.

2.5 An indication of how an initial level of proficiency with regard to self-reflective[5] use of social work values, knowledge and skills is to be attained by social work students.

2.6 An indication of how the programme meets the requirements of nationally and/or regionally/internationally defined professional goals, and how the programme addresses local, national and/or regional/international developmental needs and priorities.

2.7 As social work does not operate in a vacuum, the programme should take account of the impact of interacting cultural, economic, communication, social, political and psychological global factors.

2.8 Provision of an educational preparation that is relevant to beginning social work professional practice with individuals, families, groups and/or communities in any given context.

2.9 Self-evaluation to assess the extent to which its programme objectives and expected outcomes are being achieved.

2.10 External peer evaluation as far as is reasonable and financially viable. This may be in the form of external peer moderation of assignments and/or written examinations and dissertations, and external peer review and assessment of curricula.

2.11 The conferring of a distinctive social work qualification at the certificate, diploma, first degree or post-graduate level as

approved by national and/or regional qualification authorities, where such authorities
exist.

3. Standards with Regard to Programme Curricula Including Field Education

With regard to standards regarding programme curricula, schools should consistently aspire towards the following:

3.1 The curricula and methods of instruction being consistent with the school's programme objectives, its expected outcomes
and its mission statement.

3.2 Clear plans for the organisation,
implementation and evaluation of the theory and field education components of the
programme.

3.3 Involvement of service users in the
planning and delivery of programmes.

3.4 Recognition and development of
indigenous or locally specific social work
education and practice from the traditions
and cultures of different ethnic groups and
societies, insofar that such traditions and
cultures do not violate human rights.

3.5 Specific attention to the constant
review and development of the curricula.

3.6 Ensuring that the curricula help social
work students to develop skills of critical
thinking and scholarly attitudes of reasoning,
openness to new experiences and paradigms,
and commitment to life-long learning.

3.7 Field education should be sufficient in
duration and complexity of tasks and learning opportunities to ensure that students are
prepared for professional practice.

3.8 Planned co-ordination and links
between the school and the agency/field
placement setting.

3.9 Provision of orientation for fieldwork
supervisors or instructors.

3.10 Appointment of field supervisors or
instructors who are qualified and experienced, as determined by the development
status of the social work profession in any
given country, and provision of orientation
for fieldwork supervisors or instructors.

3.11 Provision for the inclusion and participation of field instructors in curriculum
development.

3.12 A partnership between the educational institution and the agency (where
applicable) and service users in decision-
making regarding field education and the
evaluation of student's fieldwork performance.

3.13 Making available, to fieldwork
instructors or supervisors, a field instruction manual that details its fieldwork standards, procedures, assessment standards/cri-
teria and expectations.

3.14 Ensuring that adequate and appropriate resources, to meet the needs of the
fieldwork component of the programme,
are made available.

4. Standards with Regard to Core Curricula

In respect core curricula, schools should
aspire toward the following:

4.1 An identification of and selection for
inclusion in the programme curricula,
as determined by local, national and/or
regional/international needs and priorities.

4.2 Notwithstanding the provision of 4.1
there are certain core curricula that may be
seen to be universally applicable. Thus the
school should ensure that social work students, by the end of their first Social Work

professional qualification, have had exposure to the following core curricula which are organised into four conceptual components:

4.2.1 Domain of the Social Work Profession:

• A critical understanding of how socio-structural inadequacies, discrimination, oppression, and social, political and economic injustices impact human functioning and development at all levels, including the global. • Knowledge of human behaviour and development and of the social environment, with particular emphasis on the person-in-environment transaction, life-span development and the interaction among biological, psychological, socio-structural, economic, political, cultural and spiritual factors in shaping human development and behaviour. • Knowledge of how traditions, culture, beliefs, religions and customs influence human functioning and development at all levels, including how these might constitute resources and/or obstacles to growth and development. • A critical understanding of social work's origins and purposes.

• Understanding of country specific social work origins and development. • Sufficient knowledge of related occupations and professions to facilitate inter-professional collaboration and teamwork. • Knowledge of social welfare policies (or lack thereof), services and laws at local, national and/or regional/international levels, and the roles of social work in policy planning, implementation, evaluation and in social change processes. • A critical understanding of how social stability, harmony, mutual respect and collective solidarity impact human functioning and development at all levels, including the global, insofar as that stability, harmony and solidarity are not used to maintain a status quo with regard to infringement of human rights.

4.2.2 Domain of the Social Work Professional:

• The development of the critically self-reflective practitioner, who is able to practice within the value perspective of the social work profession, and shares responsibility with the employer for their well being and professional development, including the avoidance of 'burn-out'. • The recognition of the relationship between personal life experiences and personal value systems and social work practice. • The appraisal of national, regional and/or international social work codes of ethics and their applicability to context specific realities. • Preparation of social workers within a holistic framework, with skills to enable practice in a range of contexts with diverse ethnic, cultural, 'racial'[7] and gender groups, and other forms of diversities. • The development of the social worker who is able to conceptualise social work wisdom derived from different cultures, traditions and customs in various ethnic groups, insofar that culture, tradition, custom and ethnicity are not used to violate human rights. • The development of the social worker who is able to deal with the complexities, subtleties, multi-dimensional, ethical, legal and dialogical aspects of power.[8]

4.2.3 Methods of Social Work Practice:

• Sufficient practice skills in, and knowledge of, assessment, relationship building and helping processes to achieve the identified goals of the programme for the purposes of social support, and developmental, protective, preventive and/or therapeutic intervention—depending on the particular focus of the programme or professional practice orientation. • The application of social work values, ethical principles, knowledge and skills to confront inequality, and social, political and economic injustices. • Knowledge of social work research and skills in the use of research methods, including ethical use of relevant research paradigms, and critical appreciation of the use of research and different sources of knowledge[9] about social work practice. • The application of social work values, ethical principles, knowledge and skills to promote care, mutual respect and mutual responsibility amongst members of a society. * Supervised fieldwork education, with due consideration to the provisions of Item 3 above.

4.2.4   Paradigm of the Social Work Profession:

Of particular current salience to professional social work education, training and practice are the following epistemological paradigms (which are not mutually exclusive), that should inform the core curricula:

• An acknowledgement and recognition of the dignity, worth and the uniqueness of all human beings. • Recognition of the interconnectedness that exists within and across all systems at micro, mezzo and macro levels. • An emphasis on the importance of advocacy and changes in socio-structural, political and economic conditions that disempower, marginalise and exclude people. • A focus on capacity-building and empowerment of individuals, families, groups, organisations and communities through a human-centred developmental approach. • Knowledge about and respect for the rights of service users. • Problem-solving and

anticipatory socialisation through an understanding of the normative developmental life cycle, and expected life tasks and crises in relation to age-related influences, with due consideration to socio-cultural expectations. • The assumption, identification and recognition of strengths and potential of all human beings. • An appreciation and respect for diversity in relation to 'race', culture, religion, ethnicity, linguistic origin, gender, sexual orientation and differential abilities.

5.   Standards with Regard to Professional Staff

With regard to professional staff, schools should aspire towards:

5.1   The provision of professional staff, adequate in number and range of expertise, who have appropriate qualifications as determined by the development status of the social work profession in any given country. As far as possible a Masters level qualification in social work, or a related discipline (in countries where social work is an emerging discipline), should be required.

5.2   The provision of opportunities for staff participation in the development of its core purpose or mission, in the formulation of the objectives and expected outcomes of the programme, and in any other initiative that the school might be involved in.

5.3   Provision for the continuing professional development of its staff, particularly in areas of emerging knowledge.

5.4   A clear statement, where possible, of its equity-based policies or preferences, with regard to considerations of gender, ethnicity, 'race' or any other form of diversity in its recruitment and appointment of staff.

5.5   Sensitivity to languages relevant to the practice of social work in that context.

5.6   In its allocation of teaching, fieldwork instruction, supervision and administrative workloads, making provision for research and publications.

Adopted at the General Assemblies of IASSW and IFSW, Adelaide, Australia in 2004.

5.7   Making provision for professional staff, as far as is reasonable and possible, to be involved in the formulation, analysis and the evaluation of the impact of social policies, and in community outreach initiatives.

6.   Standards with Regard to Social Work Students

In respect of social work students, schools should endeavor to reach the following:

6.1   Clear articulation of its admission criteria and procedures.

6.2   Student recruitment, admission and retention policies that reflect the demographic profile of the locality that the institution is based in with active involvement of practitioners and service users in relevant processes. Due recognition should be given to minority groups[10] that are under-represented and/or under-served. Relevant criminal convictions, involving abuse of others or human rights violations, must be taken into account given the primary responsibility of protecting and empowering service users.

6.3   Provision for student advising that is directed toward student orientation, assessment of the student's aptitude and motivation for a career in social work, regular evaluation of the student's performance and guidance in the selection of courses/modules.

6.4   Ensuring high quality of the educational programme whatever the mode of delivery. In the case of distance, mixed-mode, decentralised and/or internet-based teaching, mechanisms for locally-based instruction and supervision should be put in place, especially with regard to the fieldwork component of the programme.

6.5   Explicit criteria for the evaluation of student's academic and fieldwork performance.

6.6   Non-discrimination against any student on the basis of 'race', colour, culture, ethnicity, linguistic origin, religion, political orientation, gender, sexual orientation, age, marital status, physical status and socio-economic status.

6.7   Grievance and appeals procedures which are accessible, clearly explained to all students and operated without prejudice to the assessment of students.

7.   Standards with Regard to Structure, Administration, Governance and Resources

With regard to structure, administration, governance and resources, the school and/or the educational institution should aspire towards the following:

7.1   Social work programmes are implemented through a distinct unit known as a Faculty, School, Department, Centre or Division, which has a clear identity within the educational institution.

Adopted at the General Assemblies of IASSW and IFSW, Adelaide, Australia in 2004.

7.2   The school has a designated Head or Director who has demonstrated administrative, scholarly and professional competence, preferably in the profession of social work.

7.3   The Head or Director has primary responsibility for the co-ordination and professional leadership of the school, with sufficient time and resources to fulfil these responsibilities.

7.4   The school's budgetary allocation is sufficient to achieve its core purpose or mission and the programme objectives.

7.5   The budgetary allocation is stable enough to ensure programme planning and sustainability.

7.6   There are adequate physical facilities, including classroom space, offices for professional and administrative staff and space for student, faculty and field-liaison meetings, and the equipment necessary for the achievement of the school's core purpose or mission and the programme objectives.

7.7   Library and, where possible, internet resources, necessary to achieve the programme objectives, are made available.

7.8   The necessary clerical and administrative staff are made available for the achievement of the programme objectives.

7.9   Where the school offers distance, mixed-mode, decentralised and/or internet-based education there is provision of adequate infrastructure, including classroom space, computers, texts, audio-visual equipment, community resources for fieldwork education, and on-site instruction and supervision to facilitate the achievement of its core purpose or mission, programme objectives and expected outcomes.

7.10   The school plays a key role with regard to the recruitment, appointment and promotion of staff.

7.11   The school strives toward gender equity in its recruitment, appointment, promotion and tenure policies and practices.

7.12   In its recruitment, appointment, promotion and tenure principles and procedures, the school reflects the diversities of

the population that it interacts with and serves.

7.13   The decision-making processes of the school reflect participatory principles and procedures.

7.14   The school promotes the development of a cooperative, supportive and productive working environment to facilitate the achievement of programme objectives.

7.15   The school develops and maintains linkages within the institution, with external organisations, and with service users relevant to its core purpose or mission and its objectives.

8.   Standards with Regard to Cultural and Ethnic Diversity and Gender Inclusiveness

With regard to cultural and ethnic diversity schools should aspire towards the following:

8.1   Making concerted and continuous efforts to ensure the enrichment of the educational experience by reflecting cultural and ethnic diversity, and gender analysis in its programme.

8.2   Ensuring that the programme, either through mainstreaming into all courses/modules and/or through a separate course/module, has clearly articulated objectives in respect of cultural and ethnic diversity, and gender analysis.

8.3   Indicating that issues regarding gender analysis and cultural and ethnic diversity, are represented in the fieldwork component of the programme.

8.4   Ensuring that social work students are provided with opportunities to develop self-awareness regarding their personal and cultural values, beliefs, traditions and biases and how these might influence the ability to develop relationships with people, and to work with diverse population groups.

8.5   Promoting sensitivity to, and increasing knowledge about, cultural and ethnic diversity, and gender analysis.

8.6   Minimising group stereotypes and prejudices[11] and ensuring that racist behaviours, policies and structures are not reproduced through social work practice.

8.7   Ensuring that social work students are able to form relationships with, and treat all persons with respect and dignity irrespective of such persons' cultural and ethnic beliefs and orientations.

8.8   Ensuring that social work students are schooled in a basic human rights approach, as reflected in international instruments such as the Universal Declaration on Human Rights, the United Nations Convention on the Rights of the Child (1989) and the UN Vienna Declaration (1993).[12]

8.9   Ensuring that the programme makes provision for social work students to know themselves both as individuals and as members of collective socio-cultural groups in terms of strengths and areas for further development.

9.   Standards with Regard to Values and Ethical Codes of Conduct of the Social Work Profession

In view of the recognition that social work values, ethics and principles are the core components of the profession, schools should consistently aspire towards:

9.1   Focused and meticulous attention to this aspect of the programme in curricula design and implementation.

9.2   Clearly articulated objectives with regard to social work values, principles and ethical conduct.

9.3   Registration of professional staff and social work students (insofar as social work students develop working relationships with people via fieldwork placements) with national and/or regional regulatory (whether statutory or non-statutory) bodies, with defined codes of ethics.[13] Members of such bodies are generally bound to the provisions of those codes.

9.4   Ensuring that every social work student involved in fieldwork education, and every professional staff member, is aware of the boundaries of professional practice and what might constitute unprofessional conduct in terms of the code of ethics. Where students violate the code of ethics, programme staff may take necessary and acceptable remedial and/or initial disciplinary measures, or counsel the student out of the programme.

9.5   Taking appropriate action in relation to those social work students and professional staff who fail to comply with the code of ethics, either through an established regulatory social work body, established procedures of the educational institution, and/or through legal mechanisms.

9.6   Ensuring that regulatory social work bodies are broadly representative of the social work profession, including, where applicable, social workers from both the public and private sector, and of the community that it serves, including the direct participation of service users.

9.7   Upholding, as far as is reasonable and possible, the principles of restorative rather than retributive justice[14] in disciplining either social work students or professional staff who violate the code of ethics.

For additional information: http://www.iassw-aiets.org/

APPENDIX A: THE PROCESS OF AND UNDERLYING APPROACH TO DEVELOPING GLOBAL STANDARDS FOR THE EDUCATION AND TRAINING OF THE SOCIAL WORK PROFESSION

The Global Minimum Qualifying Standards[15] Committee was formally established as a joint initiative of the International Association of Schools of Social Work (IASSW) and the International Federation of Social Workers (IFSW) at the joint IASSW/IFSW Conference in Montreal, Canada in July 2000 (see Appendix C for a list of the Committee members). This discussion document was put together with the input of various Committee members, a review of relevant documents, e-mail consultations, and personal consultations with colleagues wherever possible

On the whole there was a favourable response to IASSW and IFSW developing a standards setting document that elucidates what social work represents on a global level. This document that identifies certain universals, may be used as a guideline to develop national standards with regard to social work education and training. Such a document should reflect some consensus around key issues, roles and purposes of social work. However, given the profession's historically fragmented strands; the contemporary debates around social work's intra-professional identity; its identity vis-à-vis other categories of personnel in the welfare sector such as development workers, child care workers, probation officers, community workers and youth workers (where such categories of personnel are differentiated from social work); and the enormous diversities across nations and regions, there was some

scepticism about the possibility of identifying any such 'universal'. The suggestion was that such a document must be sufficiently flexible to be applicable to any context. Such flexibility should allow for interpretations of locally specific social work education and practice, and take into account each country's or region's socio-political, cultural, economic and historical contexts while adhering to international standards.

The main reasons for the development of global standards were to (stated in no particular order of priority):

- Protect the 'consumers', 'clients' or 'service users'[18] of social work services;
- Take account of the impact of globalisation on social work curricula and social work practice;
- Facilitate articulation across universities on a global level;
- Facilitate the movement of social workers from one country to another;
- Draw a distinction between social workers and non-social workers;
- Benchmark national standards against international standards;
- Facilitate partnerships and international student and staff exchange programmes;
- Enable IASSW and IFSW, in developing such guidelines, to play a facilitative role in helping those faculties, centres, departments or schools of social work that lack resources to meet such guidelines.
- Give practical expression to the aim of IASSW as some saw the formulation of international guidelines for social work education and training to be the core business of IASSW.

Clearly not all of the above expressed purposes are feasible, e.g. it is not feasible via such an endeavour to draw a clear distinction between social workers and non-social workers, neither might we be able to realise the objective of protecting 'clients' through the standards. Facilitating the movement of social workers from one country to another is a contentious issue in view of the direct recruitment of social workers from some countries to others, e.g. from South Africa and the Caribbean to the United Kingdom to the disadvantage of South Africa and the Caribbean. However, from an ethical point of view the migration of those social workers that wish to practice in another country should be enabled and not blocked. The retention of social work skills within countries is dependent on such factors as service conditions, salaries and validation of the profession which need to be addressed on national levels.

A few participants expressed the view that the document should go further to include more practical guidelines. These practical guidelines should include: a multi-tiered classification for the basic qualification, e.g. with a range from the number of years of basic schooling, plus at least one year of full time social work education to a degree with 3 or 4 years of social work education (the minimum period of practical training should be specified in such a classification); the acknowledgement and recognition of prior learning experiences; and the identification of core competencies, knowledge and skills as applied to context-specific realities. A very small minority went as far as asking for the global standards to prescribe texts and minimum number of hours that students need to spend on reading. This was clearly an impossible request to include

at the global level as it would entail a complete denial of context-specific realities. Indeed, it would perhaps be impossible to entertain such a request even at local or national levels, as it would contribute to the curtailment of academic freedom, restrict knowledge development and constrain the development of critical thinking. Other participants expressed concern that the proposed multi-tiered system may appear to be far too elitist, with perhaps social workers from the Two-Thirds World[20] being more likely to be categorised into the lower ranks. Prescribing the duration of training or the number of course credits is problematic, given the variations of the academic year across countries and regions, and the diversities in crediting courses in different contexts. Also, for example, a six to twelve month intensive social work programme, with careful selection of mature students with appropriate prior learning experiences and/or related qualifications, might prove to be as valuable as a first degree social work programme with school leaving students. It is the quality of the educational programme that must not be compromised. From available information, it would appear that the academisation of social work is becoming the norm, with many countries opting for either a three or four-year Bachelors degree in Social Work, with a few countries, like Chile, being an exception with a five-year Bachelors degree.

A minority view was that IFSW and IASSW begin with no document; that a grassroots approach be used in encouraging national bodies to formulate their own standards. These national standards, formulated for example via a five-year action plan, could then be processed into global standards. However, one does not have to adopt an either/or approach to the development of global standards. If we accept the premise that such standards do not represent a finite or static product, but a dynamic process through which we continue building a framework that we aspire towards, then we accept that such an endeavour would involve a global-regional-national-local dialectical interaction. This must involve cross-national and cross-regional dialogue.

In developing global standards, care needed to be taken that we did not further fragment and de-professionalise social work, as so clearly elucidated by Dominelli (1996) in her discussion on the impact of the competencies-based approach to social work education and practice. This view was supported by Lorenz (2001:19), who, while not invalidating the need for quality control[21] by having some benchmark criteria, warned that it might "trivialise social work skills even further". To circumvent this possibility we made concerted efforts to transcend the kind of reductionist language used within many national/regional contexts in their development of unit standards, designed to meet criteria for the competencies-based approach that fragments social work skills and roles into minute, constituent parts. We acknowledge that there might be merits to the competencies-based approach on national/regional levels. However, this is seen to be far too specific to be applied to the global level.

During consultations questions were raised regarding 'minimum' by whose or what standards? Is it possible that 'minimum standards' could decrease rather than enhance the profession's standards? An alternative argument was that as 'standards' represent an ideal, they could, in effect, come to be 'maximum standards' that all schools of social work in all countries and regions are put under pressure to attain. The experience of South Africa in the early 1990s is a case in point. The then Council for Social Work, which was actually a State apparatus designed to uphold the ideology of apartheid, proposed what it called 'minimum standards'. However, the document actually reflected superior standards and proposed control mechanisms, which, if accepted, would have jeopardised the position and, perhaps, the very existence of schools of social work at the historically disadvantaged black institutions, which were poorly resourced compared with the white universities. Fortunately there was sufficient solidarity among social work educators who rejected the document, so it did not become part of the statutory requirement. These concerns provided further ground for omitting the 'minimum' from this document, and to move toward the use of: "global standards for the education and training of the social work profession". This document does not purport to reflect minimum standards, but ideals that schools of social work should consistently aspire towards.

Some colleagues who engaged in the consultation process also expressed concern about the possibility of a western domination. Given the western hegemony in social work education and practice, and that "Western European countries and the USA perhaps have fairly settled views of what social work is and what it means to provide good social work education" (Payne, 2001:41—our emphasis), such fears are not merely speculative. We acknowledge that the claim to what constitutes good social work education in Western Europe and the USA may be based on ill-founded premises.[22] Australia and Canada also seem to have made a great deal of progress in the development of national standards. In order to prevent such a western domination, the following were considered, and must continue to be considered in relation to the global standards:

- Ensuring representation from different regions of the world on the Committee in the formulation of the standards.
- Facilitating as much consultation and inclusion in the process as possible.
- Ensuring that the global standards take into account a country's unique historical, political, cultural, social and economic contexts.
- Ensuring that the unique developmental needs of countries are considered in relation to the global standards.
- Ensuring that the profession's developmental status and needs in any given country are considered while encouraging schools to secure adequate resources to the extent possible, that we ensure that there is no assumption that schools with lesser resources provide poorer quality programmes.
- Facilitating open dialogue across national and regional boundaries.

Amongst those who participated during consultations, there was overwhelming concern that context-specific realities, and the resources available to individual institutions to meet the global standards, are taken into consideration. In the development of global standards we should not create unintended consequences by disadvantaging some educational institutions. As much as global standards may be used to benchmark

national norms and standards, as far as possible, national and regional experiences and practices (even where formal standards do not exist) were incorporated into the formulation of the global standards. Where national or regional standards do not exist, IASSW and IFSW should collaborate to facilitate the development of such standards. The circular, interactive and discursive processes in developing national and global standards can, in these ways, become and remain continuous and dynamic. The process-product dialectic, in the formulation of the global standards, has been vital. While we had necessary pre-determined time frames, we tried, as far as possible, not to compromise consultation processes.

Two participants during consultations recommended a two-phased process; the first would involve consultations to "get everyone on board" that might span a two to six year period. The second phase would consist of submissions by each region/national body to IASSW to ensure compliance. The recommendations ranged from bi-annual submissions to submissions once in five years. The majority believed that, beyond the formulation of a standards document, IASSW/IFSW could play no role, and that these bodies could not really effect any mechanisms to "ensure compliance". Monitoring, conforming to the global standards and the possibility of downgrading or up grading of educational institutions were not seen as the tasks of IASSW/IFSW. The roles of IASSW and IFSW should be facilitative and supportive. Payne (2001) pointed out that by virtue of membership with IASSW, educational institutions had to uphold at least the following minimum criteria:

- That social work education takes place after a school leaving certificate has been obtained; and that
- Social work education takes place at the tertiary level.

While these two criteria were accepted as valid for the purpose of this document, it must be remembered that various educational institutions do recognise prior learning experiences in the selection of students, where a school-leaving certificate has not been obtained. Where recognition of prior learning experiences is implemented (generally with policy or criteria determined at school, local or national levels), this needs to be accepted and respected.

APPENDIX B: CONCLUDING COMMENTS AND CAUTION IN THE USE OF THE DOCUMENT

The development of global standards, by their very nature, generally tends to fall within the prescriptive, reductionist, logical-positivist paradigm. Efforts have been made to adopt an alternative and a more empowering, non-prescriptive language in this document. The main aim is to enhance social work education, training and practice on a global level, by facilitating dialogue within and across nations and regions. The document reflects global standards that schools of social work should consistently aspire towards, which (collectively, and if met) would actually provide for quite sophisticated levels of social work education and training. This is, as it ought to be: the provision of the best possible education and training for social work students who, after qualifying, bear enormous responsibilities in their communities.

The extent to which schools of social work meet the global standards will depend on the developmental needs of any given country/region and the developmental status of the profession in any given context, as determined by unique historical, sociopolitical, economic and cultural contexts. These are given due consideration throughout the document. It is accepted that, while some established schools might have surpassed the standards contained in this document, other schools might be in the process of beginning social work programmes. The document details ideals regarding what schools, such as the latter, might aspire towards, even if it takes the next twenty or more years to reach them. In specifying the standards, there is no expectation that all schools in all parts of the world would measure up to them on an immediate level. Also, whether or not schools measure up to them will not be determined at the international level. A school may engage in self-assessment to determine the extent to which its programme is consistent with the standards elucidated in this document. Quality assurance and accreditation criteria and procedures will have to be determined at national and/or regional levels. There is undoubtedly, on a global level, a move toward the creation of national and regional qualification frameworks (Department of Education and Department of Labour, 2003).

In formulating the global standards, care was taken to ensure that we do not take on the dominant language of managerialism (this does not mean the negation of sound management) and marketisation, which is seen to be inconsistent with the core values and purposes of social work. By locating the global standards against the international definition of social work and the core purposes of social work, the document ensures an approach to education and training that supports human rights, social justice, and an essential commitment to caring for, and the empowerment of individuals, groups, organisations and communities. It also reflects a commitment to the personal and professional development of social work students, with particular emphases on the development of the critically self-reflective practitioner, and the place of values and ethics in social work education and training. In the formulation of the global standards, the challenge has been for them to be specific enough to have salience, yet broad enough to be relevant to any given context. While the standards have been formulated at the global level, the document allows for sufficient interpretation and application at the local levels. What would be a distinctive advantage is empirically-based comparative international research involving the application and evaluation of the standards in different contexts. This would help in identifying gaps and limitations of the current document and for further revision and refinement.

Given the number of concerns that were raised in the preamble to this document and some additional issues that arose as the consultations proceeded, caution must be exercised in how the document should and should not be used. There was some concern raised during the consultation process from a colleague in Canada, that the development of global standards may be used for international trade purposes in relation to the Agreement on Trade in Service (GATS). IASSW and IFSW categorically assert that the standards are not to be used for such a purpose. Neither of these

international bodies is bound to GATS regulations, and there was no external funding to the development of the global standards. The formulation of the standards represents the attempt to uphold the best possible standards for the social work profession on a global level, and to facilitate dialogue and debate within and across national and regional boundaries and is in no way linked to international trade in services. The intention is to enhance academic freedom and promote the development of locally specific theory and practice, rather than inhibit or constrain such development. We concur with the view of Rossiter (undated, p. 5) that there is a need to mobilise against such trade agreements as "they 1) increase poverty, 2) contribute to environmental degradation, 3) reduce the power of labour, 4) contribute to national and international inequality, 5) constitute an un-elected, non-transparent series of agreements that weaken local power and government power to regulate economies towards human need rather than profit". Such agreements also reduce the power of individuals to control their own working and welfare environment.

In the elucidation of standards on structure, administration, governance and resources, neither IASSW nor IFSW endorses that view that those schools that lack material and infrastructural resources have poorer quality programmes. However, it is accepted that adequate human and material resources do facilitate easier achievement of programme purposes and objectives. Some colleagues in the Asia-Pacific, the African and the Nordic regions have indicated that they have used the draft document as leverage to lobby for more adequate resources from their institutions. That the document, even in its draft form and without adoption at the international level, was used for such a purpose is clearly an advantage. However, it must be borne in mind that such pressure from external sources may offend some educational institutions in other regions of the world. Thus, whether or not the document is used for the purpose of lobbying for adequate resources, or how this is done, should rest at the discretion of the individual school.

In formulating global standards for the education and training of the social work profession, neither the IASSW nor the IFSW will play any monitoring, control or accreditation function at the level of the school. Whether or not IASSW and IFSW would play any significant role at the national or regional level in the future will depend on how the document is interpreted in different contexts, how it is operationalised in different parts of the world, and on the requirements and expectations of its membership. One of the fears in producing a document such as this is that we recognise that a text, once written, is outside of the control of its authors.[23] The roles of IASSW and IFSW are intended to be supportive and facilitative. There must be clear mechanisms of communication across national and/or regional social work educators' associations and IASSW. Part of the developmental objective to the global standards, should be IASSW's and IFSW's commitment to developing guidelines about mechanisms to facilitate such communication. One of the objectives is that, through the assistance of the Census Commission, IASSW will develop a data bank containing the details and programmes of member schools and of national and/or regional standards and systems of quality

assurance and accreditation. Such information may be shared on an international level on request and/or via the websites of IASSW and IFSW. It is hoped that such sharing would provide the impetus for schools of social work to aspire towards the global standards for professional social work education and training elucidated in this document. The document is not intended to be a fixed, timeless product; it is a dynamic entity subject to review and revision as and when the need arises. This can only be achieved with continued critical debate and dialogue within the profession on local, national, regional and global levels.

APPENDIX C

The Committee consists of the following members:

IASSW Representatives

- Vishanthie Sewpaul from South Africa (Chair of the Committee since January 2001); Lena Dominelli (Chair until January 2001 and then ex-officio as President of IASSW)
- Sven Hessle from Sweden
- Karen Lyons from the United Kingdom
- Denyse Cote from Canada
- Nelia Tello from Mexico
- Barbara White from the United States
- Hoi Wa Mak from Hong Kong

IFSW Representatives

- David Jones (Co-Chair of the Committee from the United Kingdom)
- Ngoh-Tiong Tan from Singapore
- Richard Ramsay from Canada
- Juan M.L. Carvajal from Columbia
- Charles Mbugua from Kenya

- Sung-Jae Choi from Korea
- Imelda Dodds (ex-officio as President of IFSW)
- Lynne Healy from the United States served as consultant

N.B. This is the final document adopted at the IASSW and IFSW General Assemblies in Adelaide, Australia, 2004. However, as the use, implementation and review of the Global Standards is to remain a dynamic process, please send your comments or recommendations to Vishanthie Sewpaul.

E-mail: sewpaul@ukzn.ac.za

Fax: Address: 27-31-2602700

Address: School of Social Work and Community Development, University of Kwa Zulu Natal, Howard College Campus, Durban

REFERENCES

Department of Education and Department of Labour. (2003). *An Independent National Qualifications Framework System Consultative Document.* Pretoria, South Africa.

Dominelli, L. D. (1996). Deprofessionalising social work: Anti-oppressive practice competencies and post-modernism. *British Journal of Social Work, 26,* 153–175

Dominelli, L. D. (2004). *Social work: Theory and practice for a changing profession.* Cambridge, MA: Polity Press.

Lorenz, W. (2001). Social work in Europe— Portrait of a diverse professional group. In Hessle, S. (Ed.), *International standard setting of higher social work education.* Stockholm University, Stockholm Studies of Social Work.

Pawson, R. et. al. (2003). Types and quality of knowledge in social care. London: Social Care Institute for Excellence. http://scie.org.uk/scieproducts/knowledgereviews/KRO3summary onlineversion07 1103.pdf

Payne, M. (2001). Social work education: International standards. In Hessle, S. (Ed.), *International standard setting of higher social work education.* Stockholm University, Stockholm Studies of Social Work.

Pozutto, R. (2001). Lessons in continuation and transformation: The United States and South Africa. *Social Work/ Maatskaplike werk, 37*(2), 154–164.

Ramsay, R. (2003). Transforming the working definition of social work into the 21st century. *Research on Social Work Practice, 13*(3), 324–338.

Rossiter, A. (n.d.). A response to Anne Westhue's Reflections on the Sector Study. Unpublished paper received by e-mail on 27/03/03: Toronto: York University.

Williams, L. O., & Sewpaul, V. (2004). Modernism, postmodernism and global standards setting. *Social Work Education, 3*(5), 555–565.

NOTES

1. All reference to "social work" in this document is to read as the "social work profession", and reference to the "social worker" is to read as the "social work professional"

2. Some colleagues have criticised this definition, expressing the view that it did not adequately cover their contexts. A colleague from the Hong Kong Polytechnic University, expressed concern about the lack of emphasis on responsibility and the collective within the western paradigm. He proposed the following additions to the definition (written in bold italics): "The social work profession promotes social change as well as social stability, problem solving as well as harmony in human relationships, and the empowerment and liberation of people to enhance well-being. Utilising theories of human behaviour and social systems and respecting unique traditions and culture in different ethnic groups, social work intervenes at points where people interact with their environments and where individuals go

well with their significant others. Principles of human rights and social justice as well as responsibility and collective harmony are fundamental to social work in various countries."

3. Such concepts lack clear definition. Persons who fall into the categories of being 'marginalised', 'socially' 'excluded', 'dispossessed', 'vulnerable' and/or 'at risk' may be so defined by individual countries and/or regions.

4. Stakeholders include the educational institution itself; the 'profession', however organised or informal, including practitioners, managers and academics; social work agencies as potential employers and providers of fieldwork learning opportunities; users of social work services; students; the government, where this funds the institution and/or sets standards and the wider community.

5. Self-reflexivity at the most basic level means the ability to question: What are we doing? Why are we doing it? Is it in the best interests of the people whom we are working with? Such reflexivity is necessary and desirable irrespective of the context one practices in, whether the emphasis is on, e.g. liberal democracy, communitarianism, autocracy or authoritarian socio-cultural systems or democratic socialism.

6. Field placements take place in different settings, within formal organisations or through direct links with communities, which may be geographically defined or defined by specific interests. Some schools have established independent student units in communities, which serve as the context for fieldwork.

7. The concepts 'racial' and 'race' are in inverted commas to reflect that they are sociostructural and political constructs, wherein biological differences amongst people are used by some dominant groups to oppress, exclude and marginalise groups considered to be of minority status.

8. Quoted from Dominelli, L. (2004) Social Work: Theory and Practice for a Changing Profession. Polity Press, Cambridge.

9. Pawson, R. et. al. (2003). Types and quality of knowledge in social care. Social Care Institute for Excellence. http://scie.org.uk/scies products/knowledgereviews/KRO3summary onlineversion071103.pdf

10. "Minority groups" may be defined in terms of numerical representation and/or "minority" in terms of socio-economic and/or political status. It remains an ambiguous and contested concept and needs to be defined and clarified within specific social contexts.

11. While cultural sensitivity may contribute to culturally competent practice, the school must be mindful of the possibility of reinforcing group stereotypes. The school should, therefore, try to ensure that social work students do not use knowledge of a particular group of people to generalise to every person in that group. The school should pay particular attention to both in-group and inter-group variations and similarities.

12. Such an approach might facilitate constructive confrontation and change where certain cultural beliefs, values and traditions violate peoples' basic human rights. As culture is socially constructed and dynamic, it is subject to deconstruction and change. Such constructive confrontation, deconstruction and change may be facilitated through a tuning into, and an understanding of particular cultural values, beliefs and traditions and via critical and reflective dialogue with members of the cultural group vis-à-vis broader human rights issues.

13. In many countries voluntary national professional associations play major roles in enhancing the status of social work, and in the development of Codes of Ethics. In some countries voluntary professional associations assume regulatory functions, for example disciplinary procedures in the event of professional malpractice, while in other countries statutory bodies assume such functions.

14. Restorative justice reflects the following: a belief that crime violates people and relationships; making the wrong right; seeking justice between victims, offenders and communities; people are seen to be the victims; emphasis on

participation, dialogue and mutual agreement; is oriented to the future and the development of responsibility. This is opposed to retributive justice which reflects: a belief that crime violates the State and its laws; a focus on punishment and guilt; justice sought between the State and the offender; the State as victim; authoritarian, technical and impersonal approaches; and orientation to the past and guilt.

15. As 'minimum standards' appeared to be too prescriptive, the suggestion at the IASSW Board meeting in Chile in January 2002, was that we refer to "Global Qualifying Standards for Social Work Education and Training". This was considered a more appealing alternative in view of the main paradigm adopted in the document. Also while each component of the 'standards' may represent a minimum, put together, the document reflects quite a sophisticated level of education and training. A first draft was debated in the IFSW General Meeting in 2002, leading to specific proposals which were reported at the Montpellier conference. As consultations proceeded a preference seemed to emerge for the use of 'International Guidelines for Social Work Education and Training.' This was on account of linking the concept 'global' with 'globalisation', with all of the latter's negative connotations and hegemonic discourses. However, on producing the fourth draft of the document as 'international guidelines' and on receiving further feedback, some colleagues reflected a clearer preference for 'Global Standards'. The pattern that emerged was interesting as the more developed Western schools seemed to prefer 'international guidelines' while developing schools preferred that we retain 'Global Standards'. This warrants further discussion and research. Colleagues from developing schools expressed the view that 'Global Standards' were more substantive and might contribute to the development of their schools and curricula by allowing them more bargaining power within their institutions. Given that we were always

mindful of reinforcing a Western hegemonic discourse, and that the standards must serve the needs of developing schools we decided to revert to the earlier decision and adopt the term 'Global Standards.' It is unacceptable that a Western hegemony prevails, simply because the West might have more presence and voice at international gatherings. Furthermore, IFSW, representing a practitioner-based body, was quite categorical in its rejection of the use of 'international guidelines'. The concept 'global' was debated at different times within both IFSW and IASSW. Both organisations concluded that 'global' was an inclusive concept referring to all regions and all countries of the world, while international may refer to two or more countries. As the standards are intended to be applicable to all schools of social work on a global level, the use of 'global' is more appropriate. According to Payne (2001) a standard refers to a pointer towards something distinctive or an ideal. A standard is defined as a "rallying principle", "a degree of excellence required for a particular purpose" or something "recognised as (a) model for imitation", "recognised as possessing merit or authority" (Oxford Dictionary). Given that we depict ideals that we aspire towards, non-prescriptive 'standards' would be more appropriate than 'guidelines'. As 'qualifying' is self-evident and perhaps redundant, it was dropped from the title.

16. The Chair of the Committee consulted with Faculty from Grand Valley State University, Grand Rapids, Michigan; representatives from Michigan State University, Hope College and Calvin College, Michigan; representatives from Social Work and the Social Welfare Training Institute—University of the West Indies, Mona Campus, Jamaica; and with the Joint Universities Committee (JUC) on Social Work Education, South Africa. The document was shared with colleagues at a seminar in Santiago, Chile in January 2002. A plenary consultation session was held at the IASSW conference in Montpellier, France in July 2002, with

educators and practitioners in New Zealand in January 2003, and in February 2003 a consultation session was held at the CSWE conference in Atlanta. A consultation session was held at the Association of Caribbean Social Work Educators in Barbados, July–August 2003, with colleagues in Estonia in August 2003 (by Lena Dominelli), and a plenary consultation session at the JUC conference in South Africa in October 2003. The first draft was debated in the IFSW General Assembly in 2002 leading to proposals that were reported to the Montpellier conference. Since the development of the first draft the document has been available on the IASSW and the IFSW web-sites. In addition both IASSW and IFSW colleagues have discussed the document at various forums in the Asia Pacific Region, Eastern Europe, the U.K., North America and Canada, Africa and in Latin America. In an effort to broaden consultation the fourth reviewed document was sent to all delegates (who had e-mail addresses) that attended the IASSW conference in Montpellier (2002). The document has been translated into French, Spanish, Swedish, Serbo-Croatian, Russian, Danish and Italian and is available in these languages on the web-sites. The publication of the document in the journal Social Work Education was a further attempt at consultation and inclusion. The document has been sent to various colleagues in different parts of the world requesting their input and comments. All feedback was considered and, as far as was reasonable and possible, was reflected in the reviews of the document. The overall response to the document has been overwhelmingly positive, with some colleagues commenting that as a global standards document, it is the best it could be. All responses received, from very diverse contexts such as Mexico, Chile, Mauritius, China, the Philippines, Russia, Armenia, Croatia, Australia, Africa and the U.K. indicated that the standards support, and would strengthen, national initiatives and would not negatively impact on the development of locally specific social work education, training and practice.

17. Continued and vibrant discourse is encouraged and welcomed on the transformational changes necessary for the social work profession to achieve the aspiration of a comprehensive and common scope that has the desired flexibility to accommodate local interpretations of social work education and practice in diverse contexts, while adhering to international standards and core components.

18. The concepts suggested here are problematic as they reflect the traditional biomedical model, which supports the notion of the service user as a passive recipient of social work services with the social worker as 'expert' who knows best, and an implication of a hierarchical worker-client relationship, characterised by a so-called neutrality. It is antithetical to the holistic bio-psychosocial, spiritual model which views people as active agents in change processes and structures, and to empowerment based practice, which calls for active involvement, rather than a detached neutrality, on the part of practitioners. A suggestion has been made for the use of 'participants in social services.' However, this alludes to an ideological position that is inconsistent with current realities of practice, which is indeed based on skewed power relationships, where service users are not fully integrated as equal participants in social work processes, delivery mechanisms and structures. Given the contemporary ethos of practice it is perhaps more ethical and realistic to retain the concepts 'service users', 'clients' or 'consumers', despite their limitations. An alternate suggestion was for the use of 'people who access social services'. But this is too awkward and cumbersome for consistent use.

19. For the purpose of convenience, the document shall refer to 'the school' or 'schools' even where the context of study is a faculty, centre or department.

20. Given the limitations of dichotomies, and the linear modernist implications of the use of

words 'under-developed', 'developing' or 'developed' there is preference for the use of the concept 'Two Thirds World'. The concept reflects, numerically, the majority of the world's population that lives in poverty and deprivation, and it does not imply any evaluative criteria with regard to superiority/inferiority.

21. It is envisaged that such quality control will not be instituted at the international level, but at local, national and/or regional levels.

22. See, e.g., Pozutto (2001) who in comparing the possible lessons that South African social work has for other parts of the world, concluded that, ". . . [For] the most part, US social workers envision the social order as a given, largely unchangeable entity. . . . Much of the American social work profession has accepted the 'knowledge' that legitimates the American social order. The drive to professionalism was . . . an early step in that direction. . . . [The] function of much of contemporary social work is to 'normalise' the population. . . . [Social] work is a form of social control contributing to the legitimisation of the current social order." (Pozutto, 2001, pp. 157–158).

23. For a discussion on this and debates around totalising discourses; representation; the universal and the particular; and knowledge, power and discursive formations see Williams and Sewpaul's article on Modernism, Postmodernism and Global Standards Setting published in Social Work Education 2004, vol. 23, No. 5: 555–565.

APPENDIX C

NATIONAL ASSOCIATION OF BLACK SOCIAL WORKERS, CODE OF ETHICS

In America today, no Black person, except the selfish or irrational, can claim neutrality in the quest for Black liberation nor fail to consider the implications of the events taking place in our society. Given the necessity for committing ourselves to the struggle for freedom, we as Black Americans practicing in the field of social welfare, set forth this statement of ideals and guiding principles.

If a sense of community awareness is a precondition to humanitarian acts, then we as Black social workers must use our knowledge of the Black community, our commitments to its self-determination, and our helping skills for the benefit of Black people as we marshal our expertise to improve the quality of life of Black people. Our activities will be guided by our Black consciousness, our determination to protect the security of the Black community, and to serve as advocates to relieve suffering of Black people by any means necessary.

Therefore, as Black social workers we commit ourselves, collectively, to the interests of our Black brethren and as individuals subscribe to the following statements:

- I regard as my primary obligation the welfare of the Black individual, Black family, and Black community and will engage in action for improving social conditions.
- I give precedence to this mission over my personal interest.
- I adopt the concept of a Black extended family and embrace all Black people as my brothers and sisters, making no distinction between their destiny and my own.
- I hold myself responsible for the quality and extent of service I perform and the quality and extent of service performed by the agency or organization in which I am employed, as it relates to the Black community.
- I accept the responsibility to protect the Black community against unethical and hypocritical practice by any individual or organizations engaged in social welfare activities.
- I stand ready to supplement my paid or professional advocacy with voluntary service in the Black public interest.

I will consciously use my skills, and my whole being as an instrument for social change, with particular attention directed to the establishment of Black social institutions.

For additional information: http://nabsw.org/

APPENDIX D
NORTH AMERICAN ASSOCIATION OF CHRISTIANS IN SOCIAL WORK

Mission

The mission of the North American Association of Christians in Social Work (NACSW) is to equip its members to integrate *Christian faith* and professional social work practice.

By Christian faith, NACSW means historic Christian faith as expressed, for example, in statements such as the following: The Apostle's Creed, The Nicene Creed, and NACSW's Statement of Faith and Practice. Members of NACSW are individuals who self-identify as Christians. The members of NACSW represent a rich diversity of Christian denominations and traditions. NACSW recognizes that different Christian denominations and traditions use different language to express the heart of historic Christian faith.

For additional information: http://www.nacsw.org/index.shtml

INDEX

ABOUT THE AUTHORS

Ira Colby, DSW, MSW, is dean emeritus of social work at the University of Houston. He served as dean of the Graduate College of Social Work for fifteen years as well as developing and directing the baccalaureate social work program at Ferrum College, Ferrum, VA. He was a faculty member at at the University of Texas at Arlington, and directed a new school of social work at the University of Central Florida. Colby has held many positions nationally, including past president of the Council on Social Work Education, and internationally, serving on the International Association of Schools of Social Work board of directors. He received his BS degree from Springfield College, his MSW from Virginia Commonwealth University, and his DSW from the University of Pennsylvania. He is widely published and has presented papers at state, national, and international meetings and forums. His passions are golf, running, and family, not necessarily in that order.

Sophia F. Dziegielewski, PhD, MSW, LCSW, is professor in the School of Social Work at the University of Central Florida. She also is chair of the Institutional Review Board for this large metropolitan university of over 60,000 students. Previously, she served as dean of the School of Social Work at the University of Cincinnati, Cincinnati, OH, and taught in the School of Social Work at the University of Alabama, the Departments of Family and Preventive Medicine and Psychiatry at Meharry Medical College, the School of Social Work at the University of Tennessee, and the U.S. Army Military College at Fort Benning, GA. She also serves as editor for the *Journal of Social Service Research.* She is widely published with over 135 publications to her credit including eight textbooks and numerous articles and book chapters.